Lecture Notes in Computer Science   4018

Commenced Publication in 1973
Founding and Former Series Editors:
Gerhard Goos, Juris Hartmanis, and Jan van Leeuwen

Vincent Wade   Helen Ashman
Barry Smyth (Eds.)

Adaptive Hypermedia and Adaptive Web-Based Systems

4th International Conference, AH 2006
Dublin, Ireland, June 21-23, 2006
Proceedings

 Springer

Volume Editors

Vincent Wade
Trinity College Dublin, O'Reilly Institute, Department of Computer Science
Dublin 2, Ireland
E-mail: vincent.wade@cs.tcd.ie

Helen Ashman
University of Nottingham, School of Computer Science and Information Technology
Jubilee Campus, Nottingham NG8 1BB, UK
E-mail: hla@cs.nott.ac.uk

Barry Smyth
University College Dublin, UCD School of Computer Science and Informatics
Belfield, Dublin 4, Ireland
E-mail: barry.smyth@ucd.ie

Library of Congress Control Number: 2006927237

CR Subject Classification (1998): H.5.4, H.4, H.5, H.3

LNCS Sublibrary: SL 3 – Information Systems and Application, incl. Internet/Web
and HCI

ISSN 0302-9743
ISBN 978-3-540-34696-8 Springer Berlin Heidelberg New York

Springer is a part of Springer Science+Business Media

springer.com

© Springer-Verlag Berlin Heidelberg 2006

Typesetting: Camera-ready by author, data conversion by Scientific Publishing Services, Chennai, India
Printed on acid-free paper   SPIN: 11768012   06/3142   5 4 3 2 1 0

Preface

We live in a world of dynamic information a world of portals and search engines, of Web pages and e-mails, blogs and e-commerce sites, online courseware and interactive tour guides. However, even though we can now avail of unprecedented levels of access to this information world, it is becoming increasingly difficult for users to locate quickly and easily the right information at the right time. For instance, even conservative estimates of the Web's current size speak of its 10 billion documents and a growth rate that tops 60 terabytes of new information per day. To put this into perspective, in 2000 the entire World-Wide Web consisted of just 21 terabytes of information. Now it grows by 3 times this figure every single day.

Adaptive Hypermedia and Adaptive Web Systems represent a critical and rapidly growing area of ICT research. Its focus on pioneering theories, techniques and innovative technologies to provide dynamic personalization, adaptation and contextualization of hypermedia resources and services has singled out the AH Conference series as the premier research event for adaptive Web systems. The conference combines state-of-the-art research investigations with industrial verification and evaluation to provide a unique event for researchers and practitioners alike. The conference series attracts researchers from the areas of knowledge engineering, artificial intelligence, Web engineering, Semantic Web, systems integration and security. In addition to these technology-and theory-oriented researchers, AH also attracts industrial and academic researchers in areas of key vertical markets such as interactive TV, e-learning, Web system, e-commerce and e-government.

It is important to note that research first heralded during the AH Conference series has often become deeply engrained in next-generation Web applications, e.g., personalized e-learning and adaptive information kiosks, personalized mo bile portals, and adaptive Web search facilities. The main professional organizations most related to adaptive hypermedia/adaptive Web system have again endorsed the AH Conference Series: International World-Wide Web Conference Committee (IW3C2), the Association for Computing Machinery (ACM), and in particular SIGWEB, SIGIR, AIED Society and User Modelling Inc.

This year's conference saw the continued growth in quantity and quality of research in this key technological area. From the 122 papers submitted to the conference, the Program Committee, after rigorous review, selected 22 submissions as full papers (i.e., 18% acceptance rate) and 19 (i.e., 15%) as short papers. The conference also solicited a Doctorial Consortium to encourage early-stage researchers to present their ideas and proposals within an expert forum. The Doctorial Consortium attracted 26 submissions of which 15 were selected for presentation at the conference. This is a significant increase over previous AH

Conferences and should provide an excellent showcase and feedback opportunity for these young researchers.

Organizing a conference such as AH2006 is a challenging task and we are very grateful to the Program Committee and external reviewers who provided such insightful review comments and constructive feedback on all submissions. This year full paper submissions received four independent reviews, with short papers each receiving three reviews. We would like to sincerely thank the entire Program Committee and external reviewers for ensuring a high-quality conference which will hopefully be enjoyed by both attendees and readers of this proceedings.

A subset of the Program Committee focused on the Doctorial Consortium submissions and provided extensive, formative feedback to all DC submission authors. We would like to single out the effort of the DC Chairs (Peter Brusilovsky and Lorraine McGinty) for their excellent work in both promoting the Doctorial Consortium and stewarding their review feedback. This year's conference also saw a strong portfolio of workshops in key areas of emerging adaptive technology research. Again our thanks to the workshop Chairs, Alexandra Cristea and Stephan Weibelzahl, for their organization of these events.

Local organization of international conferences is a very difficult task and we would like to thank our fellow Organizing Committee members. In particular would like to mention Declan Kelly (Local Chair), Shauna Cassidy (Local Administrator), Eugene O'Loughlin (Industrial Chair), and Mark Melia (AH Website Administrator) for all their efforts in making AH2006 a success. We would also like to thank Alex O'Connor, Shay Lawless and Ian O'Keeffe for their help in finalizing the typesetting of the proceedings and indexes.

And finally to you, the delegate and reader of this volume. The research presented in this book represents a wide and insightful view of the direction and state of the art in personalization and adaptivity of hypermedia and Web-based systems. We hope that you enjoy the papers and that they provide a considerable contribution to your interest and future endeavors.

June 2006

Vincent Wade
Helen Ashman
Barry Smyth

Organization

AH2006 was jointly organized by Trinity College, Dublin, University College Dublin and the National College of Ireland (Dublin).

General Chair

Barry Smyth (University College Dublin)

Program Chairs

Vincent Wade (Trinity College, Dublin)
Helen Ashman (University of Nottingham)

Local Chair

Declan Kelly (National College of Ireland)

Doctoral Consortium

Peter Brusilovsky (University of Pittsburgh)
Lorraine McGinty (University College Dublin)

Workshops and Tutorials

Alexandra Cristea (Technical University Eindhoven)
Stephan Weibelzahl (National College of Ireland)

Industry Chair

Eugene O'Loughlin (National College of Ireland)

Program Committee

Ignaceo Aedo, Universidad Carlos III de Madrid, Spain
Elisabeth Andre, University of Augsburg, Germany
Liliana Ardissono, University of Turin, Italy
Lora Aroyo, Eindhoven University of Technology, The Netherlands
Helen Ashman, University of Nottingham, UK
Mark Bernstein, Eastgate, USA
James Blustein, Dalhousie University, Canada
Tim Brailsford, University of Nottingham, UK
Peter Brusilovsky, University of Pittsburgh, USA
Ricardo Conejo, Universidad de Málaga, Spain

Owen Conlan, Trinity College Dublin, Ireland
Alexandra Cristea, Eindhoven University of Technology, The Netherlands
Paul Cristea, Politehnica University Bucharest, Romania
Hugh Davis, University of Southampton, UK
Paul De Bra, Eindhoven University of Technology, The Netherlands
Vania Dimitrova, University of Leeds, UK
Peter Dolog, University of Hannover, Germany
Erich Gams, Salzburg Research, Austria
Franca Garzotto, Politecnico di Milano, Italy
Mehmet Goker, PricewaterhouseCoopers Center for Advanced Research, USA
Wendy Hall, University of Southampton, UK
Nicola Henze, University of Hannover, Germany
Geert-Jan Houben, Vrije Universiteit Brussel, Belgium
Anthony Jameson, International University, Germany
Judy Kay, University of Sydney, Australia
Declan Kelly, National College of Ireland, Ireland
Peter King, University of Manitoba, Canada
Alfred Kobsa, University of California, Irvine, USA
Rob Koper, Open Universiteit Nederland, The Netherlands
Milos Kravcik, Fraunhofer Institute FIT, Germany
Henry Lieberman, MIT, USA
Paul Maglio, IBM Almaden Research Center, USA
Lorraine McGinty, University College Dublin, Ireland
Alessandro Micarelli, University of Rome III, Italy
Maria Milosavljevic, HCRC, Uni. of Edinburgh, UK
Antonija Mitrovic, University of Canterbury, New Zealand
Dunja Mladenic, Jozef Stefan Institute, Slovenija
Adam Moore, University of Nottingham, UK
Wolfgang Nejdl, University of Hannover, Germany
Jon Oberlander, University of Edinburgh, UK
Jose-Luis Perez-de-la-Cruz, Universidad de Málaga, Spain
Gustavo Rossi, Universidad Nacional de la Plata, Argentina
Lloyd Rutledge, CWI, The Netherlands
Demetrios Sampson, University of Piraeus & CERTH, Greece
Vittorio Scarano, University of Salerno, Italy
Frank Shipman, Texas A&M University, USA
Alan Smeaton, Dublin City University, Ireland
Barry Smyth, University College Dublin, Ireland
Marcus Specht, Open Universiteit Nederland, The Netherlands
Craig Stewart, University of Nottingham, UK
Carlo Strapparava, ITC-IRST Trento, Italy
Carlo Tasso, Universitá degli Studi di Udine, Italy
Jacco van Ossenbruggen, CWI, The Netherlands
Fabio Vitali, University of Bologna, Italy
Vincent Wade, Trinity College Dublin, Ireland

Gerhard Weber, PH Freiburg, Germany
Stephan Weibelzahl, National College of Ireland, Ireland
Ross Wilkinson, CSIRO, Australia
Massimo Zancanaro, ITC-IRST Trento, Italy

External Reviewers

Alia Amin, CWI, The Netherlands
Keith Bradley, University College Dublin, Ireland
David Bueno, Universidad de Málaga, Spain
Arthur Cater, University College Dublin, Ireland
Declan Dagger, Trinity College, Dublin, Ireland
Sarah Jane Delany, Dublin Institute of Technology, Ireland
Michiel Hildebrand, CWI, The Netherlands
Jure Ferlez, Jozef Stefan Institute, Slovenija
Miha Grcar, Jozef Stefan Institute, Slovenija
Eduardo Guzman, Universidad de Málaga, Spain
Jure Leskovec, Carnegie Mellon University, USA
Eleni Mangina, University College Dublin, Ireland
Eva Millan, Universidad de Málaga, Spain
Gabriel-Miro Muntean, Dublin City University, Ireland
Alexander O'Connor, Trinity College Dublin, Ireland
Noel O Connor, Dublin City University, Ireland
Cesare Rocchi - ITC-IRST Trento, Italy
Bernard Roche, University College Dublin, Ireland
Monica Trella, Universidad de Málaga, Spain
Miha Vuk, Jozef Stefan Institute, Slovenija
David Wilson, University of North Carolina, USA

Organizing Committee

Helen Ashman, University of Nottingham, UK
Peter Brusilovsky, University of Pittsburgh, USA
Shauna Cassidy, National College of Ireland, Ireland
Alexandra Cristea, Technical University Eindhoven, The Netherlands
Declan Kelly, National College of Ireland, Ireland
Lorraine McGinty, University College Dublin, Ireland
Eugene O'Loughlin, National College of Ireland, Ireland
Barry Smyth, University College Dublin, Ireland
Vincent Wade, Trinity College, Dublin, Ireland
Stephan Weibelzahl, National College of Ireland, Ireland

Table of Contents

Keynote Speakers

Full Papers

Short Papers

Posters

Doctoral Consortium

Knowledge-Driven Hyperlinks: Linking in the Wild

Sean Bechhofer[1], Yeliz Yesilada[1], Bernard Horan[2], and Carole Goble[1]

[1] University of Manchester, UK
{sean.bechhofer, yeliz.yesilada, carole.goble}@manchester.ac.uk
http://www.manchester.ac.uk/cs
[2] Sun Microsystems Laboratories
bernard.horan@sun.com
http://research.sun.com

Abstract. Since Ted Nelson coined the term "Hypertext", there has been extensive research on non-linear documents. With the enormous success of the Web, non-linear documents have become an important part of our daily life activities. However, the underlying hypertext infrastructure of the Web still lacks many features that Hypertext pioneers envisioned. With advances in the Semantic Web, we can address and improve some of these limitations. In this paper, we discuss some of these limitations, developments in Semantic Web technologies and present a system – COHSE – that dynamically links Web pages. We conclude with remarks on future directions for semantics-based linking.

1 Introduction

The World Wide Web (Web) is the most successful hypertext ever, with recent figures[1] suggesting that more time is now spent in the UK surfing the Web than watching television. It is only natural and appropriate that hypertext research, and its researchers, would thus adapt to the Web and its ways, despite the fact that the underlying hypertext infrastructure is simple (good) and limited (bad). The model is based almost entirely around nodes with links playing second fiddle – embedded and difficult to author, maintain, share and adapt. Approaches such as Open Hypermedia go some way toward addressing this issue.

The Semantic Web (SW) is based on the notion of exposing metadata about resources in an explicit, machine-processable way. By doing so, we open up the possibility of using machine processing in order to help us search, organize and understand our data. So far this has largely been used to provide more effective search, describe Web Services and drive applications like enterprise integration. We must not forget, however, that the Semantic Web is still a *Web* and that query by navigation, via links between documents, is still fundamental to the

---

[1] e.g. see The Guardian March 8, 2006:
http://technology.guardian.co.uk/news/story/0,,1726018,00.html

V. Wade, H. Ashman, and B. Smyth (Eds.): AH 2006, LNCS 4018, pp. 1–10, 2006.

way in which we interact with the Web. Serendipitous linking, where unforeseen connections are uncovered between resources, is complementary to directed search.

A key driver for Semantic Web advances is to improve machine processing on the Web. However, including *semantics* for machine-processing can also be used to improve the linking and navigation of Web pages intended for human end-users. Semantic Web components can be used to add links dynamically between resources using the existing infrastructure of the Web.

Semantic Web technologies can be used to adapt and evolve the embedded link structure of the Web, effectively building a semantically-driven dynamic open hypermedia system. Additional metadata and reasoning components add links dynamically between resources, potentially improving the linking and navigation of Web pages intended for end-users. Different knowledge resources can be used to personalise links, providing better relations, presentations and links that are more relevant to users. Systems such as COHSE [8] and Magpie [15] have pioneered these ideas, and can be presented as allies to the notions of semantic wikis and social tagging. Thus they bridge between the high-brow world of Semantic Web as perceived by the Artificial Intelligence community, the low-brow world of "collective intelligence" as perceived by the Web 2.0 community, the Web designers' world of content and link creation and the users' experience of hypermedia navigation.

2   Hypertext and the Web

The theoretical foundation of the Web is the concept of linked resources [5]. There has been extensive research on Hypertext and Hypermedia; different information models have been introduced and extensive work has been done on engineering hypermedia, navigation and browsing models, design methodologies, etc [23]. With its simple infrastructure, the Web as Hypertext fails to support some of the features introduced in Hypertext research. For example, it does not support generic linking.

Links between documents provide utility (to both humans and machines). Typically, links between documents on the Web are embedded within those documents. Although the approach of embedding links is simple and scalable, there are a number of well-known limitations [11, 12]:

Hard Coding: Links are hard coded and often hand-crafted in the HTML encoding of a document.

Format Restrictions: Documents need to be written in a particular format (e.g. HTML or PDF) in order to support the addition of links.

Ownership: Ownership of a document is required in order to place an anchor in it.

Legacy resources: It can be difficult to deal with legacy material – when the view of a world changes, old documents might need to be updated with new links. It can also be difficult to create multiple views (as suggested by links) over documents.

Maintenance: There is a weight of maintenance in creating and updating links in documents. This is due in part to the hard coding and ownership issues described above.

Approaches such as Open Hypermedia [18, 25] have sought to address some of these problems. Rather than embedding links in the documents, links are considered *first class citizens*. They are stored and managed separately from the documents and can thus be transported, shared and searched separately from the documents themselves. The emergence of the Semantic Web also offers potential for addressing the issue of linking.

3   Semantic Web

HTML is a simple authoring language and this simplicity contributed enormously to the success of the Web. However, HTML focuses on document structure and thus provides little knowledge about the document content. For humans, who in general access this content visually, this is fine, for machine automation, however, something more is needed.

The Semantic Web vision, as articulated by Tim Berners-Lee [5], is of a Web in which resources are accessible not only to humans, but also to automated processes, e.g., automated "agents" roaming the Web performing useful tasks such as improved search (in terms of precision) and resource discovery, information brokering and information filtering. The automation of tasks depends on elevating the status of the web from machine-readable to something we might call machine-understandable.

The Semantic Web is thus based on the notion of exposing metadata about resources in an explicit, machine-processable way. The key idea is to have data on the web defined and linked in such a way that its meaning is explicitly interpretable by software processes rather than just being implicitly interpretable by humans. By doing so, we open up the possibility of using machine processing in order to help us search, organize and understand our data. So far this has largely been used to help in provide more effective search, describing web services and driving applications like enterprise integration. Semantic Web technologies also offer the potential, however, for evolving the link structure of the Web.

We suggest that building a Semantic Web involves tying together three aspects (See Fig. 1).

Semantics: Providing machine processable representations of conceptual models and content;
Hypertext Architecture: A model of links and nodes;
Web Framework: Building on existing standards and infrastructure.

We can observe combinations of these aspects in existing work such as Open Hypermedia, early Semantic Web research and Conceptual Hypermedia.

The Distributed Link Service (DLS)[7], developed by the University of Southampton is a service that adopted an Open Hypermedia approach, and provided

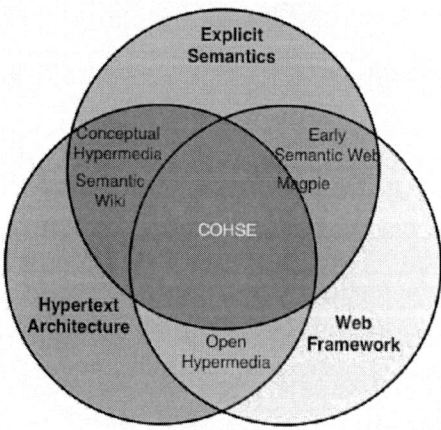

Fig. 1. Three Pillars of the Semantic Web

dynamic linking of documents. Links are taken from a link base, and can be either *specific*, where the source of the link is given by addressing a particular fragment of a resource, or *generic*, where the source is given by some selection, e.g. a word or phrase. Documents and linkbases are dynamically brought together by the DLS, which then adds appropriate links to documents. The DLS thus combines a hypertext architecture within the web framework, but brings little in terms of explicit semantics.

The focus of Semantic Web research has largely been on the development of standards to support document metadata, positioned within the context of web standards. Thus DAML+OIL [9], RDF(S) [6] and latterly OWL [13] provide knowledge representation functionality in languages fitting into the Web Stack. Applications such as SHOE [21] and OntoBroker [14] provided early mechanisms for annotating documents, with the annotations kept in some central store for later query. This focus is changing – for example the recent call for the Semantic Web track of the World Wide Web Conference 2006 explicitly ruled out of scope papers that didn't take account of Web aspects. Applications like Haystack [26] and PiggyBank [22] have carried these ideas further into the Web arena. PiggyBank uses a number of mechanisms for harvesting metadata associated with web resources, for example using screen scraping or explicit RDF files associated with the resources. This is thus a use of metadata and semantics within the Web framework, but PiggyBank is not a hypertext system – it supports tagging of web pages with metadata and then allows the user to search and browse through this metadata, but the emphasis is not on linking (in a hypertext sense).

Conceptual Hypermedia systems sought to bring conceptual models to bear in order to support linking. However, systems such as MacWeb [24] and SHA [10] provided closed systems rather than supporting linking in the wide (and wilder) world of the Web. Semantic Wikis (e.g., Platypus Wiki[2].)) also introduce explicit models of knowledge in support of management of content. This combines

---

[2] Platypus Wiki, `http://platypuswiki.sourceforge.net/`

hypertext and metadata, but is again primarily concerned with organising and managing resources under a single point of control (albeit control by a collection of individuals).

Magpie [15], from the Open University, supplies what we might call a Semantic Web Browser. Rather than placing an emphasis on hypertext linking though, Magpie integrates Semantic Services that provide on-demand added value based on the content of the pages.

The Conceptual Open Hypermedia Service (COHSE) project brought all three aspects together, marrying the DLS with Ontological Services. COHSE provides a framework that integrates an ontology service and the open hypermedia link service to form a conceptual hypermedia system enabling documents to be linked via ontologies [8]. Through the use of different domain ontologies, COHSE can provide different hypertext views of Web resources. For instance, [3] presents how the COHSE system is used in Bioinformatics to link biology resources by using the Gene Ontology[3] and [4] presents how Sun's Java tutorial[4] pages are augmented using a Java and programming ontology.

COHSE extends the DLS with *ontological services*, providing information relating to an ontology. These services include mappings between concepts and lexical labels (synonyms). Giving an example based on Sun's product catalogue, the ontology tells us that Campfire Rack+ is a synonym of Sun Enterprise 5500 Server. In this way, the terms and their synonyms in the ontology form the means by which the DLS finds lexical items within a document from which links can be made (providing *generic* links). The services also provide information about relationships, such as sub- and super-classes – here Sun Enterprise 5500 Server is a kind of System. The use of an ontology helps to bridge gaps [1] between the terms used in example web pages (e.g. in this case Campfire Rack+), and those used to index other resources, such as sites providing trouble-shooting support.

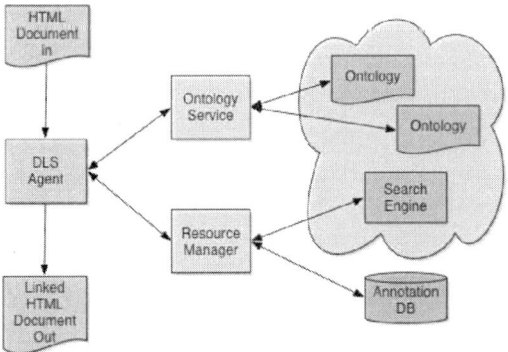

Fig. 2. The COHSE architecture

---

[3] Gene Ontology (GO), http://www.geneontology.org/.
[4] The Java Tutorial, http://java.sun.com/.

COHSE's architecture (See Fig. 2) is composed of a COHSE Distributed Links Service (DLS) agent and two supporting services: an Ontology Service (OS) and a Resource Manager (RM).

Ontology Service (OS): supports interaction with ontologies by providing services such as mapping between concepts and lexical labels (synonyms), providing information about specialisation (sub-classes) and generalisation (super-classes) of concepts, descriptions of concepts, etc. [2]. The service has a simple HTTP interface and can host third party ontologies represented using OWL – we return to this point later. Reasoning about the ontologies (e.g., the construction of classification hierarchies or the classification of arbitrary conceptual descriptions) can be performed through the use of an OWL Reasoner.

Resource Manager (RM): manages resources. One function of the RM is to maintain and store annotations of resources – mappings between concepts in an ontology and a resource fragment such as a paragraph in an XHTML document (i.e. semantic annotation [19]). These annotations may be produced by parties other than the document owners or users of the COHSE system. The annotations are used in two ways: the concept to resource mapping provides candidate targets for links and the resource to concept mapping provides candidate source anchors for links. Therefore, the RM is used for both source anchor identification and discovery of possible target anchors.

DLS agent: responsible for modifying pages and adding links depending on information provided by the OS and RM. The agent processes documents and inserts link source anchors into the document along with the possible link targets. The system has, in the past, been deployed as a browser extension (based on Mozilla) or as a proxy through which HTTP requests are routed. We are currently also exploring a portal based implementation. A portal provides a framework for aggregating content from different sources, and supports storage of user profiles, customisation and personalisation [17], all of which contribute to a flexible, adaptive system.

COHSE uses these components to provide two different link types based on the way the source anchors are discovered. In both, target anchors are identified by the RM.

1. *Generic Links* A set of conditions are specified that must be met in order to insert a source anchor [27]. For example, source anchors are identified by analysing a document with a lexical matching algorithm using the terms from an ontology which are provided by the OS.
2. *Specific Links* Source anchors are stored explicitly via a reference mechanism [23]. Source anchors are identified using an RM that maintains external annotations populated using various techniques.

COHSE thus extends the notion of generic linking – the key point being that the ontology provides the link service with more opportunities for identifying link sources. As the ontology contains the terms that inform the DLS about the lexical items that may become links, there is no longer a need to own the page in order to make the link from the source to the target – this is taken care of by the DLS. Furthermore, the effort in providing the source of links moves from the document author to the creator(s) of the ontologies and annotations that are used by COHSE.

4   Web 2.0: The Rise of the Scruffies

Languages like OWL [13] provide representations that support detailed, formalised conceptual models. They come with a well-defined formal semantics that tell us *precisely* how composite concept descriptions should be interpreted. These formal semantics can help to drive the machine-processing that will underpin the Semantic Web and are vital if we are to support machine to machine communication. However, such an approach comes with an associated cost. OWL ontologies can be hard to build, hard to maintain, and hard to use. In domains such as medicine or bioinformatics, formal ontologies help to ensure interoperability between applications and the use of logic-based classifiers also helps in building and maintaining consistent vocabularies [28]. Ontologies have also proved of use in our work supporting accessibility, as shown in the DANTE [29] and SADIe [20] projects. Here, annotations provide extra information as to the role played by objects in a web page. This information can then be used to transcode pages, producing versions that are more accessible to users employing assistive technologies.

A key point here is that in the above applications, the knowledge models are being used by some process or program in order to perform a task for the user. Thus the content must be unambiguously and explicitly represented (hence the need for languages such as OWL).

In some situations, this "high-pain, high-gain" approach of detailed and formal semantics may not be necessary. For example, supporting navigation (as in COHSE) does not necessarily require that the relationships that we use for navigation are strict super or subclass relationships. Rather, we can look towards the approaches espoused in what has become known as Web 2.0, with its emphasis on social networking, tagging and "folksonomies". Here, the knowledge models are lightweight. There is little control over the vocabularies used, and there is little structure provided (in the sense of, say, formal relationships between terms in the vocabulary).

Folksonomies are easy to build, and represent some notion of collective intelligence. Although the knowledge models are shallow, their power lies in their shared use by a community of users. Folksonomies do well in supporting the kind of unfocused, undirected browsing supported by collections such as flickr[TM]– "I'd like to find some nice pictures of whales"[5] .

In Fig. 3 we see two axes representing an increase in expressive power: Artificial Intelligence[6], and community: Collective Intelligence (as exemplified by Web 2.0) along with a positioning of Semantic Web advances.

---

[5] http://www.flickr.com
[6] Or perhaps more accurately Knowledge Representation.

Artificial Intelligence

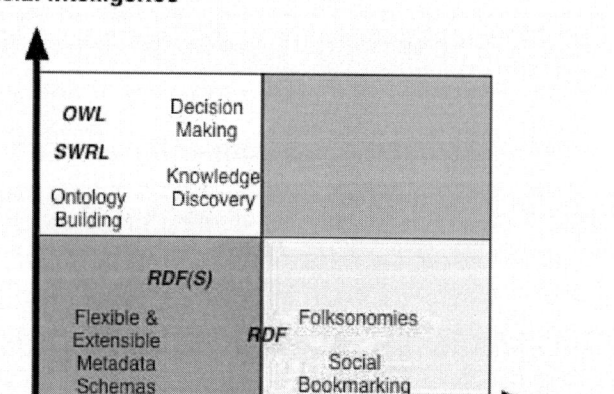

Fig. 3. The Semantic Web Landscape

5   Looking Forward

COHSE allowing interlinking between distinct web sites based on some conceptual model. However, with hindsight, our implementation and architecture were bound too tightly to the representation used for the knowledge – the OWL ontologies. We effectively provide a model-based approach to hypermedia, with the model being the ontology. Navigation was then based largely on the *clustering* of resources that OWL classification gave us along with query expansion driven by traversal of hierarchical relationships. This supports open, flexible linking, but required us to represent our knowledge using a particular approach, concentrating heavily on subsumption (as defined in OWL).

Our experience in trying to make use of knowledge sources such as product catalogues from Sun suggested that this concentration on classification resulted in an ontology that was artificially "forced" into a hierarchy. Relationships which were not strictly super/subclass were represented as such. More flexibility and the ability to move away from such formalised relationships is needed, along with the possibility to make use of other lightweight knowledge sources such as folksonomies. This is not to say that linking should be a "free-for-all" – a principled approach is still required.

Dynamic linking based on semantics (as espoused by COHSE) is an attractive prospect, supporting open, flexible linking across multiple sites. To achieve this however, we need to answer a number of questions.

– What are appropriate models for intersite linking?
– How best do we separate the ontology/knowledge from the navigation?
– How might we map from our diverse knowledge structures (and their associated annotations) into the navigational models?

Acknowledgements

Yeliz Yesilada is funded by Sun Microsystems Laboratories, whose support we are pleased to acknowledge.

References

1. Marcia J. Bates. Indexing and Access for Digital Libraries and the Internet: Human, Database and Domain Factors. *JASIS*, 49(13):1185–1205, 1998.
2. S. Bechhofer and C. Goble. Delivering Terminological Services. *AI*IA Notizie, Periodico dell'Associazione Italiana per l'intelligenza Artificiale.*, 12(1), March 1999.
3. S. Bechhofer, R. Stevens, and P. Lord. Ontology driven dynamic linking of biology resources. *Journal of Web Semantics (JWS)*. Accepted for Publication.
4. Sean Bechhofer, Carole Goble, Leslie Carr, Simon Kampa, and Wendy Hall. COHSE: Conceptual Open Hypermedia Service. In Siegfried Handschuh and Steffen Staab, editors, *Annotation for the Semantic Web*, volume 96 of *Frontiers in Artifical Intelligence and Applications*. IOS Press, 2003.
5. T. Berners-Lee. *Weaving the Web*. Orion Business Books, 1999.
6. Dan Brickley and R.V. Guha. RDF Vocabulary Description Language 1.0: RDF Schema. W3C Recommendation, World Wide Web Consortium, 2004. http://www.w3.org/TR/rdf-schema/.
7. Les A. Carr, David C. DeRoure, Wendy Hall, and Gary J. Hill. The Distributed Link Service: A Tool for Publishers, Authors and Readers. In *Fourth International World Wide Web Conference: The Web Revolution, (Boston, Massachusetts, USA).*, pages 647–656. O'Reilly & Associates, December 1995. Appears in World Wide Web Journal issue 1, ISBN 1-56592-169-0, ISSN 1085-2301.
8. Leslie Carr, Sean Bechhofer, Carole Goble, and Wendy Hall. Conceptual Linking: Ontology-based Open Hypermedia. In *WWW10, Tenth World Wide Web Conference*, May 2001.
9. Dan Connolly, Frank van Harmelen, Ian Horrocks, Deborah L. McGuinness, Peter F. Patel-Schneider, and Lynn Andrea Stein. DAML+OIL (March 2001) Reference Description. W3C Note, World Wide Web Consortium, 2004. http://www.w3.org/TR/daml+oil-reference.
10. D. Cunliffe, C. Taylor, and D. Tudhope. Query-based Navigation in Semantically Indexed Hypermedia. In *Proceedings of HT97, the Eighth ACM International Hypertext Conference.*, 1997.
11. H. Davis. To embed or not to embed. *Communications of the ACM*, 38(8):108–109, 1995.
12. H. Davis. Referential integrity of links in open hypermedia systems. In *Proceedings of the Ninth ACM Conference on Hypertext*, pages 207–216. ACM, 1998.
13. Mike Dean and Guus Schreiber. OWL Web Ontology Language Reference. W3C Recommendation, World Wide Web Consortium, 2004. http://www.w3.org/TR/owl-ref/.
14. S. Decker, M. Erdmann, D. Fensel, , and R. Studer. Ontobroker: Ontology Based Access to Distributed and Semi-Structured Information. In R. Meersman, Z. Tari, and S. Stevens, editors, *Semantic Issues in Multimedia Systems. Proceedings of DS-8*, pages 351–369. Kluwer Academic Publishers, 1999.
15. Martin Dzbor, John Domingue, and Enrico Motta. Opening Up Magpie via Semantic Services. In *Proceedings of WWW2004, Thirteenth International ACM World Wide Web Conference*, 2004.

16. Dieter Fensel, Katia Sycara, and John Mylopoulos, editors. *Proceedings of the 2nd International Semantic Web Conference, ISWC2003*, volume 2870 of *Lecture Notes in Computer Science*. Springer, October 2003.

17. N. Ferguson, S. Schmoller, and N. Smith. Personalisation in presentation services. Technical report, The Joint Information Systems Committee, 2004.

18. K. Grønbæk, L. Sloth, and Orbæk P. Webvise: Browser and Proxy Support for Open Hypermedia Structuring Mechanisms on the WWW. In *Proceedings of the Eighth International World Wide Web Conference*, pages 253–268, 1999.

19. S. Handschuh and S. Staab. *Annotation for the Semantic Web*, volume 96 of *Frontiers in Artificial Intelligence and Applications*. IOS Press, 2003.

20. Simon Harper and Sean Bechhofer. Semantic Triage for Accessibility. *IBM Systems Journal*, 44(3):637–, 2005.

21. J. Heflin. *Towards the Semantic Web: Knowledge Representation in a Dynamic, Distributed Environment*. Phd, University of Maryland, College Park, 2001.

22. David Huynh, Stefano Mazzocchi, and David Karger. Piggy Bank: Experience the Semantic Web Inside Your Web Browser. In Yolanda Gil, Enrico Motta, V. Richard Benjamins, and Mark Musen, editors, *Proceedings of the International Semantic Web Conference, ISWC2002*, volume 3729 of *Lecture Notes in Computer Science*. Springer-Verlag, November 2005.

23. David Lowe and Wendy Hall. *Hypermedia and the Web: An Engineering Approach*. John Wiley and Sons, 1999.

24. Jocelyne Nanard and Marc Nanard. Using structured types to incorporate knowledge in hypertext. In *HYPERTEXT '91: Proceedings of the third annual ACM conference on Hypertext*, pages 329–343, New York, NY, USA, 1991. ACM Press.

25. K. Osterbye and U Wiil. The Flag Taxonomy of Open Hypermedia Systems. In *Proceedings of the 1996 ACM Hypertext Conference*, pages 129–139, 1996.

26. Dennis Quan, David Huynh, and David R. Karger. Haystack: A Platform for Authoring End User Semantic Web Applications. In Fensel et al. [16].

27. E. Wilde and D. Lowe. *XPath, XLink, XPointer, and XML: A Practical Guide to Web Hyperlinking and Transclusion*. Addison Wesley, 2002.

28. C.J. Wroe, R.D. Stevens, C.A. Goble, and M. Ashburner. A Methodology to Migrate the Gene Ontology to a Description Logic Environment Using DAML+OIL. In *8th Pacific Symposium on biocomputing (PSB)*, pages 624–636, 2003.

29. Yeliz Yesilada. *Annotation and Transformation of Web Pages to Improve Mobility for Visually Impaired Users*. PhD Thesis, University of Manchester, 2005.

Scrutable Adaptation: Because We Can and Must

Judy Kay

Smart Internet Technology Research Group
School of Information Technologies
University of Sydney
Australia 2006

Abstract. Beginning with the motivations for scrutability, this paper introduces PLUS, a vision of Pervasive Lifelong User-models that are Scrutable. The foundation for PLUS is the Accretion/Resolution representation for active user models that can drive adaptive hypermedia, with support for scrutability. The paper illustrates PLUS in terms of its existing, implemented elements as well as some examples of applications built upon this approach. The concluding section is a research agenda for essential elements of this PLUS vision.

1 Introduction

Adaptive hypermedia aims to adapt to the user's current needs, knowledge, goals, preferences and other attributes. Essentially, this means that different people will typically have a different experience when they encounter the same adaptive hypermedia application. We are beginning to explore ways to exploit the power of computation that is increasingly integrated into pervasive or ubiquitous, context-aware personalised environments. So, for example, we might envisage information about this conference being available, in personalised form at convenient places in our environment.

My own version of this information might be delivered to my kitchen table, a tabletop display that I can interact with using finger gestures. It might have the following main links for me to expand:

- Registration
- Cheap hotels (less than 10 minutes walk from conference site)
- Excellent coffee shops (within 20 minutes walk of it)
- Inexpensive restaurants (within 20 minutes walk of it)
- Other
- History

where the registration link is at the top because I still need to register and the early deadline is fast approaching. (Later, it would be relegated to details within the History.) Note that there is a common thread to the second to fourth items: all refer to low cost options, befitting the preferences of an academic. These three also reflect the distance I am willing to walk for each of these services.

Typically, I will interact with this system to achieve goals like planning my finances for the trip, checking out hotel options and planning my time. Sometimes, however, I may want to know why the personalization has delivered this information,

V. Wade, H. Ashman, and B. Smyth (Eds.): AH 2006, LNCS 4018, pp. 11 – 19, 2006.
© Springer-Verlag Berlin Heidelberg 2006

in this form. I want to be able to scrutinise the adaptive hypermedia, where scrutable adaptive hypertext is: "Capable of being understood through study and observation; comprehensible"[1] and "understandable upon close examination"[2]. This means that, if and when I am prepared to invest a little effort, I can get answers to questions like:

- What information does the system collect about me to drive this personalisation?
- What does this system do with that information?
- With whom does it share the information?
- What information is in this part of my environment?
- How is it combined with other information about me?
- What is the meaning of "prefers low cost travel"?
- How did the system conclude that I prefer to travel at low cost?
- How can I get a big picture of the models related to my travel?
- How did the system choose to put this information here and now?
- What did it present a week ago?
- What would it present if I were a rich man?
- How do I change any of the above processes?

Why scrutability?
Briefly, motivations for scrutability include:

- The user's right to see and appreciate the meaning of personal information the computer holds about them in a user model;
- The possibility of users correcting errors in the model;
- Confirming the role of the machine as the servant or aid of the user;
- Programmer accountability for the personalisation;
- Enabling users to have a sense of control over the adaptation of systems by controlling the user model, the way that the model is interpreted and the way that it used to perform the personalisation;
- Helping people become more self-aware and to avoid self-deception, because their user model mirrors their real actions;
- In the case of teaching systems, the potential to encourage metacognition and deeper learning;
- Helping people monitor their progress and plan, especially in the case of learning;
- Motivate people to share user model data because they feel confident about its meaning and use;
- As an aid to collaboration where team members can learn relevant information about each other and can help each other more effectively.

The first two motivations relate to personal information and its use. This is captured in the spirit of emerging legislation [1]. The next three elements relate to user control over their adapted environment. This is a rather neglected but important area of effective use of technology, with wide recognition of its importance. The next three elements are

---

[1] http://www.thefreedictionary.com/scrutable 4 April, 06.
[2] http://www.tiscali.co.uk/reference/dictionaries/difficultwords/data/d0011288.html 4 April, 06.

associated with self-awareness. Essentially, user models have an outstanding potential to help people see themselves in terms of how they have behaved in the long term as they interacted with the various collectors evidence about them. The emerging research community called LeMoRe[3] (Learning Modelling for Reflection) is exploring this aspect in relation to learning contexts. But it has much broader applicability for the very important goals of learning from experience and planning the future. The last two aspects relate to the critical role of scrutability in making it acceptable to share one's user model for benefits. These mean that user models may have the potential to improve services, social interaction and collaborative learning.

2   PLUS: Pervasive Lifelong User-Models That Are Scrutable

There is already considerable personalisation of web applications [2]. Typically, these are independent applications, each with their own user models. There are serious challenges to going beyond this to longer term user models that can be effectively put into service for many applications. It is worth finding ways to overcome these as there are potential benefits, especially in terms of support for awareness and effective sharing of user models with other people. Scrutability is key to enabling such reuse and sharing of user model data.

In teaching systems, reuse of user models across applications means that each teaching system can start with a substantial user model, based on past user activity. Essentially, this is similar to a teacher studying a student's history as a starting point for teaching. In other applications, for example, those with models of user preferences, a person may benefit from reuse of their profile from one application, such as Amazon, taking it to the bookshop of their choice. Equally, my machine preferences, in terms of fonts, numbers of virtual desk tops and the like constitute information about me that I may like to make available, with minimal effort, to new machines.

PLUS, Pervasive Lifelong User-models that are Scrutable is a vision for achieving long term models that are associated with a person, rather than an application. PLUS is based on a view of personalised systems, shown in **Fig. 1**, where user models are seen as long term repositories of evidence about people.

The figure has the user at the top, their long term user model at the bottom and the layer in between shows the user modelling processes that provide that evidence. At the very bottom is the user model ontology. This poses challenges for scrutability: if the user model represents aspects about the user, one of the obvious things a user might want to know is the meaning of the aspects modelled. If the model includes aspects the user does not know about, it may not be trivial to explain this.

Lines leading into the user model show evidence sources that contribute to reasoning about the user. The thinner lines emanating from the user model indicate where the model is used: as input to the user model interface; driving the personalisation of applications; as data for the triggers on stereotypes and knowledge-based inference.

Central to Figure 1 is the role of evidence about users. The potential sources of such evidence are shown in the heavy lines that flow down the figure. At the left, the

---

[3] http://www.eee.bham.ac.uk/bull/lemore/ 4 April, 06.

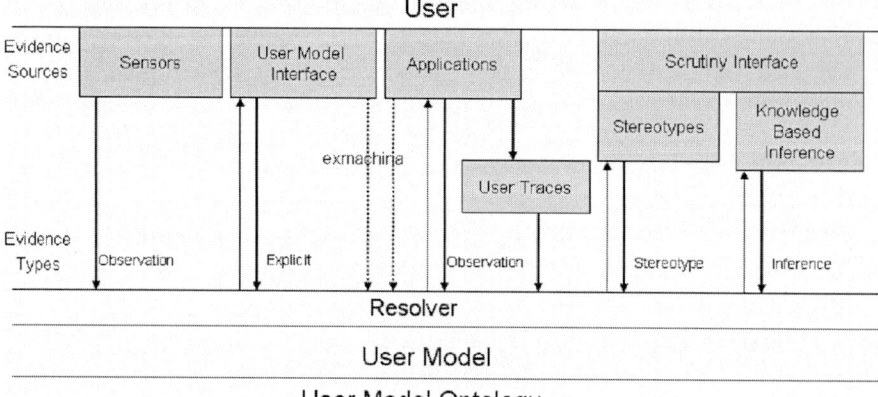

Fig. 1. PLUS Framework

figure shows sensors, programs that observe the user unobtrusively and add evidence to the user model. In a pervasive computing environment, these sensors might be Bluetooth, Wiki, Infrared or other quite subtle sensors.

The next source of evidence comes from the user interacting with an interface that explicitly elicits and interacts with a user model. Interfaces like this are common for managing user profiles in many applications, with the important difference that PLUS envisages that all such interfaces be treated as evidence sources for a person's user model (rather than a set of flags for a particular application or machine).

The third class of evidence sources is the applications that people use for a diverse set of activities such as reading email or browsing the web. If these are personalised, they need to access the user model and may also contribute evidence directly to it. Conventional applications without personalisation may have no direct connection to the user model but they typically do leave electronic traces and these may be mined to provide user modelling evidence.

It is useful to distinguish two types of evidence from the sources described so far. Evidence from direct interaction with the user is *explicit* while evidence collected unobtrusively is of type *observation*. The important distinction is that if the user has a direct role, explicitly providing the evidence, they are more likely to be aware of it. The third class of evidence, *exmachina* comes from the machine's actions. For example, if a teaching system tells the student a fact, evidence about this suggests the student knows the fact. At the very least, the application may take account of what it has told the user so that it is not repetitive. The two other sources of evidence are *stereotypic* reasoning and knowledge-based *inference*. These are not normally connected to the outside world, or the user, making them quite different ground inferences based on evidence from user actions.

PLUS is based on *accretion/resolution*, a minimalist approach to managing long term user models [3, 4]. There are two basic operations: *accretion* describes the collection of evidence about the user from sources allowed to contribute to it. When an application needs to query the user model, the available and relevant evidence needs to be interpreted: this is *resolution*. The resolution confers considerable flexibility.

For the purposes of supporting user control, it is useful to identify the points in Figure 1 where the user may wish to exercise control. First, the user can exercise control at points shown by the lines flowing *into* the model: defining which evidence sources may contribute to their user model. The user may also control the classes of evidence allowed: explicit, observation, exmachina, stereotype and inference. The user can control the *outflow* arrows of the diagram. One mechanism operates in terms of which resolvers are available to an application. The user can also control which applications have access to particular classes of evidence, just as on the control of evidence into the model. For example, the user may allow an application to access only explicit evidence: then, the resolution process for that application only sees that class of evidence. Another level of control is in terms of the parts of the model, the components. Applications will typically be restricted to subsets of the components in the model. The user may also want to be able to scrutinise how the model was used in the past and what values its components had in the past: for this the resolver opereates as it did at that time, ignoring later evidence.

Although the basic ideas of accretion and resolution are quite simple, effective user interfaces to support it are not easy to build. They need to be designed so that they do not get in the way of the user's main goals and, at the same time, when the user wants to scrutinise, this has to be possible. Moreover, we would expect that most people will scrutinise their user models infrequently. The means the interface supporting scrutiny must be easy to learn.

Finally, Figure 1 shows personalised applications, which employ parts of the user model information to drive their interaction with the user. If a user is to be in control, they need to be able to scrutinise the way this personalization process operates, as well as the user model. This also poses interface design challenges, especially where the personalisation is complex.

3   Some Existing Elements of PLUS

The long term vision for PLUS is that the many sources of evidence about the user should be collected in that person's long term user model, with the user in control of what is allowed into the model as well as what and who can access it. In addition, the user model should be structured and, potentially, distributed with partial models available at the places that they are needed. We also need a collection of tools to support scrutability effectively, both for the user model itself and for personalised applications. It will also be critical to find ways to support the adaptive hypermedia author to create scrutably personalised systems. This section describes some elements we have so far created as part of this vision.

PLUS element: Personis-lite
Early implementations of the core of accretion/resolution are described in [3, 4]. More recently, we have created a light-weight implementation which we call Personis-lite. It operates as a library, used within applications. It has just two core operations: *ask* to request a resolved set of component values, where these can be arbitrary lists; *tell* to provide a piece of evidence for a component of the model, within a nominated user-model context.

PLUS element: Personis-plus
Although Personis-lite is very simple, it has been used in several projects, some of which are described in the next section. Personis-plus provides two important extensions. First it make the user model available as a server, essentially a new light-weight Personis [4], omitting its security model. This supports construction of a collection of distributed models. Personis-plus also offers active models: an active component has one or more rules associated with it. When the component changes, the triggers are evaluated, testing for an arbitrary pattern across any user model components. On a match, the rule action can be either a *tell*, adding evidence to a component of a model or a *notify*, which sends a message to a server, for example, informing an application of relevant changes in the model. In parallel with these enhancements on Personis-lite, we have applied the same approach to modelling the elements of a ubiquitous computing environment: sensors, devices, services and places [5].

PLUS element: VCM
VCM, the verified concept mapper [6] is an example of an elicitation interface. Essentially, it is similar to a conventional concept mapping interface with some added functions. When the user reaches a stopping point in the mapping process, they request analysis of the map. VCM then asks them questions about aspects that are important and appear to be missing. It also summarises its conclusions about the user. The principle is that, once the user has completed the map, they are explicitly told what has been inferred about them, from that map.

PLUS element: SIV
SIV, Scrutable Inference Viewer [7], is our most mature exploration of an interface to a large user model. It has been built upon VLUM, Very Large User Model Viewer [8], which has been demonstrated as an effective interface to models with up to 700 concepts presented on the screen at once. SIV is structured by an ontology, providing a more effective and intuitive organisation of the display. It also supports ontological inference: in learning contexts, it is common to have much fine grained user modelling evidence and the ontology enables the learner to see inferred models of coarser grained aspects. This work is just one part of an increasing exploration of a variety of interfaces and visualisations for user models [9].

PLUS element: METASAUR
This is a tool for marking up the metadata on learning objects. It makes use of SIV.. It is tightly linked to the user modelling, since it is helpful if there is a close correspondence between the metadata and the user models created when learners interact with the associated learning objects.

PLUS application: SASY, scrutably adaptive hypermedia
SASY [10] has explored the challenges of supporting scrutable adaptation in hypermedia where the adaptation process selectively includes or excludes content or links, based on boolean expressions on the user models. Each SASY web page has a cell at the right showing the parts of the model that played a role in the personalisation on the current page. Each of these has a link labelled, *Why?* This brings up the Evidence Tool which gives an explanation of the value of the component in terms of the evidence that

determines its value. The Highlight Tool, also available at the right of each screen, changes the main adapted page to show which aspects were included for this user, along with the condition that caused the selection. Similarly, omitted sections are indicated. The profiles tool shows the user model, its possible resolved values, current value and an explanation of the meanings of the values. SASY content is created in its own XML variant called ATML, Adaptive Tutorial Markup Language. SASY provides a shell for creating adaptive hypertext which supports both scrutiny of the user model and the personalisation built upon it.

PLUS application: JITT SATS
SATS, Scrutably Adaptive Teaching System is a framework for building a tutor with variable teaching strategies and support for scrutiny of the teaching strategy as well as the user model. It was used as a base for JITT, the Just in Time Teaching System [11] which uses a workflow of a process in a workplace to structure delivery of learning content. The goal is that as people in an organisation need to know some aspect, as modelled in the workflow of a process they are working through, JITT presents the relevant material. If there are multiple paths through the workflow, the employee need only learn those aspects needed for the paths relevant to them. JITT has a scrutable user model on its profile page. For each workflow, it shows the associated concepts and a skillometer for the employee's knowledge of each. Alongside each is a link to a screen with the evidence for each and an explanation of how it was interpreted. JITT offers the user the option of changing the resolver, so that evidence is interpreted differently. For example, one person may decide that certain classes of evidence are less important for them. JITT also offers the option of changing the teaching agent, selecting one from a set available. Like SASY, SATS is a step beyond just scrutability of the user model, in this case supporting scrutability and control over the teaching strategy.

4   Demonstrator Applications

This section describes some of the demonstrator applications that have been built with existing PLUS tools and the accretion/resolution approach.

PLUS application: Reflect
Reflect [12] is a particularly interesting exploration of scrutability. It adds a knowledge layer to a teaching tool, Assess, which aimed to help students learn a complex design skill. It has two main parts: synthesis and analysis. The synthesis stage requires a learner to solve a program, for example writing a small program. In the analysis stage, the learner assesses this solution according to teacher-specified criteria. The learner then reads a set of example answers, assessing each of these. The system compares student answers against those expected by the teacher, using this to model the learner's knowledge. Reflect makes use of Personis-Lite for the modelling and SIV to display one form of the learner model.

PLUS element: MyPlace
When people come to an unfamiliar place, they need information about the relevant elements in it. MyPlace is a mobile adaptive hypertext that provides a personalised

view of the relevant parts of a pervasive computing environment [5, 13]. Depending upon the user's existing knowledge of the environment and the aspects that they are interest in, MyPlace can present details of nearby sensors, such as Bluetooth sensors, services, such as printers the person is allowed to use, places, such as the rooms they need to know about and people they know. It allows blurring of people's location information if they want that.

5 Research Agenda and Conclusions

This brief outline of PLUS has concentrated on the underpinnings and the elements we have already built. There is much yet to be done:

- Privacy and security are essential elements [1] and these will be very difficult to deal with effectively, with research needed to find suitable user interfaces and interaction mechanisms that are practical and effective;
- Machine learning to build scrutable stereotypes since these are so useful and powerful for personalisation [14-17];
- Pervasive computing, with user evidence, and possibly user models, embedded within environments is largely uncharted territory [18];
- Ontologies will need to play a critical role, especially in supporting explanations to users about the meaning of the user model components, as well as the more classical role of combining evidence by harmonising ontologies and providing scrutability of this;
- Interfaces to the details of the user model as we have begun to explore in SIV and others have been exploring [19, 20];
- Interfaces to the user modelling evidence as JITT has partly done;
- Interfaces to the personalisation processes as in SASY and as has been done by Bull et al [19];
- Tools to support authors of personalised hypermedia so that they can be scrutable;
- Scalability and efficiency of the modelling, including management of deletion;
- Evaluation of the effectiveness of scrutability [21].

The core of scrutability is that people should be able to scrutinise their user model and to determine what is being personalised and how. Hand-in-hand with supporting scrutability is the possibility for user control. Essential for achieving scrutability is that systems are designed, at all levels, so that scrutability is kept in mind and the designer is aware of trade-offs that include scrutability.

References

1. Kobsa, A.: Personalized Hypermedia and International Privacy. Communications of the ACM **45** (2002) 64-67
2. Kobsa, A., Koenemann, J., Pohl, W.: Personalized hypermedia presentation techniques for improving online customer relationships. The Knowledge Engineering Review **16** (2001) 111-155
3. Kay, J.: The um toolkit for cooperative user modelling. User Modeling and User-Adapted Interaction **4** (1995) 149-196

4. Kay, J., Kummerfeld, B., Lauder, P.: Personis: a server for user models. In: Bra, P.D., Brusilovsky, P., Conejo, R. (eds.): Adaptive Hypertext 2002. Springer (2002) 203 - 212
5. Carmichael, D.J., Kay, J., Kummerfeld, B.: Consistent Modelling of Users, Devices and Sensors in a Ubiquitous Computing Environment. User Modeling and User-Adapted Interaction **15** (2005) 197-234
6. Cimolino, L., Kay, J.: Verified Concept Mapping for Eliciting Conceptual Understanding. In: Aroyo, L., Dicheva, D. (eds.): ICCE Workshop on Concepts and Ontologies in Web-based Educational Systems, ICCE 2002, International Conference on Computers in Education. CS-Report 02-15 Technische Universiteit Eindhoven (2002) 9-14
7. Kay, J., Lum, A.: Exploiting readily available web data for scrutable student models. 12th International Conference on Artificial Intelligence in Education, Amsterdam, Netherlands (2005) 338-345
8. Uther, J., Kay, J.: VlUM, a web-based visualisation of large user models. User Modeling 2003 (2003) 198-202
9. Bull, S., Kay, J.: A framework for designing and analysing open learner modelling. In: Kay, J., Lum, A., Zapata-Rivera, D. (eds.): 12th International Conference on Artificial Intelligence in Education (AIED 05) Workshop 11, Amsterdam (2005) 81-90
10. Czarkowski, M., Kay, J.: Giving learners a real sense of control over adaptivity, even if they are not quite ready for it yet. In: Chen, S., Magoulas, G. (eds.): Advances in web-based education: Personalized learning environments. IDEA (2006) 93-125
11. Holden, S., Kay, J., Poon, J., Yacef, K.: Workflow-based personalised document delivery. International Journal on e-Learning **4** (2005) 131-148
12. Li, L., Kay, J.: Assess: promoting learner reflection in student self-assessment. 12th International Conference on Artificial Intelligence in Education (AIED 05) Workshop 11, Amsterdam, the Netherlands (2005)
13. Assad, M., Kay, J., Kummerfeld, B.: Models of people, places and devices for location-aware services (To appear). Pervasive 2006 (2006)
14. Merceron, A., Yacef, K.: A web-based tutoring tool with mining facilities to improve learning and teaching. 11th International Conference on Artificial Intelligence in Education (AIED03). IOS Press, Sydney (2003)
15. Merceron, A., Yacef, K.: TADA-Ed for educational data mining. Interactive Multimedia Electronic Journal of Computer-Enhanced Learning and Instruction **7** (2005)
16. Martin, E.M.: Learning scrutable user models: Inducing conceptual descriptions Knstliche Intelligenz (2002)
17. Mazza, R., Dimitrova, V.: CourseVis: Externalising student information to facilitate instructors in distance learning. In: Hoppe, F.V., Kay, J. (eds.): Artificial Intelligence in Education. IOS Press (2003) 279-286
18. Cheverst, K., Byun, H.E., Fitton, D., Sas, C., Kray, C., Villar, N.: Exploring Issues of User Model Transparency and Proactive Behaviour in an Office Environment Control System. User Modeling and User-Adapted Interaction **15** (2005) 235-273
19. Bull, S., Brna, P., Pain, H.: Extending the scope of the student model. User Modeling and User-Adapted Interaction **5** (1995) 45-65
20. Beck, J., Stern, M., Woolf, B.P.: Cooperative Student Models. In: du Boulay, B., Mizoguchi, R. (eds.): Artificial Intelligence in Education. IOS Press, Amsterdam (1997) 127-134
21. Mitrovic, A., Martin, B.: Evaluating the effects of open student models on learning. In: de Bra, P., Brusilovsky, P., Conejo, R. (eds.): The 2nd International Conference on Adaptive Hypermedia and Adaptive Web-based Systems, Vol. 296-305. Springer-Verlag, Berlin Heidelberg (2002)

Adapting NLP to Adaptive Hypermedia

Jon Oberlander

School of Informatics
University of Edinburgh
2 Buccleuch Place
Edinburgh EH8 9LW, UK
J.Oberlander@ed.ac.uk

Abstract. Natural Language Processing (NLP) techniques ought to be really useful for people building adaptive hypermedia (AH) systems. This talk explores the gap between theory and practice, illustrating it with examples of things that do (and don't work), and it suggests a way of closing the gap. The examples are mainly drawn from collaborative work I've been involved with over the last decade, on a series of AH systems using NLP: ILEX, SOLE, M-PIRO and Methodius. In theory, NLP sub-systems should help find, filter and format information for representation in AH systems. So there ought to be lots of cross-fertilisation between NLP and AH. It is true that some projects have effectively brought them together; particularly on the formatting—or information presentation—side, natural language generation systems have allowed quite fine-grained personalisation of information to the language, interests and history of individual users. But in practice, NLP has been less useful to AH than one might have expected. Now, one reason for this is that the information to be presented has to come from somewhere, and NLP support for AH authors is not as good as it should be. Arguably, where NLP could really make a difference is on the finding and filtering side. State-of-the-art information extraction tools can increase author productivity, and help make fine-grained personalisation more practical.

V. Wade, H. Ashman, and B. Smyth (Eds.): AH 2006, LNCS 4018, p. 20, 2006.
© Springer-Verlag Berlin Heidelberg 2006

Cross-Technique Mediation of User Models

Shlomo Berkovsky[1], Tsvi Kuflik[1], and Francesco Ricci[2]

[1] University of Haifa, Haifa
slavax@cs.haifa.ac.il, tsvikak@is.haifa.ac.il
[2] ITC-irst, Trento
ricci@itc.it

Abstract. Nowadays, personalization is considered a powerful approach for designing more precise and easy to use information search and recommendation tools. Since the quality of the personalization provided depends on the accuracy of the user models (UMs) managed by the system, it would be beneficial enriching these models through mediating partial UMs, built by other services. This paper proposes a cross-technique mediation of the UMs from collaborative to content-based services. According to this approach, content-based recommendations are built for the target users having no content-based user model, knowing his collaborative-based user model only. Experimental evaluation conducted in the domain of movies, shows that for small UMs, the personalization provided using the mediated content-based UMs outperforms the personalization provided using the original collaborative UMs.

1 Introduction

The quantity of information available on the Web grows rapidly and exceeds our limited processing capabilities. As a result, there is a pressing need for intelligent systems providing personalized services according to user's needs and interests, and delivering tailored information in a way most appropriate to the user [10]. Providing personalized services to the users requires modeling their preferences, interests and needs. This data is referred in the literature as a User Model (*UM*) [8].

Typically, service providers build and maintain proprietary UMs, tailored to the application domain of the service and to the specific personalization technique being exploited. Since the accuracy of the provided personalized service heavily depends on the characteristics and quality of the UMs, different services would benefit from enriching their UMs through importing, translating and aggregating partial UMs, i.e., UMs built by other, possibly related, services. This can be achieved through *mediation* of partial UMs [2].

The main functionality of UM *mediator* [2] is to acquire partial UMs built by other service providers, and to aggregate the acquired UMs into a UM for the target service. Analysis of the state-of-the-art personalization techniques and application domains yields four groups of services that can potentially provide valuable partial UMs for building a UM for a service from domain d exploiting technique t: (1) services from d that also exploit t, (2) services from d that exploit another technique t', (3) services

V. Wade, H. Ashman, and B. Smyth (Eds.): AH 2006, LNCS 4018, pp. 21–30, 2006.

from another, relatively similar, domain d' that also exploit t, and (4) services from another, relatively similar, domain d' that exploit another technique t'.

Clearly, for the first group of services, the mediation of partial UMs is quite simple, as both the content and the representation of the UMs are similar. Although the mediation should still cope with semantic heterogeneity of the UMs, e.g., synonyms or multilinguality, this can be resolved through adapting the solutions proposed by the Data Integration community [3]. This is not the case for the second and third group of services. Mediation of the UMs, whether represented according to a different personalization technique, or representing a different application domain, requires identifying the relationships between the knowledge modeled by the source UMs and the knowledge required by the target UM. This can be achieved through exploiting a rich semantic *Knowledge Base* (KB), covering both the target and the source UMs, which will actually facilitate the translation of the 'overlapping' (i.e., stored by the source and needed by the target) parts of the UMs. The above two types of mediation will be referred to as *cross-technique* and *cross-domain* mediations[1], respectively.

This paper focuses on cross-technique mediation of partial UMs from collaborative filtering recommender systems, where a vector of explicit ratings on a set of objects is provided by a user [5], to a content-based UM, represented as a list of the user's preferences [9]. The mediation exploits a KB facilitating the identification of commonalities in positively or negatively rated objects, as derived by the collaborative filtering UM, and generalizing them into a weighted list of topics liked/disliked by the user.

The proposed mediation mechanism was implemented, and its accuracy was evaluated using EachMovie, a publicly available movie ratings dataset. IMDb database (The Internet Movie Database, *http://www.imdb.com*) was exploited for extracting the features of the rated movies, such as genre, actors, directors etc. Then, the UMs mediation was accomplished through translating the collaborative ratings, of the user to whom a recommendation is to be provided, into a weighted list of liked/disliked features. The translation was based on the assumption that user's rating on a movie steadily reflect her/his preferences of the features of the movies, such as preferred genre, or director. The generated UMs served as a basis for generating content-based predictions. Two experiments were performed. The first was designed to fine-tune and optimize the predictions generation mechanism, while the second actually evaluated the accuracy of the predictions using the well-known Mean Average Error (MAE) metric [6]. Experimental results demonstrate high accuracy of the generated predictions, validating usefulness of the collaborative to content-based translation, and demonstrating the applicability of cross-technique mediation of UMs.

The rest of the paper is organized as follows. Section 2 briefly presents prior research efforts on mediation and aggregation of UMs. Section 3 describes the proposed approach for cross-technique UM mediation and elaborates on translation of collaborative filtering UMs to content-based UMs. Section 4 presents and discusses the experimental results, and section 5 concludes and presents future research topics.

---

[1] Note that currently our research does not deal yet with a combination of cross-technique and cross-domain mediations, since this would require multiple translations of partial UMs, which may 'contaminate' the original data.

2 Mediation and Aggregation of User Models

Centralized generation of the UMs, as a composition of partial UMs stored by different personalization services, is proposed in [7]. To accomplish this, each service maintains a mechanism for extracting the relevant parts of the central UM, and updating the central UM after the service is provided. A similar approach is discussed in [11], proposing to use Unified User Context Model (UUCM) for improving the partial UMs built by individual services. To provide personalization, services extract the required data from the UUCM, deliver the service, and update the UUCM. However, the centrality of the UM poses a severe privacy problem that should be resolved.

In recommender systems, many prior works on *hybrid* recommender systems tried to integrate multiple techniques in the prediction generation process [4]. Hybrid recommenders usually combine two or more techniques to improve predictions accuracy, but they are not concerned with the conversion of UMs between the techniques. Other related approach is presented in [12], that integrates collaborative and content-based techniques by basing collaborative-based similarity assessments on the content-based UMs. In [1], the authors extract content-based UMs from collaborative UMs and use both of them for the purposes of the predictions generation. Conversely, the current work focuses on generation of pure content-based predictions, based solely on the UM provided by the mediator. As such, it can not be classified as a hybrid one.

3 Collaborative Filtering to Content-Based Translation of UMs

Collaborative filtering is probably one of the most popular recommendation techniques. It recognizes cross-user correlations and generates predictions by weighing the opinions of similar users [5]. The input for the collaborative filtering is a matrix of users' ratings on a set of items, where each row represents ratings of a single user and each column represents ratings on a single item. Thus, collaborative filtering UMs are represented as ratings vectors $UM_{CF}=\{i_1:r_1, i_2:r_2, ..., i_n:r_n\}$, where every pair $i_k:r_k$, corresponds to a real rating r_k provided by the user on an item i_k.

Content-based filtering [9] builds personalized recommendations by taking as input: (1) the features of items that have been rated by the user, and (2) the set C of available items, not yet rated by the user, i.e., the candidate recommendations. The output recommendation is a subset of C, containing items whose features match the features of items which were preferred by the user. Content-based recommenders generate recommendations based on the set of features weighed according to a predefined scale, such as like/dislike or a number between 0 and 1. Thus, content-based UMs are represented as a list $UM_{CB}=\{f_1:w_1, f_2:w_2, ..., f_n:w_n\}$, where f_k denotes one of the domain features and w_k the level of the user's preference regarding this feature.

For instance, a collaborative UM for movie recommendations is a collection of movies and their respective ratings, explicitly provided by the user. Consider the following sample $UM_{CF}=\{$"The Lord of The Rings":1, "The Matrix":0.8, "Psycho":0.2, "Friday the 13th":0, "Star Wars":0.9, "The Nightmare":0.1", "Alien":0.9}, built on a continuous scale of ratings between 0 to 1. Although a collaborative UM represents the user as a set of ratings, it can be recognized that the user likes science-fiction movies, and dislikes horror movies. Thus, content-based UM of the user may be similar to $UM_{CB}=\{science\text{-}fiction\text{:}0.9,\ horror\text{:}0.1\}$, where the genre weights are computed as an average of the ratings given to the movies in this genre. Similarly to the genre weights, also the weights of other features, such as, directors and actors can be computed.

To handle the translation of collaborative UMs into content-based UMs, a rich movies' KB is needed for identifying the content of the movies, and providing the required lists of genres, actors, directors, and so forth. In this work, an offline version of the IMDb movie database (*http://www.imdb.com*) served as the translation KB. IMDb provides information in *49* feature categories, such as genre, actors, directors, writers, cinematographers, composers, keywords, languages, etc. For the sake of simplicity, only 7 feature categories were used in this work: *genres, keywords, actors, actresses, directors, production countries* and *languages*, as these categories seem to most affect the user's decision in selecting a movie.

Translating collaborative UMs to content based UMs takes the user's ratings vector as an input. Since different users may express their ratings in different ways (e.g., rating *4*, provided by a user whose average rating is *2* should be treated differently than rating *4* provided by a user whose average is *3.5*), users' ratings were normalized in order to eliminate individual differences between users. This was done by subtracting the average rating of the user from the provided ratings.

For each movie rating in a collaborative UM, a list of a movie's features (in the above categories) was extracted from IMDb. The weights of the features were updated according to the normalized rating of the movie, provided by the collaborative vector. In other words, the normalized rating of the movie was added to the weights of all the movie genres, actors and directors involved in the movie (and similarly for all the remaining categories). In addition, the number of occurrences for each feature, i.e., the number of movies rated by the user and having that feature was recorded.

For example, consider the rating *"Star Wars":0.9*, given by a user whose average rating is *0.6*. According to the IMDb, the genres of *"Star Wars"* are *action, adventure, fantasy* and *science-fiction*. Thus, the existing weights of these four features are increased by *0.3*. Similarly, the weights of the movie director *George Lucas*, and all the actors involved in the movie are increased by *0.3*. The number of occurrences for the above genres, *George Lucas*, all the actors and other features is increased by one.

After the content-based UM is generated, the user is modeled as a set of weights $\{w_{i(1)}, ..., w_{i(k)}\}$ for a subset of size k (depending on the user) features available in the 7 categories, and corresponding feature frequencies $\{c_{i(1)}, ..., c_{i(k)}\}$. Hence, a predicted rating for a movie m can be generated by extracting from IMDb all the relevant features of m and computing the prediction as a weighted average of the weights of the features that are both in the UM and in the movie description:

$$rating(m) = \frac{\displaystyle\sum_{j \in F(u) \cap F(m)} w_j c_j}{\displaystyle\sum_{j \in F(u) \cap F(m)} c_j}$$

where $F(u)$ are the features in the user model and $F(m)$ are the features in the movie model. Finally, a movie with the highest prediction is recommended to the user.

Note that the predictions are generated solely based on content-based UM, which is derived from the collaborative UM. As such, the predictions mechanism is capable of building content-based predictions regardless of the number of ratings available for the given movie. Therefore, this approach resolves the well-known *first-rater problem* in collaborative filtering [5], where an item cannot be recommended unless it was already rated by a sufficient number of users. Nevertheless, as a pure content-based recommender, it may suffer from an inherent *serendipity problem*, i.e., it can recommend only movies that are similar to the movies already rated by the user.

3.1 Fine-Tuning of the Prediction Mechanism

Although the proposed mechanism is capable of generating predictions regardless of the number of available ratings on a movie, it may suffer from instability (i.e., undesired fluctuations affected by minor factors). Since IMDb contains a lot of information for each movie, content-based UMs built from collaborative UMs containing a dozen of ratings only include thousands of features of actors, actresses and keywords occurring only once. This is explained by the fact that hundreds of actors and actresses are involved in every movie, while the number of genres or directors is at most *3-4*. As the UM accumulates movie data, the number of such *once-occurring* features increases, and they add noise to the prediction mechanism by becoming a dominant factor and 'blurring' the important features. In addition to once-occurring features, content-based UMs typically store a large number of *neutral* features, i.e., features to which the user is indifferent, which are sometimes rated positively and sometimes negatively. As a result, their weight is close to *0*, regardless of the number of occurrences in the UM. Similarly to once-occurring features, a large number of neutral features also adds noise to the prediction mechanism by 'blurring' the *differentiating* features.

To filter the influence of once-occurring and neutral features, two thresholds were defined: (1) *min-occurs* – minimal number of occurrences for a feature, and (2) *confidence* – minimal weight of a feature. The prediction mechanism was modified to take into account only those features, that occur at least *min-occurs* times, and whose weight is above *confidence* or below *-confidence* threshold. However, the weight of a feature depends on the number of occurrences of the feature. Thus, a *normalized weight* of the features was computed by dividing the weight of a feature in the content-based UM by the number of occurrences of that feature. The following pseudo-code describes the fine-tuned recommendation generation process:

```
Recommend (Content-Based-UM u, set-of-movies M )
  foreach m∈ M
    retrieve F(m) = set-of-feature of m
    for each j∈ F(m)
      if j∈ F(u) AND |norm-w_j|>confidence AND c_j>min-occurs
        take j into account for prediction of rating(m)
    compute rating(m)
  return m with maximal predicted rating(m)
```

We note that the proposed prediction mechanism assigns equal weights for features across different categories, i.e., there is no additional weighing factor that reflects the importance of a category. Although the weighing issues are important, they fall beyond the scope of the current work.

4 Experimental Results

The above collaborative to content-based translation was tested over publicly available EachMovie dataset (*http://research.compaq.com/SRC/eachmovie/*). EachMovie is a collaborative filtering dataset, storing *2,811,983* ratings between *0* and *1* of *72,916* users on *1,628* movies. In our experiments, we selected a subset of *1,529* movies, which were identified in IMDb, and *47,988* users whose variance of ratings is not *0* (i.e., the ratings are not identical) that rated more than *10* movies. Thus, a total number of *2,667,605* ratings were obtained, producing a sparse dataset with a sparsity of *3.64%*. Most of the users in the dataset rated relatively few movies. Table 1 shows the distribution of the number of rated movies among the users:

Table 1. Distribution of ratings among the users in the dataset

rated movies	0 to 25	26 to 50	51 to 75	76 to 100	101 to 125	126 to 150	151 to 175	176 to 200	201 to 225	226 to 250	251 to 300	301 to 500	over 500
number of users	17,321	13,788	6,514	3,609	2,302	1,349	887	609	441	327	358	436	47

The first set of experiments was designed to fine-tune the prediction mechanism by selecting the most appropriate values for the *confidence* and *min-occurs* thresholds. To accomplish this, one of the thresholds was set to a constant, while the values of the second were gradually modified. For each value of the modified threshold, a subset of *1,000* users that rated at least *100* movies was selected, and for each one of them, *90%* of the ratings were defined as the training set and the remaining *10%* as the test set. Then, the collaborative UM was translated to the content-based UM, using only the ratings contained in the training part, and predictions for the movies in the test set were built according to the above prediction mechanism. Accuracy of the predictions using the given threshold values was evaluated by the well-known MAE metric [6].

To find the most appropriate value of *confidence*, *min-occurs* threshold was set to *min-occurs=2* for all the categories, and the values of *confidence* threshold were gradually increased from *0* to *0.5*. To provide an initial indication for different relative importance of different categories, the predictions were generated in two ways: (1) using features from all *7* categories, and (2) using features from all the categories, except *keywords*. We note that a high *confidence* threshold reduces the number of features in a UM and therefore ratings of some movies cannot be predicted. Hence, for each value of *confidence*, the prediction rate (i.e., the percentage of movies whose ratings were predicted) was computed. Figure 1 illustrates the results of the experiments. The horizontal axis shows the values of *confidence* threshold, and the vertical – the MAE and prediction rate values. The dotted curves show the prediction rate values, while the continuous ones the MAE. The dark curves show the results based on 7 categories, while the light curves are based on 6 categories, excluding *keywords*.

As can be seen, MAE values initially slightly decrease with the *confidence*, and then monotonically increase. This is explained by the influence of neutral features. If the *confidence* threshold is low, and neutral features are not filtered, they add noise to

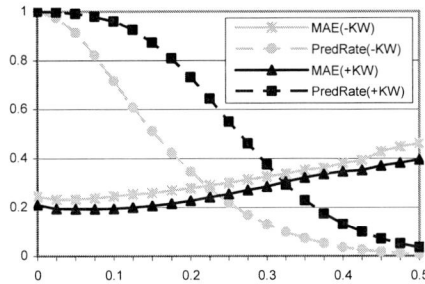

Fig. 1. MAE and prediction rate vs. *confidence* threshold

the prediction mechanism and the MAE is higher. When the *confidence* increases, neutral features are filtered and MAE decreases. However, high values of the *confidence* filter also differentiating features, and MAE increases again. Thus, *confidence=0.025* was chosen as an optimal value, where the MAE is minimal and prediction rate is high (over *0.99*). Prediction rate monotonically decreases with *confidence*, since when more features are filtered, the task of generating a prediction is harder to accomplish. Note the difference between the experiments including and excluding the *keywords* features in prediction generation. Both metrics of MAE and prediction rate show that it is beneficial to take the keywords into account.

After determining the value of *confidence* threshold it was used for choosing the optimal value of the *min-occurs* threshold. Considering *min-occurs*, we observed two different situations corresponding to two types of categories. For the first one, such as *genres* or *languages*, the number of possible features is low. As a result, the *min-occurs* threshold is relatively high. For the second, such as *actors* or *keywords*, the number of possible features is very high, and the *min-occurs* threshold is low. The categories were separated, and the same methodology was used to determine the optimal *min-occurs* value for each category. The value of the *confidence* threshold was set to *0.025*, and the values of the *min-occurs* thresholds were gradually modified to determine the optimal threshold. Note that for each category, a separate experiment was conducted where the predictions were generated based only on the features of this category, and MAE and prediction rate values were computed as a function of the *min-occurs* threshold. The experiment was conducted for the same *1,000* users that rated at least *100* movies. Due to a lack of space, figure 2 illustrates the results of the experiments for two representative categories: *genres* (left) and *keywords* (right). In both experiments, the horizontal axis shows the percentage of the rated movies containing the given feature and the vertical – the MAE and prediction rate values.

The results show that for the *genres* category, MAE monotonically increases with *min-occurs*. Thus, filtering of *genres* features hampers the accuracy of the generated predictions, and practically, any feature from this category is valuable. This means that the optimal *min-occurs* threshold for the *genres* category is 0. Conversely, the *keywords* MAE curve behaves similarly to the *confidence* curve. It initially decreases with *min-occurs*, filtering the noisy features, and then monotonically increases, as for a higher *min-occurs* threshold, also important features with a high number of occurrences are being filtered. As for the prediction rate, it monotonically decreases with *min-occurs*. Similarly to the *confidence* threshold, this is explained by the fact that the high threshold filters important features, and the prediction generations are harder.

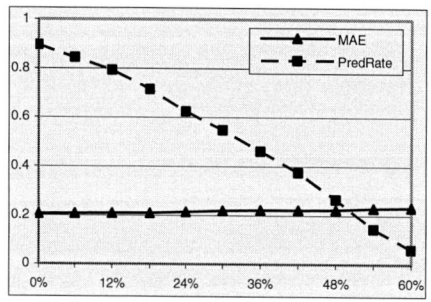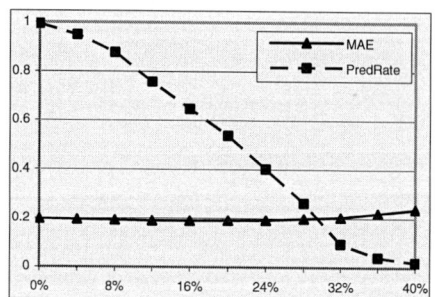

Fig. 2. MAE and prediction rate vs. *min-occurs* threshold for *genres* (left) and *keywords* (right) categories

Similar behavior was also observed for other categories. For categories with a small number of possible features, such as *production countries* and *languages*, any filtering hampers the MAE, and therefore, the optimal *min-occurs* threshold is *min-occurs=0*. For categories with a large number of features, such as *actors*, *actresses* and *directors*, initial filtering improves the MAE, whereas additional increase of *min-occurs* threshold causes the MAE to monotonically increase. The following table summarizes the optimal values of the *min-occurs* threshold for different categories:

Table 2. Values of min-occurs threshold for features from different categories

category	genres	keywords	actors	actresses	directors	countries	languages
min-occurs (%)	0	12	2	1.2	0.45	0	0

The determined *min-occurs* and *confidence* thresholds were applied in the second set of experiments, designed to compare the original collaborative and content-based recommendations. In principle, the collaborative and content-based recommenders are designed to recommend different types of movies. A collaborative recommender will recommend movies rated positively by similar users, while a content-based – movies similar to the movies that were rated highly by the user. Thus, the best experiment would be generating *sets* of recommended movies and conducting user studies evaluating these sets. Since we were unable to conduct such experiments, the accuracy of the generated predictions was compared using the MAE metric [6].

For this experiment, the users in the dataset were again partitioned into *12* groups of users, according to the number of rated movies[2]. *325* users were selected from each group, and the collaborative UM of each selected user was partitioned to *90%* training set and *10%* test set. Then, two types of predictions were generated: collaborative predictions based on the collaborative training set UM, and content-based predictions based on the translated content-based UM. For each group, collaborative and content-based

---

[2] In the first experiment, we selected *1,000* users that rated at least *100* movies. For the second experiment, we defined *12* groups of *325* users each, a total of *3,900* users. Although there is overlapping, it is partial, and it is only for groups of users with over *100* rated movies.

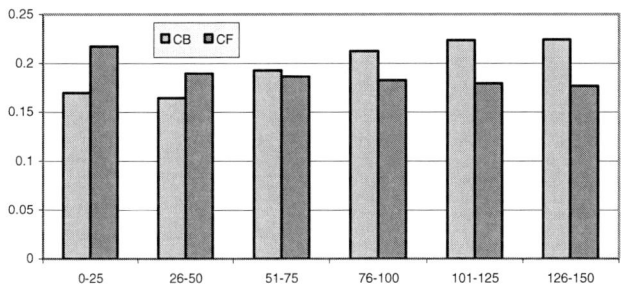

Fig. 3. MAE of content-based (left, light columns) and collaborative (right, dark columns) prediction vs. the number of rated movies in the UM

MAE values were computed. Figure 3 shows the MAE values. The horizontal axis reflects the number of users in a group, while the vertical axis stands for the MAE. Due to the lack of space, MAE values of the first 6 groups only are shown.

The chart shows that the MAE of content-based predictions for the UMs containing below 50 movies is relatively low, approximately 0.17. This is explained by the observation that for a low number of rated movies in the UM, it is easy to find the weights of differentiating content-based features, while the number of neutral features is still low, and they do not dominate in the predictions generation. For larger UMs, between 50 and 100 movies, the MAE increases with the number of rated movies. We conjecture that this happens due to a larger number of neutral features, which hamper the accuracy of the generated prediction. Finally, for UMs with over 100 rated movies, the MAE stabilizes at approximately 0.22. For most of the groups, the prediction rate is over 0.99 (except the group of less than 25 movies, where it is 0.974). This means that predictions can be computed for almost every movie.

Comparison of the content-based and collaborative MAE values shows that for below 50 rated movies in the UM, pure content-based prediction based on the translated artificial UMs outperforms collaborative predictions, based on the original UMs. According to table 1, 64.8% of the users in the dataset rated up to 50 movies. Thus, improving the predictions accuracy in this range is extremely important. Since the accuracy of the collaborative predictions for this size of the UMs is quite low, translation of the UMs and further content-based predictions provide a solid alternative technique. For a larger number of rated movies in the UMs, collaborative predictions outperform the content-based ones. However, the difference in the MAE is smaller than 0.05, which indicates a reasonable performance of content-based predictions. We conjecture that weighing categories and specific features may significantly improve the accuracy of content-based predictions also for larger UMs.

5   Conclusions and Future Research

This work presents cross-technique mediation of UMs and demonstrates the feasibility of translating from collaborative to content-based UMs, allowing a content-based recommender to generate recommendations for a new user, whose UM was imported from a collaborative recommender. The experimental study first focused on determining the thresholds which filter out irrelevant and neutral features. Then, the thresholds were applied and the accuracy of the generated content-based predictions was evaluated and compared to the accuracy of the original collaborative predictions. The experiments showed that for a small number of rated movies in the UMs (typical for most users), the accuracy of content-based predictions is higher than that of collaborative-based prediction. This leads to the conclusion that cross-technique mediation of the UMs is feasible, and can also improve the quality of the personalization provided.

The discussed prediction mechanism is quite simple, as it assigns equal weights to different categories of the UM data. In the future, we plan to exploit various learning techniques to infer the weights of the categories and specific features within the categories. We believe this will significantly improve the accuracy of the personalization provided and strengthen the proposed cross-technique mediation. We also plan to extensively evaluate the proposed approach for other cross-technique mediations (e.g., the reverse translation, from content-based to collaborative UMs) and in different application domains.

References[3]

[1] C.Basu, H.Hirsh, W.Cohen, *"Recommendation as Classification: Using Social and Content-Based Information in Recommendation"*, in proc. of the AAAI Conference, 1998.

[2] S.Berkovsky, *"Decentralized Mediation of User Models for a Better Personalization"*, in proc. of the AH Conference, 2006.

[3] P.A.Bernstein, S.Melnik, *"Meta Data Management"*, in proc. of the ICDE Conference, 2004.

[4] R.Burke, *"Hybrid Recommender Systems: Survey and Experiments"*, in User Modeling and User-Adapted Interaction, vol.12(4), p.331-370, 2002.

[5] J.L.Herlocker, J.A.Konstan, A.Borchers, J.Riedl, *"An Algorithmic Framework for Performing Collaborative Filtering"*, in proc. of the SIGIR Conference, 1999.

[6] J.L.Herlocker, J.A.Konstan, L.G.Terveen, J.T.Riedl, *"Evaluating Collaborative Filtering Recommender Systems"*, in ACM Trans. on Information Systems, vol.22(1), p.5-53, 2004.

[7] J.Kay, B.Kummerfeld, P.Lauder, *"Managing Private User Models and Shared Personas"*, in proc. of the UbiUM Workshop, 2003.

[8] A.Kobsa, *"Generic User Modeling Systems"*, in User Modeling and User-Adapted Interaction, vol.11(1-2), p.49-63, 2001.

[9] M.Morita, Y.Shinoda, *"Information Filtering Based on User Behavior Analysis and Best Match Retrieval"*, in proc. of the SIGIR Conference, 1994.

[10] M.D.Mulvenna, S.S.Anand, A.G.Buchner, *"Personalization on the Net Using Web Mining"*, in Communications of the ACM, vol.43(8), p. 123-125, 2000.

[11] C.Niederee, A.Stewart, B.Mehta, M.Hemmje, *"A Multi-Dimensional, Unified User Model for Cross-System Personalization"*, in proc. of the E4PIA Workshop, 2004.

[12] M.J.Pazzani, *"A Framework for Collaborative, Content-Based and Demographic Filtering"*, in Artificial Intelligence Review, vol.13(5-6), p.393-408, 1999.

[3] The authors would like to thank Boris Bolshem and Sveta Ogiyenko for their assistance with the implementation of the system.

Authoring Adaptive Learning Designs Using IMS LD

Adriana J. Berlanga[1], Francisco J. García[1], and Jorge Carabias[2]

[1] University of Salamanca, Department of Computer Science, Spain
{solis13, fgarcia}@usal.es
[2] Clay Formación Internacional, Salamanca, Spain
jorge@clayformacion.com

Abstract. Adaptive Educational Hypermedia Systems have the potential to deliver instruction tailored to the characteristics of each student. However, despite many years of research in the area, these systems have been used only in a few real learning situations. Reasons for this include their use of proprietary semantics in the definition of adaptivity and educational elements, and their lack of interoperation among courses and applications. We claim that an option to overcome these issues is to annotate adaptive rules, techniques, and learning elements using a common notational method, the IMS Learning Design (IMS LD). This paper presents a novel approach to define adaptive learning designs and, particularly, how adaptive hypermedia techniques and adaptive rules can be modelled by means of IMS LD.

1   Introduction

Research in the area of Adaptive Educational Hypermedia Systems (AEHS) has been conducted since 1996. Nevertheless, their application in real learning situations is rare. Reasons for this include their high cost of production, lack of credible evidence of their benefits, and limited subject matter coverage [17]. Additionally, these systems have been designed in such way that they cannot reuse or exchange educational elements, adaptive strategies, contents or adaptive rules.

An alternative to solve these problems is to model predefined rules, techniques, and learning elements using the IMS Learning Design specification (IMS LD) [11]. This will emphasize the importance of instructional strategies in AEHS, and could guide the description of pedagogical approaches tailored to both students' characteristics and knowledge properties. To support this argument, this paper outlines our work in the definition of Adaptive Learning Designs (ALD), which are designs with adaptive characteristics that can be modelled by means of IMS LD.

The rest of this paper is structured as follows: first, it reviews IMS LD and explains how it can be used to model elements and adaptive hypermedia techniques. Then, it presents the concept of ALDs, an authoring tool developed for defining them, and an evaluation performed to verify their adaptivity behaviour. Finally, it discusses the drawbacks of using IMS LD in the definition of adaptivity, mentions related work, and exposes conclusions.

V. Wade, H. Ashman, and B. Smyth (Eds.): AH 2006, LNCS 4018, pp. 31–40, 2006.

2   IMS Learning Design (IMS LD)

The objective of the IMS LD specification is to provide a framework of elements that can describe in a formal way any design of the teaching and learning process. Fig. 1 shows the hierarchically order of its main elements. The asterisk (*) represents that an element may occur more than once.

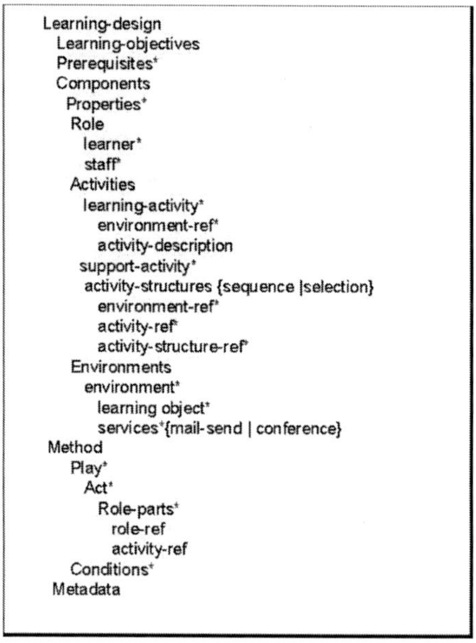

```
Learning-design
  Learning-objectives
  Prerequisites*
  Components
    Properties*
    Role
      learner*
      staff*
    Activities
      learning-activity*
        environment-ref*
        activity-description
      support-activity*
      activity-structures {sequence |selection}
        environment-ref*
        activity-ref*
        activity-structure-ref*
    Environments
      environment*
        learning object*
        services*{mail-send | conference}
  Method
    Play*
      Act*
        Role-parts*
          role-ref
          activity-ref
    Conditions*
  Metadata
```

Fig. 1. IMS LD main elements

One of the most promising features of IMS LD is its potential to annotate adaptation characteristics based on learner's preferences, pre-knowledge, and/or educational needs. This specification includes –in its Level B of compliance– elements like *properties* to store information about users, *global elements* to set and view the information of the properties, *monitor services* to read the properties, and *conditions* to manage and change the value of the properties [16]. Moreover, it includes specific elements for adapting learning activities, acts, plays, etc., such as <conditions> (which includes elements as <if>,<show>,<hide>), <when-property-value-is-set>, and <when-condition-true>.

3   AEHS and IMS LD

When IMS LD is used to structure and annotate the learning process, this specification can be seen as an ontology of the process [15], where a clear separation between the learning flow and its components (i.e. learning activities, resources, etc.) exists. Therefore, the use of IMS LD in AEHS guarantees the semantic description of its components and of the learning process. Likewise, the defined elements could be exchanged and reused among different AHES or applications compliant with IMS LD, and/or be modified, run and stored in IMS LD compliant tools.

3.1 Elements for Performing Adaptivity Using IMS LD

Elements for performing adaptivity using IMS LD are primarily a conjunction between two elements of IMS LD: <properties> and <conditions>. Table 1, which takes into account the learning conditions stated by Koper [14] and the elements for performing adaptivity proposed by Brusilovsky [4] and Kobsa *et al.* [13], presents a set of elements that can be used to perform adaptivity. Generally, these elements can be modelled using the IMS LD <property> element, but media characteristics are more suitable to be modelled using IMS LOM [12] elements, since this specification has elements that describe this kind of characteristics.

Table 1. Elements for performing adaptivity using IMS LD

Category	Options	Data type	Examples
[LO] Learning Objectives		String, Boolean	Knowledge, skills, attitude, competence
[LD] Learner Demographics	Age	Integer	
	Language	String, Boolean	Spanish, English, Dutch
[LC] Learner Characteristics	Pre-knowledge, Profile	String, Integer, Boolean, Percentage	
	Learning style	String, Boolean	Sensitive/intuitive, visual/verbal, sequential/global [9]
[LP] Learner Preferences	Level of detail	String, Boolean	Basic, medium, high
	Learning style	String, Boolean	
	Level of inter-activity type	String, Boolean	Linear/interactive
	Learning strategy	String, Boolean	Theory/practice; learning by example/learning by doing
[MC] Media Characteristics	Technical characteristics	Boolean, Integer	OS, bandwidth, hardware
	Communication	String, Boolean	Synchronous/asynchronous
	Media type	String, Boolean	Video, text, graphic
	Interactivity type	String, Boolean	Linear/interactive

3.2 Adaptive Hypermedia Techniques and IMS LD

Plays, acts, role-parts, activity sequences and learning activities can be adapted if IMS LD elements such as <conditions>, <hide>, <show>, <properties>, or <on-completion> are included to show certain learning activities, or to annotating learning sequences for adaptive navigation support (using the XHTML "class" attribute to annotate links).

For instance, Table 2 shows how some adaptive techniques [4] can be modelled using IMS LD. The elements on the third column, which contains the elements for performing adaptivity, are equivalent to those defined on Table 1 (i.e. the first column of Table 1 shows the meaning of the categories included on the last column of Table 2). Also, a prerequisite ([PRE]) element is included; this means that the adaptivity technique could be performed if the prerequisite of the learning activity has been completed.

Table 2. Adaptive Techniques and IMS LD

Adaptive Technique	Element	Elements for performing adaptivity (properties)
Direct guidance	Play I Act I Role-Part I Activity Sequence	[LO] I [PRE] I [LC] I [LP] I [LD] I [MC]
Curriculum sequencing	Play I Act I Role-Part I Activity Sequence	[LO] I [PRE] I [LC] I [LP] I [LD] I [MC]
Show/Hiding links	Play I Act I Role-Part I Activity Sequence I Learning Activities	[LO] I [PRE] I [LC] I [LP] I [LD] I [MC]
Link annotation	Play I Act I Role-Part I Activity Sequence I Learning Activities	[LO]I [PRE] I [LC] I [LP]
Inclusion of pages	Play I Act I Role-Part	[LO]I [PRE] I [LC] I [LP] I [LD]

4   Definition of Adaptive Learning Designs (ALD)

ALDs, which are semantically structured according to IMS LD, are learning designs that consider a set of predefined characteristics (i.e. knowledge, learning styles, etc.) in order to deliver personalized learning flows.

By means of a *Lego* metaphor [2], ALDs aim at combining the personalization and reusability characteristics of IMS LD. Each element of IMS LD (see Fig. 1) –such as learning objectives, prerequisites, learning activities, activity structures, methods, personalization properties, and adaptive rules (i.e. conditions)– is defined and stored as a separate object. This allows authors to reuse and interchange a complete ALD, but also each one of its elements. For instance, the learning object *LO-v* can be attached to the learning activity *LA-w* or to *LA-x*. Then, *LA-w* can be included into adaptive rule *RUL-x* or into *RUL-y*. In this manner, components can be reused and exchanged among different AEHS, applications and tools, and the definition of a new method of instruction does not imply to annotate learning activities, objectives, etc., that have been created before for other ALDs.

4.1   HyCo-LD: The Authoring Tool for ALD

In order to have an ALD authoring tool, we extended the functionality of a tool that supports the creation of hypermedia learning materials, the Hypermedia Composer (HyCo) [10]. This new tool, called HyCo-LD, follows the *Lego* metaphor explained before. Therefore, every element is defined independently from each other.

Furthermore, thanks to HyCo authoring facilities, learning objectives, prerequisites, learning activities, feedbacks, and learning contents can be defined as hypermedia resources (that could include URL, graphics, videos, and so on) and, later on, attached to ALDs elements.

For validating and running an ALD, HyCo-LD integrates the IMS LD engine CopperCore [5]. This means that HyCo-LD validates and generates the users and roles that this engine requires, and delivers an ALD through the CopperCore player. With this option designers can test how an ALD will behave, and students can have a straightforward option to interact with it.

Due to lack of space, this paper does not explain the definition of each element of ALDs. It focus on how adaptive rules can be created using HyCo-LD. A learning scenario modelled by means of an ALD can be found in [1].

4.2 Authoring Adaptive Rules for Novice Users

HyCo-LD has a wizard [3] for supporting novice users in the definition of basic adaptive techniques that can be managed as separate objects and included into learning methods. This wizard follows the definition of adaptive techniques described on Table 2, and the elements for performing adaptivity grouped on Table 1.

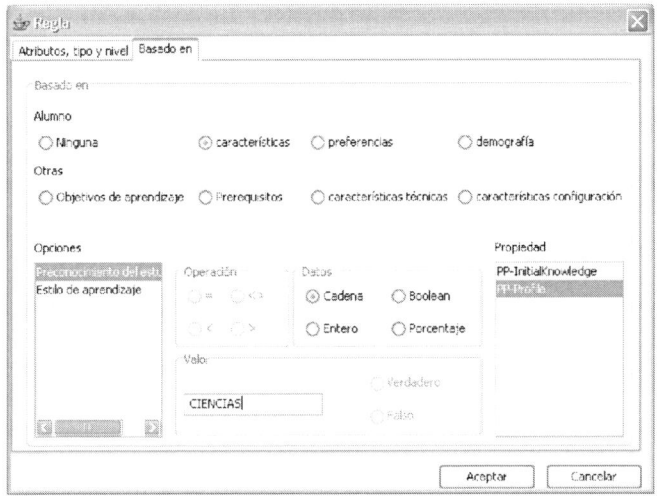

Fig. 2. Wizard to create adaptive hypermedia techniques

Fig. 2 shows the interface of the wizard. In the first tab (Attributes, type and level; "Atributos, tipo y nivel" in the interface) the type of the technique should be indicated (e.g. direct guidance) and its name and level (e.g. play, activity sequence or learning activity). Then, in the next tab, authors should select the element that will be the base of the adaptivity. The options are presented on Table 1 (elements for performing adaptivity), therefore, if the author selects a category option (i.e. second column of Table 1) (based on; "basado en" in the interface) then the list box will display the elements that contain that category (i.e. third column of Table 1). Afterwards, authors need to indicate the operation ("operación"), data ("datos") and value ("valor") of the selected element, as well as the value of the property ("propiedad") that will be taken into account to perform the adaptive technique.

4.3 Authoring Adaptive Rules for Expert Users

The definition of properties is not restricted for expert users. They can define direct guidance techniques using an expression-builder tool (see Fig. 3) that permits the creation of adaptive rules based on the IMS LD element <conditions> and its sub-elements using the following formalism (BNF notation):

$$\text{<adaptive-statement>} ::= \textbf{IF} \text{ <condition>} \textbf{ THEN } \text{<action>} \tag{1}$$

$$\text{<condition>} ::= \text{<operator-set>} [\text{ <property>} | \text{<role>}] \text{<value>} \tag{2}$$

$$\text{<action>} ::= [\textbf{<show>} | \textbf{<hide>}] \text{ <element-set>} \tag{3}$$

$$\text{<operator-set>} ::= [\text{<is member of role>} | \text{<is>} | \text{<greater than>} | \text{<divide>} | \text{<multiply>} | \text{<subtract>} | \text{<is not>} | \text{<sum>} | \text{<less than>} | \text{<no value>} | \text{<complete>}] \tag{4}$$

$$\text{<element-set>} ::= [\text{<learning activity>} | \text{<activity structure>} | \text{<play>}] \tag{5}$$

$$\text{<value>} ::= [\text{<integer>} | \text{<string>} | \text{<boolean>} | \text{<percentage>}] \tag{6}$$

Using this formalism, the expression-builder tool guides authors in the definition of adaptive rules. It shows a set of boxes that contain the operations ("operador" in the interface), properties ("propiedad"), roles ("roles"), and the elements created before that can be selected to define an adaptive rule: learning activities ("actividades de aprendizaje"), activity structures ("estructuras de actividades"), and plays ("ejecuciones"). From these boxes authors select the element they want to include in the rule. The tool guides them showing only the operator, property or element that can be chosen in each part of the rule.

4.4 Example of Authoring Adaptive Rules for Expert Users

To exemplify the creation of adaptive rules for expert users, we will define an adaptive rule that considers if the profile of the student is Sciences (e.g. s/he has studies on Computer Science) in order to present her or him a particular learning activity.

The first step is to define the personalization property that represents the variable (i.e. profile) that will be considered to adjust the learning flow, as well as the learning activity that represent the task that will be performed in order to reach a learning objective. By means of HyCo-LD authors can define these elements using the IMS LD specification [1]. To define personalization properties is necessary to indicate their title, URI, data-type, restrictions, initial-value, and metadata. For the example stated above, the title of the personalization property is "PP-Profile", its data-type "String", its restrictions "Sciences" or "Other", and its initial-value "Sciences".

To define learning activities in HyCo-LD is necessary to indicate their title, complete activity options, learning objectives, prerequisites, a description of the activity, and its feedback. For the example stated above, the title of the learning activity is "A.2. Basic concepts", it will be considered completed when the student decides, and its content and feedback have been defined as hypertexts using HyCo.

Once these elements have been created they can be included in the adaptive rule. By means of the expression-builder tool the adaptive rule can be created by selecting the personalization property defined previously ("PP-Profile") and indicating that its value ("valor" in Fig. 3) has to be "Sciences" to perform the adaptation rule

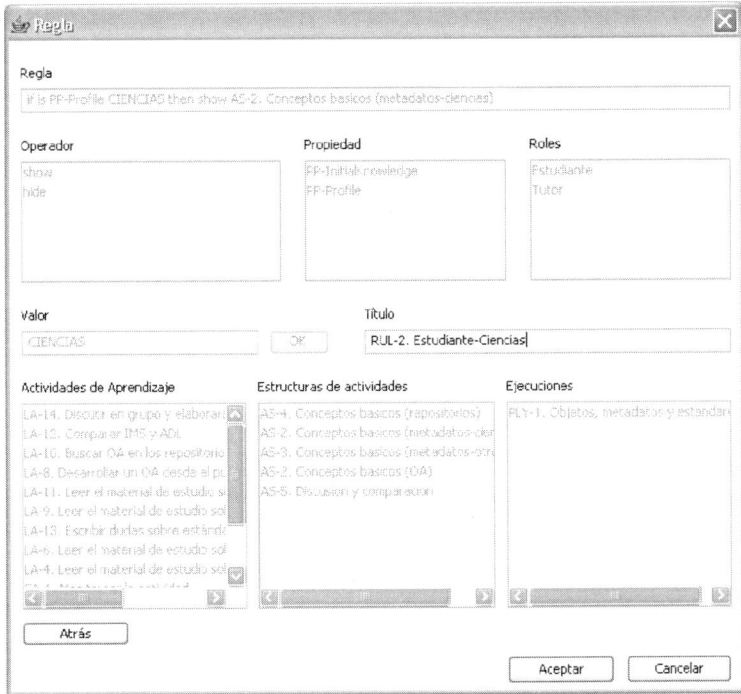

Fig. 3. Expression-builder tool to create adaptive rules

("Ciencias" in Fig. 3). Then, the learning activity "A.2. Basic concepts" ("A.2 Conceptos básicos" in Fig. 3) should be chosen. Finally, it is necessary to save the rule ("RUL-2. Estudiante-Ciencias" in Fig. 3). In this way, it can be included in different ALDs.

4.5 Evaluation of ALDs

A study to test an ALD was performed in a postgraduate course of the University of Salamanca. We choose a course directed to students from a wide range of backgrounds (e.g. computer science, education, social sciences, etc.) that will help us to test an ALD, its adaptivity behaviour, and the students' opinion about the learning experience.

We used HyCo-LD to design an ALD for the lesson "Introduction to Learning Technology". The ALD contained an act for each topic of the lesson: learning objects, metadata, repositories, and learning technology standards and specifications. Each one of them contained activity sequences that included the content of the lesson and learning activities. These activities were designed to motivate students to define examples of learning objects, to look for learning objects in repositories and to discuss the benefits and limitations of learning technologies.

We used the wizard to define a direct guidance technique that considered the prerequisites and the initial knowledge of the student, in order to present learning activities according to her/his characteristics. If the student did not have knowledge about the creation of learning materials for web-based courses then an introductory learning activity was suggested. Likewise, if the student knew markup languages (i.e. XML), then s/he had to perform a learning activity that required the use of metadata to identify a learning object according to the IMS LOM specification.

We also used the expression-builder-tool to depict an adaptive rule that showed a complementary topic once the student had finished all the learning activities of the ALD. First, the learning content of the lesson was presented and, when the student selected the option "completed", the learning activities were displayed. Once the learning activities were done, the next topic of the lesson was shown.

Students interacted with the ALD using the CopperCore player integrated in HyCo-LD. When they finished the lesson, which took them around three hours, we asked them to fill out a questionnaire aimed to collect feedback about various aspects of the ALD and its adaptivity behaviour. Out of 13 students in the class, 8 answered the questionnaire. The answers analysis established that 75% of the students regarded the lesson adequate to their initial knowledge and profile. The same percentage of students judged that the learning activities were helpful to understand the topic. However, 63% of them replied they would prefer to have control of the learning flow and be able to choose what activities perform first and in what order.

5   Discussion

Although IMS LD can be used to model ALDs, designing more complex adaptivity behaviour is not easy. For instance, the definition of the roles is static. They cannot be defined according to students' characteristics and they do not have properties that allow distinguishing between types of roles. Also, as IMS LD does not deal with content, it is not possible to define adaptive presentation techniques. Moreover, in IMS LD it is difficult to support multiple overlapping interactions, enforce the learning flow, and change the learning strategy [18] or the adaptivity conditions once a IMS LD package has been delivered (due to its "manifest-centred" representational schema).

The *Lego* metaphor and its implementation in HyCo-LD might be an option to avoid the creation of the same elements (e.g. learning activities, adaptive rules, etc.). One step further is distributing the repositories that store these elements on different servers and define adaptive conditions outside the ALDs (e.g. URL anchoring to different conditions). This might be a solution that will permit to change adaptivity conditions during the interaction and to store them outside the learning designs. In consequence, this kind of dynamic adaptation will modify the current learning design behaviour: from "system to student" to "student to system".

6   Related Work

The work presented in this paper is related to the authoring of AEHS where a separation between the learning flow and its components exists. A well known example in this domain is the LAOS model [6] that consists in five layers: domain model, goals and constraints model, user model, adaptation model, and presentation model. However, as it is based on AHAM [8], the pedagogical strategies are defined inside the adaptation model; as a result, it does not clearly separate the pedagogical strategies and the adaptation rules. Furthermore, the grammar for authoring adaptive rules [7] is proprietary – it might be difficult for authors without computer background–, and does not consider the use of learning technology specifications. Finally, it uses a set of semantics that makes impossible the reuse and interoperation of learning elements or adaptation rules among AHES or applications that do not use the proposed model.

Our approach, in contrast, uses a common notational method that separates the learning elements, adaptivity rules and pedagogical strategy in order to favour their reuse in systems and applications compliant with IMS LD. Moreover, it provides two ways for supporting novice and expert users in the definition of adaptive behaviour.

Other area related to the work presented in this paper is the use of IMS LD to create predefined rules and declarations for adaptivity. In this area, the aLFanet project [19] aim at offering intelligent adaptivity capabilities in a learning management system. Although this project investigates many aspects that are not related to our work (e.g. agents, runtime adaptation, etc.), the aLFanet LD Editor, as our proposal, closely represents the IMS LD structure. However, the authoring process does not consider the definition of adaptive techniques as our proposal does.

7   Conclusions and Future Work

A common notational method is needed for pushing forward the benefits of adaptivity and AEHS for a wide range of applications and systems. Although IMS LD is in its early phases of development and dissemination, it might be an option. One could argue that it is not intended for adaptivity and that it is more appropriated to develop a particular notational method. However, the dissemination of a particular notational method is not likely to be as widespread as specifications proposed by an international consortium, and there are fewer chances that commercial products will use it than employ IMS LD.

Currently, we are analysing the improvements HyCo-LD might need to make easier the creation of ALDs (e.g. templates, copy learning activities with other names, automatically create a learning activity from HyCo content, and so on), as well as designing new options for defining adaptivity and providing generalizations of these definitions. Then, we will perform experimental studies to evaluate the appropriateness of this tool for the authoring of ALDs.

Acknowledgements

Adriana J. Berlanga thanks the Mexican Council of Science and Technology (CONACyT) for its support. This work is partially supported by the Spanish Ministry of Education and Science (ref. TSI2005-00960).

References

1. Berlanga, A. J., García, F. J.: Authoring Tools for Adaptive Learning Designs in Computer-Based Education. In Proc. of Latin American Conference on Human-Computer Interaction. CLIHC 2005, Cuernavaca, México, vol. 124 ACM Press, New York, USA (2005) 190-201.

2. Berlanga, A. J., García, F. J.: IMS LD reusable elements for adaptive learning designs. Journal of Interactive Media in Education (Advances in Learning Design. Special Issue, eds. Colin Tattersall, Rob Koper) 11, (2005).
3. Berlanga, A. J., García, F. J.: Modelling Adaptive Navigation Support Techniques Using the IMS Learning Design Specification. In Reich, S. and Tzagarakis, M., (eds.) Proc. of Hypertext and Hypermedia. HT'05, Salzburg, Austria, ACM Press, New York, USA (2005) 148-150.
4. Brusilovsky, P.: Adaptive Hypermedia. User Modeling and User Adapted Interaction 11, (2001) 87-110.
5. CopperCore: SourceForge site, http://www.coppercore.org (2005).
6. Cristea, A. I., De Mooij, A.: LAOS: Layered WWW AHS Authoring Model with Algebraic Operators. In Proc. of 12th World Wide Web Conf. WWW2003. Alternate Paper Tracks, Budapest, Hungary, (2003).
7. Cristea, A. I., Verschoor, M.: The LAG Grammar for Authoring the Adaptive Web. In Proc. of International Conference on Information Technology, ITCC'04, Las Vegas, USA, IEEE Computer Society Press, Los Almitos, USA (2004) 382-386.
8. De Bra, P., Houben, G. J., Wu, H.: AHAM: A Dexter-based Reference Model for Adaptive Hypermedia. In Proc. Hypertext and Hypermedia. HT'99, ACM Press, New York, USA (1999) 147-156.
9. Felder, R. M., Silverman, L. K.: Learning and Teaching Styles in Engineering Education. Engineering Education 78,7, (1988) 674-681.
10. García, F. J., García, J.: Educational Hypermedia Resources Facilitator. Computers & Education 3, (2005) 301-325.
11. IMS LD: Learning Design specification v1, http://www.imsglobal.org/learningdesign (2003).
12. IMS LOM: Learning Resource Metadata specification v1.1.2, http://www.imsglobal.org/metadata (2001).
13. Kobsa, A. Koenemann, J., Pohl, W.: Personalized Hypermedia Presentation Techniques for Improving Online Customer Relationships. The Knowledge Engineering Review 16,2, (2001) 111-155.
14. Koper, R.: An Introduction to Learning Design, in *Learning Design. A Handbook on Modelling and Delivering Networked Education and Training*, Koper, R. and Tattersall, C., (eds.), Springer Verlag, The Netherlands (2005) 3-20.
15. Koper, R.: Use of the Semantic Web to Solve Some Basic Problems in Education. Journal of Interactive Media in Education. Special Issue on Reusing Online Resources 6, (2004).
16. Koper, R., Burgos, D.: Developing Advanced Units of Learning Using Learning Design Level B. International Journal on Advanced Technology for Learning 2,3, (2005).
17. Murray, T.: Design Tradeoffs in Usability and Power for Advanced Educational Software Authoring Tools. Educational Technology 44,5, (2004) 10-16.
18. Towle, B., Halm, M.: Design Adaptive Learning Environments with Learning Design, in *Learning Design. A Handbook on Modelling and Delivering Networked Education and Training*, Koper, R. and Tattersall, C., (eds.), Springer Verlag, The Netherlands (2005) 215-226.
19. Van Rosmalen, P., Boticario, J.: Using Learning Design to Support Design and Runtime Adaptation, in *Learning Design. A Handbook on Modelling and Delivering Networked Education and Training*, Koper, R. and Tattersall, C., (eds.), Springer Verlag, The Netherlands (2005) 291-301.

Ways of Computing Diverse Collaborative Recommendations*

Derek Bridge and John Paul Kelly

University College Cork,
Cork, Ireland
{d.bridge, jpk2}@cs.ucc.ie

Abstract. Conversational recommender systems adapt the sets of products they recommend in light of user feedback. Our contribution here is to devise and compare *four* different mechanisms for enhancing the diversity of the recommendations made by collaborative recommenders. Significantly, we increase diversity using collaborative data only. We find that measuring the distance between products using Hamming Distance is more effective than using Inverse Pearson Correlation.

1 Introduction

Recommender systems suggest products, services or information sources to their users. They differ in the way they find the items they recommend:

Content-based systems: The system stores a description of each available item. A user describes the item that she wants as a query or she describes the kinds of items that she likes as entries in a user profile. The system compares the user's descriptions against the store of item descriptions and recommends items that match.

Collaborative systems: Item descriptions are not used. A user's profile stores user opinions against item identifiers. The system compares other users with the active user and recommends items that were liked by users whose profiles are similar to the active user's profile.

Recommender systems differ also by the extent to which they engage in dialogue with the user:

Single-shot systems: In response to a user request, the system delivers a set of recommendations. Each request is treated independently of previous ones.

Conversational systems: Users elaborate their requirements over the course of an extended dialogue. In particular, the user can supply feedback on the recommended items. Her feedback influences the next set of recommendations.

---

* This material is based on works supported by Science Foundation Ireland under Grant No. 03/IN.3/136. We are grateful to Professor Barry Smyth for his advice and to the GroupLens project team for making their data available.

V. Wade, H. Ashman, and B. Smyth (Eds.): AH 2006, LNCS 4018, pp. 41–50, 2006.

Table 1. A ratings matrix

	Ann	Bob	Col	Deb	Edd	Flo
Cape Fear	$\perp$	$\perp$	3	5	5	5
Naked Gun	3	2	$\perp$	2	4	$\perp$
Aliens	$\perp$	5	$\perp$	$\perp$	2	4
Taxi Driver	$\perp$	$\perp$	3	4	3	$\perp$

Conversational systems can more easily adapt their recommendations to the user's short-term interests. By dint of mood changes or other special circumstances, short-term interests may not coincide with long-term interests.

There is a mature body of research on conversational *content-based* systems. But research into *collaborative* systems has focused on single-shot recommenders. The work of Rafter & Smyth [1] is a recent exception. Section 3 describes their work on conversational collaborative recommenders. Section 4 describes how we have enhanced the diversity of the recommendations made by a conversational collaborative recommender. Doing this requires a way of measuring the distance between two products; Section 5 proposes four ways of doing this using collaborative data only. Section 6 compares the diversity-enhanced conversational collaborative recommenders with a single-shot recommender and with a standard conversational collaborative recommender. But first Section 2 summarises the operation of the class of collaborative recommenders used in this work.

2   Single-Shot Collaborative Recommender Systems

In a collaborative recommender, given m items, $I = \{i : 1 \ldots m\}$, and n users, $U = \{u : 1 \ldots n\}$, preferences are represented using a $m \times n$ matrix of ratings $r_{i,u}$. Note that it is possible and common that $r_{i,u} = \perp$, signalling that the user has not yet rated that item. An example of a ratings matrix for movies is shown as Table 1. Each column in the matrix is a user's long-term profile. We will write u^{LT} for the item identifiers that have non-$\perp$ ratings in user u's long-term profile. For example, $\mathrm{Bob}^{LT} = \{\mathrm{Naked\ Gun, Aliens}\}$. We will write u^{LT^+} for the set of items in u's long-term profile for which the rating is greater than or equal to the mid-point of the rating scale. For example, assuming a 5-point rating scale, $\mathrm{Edd}^{LT^+} = \{\mathrm{Cape\ Fear, Naked\ Gun, Taxi\ Driver}\}$.

There are many ways of building collaborative recommenders, most of which are compatible with the research reported in this paper. Here we describe just the one we have implemented; for details, see [2]:

- The similarity $w_{u_a,u}$ between the active user u_a and each other user, $u \neq u_a$, is computed using Pearson Correlation, $\mathrm{correl}(u_a, u)$, over their co-rated items.
- After computing the similarity between u_a and each other user, u, the N (in our case, 20) *nearest neighbours* are selected, i.e. the N for whom $w_{u_a,u}$ is highest.

- For each item i that has not been rated by u_a but has been rated by at least one of the neighbours, u_a's rating for i is predicted, p_{i,u_a}. This is essentially an average of the neighbours' ratings for item i weighted by the values for correl(u_a, u).
- These items are then sorted into descending order of p_{i,u_a}. This is the order in which items will be recommended. For example, if in a single-shot system we want to recommend three items, then the first three items in this sorted list are selected.

3   Conversational Collaborative Recommender Systems

In 2004, Rafter & Smyth described their conversational collaborative recommender: the system recommends items to the user; the user gives feedback on the recommendations; and the feedback influences the next set of recommendations [1]. We use CCR$^+$ to designate our implementation of their ideas [3].

In CCR$^+$, the active user has a long-term profile (based on a column in the ratings matrix), u_a^{LT}, as do all other users. But, for the duration of her interaction with the system, the active user also has a short-term profile, $u_a^{ST^+}$.

Initially, the short-term profile is empty and the first set of k (typically, three) recommendations is made in the fashion described in Section 2. At this point, the system solicits user feedback. The user can terminate the dialogue, with or without having chosen an item for purchase or consumption. Or, if she wishes to continue the dialogue, she can optionally indicate which recommended item best matches her short-term interests. If she does, the selected item's identifier is added to her short-term profile, $u_a^{ST^+}$. Nothing is done with the other items.

If the dialogue has not been terminated, the system now recommends another set of items. New recommendations never repeat ones made previously in the dialogue. But, additionally, through the way it computes user similarity, the system attempts to steer new recommendations towards the kind of items in $u_a^{ST^+}$; see below for details. This recommendation-and-feedback cycle continues until either the user finds an item she wishes to consume, she abandons the dialogue having found no such item, or the system can make no fresh recommendations.

It remains to say how $u_a^{ST^+}$ influences subsequent recommendations. When finding neighbours, the similarities between users will no longer be based just on the Pearson Correlation between their long-term profiles. The idea in conversational collaborative recommending is that the selection of nearest neighbours is "...directed towards users that have liked the items in the target user's [short-term profile]" [1, p.152]. Specifically, correl(u_a, u), the correlation between the long-term profiles of the active user u_a and each other user u, will be boosted by an amount based on the size of the intersection between u's long-term positive profile u^{LT^+} (the item's in u's long-term profile for which the rating equals or exceeds the mid-point of the rating scale) and u_a's short-term profile u_a^{ST} [3].

We have found that enhancing the diversity of the recommendations improves results (Section 6), so this is the topic of the next section.

4 Diversity-Enhanced Conversational Collaborative Recommender Systems

This section introduces the $CCR^+Div(b, k)$ system. In its name, Div indicates a concern for the diversity of recommendations; b and k are parameters, which are explained below.

For *content-based* recommender systems, the argument has been convincingly made that items should be selected for *diversity* (relative to each other) as well as *similarity* (to the query or the user's profile) [4]. Too much similarity between the recommended items (e.g. three Woody Allen movies) can be undesirable. But, when recommendations are diverse, if the user is not satisfied with the most highly recommended item, for example, the chances of her being satisfied with one of the alternative recommendations is increased.

There is a body of research that addresses diversity for *content-based* recommenders, e.g. [4, 5, 6]. It is only now that we are seeing the first work that attempts to improve the diversity of the items recommended by *collaborative* recommenders [3, 7]. We hypothesise that a direct concern for diversity may be important, especially in *conversational* collaborative systems: diverse recommendations increase the chances of positive feedback (where an item is preferred over the others), and this helps the system target the recommendations towards the user's short-term interests.

To investigate this, we implemented the Bounded Greedy selection algorithm (henceforth BG) from [4]. To recommend k items, BG finds bk items. In [4], these are the bk items that are most similar to the query (content-based recommending). Here, they are the bk items with the highest prediction values p_{i,u_a} (where neighbours are computed by the CCR^+ system). From these bk items, BG selects k to recommend to the user. It selects the k in a greedy fashion, based on ones selected so far; see Algorithm 1.

In the algorithm, the quality of item i relative to the result set so far R is defined as follows:

$$Quality(i, R) =_{\text{def}} (1 - \alpha) \times p_{i,u_a} + \alpha \times RelDiv(i, R) \qquad (1)$$

i.e. it is a weighted combination of the predicted rating for item i and the diversity we will attain if we include i in R. α is a factor that allows the importance of the predicted rating and relative diversity to be changed. In this paper, we

---

Algorithm 1. The Bounded Greedy selection algorithm. Adapted from [4].

Candidates $\leftarrow$ bk items recommended by CCR^+
$R \leftarrow \{\}$
for $j \leftarrow 1$ to k **do**
    best $\leftarrow$ the $i \in$ *Candidates* for which $Quality(i, R)$ is highest
    insert *best* into R
    remove *best* from *Candidates*
end for
return R

---

only investigate the case where the two factors are given equal weight. Hence, we normalise both factors so that they fall in $[0, 1]$ and we then use $\alpha = 0.5$.

Diversity relative to the result set so far is defined as the average distance between i and the items already inserted into R:

$$RelDiv(i, R) =_{\text{def}} \begin{cases} 1 & \text{if } R = \{\} \\ \frac{\sum_{j \in R} \text{dist}(i,j)}{|R|} & \text{otherwise} \end{cases} \quad (2)$$

This will lie in $[0, 1]$ provided each $\text{dist}(i, j)$ lies in $[0, 1]$.

This leaves the issue of how to measure distance *between items* in Equation 2. In [4], the distance between items is the inverse of the *content-based* similarity. If item descriptions are available, the same approach can be used to enhance the diversity of collaborative recommendations. Ziegler, for example, uses taxonomic knowledge in his system [7]. But we choose to proceed on the assumption that item descriptions are not available. We enhance diversity using a measure of distance that is calculated using *collaborative data only*, i.e. we use only the ratings matrix.

Our approach to distance using collaborative data only is based on the following heuristic:

Two items are different if the users who rated them are different.

The intuition is that the community of users who have rated item i have a certain set of tastes. The more the membership of the community who rated item i differs from the membership of the community who rated item j, the more likely i and j satisfy different tastes and are different kinds of items. For example, according to this heuristic, a movie that is liked exclusively by adolescent males is likely to be distant from one that it liked exclusively by middle-aged women. (We stress, however, that, just as we are not using content-based data, we are not using demographic data either: our ways of computing distance will make use only of the ratings matrix.)

There are numerous ways to make this informal heuristic into something that can be implemented. We described one such way in [3], showing that it outperformed Rafter's & Smyth's original system, our minor variant of their system (CCR$^+$), and a system that enhances diversity by choosing items at random from the bk items with the highest prediction values. The contribution here is to compare that approach with three other ways of implementing the heuristic.

5   Definitions of Item Distance

In this section, we look at four ways of defining the distance between pairs of items, for use in Equation 2. The four definitions differ on two dimensions, which we explain below.

Nearest Neighbours or All Users. The first dimension is the way we choose the set of users on which the communities are defined. One possibility is to confine attention to the active user's nearest neighbours (NN). We could instead define the communities over the set of *all* users known to the system (All). In other words, in the former, distance is computed between vectors of length N, where N is the number of nearest neighbours; in the latter, distance is computed over vectors of length n, where n is the size of U.

Hamming Distance or Inverse Pearson. The second dimension is the way in which we compute by how much two communities differ.

One possibility is to define the distance between two items to be inversely related to the size of the intersection of the sets of users who rated the two items. This definition of distance can be computed quite efficiently using bit-vectors. In detail, then, we compute dist(i, j) as follows:

- For both i and j, we create bit vectors I and J of length N (in the case where only nearest neighbours are being used) or n (in the case where all users are being used). Digit d in vector I is set if user d has a non-$\perp$ rating for item i; similarly for bits in J.
- dist(i, j) is computed as the Hamming Distance (HD) between I and J, i.e. a count of the number of positions in which their bits differ. This value is normalised, so that it falls within $[0, 1]$, by dividing it by N or n as appropriate.

Figure 1 illustrates this process; it shows Naked Gun to be more different from Cape Fear than Taxi Driver is. In the figure, we are using NN, the nearest neighbours; we take the number of these to be three; and we assume these are Ann, Col and Deb. We take their ratings from Table 1 and set bits to show who rated what.

	Ann	Col	Deb
Cape Fear	0	1	1
Naked Gun	1	0	1

Hamming Distance: 2
Normalised: $\frac{2}{3}$

	Ann	Col	Deb
Cape Fear	0	1	1
Taxi Driver	0	1	1

Hamming Distance: 0
Normalised: $\frac{0}{3}$

Fig. 1. Hamming Distances

This definition takes no regard of the magnitudes of the ratings. It considers only whether a user has rated an item or not; it counts how many of the users have rated one of the two items but not the other.

We could instead compute the Inverse of Pearson Correlation (IP) between the users' ratings of the two items. Effectively, this means computing Pearson Correlation between *rows* rather than columns in the ratings matrix (Table 1), takings its inverse, and normalising so that it falls within $[0, 1]$. This would have the seeming advantage of being sensitive to the magnitudes of the ratings.

Table 2. Four definitions of item distance, using collaborative data only

	Nearest Neighbours	All Users
Hamming Distance	HD-NN	HD-All
Inverse Pearson	IP-NN	IP-All

Summary. Two binary dimensions gives four definitions, as shown in Table 2. We emphasise that in all other respects these four systems are identical: only their computation of item-item distance within the definition of relative diversity varies.

6   Empirical Evaluation

To evaluate the systems that we have described, we adopt Rafter's & Smyth's methodology [1]. One hundred user profiles are selected at random and removed from the '100K MovieLens Dataset'[1]. Each of these acts in turn as an (artificial) active user. The item that the user is seeking is obtained through the leave-one-in methodology, i.e. given the active user's long-term profile, each item in turn is treated as the target item. Each of the systems that we evaluate repeatedly recommends sets of three items to the user until either the target item is one of the recommended items, there have been 100 recommendation cycles, or no further recommendations can be made to this user, whichever comes soonest. If the target item is recommended within 100 cycles, the number of items recommended is recorded. Results are subjected to three-fold validation, with a different 100 active users in each fold.

In each recommendation cycle, the (artificial) user's feedback needs to be simulated. For each movie, the MovieLens datasets record a set of genres, which allows a simple-minded content-based approach. If the target item's set of genres is G_t and a recommended item's set of genres is G_r, we compute $\frac{|G_t \cap G_r|}{|G_t \cup G_r|}$. If all recommended items score zero, then none is taken to match the user's short-term interests; otherwise, the highest-scoring item (with random tie-breaking) is taken to match the user's short term-interests and is inserted into u_a^{ST+}.

In the diversity-enhanced systems, we have taken $k = 3$ and $b = 15$. In other words, a set of three items is chosen greedily from 45 candidates. In previous work, we have partially explored what happens when different values of b are chosen [3]. There we found better results for $b = 15$ than $b = 5$ and $b = 10$. Of course, it does not follow that results will continue to improve with ever larger values of b: at some point, the set of candidates will be so large that it will include items whose predicted ratings are so low that they will not be valuable recommendations. In future work, we need to find the values of b for which this is the case.

Figure 2 shows, as a percentage of a total of 34759 dialogues, how often the target item was found. In addition to CCR$^+$ and the four versions of CCR$^+$Div(15, 3),

---

[1] www.grouplens.org

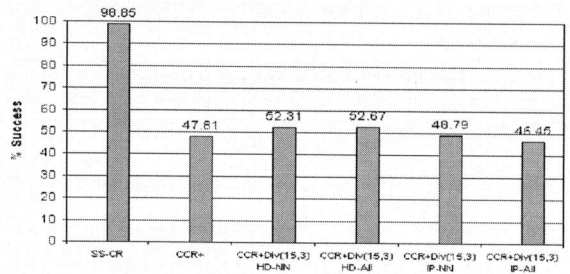

Fig. 2. Success rates

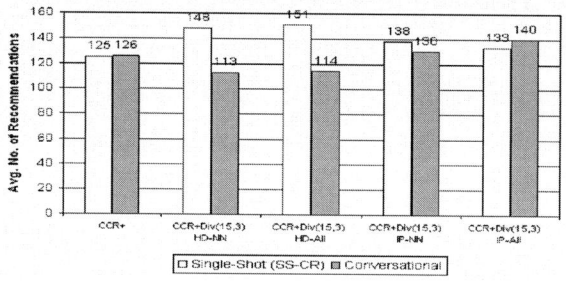

Fig. 3. Average number of recommendations

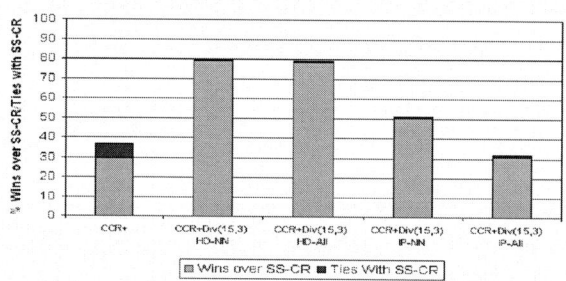

Fig. 4. Wins over SS-CR and ties with SS-CR

we show the results for SS-CR, a single-shot recommender, which computes a ranked list of items in the way described in Section 2, and recommends them in decreasing order of predicted rating, k $(= 3)$ items at a time. We regard SS-CR as successful if the target item is among all the possible recommendations it can make to the active user. The other systems are successful if the target item is recommended within 100 cycles of three recommendations each. Unsurprisingly, SS-CR has by far the highest success rate; encouragingly, most of the diversity-enhanced systems have higher success rates than CCR$^+$. Of the diversity-enhanced systems, the ones that use Hamming Distance are more successful than those that use Inverse Pearson Correlation.

Table 3. Winning and losing margins

	Win	Lose
CCR$^+$	46	24
CCR$^+$Div(15, 3) HD-NN	51	29
CCR$^+$Div(15, 3) HD-All	56	33
CCR$^+$Div(15, 3) IP-NN	48	33
CCR$^+$Div(15, 3) IP-All	59	37

Figure 3 shows how many items are recommended, on average, before the system recommends the target item. In this figure, each system is compared with the SS-CR in cases where both were successful in finding the target item. We see that SS-CR can rival CCR$^+$, which suggests that the user feedback has little value in CCR$^+$. The diversity-enhanced systems all outperform SS-CR and CCR$^+$, which confirms that diverse recommendations can elicit more useful user feedback. Of the diversity-enhanced systems, the ones that use Hamming Distance are by far the most successful; they require about 35 fewer recommendations to reach the target item than SS-CR.

Figure 4 shows how often each of the conversational systems makes the same or fewer recommendations than SS-CR (when both are successful). We see that the diversity-enhanced systems that use Hamming Distance make fewer recommendations than SS-CR nearly 80% of the time; the other systems are competitive with SS-CR between 30% and 50% of the time.

Finally, Table 3 shows winning and losing margins. The table shows, for example, that, when CCR$^+$ wins against SS-CR, it makes on average 46 fewer recommendations and, when CCR$^+$ loses against SS-CR, it makes on average 24 more recommendations. We see that IP-All wins by most when it wins but it also loses by most when it loses. By this measure, the systems that use Hamming Distance do well: when they win, they win by a respectable margin; when they lose, they lose by some of the smaller amounts.

7 Conclusions

Building on the seminal work reported in [1], we have developed a number of conversational collaborative recommender systems. In all these systems, the selection of neighbours is guided by overlap with the active user's short-term profile. In CCR$^+$Div(b, k), we introduce an explicit mechanism that uses collaborative data only to enhance the diversity of recommendations made by (conversational) collaborative recommender systems.

We have experimented with four definitions of distance, for use when computing relative diversity. We found, perhaps counter-intuitively, that approaches based on Hamming Distance work better than those based on Inverse Pearson Correlation. This is surprising: ignoring the magnitudes of the ratings is better than taking them into account! We suspect that this is because Hamming Distance, being more discrete, sharpens the definitions of the communities, which is important in our heuristic definition of item diversity, whereas Inverse Pearson, being more continuous, de-emphasises community differences.

In terms of success rates and average numbers of recommendations, there is little to choose between Hamming Distance over NN and Hamming Distance over All Users. More research, focusing on their relative efficiencies, is needed to choose between these two.

Conversational collaborative recommenders are a new line of research, and enhancing the diversity of their recommendations is a new departure too. Future work could include more systematic investigation of good values for α, b and k, and validation of our results on other datasets. It would also be interesting to compare content-based approaches to the approaches that we have reported in this paper, which use purely collaborative data. We would also like to investigate the role of diversity over the course of the dialogue. Diversity can be helpful in early cycles, when the user is exploring the space and making her short-term interests known; but in later cycles, when the user is homing in on a suitable item, diversity may be less appropriate [8].

References

1. R. Rafter and B. Smyth. Towards conversational collaborative filtering. In L. McGinty and B. Crean, editors, *Procs. of the 15th Artificial Intelligence and Cognitive Science Conference*, pages 147–156, 2004.
2. J. L. Herlocker. *Understanding and Improving Automated Collaborative Filtering Systems*. PhD thesis, University of Minnesota, 2000.
3. D. Bridge and J. P. Kelly. Diversity-enhanced conversational collaborative recommendations. In N. Creaney, editor, *Procs. of the 16th Irish Conference on Artificial Intelligence & Cognitive Science*, pages 29–38. University of Ulster, 2005.
4. B. Smyth and P. McClave. Similarity vs. diversity. In D. W. Aha and I. Watson, editors, *Procs. of the 4th International Conference on Case-Based Reasoning*, pages 347–361. Springer, 2001.
5. D. Bridge and A. Ferguson. Diverse product recommendations using an expressive language for case retrieval. In S. Craw and A. Preece, editors, *Procs. of the 6th European Conference on Case-Based Reasoning*, pages 43–57. Springer, 2002.
6. D. McSherry. Diversity-conscious retrieval. In S. Craw and A. Preece, editors, *Procs. of the 6th European Conference on Case-Based Reasoning*, pages 219–233. Springer, 2002.
7. C.-N. Ziegler, S. M. McNee, J. A. Konstan, and G. Lausen. Improving recommendation lists through topic diversification. In *Procs. of the 14th International World Wide Web Conference*, pages 22–32. ACM Press, 2005.
8. L. McGinty and B. Smyth. On the role of diversity in conversational recommender systems. In K. Ashley and D. Bridge, editors, *Procs. of the 5th International Conference on Case-Based Reasoning*, pages 276–290. Springer, 2003.

Addictive Links: The Motivational Value of Adaptive Link Annotation in Educational Hypermedia

Peter Brusilovsky, Sergey Sosnovsky, and Michael Yudelson

School of Information Sciences
University of Pittsburgh, Pittsburgh PA 15260, USA
peterb@pitt.edu, sas15@pitt.edu, mvy3@pitt.edu

Abstract. Adaptive link annotation is a popular adaptive navigation support technology. Empirical studies of adaptive annotation in the educational context have demonstrated that it can help students to acquire knowledge faster, improve learning outcome, reduce navigation overhead, and encourage non-sequential navigation. In this paper we present our study of a rather unknown effect of adaptive annotation, its ability to significantly increase student motivation to work with non-mandatory educational content. We explored this effect and confirmed its significance in the context of two different adaptive hypermedia systems. The paper presents and discusses the results of our work.

1 Introduction

Adaptive link annotation is a popular adaptive navigation support technology. The idea of adaptive annotation is to augment links with personalized hints that inform the user about the current state of nodes behind the annotated links. Usually, these annotations are provided in the form of visual cues employing, for example, contrasting font colors, font sizes, font types for the link anchor or different icons next to the anchor [1]. Adaptive annotation is especially popular in educational hyper-media. A range of annotation approaches has been introduced and explored in adaptive educational hypermedia systems [2, 3, 7, 8, 11, 13]. Empirical studies of adaptive annotation in the educational context have demonstrated that it can help students acquire knowledge faster, improve learning outcome, reduce navigation overhead, and encourage non-sequential navigation [2, 3, 6, 9, 12]. These effects are frequently cited as the *value* of adaptive annotation.

In this paper we present our recent work on a rather unknown effect of adaptive annotation, its ability to significantly increase student motivation to work with non-mandatory educational content. This effect was first discovered during out-of-the-classroom studies of the ELM-ART system [13]. ELM-ART, an adaptive Web-based system for learning the LISP programming language was (and still is) freely available on the Web for anyone interested in learning LISP. The use of the system was not mandatory for any of the users – they worked with the system only as long as they were interested and motivated. The log analysis demonstrated that subjects who were familiar with at least one other programming language visited visibly more pages and solved more exercises and problems when they were working with adaptive link

V. Wade, H. Ashman, and B. Smyth (Eds.): AH 2006, LNCS 4018, pp. 51 – 60, 2006.

annotations. However, the effect was not statistically significant and the motivational value of adaptive annotation went unnoticed by the community.

We re-discovered the motivational value of adaptive annotation in a classroom study of QuizGuide, an adaptive hypermedia service developed to guide students to the most relevant self-assessment quizzes [5]. The use of self-assessment quizzes was not mandatory – the students were allowed to use them as much as they wanted, in order to check the level of their knowledge and to prepare for classroom quizzes and exams. The original goal of QuizGuide was to increase the quality of learning. While this goal has been achieved, the most striking effect of adaptive annotation we discovered in the study was the remarkable increase of student motivation to work with self-assessment quizzes. With QuizGuide, the students explored more questions, worked with questions more persistently, and accessed a larger diversity of questions. In some sense, adaptive annotations made the quiz work almost addictive: Once the students started a session, they stayed with the system much longer. Average session length and average number of questions attempted during a semester increased significantly [4].

Despite the obvious importance of the motivational value of adaptive annotation, a single study was not deemed sufficient to publicly announce our new respect for adaptive annotations. We spent an additional year exploring this effect and measuring its significance. To check the stability of the motivational effect, we ran another semester-long study of QuizGuide. To check its transfer, we attempted to replicate this effect using different kinds of adaptive annotations and different educational content – program examples. Our studies confirmed our original observations in both explored contexts, demonstrated the significance of the observed effect, and brought a better understanding of some underlying mechanisms. This paper reports on our exploration of the motivational effect of adaptive annotation. We start by introducing the systems that were used as the initial platform for our study, present the results of the study, discuss its importance, and chart some directions for future work.

2   QuizGuide – Adaptive Annotation for Self-assessment Quizzes

QuizGuide [5] is an adaptive hypermedia service for personalized access to self-assessment quizzes, served by the previously developed system, QuizPACK. It informs students about their current knowledge and learning goals by giving adaptive annotations along with the links to quizzes. QuizGuide groups quizzes available to students into coarse-grained topics (Fig. 1). The link to each topic is annotated with an icon showing a target with (or without) arrows. The number of arrows (from 0 to 3) reflects the student's performance on the quizzes of that annotated topic (no arrows represent no or very little progress, three arrows representing good comprehension). The color of a target encodes the relevance of a topic to the current learning goal of the class. The topics form a prerequisite-outcome structure. Every time new topics are introduced in a lecture, they are annotated with a bright-blue target. Topics that serve as prerequisites for any of the current topics have a pale-blue target. Completed topics are assigned grey targets. Finally, topics that belong to learning goals not yet covered in class are annotated with crossed targets.

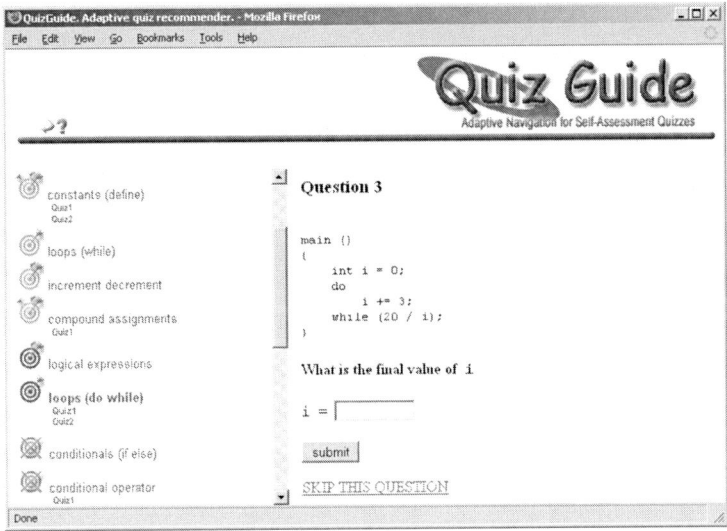

Fig. 1. The Student Interface for QuizGuide

3   NavEx – Adaptive Guidance for Annotated Code Examples

The NavEx system [14] provides adaptive access to a relatively large set of interactive programming examples. It is built as an adaptive, value-added service for a non-adaptive system, WebEx, which delivers selected examples. The added value of NavEx is that it gives adaptive visual cues for every example link. The NavEx window consists of a navigation frame (on left) and the content area (Fig. 2). Adaptive link annotations presented in the navigation frame integrate several kinds of information about examples and express it through the icon and the font type.

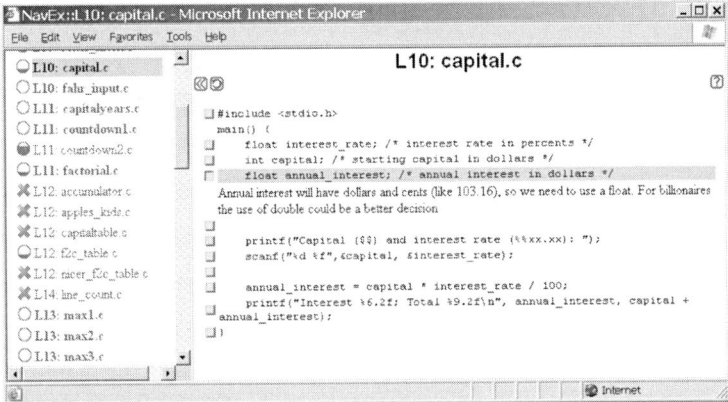

Fig. 2. The Studentf NavEx

The icon/font combination displayed by NavEx performs three functions:

1. categorize examples as ones the student is ready (annotated with green bullets) or not yet ready to explore (annotated with red X icons);
2. reflect the student's progress within each example (displayed as a gradual filling of the green bullet); and
3. emphasize with bold font the most relevant examples to explore.

4   A Study of the Motivational Effect in Two Systems

We performed a number of classroom studies of the non-adaptive systems QuizPACK and WebEx, and adaptive value-added services QuizGuide and NavEx. The studies were done in the context of an undergraduate programming course at the School of Information Sciences, University of Pittsburgh, from the Spring 2003 to the Fall 2005 semesters. The non-adaptive systems, QuizPACK and WebEx, were accessible to students starting in the Spring 2003 semester. QuizGuide was introduced in Spring 2004 and NavEx followed in Fall 2004. After students gained access to adaptive services, non-adaptive systems were still available. Students were able to access the content through the adaptively annotated links provided by new services or in the "old way" - through non-annotated links in the course portal. The set of quizzes and code examples remained to a great extent unchanged across semesters. The setup of the course remained the same across all those semesters, including lectures' content, the scope of home assignments and in-class quizzes.

The introduction of each of the adaptive services caused an impressive increase of student interaction with the supported content (quizzes for QuizGuide and examples for NavEx) as compared to their work with non-adaptive interfaces in previous semesters. Since work with this educational content continued to be non-mandatory, we refer to the observed phenomenon as the motivational effect of adaptive link annotation. The following subsections present some results derived from our study of the motivational effect in the context of QuizGuide and NavEx. Section 4.1 reports the magnitude and the significance of the increase, using several usage parameters, while section 4.2 attempts to look deeper into the process in order to uncover some mechanisms behind this effect.

4.1   Bottom-Line Data and Significance

In this section, we will present our quantitative analysis of the added value that the adaptive annotations in QuizGuide and NavEx have over the non-adaptive access in QuizPACK and WebEx. The source data for the analysis were the activity logs collected by the systems. The logs recorded every user click (i.e., submitting an answer to a question or clicking on a line of example code). Data collection procedures did not differ across discussed semesters and were not dependent on method of student access to quizzes or code examples (whether via adaptive or non-adaptive systems). Student work with any of the discussed systems was included equally for user modeling. Log data gave clear evidence as to whether a student accessed quizzes or examples through the adaptive service or not.

We used three variables to parameterize student performance:

1. activity: the number of clicks on lines of code (in the case of WebEx and NavEx) or attempts to answer a quiz question (in the case of QuizPACK and QuizGuide) -- later referred to as clicks or actions;
2. quantity: the number of examples explored (WebEx and NavEx) or quizzes taken (QuizPACK and QuizGuide) --later referred to as examples or quizzes, and
3. coverage: the number of lectures that the reviewed examples or attempted quizzes were drawn from (later referred to as lectures).

Each of these variables was aggregated on two levels:

1. overall performance level – the total number of clicks made, examples/quizzes explored, and lectures covered by each user over the course of the semester; and
2. session performance level – the average number of clicks made, examples/quizzes explored, and average number of lecture topics explored per session by a user.

Our objective was to support our subjective observation that adaptive guidance does make a difference, i.e. to determine whether activity, quantity and coverage of topics were higher for students who were exposed to QuizGuide and NavEx than for those who used the non-adaptive QuizPACK and WebEx format. The results of our comparison clearly demonstrated the value of adaptive navigation support in motivating students to interact more with quizzes and examples.

In our analysis of the value of QuizGuide we compared two semesters (Spring 2003 and Fall 2003) when only QuizPACK was used to access quizzes with two semesters when both QuizGuide and QuizPACK were available to students (Spring 2004 and Fall 2004). When examining the adaptive value of NavEx, we compared two semesters when only WebEx was used by students to access annotated code examples (Fall 2003 and Spring 2004) with one semester during which students could also retrieve examples via WebEx or NavEx (Fall 2004).

During our analysis we inspected about 18,300 QuizPACK and QuizGuide user actions (question attempts) and nearly 3,400 WebEx and NavEx actions (requests for comments about lines of code). Prior to data examination, we performed outlier filtering of individual clicks according to the overall user number of clicks variable. The filtering was done by setting a plus-minus three-sigma interval around the overall number of clicks mean in each of the four semesters. The distributions of data across all our variables were severely skewed because there were a number of not very active students (in terms of clicks made, examples reviewed etc), fewer were moderately active students, and very few very active students. This, along with heterogeneity of variances, prevented us from applying parametric statistical tests to the comparison of usage data. Instead we employed Mann-Whitney tests as t-tests' substitutes.

The results of these tests have revealed that for nearly all variables and aggregation levels, users exposed to the adaptive features of QuizGuide/NavEx achieved significantly higher results (Table 1). First of all, for the QuizGuide+QuizPACK combination vs. the use of QuizPACK alone: In a comparison of the levels of overall parameters, users working with adaptive guidance were making twice as many question attempts a semester (an average of roughly 260 vs. 128), and working with almost twice as many quizzes (an average of roughly 24 vs. 13). This remarkable increase of non-mandatory activity measured by these parameters in combined

QuizGuide+QuizPACK over QuizPACK alone was statistically significant. The increase of course coverage was visible, but not statistically significant. Unlike other usage parameters, course coverage has a natural maximum boundary – the total number of lectures in the course. The lack of significant difference shows that students are able to do more work with quizzes while having the same volume of quiz material available. On the level of average user session statistics across all variables, the parameters of QuizGuide+QuizPACK combined were all roughly 1.5–2 times higher then those of QuizPACK alone. All of the observed increases were significant.

Table 1. Comparing the means of the variables for semesters when adaptive systems (NavEx, QuizGuide) were used in combination with non-adaptive ones (WebEx, QuizPACK) with semesters when only non-adaptive systems were used

		QuizPACK	QuizGuide + QuizPACK	p-value
Overall user statistics	Clicks	127.68±15.97	261.21±53.15	**0.023***
	Quizzes	13.11±1.06	23.97±1.96	**<0.001**
	Lectures	8.70±0.64	10.18±0.61	0.188
Average user session statistics	Clicks	10.48±1.32	17.19±2.03	**<0.001**
	Quizzes	1.87±0.10	3.64±0.49	**<0.001**
	Lectures	1.40±0.05	2.09±0.27	**<0.001**
		WebEx	NavEx + WebEx	p-value
Overall user statistics	Clicks	34.76±6.66	171.90±65.56	**<0.001**
	Examples	5.66±0.87	18.10±4.32	**<0.001**
	Lectures	3.52±0.42	8.20±1.23	**<0.001**
Average user session statistics	Clicks	7.85±0.87	9.49±1.28	0.122
	Examples	1.56±0.12	2.03±0.22	**0.013**
	Lectures	1.20±0.05	1.37±0.10	**0.020**

* boldface indicates p-value less then 0.05

Second, for the NavEx+WebEx vs. WebEx comparison on the level of overall parameters, users exposed to adaptive guidance were making 5 times more clicks a semester (an average of roughly 170 vs. 35), reviewing almost thrice as much code examples (an average of roughly 18 vs. 6), and covering almost twice as larger scope of lectures (an average of 8 lectures vs. 3.5). All of the mentioned advantages on the level of overall user statistics are significant. On the level of average user session statistics the number of clicks users made was higher for those users who were able to use adaptive guidance but not significantly higher. However the number of examples reviewed and number of lectures they were drawn from were significantly higher for users of adaptive guidance.

To ensure that the observed difference in motivation is not explained by differences in student population across semesters, but indicates the added value of adaptive annotation, we analyzed students' initial programming experience and gender across semesters. The results of Chi-Square test show that there was no significant difference between QuizPACK and QuizGuide groups in gender distribution (Pearson Chi-Square = 0.718, p-value = 0.397) or initial experience distribution (Chi-Square = 4.263, p-value = 0.119). Similar results were obtained for WebEx and NavEx groups for both gender (Chi-Square = 1.720, p-value = 0.268) and initial experience (Chi-Square = 0.704, p-value = 0.703).

4.2 A Deeper Look at the Usage Profile

While comparing student work with adaptive and non-adaptive versions, we noticed that typical QuizGuide and NavEx sessions are both *longer* and *more diverse* than QuizPACK and WebEx sessions alone are, correspondingly. Students attempted more questions through QuizGuide and explored a larger number of examples through NavEx. In addition, in both adaptive systems, students more frequently accessed activities corresponding to different lectures within the same session.

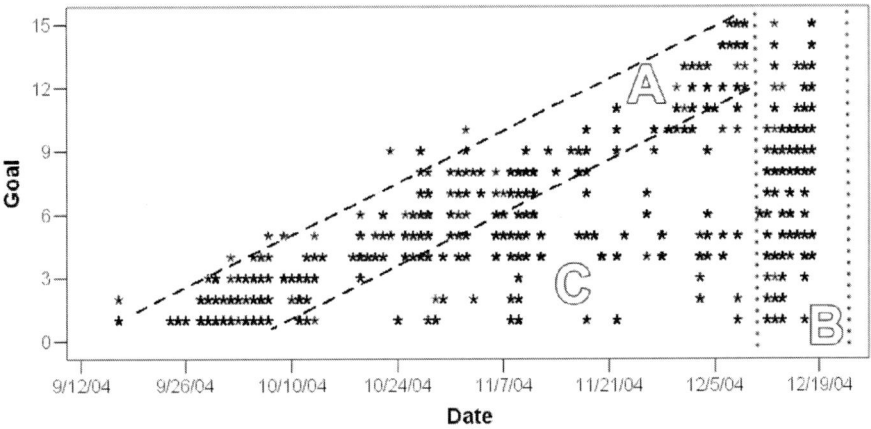

Fig. 3. Time distribution of all actions performed by students with QuizGuide and QuizPACK in Fall 2004 semester. Zone "A" – lecture *stream*, zone "B" – final exam *cut*, and zone "C" – *self-motivated* work with the material of earlier lectures.

To take a closer look at the nature of these results, we performed a deeper analysis of student activity, by taking into account lecture coverage included in all students' actions. Every selection of an example of a question was attributed to the lecture (or the learning goal) it belongs to. For example, Fig. 3 visualizes over 5,500 question-attempts performed by students using QuizGuide or QuizPACK in the Fall 2004 semester. 15 lectures form the vertical axis. The time of the action is marked on the horizontal axis. We can detect three zones of activity. The zone "A" contains all of the "current" activity that students perform along the lecture stream of the course. It is fairly broad, since home assignments and in-class quizzes introduce 1-2 weeks delay in shifting the students' focus from the previous topics. Zone "B" contains a period of preparation for the final exam. The pattern of work with our systems is totally different during this stream of time. Finally, zone "C" contains all actions that students performed during the regular part of the semester, for topics laying far from the "current" lectures. This is the zone we were particularly interested in. All actions here are not directly motivated by the "current" course situation, but rather initiated by the students themselves, possibly in an attempt to bridge the gap in their knowledge that should have been acquired earlier.

We used two measures to assess the intensity of students' *self-motivated* activity: the number of actions in the zone "C" divided by the total number of actions and the average distance between the learning goal which is current at this time and their current activity. For the calculation of the second measure, we used zones "A" and "C".

For all students we calculated an average "C"-ratio and goal distance for quizzes and examples. To evaluate the influence of QuizGuide on motivated activity, we again divided students into two groups: *adaptive* (Spring 2003 and Fall 2003) and *non-adaptive* (Spring 2004 and Fall 2004). Since assumptions of homogeneity of variance and normality were violated, we had to perform nonparametric Mann-Whitney's test. As shown by Table 2, both measures are significantly higher for the adaptive group, which means that students in the semesters when QuizGuide was available more willingly accessed non-current activities. The same analysis was performed for the WebEx/NavEx systems. Their adaptive groups included students of the Fall 2004 semester; while the non-adaptive group combined the Fall 2003 and Spring 2004 semesters. As you can see from the bottom rows of the Table 2, both measures are significantly higher for WebEx+NavEx than for WebEx alone.

Table 2. These parameters characterize the *self-motivated* activity of students with and without adaptive annotations: The "C"-ratio estimates the percentage of students' activity performed outside the current course focus, while the Goal distance assesses how broadly roams (in terms of learning goals) the voluntary interest of a student who is working with the system

		Non-adaptive	Adaptive	p-value
Quizzes	"C" ratio	0.20±0.03	0.28±0.04	**0.025**
	Goal distance	5.89±0.84	9.56±1.61	**0.026**
Examples	"C" ratio	0.24±0.05	0.51±0.08	**0.005**
	Goal distance	8.73±1.90	17.64±2.51	**0.002**

The observed effect can be explained by the fact that progress-based and prerequisite-based adaptive annotations generated by QuizGuide and NavEx directed students' attention to the material related to earlier lectures, which they did not understand well. In QuizGuide, this guidance is very soft. The zone of recommended work is moving along *class progress* – topics are annotated as ready and current in the week they are presented in a lecture. On the other hand, topics that are prerequisite to current are clearly shown, along with their progress. Student struggling with a current topic can easily focus on prerequisite topics that were not well understood, according the arrow progress measure. The guidance in NavEx is stricter: the zone of recommended work is adapted to the student's *individual progress*. It provides a stronger push to explore insufficiently learned prerequisite concepts in previous examples. This stronger push may cause the observed higher increase of work with non-current activities in NavEx.

5 Discussion

The ability of adaptive annotations to increase student motivation to work with non-mandatory educational content is very important in the context of modern E-Learning. Over the last decade, researchers and practitioners have developed a range of advanced Web-based educational tools such as educational animations and simulations, on-line labs, tutorials, and self-assessment questions. Many developed tools have been evaluated in the lab and small-scale classroom studies and proven to be useful. However, we have now learned that the mere availability of a good tool, although known as beneficial for students, is not enough to ensure its broad educational impact [10]. An important challenge for those who research the use of computers in education is to increase the *effective* use of *student-driven* educational tools. Student-driven tools are created to assist student learning, yet their use is not required and does not count towards the student's course grade. Unlike a variety of assessment-driven tools that the students are required to use in order to complete their assignments, it is up to the students to decide to what degree and how frequently they use the student-driven tools. An instructor might work hard to provide a good set of educational tools of known benefit to the students, only to discover that these tools are dramatically underused. Our work has demonstrated that adaptive annotation can be instrumental in motivating the student to do more work with non-mandatory educational tools which is likely, in turn, to lead to better learning outcomes.

6 Conclusions and Future Work

The results of our studies reported in this paper confirm the motivational effect of adaptive link annotation in educational hypermedia, demonstrate its magnitude and significance, and shed some light on the mechanisms of this effect. We were able to demonstrate this effect in the context of two different personalized access systems. The presence of adaptive annotations caused the increase of several usage parameters. Accessing non-mandatory educational activities through adaptively annotated links, the students explored significantly more activities, worked with them more persistently, and accessed items more broadly distributed over the course lectures.

Added to the earlier report of a similar effect of adaptive annotation in the context of ELM-ART study, our results allowed us to generalize the observations and talk about the motivational value of adaptive link annotation. We consider the results we obtained as both exciting and important. First, it is always exciting to discover new value in a popular technology. Secondly, the ability to significantly increase student motivation to interact more with non-mandatory educational activities turns adaptive annotation into a technology that may become critical to the practical success of a wide range of beneficial educational technologies.

More work is required to determine the borders of the motivational effect and to master its practical use. While this effect was observed with three different kinds of adaptive annotations, the mechanisms were conceptually similar, in that they combined *appropriateness* (too early, too late, just right) and *progress-based* (how much is already done) annotations. While we argue that both mechanisms contributed to the motivational value, we do not have data to confirm it. It is also not clear whether the observed effect is specific to these two annotation mechanisms or can be generalized to other kinds of adaptive annotations (and possibly to other kinds of adaptive navigation support). To answer these questions, we intend to continue our exploration of the motivational value of adaptive link annotation.

Acknowledgements

This material is based upon work supported by the National Science Foundation under Grants No. 0310576, 042602, and 0447083.

References

[1] Brusilovsky, P.: Methods and techniques of adaptive hypermedia. User Modeling and User-Adapted Interaction **6**, 2-3 (1996) 87-129

[2] Brusilovsky, P. and Eklund, J.: A study of user-model based link annotation in educational hypermedia. Journal of Universal Computer Science **4**, 4 (1998) 429-448

[3] Brusilovsky, P. and Pesin, L.: Adaptive navigation support in educational hypermedia: An evaluation of the ISIS-Tutor. Journal of Computing and Information Technology **6**, 1 (1998) 27-38

[4] Brusilovsky, P. and Sosnovsky, S.: Engaging students to work with self-assessment questions: A study of two approaches. In: Proc. of ITiCSE'2005, Monte de Caparica, Portugal, ACM Press (2005) 251-255.

[5] Brusilovsky, P., Sosnovsky, S., and Shcherbinina, O.: QuizGuide: Increasing the Educational Value of Individualized Self-Assessment Quizzes with Adaptive Navigation Support. In: Nall, J. and Robson, R. (eds.) Proc. of World Conference on E-Learning, E-Learn 2004, Washington, DC, USA, AACE (2004) 1806-1813.

[6] Davidovic, A., Warren, J., and Trichina, E.: Learning benefits of structural example-based adaptive tutoring systems. IEEE Transactions on Education **46**, 2 (2003) 241-251

[7] De Bra, P. and Calvi, L.: AHA! An open Adaptive Hypermedia Architecture. The New Review of Hypermedia and Multimedia **4** (1998) 115-139

[8] Henze, N. and Nejdl, W.: Adaptation in open corpus hypermedia. International Journal of Artificial Intelligence in Education **12**, 4 (2001) 325-350.

[9] Masthoff, J.: Design and evaluation of a navigation agent with a mixed locus of control. In: Cerri, S. A., Gouardères, G. and Paraguaçu, F. (eds.) Intelligent Tutoring Systems. Lecture Notes in Computer Science, Vol. 2363. Springer-Verlag, Berlin (2002) 982-991

[10] Naps, T. L., Rößling, G., et al. Exploring the role of visualization and engagement in computer science education. ACM SIGCSE bulletin **35** (2003) 131-152.

[11] Papanikolaou, K. A., Grigoriadou, M., Kornilakis, H., and Magoulas, G. D.: Personalising the interaction in a Web-based Educational Hypermedia System: the case of INSPIRE. User Modeling and User Adapted Interaction **13**, 3 (2003) 213-267.

[12] Specht, M.: Empirical evaluation of adaptive annotation in hypermedia. In: Ottmann, T. and Tomek, I. (eds.) Proc. of ED-MEDIA/ED-TELECOM'98 - 10th World Conference on Educational Multimedia and Hypermedia, Freiburg, Germany, (1998) 1327-1332.

[13] Weber, G. and Brusilovsky, P.: ELM-ART: An adaptive versatile system for Web-based instruction. International Journal of Artificial Intelligence in Education **12**, 4 (2001) 351-384, available online at http://cbl.leeds.ac.uk/ijaied/abstracts/Vol_12/weber.html

[14] Yudelson, M. and Brusilovsky, P.: NavEx: Providing Navigation Support for Adaptive Browsing of Annotated Code Examples. In: Looi, C.-K., McCalla, G., Bredeweg, B. and Breuker, J. (eds.) Proceedings of AI-ED'2005. IOS, Amsterdam (2005) 710-717

An Adaptive Personalized Recommendation Strategy Featuring Context Sensitive Content Adaptation

Zeina Chedrawy and Syed Sibte Raza Abidi

Faculty of Computer Science, Dalhousie University, Halifax B3H 1W5, Canada
{chedrawy, sraza}@cs.dal.ca

Abstract. In this paper, we present a new approach that is a synergy of item-based Collaborative Filtering (CF) and Case Based Reasoning (CBR) for personalized recommendations. We present a two-phase strategy: in phase I, we developed a context-sensitive item-based CF method that leverages the original past recommendations of peers via ratings performed on various information items. In phase II, we further personalize the information items comprising multiple components using a CBR-based compositional adaptation technique to selectively collect the most relevant information components and combine them into one composite recommendation. In this way, our approach allows fine-grained information filtering by operating at the constituent elements of an information item as opposed to the entire information item. We show that our strategy improves the quality and relevancy of the recommendations in terms of its appropriateness to the user's needs and interests, and validated by statistical significance tests. We demonstrate the working of our strategy by recommending personalized music playlists.

1 Introduction

The volume of information over the Internet is increasing at a tremendous rate, and as a consequence the search for 'relevant' and 'useful' information is becoming proportionally difficult. Adaptive recommender systems—a class of adaptive hypermedia systems—act as mediators between information sources and information seekers [6], as they exploit the user's current specific interests and needs to (a) regulate the flow of information to users; and (b) direct users to the right information—i.e. personalized information selection and filtering [3]. Adaptive recommender systems are applied in a variety of application domains, including healthcare [15], business [14], education [16], entertainment [17], and so on.

Adaptive recommender systems use a variety of methods, spanning from adaptive hypermedia to information retrieval to machine learning to artificial intelligence, in order to determine the *relevance* and *utility* of any given information item with respect to the user's model/profile that characterizes the user's information needs, interests, preferences, demographics and consumption capacity. Functionally speaking, if an information item—which can be a document, news item, music compilation, movie, educational module, shopping list, activity plan, and so on—is deemed as relevant to the user then it is recommended to him.

V. Wade, H. Ashman, and B. Smyth (Eds.): AH 2006, LNCS 4018, pp. 61–70, 2006.

In our approach to offering personalized recommendations, we extend the functionality of current adaptive recommender systems by pursuing (a) *context-sensitive information selection*; and (b) *compositional information personalization*.

Context-sensitive information selection involves the characterization and use of the context in which a recommendation is sought, processed and offered. We argue that in a collaborative filtering setting it is important to know why did a user recommend (or otherwise) a particular information item, as opposed to just tracking that the user has given a recommendation for the information item. For instance, in recommending a music CD, one user's recommendation can be due to his/her approval of the lyrics, tunes and vocals—these can be regarded as *recommendation perspectives*—whereas another user may recommend the same music CD along the recommendation perspectives of lyrics, directorship and performance. Although both users recommend the same music CD, yet the recommendation is due to different reasons or under different *contexts*. We argue that since collaborative filtering is guided by user's ratings of items it is useful to exploit the context of the rating of one user in making recommendations for other similar users. Context, for our purposes, implies a generalized set of relationships between a set of recommendation perspectives along which an information item can be rated [4]. Subsequent recommendation of the information item should be dictated by the similarity between the contexts of the recommender and the information seeker.

Compositional information personalization involves the fine-grained selection of individual components of an information item in response to a user model. An information item can be a music CD with its constituent components being the individual songs, or an E-learning module is an information item and the individual lessons are its constituent components. Compositional information personalization, therefore, involves firstly the selection of relevant information items and secondly the selection of the most salient individual components from the relevant information items [2]. A systematic compilation of these individual components, originating from different yet relevant sources, yields a fine-grained personalized information item that is much closer to the user-model as opposed to actual information items that may have some components that are not necessary of interest to the user.

We have devised a two-stage hybrid information recommendation strategy: Stage 1 uses item-based Collaborative Filtering (CF) to identify the information items that are relevant to the user-model; and Stage 2 uses compositional adaptation, in the realm of Case-Based Reasoning (CBR), to select the most salient information components (from a set of relevant information items) to dynamically compose a fine-grained personalized recommendation for the user. We extended the traditional item-based CF method [6] to establish the notion of context, whereby users are able to rate an item along multiple perspectives to elicit the basis of their recommendation. Our strategy is a hybrid of information retrieval viz. CF methods and artificial intelligence viz. CBR based compositional adaptation. It is important to note that the CF method in the first stage serves as the case retrieval mechanism vis-à-vis the CBR approach that we use to adapt the information items (or past cases) in stage 2 (Fig.1).

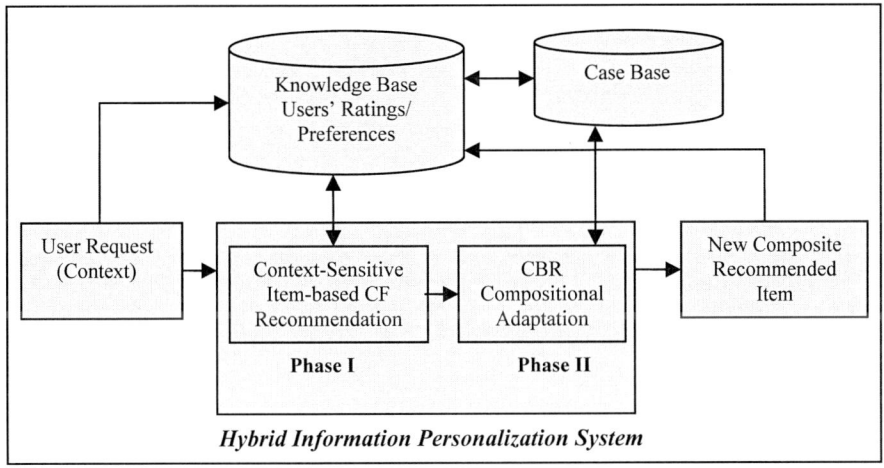

Fig. 1. PRECiSE Framework

2   Related Work

Recommender Systems (RS) are used to customize information content upon an individual's needs and interests to provide the most "*relevant*" and "*precise*" information. Since RS are grounded to solve real world problems, they have been adopted in both business and academic domains. One way to recommend objects is based on the explicit ratings of other people who have rated/purchased the objects in the past. Collaborative Filtering (CF) does this by first asking people to rate given items and recommending new items that have been highly rated by similar users. CF systems are the most widely used recommender systems [6]. Recently, integrating CBR in CF has gained a lot of attention and success [18] because the problem-solving principles of CBR make them an interesting candidate for integration with similarity based information filtering methods, such as CF methods [20]. As a matter of fact, hybrid recommendations were extended to contain knowledge-based techniques such as Case Based Reasoning for the purposes of improving the quality of recommendations and reducing the effect of the traditional CF cold-start problem. PTV [9] is a hybrid recommender system of which operates in the TV listings domain to recommend TV programs and produce personalized TV guides for active users. CoCoA [17] is a recommendation system for music compilation. It uses a case-based retrieval engine based on the CF users' ratings to propose an existing collection of sound tracks. Other hybrid systems were also developed such as Tapestry [21], GroupLens [5].

We present our adaptive recommendation system—*PRECiSE (Personalized Recommendations in a Context-Sensitive Environment)*, that combines item-based CF and CBR techniques to generate fine-grained personalized information and demonstrate its working through an exemplar application for recommending a personalized music playlist.

3   Experimental Design

Our experimental dataset contains 100,000 ratings performed by 943 users on 1682 music compilations where each compilation is a collection of 10 songs. Each user in the dataset has rated a number of compilations along three pre-defined perspectives *song lyric, singer performance* and *song rhythm*. The dataset is divided into training (80%) and test sets (20%). The training set is used to identify the N ($N=10$) recommended items while the test set is used to measure the quality of the recommendation in terms of the F1-metric (F_1) and the appropriateness degree (AD). The F1-metric combines recall (R) and precision (P) at similar weights as defined in [7]. Let *hits* be the total number of recommended items that were really rated by any of the users but were excluded from the training set to be part of the test set; when a set of recommended items is generated for a user, if the rated item in the test set exists in the recommended set, then a hit is recorded. Let t be the total number of users in the test set and N the total number of recommended items. Therefore,

$$R = \frac{hits}{t}; P = \frac{hits}{N}; F_1 = \frac{2 * R * P}{R + P} \qquad (1)$$

The appropriateness degree (AD) determines the degree of similarity between a recommended item and a user profile. The calculation of the (AD) is detailed in Section 5.2.

Given a database of preferences that contains users' ratings on items along multiple perspectives. A user, who is seeking for advice, specifies the perspectives he is interested in and the relevance of each perspective is expressed in terms of weight values denoting the contribution of each perspective in the recommendation based on the user's interests. The system then recommends music compilations well-focused towards the user needs.

4   PRECiSE Methodology

4.1   Phase I: Item-Based CF Recommendation

The first phase of our strategy involves item-based CF recommendation to select a set of information items based on the ratings/recommendations of like-minded peers. Information filtering is pursued via collaboration based approaches, including CF, that filter information by making use of the opinions of peers with similar interests—peers critique the information items by rating them along a number of dimensions that reflect the quality and utility of the item.

We believe that the role of context in generating personalized recommendations is paramount as it determines both the relevance and usefulness of the recommended information. Note that the traditional CF approaches compare items along a single perspective—i.e. whether the item was liked/disliked by the user, without recourse to what perspectives of the item were rated and how were they rated. Original Item-based CF algorithms compare the user model of a user with the user models of other peers to recommend items that may be of interest to the user. The user model is expressed as a vector of attribute/value pairs defining items rated by the user, and the corresponding ratings' values with respect to all given perspectives. In our frame-work, we create a context for information filtering where a user can rate an item along multiple pre-defined perspectives. The rating on these perspectives is subsequently used to recommend the item to similar users. Hence, we extended the item-based CF method proposed by Sarwar et al. [6] so that, instead of having one similarity value for two items i and j, a similarity vector of dimension P is generated (P is the total number of perspectives available for a user to rate an item). The components of this vector are the individual similarities calculated based on the perspectives selected by a user. For instance, for a music playlist compilation problem the set of perspectives can be lyrics, tunes, band, vocals, direction, video, etc. Based on the user's context—i.e. a selection of perspectives—we compare the compilations that have been previously rated by other users and compute the degree of similarity between them.

Our context-based CF algorithm is described below:

1. The user chooses the relevant perspectives along which similarity between items is desired. Preferences of all users are induced through previous ratings along multiple perspectives on chosen items that are expressed as numerical scores. A separate rating matrix $M_p(u,i)$ is generated for every perspective, where $M_p(u,i)$ is the rating of user u on item i for perspective p.
2. We identify and isolate users that have rated both items and then we apply the similarity technique proposed by [6]. Let $PS_p(i,j)$ be the *Perspective Similarity* between two co-rated items i and j with respect to perspective p, and is calculated using (Eq.2).

$$PS_p(i,j) = \frac{\sum_{u \in U}(M_p(u,i) - \overline{M}_p(u))(M_p(u,j) - \overline{M}_p(u))}{\sqrt{\sum_{u \in U}(M_p(u,i) - \overline{M}_p(u))^2}\sqrt{\sum_{u \in U}(M_p(u,j) - \overline{M}_p(u))^2}} \tag{2}$$

where $\overline{M}_p(u)$ is the average rating of user u on all rated items. U is the set of all users in the CF knowledge base. Let W_p the weight assigned to perspective p; the Contextual Similarity $CS(i,j)$ between items i and j is then computed as:

$$CS(i,j) = \frac{\sum_{p=1}^{P} W_p * PS_p(i,j)}{\sum_{p=1}^{P} W_p} \tag{3}$$

When a user selects a specific context for similarity computation, the summation in (Eq.3) is achieved over the selected perspectives only.

3. Let the set I_u contains all items that have been rated by user u. For every item $i \in I_u$, we find the set of k most similar items (K_u). The set K_u excludes any item that has been rated/preferred by u and hence belong to the set I_u.
4. For every item $i \in K_u$, we compute its similarity $S\text{-}set(i,I_u)$ to the set I_u. This similarity is the sum of the similarities (calculated in *Step 2*) between all items rated by user u and item i.

$$S - set(i \in K_u, I_u) = \sum_{j \in I_u} CS(i, j) \tag{4}$$

5. We sort the set K_u by the similarity $S\text{-}set(i,I_u)$ in decreasing order and select the top N items. The selected N items/compilations would most likely interest the user.

4.2 Phase II: CBR-Mediated Compositional Adaptation

Case adaptation in a CBR cycle allows for the adaptation of past cases (or solutions) in line with the description of the current problem [1, 11]. In our approach, we regard an information item (comprising a set of individual components) as a past case. The case selection process is achieved by the CF method in phase I of our strategy. Here, we apply a compositional case adaptation method to select the most pertinent constituent components of a composite information item [8]; provided the information components are mutually independent and compatibility between components is not an issue. The adapted case—i.e. a set of information components selected from the multiple information items—represents a fine-grained information item [12].

The basis for our adaptation strategy is defined by (a) the frequency of occurrence of a solution component in the similar cases and, (b) the degree of similarity between the user request and the retrieved case (measured in terms of the *appropriateness degree*). Our compositional adaptation of past cases is achieved as follows:

1. Given that a case is an item comprising multiple components. The similarity between a retrieved case C and a user u is calculated as shown in Eq.4. The similarity $S(u,C)$ between user u and every retrieved case C as $S(u,C)=S\text{-}set(i,I_u)$.
2. For every similar item case C_i, the Normalized Similarity (NS) of C_i to user u over the entire set of retrieved cases (RC) is calculated as follows:

$$Temp = \sum_{i=1}^{RC} 1/S(u, C_i) \tag{5}$$

$$NS(u, C_i) = 1 - 1/(S(u, C_i) * Temp) \tag{6}$$

3. Let $Comp_{C_i}$ be a component of the solution derived from a past case C_i, and $AD_u^{Comp_{C_i}}$ be the appropriateness degree for $Comp_{C_i}$, then

    For every user u in the test set,
     For i = 1 to RC
      If $Comp_{C_i}$ exists in the solution of the similar case C_i

$$AD_u^{Comp_{C_i}} = AD_u^{Comp_{C_i}} + NS(u, C_i) \tag{7}$$

In order to compute the Appropriateness Degree (AD) of each component, the normalized similarities of the similar cases that contain this component are added to one another.

4. We sort the distinct components of the N items by their AD, and select the M top components—i.e. the components that are most similar to the user. The value for M can be specified by the user.

5. The *M* selected components are amalgamated into one information item (or a new adapted case) that is recommended to the user.

Note that the application of the compositional adaptation method not only takes into account the global similarity between the present and past cases, but it is additionally driven by an attribute-level similarity between the current and retrieved cases.

5 Empirical Results

5.1 Performance of the Contextual Similarity in CF Recommendation

The quality of our item-based CF recommender system depends on how accurately it captures the user's preferences (ratings) as well as its ability to accurately match those preferences with similar users. Our experiments show that as we increase the number of perspectives, the F1-metric and the appropriateness degree increase and as a consequence a more personalized recommendation is provided. In fact, the appropriateness degree increases significantly by 52% when we apply 3 perspectives instead of only one perspective. Our conclusion is grounded in the observation that when the similarity is based on fewer perspectives, the similar item space which includes all items similar to the target item is large and contains items that are of potentially of little interest to the target user.

We performed statistical tests to study whether the difference between the means F1-metric for all three alternatives (1, 2, and 3 perspectives) is significant. In this regards, we used the General Linear Model approach [13] to perform the statistical test. The null hypothesis for the test is that all means are the same. Our test gave strong evidence against the null hypothesis (p-value, which denotes the probability that the null hypothesis is true, is much less than 0.001); hence, we conclude that the difference between the three F1-metric means is statistically significant.

5.2 Performance of the Compositional Adaptation Technique

The *AD* computed in (Eq.7) is used as a measure for the efficiency of our compositional adaptation technique. We calculate the *AD* of the newly adapted item which reflects the similarity degree between the adapted item and the individual user's preferences (represented by the set of items rated by the user). Basically, the *AD* of the final solution is the average sum of the *AD*s of the *M* (most relevant) components that constitute the final personalized information item.

In Fig.2, we note an increase in the appropriateness degree from phase I to phase II for selected users. An average percent increase of 61% was recorded for all users in the test dataset. The composite solution is more appropriate to the user's preferences than the items recommended through the CF phase; we conclude that our CBR-based compositional adaptation has provided the opportunity to pursue personalized information content more focused toward an individual user's interests.

In order to show that the difference in the appropriateness degree between phase I and phase II is statistically significant, we apply the General Linear Model approach

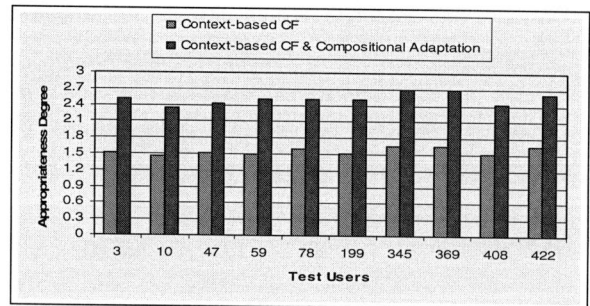

Fig. 2. Impact of the compositional adaptation on the appropriateness of the final solution

for testing whether the 2 mean values in appropriateness degree over all test users between phase I and phase II are different. The null hypothesis of the statistical test is that the 2 means are the same. Our test provided strong evidence against the null hypothesis (p-value < 0.001); we conclude that the 2 mean *AD*s are statistically different.

6   Working Example

We present a working example for recommending personalized music playlists. The user *u* has rated a set of CD compilations (see Fig. 3), where each compilation consists of 10 songs. The hit set contains those compilations that are recommended and were rated by *u* but were excluded from the training set for testing purposes. Note that users, music compilations (i.e. items) and songs (i.e. components) are represented by their IDs. The output of Phase I and Phase II is shown below.

User ID	Compilations (Information Items)				
130	1	17	42	96	159
	328	444	578	892	1095

Fig. 3. Preferred music compilations for user ID '130'

- *Output from Phase I:* CF is applied with a context of 3 perspectives yields a hit set containing 6 compilations (see Fig.4). The appropriateness degree (AD) is averaged over the 10 recommendations. The F1-metric with a context (i.e. 0.34) is found to be better than without context (i.e. 0.76).

User ID	Compilations (Information Items)					F1 Metric	AD
130	47	92	295	331	332	0.34	1.134
	348	379	876	1012	1197		

Fig. 4. *N* Recommended music compilations (Phase I). Hit List is shaded grey. *N=10.*

- *Output from Phase II:* We apply compositional adaptation to recommended compilations (in Fig.4). Fig. 5 shows a sample of the recommended items together with their components. The components selected in phase II are shaded in Fig. 5, whereas Fig. 6 shows the final personalized recommended music playlist.

User ID	Item ID	Songs (Components)					AD
	332	2	26	46	63	88	
	348	22	35	104	125	187	
130	379	2	20	41	110	128	1.801
	876	20	25	125	196	198	
	1012	24	35	113	161	198	

Fig. 5. A sample of the 10 recommended compilations and their constituent songs. Shaded songs are the most relevant to the user.

User ID	Personalized Music Playlist				
130	2	20	22	25	46
	71	104	125	187	198

Fig. 6. New composite recommendation comprising the 10 most relevant songs for user ID '130'

We note an improvement in the quality of the final personalized recommendation in terms of the *F1-metric*, and the *appropriateness degree* that has increased significantly by 58.8%. The personalized music playlist, originating from different items, will be presented to the user as being most relevant to his/her interest.

7   Concluding Remarks and Future Work

In this paper, we have introduced a new personalized recommendation strategy featuring a unique hybrid of item-based Collaborative Filtering and Case Based Reasoning— i.e. a hybrid of information retrieval and artificial intelligence methods. We addressed personalization at a fine-grained level, whereby in the first stage the collaborative information filtering strategy initiates the process guided by peer based recommendations for pertinent information items. Next, in the second stage, the compositional adaptation method takes into account the degree of relevance of the retrieved information items and the weighted frequency of the recurring constituent information components in order to select the most appropriate information components. We introduced the notion of context—basically rating an item along distinct perspectives, where the more perspectives are used to rate the item the more focused and appropriate the retrieved information items would be to the user. This is an improvement from the single-dimensional binary rating scheme observed by CF systems. Our empirical results show that the usage of context as well as the compositional adaptation has provided more precise personalized recommendations in line with the user's needs.

For future work, we plan to explore quantifying the users' ratings based on the Multi-Attribute Utility Theory [19]. For instance, we evaluate initially the overall rating value on every rated item as a weighted addition of its ratings along the multiple perspectives, and finally we compute the similarity between rated items.

References

1. Aamodt, A., Plaza, E.: Case-Based Reasoning: Foundational Issues, Methodological Variations, and System Approaches. AI Communication, IOS Press (1994)

2. Abidi, S.S.R.: Designing Adaptive Hypermedia for Internet Portals: A Personalization Strategy Featuring Case Based Reasoning with Compositional Adaptation. Lecture Notes in Artificial Intelligence 2527, Springer-Verlag, Berlin (2002)
3. Belkin, N. J., Croft, W.B.: Information Filtering and Information Retrieval; Two Sides of the Same Coin. Communications of the ACM, Vol. 35. (1992) 29-38
4. Dilley, R.: The problem of Context. Berghahn Books, New York (1999)
5. Resnick, P., N. Iacovou, M. Suchak, P. Bergstrom, and J. Riedl: GroupLens: An Open Architecture for Collaborative Filtering of Netnews, Proceedings of ACM 1994 Conference on Computer Supported Cooperative Work: Chapel Hill, NC (1994) 175-186
6. Sarwar, B., Karypis, G., Konstan, J., Riedl, J.: Item-based Collaborative Filtering Recommendation Algorithms. Proceedings of the International WWW Conference (10). Hong Kong (2001)
7. Sarwar, B., Karypis, J., Konstan, J., Riedl, J.: Analysis of Recommendation Algorithms for E-Commerce. 2nd Conf. on Electronic Commerce (EC'00), New York (2000)
8. Wilke, W., Bergmann, R.: Techniques and Knowledge Used for Adaptation During Case-Based Problem Solving. Proceedings of the 11th International Conference on Industrial and Engineering Applications of Artificial Intelligence and Expert Systems (1998)
9. Cotter, P. and B. Smyth: PTV: Intelligent Personalized TV Guides, Proceedings of the Seventeenth National Conference on Artificial Intelligence and Twelfth Conference on Innovative Applications of Artificial Intelligence. AAAI Press, MIT Press (2000) 957-964
10. Geong, Y. Y.: An Analysis of Collaborative Filtering Systems. KMS Research Paper, School of Information, University of Texas, Austin (2003)
11. Schmidt, R., Vorobieva, O., Gierl, L.: Case-Based Adaptation Problems in Medicine. Proceedings of WM2003: Professionelles Wissensmanagement, Kollen-Verlag Bonn (2003)
12. Reyhani, N., Badie, K., Kharrat, M.: A New Approach to Compositional Adaptation Based on Optimizing the Global Distance Function and Its Application in an Intelligent Tutoring System. Proceedings of 2003 IEEE Intl. Conf. on Information Reuse and Integration, Las Vegas, USA (2003) 285-290
13. Daniel Wayne W.: Biostatistics, A Foundation for Analysis in the Health Sciences. Wiley (1987)
14. Kobsa A.: Customized Hypermedia Presentation Techniques for Improving Online Customer Relationships. Knowledge Engineering Review, Vol. 16(2). (1999) 111-155
15. Abidi, S.S.R., Chong, Y., Abidi, S.R.: Patient Empowerment Via 'Pushed' Delivery of Customized Healthcare Educational Content Over the Internet. 10th World Congress on Medical Informatics, London (2001)
16. Henze, N., Nejdl, W.: Extensible Adaptive Hypermedia Courseware: Integrating Different Courses and Web Material. In P. Brusilovsky, O Stock & C Strappavara (Eds.) Adaptive Hypermedia and Adaptive Web-based Systems, Springer-Verlag (2000) 109-120
17. Aguzzoli, S., Avesani, P., Masssa, P.: Compositional CBR via Collaborative Filtering. Proceedings of ICCBR'01 Workshop on CBR in Electronic Commerce, Vancouver, Canada (2001)
18. Burke, R.: A Case-Based Approach to Collaborative Filtering. Advances in Case-Based Reasoning, 5th European Workshop EWCBR 2000. Springer-Verlag, New York (2000)
19. Winterfeld, D. von, Edwards, W.: Decision Analysis and Behavioral Research. Cambridge, England, Cambridge University Press (1986)
20. Goker, M. H. and B. Smyth: Workshop on Case Based Reasoning and Personalization, 6th European Conference on Case Based Reasoning ECCBR, Aberdeen, Scotland (2002)

An Empirical Study About Calibration of Adaptive Hints in Web-Based Adaptive Testing Environments

Ricardo Conejo, Eduardo Guzmán, José-Luis Pérez-de-la-Cruz, and Eva Millán

Departamento de Lenguajes y Ciencias de la Computación,
Universidad de Málaga,
Bulevar Louis Pasteur, 35,
Málaga, 29071, Spain
{conejo, guzman, perez, eva}@lcc.uma.es

Abstract. In this paper we present a proposal for introducing hint adaptive selection in an adaptive web-based testing environment. To this end, a discussion of some aspects concerning the adaptive selection mechanism for hints is presented, which results in the statement of two axioms that such hints must fulfil. Then, an empirical study with real students is presented, whose goal is to evaluate a tentative bank of items with their associated hints to determine the usefulness of such hints for different knowledge levels and to calibrate both test items and hints.

1 Introduction

Testing is commonly used in many educational contexts with different purposes: grading, self-assessment, diagnostic assessment, etc. In order to improve the efficiency of the diagnosis process, adaptive testing systems select the next best question to be asked according to the relevant characteristics of the examinee. In this way, higher accuracy can be reached with a significant reduction in test length. In literature, there are different proposals for adaptive testing [1], [2]. One of the most commonly used is the *Item Response Theory* (IRT) [3], which has a well-founded theoretical background which assumes that the answer to a question depends on an unknown latent numerical trait. The latent trait θ represents a psychological factor that we want to measure and that is not directly observable. In educational environments, the latent trait corresponds to the knowledge of the subject being tested.

In any adaptive educational system, it is necessary to have accurate estimations of the student's knowledge level in order to take the most suitable instructional action. In this sense, *Computerized Adaptive Tests* (CATs) [4] based on IRT provide a powerful, efficient and reliable diagnosis tool. SIETTE [5], [6] is a web-based assessment environment that allows the construction and administration of conventional tests and CATs based on a discretization of IRT. One of the most relevant characteristics of SIETTE is that it is an open assessment tool, i.e, it can be easily integrated into any web-based learning system. In this

V. Wade, H. Ashman, and B. Smyth (Eds.): AH 2006, LNCS 4018, pp. 71–80, 2006.

way, SIETTE can be responsible for all the tasks concerning student modelling (basically creation and maintenance of the student model). This system can be accessed at *http://www.lcc.uma.es/SIETTE*.

One of the contributions to educational psychology in the XX century is Vigotskii's *Zone of Proximal Development* (ZPD) [7], defined as "the distance between the actual developmental level as determined by independent problem solving and the level of potential development as determined through problem solving under adult guidance or in collaboration with a more capable peer". A short operational definition useful for our purposes is given in [8]: the zone defined by the difference between a child's (in our case, person's) test performance under two conditions: with or without assistance.

Soon after the definition of the ZPD, attempts to apply this concept were made in the context of the test administration, under the two conditions described (with or without assistance), typically with the aim of classifying students in order to allocate them in the most appropriate educational program. But the main goal of the work presented here is different: to build a model that allows the integration of adaptive assistance in the adaptive testing procedure within the SIETTE system.

Hinting can be considered a general and effective tactic for human tutoring. In this sense, some researchers have put the emphasis on the mechanisms used by students to request hints when needed [9, 10]. On the other hand, many Intelligent Tutoring Systems also give hints to the student, like for example, ANDES [11], which calculates the score according to the correctness of the student's answer and the number of hints received; or AnimalWatch [12], which has different types of hints available (highly/low interactive and specific/symbolic hints) and adapts such hints to relevant features of the student such as the level of cognitive development and gender. It can be observed that human tutors maintain a rough assessment of the student's performance (the trait in our approach) in order to select a suitable hint [13].

Consequently, we will assume that assistance is represented by hints, h_1,..., h_n that provide different levels of support for each test question (commonly known as *items* in adaptive testing environments). By adaptive assistance we mean that the hint to be presented will be selected by the system depending on where the item is in the ZPD, in such a way that it provides the minimal amount of information and yet the student will still be able to correctly answer such an item.

The work presented here further extends our investigation about introducing hints and feedback in adaptive testing, presented in [12]. Now, our main objectives are:

- Definition of a theoretical framework for adaptive hinting selection.
- Empirical study of the feasibility of the approach. To this end, an item bank has been developed for a course. Each item had a set of hints assigned. This bank has been tested in several experiments, all of them with real students. The final goal of these experiments was to validate the hints developed.

A further issue considered in paper is the calibration of the pairs of item-hints. Once this procedure has been accomplished, it will allow tests to be delivered in which both items and hints are adaptively selected according to the current estimation of the student's knowledge level.

2   Computerized Adaptive Testing and Item Response Theory

The CAT theory when combined with IRT allows a well-founded administration of adaptive tests. A *Computerized Adaptive Test* is a computer-based test where the decision to present a test item and the decision to finish the test are dynamically made depending on the examinee's performance in previous answers. If the CATs of two examinees are compared, each one of them will usually receive different sequences of items, and even different items. To properly administrate a CAT, each item i in the item bank is assigned an *Item Characteristic Curve* (ICC). An ICC is a function representing the probability of a correct answer to that item given the student's knowledge level θ, which is unknown but supposed to be constant during the whole test. The probability P_i of succeeding when answering a test item ($u_i = 1$) can be computed as $P_i = P(u_i = 1|\theta)$, and the probability Q_i of failing as $Q_i = P(u_i = 0|\theta) = 1 - P(u_i = 1|\theta)$. If the test is composed of n items, knowing their ICCs, and assuming local independence of items, a likelihood function L can be constructed as shown below:

$$L(u_1, u_2, ..., u_n|\theta) = \prod_{i=1}^{n} P^{u_i} Q^{1-u_i} \tag{1}$$

The maximum of this function gives an estimation of the most likely value of θ. A probability distribution of θ can be obtained by applying Bayes' rule n times. It is usually assumed that ICCs belong to a family of functions that depend on one, two or three parameters. These functions are constructed based on the normal or the logistic distribution functions. For example, in the three-parameter logistic model (3PL)[14] the ICC is described by:

$$CCI_i(\theta) = c_i + (1 - c_i)\frac{1}{1 + e^{-1.7a_i(\theta - b_i)}} \tag{2}$$

where c_i is the *guessing factor*, b_i is the item *difficulty* and a_i is the *discrimination factor*. The *guessing factor* is the probability that a student with no knowledge at all answers the item correctly. The question *difficulty* represents the knowledge level in which the student has equal probability of answering or failing the item, in addition to the guessing factor. The *discrimination factor* is proportional to the slope of the curve.

Based upon the IRT and the CAT theory, our group has developed and implemented the SIETTE for adaptive testing construction and administration via the Web. In contrast with traditional IRT-based proposals, the knowledge level in SIETTE is a discrete variable that can take $n + 1$ values $v_0 < v_1 < ... < v_n$

(in the sections which follow, we will represent these values as $0, 1, ..., n$). In this way, in SIETTE ICCs are represented by vectors of $n + 1$ elements. Hence, computation of Bayes' rule is simply turned into a product of $n + 1$ values plus a normalization procedure. The main advantage of this discretization is that it improves the computational efficiency of the calculus, turning SIETTE into a scalable system. However, this entails a slight loss of accuracy in estimations.

3 Introducing Hints in an Adaptive Testing-Based Assessment Model

To introduce hints in the model, let us first define some terms:

- *Item.* We use this term to generically denote a question or exercise posed to a student. The solution of such task or question could be provided in different manners: by selecting one or more choices available within the item, or even allowing the examinee to write a brief text.
- A *test* is a sequence of items.
- *Hint.* A hint is an additional piece of information that is presented to the student after posing an item and before he/she answers it. Hints may provide an explanation of the stem, clues for rejecting one or more choices, indications on how to proceed, etc. Hints can be invoked in two different ways: a) *actively*, i.e., when the examinee asks for the hint by clicking a button; or b) *passively*, that is, when the hint is triggered as a consequence of his/her behavior while answering the item, indicating that the student has reached an impasse (for example, too much time waiting).

Let us see a simple example. Consider the following test item:

```
What is the result of the expression: 1/8 + 1/4?
   a) 3/4  b)2/4   c)3/8   d)2/8
```

Possible hints may be:

```
Hint 1. 1/4 can be also represented as 2/8.
Hint 2. First, find equivalent fractions so they have
the same denominator.
Hint 3. Once fractions have the same denominator,
sum up numerators.
```

In the work presented here, a simplifying assumption is that *hints do not modify student's knowledge* (i.e., no student learning occurs either while testing or when receiving hints). This assumption is usual in adaptive testing (the trait θ remains constant during the test), and makes the model computationally tractable. In our case, this hypothesis means that hints do not cause a change in examinee's knowledge, but there is a change in the ICC shape. In this way, the hint brings the question from the ZPD to the student's knowledge level. In this sense, the combination of the item plus the hint can be considered as a new item. This new (virtual) item can be treated and measured in the same way as the other items in the test: the new item is represented by a new ICC whose parameters can be estimated using the traditional techniques. However, both ICC's are not independent of each other. First of all, the use of a hint should make the question easier. This condition can be stated in mathematical terms by the following:

Axiom 1. Given an item q and a hint h, for all knowledge levels k, the following constraint must be fulfilled: $CCI_q(k) \leq CCI_{q+h}(k)$. ICC_q represents the original item characteristic curve and ICC_{q+h} represents the characteristic curve of the item with the hint.

If the examinee uses a combination of hints, the question should become even easier. Mathematically this condition can be written as follows:

Axiom 2. Given an item q, a set of hints H and a hint $h \notin H$, for all knowledge levels k, the following constraint must be fulfilled: $CCI_{q+H}(k) \leq CCI_{q+H+\{h\}}(k)$.

For a set of items and their corresponding hints, after the ICC parameters calibration[1] (of the real and virtual items), if the resulting ICCs do not satisfy the axioms above, it means that the piece of information given is a misleading element instead of a hint; therefore, it should be rejected. This simple approach provides us with a useful empirical method that allows validation of the proposed hints.

In adaptive environments, it makes sense to look for a criterion for adaptively selecting the best hint to be presented (from a set of available hints). Under the ZPD framework, if the student is not able to solve the item but this item is in his/her ZPD, the best hint to be presented would be the one that brings item I from the ZPD to the zone of the student's knowledge, and of course it will depend on how far on the ZPD the item is located. So, for example, if an item I has three associated hints h_1, h_2 and h_3 at different levels of detail, it means that each hint is suitable for a different part of the ZPD.

Therefore, the selection of h_i as the best hint to be presented would mean that the item I lies in ZPD_i for this particular student. A possibility for adaptive selection of hints is to use classical adaptive item selection mechanisms, e.g. given the knowledge estimation $\theta(k)$ for a student, and given two hints h_1, h_2, with $ICC_{q+\{h1\}}(k)$ and $ICC_{q+\{h2\}}(k)$, the best hint to use is the one that minimizes the expected variance of the posterior probability distribution. This mechanism is simple to implement and does not require substantial modifications in the adaptive testing procedure, because the test is only used for assessment and not as a learning tool. However, the use of adaptive hints in this context can provide positive stimuli and, as a consequence, increase student self-confidence.

---

[1] The calibration process consists of inferring ICCs from the student initial score. As a result, a first estimation of the student knowledge θ can be computed from these ICCs. This procedure will iterate until an equilibrium is reached. Therefore, students having asked for more hints (i.e., those students which presumably answered "easier" items), obtain a score which is very close to the one obtained when no hints are requested. ICCs take into account the lower or greater item "difficulty".

4   Experiments with Real Students

An important first step towards the integration of this new adaptive hints approach into the SIETTE system is the calibration of the virtual items resulting from the combination of items and hints. Calibration of hints is a difficult goal, and, to this end, a methodology composed of several steps must be observed:

1. First of all, an item bank must be developed. Each item must also have several hints assigned.
2. Second, items must be administered to a student sample by means of a conventional (i.e. non-adaptive) test. After that, characteristic curves of real and virtual items must be calibrated.
3. Finally, once the ICCs have been inferred, adaptive administration of the test and the hints assigned with its items can be accomplished.

Regarding the first step, an item bank relating to a course of *Language Processors* has been developed. This course is taught at the Computer Science School in the University of Málaga (Spain). Each item has 2, 3 or 4 associated hints. Examples of such items are:

```
1. What is the output of the following LEX program with input abc?
     ab/c  { printf(''one'');    }
     c     { printf''two'');     }
     abc   { printf(''three''); }

   a) three b) one two  c) one  d) one two three

   Hint 1. yytext does not contain the characters on the right
   hand side of the lookahead operator ''/''.
   Hint 2. When the regular expression includes a lookahead
   operator, the length of the string matched corresponds to the
   part of the expression on the left of the operator.

2. Let T be the set of all ASCII characters from 0 to 127. The set
of all strings that can be formed with the symbols of T, can be
represented in LEX by the regular expression:

   a)(.|\n)*   b)[a-zA-Z0-9]*  c).*   d)[.]*

   Hint 1. The .(dot) operator represents any ASCII
   character, except the end of the line.
   Hint 2. The .(dot) operator does not have any special
   meaning when it is used inside the brackets [].
   Hint 3. The ASCII alphabet includes more than letters and
   digits, it also includes operators, punctuation symbols,
   parenthesis, and other special characters.
```

In the second step, three experiments have been carried out, with a total number of 263 individuals. Experiments included students taking the *Language Processors* course during 2003/04, 2004/05 and 2005/06. The sample size was 100, 80 and 83 students, respectively. All students were graded by means of a non-adaptive test-based exam composed of 20 items. These tests were administered using the SIETTE system. Students had a time limit of 45 minutes available to complete the test. The majority of students (87%), completed the test. 97% of them answered at least 18 items. All these data were used in the analysis described in this paper. For each test item, students were given the possibility of requesting a hint. It was a heterogeneous test where several types of items were combined (multiple-choice with just one correct choice, multiple-choice with more than one correct choice and fill-in-the-blank items). The same 20 items were posed to all students, but in a different order, in order to avoid cheating. Once a student requested a hint, it was randomly selected from the pool of hints assigned to the item.

The scoring method differed according to the experiment. In all of them, for each correctly solved, the student was awarded 1 point (in order to pass the exam students needed a minimum of ten points). However if a hint had been used, the correct solution only gave 0.5 points in the first experiment, 0,75 in the second, and 1 (i.e., no penalization) in the third one.

Table 1. Portion of students answering correctly

Item 1	*No hint*	*Hint 1*	*Hint 2*	**Item 2**	*No hint*	*Hint 1*	*Hint 2*	*Hint 3*
Correct	108	20	25	*Correct*	134	20	13	20
Total	198	29	34	*Total*	176	31	26	27
Percentage	54,5%	68,9%	73,5%	*Percentage*	76,1%	64,5%	50%	74%

Table 1 collects the results for items 1 and 2. It shows the number of students who correctly answered the corresponding item. The second row contains the portion of students, and the third row the corresponding percentage. For instance, the pair 108/198 in the first position of the first row, indicates that 198 individuals answered item 1 without asking for hints, and from this set, only 108 students gave the correct answer.

Fig. 1 shows the total percentage average of hints requested for each item and experiment. The total use of hints was 8, 7 and 53%, respectively. This suggests students only perceived qualitatively the penalty applied for hint requesting, since there are not significant differences between the first two experiments, in spite of the fact that the penalization in the second experiment was lower. The use of hints was much more frequent in the third experiment because, as explained before, they were not penalized. Still, there were students that decided not to ask for hints, probably because they knew (or thought they knew) the correct answer or because the time of the test was limited and they did not want to waste time reading the hint.

With regarding to the real usefulness of hints, which we define as the percentage of items successfully answered after requesting a hint, this was around 50% (more specifically, 38%, 47% and 56% in each of the three experiments).

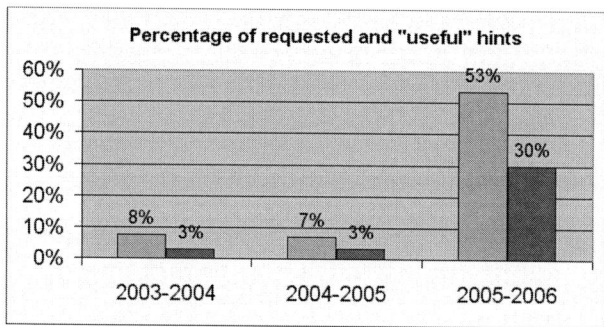

Fig. 1. Results about the use of hints in the three experiments

4.1 Item Calibration Under the 3PL Model Analysis

Much more interesting is a whole analysis of the ICC achieved using the IRT. For this purpose, we will assume all ICCs follow the 3PL model, formerly expressed in equation 2.

In this new experiment, 81 ICCs have been calibrated: 20 curves corresponding to the real items, and in addition, the curves of the 61 virtual items obtained from the combination of each pair *item+hint*. To this end, we have used one of the most popular item calibration tools in IRT, i.e., MULTILOG [15]. Results

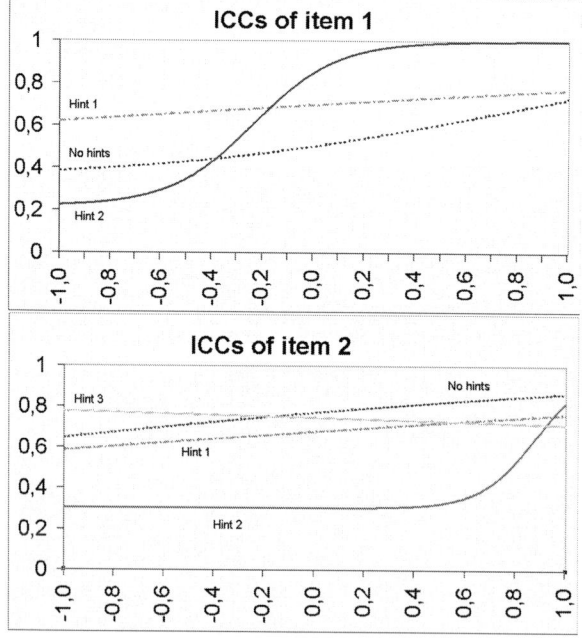

Fig. 2. ICCs of items 1 and 2

show that student knowledge level distribution (θ) is normal with a mean of $0,018$ and standard deviation of $0,337$. That is, $99,7\%$ of the sample exhibit θ values located at the interval $[-1,1]$. Fig. 2 depicts the results for items 1 and 2 in this interval. The horizontal axis displays the knowledge level (θ), and the vertical axis the probability of correctly answering the item. The calibrated ICCs of the items without hints are represented by a dotted line.

As can be seen, after this analysis, hints of item 1 are useful only from a certain knowledge threshold. This threshold is located at the intersection of both curves. Hint 1 is useful for the majority of students but, in contrast, hint 2 is only useful for those whose knowledge level satisfies the following constraint: $\theta > -0,35$, i.e., for the 84% of the sample individuals. Regarding item 2, observe that hint 1 does not provide any improvement in the success percentage, and its curve is very close to the one corresponding to the original item. Consequently, we can infer that it does not contain relevant information to help students solve the item. Likewise, hint 2 is counterproductive for the majority of students. Finally, hint 3 is as a misleading element (note that the slope of the ICC is negative) so this hint should be discarded.

5   Conclusions and Future Work

This paper has presented some ideas about hint adaptive selection in an adaptive testing environment, based upon IRT constructs. Hints are considered not as knowledge modifiers, but as modifiers of the ICC of an item. Some formal axioms that every model of hints must satisfy have been stated and informally justified.

We have also described the three different experiments with real students which we carried out between 2003 and 2006. In those experiments three student samples took a test composed of the same items. Once an item was posed, students were given the possibility of asking for a hint. Depending on the experiment, the use of a hint was penalized.

Finally, we have performed the ICC calibration based on well founded IRT based techniques. Calibration was done for each item, and also, for each virtual item, resulting from each pair *item+hint*. The input data used for calibration was the performance of real students who took the test in the three former experiments. Thanks to the ICCs inferred from calibration, we have got not only a set of calibrated ICCs, but a mechanism to discern between useful and useless hints, and to remove those hints that confuse the students.

Plans for immediate future work involve the adaptive administration of both items and hints and, accordingly, the evaluation of the benefits of our proposal.

References

1. Rudner, L.M.: An Examination of Decision-Theory Adaptive Testing Procedures. In: Annual meeting of the American Educational Research Association. (2002)
2. Chua Abdullah, S.: Student Modelling by Adaptive Testing - A Knowledge-based Approach. PhD thesis, University of Kent, Canterbury (2003)

3. Hambleton, R.K., Swaminathan, J., Rogers, H.J.: Fundamentals of Item Response Theory. Sage publications (1991)

4. Wainer, H.: Computerized Adaptive Testing: A Primer. Lawrence Erlbaum, Hillsdale, NJ (1990)

5. Conejo, R., Guzmán, E., Millán, E., Trella, M., Pérez de la Cruz, J.L., Ríos, A.: SIETTE: a Web-based tool for adaptive testing. Journal of Artificial Intelligence in Education **14** (2004) 29–61

6. Guzmán, E., Conejo, R.: A brief introduction to the new architecture of SIETTE. In Bra, P.D., Nejdl, W., eds.: Proceedings of the IIIth International Conference on Adaptive Hypermedia and Adaptive Web-Based Systems(AH 2004). Lecture Notes in Computer Science. Number 3137. New York: Springer Verlag (2004) 405–408

7. Vygotskii, L.:   Mind in Society: The Development of Higher Psychological Processes. Cambridge, MA: Harvard University Press (1978)

8. Wells, G.:   Dialogic Inquiry: Towards a Socio-Cultural Practice and Theory of Education. New York: Cambridge University Press (1999)

9. Luckin, R., Hammerton, L.: Getting to know me: Helping learners understand their own learning needs through meta-cognitive scaffolding. In: Proceedings of the 6th World Conference of Intelligent Tutoring Systems. ITS'02. Springer-Verlag (2002) 759–771

10. Aleven, V., McLaren, B., Roll, I., Koedinger, K.: Towards tutoring help seeking: Applying cognitive modeling to meta-cognitive skills. In: Proceedings of the 7th World Conference of Intelligent Tutoring Systems. ITS'04. Springer-Verlag (2000) 227–239

11. Gertner, A.S., Conati, C., VanLehn, K.: Procedural Help in Andes: Generating Hints Using a Bayesian Network Student Model. In: Proceedings of the 15th National Conference on Artificial Intelligence. Madison, Wisconsin (1998)

12. Arroyo, I., Beck, J.E., Woolf, B.P., Beal, C.R., Schultz, K.: Macroadapting Animalwatch to gender and cognitive differences with respect to hint interactivity and symbolism. In: Proceedings of the 5th World Conference of Intelligent Tutoring Systems. ITS'00. Springer-Verlag (2000) 604–614

13. Hume, G.D., Michael, J., Rovick, A., Evens, M.W.: Hinting as a tactic in one-on-one tutoring. Journal of Learning Sciences **5**(1) (1996) 23–47

14. Birnbaum, A.: Some Latent Trait Models and Their Use in Inferring an Examinee's Mental Ability. In: Statistical Theories of Mental Test Scores. Reading, MA: Addison-Wesley (1968)

15. Thissen, D.: MULTILOG: Multiple, categorical item analysis and test scoring using item response theory (version 5.1) (1988)

Combining Adaptive Hypermedia Techniques and Ontology Reasoning to Produce Dynamic Personalized News Services

Owen Conlan, Ian O'Keeffe, and Shane Tallon

Knowledge and Data Engineering Group, Department of Computer Science,
Trinity College, Dublin 2, Ireland
{Owen.Conlan, Ian.OKeeffe, stallon}@cs.tcd.ie
http://kdeg.cs.tcd.ie

Abstract. Applying traditional Adaptive Hypermedia techniques to the person-alization of news can pose a number of problems. The first main difficulty is the fact that news is inherently dynamic, thus producing an ever shifting pool from which content can be sourced. The second difficulty arises when trying to model a users interests and how they may be related to the available news items. This paper investigates the use of ontologies as a means of providing se-mantic bridges between available news items from RSS [1] news feeds and the interests of a user. Specifically, it investigates the combination of AH tech-niques with the ideas of loose and strict ontologies as the basis for personaliza-tion. This combination is highlighted through the design, development and evaluation of the Personalized News Service (PNS), which is based on the APeLS architecture [2].

1 Introduction

The personalization of information for each user is an area of research which provides an alternative to the "one-size fits all" [3] view of today's World Wide Web. Such personalization of information allows the users of a system to have tailored experi-ences where they are only presented with information which is of interest to them. The majority of personalization systems [4] [5] [2] work on a closed world model, where the information which is personalized is defined and marked-up with appropri-ate metadata before adaptation occurs. This step is often seen as necessary as is en-sures there are semantic relationships between the content in the information space, the adaptation logic and the models (usually the user model) upon which the adapta-tion is based [6] [2]. Alternatively, many older Adaptive Hypermedia Systems [4] [5] explicitly refer to content in their adaptive logic in order to facilitate personalization.

Applying such approaches to the personalization of news content, however, would prove difficult. News is highly dynamic and users' interests in it can be fickle. The application of a closed world approach does not lend itself to the dynamism of news as the definition, classification and mark-up of individual news items would prove cum-bersome. More significantly, the development of appropriate adaptive logic would need to be carried out on a continuous basis. Therefore, there exists a potential seman-tic gap, brought about by the dynamism of news, between the expression of a users

V. Wade, H. Ashman, and B. Smyth (Eds.): AH 2006, LNCS 4018, pp. 81–90, 2006.

interests and the ever changing news domain. For example, if, as a consumer of news, I said in 1998 that I was interested in Bill Clinton, what does that mean? It could be interpreted that I have a general interest in the office of President of the USA. Alternatively, it could have been a passing interest in the impeachment proceedings initiated in that year. Then again it could be a specific interest in his family. This example is indicative of the problem faced in applying current AHS techniques to such a dynamic and complex domain as news. This paper investigates the application of ontologies to help bridge the semantic gap between news items and user interests.

Ontologies provide a structured, semantically rich way of modeling a domain. They are frequently defined using the eXtensible Markup Language (XML) and can be built using definition languages such as OWL [7], and DAML+OIL [8]. Ontologies count classes, inheritance, relationships between classes and instances as some of their major components. The ability to reason over relationships defined in an ontology and, therefore, relate instances to their abstracted types is the primary benefit to using ontologies. From the example above, we may be able to reason that Bill Clinton (an instance) is the President (a class) of the USA (an instance of class Country) through the relationships in an ontology. Furthermore, we may be able to determine that he is married to (a relationship) Hilary Clinton.

This paper proposes the application of ontologies as a means of achieving semantic precision between a user's interests and the news items available. It investigates the issues surrounding building different types of ontologies, modeling user interests and achieving effective personalization. Specifically, it presents the Personalized News Service, a service developed in Trinity College Dublin, as the embodiment of these principles. Section two gives an overview of existing personalized news/information systems; section three follows with a discussion on designing ontologies for personalized news; section four describes user modeling issues and the architecture of the PNS; and section five presents the evaluation results of the trial of PNS.

2 Overview of Existing Systems

This section will briefly review a number of existing personalized news/information systems. The goal of this overview is to provide a backdrop upon which design decisions in the Personalized News Service may be based.

In Merialdo et al. [9] deals with the adaptation of video. The approach taken is not very different to adaptive insertion/presentation of text found in many AHS, as the video is indexed or annotated with metadata providing a good source of uniqueness of the data stream. Of more interest to this work is the fact that the project deals with a very large scope of news, including international politics, national politics, international society, national society, economy, culture and sport. The user model provided by the system combines a level of interest in a category (or multiple categories), and uses a labeling mechanism to annotate a story with an associated importance level. By combining the two, and using a probabilistic formulation, a simple yes or no answer can be given to determine a user's interest in a particular story. Articles of interest are compiled together so the user can view the combined video articles. A basic approach of providing a level of interest in particular topics was used to model the users. Yet the simple user model did not detract from the quality of personalized news that was provided for the users. The domain models were also relatively simple, being divided into several categories. Each article was then associated with a category and given a weighting from 1 to 100. This approach allowed for a good probabilistic chance that the user would not receive information which they would deem unsuitable to their needs.

In Jokela et al. [10], structured content, in the form of domain ontologies, are used. News content is provided with a semantic structure, which is then compared to a user profile to establish the relevancy of news articles. It is noted however, that interests can change and shift over time, and to provide a mechanism to adapt to such changes, user feedback is employed. In gathering user feedback, the ontologies can change, and become even more powerful than static ontologies. SmartPush [10] aims to get rid of some of the shortcomings available in commercial systems, such as the lack of customizable ontologies and relative depth for experts. The SmartPush system applies weights to semantic relationships between objects, culminating in more power and expressiveness in the system. The domain model, was represented as an ontology, providing semantic meaning to the domain model. As the concepts carried weights, to distinguish between important and unimportant concepts, the domain model had more power over the information provided by the content.

SeAN [11] is an adaptive system which starts by classifying documents into a tree, made up of sections and subsections. The hierarchical nature of the system is in parallel with the same kind of structure associated with newspaper editorial systems. SeAN attempts to be able to personalize the detail level of a news document based on the user model. The user model is an ontology, which is rather different to most ontologies, as most ontologies represent content or conceptual domains. The user model is broken down into different dimensions, providing an altogether different view of a user than is usual. These dimensions are Interests, Expertise, Cognitive Characteristics and Lifestyle. Behavior tracking is used to a great extent in the system also. Such behavior as the time spent reading a news article, false positives and misses are taken into account, and these instances are learned from. User axes such as preferences, cognitive style, and domain knowledge form the basis of the user modeling approach. Stereotypes such as these can provide the system with enough knowledge to base its first few adaptations, with adaptability becoming more focused as more use is made of the system. Due to the domain being represented as a hierarchical structure of articles, from high level concepts to lower level niche topics, adaptive presentation is used where only information relating to the user model is provided, and other redundant information is not presented to the user.

PIN [12] is an adaptive system which uses neural networks to learn user profiles. User profile learning is done quickly and easily using this method. User profiles grow and adapt to new interests of the user. User feedback also helps with the dynamism of the user models. Adaptive Navigation forms the basis of the adaptive techniques used in PIN. Links are sorted based on relevance, in decreasing order. Users are modeled by associating concepts from the domain, with interest weights provided for those concepts. Concepts have semantic meaning, providing more weight for the information which is of interest to the user. User Models are also updated "on the fly" as the system is being used, providing an adaptive user model, which is of better use than a static model.

3   Designing Ontologies for Personalized News

As part of this research two different forms of ontologies were proposed as a basis for personalization. These were termed the *strict* and *loose* ontologies. This section describes the rationale behind their design and the impact of gathering and using these ontologies. Personalization is facilitated through using these ontologies as semantic bridges between the general interests of a user and the specific instances of the domain from whish the news is taken.

3.1   Influences from State of the Art

Ontologies provide the semantic relationships between objects and instances in a particular domain. In order to ensure the use of ontologies is viable they should be as easy to maintain as possible. Lightweight ontologies make this feasible. Using a tool such as Protégé [14] allows the manual maintenance and updating of an ontology in a relatively easy manner. Classes, relationships and instances can be added and deleted as needs be.

Jokela et al. [10] make use of an ontology to describe the domain. The domain ontology provided a structured view of the domain, with concepts carrying weights to determine their importance within the domain. The weights allow even more inferences to be made about the suitability of a news article when combined with the user model. The weighting in the domain model, however, is a little restrictive as it assumes all users place the same importance on the relative relationships. In using an ontology to represent a user model such as SeAN [11], an overall, structured, and weighted view can be placed on the user's interests. The structure and the semantic meaning which an ontology can provide gives a view of a domain which would be similar to that of a human's view. For example, knowing which are the more important concepts in a domain, the important relationships between concepts and the weight the concepts carry within the domain are examples of a persons view of that domain. However, there is a potential for high overhead in the maintenance of an ontology per user as the user model could grow quite large. There is also the possibility that the relationships in personal ontologies will become so idiosyncratic that they cannot be reconciled by the adaptive mechanisms used.

The Metasaur system [14] performs automated ontology building. The system allows the insertion of objects into a data dictionary, which is analyzed and incorporated into a domain ontology. This kind of automatic creation provides the developer with a much less time consuming method of creating a domain ontology. This method also removes the restricted ontology problem, which is when all the concepts in the domain are not available for markup. The disadvantage with this method, is that while it provides an ontology, there is little or no semantic meaning within the ontology. The domain is trawled, and links are inferred from objects, which lead to relationships being provided between those objects. Without much semantic meaning however, objects which have a higher importance than others can only be inferred by the number of related objects.

3.2 Defining the Types of Ontologies

There are primarily two methods of constructing ontologies, being manual creation and automatic creation. Manually building an ontology requires the identification of concepts and properties within the domain of the ontology. There is also the need to populate this ontology with instances of the classes (and possibly properties), which are generally temporal instances specific to the ontologies content domain. The primary type of ontology defined by manual ontology construction is a strict ontology, or an ontology rich with semantics.

The other method of ontology construction is automatic or semi automatic ontology creation, similar to that applied in the Mercureo [15] and Metasaur [14] systems. Semi automatic ontology construction can be implemented by trawling hyperlinked web resources attempting to determine concepts and relationships. The relationships derived however, have little meaning associated with them, as the nature of relationships through trawling are difficult to obtain. This can result in what can be termed a *loose* ontology, or an ontology with little semantic meaning between the relationships.

The ontology can then be considered in two forms, a strict ontology and a loose ontology. The strict ontology provides meaning for things and their relationships. such as a driver is a sub class of a person, as is a team technical director. A loose ontology may be derived by stripping the meaning from a strict ontology, leading to a mass of things and relationships, but little or no explicit meaning for those things and relationships. Instances may also be included in the loose ontology. With so little semantic meaning in the loose ontology a position could be argued for not counting it as an ontology at all. It could be considered a linked taxonomy.

3.3 Building the Experimental Ontologies

Strict and loose ontologies present significantly different challenges in their creation, i.e. loose ontologies may be created in an automated or semi automated fashion, while currently the only way to create a strict ontology is to build it manually. Since news is a highly dynamic domain there are significant arguments for an automated approach to building ontologies, and thus basing personalization on loose ontologies. As part of this work two ontologies were developed – one strict and one loose. The first ontology provides a domain model which is semantically rich in meaning and relationships. For the experiment this strict ontology is created manually using Protégé and exported into OWL. The other, loose, ontology provides a domain model which has no semantic meaning and is created from the strict ontology by stripping out the class and relationship information. The goal of creating two ontologies is to investigate the relative benefits of rich semantics versus weak semantics. For example, the strict ontology will note that Michael Schumacher is a Driver and that Ferrari is a Team. It will also note that there is a reciprocal relationship of drivesFor/isDriverOf between these instances. In the loose ontology Michael Schumacher is a Thing, as is Ferrari and they are related. As may be gathered from this example the domain modeled for the experiment is that of Formula One.

One important point to note about the strict ontology is that the classes and relationships are not likely to be subject to temporal change. In other words, the structure of the domain does not change much with time. Formula One has not changed significantly in structure in the last fifty years, i.e. there were still drivers who drove for teams, team cars had to have tyres, an engine and a chassis etc. What has changed, and is the main source of dynamism in this news domain, are the instances (and possibly number of instances). For example, the driver line ups of teams change year on year. In this sense, ontologies are an effective way of describing a domain, especially in terms of sport, as structurally is remains quite consistent.

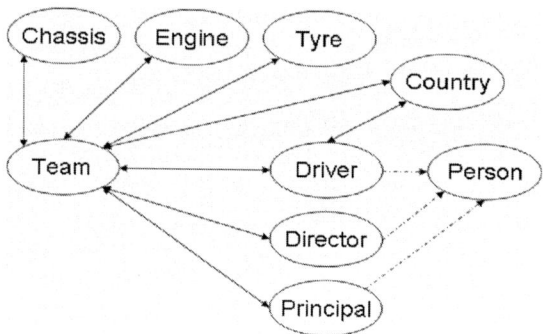

Fig. 1. Strict Ontology Classes and Relationships

Figure 1 shows the classes provided by the strict ontology and which classes are related to each other. The broken line between Person to the Driver, Principal and Director imply that the three classes are a subclass of the class Person. The relationships (which are not explicitly named in Figure 1) between classes are symmetric. For example, if a driver drives for a team, then the team employ that driver. Transitive relationships may be inferred from the strict ontology, i.e. you may wish to determine which Drivers drive on which Tyres.

4   Design and Implementation of the Personalized News Service

This section details the architecture Personalized News Service (PNS) that supports the use of ontologies as the basis for news personalization. It begins with an overview of the how ontologies and the user's interests, and their level of interest, are related. It then presents the suite of services that comprises the architecture of the PNS.

4.1   Modeling the User's Interest and Level of Interest

Separating the interests of a user from their level of interest provides independence for the user model. This independence can be very useful when presented with users who would define these levels differently and also when presented with different domains. By having the interests separated from the level of interest there is the opportunity to provide users with control over their level of interest. From a domain perspective it enables there to be multiple definitions of medium interest. In the case of Formula One a user with a medium interest in Michael Schumacher may be interested in his Team and Team Mate also. In this example, the user model would simply state that the user has a medium interest in Michael Schumacher. The (separate) level of interest model would define interest in a Driver as being interested in his Team and Team Mate. The benefit of separating interest from the level of interest means that the user model does not become cluttered with unnecessary instance information. Continuing the example, the user model does not say that the user is also interested in Rubens Barrichello and Ferrari. This instance information is temporal and may become stale (e.g. Rubens is no longer Michael's team mate).

User modeling is achieved by presenting the user with a web-based instrument, derived from the domain ontology, that lists the instances of the domain by type and asks the user to grade their interest on the scale: none, low, medium and high.

4.2 Architecture

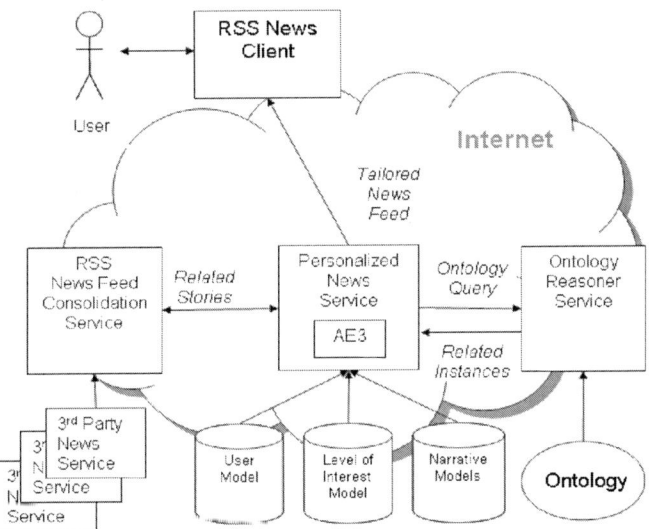

Fig. 2. Service Architecture

The Personalized News Service is actually the combination of three services – the RSS News Feed Consolidation Service, the Ontology Reasoner and the Personalized News Service itself. All threes services are implemented as Java web services and have associated Web Service Description Language (WSDL) descriptions. The RSS News Feed Consolidation Service is the most basic of the three. It provides a means of registering third party news feeds, such as those offered by most commercial news sites, and of performing keyword queries on the articles available from those services.

The Ontology Reasoner Service is based on Jena [16] and exposes a WSDL interface over which RDQL (RDF Data Query Language) [17] queries may be passed using SOAP. Jena provides an open source ontology reasoner and can be used to reason over OWL DL [7] ontologies. Jena allows the checking of consistency of ontologies, classification of ontologies and answering a subset of RDQL queries. The Ontology Reasoner Service simply exposes this functionality.

The central service is that of the Personalized News Service. This service is built on top of the Adaptive Engine (AE3) used by the Adaptive Personalized eLearning Service (APeLS) [2]. The AE3 provides specific adaptive functionality that is suitable for this form of personalization. The model-driven approach used by the engine, and its ability to strategically reconcile these models at runtime through narrative, means that it can be used to generate queries (in RDQL). Furthermore AE3 has built in support for accessing and invoking external web services. Using this functionality the RDQL query, which has been adaptively composed, using the narrative to examine the user's interests and level of interests, is passed to the Ontology Reasoner Service. In this way AH techniques are used in conjunction with ontology reasoning. Through this step the reasoner can determine what other instances would be of interest to the user. For example, if the user model states that the user is highly interested[1] in Michael Schumacher the following steps are carried out: 1) The Personalized News Service determines what a high interest in a Driver means, i.e. what relationships are of interest; 2) It assembles an appropriate RDQL query to request the associated instances along those relationships; 3) Invokes the Ontology Reasoner Service; 4) Receives a result set with a list of related instances. In the case of Michael Schumacher this may include Ferrari (Team), Felipe Massa (Driver associated with Ferrari), Bridgestone (Tyre) etc.

Once the appropriate related instances have been determined the Personalized News Service then invokes the RSS News Feed Consolidation Service to search for appropriate articles. These articles are then assembled, again using narrative, into a tailored news feed which may be accessed from any appropriate RSS Reader.

5   Evaluation of PNS

The evaluation of the Personalized News Service was carried out by conducting a user trial. Users were presented with three news feeds: a personalized news feed based on their interests, level of interest and using the strict ontology; a personalized news feed based on their interests, level of interest and using the loose ontology; and a consolidated non-personalized news feed that showed all of the articles that were available. The trial was conducted with ten users, with varying degrees of interest in Formula One, over a period of four weeks. The news feed, upon which the personalized services operated, was taken from www.itv-f1.com. The objective of the trial was to see if the strict ontology and loose ontology based services produce dramatically different personalized user experiences.

Each user was asked to complete the web-based instrument to solicit their interests and levels of interest in Formula One. Once this step was completed they were asked to access three feed URLs, corresponding to the three services above, daily using their preferred RSS news reader. The feeds were identified as Feed One, Feed Two and Original Feed. Feed One corresponded to the personalized service using the strict ontology and Fees Two to that using the loose ontology, however, the users were not told this.

---

[1] When reconciling level of interest using the loose ontology semantic relationships are meaningless (as they don't exist in the loose ontology). Conceptual distance (one relationship away, two relationships away, etc.) was used instead for the loose ontology.

Following the trial each user was interviewed, with a specific set questions relating to usability and quality of experience being asked. The qualitative results obtained indicated that all of the users found the services easy to use as, for them, it simply meant completing a web-based instrument and then pointing their RSS reader at the generated feeds. In general the two personalized news feeds presented articles that the users believed appropriate. Occasionally, through looking at the static news feed, the users identified articles that the loose-ontology service missed. When asked if they perceived differences between Feed One and Feed Two, only one person felt there were Major differences, with the remainder of the users perceiving only minor or no differences. The user who experienced major differences was also the user with the lowest overall interest in Formula One.

6 Conclusion

The evaluation showed that end users perceived little difference in experience and satisfaction between the two personalized services. This is an interesting result as the level of semantic matching carried out when using the strict ontology is much higher, compared to that of the loose ontology. The strict ontology, however, is much more time consuming to generate and maintain as automated approaches are not viable. This is an encouraging result as systems such as Mercureo and Metasaur produce ontologies that are not dissimilar to the loose ontology used in the experiment, pointing to the viability of this approach.

The overall approach of using ontologies to bridge the semantic gap between user model and the content available proved successful. The ability to keep the user model minimal and only containing the items the user was centrally interested coupled with their level of interest meant the user model was not full of tangentially interesting concepts. The danger of such concepts in a dynamic domain such as news is that they may become *stale* quickly.

The approach of using the narrative to compose the query leaves open the opportunity to extend the service to cater for other axes of adaptivity. For example, the number, quality and source of news articles could all be personalized. Another feature of narrative as it is supported by the AE3 is the possibility to invoke services as part of a service oriented approach. This capability means that the adaptive systems can be broken up into logical (and reusable) services.

References

1. Really Simple Syndication (RSS) Specification v2.0, Available online at http://blogs.law.harvard.edu/tech/rss
2. Owen Conlan, Vincent Wade, Catherine Bruen,, Mark Gargan: Multi-model, Metadata Driven Approach to Adaptive Hypermedia Services for Personalized eLearning. In: AH '02: Proceedings of the Second International Conference on Adaptive Hypermedia and Adaptive Web-Based Systems, London, UK, Springer-Verlag (2002) 100–111
3. Conklin J. (1987). Hypertext: An Introduction and Survey. IEEE Computer, 20(9), 17-41

4. Paul De Bra, Ad Aerts, Bart Berden, Barend de Lange, Brendan Rousseau, Tomi Santic, David Smits, Natalia Stash, AHA! The Adaptive Hypermedia Architecture, in Proceedings of the ACM Hypertext Conference, Nottingham, UK, pp 81-84
5. Peter Brusilovsky, Elmar Schwarz, Gerhard Weber, ELM-ART: An Intelligent Tutoring System on World Wide Web, in Third International Conference on Intelligent Tutoring Systems, ITS-96, Montreal, 1996
6. Marcus Specht, Milos Cravcik, Leonid Pesin, Roland Klemke, Authoring Adaptive Educational Hypermedia in WINDS, in Proceedings of ABIS2001, Dortmund, Germany, October, 2001, pp 1-8
7. Web Ontology Language (OWL) Reference, Available online at http://www.w3.org/TR/2004/REC-owl-ref-20040210/
8. DAML+OIL (March 2001) Reference Description, Available online at http://www.w3.org/TR/daml+oil-reference
9. Bernard Merialdo, Kyung Tak Lee, Dario Luparello, Jeremie Roudaire, Automatic Construction of Personalised TV News Programs, in ACM Multimedia '99, October 99, Orlando, Florida, USA, pp 323-331
10. Sami Jokela, Marko Turnpeinen, Teppo Kurki, Eerika Savia, Reijo Sulonen, The Role of Structured Content in a Personalised News Service, in Proceedings of the 34th Hawaii International Conference on System Sciences 2001, pp 1-10
11. Liliana Ardissono, Luca Console, Iliara Torre, An Adaptive System for the Personalised Access to News, in AI Communications 14: pp 129-147, 2001
12. Ah-Hwee Tan, Christine Teo, Learning User Profiles for Personalised Information Dissemination, in Proceedings of International Joint Conference on Neural Network 1998, pp 183-188
13. The Protégé Ontology Editor and Knowledge Acquisition System, Available online at http://protege.stanford.edu
14. J Arjona, R Corchuelo, A Ruiz, M Toro, Automatic Extraction of Semantically-Meaningful Information from the Web, in Adaptive Hypermedia 2002, LNCS 2347, pp 24-35
15. Trent Apted, Judy Kay, Andrew Lum, Supporting Metadata Creation with an Ontology Built from an Extensible Dictionary, in Adaptive Hypermedia 2004, LNCS 3137, pp 4-13
16. Jena Semantic Web Framework, Available online at http://jena.sourceforge.net/
17. RDQL, A Query Language for RDF, Available online at http://www.w3.org/Submission/2004/SUBM-RDQL-20040109/
18. Yannis Kalfoglou, John Domingue, Enrico Motta, Maria Vargas-Vera, Simon Buckingham Shum, myPlanet: An Ontology-Driven Web-Based personalised news service, in Proceedings IJCAI 2001 Workshop on Ontologies and Information Sharing, Seattle USA, pp 140-148

Social Navigation Support in a Course Recommendation System

Rosta Farzan[1] and Peter Brusilovsky[1,2]

[1] Intelligent Systems Program and [2] School of Information Sciences
University of Pittsburgh, Pittsburgh PA 15260, USA
rosta@cs.pitt.edu, peterb@pitt.edu

Abstract. The volume of course-related information available to students is rapidly increasing. This abundance of information has created the need to help students find, organize, and use resources that match their individual goals, interests, and current knowledge. Our system, CourseAgent, presented in this paper, is an adaptive community-based hypermedia system, which provides social navigation course recommendations based on students' assessment of course relevance to their career goals. CourseAgent obtains students' explicit feedback as part of their natural interactivity with the system. This work presents our approach to eliciting explicit student feedback and then evaluates this approach.

1 Introduction

Information technology (IT) has rapidly changed many aspects of receiving a college education. The volume of course-related information available to students is rapidly increasing. This abundance of information has created the need to help students find, organize, and use resources that match their individual goals, interests, and current knowledge. One of the concerns students have is to make decisions about which courses to take. The concern is more serious for graduate students who have more freedom to choose courses while they care more about taking courses that contribute to their progress towards career goals. To make these decisions, they use information from course catalogs and schedules, consult with their advisors, and seek guidance from their classmates, especially those with similar interests. To give better decision-making support to students who wish to make relevant course choices, we have developed a course recommendation system, CourseAgent, which integrates all available information about courses and provides personalized access to it.

CourseAgent is a community-based recommendation system that employs *social navigation* [5] to tackle the problem of information overload. Community-based systems integrate explicit and implicit feedback provided by the community of users regarding information items and distill the collective wisdom of the community to help individuals. *Explicit feedback* is registered when a user rates an item as interesting or relevant. *Implicit feedback* is extracted from user actions that indirectly provide some evidence about item quality or relevance - such as link selection, reading time, bookmarking, etc. A challenge for recommendation systems is to encourage users to provide explicit feedback. Explicit feedback is considered the most

V. Wade, H. Ashman, and B. Smyth (Eds.): AH 2006, LNCS 4018, pp. 91–100, 2006.

reliable source of information for personalization; however, users rarely provide it since they don't perceive this activity as essential to their work with the system [4].

CourseAgent provides community-based recommendations of courses using explicit feedback - students' assessment of course relevance to their various career goals. To elicit feedback from users, the system employs a specific "do-it-for-yourself" approach. The main theme of this approach is to obtain students' explicit feedback *implicitly*, as part of their natural interaction with the system. This research study presents our approach for eliciting feedback from the students, and then evaluates our approach. The rest of the paper is organized as follows: section 2 describes background information and related work, section 3 provides details about different parts of CourseAgent system, details on adaptation and social recommendation, and our approach for eliciting user feedback. Section 5 presents our evaluation methods and the results of this evaluation. We conclude the paper in section 6 and provide several ideas for the future direction of this work.

2   The Under-Contribution Problem in Adaptive Community-Based Systems

There is an increasing focus on creating community-based adaptive Web systems that provide navigation support or collect recommendations based on feedback from the users of the system. Amazon.com recommends items to buy based on activities of other users. MovieLens [9] recommends movies to watch based on the feedback provided by similar users. The I-Spy search engine uses the information provided by their community to re-rank search results [6]. The functionality and precision of these community-based systems is strongly dependent upon the amount of feedback provided by users of the systems. In many cases, the insufficient quantity of contributions from users has damaged the value of these systems. Encouraging users to contribute has become one of the most important challenges to this field.

Since the discovery of the "users do not like to rate" phenomenon, different systems have tried different approaches to collecting user feedback, in order to fuel the recommendation mechanisms. Early works focused on substituting *explicit* feedback, such as relevance rating, with *implicit* feedback, such as time spent reading a page, time spent scrolling a page, or number of clicks [4]. While several studies have demonstrated the potential of implicit feedback in several contexts, it has not emerged as the ultimate solution. In many cases, implicit feedback lacks the required accuracy, damaging the system's precision.

The idea of a more recent "economy" approach is to encourage users' explicit contribution by building a reward mechanism into the system. In their early work, Bretzke and Vassileva [1] tried several reward mechanisms for encouraging contributions to their system resource-sharing system COMTELLA. The system rewards more cooperative users by such incentives as more bandwidth for download, or higher visibility in the community. More recent version of COMTELLA used the rewarding mechanism to regulate the quality of participation [3]. Harper et al. [7] designed an economic model to analyze users' contributions to a movie recommendation web site. The model compares the effort required for providing ratings with the direct and indirect benefits of the contribution. The model provides ideas on how to motivate users' ratings, such as improving the interface to increase the fun and non-predictable personal benefits of rating, and improving the interface for browsing collections of one's own ratings. Ling et al [8] employed social psychology theories to address the problem of under-contribution in online movie recommender community. The results of their study show that uniqueness of contribution can play an encouraging role for the users. Moreover, they found that users are more likely to contribute when the goal is very specific and challenging.

Our work explores an alternative approach to eliciting user feedback that we call "do-it-for-yourself." The main theme of this approach is to encourage users' participation by turning their feedback into an activity that is important and meaningful to them. In other words, we make the achievement of a personal goal dependent upon their contribution to the community. This approach stands somewhat between the two approaches analyzed above. On one hand, we encourage users to provide reliable explicit feedback. On the other hand, this feedback might be considered implicit by a recommendation system since it was provided not for the system (as in the "economy" approach), but rather to achieve the users' own goals.

3   CourseAgent

CourseAgent is an adaptive community-based hypermedia system that provides personalized access to information about courses. CourseAgent was developed for students and instructors in the School of Information Sciences at the University of Pittsburgh and incorporates information about courses offered at the School. However, it can easily be adopted for different programs by merely integrating the program-specific course data into the system.

3.1   Social Recommendation in CourseAgent

CourseAgent is a social navigation support system. It provides recommendation in the form of in-context adaptive annotations instead of generating an out-of-context sorted list of recommended courses. Course information is annotated with adaptive visual cues that help students to select their most appropriate courses. Fig. 1 demonstrates the use of in-context adaptive community-based annotations on the Schedule screen of CourseAgent. The Schedule screen provides different information about courses offered in a specific semester. As does any course schedule, it provides various information about each offered course, such as course number, course title, date and time, location, and information about the instructor. If the student finds a specific course relevant and interesting, she can use the provided link to register for this course or to plan to pursue this in the future (right column). To help the student register and plan decisions, the system attempts to enhance each link with two kinds of community-based annotation displayed as icons to the left of the links. One icon expresses the expected course workload (one shovel for low, two for average and three for a high workload). The other icon expresses the expected relevance of the course to the career goals of the given student (from one thumb up for a relevant course to three for a highly relevant course). The estimated workload and relevance of a specific course is calculated using community feedback about past offerings of this course, as taught by the same instructor. In addition, another kind of icon in the relevance column indicates that the student's advisor considers this course to be relevant for the given student.

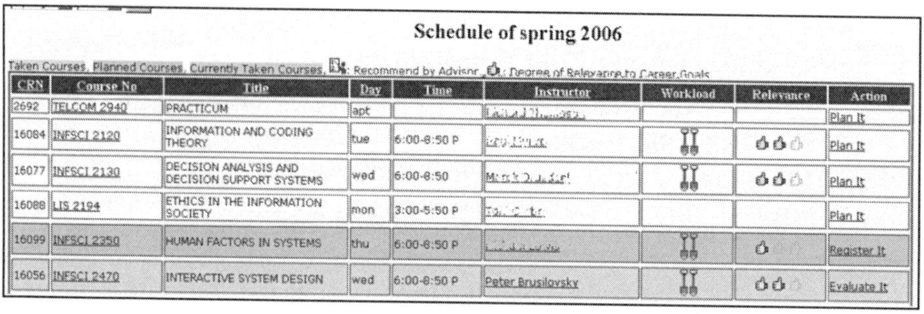

Fig. 1. Checking the schedule in CourseAgent

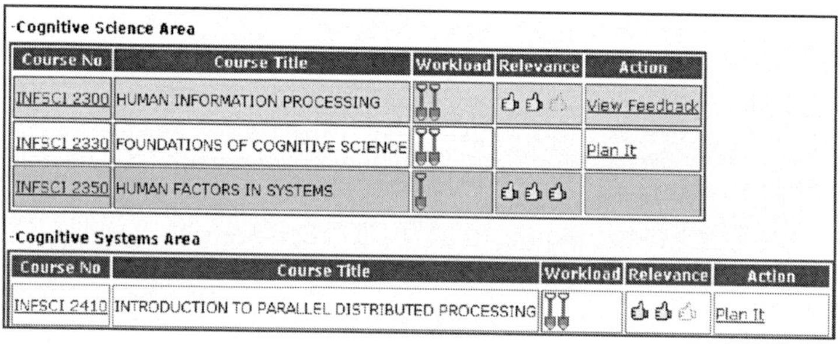

Fig. 2. The Course Catalog screen in CourseAgent

Similar social navigation support is provided in the Course Catalog screen of the system. In this screen, courses are grouped by *areas of study* defined by the program as shown in Fig. 2. For example, an Information Science degree includes areas such as Cognitive Science, Cognitive Systems, and Mathematical and Formal Foundation. Each course in the catalog is annotated with social recommendation information representing the relevance and workload of the course. However, since different instructors might teach the same course, the average relevance and workload of each course is based upon the average score over all instructors who taught the course.

3.2 Providing Feedback

CourseAgent provides social navigation support by collecting three kinds of information from the community of students: a) the student's self-selected career goals, b) the students' explicit evaluation of course workload, and c) the student's personal rating for career goal relevance for the courses that they have already taken. We have defined an extendable list of 22 career goals that cover different ranges of careers related to the information science field. Students are able to add career goals that they wish to pursue to their profile. In addition, the system provides an interface to evaluate courses already taken. Students are asked to evaluate the relevance of each taken course to each of their career goals on a scale of 1 to 5 and to evaluate the workload of the course on a scale of 1 to 3. Fig. 3 presents the evaluation interface .

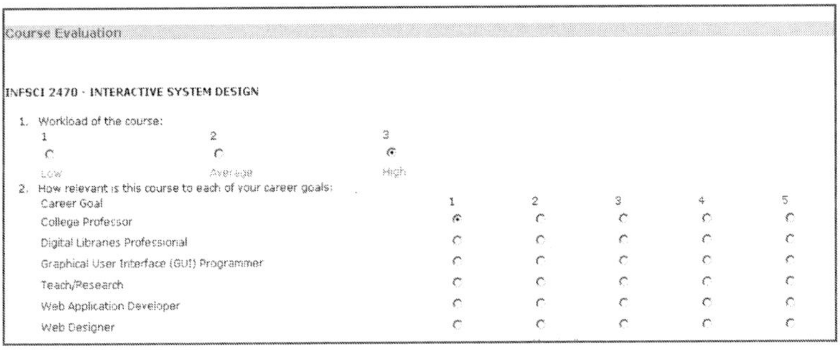

Fig. 3. Evaluation interface of the CourseAgent system

The collected information is used to deliver adaptive annotations presented in the previous section. The overall workload level of the course is computed by simply averaging all ratings provided by the students. The relevance of a course to a student is computed based on the relevance of the course to each of the student's career interests. To compute total relevance, we cannot easily average the relevance to all career goals of the student: A worthy course might be irrelevant to most of the students' career goals while being critical to only one goal. In this case, a simple average will give this a poor relevance rating, while the student might actually be especially interested in taking the course since it is essentially relevant to one of his career goals. To overcome this, we designed a simple algorithm to compute course relevance. The relevance of a course to each career interest of the student ranges from 1 to 5 - where 1 is not relevant and 5 is relevant in an essential way. Courses with a relevance level of 3 and above to at least one of the student's career goals contribute to the overall relevance of the course to the student. The relevance of the course to the student is visualized with a thumb-up icon (1 icon means reasonable relevance and 3 means the highest relevance). Table 1 presents part of our algorithm for computing course relevance. For example, if a course is essentially relevant (relevance level of 5) in 2 of the student's career goals, the course will be considered highly relevant to the student. The complete set of rules consists of 16 cases. The current version of the algorithm is derived from our preliminary assumptions and needs to be evaluated with real users. The evaluation of this algorithm is part of our future work.

Table 1. The Algorithm for computation of course relevance

# of career goals with Relevance 5	# of career goals with Relevance 4	# of career goals with Relevance 3	Total Relevance
>=2	*	*	 👍👍👍
1	>1	*	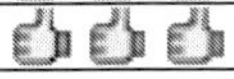 👍👍👍
....			
0	1	0	👍
0	0	2	👍

3.3 Motivation for Providing Feedback

Similar to any other community-based adaptive system, the success of CourseAgent is highly dependent upon the feedback provided by the community. Course recommendation is a good example of a domain where community-based recommendation is useful while item-based recommendation [10] is not, since students are typically interested in taking courses that are *different* from those already taken, in order to learn the wide variety of knowledge that will be relevant for a career in this field. Moreover, unlike some community-based recommenders, such as MovieLens [9], recommendations that are provided to a specific student do not take into account her own ratings, but only the ratings of students who took potentially interesting courses earlier. As a result, ratings provided by the students in CourseAgent are beneficial solely to the community but not to the author of the ratings. This typical contradictory situation requires us to find some way for the system to encourage students to provide explicit feedback. As explained in the introduction, our goal has been to use a "do-it-for-yourself" approach. Therefore, our challenge has been to design an activity that is both attractive and meaningful for the students and can use course ratings provided by the student for the benefit of the author of the ratings. In our context, career planning looks like an attractive candidate for this kind of activity. To integrate career planning with student course evaluation, we developed the Career Scope interface, which is presented in this section.

In Career Scope, students can view the progress they have made towards each career goal. Courses they have taken and evaluated are used to compute their progress towards the career goal. The more relevant the course to the career goal, the more progress they will make towards the goal. Also, the difficulty level of the course will affect this rating. A low-load course would not necessarily cause the same progress as a high-load course. To visualize progress, we have assumed that a specific career goal can be "covered" by taking four relevant courses with medium level difficulty. More difficult courses with higher relevance contribute more to "covering" a career goal while courses with less relevance contribute less. To give more weight for courses taken earlier, we chose to use a logarithmic contribution function instead of a linear one. The current contribution function and all the parameters are considered to be pilot settings that will need to be validated with real users.

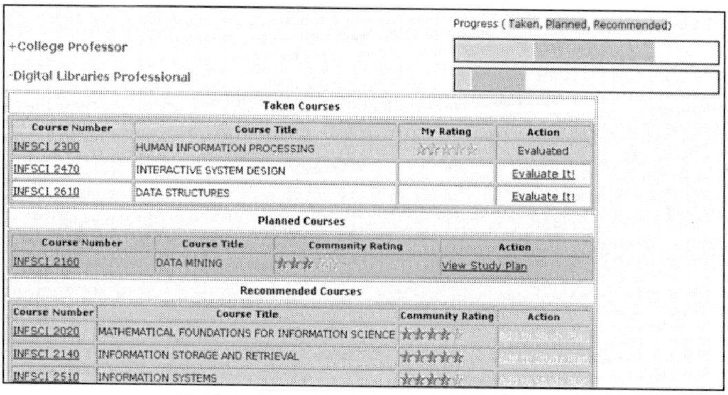

Fig. 4. Career Scope in CourseAgent

Fig. 4 shows a screenshot of the Career Scope section. For each specified career goal, the Career Scope section displays a progress bar that displays the contribution of relevant taken and planned courses towards achieving this goal. A taken course contributes to a career goal if the student rated it as being relevant to this goal. The amount of contribution depends upon the relevance and workload rating. The total contribution of the students' planned courses is computed from the average relevance and average difficulty level provided by the community of students. To distinguish actual progress from future progress, the contribution of planned courses is shown in the progress bar with a different color.

As shown in Fig. 4, the system lists three possible groups of courses for each career goal: taken, planned, and recommended. The students are able to see their own evaluation of taken courses. Taken but not evaluated courses are presented in the Taken Courses table with a lighter background. This prompts the students to evaluate the course (using the link to the right) in order to be count as a part of progress toward the career goal. Students can also re-evaluate the courses they have previously evaluated by clicking on the original rating. They are also able to view the community's evaluation of their planned courses, as rated by relevancy to each specific career goal. The list of recommended courses (based on the community's evaluation) is provided for each specific career goal and students are able to plan any of the recommended courses.

The design of Career Scope is based upon the assumption that the main goal of students is to take courses that will help them to find an interesting career in the future. By rating the relevance of courses, students are better able to take advantage of the system and observe their progress towards each of their career goals. This employs the methodology of "do-it-for-yourself" that is the main focus of our current work. By visualizing the contribution of planned courses to students' progress, we tried to encourage students to specify courses they plan to take. Specifying planned courses can then serve as implicit feedback for generating recommendations for the community. Social navigation support provided by the current version of the system does not take into account implicit feedback. As future work, we are planning to add implicit feedback into social navigation support.

4 Evaluation

We have completed the first study of the CourseAgent system at the School of Information Sciences in the University of Pittsburgh. The main goal of the study was to assess whether "do-it-for-yourself" approach increases student contribution to the system. To evaluate this hypothesis, we prepared two different versions of the system. The controlled version does not include the Career Scope screen that was designed to provide motivation to rate and plan courses. The rest of the system is exactly the same for both versions. The system was advertised to graduate students of the School of Information Sciences for two weeks before the registration deadline. When a student requested to use the system, they were randomly assigned to one of the two groups. For evaluation purposes, we logged all user interactions with the system.

We hypothesized that students in the control group would provide fewer evaluations and career interests, plan fewer courses to take in the future, and provide fewer taken courses. To evaluate our hypothesis, we looked at the average number of times that each group saved an evaluation, added a course, planned a course, and added a career interest. Table 2 presents the result. As shown in the table, the control group has planned fewer courses, added fewer career interests, and provided less evaluation. This means that the control group has provided less implicit and explicit feedback. However, the difference is not significant.

Table 2. Contribution of users in from the control and experimental group

	# of students	Average # of added courses	Average # of planned courses	Average # of added career interests	Average # of saved evaluations
Control	11	5	2	0.91	4.55
Experimental	9	5.89	5	2.22	6.22

For a deeper analysis, we looked at the usage of Career Scope by the experimental group. We observed that about half of the students in the experimental group did not actually use Career Scope. This might be due to interface problems such as the name of the section or the position of the section in the system. Also users might be lacking a good description of this part of the system. (We will investigate this issue as part of our future work.) As a result, for better analysis of the effect of Career Scope, we divided the users into 3 groups: control group, experimental group I who did not use Career Scope, and an experimental group II who used Career Scope. Table 3 presents the same result as Table 2 for these 3 groups. As shown in the table, the contribution of users from experimental group who did not actually use Career Scope is close to the contribution of users from the control group. The data shows that students who actually used Career Scope contributed significantly more to the system by providing more evaluations, planning more courses, and adding more career interests and taken courses. In all cases, the difference is statically significant (t-test, α=0.05).

Table 3. contribution of users with respect to usage of Career Scope

	# of students	Ave. # of added courses	Ave. # of planned courses	Ave. # of added career interests	Ave. # of saved evaluation
Control Group	11	5	2	0.91	4.55
Experimental group I	4	2.25	1.5	1.25	3.75
Control + Experimental I	15	4.27	1.87	1	4.33
Experimental group II	5	8.8	7	3	8.2

We were also interested in observing the activity patterns among these three groups. We looked at the fraction of providing feedback (explicit & implicit) compared to other actions, to measure the extent that the rating had been encouraging. The following graph presents the percentage of different types of activity among the three groups. The results suggest that the experimental group II, who received more encouragement for providing feedback, spent a higher fraction of their time on activities that would provide feedback to the system. This result is another indication that the encouragement caused by presenting career progress was beneficial to creating more feedback.

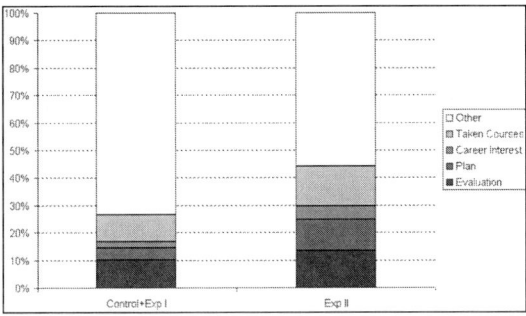

Fig. 5. Activity analysis of 3 groups

5   Discussion and Future Work

CourseAgent is a social navigation system that strives to automate "word of mouth" to help students making decision about courses to take [11]. Similar to any other community-based adaptive system, the success of CourseAgent is highly dependent on the feedback provided by the community. In CourseAgent we have tried to address the problem of under-contribution by employing a "do-it-for-yourself" approach and emphasizing the direct benefit of providing feedback. In CourseAgent, students are able to provide feedback in implicit and explicit ways. They can directly evaluate courses with respect to the relevance to each career goal as well as the difficulty level of the course. They are also providing implicit feedback when they plan or register for a course. Registering or planning a course represents an implicit interest in the course, which may be due to the relevance of the course to the students' career goals. The basic and obvious benefit of the system to the students is as a course management system that keeps information about courses they have taken and facilitates communication with their advisors. Providing social navigation support and community-based recommendation provides more benefit and encouragement to use the system. However, to encourage students to evaluate the courses they have taken, we have designed the Career Scope section of the system. Our results suggest that the "do-it-for-yourself" approach succeeds in providing more course recommendations. Observing progress toward each career goal is an important motivation for the students to use the system while also providing more explicit and implicit feedback to the system.

Currently, we are trying to advertise the use of this system among a larger number of students in the School of Information Sciences at the University of Pittsburgh, to validate our hypotheses with a larger number population. We have also designed a user study to conduct interviews and surveys. We plan to collect subjective feedback from students about the community-based support provided by CourseAgent. Using subjective data from real users, we will adjust our adaptation algorithm and different parameters used in the algorithms. We plan to modify the constant parameters in the algorithms (e.g. number of courses to cover a career goal) to variable parameters that are adjustable to students' goal and interests and specification of the area of the study. In the next version of the system we plan to improve the adaptation algorithm by taking into account the implicit feedback such as course planning. We hope that extending the development of this system and its evaluation will provide us with more ideas, in order to improve our approach for eliciting user feedback, an essential tool for building community-based adaptive hypermedia systems.

Acknowledgement

This research is supported by the National Science Foundation under Grant No. 0447083 and the National Science Foundation graduate fellowship. We would also like to thank Li-Chen Mao for developing the earlier version of the system.

References

1. Bretzke H. and J. Vassileva (2003). Motivating cooperation on peer to peer networks. Proceeding of 9th International Conference on User Modeling .
2. Brusilovsky, P. (2001). Adaptive hypermedia. User Modeling and User Adapted Interaction 11(1/2): 87-110.
3. Cheng, R. and Vassileva, J. (2005) Adaptive Reward Mechanism for Sustainable Online Learning Community. In Proceedings of 12th International Conference on Artificial Intelligence in Education, AIED'2005.
4. Claypool, M., Le, P., Waseda, M., and Brown D. (2001). Implicit interest indicators. In Proceedings of ACM Intelligent User Interfaces (IUI'01).
5. Dieberger, A., Dourish, P., Höök, K., Resnick, P., and Wexelblat, A (2000). Social navigation: Techniques for building more usable systems. Interactions, 7(6), 36-45.
6. Smyth, B., E. Balfe, Freyne, J., Briggs, P., Coyle, M., and Boydell, O. (2004). Exploiting Query Repetition and Regularity in an Adaptive Community-Based Web Search Engine. User Modeling & User-Adapted Interaction 14(5): 383-423.
7. Harper F. M., Li X., Chen Y., and Konstan J. (2005). An economic model of user rating in an online recommender system. In Ardissono L., Brna P., and Mitrovic A. (Eds.), Proceedins of 10th International Conference on User Modeling (UM 2005), Edinburgh, Scotland, UK.
8. Ling, K., Beenen, G., Ludford, P., Wang, X., Chang, K., Li, X., Cosley, D., Frankowski, D., Terveen, L., Rashid, A. M., Resnick, P., and Kraut, R. (2005). Using social psychology to motivate contributions to online communities. Journal of Computer-Mediated Communication, 10(4), article 10.
9. Miller, B., Albert, I., Lam, S.K., Konstan, J., and Riedl, J. (2003). MovieLens Unplugged: Experiences with a Recommender System on Four Mobile Devices, Proceedings of the 17th Annual Human-Computer Interaction Conference.
10. Sarwar, B., Karypis, G., Konstan, J., and Riedl J. (2001) Item-based Collaborative Filtering Recommendation Algorithms, In proceedings of 10th International World Wide Web conference.
11. Shardanand, U. and Maes, P. (1995). Social information filtering: Algorithms for automating 'word of mouth'. In Proceedings of Computer Human Interaction.

Cooperating Search Communities

Jill Freyne and Barry Smyth

School of Computer Science and Informatics,
University College Dublin, Belfield, Dublin 4, Ireland
{Jill.Freyne, Barry.Smyth}@ucd.ie*

Abstract. Collaborative Web Search (CWS) seeks to exploit the high degree of natural query repetition and result selection regularity that is prevalent among communities of searchers. CWS reuses the search experiences of community members, to promote results that have previously been judged relevant for queries. This facilitates a better response to the type of vague queries that are commonplace in Web search and allows a generic search engine to adapt to the preferences of communities of individuals. CWS contemplates a *society* of search communities, each with its own repository of experience. In this paper we describe and evaluate a new technique for leveraging the search experiences of related communities as sources of additional search knowledge.

1 Introduction

Web search is challenging for many reasons, not least of which is the sheer scale and heterogeneity of the Internet. In addition, the average searcher is not the information retrieval expert assumed by the techniques that underpin today's search engines. Most Web search queries are vague and under-specified, containing an average of only 2-3 terms [1] which are often poorly chosen with respect to the documents being sought [2]. As a result, even leading search engines struggle to effectively cope with many search queries [3].

Collaborative Web Search (CWS) takes advantage of query repetition and selection regularity among communities of like-minded searchers. For example, a community of motoring fans is likely to be looking for car-related results for the query '*jaguar*', whereas searchers with an interest in wildlife are likely to be interested in the wildcat. Generic search engines like Google do not attempt to resolve these differences at search time, preferring to present the searcher with the more likely interpretation or a mixture of different result types. CWS addresses this problem by recording and reusing search histories thus learning a preference model for a community. We view CWS as a form of case-base reasoning (CBR) with new search problems (queries) being solved by retrieving and adapting the results of previous search cases; see [4, 5]. Each community's preference model is essentially a *case-base* of *search cases* with each case containing a search query and a set of selected results with their selection frequencies.

* The support of the Informatics Research Initiative of Enterprise Ireland is gratefully acknowledged.

V. Wade, H. Ashman, and B. Smyth (Eds.): AH 2006, LNCS 4018, pp. 101–110, 2006.
© Springer-Verlag Berlin Heidelberg 2006

When responding to a query, CWS retrieves the most similar search cases to the query and rank-orders their previously selected results using a weighted model of relevance, based on the selection frequency data within the cases.

CWS contemplates a society of community-based search engines, each with its own community specific search knowledge. These communities can be loosely or more formally defined and the I-SPY implementation of CWS (see *ispy.ucd.ie*) offers a range of community formation features. For example, an ad-hoc community might be made up of searchers that use a search box on a motoring Web site. Alternatively, a search community may be more formally defined, for example, a set of employees working in the IT department of some organisation. The point is that we can expect these communities to display a high degree of local repetition and regularity in their search behaviour [6], which can be exploited by CWS to deliver more relevant results to each community.

Ordinarily the searches of a specific *host* community are answered with reference to their local case-base. However, in this work we consider the possibility of leveraging the search experience of other related communities when responding to the queries of a host community. Consider the example above of a general motoring Web site. For the query *'jaguar'* this (host) community might promote pages to do with Jaguar cars. However, there may be a more specialised community based around *Jaguar-Enthusiasts.com* whose search case-base may have other results that are likely to be more specialised, but which are also likely to be relevant to at least some searchers within the host community. In this paper, after discussing some related work we provide a brief review of CWS, we describe the adaptations necessary to take advantage of multiple communities and finally we describe the results of a recent real-user evaluation.

2   Related Work

The work presented in this paper touches on a number of areas of related research. Of particular importance is the idea that Web search experience can be usefully captured as a case-base of reusable cases and that this experience can be distributed across multiple case-bases which correspond to the needs of communities of searchers; see [7, 8, 9] for related ideas in the CBR community.

With the popularity of networked services the practice of distributed information retrieval (DIR) has come to the fore. DIR involves examining locally or geographically separated information sources to satisfy an information need. One of the principle concerns of DIR systems is the routing of queries to appropriate sources. Early systems such as STARTS [10] made routing decisions based on the content of an information source. Recently, more sophisticated techniques for making routing decisions involve exploiting the performance of the sources for past searches. The uniqueness of these systems is that they do not require any knowledge of the content of each source corpus. For example, NeuroGrid [11] is an approach to DIR involving the adaptation to ongoing network activity. User responses (i.e. evidence of clicking or book-marking or lack thereof) are stored and used to update the information on which the routing decisions are made.

Similar, but based on the World Wide Web is the SavvySearch system [12]; a meta-search engine that selects which search engines to use based on a query and each engine's past performance when faced with this query.

Finally it is worth commenting on result clustering work in Web search. The ranked-list presentation format that has been almost universally adopted by Web search engines makes it quite inefficient for users to quickly assess the relevance of retrieved results. A solution that has attracted considerable attention is that of result clustering, where result-lists are organised into clusters of semantically related results [13]. A range of efficient algorithms have been developed for the rapid clustering of search results [14, 15]. The traditional approach involves an analysis of the contents of result pages or associated snippet texts. This is computationally expensive and accurate clustering is often compromised for reasons of response-time. Our extension is a form of result clustering, in the sense that each community acts as a cluster of results, but without the need for result-based analysis. Moreover, our clusters relate to genuine groups of interest.

3   A Review of Collaborative Web Search

The CWS technique is a form of meta-search that focuses on the post-processing of search results in response to a learned model of community preferences; see Figure 1. Each query, q_T, is submitted to a set of underlying search engines], $S_1,..S_n$, and their results form a meta-search result-list, R_M. The key novelty of CWS is the production of a new result-list, R_T, that reflects the preferences of the community. This involves the promotion of results which were frequently selected by the community's members in the past for similar queries.

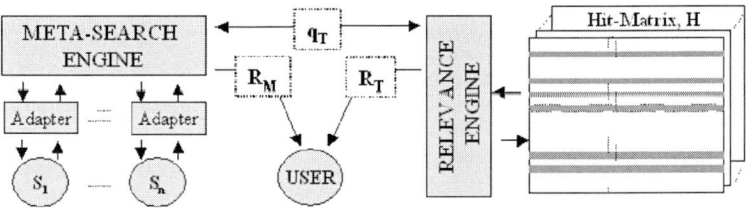

Fig. 1. CWS as implemented in I-SPY (*ispy.ucd.ie*)

3.1   Profiling Community Preferences

These results are stored in the *hit-matrix, H*, which is the key data structure that relates page selections to past queries for a given community of users. H_{ij} is the number of times that page p_j has been selected for query q_i. The hit-matrix forms the basis for each community case-base. From a CBR perspective each row corresponds to an individual search case (Equation 1) made up of the query component plus k result-pairs (page-id & relevance score (See Equation 4)). The *problem specification* part of a case (Equation 2) corresponds to the query terms and the *solution* part (Equation 3) to the result-pairs; that is, the set of page selections that have been accumulated as a result of past query submissions. The *target problem* is represented by the target query terms.

$$c_i = (q_i, (p_1, r_1), ..., (p_k, r_k)) \tag{1}$$

$$Spec(c_i) = q_i \tag{2}$$

$$Sol(c_i) = ((p_1, r_1), ..., (p_k, r_k)) \tag{3}$$

3.2 Retrieving Similar Search Cases

For each target query, q_T, we retrieve a set of similar search cases to serve as a source of relevant results. Case similarity is measured by examining the overlap in query terms of the target case and past search cases. During the retrieval stage, this allows collaborative search to rank-order past search cases according to their similarity to the target query so that all, or a subset of, these cases might be reused during result ranking.

3.3 Case Reuse and Result Ranking

Consider a page, p_j, that is part of the solution of a case, c_i, with query, q_i. The relevance of p_j to this case is given by the relative number of times that p_j has been selected for q_i; see Equation 4. And the relevance of p_j to the new query q_T is the combination of the individual $Rel(p_j, q_i)$'s across all cases $c_1, .., c_n$ that contain a query that is deemed similar to q_T; see Equation 5. Essentially each $Rel(p_j, q_i)$ is weighted by $Sim(q_T, c_i)$ to discount the relevance of results from less similar queries; $Exists(p_j, c_i) = 1$ if $H_{ij} <> 0$ and 0 otherwise. This relevance metric is used to rank-order the promotion candidates which are then recommended ahead of the remaining meta-search results.

$$Rel(p_j, q_i) = \frac{H_{ij}}{\sum_{\forall j} H_{ij}} \tag{4}$$

$$WRel(p_j, q_T, c_1, ..., c_n) = \frac{\sum_{i=1,...,n} Rel(p_j, c_i) \bullet Sim(q_T, c_i))}{\sum_{i=1,...,n} Exists(p_j, c_i) \bullet Sim(q_T, c_i)} \tag{5}$$

4   Communities, Collaboration and Cooperation

CWS obviously assumes that each community preference model (hit-matrix) reflects some relatively uniform domain of interests. This is a crucial assumption and not one that will be tested here. However, it has been validated in a variety of search scenarios [6, 3]. In this work we will consider how communities might cooperate and collaborate during Web search. Our proposed community cooperation technique (CC) looks at a straightforward adaptation of the CWS concept and proposes how groups of related communities can contribute potentially relevant results to the result-list of a host community. Thus, when a target query, q_T, is submitted by a searcher from some host community, C_h, a result-list is generated in the usual way by C_h, but in addition extra results are also promoted from the recommendations of a set of related communities, $C_1, .., C_k$.

4.1   Collaborating Communities

Recent work in distributed CBR suggests that it is often worthwhile considering the knowledge contained in similar case-bases when solving some problem in a related task context [7, 8]. Similar benefits may be available within our Web search application by including the recommendations from similar communities within the result-list returned to the searcher. We hope that if there are strong similarities between communities then the results from the related community will be relevant and may even offer the searcher a different perspective.

How then can we measure community similarity? We start by supposing that if two communities have similar query term distributions then they might reflect the interests of similar communities of users. Here we use a simple model of community similarity based on the percentage of overlapping query terms for a host community, C_h, and another community, C_r; Equation 6.

$$CommunitySim(C_h, C_r) = \frac{|QueryTerms(C_h) \cap QueryTerms(C_r)|}{|QueryTerms(C_h)|} \qquad (6)$$

It makes sense to consider community similarity as a function of both result overlap and query overlap. However, we will leave these enhancements as future work and proceed with the simple model of community similarity above.

4.2   Result Clustering and Ranking

Once a set of similar communities has been identified they can each be used to produce a set of results in response to the target query, q_T, from the host. For each of these related communities we retrieve the set of result recommendations coming from their respective case-bases. In other words, they do not initiate full searches by submitting queries to their own underlying search engines but only perform what is effectively a local search of their own search knowledge. Thus, each related community, C_i, produces its own set of recommended results, R_i.

In this paper we propose displaying separate community result-lists, with separate recommendations under their respective community headings. Essentially this is a type of result clustering and we argue that it has the advantage of preserving the association between related communities and their recommended results to provide the searcher with useful context information when it comes to understanding these recommendations. An example of this approach is presented in Figure 2 for a collection of search communities related to the sport of Rugby. The target query, *'6 nations'* (referring to the annual competition), is submitted by a member of the host community, *Rugby Union*, and its results are shown in Figure 2. The top-half of the result-list presents the recommendations from the host community and they are followed by results that have been returned by the meta-search engine. At the top of the page is a set of tabs, each containing the title of a related community, plus the number of results it has provided. Selecting a tab will show the results from this particular community. Inset to the right of the figure is a section of the recommendation page from the *Irish Rugby* community. Notice how these recommendations are different from those

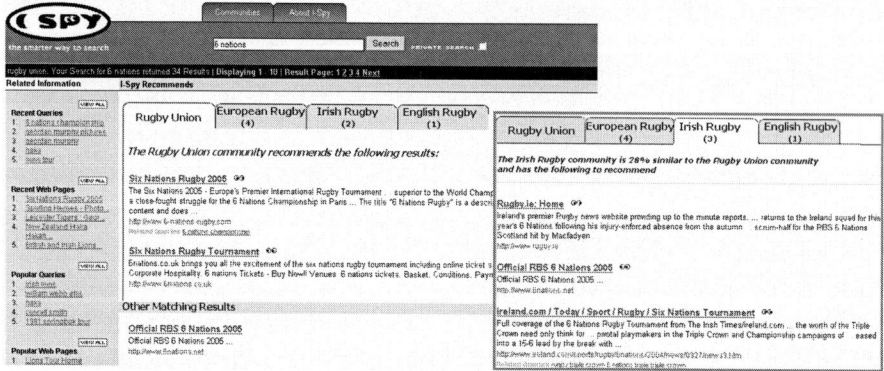

Fig. 2. The results page for the related Irish Rugby community

of the host, although still clearly relevant to the target query. Notice too how 2 of the 3 recommendations have an Irish angle; one is from an Irish rugby site (*Rugby.ie*) and the other from *Ireland.com* the Web site of an Irish newspaper.

5   Evaluation

In this paper we have hypothesised about the value of leveraging the search knowledge of multiple communities when responding to a host's query. We suggested that if similar communities can be identified, then their recommendations are likely to be relevant and may even complement the results recommended by the host. Our previous work demonstrates this potential through a limited artificial search scenario [16]. Here we focus on a real-user evaluation and show how similar performance improvements can be achieved in a realistic search setting.

5.1   Set-Up and Methodology

This evaluation is based on 9 weeks of search data collected by monitoring the search habits of a Dublin software company. 1986 individual search sessions, each containing an IP addresses, a query, and at least one result selection, $(ip, q, r_1$-$r_n)$ were collected. This data was used to populate a set of search communities, each made up of the employees of a different department within the company. We evaluate our new CC approach by examining and judging each community's coverage and precision scores for the result-lists produced for a set of queries.

Community Creation. In total, 7 separate communities were created, each with their own employees, focus and search history size. These communities ranged from the large *Development B* community, made up of software developers, and comprising 749 queries to the much smaller *Marketing* community of only 54 queries; see Table 1. The queries contained on average 2.66 terms and were a mix of general and computing related queries; for example *"public holidays Ireland"* and *"jprofiler 3.0 linux installation"*.

Community Training and Relevance Testing. Populating the case-bases (hit-matrices) for each community was a straightforward task: the first 80% of each community's search data was used as the basis for each community's search cases. This left the remaining 20% of search sessions as a basic test set (403 in total) to use as the basis for our relevance evaluation. The pairwise similarity scores for each of the resulting communities is presented in Table 1.

Table 1. Pairwise community similarities

Community (sessions)	Web Devel.	Marketing	Proj. Man.	Devel. A	QA	Finance	Devel. B
Web Devel(58)		0%	15%	19%	22%	3%	33%
Marketing (54)	0%		9%	25%	13%	11%	20%
Proj Man (204)	3%	2%		17%	20%	4%	29%
Devel A (370)	3%	3%	12%		21%	3%	29%
Quality A (486)	3%	1%	11%	17%		3%	28%
Finance (53)	3%	8%	17%	18%	22%		24%
Devel B (749)	2%	1%	10%	15%	18%	2%	

Table 2. Technique performance

	Traditional CWS	Community Cooperation model
Recommendations	82	130
Successful Queries	54	69

We evaluated the performance of a community's response to its own test queries and separately its response to the test queries from other communities. We were primarily interested in the relevance of the result-lists produced. Although we have access to the results that the original searchers selected, it does not follow that we can assume that unselected results are irrelevant. For our evaluation we needed some way of identifying other results as potentially relevant. Our solution was to use Google's "similar pages" feature as a means to generate lists of results that are similar to those selected by the original searchers (the *seed pages*). This allowed us to generate a list (on average 15.15 results) of *relevant candidates* for each search session from its seed pages. We deemed a result page to be 'relevant' to some target query, q_T, if (1) the result was actually selected by a searcher for q_T (seed page); or (2) the results was at least 30% similar to a seed result; or (3) the result was at least 50% similar to one of the pages Google deemed to be similar to a seed.

5.2   Query Coverage

In our first test we looked at the number of queries for which recommendations could be generated by CWS in comparison to the CC approach. It is important to realise that when we talk about a *recommendation* being generated, we are referring to the promotion of a specific search result based on its previous selection history. Table 2 shows that the CC approach enjoys a clear advantage over the standard CWS approach. Only 82 (20%) of the 403 queries submitted to the standard CWS system resulted in recommendations being generated compared to 130 queries for the CC approach, representing a relative increase in recommendation coverage of more than 58% for the CC approach.

5.3   Result Relevance

Of course query coverage is not a very revealing quality measure as it says nothing about recommendation relevance. Thus, we look at the quality of the recommendations generated by each approach. Specifically, we look at the number of queries for which at least one *relevant* recommendation was generated—*successful queries*. The results presented in Table 2 again speak to the benefits of the CC approach, which delivers 69 successful queries against CWS's 54; a relative increase of 27% for the CC approach over standard CWS.

166 relevant results were promoted by the traditional CWS technique across its 54 successful queries. When we look at the similar-community recommendations generated for these queries we find 45 relevant results. However crucially, we see that 38 of these 45 relevant recommendations are unique. In other words, over 84% of the relevant recommendations that originate from similar communities are different from the recommendations generated by the host community. It is worth noting that the community with the greatest similarity to the host in most cases, the *Development B* community, did not contribute any unique results to this set, thus showing that communities that are very similar to a host often do not contribute as many unique results as less similar communities.

5.4   Result Precision

Figure 3 shows the precision scores for a selection of the communities for different recommendation set sizes (k). Each graph shows the precision of the host community's recommendations as well as the precision of the recommendations that are generated by the remaining 6 communities. The relevance of a recommendation is judged with respect to the host community only. The low precision performance here is attributed to our strict relevance notion rather than the CWS techniques; see [3, 6] for live-user trial results. In 3 out of the 7 communities tested (*Project Management, Finance & Development B*) the host community performs best returning more relevant results than any partner communities. Interestingly, in the remaining communities the host community's precision scores are outperformed by a partner community. In the cases where this occurs the more mature *Development B* community returns more relevant results than a less mature host. This can be attributed to the high similarity (24%-34%) of the *Development B* community to the host community in each case. The *Development A* and *Quality Assurance* communities also perform quite well in these cases, again owing to their maturity and high similarity to the host community. Examining the correlation coefficient between precision (k=5) and similarity for each community shows an average correlation coefficient of 0.67. This supports our hypothesis that similar communities tend to provide the more relevant results.

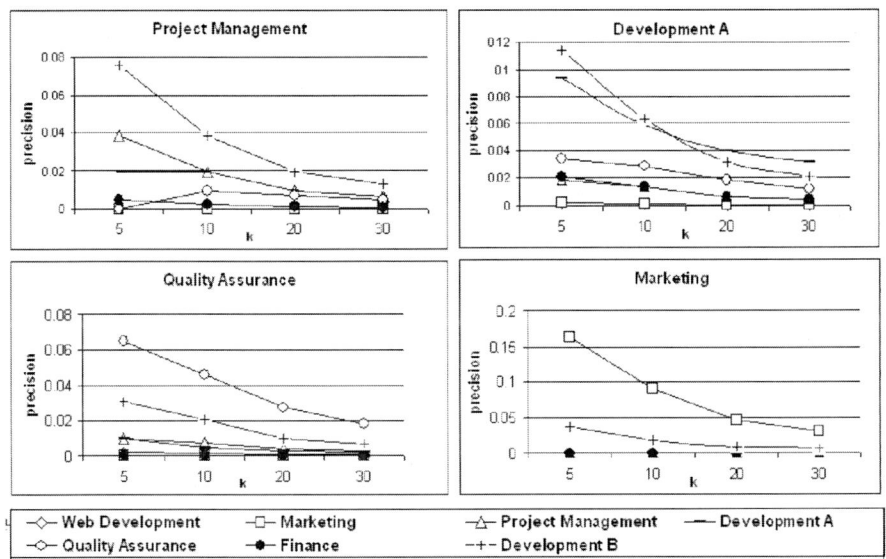

Fig. 3. Precision graphs for the 4 out of 7 communities

6   Conclusions

In this paper we described how our CWS approach can be extended to facilitate cooperation between search communities so that searchers from one community can benefit from the search experience of another similar community. The results of a real-user evaluation support the value of this idea and indicate that similar communities can serve as an important source of search knowledge and that their recommendations can improve the quality of result-lists returned to searchers.

References

1. Lawrence, S., Giles, C.L.: Context and Page Analysis for Improved Web Search. IEEE Internet Computing **July-August** (1998) 38–46
2. Furnas, G.W., Landauer, T.K., Gomez, L.M., Dumais, S.T.: The vocabulary problem in human-system communication. Communications of the ACM **30** (1987) 964–971
3. Smyth, B., Balfe, E., Boydell, O., Bradley, K., Briggs, P., Coyle, M., Freyne, J.: A Live-User Evaluation of Collaborative Web Search. In: Proceedings of the 19th International Joint Conference on Artificial Intelligence (IJCAI '05), Edinburgh, Scotland (2005) 1419–1424
4. Kolodner, J.: Case-Based Reasoning. Morgan Kaufmann (1993)
5. Aamodt, A., Plaza, E.: Case-based reasoning: Foundational issues, methodological variations, and system approaches. AI Communications **7** (1994) 39 – 59
6. Smyth, B., Balfe, E., Freyne, J., Briggs, P., Coyle, M., Boydell, O.: Exploiting Query Repetition and Regularity in an Adaptive Community-Based Web Search Engine. User Modeling and User-Adapted Interaction **14** (2004) 383–423

7. Leake, D.B., Sooriamurthi, R.: When Two Case-Bases Are Better than One: Exploiting Multiple Case Bases. In Aha, D.W., Watson, I., eds.: Proceedings of the 4th International Conference on Case-Based Reasoning. Volume 2080 of Lecture Notes in Computer Science., Springer (2001) 321–335

8. McGinty, L., Smyth, B.: Collaborative Case-Based Reasoning: Applications in Personalised Route Planning. In Aha, D.W., Watson, I., eds.: Proceedings of the 4th International Conference on Case-Based Reasoning (ICCBR '01). Volume 2080 of Lecture Notes in Computer Science., Springer (2001) 362–376

9. Prasad, M.N., Plaza, E.: Corporate Memories as Distributed Case Libraries. In: Proceedings of the Corporate Memory and Enterprise Modeling Track in the 10th Knowledge Acquisition Workshop. (1996)

10. Gravano, L., Chang, C.C.K., García-Molina, H., Paepcke, A.: STARTS: Stanford proposal for Internet meta-searching. In: Proceedings of the 1997 ACM SIGMOD Conference, 1997. (1997) 207–218

11. Joseph, S.: NeuroGrid: Semantically Routing Queries in Peer-to-Peer Networks. Lecture Notes in Computer Science **2376** (2002) 202–214

12. Dreilinger, D., Howe, A.E.: Experiences with Selecting Search Engines Using Meta Search. ACM Transactions on Information Systems **15(3)** (1997) 195–222

13. Zamir, O., Etzioni, O.: Grouper: Dynamic Clustering Interface to Web Search Results. Computer Networks **31(11-16)** (1999) 1361–1374

14. Zhang, D., Dong, Y.: Semantic, Hierarchical, Online Clustering of Web Search Results. In: Proceedings of the 6th Asia Pacific Web Conference (APWEB), Hangzhou, China (2004) 69–78

15. Hamilton, N.: The mechanics of a Deep Net Metasearch Engine. In: Proceedings of the 12th International World Wide Web Conference, Budapest, Hungary (2003)

16. Freyne, J., Smyth, B.: Communities, Collaboration and Cooperation in Personalized Web Search. In: Proceedings of the 3rd Workshop on Intelligent Techniques for Web Personalization (ITWP'05) in conjunction with the 19th International Joint Conference on Artificial Intelligence, Edinburgh, Scotland (2005) 73–80

Temporal Rules for Predicting User Navigation in the Mobile Web

Martin Halvey, Mark T. Keane, and Barry Smyth

Adaptive Information Cluster, School of Computer Science and Informatics,
University College Dublin, Dublin 4, Ireland
{martin.halvey, mark.keane, barry.smyth}@ucd.ie

Abstract. Numerous systems attempt to predict user navigation on the Internet through the use of past behavior, preferences and environmental factors. However many of these models have shortcomings, in that they do not take into account that browsers may have several different sets of preferences. Here we investigate time as an environmental factor in predicting user navigation in the Internet. We present methods for creating temporal rules that describe user navigation patterns. We also show the advantage of using these rules to predict user navigation and also illustrate the benefits of these models over traditional methods. An analysis is carried out on a sample of usage logs for Wireless Application Protocol (WAP) browsing, and the results of this analysis verify our theory.

1 Introduction

The ultimate aim of total personalization for adaptive hypermedia hinges on discovering all of the factors that impact user activities in different contexts. Some of these factors are quite obvious, like explicitly stated user preferences, while others are less obvious, for example implicit preferences, patterns of past behavior, and the physical environment. The challenge facing adaptive hypermedia is to properly recognize these factors, the way in which they influence behavior and the degree of that influence. Previously we have identified time as an important environmental factor that impacts user navigation behavior in a mobile-internet portal [7,11]. However, this work was not fully automated and required a number of knowledge engineering steps to segment the log date. In this paper, we develop an automated method for determining temporal rules that describe user navigation. We use these methods to describe user navigation with respect to URL's selected during navigation. We find that the methods that we describe in this paper learn a greater number of high confidence rules than traditional association rule mining methods. The next section provides some related work. Section 3 gives some context to the problem that we are trying to solve. Section 4 gives an overview of the techniques we are implementing. Section 5 provides an experimental evaluation of our techniques. Section 6 shows the effectiveness of our techniques for predicting user navigation. The final section provides a conclusion and some ideas for future work.

V. Wade, H. Ashman, and B. Smyth (Eds.): AH 2006, LNCS 4018, pp. 111 – 120, 2006.

2 Background Reading

2.1 Mobile Web Navigation

Buchanan et al [6] believe the biggest problem that remains in the mobile Internet is the problem of navigation and site structure and they present alternate methods for presenting information in wireless device interfaces. Billsus et al [5] also note that it is essential to have some sort of adaptive interface for users of the mobile Internet to overcome its shortcomings [6,16] and use a combination of similarity-based, Bayesian and collaborative techniques to allow systems to adapt to users' changing interests. Anderson et al [2] also present a method for creating adaptive web pages for wireless devices. Their MINPATH algorithm makes use of "expected savings" to recommend pages to users. Smyth and Cotter have supported adaptability in the mobile Internet domain by learning probabilistic models of page accesses in order to guide promotion of pages within mobile portals [17]. However, this work has not looked at the role that temporal patterns might play; an issue to which we now turn.

2.2 Temporal Analysis

In recent times there has been an interest in time-based usage patterns in office environments. For example, Begole et al [3] attempt to detect and model rhythms of work patterns in an office. Horvitz et al [12] use Bayesian networks built over log data to model time-based regularities in work patterns in order to predict meeting attendance and interruptability. Time-based analyses of web searching have also been carried out. With the aim of supporting users, Lau and Horvitz [13] have constructed probabilistic models centering on temporal patterns of query refinement to predict how a user would continue their search. Beitzel et al [4] have analyzed search engine queries with respect to time and found that some topical categories vary substantially more in popularity throughout the day; they also found that query sets for different categories have differing similarity over time. Halvey et al [8,9] have provided temporal analysis of mobile web navigation and have shown temporal predictive models to be more accurate at predicting user navigation than similar standard predictive models. Their models segregate the log files before predictive Markov chain models are created. Data is segregated based on the results of hierarchical clustering methods [8] and also segregated by exploiting the fact that user navigation patterns are not distributed uniformly throughout time periods [9]. The following section provides some context and further background for our current work.

3 Task Context

While people have been surfing the World Wide Web (WWW) by traversing hyperlinks for over 15 years, surfing the mobile-Web is a relatively more recent experience for most. In Europe, some of the first versions of the mobile-Web have been available through WAP enabled phones. WAP devices provide access to specifically tailored mobile portals with various services (e.g., email, betting) and information on diverse topics (e.g., TV listings, entertainment guides, sport). Presumably, as 3G phones become commonplace, this particular type of mobile surfing will become more prevalent. While the distribution of navigation patterns of mobile-Internet users still conforms to the Universal Law of Surfing [10] observed in WWW users [15], the way people navigate is quite different. Surfing mobile portals on a WAP phone is not the same as surfing the WWW on a PC. The screen real-estate of these devices is limited to displaying a few lines of text (or links), input capabilities are restricted, download times are slow and governed by incremental billing [16] and specific interface restrictions constrain user behavior in several ways. Specifically, mobile users tend to scroll and click through menu hierarchies rather than using jump-off points for link traversal from search-engine query result lists. One major consequence of this navigation style is that the depth of items in the menu hierarchy has profound effects on access times to a given page and, indeed, on the cost to the user of access. As such, the mobile-Web domain presents a classic personalization problem, where the exploitation of user navigation patterns could be used to re-order menu hierarchies to better deliver sought-for pages quickly and easily.

Halvey et al [7,11] have extended this type of personalization through menu re-ordering by exploiting time-of-the-week factors. The intuition guiding this work is that users' navigation on the weekend when they have leisure time should differ from their navigation on weekdays when they are at work for example, users will have different goals and desires in these different time periods. For instance, a stockbroker may be interested in business web pages during work hours but entertainment pages during leisure time, as he/she is an avid cinema fan. Users may also have different goals and desires in different locations. Halvey et al. [7,11] have confirmed the temporal part of this hypothesis by showing that predictive Markov models based on slices of log data cut from weekdays, evenings and weekends are better predictors of navigation behavior than the same log data as an undifferentiated whole. Furthermore, the weekend models were shown to predict the weekend best, the evening models the evening best and so on, showing that navigation patterns within each period had a distinctive shape. Halvey et al. [7,11] relied on intuition and informal data analysis. It would clearly be better if we could automate this step, taking the art out of the process. The following section provides a possible solution to the problem, where we outline some methods for learning temporal rule based user profiles.

4   Time Based User Profile

The problem of mining association rules can be formalized as follows [1]. Let $I = \{i_1, i_2, \ldots, i_m\}$ be a set of literals, called items. Let D be a set of transactions, where each transaction T is a set of items such that $T \subseteq I$. Associated with each transaction is a unique identifier, called its TID. We say that a transaction T contains X, a set of some items in I, if $X \subseteq T$. An association rule is an implication of the form $X \rightarrow Y$, where $X \subset I$, $Y \subset I$, and $X \cap Y = 0$. The rule $X \rightarrow Y$ holds in the transaction set D with confidence c if c% of transactions in D that contain X also contain Y. The rule $X \rightarrow Y$ has support s in the transaction set D if s% of transactions in D contain $X \cup Y$.

Our proposal is that each transaction T has associated with it a timestamp t. So for some rules R of the from $X \rightarrow Y$, the rule could be refined to R' of the form $X \cup t \rightarrow Y$ such that c of $X \rightarrow Y$ for transactions that take place in transaction set D during times t is greater than confidence c over all of the transaction set D. Time periods can be determined at the start of the process and can be any period less than the total time period over which the data can be collected, i.e. seconds, years, days or hours could be used provided they are not longer than the total time period. We are proposing four methods to determine these temporal types of rules:

- **Point Better:** For each point in the time period that the confidence c is improved we create a new rule. Point in the time period will depend on how time is being measured, for example days or hours etc.
- **Point Threshold:** This is a refinement of the point better method. For each point in the time period that the confidence c is above a certain threshold we create a new rule. This may require learning some initial rules that are below the threshold value so that the improvement may be above the threshold value. Point in the time period will depend on how time is being measured, for example days or hours etc.
- **Sequence Better:** This is a refinement of the point better method. For each sequence in the time period that the confidence c is improved we create a new rule. By sequence we mean a consecutive period of one or time points.
- **Sequence Threshold:** This is a refinement of the sequence better method. For each sequence in the time period that the confidence c is above a certain threshold we create a new rule. This may require learning some initial rules that are below the threshold value so that the improvement may be above the threshold value. By sequence we mean a consecutive period of time points.

Each of these methods requires an existing algorithm to learn an initial set of rules and each of these methods may also require multiple scans of the data set or initial set of rules.

5   Experimental Evaluation

5.1   Measurement of Effectiveness of Algorithms

There are a number of different metrics for measuring the effectiveness of a rule. The main metrics for association rules are confidence and support and they are defined as follows. The confidence of a rule R = "A and B ➜ C" is the support of the set of all items that appear in the rule divided by the support of the antecedent of the rule, i.e. confidence(R) = (support ({A, B, C}) / support ({A, B})) *100%. The support of a rule "A and B ➜ C" is the support of the set {A, B, C}. Here we provide some variations on these metrics to illustrate the benefit of our techniques and also the differences between the rules they determine and the rules that traditional methods determine. These metrics are:

- **Confidence in specific time period:** This is the confidence of a rule in the time period when it is applied. For example for a normal rule this would be the confidence over the entire time period, for a refined rule this would be the confidence over the period t.
- **Support in a specific time period:** This is the support of a rule in the time period when it is applied. For example for a normal rule this would be the support

over the entire time period, for a refined rule this would be the support over the period t.

- **Confidence over all time:** This is the confidence of a rule over the entire time period over which rules are determined.
- **Support over all time:** This is the support of a rule over the entire time period over which rules are determined.

For rules without the temporal refinement, the support over all time and the support in a specific time period are equivalent, and the confidence over all time and the confidence in a specific time period are equivalent. The purpose of these metric refinements is to illustrate fully the difference in the type of rules determined by these temporal methods and traditional association rule mining algorithms.

5.2   Temporal Rules for URL's

The methods outlined in section 4 were applied to web logs from a mobile Internet portal of a major European operator. This data, gathered in September 2002, involved 1,168 users and almost 147,700 individual user sessions. The average number of user sessions for a user in the time period was 126.45, with a maximum of 873 for a single user and a minimum of 19. The portal in which the users browsed contained 256 unique URL's. During the time period users accessed on average 40.92 URL's, with a maximum of 122 accesses for a single user and a minimum of 4. In this sub-section we will investigate the patterns that existed in the pages that users visited. The baseline algorithm that was used for this was Apriori [1], using Apriori rules were discovered with minimum confidence of 0.01 and a minimum support of 0.01 for up to a maximum of 100 rules for all users. The methods outlined in section 4 were then applied to see how the confidence and support were affected. The time points that were used for these methods were hours in a day and days in a week. The following figures illustrate our results with respect to days, for reasons of space we do not show the results for hours.

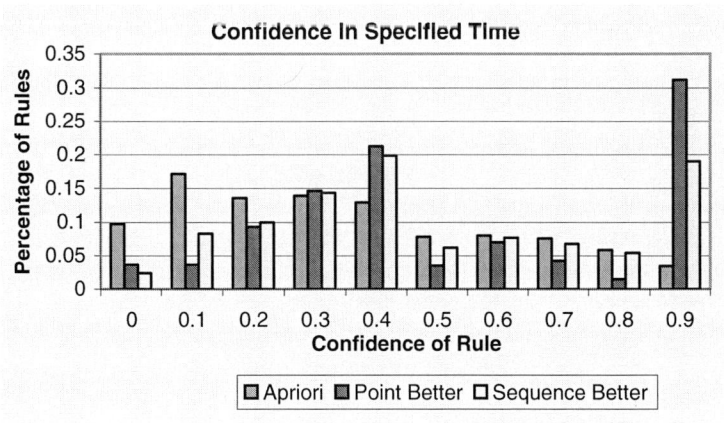

Fig. 1. Graph illustrating the confidence for rules concerning URLs over a specific time period for Apriori, point better and sequence better with days as time points

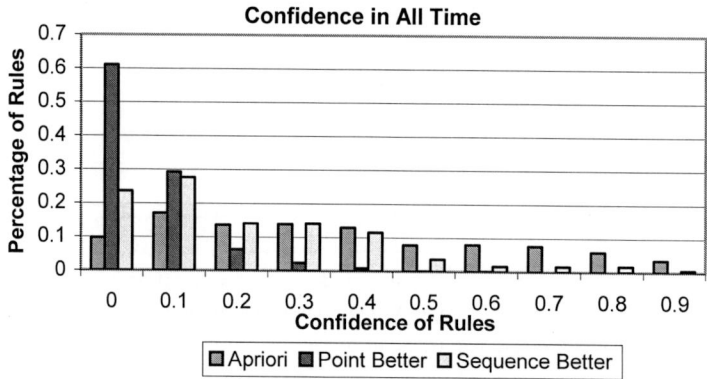

Fig. 2. Graph illustrating the confidence for rules concerning URLs over the entire time period for Apriori, point better and sequence better with days as time points

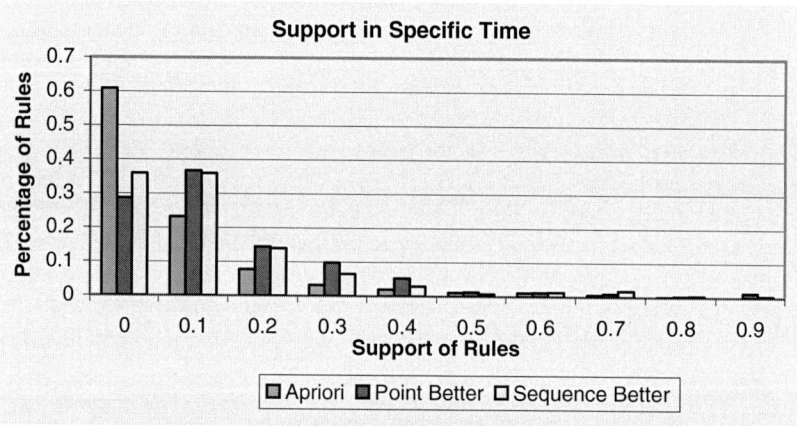

Fig. 3. Graph illustrating the support for rules concerning URLs over a specific time period for Apriori, point better and sequence better with days as time points

We find that using the temporal rules result in rules with in general greater levels of confidence and support (Figure 1 and Figure 2), and that using the entire time period Apriori has rules with greater confidence and support (Figure 3 and Figure 4), but that the amount by which it out-performs the temporal methods is not huge. Table 1 provides further evidence that the temporal rules are better indicators of user navigation. Table 1 shows for different levels of confidence and the average number of rules that are learned for each. The temporal methods once again out-perform Apriori, they created a much larger number of rules with high confidence values. The following section will provide an analysis and experimental evaluation of using the methods outlined in the last two sections for personalization.

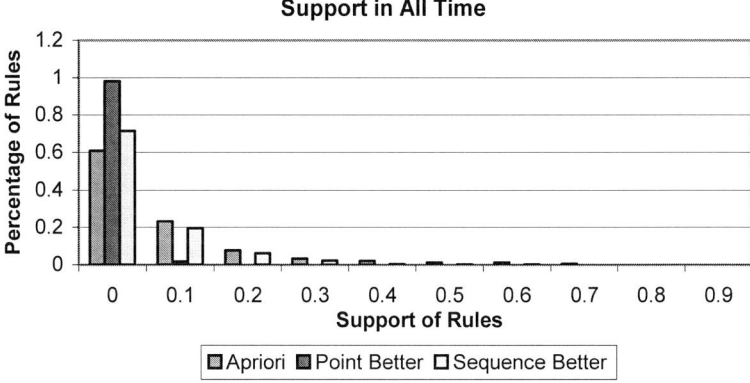

Fig. 4. Graph illustrating the support for rules concerning URLs over the entire time period for Apriori, point better and sequence better with days as time points

Table 1. Table illustrating the average number of rules returned for each user by the Apriori and the Threshold methods with respect to both days and hours for web pages

Confidence	>0.7	>0.8	>0.9
Apriori Day	7.83	4.33	1.61
Apriori Hour	29.75	16.67	5.91
Point Thres Day	52.32	46.28	44.17
Point Thres Hour	212.31	202.33	193.18
Seq Thres Day	28.79	22.53	17.51
Seq Thres Hour	55.27	52.33	45.22

6   Predicting User Navigation Using Time Based User Profiles

To evaluate the effectiveness of the techniques that we have outlined in this paper for personalization, the data set was segmented into four parts, each part is the equivalent of 1 weeks browsing on the WAP portal. In turn each possible combination of 3 weeks was used to learn rules using Apriori. The point threshold and sequence threshold methods were then applied to each of the possible combination of 3 weeks. Each of the rule sets was then used to try and predict user navigation in the 4th week. Here we compare results based on accuracy of predictions, number of predictions made and number of applicable rules that may be applied for each user. Initially we had hoped that we could compare our techniques with an existing algorithm (i.e. Apriori). However the algorithm did not learn a sufficient number of high confidence rules for a fair comparision to take place. In fact for a majority of users no rules were learned in the 0.6 – 1 confidence range. However in the figures below we can see the results of a comparison between the point threshold method applied to days (PTD) and hours (PTH), and the sequence threshold method for days (STD) and for hours (STH).

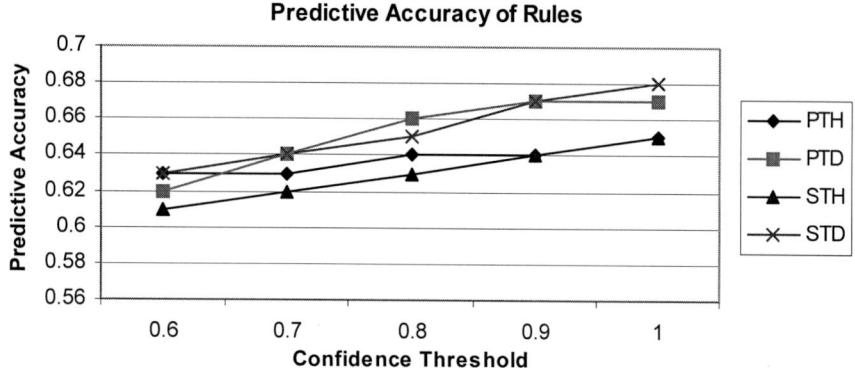

Fig. 5. Predictive Accuracy for each user for each of the four methods

Figure 5 shows the predictive accuracy of the rules. The predictive accuracy of the rules is in the range of 60%-70%. This is surprising given that many of the rules have high confidence values. In general it can be seen that the rules learned using days, as time periods are more accurate than those using hours. We can draw the conclusion that days are better time points than hours, which appear to be to fine grained. In general for each user less rules were learned using days as time points, we found that the rules are applied more often and the rules are more accurate for predicting user navigation. A possible solution would be to use periods of hours rather than single hours as time points in some sort of sliding window technique.

7   Conclusions and Future Work

User navigation in the Internet can be time dependent; users have different desires and goals at different times. As such we have presented a number of methods for learning rules that can be applied during particular time periods, during which users in general have different goals. We have analyzed our methods with respect to pages that users have visited and found that a greater number rules with high confidence and high support values were discovered. We then used our methods to try and predict user navigation in a WAP portal by using a number of weeks of navigation to predict subsequent weeks navigation. We found that, for each user, the average number of rules found, and the number of times that those rules could be applied, was greater for the temporal rules learned using our methods than those learned using a traditional association rule mining algorithm. Subsequently as high confidence rules were applied more often we have shown that these methods can potentially be of great benefit to users who navigate on mobile devices and aid their experience. As this is an initial attempt at learning temporal rules and models of user navigation in mobile devices there are, of course, other extensions that can be made to this work. Firstly we hope to investigate the use of categories to predict user navigation and indeed use these temporal models in conjunction with such a method to improve the user browsing experience. Secondly we hope to develop more sophisticated algorithms to create temporal rules and models of user navigation to predict and aid user navigation. This study is a new direction in mobile-Internet navigation and will hopefully lead to the way for future work and improve navigation for users on mobile devices. Integrating this knowledge with some existing techniques as has been outlined can benefit users who access the Internet on all manner of devices.

Acknowledgements

This research was supported by the Science Foundation Ireland under Grant No. 03/IN.3/I361 to the second and third authors.

References

1. Agrawal R. & Srikant R. Fast Algorithms for Mining Association Rules in Large Data-bases, In Proceedings of the 20th International Conference on Very Large Databases, VLDB 1994, P.P. 487 – 499.
2. Anderson C.R., Domingos P. & Weld D.S. Adaptive Web Navigation for Wireless Devices, In Proceedings of the 17th International Joint Conference on Artificial Intelligence, IJCAI 2001, P.P. 879 – 884.
3. Begole J., Tang J.C. & Hill R. Rhythm Modeling, Visulizations and Applications, In Proceedings of the 16th Annual ACM Symposium on User Interface Software and Technology, UIST 2003, P.P. 11-20.
4. Beitzel S.M.,Jensen E.C., Chowdhury A., Grossman D., and Frieder O. Hourly analysis of a very large topically categorized web query log. In Proceedings of the 27th Annual ACM Conference SIGIR 2004. P.P. 321 – 328, 2004.
5. Billsus D., Brunk C., Evans C., Gladish B., & Pazzani M.J. Adaptive Interfaces for Ubiquitous Web Access, Communications of the ACM 45(4) P.P. 34 – 38, 2002.
6. Buchanan G., Farrant S., Jones M., Thimleby H.W., Marsden G. & Pazzani M.J. Improving Mobile Internet Usability, In Proceedings of the 10th World Wide Web Conference, WWW 2001, P.P. 673 – 680.
7. Halvey M., Keane M.T. & Smyth B. Predicting Navigation Patterns on the Mobile-Internet Using Time of the Week, WWW (Special Interest Tracks and Posters) 2005, P.P. 958 – 959.
8. Halvey M., Keane M.T. & Smyth B. Birds of a Feather Surf Together: Using Clustering Methods to Improve Navigation Prediction from Internet Log Files, Lecture Notes in Computer Science, Volume 3587, P.P. 174 – 183.
9. Halvey M., Keane M.T. & Smyth B. Time Based Segmentation of Log Data for User Navigation Prediction in Personalization, In Proceedings of the 3rd International Conference on Web Intelligence, WI 2005, P.P. 636 – 641.
10. Halvey M., Keane M.T., & Smyth B. Mobile Web Surfing is the same as Web Surfing. Communications of the ACM, Volume 49, Issue 3, P.P. 76-81.
11. Halvey M., Keane M.T. & Smyth B. Time Based Patterns in Mobile-Internet Surfing, In Proceedings of CHI 2006, (Accepted; In Press).
12. Horvitz E., Koch P., Kadie C.M. & Jacobs A. Coordinates: Probabililistic Forecasting of Presence and Availability, In Proceedings of the 18th Conference in Uncertainty in Artificial Intelligence, UAI 2002, P.P. 224 – 233.

13. Lau T. & Horvitz E. Patterns of Search: Analyzing and Modeling web Query Refinement, In Proceedings of the 7th International Conference on User Modeling, UM 1999, P.P. 119 – 128.
14. Perkowitz M. & Etzioni O. Towards Adaptive Web Sites: Conceptual Framework and Case Study. Artificial Intelligence 118(1-2), P.P. 245 – 275.
15. Pirolli P. Distributions of Surfers' Paths through the World Wide Web: Empirical Characterizations. *The Web Journal*, 2 (1998):P.P. 29-45.
16. Ramsay M, and Nielsen J. Nielsen Report: WAP Usability Deja Vu: 1994 All Over Again, 2000.
17. Smyth B. & Cotter P. The Plight of the Navigator : Solving the Navigation Problem for Wireless Portals, AH 2002, P.P. 328 – 227.

The Value of QoE-Based Adaptation Approach in Educational Hypermedia: Empirical Evaluation

Cristina Hava Muntean and Jennifer McManis

Performance Engineering Laboratory, School of Electronic Engineering
Dublin City University, Glasnevin, Dublin 9, Ireland
{havac, mcmanisj}@eeng.dcu.ie

Abstract. This paper reports the results of a comparison-based empirical study on the applicability of the end-user Quality of Experience-based content adaptation mechanism in adaptive educational hypermedia. The focus of the paper will be the experiment itself: the initial settings, testing scenarios and the results. We will show that for low bit rate connections the QoE-based adaptation decreases study session time, information processing time per page and the number of re-visits to a page, it maintains similar learning outcomes while also improving the user quality of experience and satisfaction with the system. Finally we will comment on the results and interpret them.

1 Introduction

New communication technologies can enable Web users to access personalised information "anytime, anywhere". However, the network environments used for accessing the information may have widely varying performance characteristics (e.g bandwidth, level of congestion, mobility support, cost of transmission, etc). It is unrealistic to expect that the quality of delivery of content can be maintained at the same level in this variable environment. Rather an effort must be made to fit the content served to the current delivery conditions, thus ensuring high Quality of Experience (QoE) to the users. Currently, the adaptive hypermedia research places very little emphasis on end-user QoE and performance. However, it should be noted that some Adaptive Hypermedia Systems (AHS) have taken into consideration some performance features such as device capabilities (GUIDE [1], MP^3 [2]), the type of the access, communication protocol (SHAAD [3]), state of the network (SHAAD [3]) etc. in order to improve the end-user QoE. However, these account for only a limited range of factors affecting QoE. In order to respond to this problem we have conducted a more complete analysis of the key factors that affect QoE. We also proposed a QoE adaptation layer that extends the adaptation functionally of the AHS and ensures high level of QoE when users access personalised material via various connectivity network environments [4].

This paper presents an empirical-analysis of the experimental study conducted applying QoE layer in adaptive educational hypermedia to ascertain its effects on the learning process. The analysis compares learner outcome, learning performance, usability and visual quality for an AHA! [5] courseware application with and without application of the QoE adaptation layer.

V. Wade, H. Ashman, and B. Smyth (Eds.): AH 2006, LNCS 4018, pp. 121–130, 2006.
© Springer-Verlag Berlin Heidelberg 2006

2 End-User QoE-Based Adaptation Overview

Most of the AHS proposed in the literature follow the abstract representation of the adaptation process illustrated in the AHAM [6] model. They construct and maintain a Domain Model (DM), a User Model (UM) and an Adaptation Model (AM). Starting from this simple abstract representation we extended the adaptation functionality with a novel content-based adaptation mechanism (called QoE Layer) that improves the end-user Quality of Experience (QoE) [7] when the Web browsing process takes place over heterogeneous and changeable network environments. While the AHS's main role of delivering personalised content is not altered, its functionality and performance is improved and thus the user satisfaction with the service provided.

To better understand the framework for our experiment, a brief presentation of the QoE layer architecture is presented next. More details were provided in other papers [4, 7, 8]. The QoE layer includes the following components: Perceived Performance Model (PPM), Performance Monitor (PM) and Adaptation Algorithm (AA). PM monitors different performance metrics (e.g. download time, round-trip time, throughput, user tolerance for delay) and user behaviour-related actions (e.g. abort request) in real-time during user navigation and delivers them to the PPM. The PPM models this information using a stereotype-based technique and probability and distribution theory [8], in order to learn about the user's operational environment characteristics, about changes in the network connection and the consequences of these changes on the user's quality of experience. Based on this information the PPM suggests optimal Web content characteristics (e.g. the number of embedded objects in the Web page, the dimension of the based-Web page without components and the total dimension of the embedded components) that will provide a satisfactory QoE. The Adaptation Algorithm uses PPM's content-related suggestions and applies various transformations [4] (e.g. modifications in the properties of the embedded images and/or elimination of some of them and placing a link to the image) to the personalised Web page (designed by the AM based on a user profile).

In this context, the adaptation process of an AHS allows for both *user-based* and *QoE-based* adaptations. *User-based* adaptation selects the fragments of information from the DM for inclusion in a user-tailored performance-orientated document, based on the user profile (UM). *QoE-based* adaptation is applied when the delivery of the personalised document over a given connectivity environment would not provide a satisfactory end-user QoE. In this case, the AA adjusts the characteristics of the personalised document.

In conclusion, the main goal of a QoE-aware AHS is to provide personalised material that suits both user's individual characteristics (e.g. goals, knowledge) and the delivery environment in order to ensure high QoE.

3 Context of the Study

As already mentioned, QoE layer aims at enhancing the adaptation functionality in order to improve the overall user experience with AHS when the user's operational environment has widely varying performance characteristics (e.g. bandwidth, delay, level of congestion, mobility support) that may affect the QoE. Therefore, the evaluation of the

QoE layer involved its deployment on the open-source AHA! system, creating QoEAHA. QoEAHA was applied in the educational area as an adaptive courseware application in order to test user perception of content delivery and its effect on learning outcome. The empirical study presented in this paper aims at a comparison-based evaluation of the QoEAHA in a home-like operational environment.

The subjects involved in the experiment were comprised of sixty-two post-graduate students from Faculty of Engineering and Computing at Dublin City University, randomly divided in two groups. They were required to perform two sets of task-based scenarios. Learning outcome, learning performance, system's usability and effectiveness, correlation analysis as well as assessment of the visual quality of the content and user satisfaction were analysed when using QoEAHA and the AHA! system. The impact of the end-user QoE on the student learning performance was also investigated.

4   Design of the Empirical Evaluation

The experiment took place in the Performance Engineering Laboratory, Dublin City University. Two sets of task-based scenarios ("interactive study" and "search for information") were developed and carried out. The first group of subjects used QoEAHA, whereas the second group used AHA!. The subjects were not aware of the type of the system they were using. The educational material consisted of an adaptive tutorial on the AHA! v.2.0 [5] application. None of the students had accessed the material prior the tests. No time limitation was imposed on the execution of tasks.

For both groups the same network conditions were emulated between the subjects' computers and the two systems. NISTNET, a network emulator that allows for the emulation of various network conditions characterised by bandwidth, delay, and loss was used to create low bit rate home-like Internet environments with network speed between 28 kbps and 128 kbps.

4.1   Scenario 1: Interactive Study

Scenario One covered an interactive study session on chapter one from the adaptive tutorial over various connection types. At the start of the study session the subjects were given a short explanation of both system usage and their required duties such as:

- *complete an on-line pre-test questionnaire* [9] with six questions related to the learning topic that aims at assessing subjects' prior knowledge on studied domain.
- *log onto the system* and proceed to browse and *study the material*. Back and forward actions through the studied material were permitted.
- at the end of the study period, *complete a post-test questionnaire* [9] consisting of fifteen questions that tests recollection of facts, terms and concepts as well as knowledge level after completing a study session.
- *Answer an usability questionnaire* [9] consisting of ten questions categorised into navigation, accessibility, presentation, performance and subjective feedback.

In order to fully assess the subjects learning outcome, both pre- and post-tests were such devised that consisted of a combination of four different types of test-items, commonly used in the education: "Yes-No", "Forced-Choice", "Multi-Choice" and "Gap-Filling" test items [10]. Each test-item type has different degree of difficulty and therefore a different weight in the final score is assigned for a correct answer. The final scores were normalised in the 0-10 range. Learning outcome, learning performance and system usability were assessed and forty-two students took part in this scenario.

4.2 Scenario 2: Search for Information

This scenario involves visual quality assessment that makes use of an evaluation criteria often used in the educational area: time taken to search for a term described in a page. Since the QoE adaptation mechanism involves applying various modifications on the properties of the embedded images, this scenario has an important role. The goal is to assess whether the quality of images is good enough to perform the required task.

The subjects were asked to look up two different terms and to answer two questions related to these terms. The terms were located on two pages of the tutorial, more precisely, in the embedded images. As these pages include the largest number of embedded images, the highest image quality degradation was caused when using QoEAHA in the tested conditions.

Objective and subjective visual quality assessments were performed involving twenty students. Time taken to complete the task and questionnaire-based evaluation techniques were used. The subjective visual quality assessment on a five-point quality scale (1-"bad", 2-"poor", 3-"fair", 4-"good", 5-"excellent") ascertained the impact of QoE-based content adaptation on user experience.

5 Results

5.1 Assessment of the Learning Outcome

Learning outcome provided by an e-learning technology relates to the degree of knowledge accumulation by a person after studying certain material. It is analysed in form of course grades, pre/post-test scores or standardised test scores. In our experiment learning outcome was analysed in term of pre-test/post-test scores of the two groups after a study session. Pre-test scores (AHA_{mean}= 0.35, $QoEAHA_{mean}$= 0.30) showed that both groups of students had the same prior knowledge on the studied domain.

The mean scores for the post-test were 7.05 for the subjects that used QoEAHA and 6.70 for the AHA! group. A two-sample T-Test analysis on these values does not indicate a significant difference in the marks received by the two groups of subjects. (α =0.05, t = -0.79, t-critical =1.68, p(t) = 0.21).

In conclusion, results indicate no significant difference in the learning outcome of the two groups, regardless of the characteristics of the operational environment. Thus, the degradation of image quality does not adversely affect student's learning outcome and QoEAHA offers similar learning capabilities to the AHA! system.

5.2 Impact of QoE-Based Adaptation on Learning Performance

Learning performance is another important barometer used to assess the utility and value of an e-learning system. In general the term refers to how fast a required task (e.g. studying, searching for information or memorising information displayed on the screen) is performed. The most common metric used in the educational area for measuring learning performance is *Study Session Time (SST)* [11, 12]. Apart of this, other metrics such as *Information Processing Time per page (IPT/page)* and *Number of Accesses to a Page (NoAccesses/page) performed by a person* were measured in our study. These metrics were analysed and compared for both group of subjects.

In the following, results for a 56 kbps emulated network environment are presented. Tests involving various low rate network environments in the range of 28 – 128 kbps provided similar outcomes as the 56 kbps case. These tests were for the first scenario.

5.2.1 Study Session Time (SST)

SST is measured from the moment when the subject logs into the system and proceeds to study, until s/he starts answering the post-test questions.

An analysis of the SST for the two groups, shows that on average students that used QoEAHA (SST_{Avg} = 17.77 min) performed better than the ones that used AHA! (SST_{Avg} = 21.23 min), leading to 16.27% improvement. This fact was confirmed with 99% confidence level by the T-Test analysis. The very large majority of the students that used QoEAHA (71.43 %) performed the study task in up to 20 min. with a large number of students (42.87 %) requiring between 15 min and 20 min of study time. When the AHA! system was used, only 42.85 % of the students succeeded in finishing the task in 20 min. The majority of them (71.42 %) required up to 25 min. with the largest number of students (28.57 %) in the interval 20-25 min (Fig. 1).

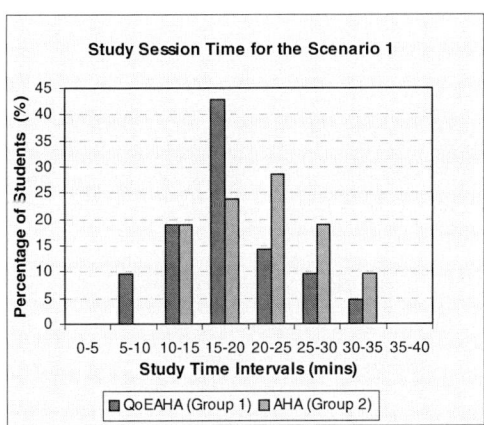

Fig. 1. Distribution of the Study Session Time for the two groups of subjects when performing Scenario 1 over a 56 kbps connection speed

5.2.2 Information Processing Time per Page (IPT/page)

IPT represents the time taken by a student to read and assimilate the information displayed on a Web page. It is measured from the moment when the Web page is delivered and displayed on the computer screen until the user sends a request for another page. The pages were not loaded in a progressive way. The results indicate that on average a lower time per page (IPT = 4.31 min) was spent by a student to process the information delivered through the QoEAHA system, in comparison to the case when AHA! was used (IPT = 4.95 min).

5.2.3 Number of Accesses to a Page (NoAccesses/page)

NoAccesses/page provides an indication of the quality of the learning process. Any re-visit to a page may indicate that the student was not able to recall the information provided in that page and thus the learning process was of poor quality. On average, subjects from the QoEAHA group performed a smaller number of re-visits (NoAccesses/page$_{Avg}$ = 1.40) than those from the AHA! group (NoAccesses/page$_{Avg}$ = 1.73). An unpaired two-tail T-Test with unequal variance assumed, confirmed with 92% confidence that there is a significant difference in the number of visits to a page measured for the two group of subjects.

How the content delivery performance of the two systems has affected *NoAccesses/page* was investigated by analysing the variability of the test-samples. The results for the *NoAccesses/page* showed that the variance for Group 1 (QoEAHA) (σ^2 =0.35) was lower than the variance for Group 2 (AHA!) (σ^2 =0.75). A F-Test analysis confirms with a 95% confidence level that Group 1 and Group 2 do not have the same variance and the difference between the two groups' variances is statistically significant. Therefore, one can conclude that Group 2 has a higher dispersion than Group 1. This indicates that a larger number of students (an average of 55 %) that used the AHA! system required more than one access per page for learning process. At the same time, the majority of students (an average of 65 %) that used the QoEAHA performed only one access per page showing that in general these students succeeded to focus better on the studied material.

Summarising the results, students from the QoEAHA group had shorter *Study Session Times* than those that used the AHA! system. A 16.27 % improvement of SST was obtained with the QoEAHA system. Since the download time per page provided by QoEAHA does not exceed the user tolerance for delay threshold [4] (12-15 sec is considered satisfactory for the Web users by the research community [13]), the students were constantly focused on required task. On average, an improvement of 26.5% [4] on the download time per page was obtained in comparison to the AHA system. Therefore, the QoE-aware system has ensured a smooth learning process. This observation is confirmed when assessing *NoAccesses/page* (on average19% decrease with QoEAHA) and *IPT/page* (on average13% decrease provided with QoEAHA).

5.3 Usability Evaluation

The goal of the usability evaluation was to measure and compare the usability, effectiveness and performance of the two systems. The methodology used for the experiment involves an online questionnaire. Questionnaires are the most widely used method in the education area with other alternatives being interviews, heuristic evaluations, subjects' observation through adequate equipment [8].

Scenario 1 required the subjects to complete an online usability questionnaire consisting of ten questions related to key usability aspects and performance issues. The answers were given on the Likert five–point scale: 1-poor, 2-fair, 3-average, 4-good,

5-excellent. The questions were categorised into: navigation, presentation, subjective feedback, accessibility and user perceived performance. The accessibility and user perceived performance questions assessed the end-user QoE. Four questions of the survey related to this and assessed user opinion about overall information delivery speed (Q6), download time in the context of browsing experience (Q7), user satisfaction in relation to the perceived performance (Q9) and whether the slow access to the content has inhibited them or not (Q5).

The results for 56 kbps connection case are briefly presented. More details on usability assessment were presented in [7]. Fig.2 shows that the QoEAHA system provided better end-user satisfaction (above the "good" level for all questions), than the AHA! system that scored just above the "average" level. This good performance was obtained in spite of the subjects using slow connection (56 kbps) during the study session and not being explicitly informed of this. Overall, the mean value of QoE usability assessment was 4.22 for QoEAHA and 3.58 for AHA!. This leads to a QoE improvement of 17.8 % for the QoEAHA system.

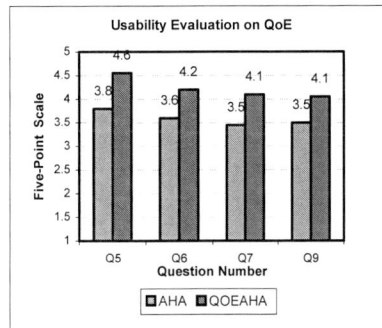 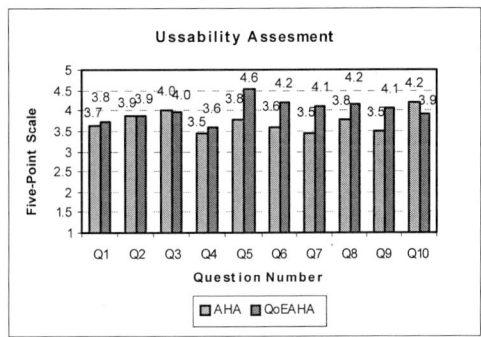

Fig. 2. Usability evaluation marks on questions that assessed the end-user QoE

Fig. 3. Comparative presentation of the answers from the usability questionnaire

Finally, an overall assessment when all ten questions (Fig. 3) were considered of equal importance shows that the students considered the QoEAHA (mean value=4.01) significantly more usable than AHA! (mean value=3.73). These results were also confirmed by an unpaired two-tailed T-Test (t=2.44, p<0.03) with a 97 % degree of confidence. An increase of 7.5 % in the overall QoEAHA usability was achieved due to the higher scores obtained in the questions related to end-user QoE.

5.4 Visual Quality Assessment

The scenario two involved both objective and subjective visual quality assessments. The goal was to investigate the effect of the quality degradation performed in a controlled manner by the QoE Layer on learning performance and student satisfaction.

Objective visual quality assessment involved searching for two terms and answering two questions related to the target information. Time taken to find each term was measured for both QoEAHA and AHA! groups. Results [14] showed that the measured times was similar for both groups. One aspect worth mentioning is all the subjects have successfully completed the task and answered the questions correctly.

The target information was presented in the embedded images of two pages that have the biggest content size. Thus, QoEAHA imposed the highest image quality degradation for these pages. For the worst operational environment case (28 kbps) QoEAHA applied 57 % reduction for Page 1 introducing the first term and 18 % for Page 2 (second term). The subjective-based visual quality assessment investigated through a questionnaire shows that regardless of the high content reduction the average quality grade for the AHA system was 3.9, very close to "good" perceptual level, and only 4.4% lower than the average quality grade (4.3) for AHA! [9]. This suggests that the cost of image quality reduction is not significant as far as user-perceived quality is concerned while at the same time yielding significant improvements in download time and learning performance.

5.5 Correlation Analysis

5.5.1 Correlation Between Learning Outcome and Judgment on Usability

One aspect worth examining is whether or not there is any correlation between students learning outcome (post-test marks) and their judgment on system usability (questionnaire scores). Therefore, we examined if students that performed well in the post-test evaluation, thought that the e-learning system (AHA!/ QoEAHA) was more usable, while students with lower scores expressed bad opinions.

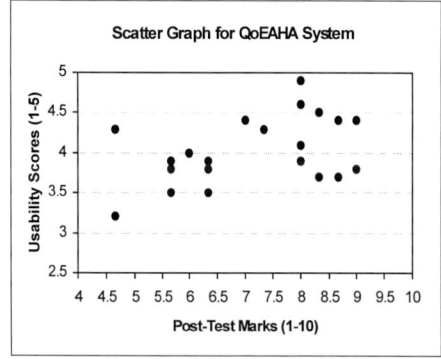
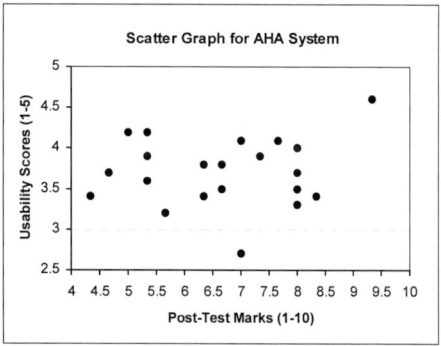

Fig. 4. Correlation analysis between learning outcome and judgment on usability for QoEAHA

Fig. 5. Correlation analysis between learning outcome and judgment on usability for AHA!

Spearman correlation coefficient (r_s) that indicates the degree of correlation between two sets of data was measured for both systems (QoEAHA: r_s=0.21, AHA!: r_s=0.03). As both values are low we can conclude that there is no strong correlation between learning performance and perception of usability. An alternative solution for examining the correlation is to represent graphically the values in a scatter plot. Fig.4 and Fig. 5 confirm again that there is no correlation.

Summarizing, no correlation has been found between the students learning outcome and their judgment on the system usability. The student opinion expressed in the usability questionnaire was not influenced by his/her mark from the post-test evaluation.

5.5.2 Correlation Analysis Between Study Session Time and Learning Outcome
This analysis aims at investigating whether the time spent studying was correlated to marks in the Post-Test evaluation. The Spearman coefficient for both AHA and QoEAHA systems was computed (QoEAHA: r_s=0.27, AHA!: r_s=0.004). As both coefficients are low value, we can conclude that there is no strong correlation between the two data sets. In consequence a low mark received by a student was not due to a short period of time allocated for the study.

6 Reflections on the Experiment Results

The aim of the experiment presented here was to investigate the usability and effectiveness of novel QoE layer enhancement for AHS, in the educational area. The choice to use AHA! as the foundation for building a QoE-aware AHS (QoEAHA), was based on issues such as availability (open-source), trust (tested), etc. However the QoE layer could be easily embedded in any AHS that respects the principles of the AHAM [5].

The QoEAHA evaluation involved a comparison with the AHA! system in home-like low-bite rate operational environments. Different educational-based evaluation techniques such as learner outcome analysis, learning performance assessment, usability survey, visual quality assessment, and correlation analysis were used in order to assess QoEAHA in comparison to AHA!. Over 60 students from Dublin City University took part in the experiment that involved two scenarios. The first scenario covered a learning session whereas the second one involved a search for information task.

Learning outcome analysis has shown that both groups of students (AHA and QoEAHA) received similar marks on the final evaluation test. Therefore, QoE layer did not affect the learning outcome and QoEAHA offers similar learning capabilities to the classic AHA! system.

Learning performance improvements in terms of Study Session Time (16.27 % decrease), Information Procession Time per page (13% decrease) and smaller number of revisits to a page were obtained with the QoEAHA system. It is noteworthy that most of the QoEAHA group students (71.43 %) finished the study in up to 20 min. while only 42.85 % of the AHA! group students finished in the same period of time.

Results on visual quality assessment confirmed that the controlled degradation of the quality of the content performed by the QoE layer did not affect the functionality of the e-learning system. Both groups of students succeeded to complete the required task in similar period of time.

The system usability investigation performed using an online questionnaire showed that students thought the QoEAHA system provided high end-user QoE. Questions related to the QoE were marked on average over the "good" level (between 4.10 and 4.55 points) while the AHA! system scored between 3.45 and 3.8. Questions related to the other aspects of the system (e.g. navigation, presentation) achieved similar marks for both systems demonstrating that the QoE layer did not affect them. Finally an overall usability assessment shows that students considered QoEAHA significantly more usable than AHA! with QoEAHA achieving a 7.5 % increase in usability due to the high marks awarded on QoE related questions.

Acknowledgement

The support of Enterprise Ireland Commercialisation Fund is gratefully acknowledged.

References

1. Smyth, B., Cotter, P.: Personalized Adaptive Navigation for Mobile Portals. 15th European Conference on Artificial Intelligence, Lyons, France (2002)
2. Cheverst, K., Mitchell, K., Davies, N.: The Role of Adaptive Hypermedia in a Context-Aware Tourist Guide. Communications of the ACM, Vol. 45 (5), (2002) 47-51
3. Merida, M., Fabregat, R., Matzo, J. L.: SHAAD: Adaptable, Adaptive and Dynamic Hypermedia System for Content Delivery. Conference on Adaptive Hypermedia and Adaptive Web-based Systems (AH2002), Malaga, Spain (2002)
4. Muntean, C, H, McManis, J.: Fine Grained Content-based Adaptation Mechanism for Providing High End-user Quality of Experience with Adaptive Hypermedia Systems. 15th Int. World Wide Web Conf. Hypermedia and Multimedia Track, Scotland (2006)
5. AHA! Project http://aha.win.tue.nl/
6. De Bra, P., Houben, G., Wu, H., AHAM: A Dexter-based Reference Model for Adaptive Hypermedia. ACM HYPERTEXT'98 Conference, Germany (1999) 147-156
7. Muntean, H. C., McManis, J.: End-User Quality of Experience Layer for Adaptive Hypermedia Systems. 3rd Int. Conf. on Adaptive Hypermedia and Web-based Systems, Workshop on Individual Differences in Adaptive Hypermedia, Eindhoven, The Netherlands (2004)
8. Muntean, C., H., McManis, J.: A QoS-aware Adaptive Web-based System. IEEE International Conference on Communications (ICC04), France (2004)
9. QoEAHA Evaluation Forms http://www.eeng.dcu.ie/~havac/QoEAHAEvalForms/
10. Muntean, C. H., McManis, J.: Adaptive E-learning Systems: Evaluation Issues. Transactions on Automatic Control and Computer Science Journal, Vol. 49 (63) 2004, 193-198
11. Weber, G., Brusilovsky, P.: ELM-ART: An Adaptive Versatile System for Web based Instruction. Artificial Intelligence in Education, Special Issue on Adaptive and Intelligent Web-based Educational Systems, Vol. 12, No. 4 (2001) 351-384
12. Ng, M. H., Hall, W., Maier, P., Armstrong, R.: The Application and Evaluation of Adaptive Hypermedia Techniques in Web-Based Medical Education. Association for Learning Technology Journal Vol. 10, No. 3 (2002) 19-40
13. Sevcik, P. J.: Understanding How Users View Application Performance. Business Communications Review, Vol. 32, No. 7 (2002) 8-9
14. Muntean, H. C., McManis, J.: QoSAHA: A Performance Oriented Learning System. AACE ED-MEDIA2004 , Lugano, Switzerland (2004)

GLAM: A Generic Layered Adaptation Model for Adaptive Hypermedia Systems

Cédric Jacquiot[1], Yolaine Bourda[1], Fabrice Popineau[1],
Alexandre Delteil[2], and Chantal Reynaud[3]

[1] Department of Computer Science, Supélec, Plateau de Moulon, 3 rue Joliot-Curie
91192 Gif-sur-Yvette CEDEX, France
{Cedric.Jacquiot, Yolaine.Bourda, Fabrice.Popineau}@supelec.fr
http://www.supelec.fr
[2] France Telecom R&D, 38 rue du général Leclerc,
92130 Issy-les-Moulineaux, France
Alexandre.Delteil@francetelecom.com
[3] Université Paris-Sud XI, CNRS (LRI) & INRIA(Futurs),
91405 Orsay, France
Chantal.Reynaud@lri.fr

Abstract. This paper introduces GLAM, a system based on situation calculus and meta-rules, which is able to provide adaptation by means of selection of actions. It is primarily designed to provide adaptive navigation. The different levels of conception, related to different aspects of the available metadata, are split in different layers in GLAM, in order to ease the conception of the adaptation system as well as to increase the potential use of complex adaptation mechanisms. GLAM uses meta-rules to handle these layers.

1 Introduction

With the development of networking technologies, and more specifically of the internet, the number of documents available both inside and outside organizations, such as companies or universities for example, has been increasing dramatically. It is commonly agreed upon that most companies' intranets are not very efficient at providing pertinent documents to the employees, let alone to order the documents or adapt them to the user's status in the company. Many Adaptive Hypermedia Systems (AHSs) have been developed in the past few years, and can provide adaptation within an annotated corpus of documents.

The problem of adaptation in AHSs has been addressed in several ways. Generally, an adaptation engine is made of adaptation data - most often a set of adaptation rules -, which can potentially be redefined by the AHS creator in order to provide different forms of adaptation, and of an inference engine, which applies the rules in order to select documents' contents and links, and in order to update the user model, i.e. mostly his knowledge, as in [1]. Some systems like [2] provide mechanisms to check if the adaptation rules are coherent and if the use of the set of rules won't result in a bad situation - like no adaptation at all for some users, or infinite loops of rules triggering each other.

V. Wade, H. Ashman, and B. Smyth (Eds.): AH 2006, LNCS 4018, pp. 131–140, 2006.

Most of these systems (cf. [2], [3]) provide adaptive navigation support and adaptive presentation, as defined in [4]. They consider fragments, atomic resources, to build up pages to provide to the user. They also modify links' visibility according to the user's model and goal.

In this paper, we focus our attention on adaptive navigation. We wish to be able to provide direct guidance, adaptive sorting and adaptive hiding. Our purpose was to create a purely declarative model, and to see how far situation calculus [5], which offers such a declarative approach, can be used as a model for adaptation in a closed-domain context [6]. Situation calculus offers a way to describe user/system interactions in an AHS very simply. Situation calculus allows us to define a model taking actions into account. An action can be "reading a document", "taking a test", "making exercises" etc. Rules classify actions according to the user's knowledge, preferences and position in the domain.

GLAM is a model for adaptation. Thus, it can be used to create different applications, in different domains. It defines a natural way to describe adaptation, thanks to the declarative aspect of situation calculus. This benefits to an AHS creator, since he has less efforts to produce in order to translate his needs into our formalism. We also provide a generic inference engine, which can take any GLAM based adaptation data into account to provide adaptation.

We also introduce a layered rule model. Usually, rules for adaptation can take into account any data relative to the user's preferences, on the one hand, and to his knowledge of the domain, on the other hand. Writing such rules can be quite complex: their premises can be numerous and of different natures. Such complex rules are hard to debug as well as to maintain, and simpler rules only offer limited adaptation. Moreover, user's preferences and knowledge are very different kinds of data about the user, thus they influence adaptation in different ways. Preferences are domain-independant. They help to choose between different kinds of documents to offer: examples, illustrations, summaries, or how fast the user can learn. On the other hand knowledge, which is domain-dependant, tells what document can or cannot be read by the user, what concept can or cannot be treated. Thus, GLAM includes a rule system layered according to the nature of the user metadata being used. The layering is achieved using meta-rules.

In section 2, we present the global architecture of GLAM In section 3, we present situation calculus and its role in our context. In section 4 we describe our adaptation model, and we detail its layered rule system. Finally we compare our approach to other well-known approaches and conclude with some perspectives about making a full generic AHS using GLAM for adaptation.

2   Global Architecture

As in most AHSs, we consider a user model, a domain model and an adaptation model. In this paper, we won't discuss the details of the user or domain models, but we focus on the adaptation model. However, we have designed GLAM in such a way that it can handle various kinds of metadata about documents and users - including relations.

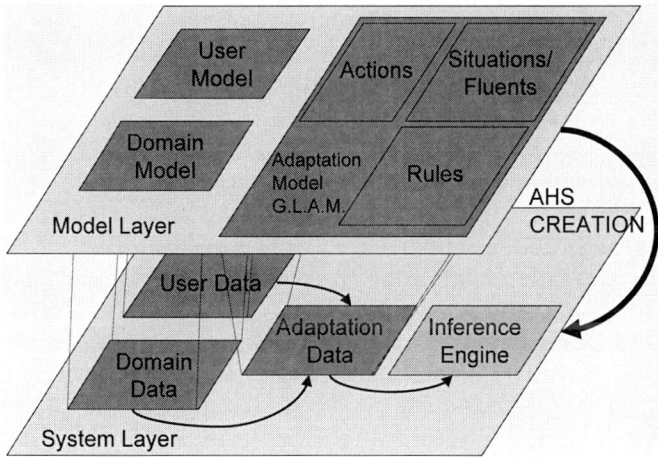

Fig. 1. GLAM's architecture

In this section, we introduce the global architecture of GLAM The way our system works is presented in figure 1. We present our architecture according to two abstraction layers. The model layer, which provides models for implementing the data into the AHS, and the system layer, which provides the data itself and the inference engine. The data is passed to the inference engine, which is able to compute the next possible step(s). As in many systems, the inference engine is reusable, since it can work with different adaptation data.

Our adaptation model is based on Sheila McIlraith's [7] adaptation of situation calculus presented in [7], and on results specific to planning techniques [8, 9]. Situation calculus provides a simple-to-understand, well-founded and expressive-enough basis for an adaptation model. Situation calculus is made of actions, situations and precondition rules (cf. section 3).

As detailed in section 4, we have enriched situation calculus in two ways. First, we have added notions related to preconditions in situation calculus, and redefined notions found in [7]. Secondly, and most importantly, we have defined a layered rule model, which replaces and enriches situation calculus's simple rule system. Criterions relative to the user are taken into account at different levels of the rule model, in order to ease the development of a system implementing potentially complex adaptation strategies.

Our inference engine uses data, described using our own version of situation calculus, to provide adaptation : it is able to tell what actions are best suited for the user's next step, according to his profile and position in the domain.

3   Situation Calculus

3.1   Why Using Situation Calculus?

Situation calculus [5] is a logic model, based on first order logic, that allows to describe observable situations modified by actions and to reason about these different items. Thus, our reasons for using situation calculus to provide adaptation are twofold. First, situation calculus allows to closely model reality : at any given time, situation calculus represents a situation as the result of a sequence of actions applied to an initial situation. Then, in any given situation, it is possible to do some actions among all existing actions. The fact that an action can or cannot be accomplished in a given situation is provided by rules, taking into account the current situation and the potential actions. Once an action is accomplished, the situation is modified according to this action.

In an AHS, a situation is given by the position of the user in the domain - which is the result of the various actions the user has achieved and of his initial knowledge and position - and by his preferences. An action in a given situation is to access a document that the user's current knowledge allows him to read. Once the user accomplishes an action, the situation is modified, i.e. his profile is updated. Thus, situation calculus is natively close from the reality of a user using an AHS and can easily be used to provide an adaptation model and the corresponding inference engine in an AHS.

3.2   Notions of Situation Calculus

Situation calculus is a formalism made of three distincts elements :

- Actions: they are the basis of situation calculus. They modify the situation when they are achieved. There are two kinds of actions : primitive actions and composite actions a.k.a procedures. In GLAM, we only focused on primitive actions, since the user takes them one at a time. One needs to declare every primitive action he intends to use using the *primitive_action* predicate. For example:
  primitive_action(read(Document)).
  primitive_action(read_about_concept(Concept, Select_Example).
  This last example shows that, if we add a document composition engine to our system layer, it is possible to achieve content adaptation on top of adaptive navigation. However, we did not address this possibility (yet).
- Fluents: they allow to observe the current situation. They are predicates defined for the initial situation, as well as for the situation resulting of an action "done" in the previous situation. The predicate *holds(Observation, Situation)* allows to describe if an *Observation* is true in a given *Situation*. The operator *do* transforms .For example:
  holds(read(Document), initial_situation) ← *false*
  holds(read(Document), do(read(Document), Previous_Situation)).
  holds(read(Document), do(read(Other_Doc), Previous_Situation)) ←
      holds(read(Document), Previous_Situation).
  means that no document has been read in the initial situation. A document is read if the last action that was "done" consisted in reading it or if it was already read in the previous situation.
- Preconditions: the *poss* operator is used to define rules that state if an action is possible or not in a given situation.

More details about situation calculus can be found in [5] and [10]. Sheila McIlraith [7] added a finer level of precondition by defining the notion of desirability. It is then possible to accomplish an action if the resources are available, and desirable to do it if the user's knowledge is sufficient. Josefina Sierra-Santibañez [9], who studied situation calculus as a way to achieve heuristic planning, refines this model by introducing a notion of order among the actions.

4   Modifying the Situation Calculus Preconditions to Match AHSs Needs

In GLAM, we decided to reuse the notions of primitive actions and fluents without redefining them. As one can define the actions and fluents he wants in a declarative manner, there appeared to be no need to redefine those notions in our context. However, preconditions are treated in a very simple manner: if a precondition rule is true, the corresponding action is possible, otherwise it is impossible. Moreover, they are described by a rule system using horn clauses, which is not especially made for AHSs (cf. 4.2). Thus we decided to redefine the notion of precondition to make it fit better in AHSs.

4.1   Redefining the Notion of Precondition

In order to redefine preconditions in situation calculus, we took ideas from [7] and [9]. We decided to use the notions of desirability and preference. These notions allow to create a double classification among actions. First, some actions are desirable, some are possible and some are bad. Secondly, within any of the previous categories, we can establish an order among actions, potentially allowing us to guide the user in a step-by-step manner. However, since we work in a closed-domain context, we did not use the same definitions as those proposed in [7]: the notion of document availability is not very useful in this context. Thus, we decided to redefine these notions so that they provide indications about the action's level of interest within the adaptation model.The notions of possibility, desirability and order are redefined as follows:

- It is possible (predicate **poss**) to accomplish an action if the user is able to understand the document that will be presented to him as a result of this action.
- It is desirable (predicate **good**) to accomplish an action if the user is able to understand the document that will be presented to him as a result of this action, and if this document leads to his goal(s).
- It is better (predicate **better**) to accomplish an action than another if it is more adapted to the learner's preferences than the other.
- It is bad to accomplish an action if it is neither desirable, nor possible. Thus, there is no predicate associated to bad actions, avoiding potential conflicts among rules.

4.2   The Layered Rule System

Layering the Adaptation Rules. AHSs can usually adapt their behavior to different aspects of the user : preferences, knowledge, goal [3, 11]. Rules in AHSs are often a mix of several different aspects [3]. In our version of situation calculus, one can describe rules for selecting good actions, possible actions, and actions better than other actions. These rules are triggered after each action is achieved, in order to compute the next possible one(s). They are independent. They cannot trigger each other. Even though they are triggered in a given order, it has no influence on the result, which is a partially ordered set of actions. Preconditions only help computing the category - bad, possible, desirable, better than - to which an action belongs. However, as in many systems, if one wishes to take several aspects of the user into account in a given rule, he has to add premises to the rule. This can lead to quite complex rules, where it becomes difficult to distinguish the different aspects of the user taken into account for adaptation. Maintaining such a rule system can be tedious.

In order to address this problem, our idea was to "adapt the adaptation" according to the user's characteristics. To do so, we define two levels for rules. First, our base rules only use data about the domain and the position of the user in this domain, i.e. domain-related knowledge. They describe different adaptation strategies, potentially incompatibles. Then, the inner characteristics of the user, like learning preferences, learning speed for example, are taken into account at the meta-level. These characteristics are domain independant, i.e. they can be reused in several domains. A set of meta-rules uses the user's characteristics to select the adaptation base rules which will be used to provide adaptation for this user. For example, some base rules can describe a linear strategy, some can add the necessity for the user to practice exercises, some rules can also indicate that the fastest way to the goal is the best way. Rules recommending exercises and rules that help to achieve the goal as fast as possible will be mutually exclusive. Thus, the meta-rules will help select the correct rules for the current user according to his profile.

This approach offers several advantages. First, the relations between the user and the domain on one side, and the inner characteristics of the user on the other side, which are often separated in the user models, are no longer mixed in the rules. They are separated at different levels of the adaptation model. The base rules provide a mean for action selection in a given position in the domain, whereas the meta-rules select the best set of adaptation rules for the current user. Maintaining the system becomes simpler since base rules and meta-rules are smaller, and thus easier to understand for the AHS creator, than classic base rules. Finally, this way of selecting rules is much finer than a classic stereotyped approach [3], since it is possible to mix up numerous characteristics about the user, and every different set of characteristics can provide a potentially different set of adaptation rules to use in the inference engine.

A Meta-rule Model. Our meta-rule model is an adaptation of a model created by Jagadish [12]. This model was originally designed for automatic database updates. It offers possibilities to help a system creator: it uses efficient algorithms to control the properties of the meta-rules.

It offers a formal approach for selecting rules according to their premises. In [12], a rule is said to be fireable if, and only if, all its premises are true. Meta-rules allow to select a subset of the set of all fireable rules, called the execution set. This set is generated using four kinds of meta-rules. Each kind of meta-rule is a binary relation between rules. The first kind of meta-rule is called requirement meta-rule, and allows to express that a rule requires another rule to be selected for execution, in order to be in the execution set. The second kind is called exclusion, and allows to describe what pairs of rules cannot be in the execution set together. The third one is called preference, and allows to describe which rule to prefer over which other rule when the two rules are exclusive from one another. Finally, the order meta-rules provide a total or partial order among the rules in the execution set.

The system also provides axioms that explain how to deduce new meta-rules from a set of given meta-rules, to detect determinism and order issues, and to select the execution rules. Thus, they can help the system creator by detecting flaws in his set of rules. For example, if a rule is exclusive from itself, the system can inform the creator that it is useless. The system can also detect cases where two rules are exclusive from one another, and yet there is no way to prefer one rule. This is called the determinism problem, and can be checked in polynomial time. If a total order among selected rules is required, the fact that the order meta-rules provide a total order for all possible fireable set can also be computed in polynomial time. All those verifications only depend of the meta-rules. They do not depend on the base rules.

Our AHS-oriented meta-rule System. We modified this system by changing the notion of fireability, which badly fit with situation calculus, and by incorporating account AHS specific notions, related to the user's capacity.

For AHSs, we define our rule system as a tuple $< V, F, M, \delta >$ where :

- V is a set of base adaptation rules, which take the form of horn clauses whose results are degrees of desirability for actions. These rules take into account the current situation and a potential action, and determine if the action is desirable (or possible, or better than another one). For example:

  $good(read(Document), Situation, User) \leftarrow$
  $not(read(User, Document)), good\_for\_partial\_goal(Document),$
  $current\_document(CDocument),$
  $prerequisite(CDocument, Document).$

  means that it is desirable to read a document if it has not already been read, if it leads to the goal and is one of the documents directly linked to the current document by a prerequisite relation. The only premises allowed for base rules are domain-related relations.
- F is a set of firing criterions. These criterions are related to the user's inner characteristics. For example : $fast\_learner = true$.
- M is a set of meta-rules. We reused the four kinds of meta-rules introduced in [12], but our meta-rules are between sets of rules instead of single rules,

allowing us to give information about all rules related to a specific user's characteristic at the same time. For example:

$\{rule1, rule2\} \supset \{rule4, rule5\}$

means that rules 1 and 2 require rules 4 and 5 to be selected for execution in order to be in this execution set.

- δ is a function that associates base rules with firing criterions. Unlike in [12], we cannot use the premises of a rule in a given situation as a firing criterion, since a rule is used several times in a give situation, according to the action that is being tested. δ allows to compute the γ function, which associates every criterion with the set of rules fireable according to this criterion. Thus, it is possible to write meta-rules about sets of rules related to a specific criterion, i.e. to write meta-rules about requirement, exclusion, preference and order between user's criterions. For example:

$\gamma(fast\_learner = false) \supset \gamma(need\_exercise = true)$

means that rules for slow users will include rules providing exercises.

Once those four elements are described, the part of the inference engine dedicated to the rule processing uses the axioms in [12] and formulas derived from these axioms, which make deductions about our meta-rules, to generate all deductible meta-rules. It checks if some rules will never be selected, if the system will always select the same set of base rules for a given set of criterions, if all rules that can be selected simultaneously are totally ordered, and if some set of criterions can lead to an empty set of adaptation rules. These verifications are intended to help the AHS creator who creates a GLAM-based AHS. They all are in polynomial time depending on the number of meta-rules. Providing meta-rules for sets of rules instead of single rules eases the creation of the system as well as it helps debugging it, since the meta-rules for set of rules are less numerous than meta-rules for single rules.

After checking all those properties, the system is ready to use. For each user, it evaluates the different firing criterions. It pre-selects the "fireable" rules related to this criterions. Then, it looks at the meta-rules to see if all rules can be put in the execution set or if some must be withdrawn, e.g. if all their prerequisites are not in the fireable set, or if they are exclusive of other preferred rules. Once the execution set is computed, it is ordered.

The decomposition of our rule model in four different parts makes it clearer to distinguish the different categories of elements to take into account. It limits the potential mix up of premises in the base rules as well as their number. Finally, it allows to add new base rules without modifying the meta-rules, thanks to the associations between rules and criterions.

5   Related Work

In this section, we discuss different approaches and how our system differs.

In AHAM [11], like in many other systems, the adaptation model relies on condition-action rules. Theses rules provide adaptation as well as user model update. Condition-action rules can trigger each other, and thus often need to be restricted to ensure termination and confluence. On the contrary, in our rule system, the nature of rules prevents us from termination problems, and we implemented a verification algorithm which can check if the system is deterministic in all cases, i.e. confluent.

The adaptation system in [13] uses TRIPLE rules for directly interrogating the user and domain data. These rules can recommend documents, which is close from action selection. Moreover, the recommendations can be more or less strong, which is close to our notion of possibility/desirability/preference. However, the layering in our system allows to separate different semantic levels in our data: preferences and knowledge are dealt with separately in GLAM, in order to simplify the conception of the system. By using distinct rule levels, we prevent an AHS creator from writing very long rules, with many premises. This layering is not arbitrary: it lies upon an intrinsic semantic separation of the nature of data manipulated to provide adaptation. Moreover, TRIPLE rules can only manipulate "subject+predicate+object" statements, whereas G.LA.M. rules can manipulate other data representation formalisms.

SCARCE [3] uses stereotypes to select the kind of adaptation to provide. In LAG and LAG-XLS [14], user-related preferences allow to select an adaptation strategy, for example, to adjust presentation of selected concept to present to the user. Our rule system goes beyond stereotypes or selection of strategy. In GLAM, one describes relations between groups of rules associated to one or more user criterion(s). These relations allow to describe the necessary rules for a strategy without having to select them manually. Moreover, a strategy can be based on several user criterions. If one takes 5 binary criterions into account, the number of potential strategies is $2^5 = 32$, which means that without meta-rules, one would have to describe 32 coherent groups of rules manually!

6   Conclusions and Future Work

In this paper, we introduced GLAM, an adaptation model for closed-content domain AHSs. We have already implemented a prototype system using this model, which is able to provide adapted navigation. We implemented the verifications for the rule system. They allowed us to check if our examples were correct and to ease the debugging process.

Using situation calculus as the core for adaptation allowed us to have a declarative representation of the system as close as possible to reality, hopefully easing the reusability of GLAM in many potential contexts. Our layered rule system introduces a way to describe adaptation by selecting adaptation strategies.

Thanks to the form of its rules, GLAM can take into account any kind of relations in the user and domain models. These models can be very different, since the different properties and relations can be different according to the domain. We now intend to provide meta-models for the user model as well as for the domain model. These meta-models are meant to help generating models fully compliant with GLAM They will also offer reusable relations and metadata, in order to ease the creation of AHSs.

References

1. DeBra, P., Houben, G.J., Wu, H.: AHAM: A dexter-based reference model for adaptive hypermedia. In: UK Conference on Hypertext. (1999) 147–156
2. DeBra, P., Aerts, A., Berden, B., de Lange, B., Rousseau, B., Santic, T., Smits, D., Stash, N.: Aha! the adaptive hypermedia architecture. In: UK Conference on Hypertext. (2003) 81–84
3. Garlatti, S., Iksal, S., Tanguy, P.: Scarce: An adaptive hypermedia environment based on virtual documents and semantic web. In: Adaptable and Adaptive Hypermedia System. (2004) 206–224
4. Brusilovsky, P.: Methods and techniques of adaptive hypermedia. User Modeling and User-Adapted Interaction 6(2-3) (1996) 87–129
5. Reiter, R.: Proving properties of state in the situation calculus. Artificial Intelligence, 64(2):337-351 (1993)
6. Jacquiot, C., Bourda, Y., Popineau, F.: Reusability in geahs. In: Proceedings of Workshops in Connection with the 4th International Conference on Web Engineering, Rinton Press (2004) 199–209
7. McIlraith, S., Son, T.: Adapting golog for composition of semantic web services. In: roceedings of the Eights International Conference on Principles and Knowledge Representation and Reasoning (KR-02). (2002)
8. Fikes, R., Nilsson, N.: Strips: A new approach to the application of theorem proving to problem solving. Artificial Intelligence 1 (1971) 27–120
9. Sierra-Santibañez, J.: Heuristic planning: A declarative approach based on strategies for action selection. Artificial Intelligence 153 (2004) 307–337
10. Levesque, H.J., et al.: Golog: A logic programming language for dynamic domains. Logic-based artificial intelligence pp 257 - 279 (2000)
11. Wu, H., de Kort, E., DeBra, P.: Design issues for general-purpose adaptive hypermedia systems. In: HYPERTEXT '01: Proceedings of the twelfth ACM conference on Hypertext and Hypermedia, New York, NY, USA, ACM Press (2001) 141–150
12. Jagadish, H.V., Mendelzon, A.O., Mumick, I.S.: Managing conflicts between rules. J. Comput. Syst. Sci. 58(1) (1999) 13–28
13. Dolog, P., Henze, N., Nejdl, W., Sintek, M.: The personal reader: Personalizing and enriching learning resources using semantic web technologies. In: Proceedings of the third International Conference on Adaptive Hypermedia and Adaptive Web-Based Sytems, Springer (2004) 85–94
14. Stash, N., Cristea, A., DeBra, P.: Explicit intelligence in adaptive hypermedia: Generic adaptation languages for learning preferences and styles. In: Proceedings of the HT 2005 CIAH Workshop. (2005)

Recomindation: New Functions for Augmented Memories

Carolin Plate, Nathalie Basselin, Alexander Kröner, Michael Schneider,
Stephan Baldes, Vania Dimitrova, and Anthony Jameson*

DFKI, German Research Center for Artificial Intelligence
Saarbrücken, Germany

Abstract. Advances in technological support for augmented personal memories make possible new ways of enhancing the process of product recommendation. Instead of simply analyzing information about a user's past behavior in order to generate recommendations, a *recominder*[1] system can additionally supply various types of information from the user's augmented memory that allows the user to take a more active role in the search for suitable products. We illustrate the paradigm of *recomindation* with reference to a prototype implementation of the system SPECTER in a CD shopping scenario and the results of a study with 20 subjects, who found most of the recomindation functionality to constitute a useful enhancement of their shopping experience.

1 An Introduction to Recomindation

One development of the past few years that promises to bring substantial innovations in the area of adaptive hypermedia (among others) concerns augmented personal memories: It is becoming feasible for a system, with the user's consent, to store a vast amount of information about the user's actions, experiences, and contexts over a long period of time (see, e.g., [1] for a pioneering effort; [2] and [3] for more recent influential projects; and [4] for a collection of recent papers). As is discussed in a recent survey by Czerwinski et al. ([5]), these technological possibilities raise the questions "Why bother?" and "What might I do with all the stuff I collect?" (p. 46). These authors list several possible answers, ranging from helping users to find lost objects to improving their time management.

The aim of this paper is to advance a new answer to this question: Augmented memories can add a new dimension to the process of product recommendation. On the one hand, most approaches to recommendation (which are surveyed, e.g., in several chapters of the edited volume [6]) rely heavily on stored information about the past behavior of the user: products purchased, ratings made, web sites visited. On the other hand, this access to information about the past occurs largely outside of the user's awareness. To be sure, the recent trend toward the explanation of recommendations sometimes

---

* This research was funded by the German Federal Ministry of Education and Research (BMBF) under contract 524-40001-01 IW C03. Vania Dimitrova participated during a sabbatical leave from the University of Leeds. The character shown in Figure 2 was designed by treschique digital arts.
[1] The third syllable is pronounced as in *remind*.

V. Wade, H. Ashman, and B. Smyth (Eds.): AH 2006, LNCS 4018, pp. 141–150, 2006.

(though by no means always; see, e.g., [7]) involves exposing the user increasingly to information about his or her past. The most familiar examples are the recommendations of amazon.com of the form "We recommend product A because you once bought product B". A different type of explanation along these lines was introduced in the *reflective history* mechanism of Zimmermann et al. ([8, 9]): When recommending a new TV show, the system would produce an explanation like "*Xena: Warrior Princess* is produced by Sam Raimi, who produced the TV show *American Gothic*", the latter TV show being one that the user has seen in the past.

We will argue that explicit reminders of the user's past experiences and behavior can enhance the recommendation process in various ways; and that, with the technical feasibility of extensive augmented memories, the time is ripe to explore these possibilities. We introduce the new term *recomindation* to capture the blend of recommendation and reminding that we propose.

We will introduce our vision concretely and concisely by describing the proof-of-concept system SPECTER that we have developed, along with a user study that reveals how people use and evaluate the new functions that SPECTER offers.[2]

2 Specter and the Method of the User Study

The basic scenario is as follows: You have been using the personal assistant SPECTER for a long time, and the system has collected information about things like CDs that you have bought and movies that you have seen. You have just received a gift certificate that entitles you to buy CDs at two music stores, called *Bonnie's* and *Clyde's*, respectively. These stores specialize in CDs of movie soundtracks. Since you are not very familiar with these genres, you decide to spend about 20 minutes browsing in the "Soundtrack CD" section of amazon.com's web site before going to the stores. SPECTER will keep a record of your browsing behavior and, once you have finished browsing, will allow you to edit this record. When you actually visit the two stores, you will be able to access SPECTER's record in various ways, even as the record is being extended with SPECTER's further observations of your behavior in the two stores.

The subjects who performed the tasks of this scenario in our user study were 20 persons between the ages of 18 and 32, 11 male and 9 female. All subjects had considerable computer experience, and 8 subjects had significant experience with PDAs.

2.1 Pre-shopping Phases

Entering of Information About Earlier Experiences. For the study, the only feasible way of finding out about relevant biographical events such as the watching of movies was to ask the subjects to enter this information via a web form before coming to participate in the experiment. Presented with a list of 100 popular movies, the subject

---

[2] An earlier presentation of SPECTER that focuses largely on other functionalities is given by [10]. An earlier version of SPECTER was tested in a similar user study with 30 subjects, whose results led to improvements in the system's design and in the method of the study described in this paper.

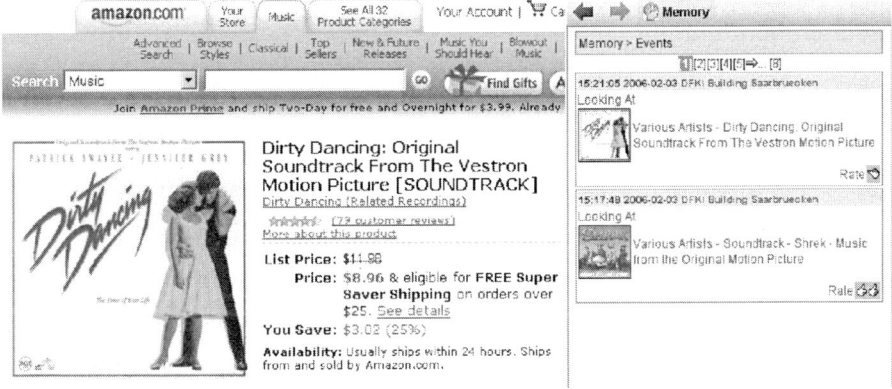

Fig. 1. Snapshot from the phase of browsing in amazon.com, with SPECTER's record of observed events shown on the right. (Ratings suggested by SPECTER have a darker background color than those made by the user herself, though this difference is barely noticeable on a monochrome printout.)

was asked to rate the movies that she[3] had seen and state when and under what circumstances she had seen them (e.g., "with friends/family"); she also answered similar questions about the soundtrack CD for the movie.

The remaining phases of the study took place at our laboratory. Before each phase, the subject was given any instructions, advice, and practice (lasting up to 30 minutes) that were necessary to enable her to operate the interfaces in question without spending much time on trial and error.

Browsing in amazon.com. As is illustrated in Figure 1, each subject spent 20 minutes browsing on a PC in the special section of amazon.com's web site for soundtrack CDs. In addition to reading texts and reviews, the subject could listen to excerpts of individual songs. In a window next to the web browser, an instantiation of SPECTER was running. Each time the subject looked at a CD's page, a record of this action was added to SPECTER's reverse-chronologically ordered list of descriptions of actions (performed by the user or by SPECTER itself). For each CD viewed, SPECTER entered an estimated rating on a 5-point scale: The highest rating of "two thumbs up" was entered if the subject spent more than 1 minute looking at the page, while "two thumbs down" was entered if they spent less time. The subject could immediately change any estimated rating; but she could also postpone such adjustments to one of the next two phases (as most subjects in fact did).

Reflecting on the Browsing Phase. In the *reflection* phase, the subject was encouraged to explore for up to 20 minutes the records that SPECTER had built up concerning the CDs that the user had encountered so far. (Most subjects did so for 5–10 minutes.) As can be seen in the right-hand side of Figure 2, each of these records refers to a particular CD—in contrast to the records shown in Figure 1, which describe actions and

---

[3] Since gender-neutral language is often imprecise and/or cumbersome, we arbitrarily use a feminine pronoun for each generic reference to a subject in the study.

Fig. 2. Screen in the reflection phase with which the user could select a subset of previously seen CDs to review. (In this case, she has chosen those rated "one thumb up".)

events). An animated character representing SPECTER encouraged the subject actively to examine various subsets of these CDs, such as the ones corresponding to the movies that the user had seen or the ones for which SPECTER had suggested a rating during the browsing phase. Here again, the subject could choose whether to change the rating estimates of SPECTER that did not reflect her actual evaluation (which tended to be numerous, because of SPECTER's crude estimation method).

2.2 Shopping in the Stores

Setup and Instructions. The final and most complex phase involved shopping for a total of 30 minutes in *Bonnie's* and *Clyde's*. Each store was mocked up with a CD rack containing 250 CD cases that looked like those found in real stores, arranged in alphabetical order by title. The two stores were mocked up on two sides of the same large room; but so that subjects could not move back and forth between them at an unrealistic rate, they were required to walk along a circuitous 50-meter trajectory to get from one store to the other.

A subset of 50 CDs was present in both stores; in each such case, the prices in the two stores differed noticeably, making it worthwhile for subjects to compare prices.

The subject was told that she was to pick out a total of 6 CDs that she would like to own; at the end of the study, two of these CDs would be picked at random by the experimenter and awarded to the subject to keep. The difference between the total price of these 2 CDs and 35 euros was paid to the subject in cash.

In this phase, the SPECTER application was operated on a PDA that was linked via Bluetooth and VNC to the central SPECTER server. Some of the functions to be described below made use of web services from amazon.com that provided information about music CDs: most importantly, a service that listed CDs that were "similar" to a given CD (or list of CDs) in the sense of amazon.com's item-to-item collaborative filtering (see, e.g., [11]): Roughly speaking, CD A is similar to CD B if customers who buy A also tend to buy B.

Table 1. Overview of functions available to the user in the hand-held SPECTER system used in stores

In any situation:	*Given a particular CD (cf. Figure 4 A)*
List all events that have occurred so far	Suggest related CDs:
List all previously encountered CDs which ...	List similar CDs in the current store
... were encountered in a given location	Give further information about the CD:
... have a price lower than a given amount	Show the details (e.g., artists) of the CD
... have a rating (by the user, by Specter, or by either one) above a particular threshold	List the prices of the CD at all places at which it has been encountered
	Show the rating of the CD (and allow the user to change it)
Given a list of CDs (cf. Figure 3 B):	List similar CDs that the user has encountered
Filter the list to keep only those which ...	List all events involving the CD
... have been encountered by the user	
... are available in the current store	*Given a list of events:*
List similar CDs which ...	Filter the list to keep only those which ...
... have been encountered by the user	... occurred in a given location
... are available in the current store	... involved a particular type of action

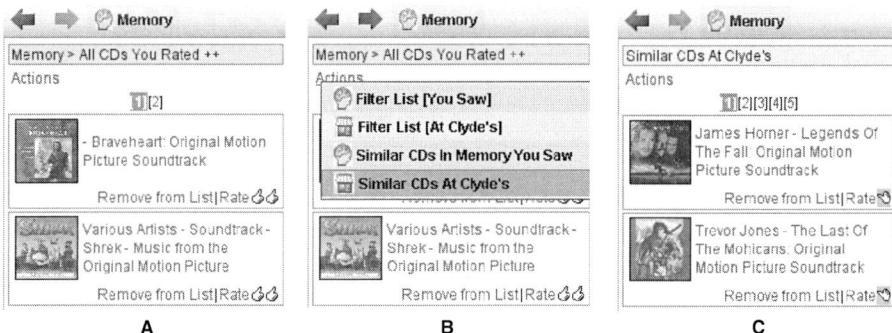

      A   **B**   **C**

Fig. 3. Sequence of screens illustrating how CDs previously rated positively can be used as a starting point for exploration in a store

Each CD case contained an RFID tag that identified the CD uniquely. When a subject removed a CD from the rack to look at the information on its cover, this action was detected by an RFID antenna that transmitted information about the action to SPECTER, allowing SPECTER to display the CD on the handheld's screen along with several options for obtaining additional information about it (see, Figure 4 A).

Functions Offered by SPECTER. Table 1 gives an overview of the functions that were made available to the user during the shopping phase. The design philosophy involved including: (a) promising novel functions that make use of SPECTER's augmented memory; and (b) a few additional functions that can make effective use of the results of the memory-related functions.

Figure 3 A illustrates how a user can acquire a starting point for exploring the current store by requesting a list of all CDs that she has previously rated very positively. As Figure 3 B shows, she could filter this list to include only CDs that are available in the current store (Clyde's); but in this example, she instead requests a list of *similar* CDs

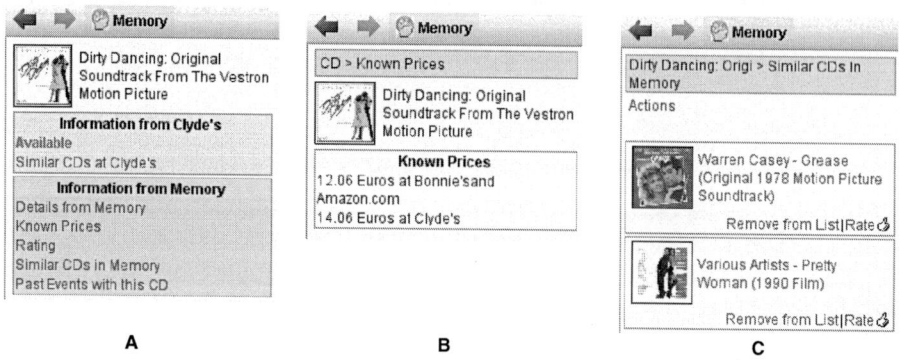

Fig. 4. Screens illustrating information from the augmented memory that the subject can request for a given CD

that are available in Clyde's. This list will probably include a number of CDs that are unfamiliar to the subject. For each such CD, the user can either (a) tap on its entry in the list or (b) retrieve the physical CD in the store and examine its contents. In either case, a screen like the one shown in Figure 4 A will appear, offering various types of additional information about the current CD, including: the prices of the CD at all locations where the user has encountered it (Figure 4 B); and a list of similar CDs that the subject has already encountered (Figure 4 C).

The potential utility of this third function may not be obvious. But consider an attentive salesperson who is aware of the customer's past purchases and can therefore introduce a new CD by pointing out that it is similar to one or more particular CDs that the customer already knows.

Another typical function is illustrated in Figure 5: For a given CD, the system lists all events that it has recorded which involve that CD. In Figure 5 A, both events occurred in Clyde's during the shopping phase. In Figure 5 B, the earlier event is the original viewing of the movie, which the user reported via the web interface. One hypothesis underlying the introduction of this function was that reminders of past experiences might bring to mind relevant thoughts, evaluations, and even emotions that the user had experienced in the past.

3   Use and Evaluation of Recomination Functionality

After this selective presentation of SPECTER's functionality, we now turn to some results about how subjects actually used and evaluated this functionality.

3.1   Responses to the Reflection Functionality

When asked "Judging from your experience, what is the reflection phase useful for?", 10 subjects noted that it was convenient to be reminded, before going into the stores, of the CDs that they had seen while browsing. Apparently, these subjects were not content simply to have SPECTER keep track of their encounters with CDs; they wanted to have

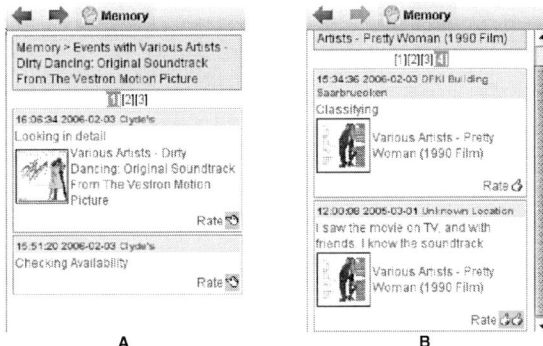

Fig. 5. Screens illustrating information about past events that can be requested for a given CD. (On the right, "Classifying" refers to the user's action of explicitly rating the CD.)

the most important CDs in their mind when they entered the stores. The other main benefit of reflection that subjects mentioned concerns the ability to adjust the tentative ratings that were made by SPECTER during the browsing phase. Subjects widely recognized that these ratings were (understandably) often inaccurate; but most of them found these tentative ratings, combined with an opportunity to revise them, to be an effective way of generating a list of promising CDs.

When asked where they would be most likely to engage in this type of reflection in everyday life, most of the subjects expressed a willingness to reflect in a bus or a train (85%), or a waiting room (75%); by contrast, only 35% expressed a willingness to do so in an office or at home in their free time. We can conclude that, despite the generally favorable response to the activity of reflection, the design of a system like SPECTER should ensure that reflection can be performed on a mobile device and in a variety of contexts.

3.2   Responses to Recomindation Functionality Used in Stores

For each of the questions represented in Figure 6, the user was asked "How often did you try to answer the following question?"; they were also asked to state which of three information sources they used (at least sometimes) to answer it: the hand-held SPECTER system, their own memory, or information available in the store. A separate question about each of the corresponding SPECTER functions asked subjects to rate its utility for their search for CDs on a scale from 1 ("not useful at all") to 5 ("very useful"). Figure 6 also shows objective data concerning the subjects' actual frequency of use of these SPECTER functions.

Use of Previously Encountered CDs as a Starting Point. As Figure 6 A shows, when subjects wanted to remember which CDs they had previously found promising, they were inclined to ask SPECTER; by contrast, remembering their previous evaluation of a given CD appears to be something that they could often accomplish with their own memory (Figure 6 B), though they still found SPECTER's automatic display of their previous ratings useful.

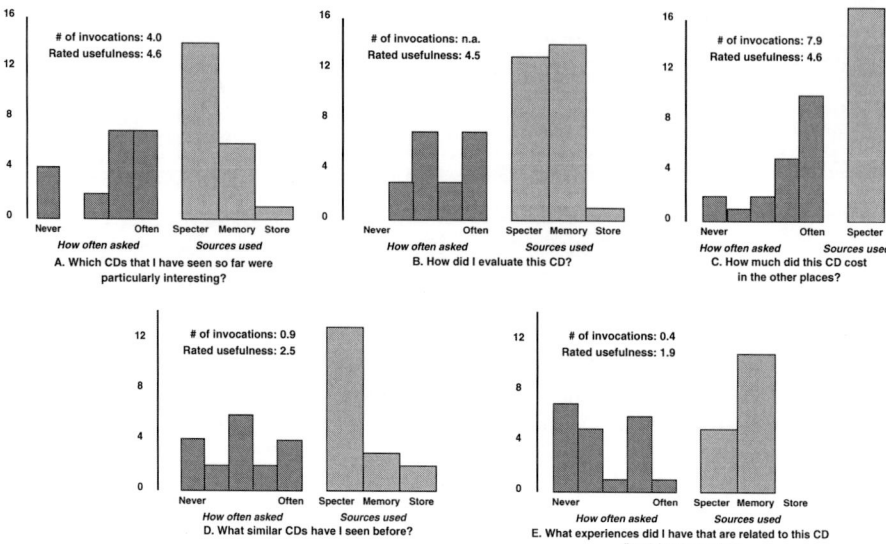

Fig. 6. Frequency distributions of subjects' estimates of how often they asked themselves particular questions during the shopping phase (left-hand side of each graph) and what source(s) of information they used (right-hand side of each graph): the SPECTER system, their own memory, or the CDs in the store. (Also given are the average number of invocations of the corresponding SPECTER function during the shopping phase, as revealed by the system logs; and the subjects' average rating of the usefulness of this SPECTER function for helping them to find appropriate CDs, on a scale from 1 (worst) to 5 (best).)

Use of Information About Known Prices. As can be seen in Figure 6 C, subjects were understandably often interested in recalling prices seen earlier, and they invariably used SPECTER, rather than their own memory, for this purpose.[4]

Use of Pointers to Previously Encountered Similar CDs. One of the more novel and less obvious functions offered by SPECTER is the one that was illustrated in Figure 4 C: informing the user about similar CDs that she has encountered before. Figure 6 D confirms that the overall frequency with which subjects considered this question was relatively low, though a few subjects did report considering it "often". Note that SPECTER offers a considerable advantage over the subject's own memory here, in that SPECTER can provide an answer even when the CD in question is totally unfamiliar to the user. It is therefore not surprising that subjects reported answering this question much more often with SPECTER than with their own memory.

Use of Representations of Past Events. When we turn to questions about specific events in the past (as shown in Figure 5), there is convergent evidence that this function

---

[4] When the subject was in a given store, her SPECTER could not access information about the availability or prices of CDs in the other store unless that information had already been retrieved and stored during a visit by the user to the other store. This restriction corresponds to a real-life situation in which each store offers complete information about its products only to customers who are physically present in the store.

was less popular than the other functions. With regard to the special case of retrieving information about movies seen at some earlier date, most subjects reported a tendency to consult their own memories rather than SPECTER (Figure 6 E). It is in fact difficult for SPECTER to compete with a user's own memory in this regard, unless it really has been collecting data about the user's movie-going behavior over a period of years, especially since all of the relevant information was supplied by the subject herself via the web interface shortly before the main part of the study.[5] On a different and more generalizable level, several subjects noted that displays such as those shown in Figure 5 are relatively cluttered, relative to the amount of useful information that they provide.

In sum, detailed representations of past events appear to have less compelling utility in the specific scenario investigated than the less concrete information about the products encountered and the ways in which they were evaluated. Any attempt to increase the utility of concrete event representations should devote more attention to ways of representing them more compactly and selectively, perhaps with some degree of aggregation. A more general lesson for research on augmented memories is that it should not be taken for granted without specific evidence that detailed representations of past events will be useful for any particular purpose.

3.3   Global Evaluations of Specter

In any user study of a novel system, global evaluations by users must be interpreted with caution (cf. [12]). Still, it is worth reporting that all of the questions that requested an overall evaluation of SPECTER yielded responses that fell mostly within the top two categories of a 5-point scale. For example, 70% of the subjects indicated that they would be interested in using a system like SPECTER for shopping if it became available.

4   Conclusions

The paradigm of *recomindation* can be seen as a way of exploiting the technological possibilities of augmented memories in such a way as to put the "mind" of the user into the process of recommendation to a considerably greater extent than has been possible so far with recommendation approaches that are based on records from the user's past. Even this selective presentation of our implementation and user feedback shows that a number of aspects of the recomindation paradigm tend to be recognized as appropriate, effective, and even enjoyable—though some limitations and preconditions have been exposed and of course no novel approach is likely to satisfy all users equally.

Comments of subjects in this and other user studies conducted within the SPECTER project have indicated that the added value of recomindation is likely to be greater in settings (such as those involving shopping for food and cooking) in which the user needs to make more complex decisions (e.g., exactly how to prepare a meal on a particular occasion) and more detailed information from the past can be usefully presented as reminders (e.g., what particular ingredients were used on previous occasions; how the diners evaluated the results). This type of scenario is currently being investigated in

---

[5] In a future study, we intend to acquire information about the subjects' past experiences in a way that will not refresh the subject's own memory of these experiences.

SPECTER's successor project SHAREDLIFE, in which the possibilities for sharing memories among friends and acquaintances (cf., e.g., [3, 4]) in the context of recomindation are also being explored.

References

1. Lamming, M., Flynn, M.: "Forget-me-not": Intimate computing in support of human memory. In: Proceedings of FRIEND21, the 1994 International Symposium on Next Generation Human Interface, Meguro Gajoen, Japan, Meguro Gajoen, Japan (1994)
2. Gemmell, J., Bell, G., Lueder, R., Drucker, S., Wong, C.: MyLifeBits: Fulfilling the Memex vision. ACM Multimedia (2002) 235–238
3. Sumi, Y., Sakamoto, R., Nakao, K., Mase, K.: ComicDiary: Representing individual experiences in a comics style. In Borriello, G., Holmquist, L., eds.: UbiComp 2002: Ubiquitous Computing. Springer, Berlin (2002) 16–32
4. Mase, K., Sumi, Y., Fels, S., eds.: Special issue of the journal "Personal and Ubiquitous Computing" on "Memory and Sharing of Experiences". Springer, Berlin (2006) In press.
5. Czerwinski, M., Gage, D., Gemmell, J., Marshall, C., Pérez-Quinones, M., Skeels, M., Catarci, T.: Digital memories in an era of ubiquitous computing and abundant storage. Communications of the ACM **49**(1) (2006) 44–50
6. Brusilovsky, P., Kobsa, A., Nejdl, W., eds.: The Adaptive Web: Methods and Strategies of Web Personalization. Springer, Berlin (2006)
7. Herlocker, J., Konstan, J., Riedl, J.: Explaining collaborative filtering recommendations. In: Proceedings of the 2000 Conference on Computer-Supported Cooperative Work, Philadelphia, PA (2000) 241–250
8. Zimmerman, J., Kurapati, K.: Exposing profiles to build trust in a recommender. In: Extended Abstracts for CHI'02, Minneapolis, MN (2002) 608–609
9. Zimmerman, J., Kurapati, K., Buczak, A., Schaffer, D., Gutta, S., Martino, J.: TV personalization system: Design of a TV show recommender engine and interface. In Ardissono, L., Kobsa, A., Maybury, M., eds.: Personalized Digital Television: Targeting Programs to Individual Viewers. Springer, Berlin (2004)
10. Schneider, M., Bauer, M., Kröner, A.: Building a personal memory for situated user support. In: Proceedings of the First International Workshop on Exploiting Context Histories in Smart Environments (ECHISE 2005) at Pervasive 2005, Munich (2005)
11. Linden, G., Smith, B., York, J.: Amazon.com recommendations: Item-to-item collaborative filtering. IEEE Internet Computing **Jan/Feb** (2003) 76–80
12. Landauer, T.: Behavioral research methods in human-computer interaction. In Helander, M., Landauer, T., Prabhu, P., eds.: Handbook of Human-Computer Interaction. North-Holland, Amsterdam (1997) 203–227

Automating Semantic Annotation to Enable Learning Content Adaptation

Jelena Jovanović[1], Dragan Gašević[2], and Vladan Devedžić[1]

[1] FON, School of Business Administration, University of Belgrade, Serbia and Montenegro
{jeljov, devedzic}@fon.bg.ac.yu
[2] School of Interactive arts and Technology, Simon Fraser University Surrey, Canada
dgasevic@sfu.ca

Abstract. This paper presents an approach to automatic annotation of learning objects' (LOs) content units that can be later assembled into new LOs personalized to the users' knowledge, preferences, and learning styles. Relying on a LO content structure ontology and some simple content-mining algorithms and heuristics, we manage to rather successfully determine the values of metadata elements aimed at annotating content units. Specifically, in this paper we present the specificities of generating metadata that describe the subject (based on a domain ontology) and the pedagogical role (based on an ontology of pedagogical roles) of a content unit. To test our approach we developed TANGRAM, an adaptive web-based educational environment for the domain of Intelligent Information system that enables on-the-fly assembly of personalized learning content out of existing content units.

1 Introduction

Personalization of the learning content stands for one of the ultimate goals of the modern web-based educational applications. Though that is a really nice idea, the present learning content standards and authoring practice impose many obstacles. First, the e-learning standards such as the IEEE Learning Object Metadata (LOM) standard are rather inflexible in terms of the variety of metadata they capture, the way they express the structure of such metadata, as well as the structure and the meaning of the learning content itself. Second, few of the metadata fields proposed by such specifications are really used in learning object repositories (LORs) to annotate the LOs, hence the possibility to retrieve and reuse LOs is reduced. This is the reason why it is very hard to enable personalized reuse of LOs or LOs' parts. To address these issues we need a set of more flexible, still more comprehensive, explicit means (such as ontologies) for describing both LOs and content units (CUs) LOs are built from. Explicitly defined structure of a LO using ontologies facilitates adaptation of the LO, as it enables direct access to each of its components and their tailoring to the specific features of a student/content author. However, as the formalization does not solve the problem of the metadata that should be collected, we still need tools that will automate that process.

This paper illustrates how Semantic Web automatic annotation techniques can be employed to mine LO content, and thus provide necessary metadata for personalized

V. Wade, H. Ashman, and B. Smyth (Eds.): AH 2006, LNCS 4018, pp. 151–160, 2006.

reuse of LO components. Relying on a profile of the IEEE LOM RDF Binding for metadata representation and a LO content structure ontology, we develop a set of automatic annotation techniques for assigning metadata to CUs. Applying these techniques, we can, for example, identify the concept of a domain ontology that describes the semantics of a CU the best, infer the educational role of the CU with respect to an ontology of pedagogical roles, generate the CU's title, description and some other metadata elements. Such annotated CUs are used in an adaptive web-based educational environment called TANGRAM. Being based on a comprehensive user model ontology and being able to directly access components of LOs (by leveraging the automatically generated metadata), TANGRAM is empowered to dynamically, on-the-fly create new, personalized learning content out of existing CUs. In this paper we illustrate how TANGRAM is used for personalization of learning content in the domain of Intelligent Information Systems (IISs). We have so far applied our approach to personalized assembling of slides and slide presentations, while the same approach can be applied to other types of LOs. In the next section we briefly describe TANGRAM and some of its functionalities in order to motivate our work.

2   The Motivation: The Personalized Learning in TANGRAM

TANGRAM provides adaptation of learning content to the specific needs of individual learners. Two basic functionalities of the system from the learners' perspective are:

- Provision of learning content adapted to the learner's current level of knowledge of the domain concept of interest, his/her learning style, and other personal preferences.
- Quick access to a particular type of content about a topic of interest, e.g. access to *example*s of RDF documents or *definition*s of the Semantic Web (both topics belong to the domain of IIS).

In this paper we focus on the former functionality and throughout the paper explain how it is realized in TANGRAM.

A learner must register with the system during the first session. Through the registration process the system acquires information about the learner sufficient to create an initial version of his/her model. The learner's learning style is determined from a simplified version of the Felder&Silverman questionnaire[1], whereas for determining the learner's initial knowledge about the IIS domain, the system relies on the learner's self-assessment.

A learning session starts after a registered learner selects a sub-domain of IIS to learn about (e.g. XML Technologies). Having verified his/her knowledge of the chosen sub-domain (in his/her user model), TANGRAM builds a visual representation of that sub-domain (i.e. its hierarchical organization of concepts) in the form of an annotated tree of links (the upper left corner of Fig. 1), exploiting link annotation and link hiding techniques [1]. Specifically, the following link annotations are used:

---

[1] The questionnaire is known as "Index of Learning Styles", and is available at
http://www.engr.ncsu.edu/learningstyles/ilsweb.html

1. blue bullet preceding a link to a domain concept denotes that the learner knows the topic that the link points to,
2. green bullet denotes a recommended domain concept, i.e. a concept that the learner has not learned yet, but has knowledge about all prerequisite topics,
3. red bullet is used to annotate a domain topic that the learner is still not ready for as (s)he is ignorant of the prerequisite topics.

The link hiding technique is used to prevent the learner from accessing topics that are too advanced for him/her. In other words, links annotated with red bullets are made inactive. Hence, the learner is free to choose one of the blue or green bulleted topics. As the selection is been made TANGRAM builds personalized content on the selected topic, 'bearing in mind' both the learner's learning style and his/her preferences regarding content authors. Having presented the assembled learning content to the student, the system updates the learner model. More details on the whole process are provided later in the paper.

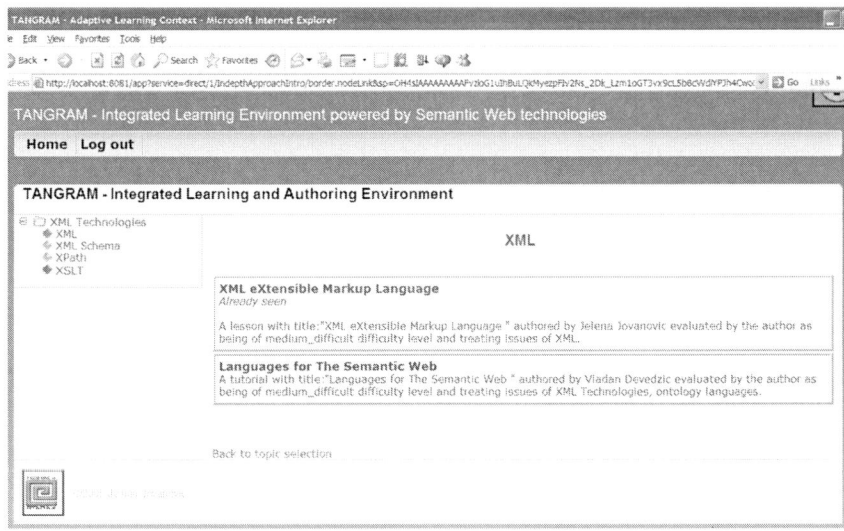

Fig. 1. A screenshot of TANGRAM after the learning topic is chosen

3   Ontological Foundation

In this section we briefly present each of the ontologies our automatic annotating approach   is   based   upon.   All   these   ontologies   are   available   at: http://iis.fon.bg.ac.yu/TANGRAM/ontologies.html. Note also that we have defined a profile of the IEEE LOM RDF Binding which is used to describe each CU. Specific metadata fields of the profile refer to these ontologies (e.g. *dc:subject* field refers to a concept from the domain ontology).

The ALOCoM Content Structure (ALOCoM CS) ontology is an extension of the Abstract Learning Object Content Model (ALOCoM) [2] with certain concepts of the

IBM's Darwin Information Typing Architecture (DITA)[2]. The ontology defines a number of concepts for different types of CUs that form the structure of a LO. The ALOCoM CS ontology distinguishes between content fragments (CFs), content objects (COs) and learning objects (LOs). CFs, formalized as instances of the *alocomcs:ContentFragment* class, are CUs in their most basic form (e.g. text, audio and video), and cannot be further decomposed. COs, formally represented as instances of the *alocomcs:ContentObject* class, aggregate CFs and add navigation. Navigational elements enable sequencing of CFs in a CO. Besides CFs, COs can also include other COs. LO (*alocomcs:LearningObject*) is conceptualized as an aggregate of COs targeted at fulfilling a single learning objective. To enable more fine grained content structuring we analyzed the structure of widely used content formats (primarily slide presentations and textual documents) and identified a number of specific content structuring types (e.g. slide, slide body, title, table). These types are included in the ontology as subclasses of the three root concepts (i.e. CFs, COs and LOs). Finally, the ontology defines aggregation and navigational relationships between CUs. Aggregation relationships are represented in the form of *alocomcs:hasPart* and its inverse *alocomcs:isPartOf* properties. Navigational relationships are specified as the *alocomcs:ordering* property that defines the order of components in a CO or a LO in the form of an *rdf:List*.

The ALOCoM Content Type (CT) ontology is also rooted in the ALOCoM model and has CF, CO and LO as the basic, abstract content types. However, these concepts are now considered from the perspective of pedagogical/instructional roles they might have. Therefore, concepts like Definition, Example, Exercise, Reference are introduced as subclasses of the CO class, whereas concepts such as Tutorial, Lesson, Test are some of the subclasses of the LO class. The CF class is not sub-classed, as according to the ALOCoM model [2], an instructional role can not be assigned to a single CF.

The domain ontology is defined using the SKOS Core ontology (http://www.w3.org/2004/02/skos/core/). Each concept of the domain is represented as an instance of the *skos:Concept* class, whereas the conceptual scheme of the domain is represented as an instance of the *skos:ConceptScheme* class. Each identified domain concept is assigned one or more aliases (i.e., alternative terms typically used in literature when referring to a concept) using the SKOS properties *skos:prefLabel*, *skos:altLabel*, and *skos:hiddenLabel*. SKOS also defines semantic properties for representing relations among domain concepts, for example a generalization hierarchy can be represented via the *skos:broader* and its inverse *skos:narrower* properties, whereas the *skos:related* property is intended for semantic relations between concepts belonging to different branches of the hierarchy.

The Learning Paths (LP) ontology defines learning trajectories through the topics from the domain ontology. We defined this ontology as an extension of the SKOS Core ontology that introduces three new properties: *lp:requiresKnowledgeOf*, *lp:isPrerequisiteFor*, and *lp:hasKnowledgePonder*. The first two are semantic properties defining prerequisite relationships between domain topics, whereas the third one defines difficulty level of a topic on the scale from 0 to 1. The LP ontology relates instances of the domain ontology through an additional set of relationships

---

[2] http://www.oasis-open.org/committees/dita

reflecting a specific instructional approach to teaching/learning. The main benefit of decoupling domain model in such a way is to enable reuse of the domain ontology – even if the applied instructional approach changes, the domain ontology remains intact.

4   Automatic Annotation Process

Metadata for a LO are mostly provided by the LO's author when uploading the LO to the repository. The challenging part is the annotation of the LO's components (COs and CFs). Peculiarities of the approach we apply to face this challenge can be summarized as follows:

- The values of some metadata elements are literally copied from LOs to their components. This is how values are assigned to *dc:creator*, *dcterms:created*, and *dc:language* metadata elements, refereeing to the author(s), date of creation and language(s) of a CU, respectively.
- Some metadata elements of the TANGRAM's LOM RDF profile are meaningful only when attached to a LO as a whole. Therefore, they are not supposed to be assigned to the components smaller than LOs (e.g. *lom-cls:accessibilityRestrictions* metadata element that refers to the learning styles a LO is particularly suitable for);
- The values of the other metadata elements are mined from a component itself, its content and presentational context.

In the rest of the section we explain our approach to automatic generation of values for metadata elements that hold ontology-based descriptions of CUs: *dc:subject* that points to a concept from the domain ontology, and *alocom-meta:type* that holds a reference to a concept form the ALOCoM CT ontology. Due to the limited size of the paper we restricted ourselves to presenting only the metadata elements that we deem as the most important for representing semantics of CUs. Similar heuristics are used for generating values of other metadata elements. For more details we refer readers to [3].

dc:subject element
To semantically annotate a CO with concept(s) from the domain ontology we applied the following approach: the domain ontology is queried for concepts that are semantically related to the domain concepts that were manually assigned to the parent LO. We assumed domain concepts as semantically related if they are interconnected via *skos:semanticRelation* property and/or its sub-properties: *skos:narrower*, *skos:broader* or *skos:related*. The retrieved concepts and their aliases, i.e. labels assigned to them as values of *skos:prefLabel*, *skos:altLabel* i *skos:hiddenLabel* properties, are stored in a hashmap and serve as the basis of the subsequent steps of the annotation process. Subsequently each component of the CO containing text is searched for the aliases stored in the hashmap, and if some of them are found, the component (i.e. CO or CF) is annotated with the domain concepts that the aliases refer to. Afterwards, we apply a *bottom-up* approach to generate a value for the CO's *dc:subject* element: the CO is annotated with a union of concepts assigned to its components. If no concept can be mined from the CO's content, the CO is annotated with concepts attached to the parent LO during the process of manual annotation.

The slide presented in Fig. 2b can help us explain another approach we employ to infer the subject of a CO - the combined *top-down & bottom-up* approach. As the figure suggests domain concept(s) that best describe the semantics of the slide's content can be inferred only from the title of the slide (it contains an alias of a domain concept). Performing the text analysis of the slide's title, XML is identified as the domain concept to be assigned to the *dc:subject* metadata element of the title (i.e. to the instance of the *alocomcs:Title* class, as its ontological equivalent). Applying the *bottom-up* approach we assign the same concept to the *dc:subject* element of the slide that aggregates the title. Next, we analyze the content of the slide's body (and each of its components) to find out that we cannot identify any concept of the domain ontology. Therefore, we apply the *top-down* approach, meaning that the XML domain concept, previously included in the slide's metadata set (via the *bottom-up* approach), is now used to semantically markup components that the slide aggregates.

For CFs that do not contain text at all, like CFs of the *alocomcs:Image* type, this approach is not applicable. Currently, in the absence of a better solution, such CFs directly inherit the value of the *dc:subject* metadata from the COs they are aggregated in.

alocom-meta:type element
This metadata element is used for annotating LOs and COs, but not for CFs, as according to the ALOCoM model an instructional role can not be assigned to a single CF.

Due to the lack of well defined formats for representing learning content of a certain instructional role (e.g. an explicit format for representing definitions), we opted for a heuristics-based approach to infer instructional role of learning CUs. The heuristics that we use are partially founded on our previous joint research efforts done with the ARIADNE group from K.U. Leuven, Belgium through the ProLearn project. Together, we did some initial research aimed at defining patterns for recognizing CUs having instructional role of *alocomct:Definition*, *alocomct:Example* and *alocomct:Reference* [4]. These patterns are defined using the experience discussed in [5]. Here, we explain how CUs of type *alocomct:Example* are recognized. Fig. 2a presents patterns that we use to check whether a CU is an example of a certain domain concept. In other words, these patterns enable us to test if a CU can be marked-up with *alocomct:Example* concept as its instructional role.

It is important to note that the patterns shown in Fig. 2a enable us to identify CUs indicating the appearance of an example. In other words, they help us recognize a CU that precedes an example. Let us consider a typical organization of a slide presenting an example of a domain concept in order to further explain the approach (Fig. 2b): the title of the slide gives information about the domain concept that the example refers to, while the slide's body actually contains the example. To be more precise, the first component of the slide's body is a list (an instance of *alocomcs:List*) with only one list item (an instance of the *alocomcs:ListItem*) that, according to the pattern number 4 from Fig. 2a, should be classified as an example (i.e. having instructional role of an example). However, it is obvious that such a conclusion is wrong. Actually, the subsequent component of the slide's body – a paragraph in this case (an instance of the *alocomcs:Paragraph*) – should be classified as an example. On the other hand, it would be hardly possible to deduce the instructional role of this paragraph just by analyzing the text it contains. Fortunately, its structural context gives us this valuable information.

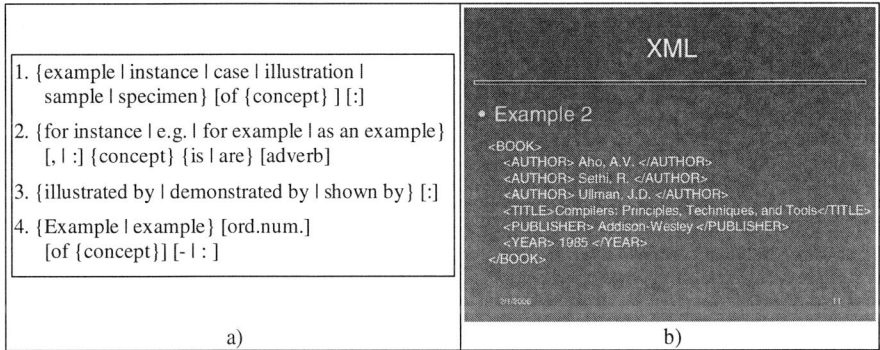

Fig. 2. The patterns applied in TANGRAM for recognizing examples (a); a typical organization of a slide presenting an example of a domain concept

Besides this pattern-based approach, we apply some simple heuristics to determine the instructional role of slides (COs of type *alocomcs:Slide*). For example, if the content of the slide's title is one of the following terms/phrases: "Bibliography", "References", "Reference list", while the content of the slide's body is structured as a list, the instructional role of the slide is presumed to be of type *alocomct:Bibliography*. Additionally, each list item appearing in the slide's body is assumed to be of *alocomct:Reference* instructional type.

The slide presented in Fig. 2b is suitable for explaining one general feature of our approach to annotation of CUs. When this slide is uploaded (as a part of the presentation that it originates from) to the TANGRAM's repository of LOs, the system actually stores an instance of the of the *alocomcs:Slide* class, as well as an appropriate ontological instance for each component constituting the structure of this slide (*alocomcs:Title*, *alocomcs:SlideBody*, *alocomcs:List*,...). Furthermore, metadata are uploaded to the repository: metadata for the slide as a whole, as well as metadata for each the slide's component that can be reused. However, metadata is not stored literally for every component of the slide. Instead, we store metadata only for those CUs that are really reusable, in the sense that we can realistically expect someone will be interested to retrieve them from the repository and reuse. For example, in the case of the slide from Fig. 2b, only metadata assigned to the slide as a whole and to the paragraph containing the text of the example will be uploaded to the repository. The rationale is that it is highly unlikely that someone would be interested in reusing a CU that contains only the text "Example 2" or a CU holding the title of the slide.

5 User Modeling and Adaptation Process

This section explains how the automatically generated semantic annotations are exploited in TANGRAM in order to provide personalized learning content. The section first explains the user model ontology, and then the implemented personalization approach.

5.1 User Model Ontology

We developed a User Model (UM) ontology to help us formally represent relevant information about TANGRAM users (content authors and students). The ontology focuses exclusively on the user information that proved to be essential for TANGRAM's functionalities. To enable interoperability with other learning applications and exchange of users' data, we based the ontology on official specifications for user modeling: IEEE PAPI Learner (http://edutool.com/papi) and IMS LIP (http://www.imsglobal.org/profiles). Furthermore, since we did not want to end up with another specific interpretation of the official specifications, potentially incompatible with existing learning applications, we explored existing solutions, like the ones presented in [6] and [7]. The result is a modular UM ontology that uses some fragments of the UM ontology developed for the ELENA project [6] and introduces new constructs for representing users' data that the official specifications do not declare and the existing ontologies either do not include at all, or do not represent in a manner compliant to the needs of TANGRAM.

The UM ontology defines formalism for representing user features common to all TANGRAM users (authors as well as learners), as well as those particular for learners. The former set of formalisms are aimed at representing the users' basic personal data (*um:PersonalInfo*), their preferences regarding language (*um:LanguagePreference*), domain topics (*um:ConceptPreference*) and authors of learning content (*um:AuthorPreference*). The latter set encompasses a number of classes and properties for representing the learners' performance, as well as their learning styles. Specifically, each learner (*um:Student*) is assigned a set of performance-related data (via *um:hasPerformance* property) represented in the form of the *papi:Performance* class and a broad set of properties aimed at capturing detailed description of a learner's performance (e.g. the *papi:learning_experience_ identifier* property identifies a CU that formed the learning material used for learning). As for representing learning styles, the ontology introduces the *um:LearningStyle* class and associates it (via the *um:hasCategory* property) with the *um:LearningStyleCategory* class that formally stands for one specific aspect (category) of the learning style. Since TANGRAM relies on the Felder & Silverman model of learning styles [8], we introduced one subclass of the *um:LearningStyleCategory* class to represent each category defined in this model (e.g. *um:LS_Visual-Verbal*). For more details on the ontology, we refer readers to [9].

5.2 Personalization of the Annotated Learning Content

A learning session starts after the user (registered and authenticated as a learner) selects a sub-domain of IIS to learn about. The system performs a sort of comparative analysis of data stored in the learner's model and in the LP ontology. Specifically, the LP ontology is queried for the set of domain concepts that are essential for successful comprehension of the topics from the chosen sub-domain (i.e. those related via *lp:requiresKnowledgeOf* property). Subsequently, the learner model is queried for the learner's level of knowledge about the selected sub-domain and the identified set of prerequisite concepts. Information resulting from this analysis is used to provide adaptive guidance and direct the learner towards the most appropriate topics for him/her at that moment. One should note that the TANGRAM does not aim to make a choice for a learner. Instead, the system provides guidance to the learner (using link annotation and hiding techniques – see Section 2), and eventually lets him/her decide on the assembly to learn from.

After the learner selects one concept from the topics tree, the system initiates the process of dynamic assembly of learning content on the selected topic. Firstly, TANGRAM's repository of LOs is queried for CUs covering the selected domain topic. The query is based on the *dc:subject* metadata element of the CUs from the repository. If the repository does not contain CUs on the selected topic, the further steps of the algorithm depend on the learner's learning style, i.e. on its Sequential-Global dimension, to be more precise[3]. If the learner belongs to the category of global learners, CUs covering advanced topics (as specified in the LP ontology) are retrieved and the algorithm proceeds normally. Otherwise, the system informs the learner that the learning content on the selected topic is currently unavailable and suggests other suitable topics. In the subsequent steps the retrieved CUs are first classified into groups according to the same parent LO criterion and then each group is sorted. The sorting procedure is based on the original order of CUs from the group, i.e. on the value of the *alocomcs:ordering* property of the parent LO. In the subsequent text we use the term *assembly* to refer to a group of CUs sorted in this manner. Each assembly is assigned a double value (relevancy) between 0 and 1 that reflects its compliance with the learner model, i.e. its relevancy for the learner (the greater the value, the higher the importance of the assembly for the student). To calculate the relevancy of an assembly we query the learner model for the data about the learner's learning style, his/her preferred author as well as his/her learning history data (already seen CUs). Subsequently, the assemblies are sorted according to the calculated relevancy and their descriptions are presented to the learner (Fig. 1). Description of an assembly is actually the value of the *dc:description* metadata element attached to the LO that the content of the assembly originates from. As soon as the learner selects one assembly from the list, the system presents its content using its generic form for presentation of dynamically assembled learning content. Finally, the system updates the learner model. Specifically, it creates an instance of the *papi:Performance* class in the learner model and assigns values to its properties (see Section on UM for details). For example, the *papi:performance_value* property is assigned a value that reflects the level of mastery of the domain topic. If it was a topic recommended by the system, the property is assigned the maximum value (1). However, if the assembly covered an advanced topic, due to the lack of more appropriate learning content, this property is set to 0.35. This approach was inspired by the work of De Bra et al [10] and is based on the assumption that the learner, due to the lack of the necessary prerequisite knowledge was not able to fully understand the presented content.

---

[3] Whereas global learners prefer holistic approach and learn best when provided with a broader context of the topic of interest, sequential learners tend to be confused/disoriented if the topics are not presented in a linear fashion (Felder & Silverman, 1988).

6 Conclusions

Using a highly structured approach to annotation of learning object's CUs as well as implementing diverse semantic annotation heuristics, we demonstrated the usefulness of such an approach for developing personalized web-based educational environments, such as TANGRAM. Although we illustrated the approach on the domain of IISs, it can be easily retargeted to any other subject domain just by using another domain ontology. A brief description and demonstration of TANGRAM as well as the ontologies referred to in the paper can be found at http://iis.fon.bg.ac.yu/TANGRAM/home.html

Beside very promising lessons we have learned in using automatic annotation approach to facilitate personalized learning content reuse, we have become aware of some important practical details concerning both sides of the proposed solution, namely automatic annotation and personalization of the learning content. On one hand, we need to empower annotation algorithm with advanced features of the state-of-the-art tools and frameworks for natural language processing (e.g. Part-of-speech taggers) and information extraction such as GATE (http://gate.ac.uk) and KIM (http://ontotext.com/kim). On the other hand, we will further explore the process of dynamic assembly of CUs originating from different sources (i.e. LOs) and dealing with the same domain concept. In our future research we address this issue by defining a richer domain ontology. Additionally, we plan to extend our solution to enable repurposing content of other types of LOs beside slide presentations.

References

1. Brusilovsky, P, "Methods and Techniques of Adaptive Hypermedia," *Adaptive Hypertext and Hypermedia*, Kluwer Academic Publishers, The Netherlands, 1998, pp. 1-43.
2. Verbert, K., Klerkx, J., Meire, M., Najjar, J., and Duval, E., "Towards a Global Component Architecture for Learning Objects: an Ontology Based Approach," *In Proc. of the OTM 2004 Worksh. on Ontologies, Semantics and E-learning,* Agia Napa, Cyprus, 2004, pp. 713-722.
3. Jovanović, J., Gašević, D., Devedžić, V., "Ontology-based Automatic Annotation of Learning Content," *Int'l J. on Sem. Web and Inf. Sys.*, Vol. 2, No. 2, 2006 (forthcoming).
4. Verbert, K., Jovanović, J., Gašević, D., and Duval, E., "Repurposing Learning Object Components," *In Proc. of the OTM 2005 Worksh. on Ontologies, Semantics and E-learning*, Agia Napa, Cyprus, 2005, pp. 1169-1178.
5. Liu, B. and Chin, C.W., and Ng, H.T., "Mining Topic-Specific Concepts and Definitions on the Web," *In Proc. of the 12th Int'l WWW Conf.*, Budapest, Hungary, 2003, pp. 251-260.
6. Dolog, P. and Nejdl, W., "Challenges and Benefits of the Semantic Web for User Modeling," *In Proc. of AH2003 Worksh. at 12th Int'l WWW Conf.*, Budapest, Hungary, May 2003.
7. Keenoy, K., Levene, M., & Peterson, D., (2003.) "Personalisation and Trails in Self e-Learning Networks", SeLeNe Working Package 4 Deliverable 4.2. [Online]. Available at: http://www.dcs.bbk.ac.uk/selene/reports/Del4.2-2.1.pdf.
8. Felder, R. and Silverman, L., "Learning and Teaching Styles In Engineering Education," *Journal of Engineering Education*, Vol. 78, No.7, pp. 674–681, 1988.
9. Jovanović, J., Gašević, D., and Devedžić, V., "Dynamic Assembly of Personalized Learning Content on the Semantic Web," *3th European Semantic Web Conf.*, Budva, Serbia & Montenegro, 2006 (submitted).
10. De Bra, P., Aroyo, L. and Cristea, A., "Adaptive Web-based Educational Hypermedia," *Web Dynamics, Adaptive to Change in Content, Size, Topology and Use*, pp. 387-410, 2004.

A Scalable Solution for Adaptive Problem Sequencing and Its Evaluation

Amruth Kumar

Ramapo College of New Jersey,
Mahwah, NJ 07430, USA

Abstract. We propose an associative mechanism for adaptive generation of problems in intelligent tutors. Our evaluations of the tutors that use associative adaptation for problem sequencing show that 1) associative adaptation targets concepts less well understood by students; and 2) associative adaptation helps students learn with fewer practice problems. Apart from being domain-independent, the advantages of associative adaptation compared to other adaptive techniques are that it is easier to build and is scalable.

Keywords: Programming tutor, Adaptive Problem Sequencing, Evaluation.

1 Introduction

Learning is most effective when it is adapted to the needs of the learner [4]. In a tutor, various aspects can be adapted to the needs of the learner, including the problem sequence, feedback type, feedback amount, and the level of detail of the open student model. Vector spaces [17] and learning spaces [10] are the popularly used mechanisms for adaptation of problem sequence in tutors. These approaches are domain-independent. But building vector spaces and learning spaces is labour-intensive. Moreover, adding new problems or concepts to a vector space or learning space entails significant redesign of the space.

Alternatively, we propose a scalable solution for adaptive problem sequencing. In this approach, we index problems by concepts. We specify proficiency criteria for each concept in the domain model and maintain the student model as an overlay of the domain model. We use simple algorithms to select the next concept for the student, and the next problem for the concept.

In this paper, we will first describe the tutors for which we developed associative adaptation. We will describe the domain and overlay student models used in these tutors. Next, we will describe the associative mechanism for adaptive generation of problems. Finally, we will describe evaluations that support our claims that associative adaptation targets concepts less well understood by students, and it helps students learn with fewer practice problems.

2 Programming Tutors

We have been developing web-based tutors to help students learn C/C++/Java/C# programming language concepts by solving problems. To date, we have developed

V. Wade, H. Ashman, and B. Smyth (Eds.): AH 2006, LNCS 4018, pp. 161 – 171, 2006.

tutors on expression evaluation, selection statements, loops, pointers in C++, parameter passing mechanisms, scope concepts and their implementation, and C++ classes. Our tutors target program analysis (solving expressions, predicting the output of programs and debugging programs) in Bloom's taxonomy [3] in contrast to program synthesis (writing a program), which has been the traditional focus of intelligent tutors (e.g., LISP Tutor [16], ELM-ART [18]).

Consider the tutor on selection statements. The tutor presents a program that involves one or more selection (if/if-else) statements, and asks the learner to predict the output of the program. The tutor grades the learner's answer. In addition, it provides explanation of the step-by-step execution of the program as part of its feedback [12].

Limited problem set has been recognized as a potential drawback of encoding a finite number of problems into a tutor [13]. Therefore, our web-based tutors generate problems as instances of parameterized templates. Each problem template is indexed by one or more concepts, and the template is used to generate problems for only these concepts.

2.1 The Domain and Student Models

We use a single unified domain model for all our programming tutors. This domain model is the concept map of the programming domain, i.e., a taxonomic map with topics as nodes, and *is-a* and *part-of* relationships as arcs. In this model, we associate two measures with each node to determine whether the student has mastered the corresponding concept:

- M_1 - The minimum number of problems the learner must solve on that concept. Typically, $M_1 = 2$.
- M_2 - The percentage of problems that the learner must solve correctly on a concept in order to be considered proficient in it. Typically, $M_2 = 60\%$.

We use an overlay of the domain model as our cognitive student model. But, instead of saving M_1 and M_2 in the student model, we save {G,A,R,W,M} to record the student's progress - the number of problems generated (G), attempted (A), correctly solved (R), incorrectly solved (W) and missed (M) by the student on that concept. Currently, our tutors use two inequalities to interpret this data and determine whether a student has mastered a concept: $A \geq M_1$ and $R / A \geq M_2$.

3   Associative Adaptation of Problem Generation

Recall that we use a concept map as our domain model, associate proficiency criteria with the concepts in the domain model, use an overlay student model, associate the student's progress statistics with the concepts in the student model, and index problem templates by concepts. We will now present the algorithm for associative adaptation of problem generation.

The Algorithm

1. Let the set of all the concepts in the topic be $C = \{C_1, C_2, ..., C_m\}$, where C_1, C_2, ..., C_m are individual concepts.
2. For each concept C_i, extract all the problem templates that match the concept. Let the resulting set of templates be $T_i = \{T_{i1}, T_{i2}, ..., T_{iq}\}$, where $T_{i1}, T_{i2}, ...,$ T_{iq} are individual templates that match C_i.
3. Identify the list of concepts that the learner has not mastered. Let this set be C_s $= \{C_1, C_2, ..., C_n\}$, $n \leq m$. If the set C_s is empty, the student has mastered this topic, exit.
4. Select the next concept C_j from the set C_s.
5. Select the next problem template T_{jk} from the set of templates T_j corresponding to the concept C_j and generate the next problem as an instance of the template.
6. After the learner has attempted the problem, update $\{G,A,C,W,M\}$ for the concept C_j in the student model, as well as any other concept affected by the template T_{jk}. Repeat from Step 3.

We define **persistence** p as the maximum number of problems a tutor generates back to back on a concept before moving on to the next concept. Persistence p affects problem generation as follows:

- $p = 1$ means that the concept is changed from one problem to the next. This may not reinforce learning due to rapid switching of concepts.
- $p = 2$ or 3 helps reinforce learning since the tutor presents 2-3 problems back to back on a concept.
- $p > 3$ may make the tutor predictable and boring. The student may begin guessing the correct answer to problems, which would negatively affect learning.

Sub-algorithm for Step 4: Given the last concept was C_i, the algorithm to select the next concept is as follows:

1. If C_i has been mastered, return the next concept C_{i+1} in the list. If $i + 1 > n$, the number of concepts not yet mastered, set $i = 1$, and return C_1
2. If p problems have been generated back to back on the concept C_i, return C_{i+1}. If $i + 1 > n$, set $i = 1$, and return C_1
3. Else, return C_i.

Sub-algorithm for Step 5: We use the round-robin algorithm for selecting the next problem template for a concept. If the last template used by the tutor for a concept is T_{ij}, the next time it revisits the concept, it uses the template $T_{i,j+1}$. If $j + 1 > q$, $j = 1$.

This associative algorithm is independent of the domain: it can be used for any domain wherein 1) appropriate concepts can be identified; 2) the student model is maintained in terms of concepts; and 3) problem templates are indexed by concepts. This associative adaptation algorithm has several advantages over vector spaces [17] and learning spaces [10] that have been popularly used to implement adaptation:

- The associative system is easier to build - there is no need to place all the problem templates in an exhaustive vector or learning space.

- The associative system is scalable - We can add new concepts and problem templates to the tutor without affecting any existing templates and/or modifying the vector/learning space.

The learning path of individual learners in the problem space is determined by matching the problem templates in the template knowledge base with the un-mastered concepts in the student model. An associative system automatically supports all the learning paths - even those that may not have been explicitly modelled in a vector or learning space. Therefore, the resulting adaptation is more flexible. Associative adaptation is similar to the adaptation mechanism used in ActiveMath [14] to determine the information, exercises, and examples presented to the learner, and the order in which they are presented.

3.1 An Example

Consider the tutor on arithmetic expressions. For this example, we will consider only the following concepts: correct evaluation and precedence of +, * and / operators. Let the following table represent the initial student model, where m / n denotes that the student has correctly solved m out of the n problems (s)he has attempted on the concept:

Student Model	+	*	/
Correct Evaluation	2/2	1/2	0/2
Precedence	0/2	2/2	1/2

Assuming $M_1 = 2$ and $M_2 = 60\%$, the student has not yet mastered the following concepts: correct evaluation of * and /, and precedence of + and /. Assume that the next problem template for the correct evaluation of * yields the expression 3 + 4 * 5, and the student correctly solves the entire expression. Since the expression includes the correct evaluation and precedence of + and * operators, the student gets credit for all four concepts:

Student Model	+	*	/
Correct Evaluation	3/3	2/3	0/2
Precedence	1/3	3/3	1/2

Since the student just mastered the correct evaluation of *, the tutor considers the next concept, viz., correct evaluation of /. Assume that the next problem template for the correct evaluation of / yields the expression 5 + 10 / 4, and the student correctly solves the entire expression. Since the expression includes the correct evaluation and precedence of + and / operators, the student gets credit for all four concepts:

Student Model	+	*	/
Correct Evaluation	4/4	2/3	1/3
Precedence	2/4	3/3	2/3

If persistence p = 2, the tutor generates a second problem on the correct evaluation of /. Note that even if the student solves the second problem correctly, correct evaluation of / will remain un-mastered (2/4 < 60%). Even so, since persistence p = 2, the tutor will pick another concept for the subsequent problem and return to the correct evaluation of / later, in a round-robin fashion.

Note that a student may master a concept without attempting any problem on it, e.g., precedence of / operator in the above example. A student could revert from mastered to un-mastered state by solving subsequent problems incorrectly.

4   Evaluation of the Adaptive Tutor

Numerous evaluations have shown that our tutors help students learn, e.g., in one controlled test comparing a tutor with a printed workbook, improvement in learning with the tutor was larger and statistically significant compared to improvement with the printed workbook [7]. Evaluations have also shown that the explanation of step-by-step execution provided as feedback by the tutors is the key to the improvement in learning [12]. We wanted to evaluate whether associative adaptation helped improve the effectiveness of the tutors. The hypotheses for our evaluations were:

1. Associative adaptation targets the concepts less well understood by students.
2. Associative adaptation helps students learn with fewer problems.

In spring and fall 2005, we evaluated our tutor on selection statements. Students used the tutor on their own time, as non-credit-bearing assignment in a course.

Protocol: We used the pre-test-practice-post-test protocol for evaluation of the tutor:

- **Pre-test** –The pre-test consisted of a predetermined sequence of 21 problems covering 12 concepts. Students were allowed 8 minutes for the pre-test. The tutor administered the pre-test. The tutor did not provide any feedback during the pre-test.

  The tutor used the pre-test to initialize the student model, as proposed by earlier researchers (e.g., [1,6]). However, the test was not adaptive as proposed by others (e.g., [2, 15]), because we wanted to compare the pre-test score with the score on a similarly constructed post test to evaluate the effectiveness of the adaptive tutor. Stereotypes [1,8] and schema-based assessment [9] are some of the other techniques proposed in literature to initialize the student model.

- **Practice** – The tutor provided detailed feedback for each problem. The tutor used the associative adaptation algorithm to present problems on only those concepts on which the student had not demonstrated mastery during the pre-test. It used persistence = 2, $M_1 = 2$, and $M_2 = 60\%$. The practice session lasted 15 minutes or until the student learned all the concepts, whichever came first.

- **Post-test** –The post-test consisted of 21 problems, covering concepts in the same order as the pre-test. Students were allowed 8 minutes for the post-test. The tutor administered the post-test. It did not provide any feedback during the post-test. The test was not adaptive.

The three stages: pre-test, practice and post-test were administered by the tutor back-to-back, with no break in between. The students did not have access to the tutor before the experiment.

Analysis: In Table 1, we have listed the average and standard deviation of the number of problems solved, the raw score, and the score per problem on the pre-test, practice and post-test for the 22 students who used the tutor in spring 2005. Note that the raw score increased by 62% (from 6.39 to 10.33) from the pre-test to the post-test. However, the number of problems solved by the students also increased by 33% (from 10.55 to 14.05), and both these increases were statistically significant (2-tailed $p < 0.05$). In order to factor out the effect of the increase in the number of problems on the increase in the raw score, we calculated the average score per problem. The average score per problem also increased by 44% from pre-test to post-test and this increase was statistically significant.

Table 1. Results from the spring 2005 evaluation of the tutor on selection statements

Spr. 05	Pre-Test			Practice			Post-Test		
N = 22	Prob.	Score	Ave	Prob.	Score	Ave	Prob.	Score	Ave
Average	10.55	6.39	0.59	17.27	9.41	0.59	14.05	10.33	0.75
Std-Dev	3.54	3.86	0.27	10.56	4.71	0.25	4.10	4.10	0.22
p-value of pre-post difference							0.0000	0.0000	0.0007

The above results do not take into account the following confounds:

- Recall that the practice provided by the adaptive tutor was limited to 15 minutes. This meant that the students often ran out of time and did not get practice on all 12 concepts.
- It was likely that students already knew some of the concepts during the pre-test – learning of these concepts could not be credited to the use of the tutor.

In order to take these into consideration, we re-analyzed the data by concepts instead of problems. For each student, and each concept, we calculated the problems solved and average score on the pre-test, practice and post-test. Next, we grouped the concepts for each student into four categories:

- **Discarded Concepts:** Concepts on which the student did not attempt any problem during the pre-test or during the post-test because of the time limit on the tests;
- **Known Concepts:** Concepts on which the student demonstrated mastery during the pre-test, i.e., attempted $M_1 = 2$ problems and solved $M_2 = 60\%$ of the problems correctly;
- **Control Concepts:** Concepts on which the student solved problems during the pre-test and the post-test, but did not demonstrate mastery during the pre-test and *did not solve any problems during practice* due to the time limit imposed on the practice session – this provided the datum for comparison of test data.
- **Test Concepts:** Concepts on which the student solved problems during the pre-test and the post-test, but did not demonstrate mastery during the pre-test and *did solve problems during practice* – since the tutor provides feedback during practice to help the student learn, data on test concepts could prove or refute the effectiveness of using the tutor for learning.

Table 2. Classifying student concepts as discarded, known, control or test

Problems Solved	Pre-Test	Practice	Post-Test
Discarded	0	*	*
Discarded	*	*	0
Known	$A \geq M_1$ & $R/A \geq M_2$	*	*
Control	+	0	+
Test	+	+	+

The four types of student concepts are summarized in Table 2, where * represents 0 or more problems solved, and + represents 1 or more problems solved. For our analysis, we ignored the discarded student concepts since they represented incomplete data. We ignored the known student concepts – the tutor cannot be credited for the learning of the concepts that the students already knew during the pre-test. On the remaining student concepts, since each student served as part of both control group (on concepts for which the student did not get practice) and test group (on concepts for which the student did get practice), we consider this a within-subjects design.

In Table 3, we have listed the average and standard deviation of the number of problems solved and the average score per problem on the pre-test, practice and post-test for the 56 control student concepts and the 135 test student concepts as defined above. Note that the average score of the control group remained steady whereas the average score of the test group increased by 48% and this increase was statistically significant. This supports the results from our prior evaluations that practicing with the tutor promotes learning.

Table 3. Control versus Test Student Concepts from spring 2005 evaluation of Selection Tutor

Spring 05	Pre-Test		Practice	Post-Test		*p*-value	
	Prob.	Ave	Problems	Prob.	Ave	Prob.	Ave
Control (N – 56 student-concepts)							
Average	1.02	0.88	0	1.11	0.87	0.02	0.68
Std-Dev	0.13	0.30	0	0.31	0.31		
Test (N = 135 student-concepts)							
Average	1.07	0.46	1.83	1.35	0.68	0.000	0.000
Std-Dev	0.26	0.47	1.14	0.48	0.43		
p-value	0.05	0.000		0.000	0.000		

Note that there is a statistically significant difference between the control and test groups on the number of problems solved and the average score on the pre-test. The average score of the test group of student concepts is significantly lower than that of the control group of student concepts. This supports our hypothesis that associative adaptation in our tutor targets the concepts less well understood by students.

Finally, we conducted a repeated measures one-way ANOVA on the average score, with the treatment (adaptive practice versus no practice) as between-subjects factor and pretest-post-test as the repeated measure. Our findings were:

- There was a significant main effect for pre-test versus post-test [$F(1,189) = 7.391$, p $= 0.007$] - post-test scored significantly higher than the pre-test.
- There was a significant interaction between the treatment (adaptive practice versus no practice) and time repeated measure [$F(1,189) = 10.211$, p $= 0.002$]: while the average score with no practice stayed steady, with adaptive practice, it showed a significant increase.

We repeated our evaluation of the tutor in fall 2005. In Table 4, we have listed the average and standard deviation of the number of problems solved, the raw score, and the score per problem on the pre-test, practice and post-test for the 16 students who used the tutor. Note that the raw score increased by 94% and the number of problems solved by the students increased by 53% from pre-test to post-test, and both these increases were statistically significant (2-tailed $p < 0.05$). The average score per problem also increased by 23% from pre-test to post-test and this increase was statistically significant.

Table 4. Results from the fall 2005 evaluation of the tutor on selection statements

Fall 05	Pre-Test			Practice			Post-Test		
N = 16	Prob.	Score	Ave	Prob.	Score	Ave	Prob.	Score	Ave
Average	7.69	5.00	0.66	15.0	11.29	0.76	11.75	9.72	0.81
Std-Dev	3.89	2.96	0.26	3.92	3.49	0.17	3.96	4.28	0.20
p-value of pre-post difference							0.0002	0.000	0.003

When we analyzed the data by student concepts instead of problems, and divided the set of student concepts into control and test groups as described earlier, we obtained the results in Table 5. On control student concepts, the average changed from 0.81 to 0.76 from the pre-test to the post-test, and the change was not statistically significant (p = 0.55). On test student concepts, the average changed from 0.61 to 0.86, and the change was statistically significant (p = 0.0000). Once again, this supports the results from our prior evaluations that the tutors promote learning.

Table 5. Control versus Test Student Concepts from fall 2005 evaluation of Selection Tutor

Fall 05	Pre-Test		Practice	Post-Test		p-value	
	Prob.	Ave	Problems	Prob.	Ave	Prob.	Ave
Control (N = 26 student-concepts)							
Average	1.15	0.81	0	1.46	0.76	0.002	0.55
Std-Dev	0.37	0.35	0	0.51	0.40		
Test (N = 87 student-concepts)							
Average	1.00	0.61	1.55	1.15	0.86	0.0000	0.0000
Std-Dev	0	0.47	1.20	0.36	0.31		
p-value	0.04	0.02		0.006	0.23		

Once again, note that there is a statistically significant difference between the control and test groups on the number of problems solved and the average score on the pre-test. The average score of the test group of student concepts is significantly lower than that of the control group of student concepts. This once again supports our hypothesis that associative adaptation in our tutor targets the concepts less well understood by students.

We conducted a repeated measures ANOVA on the percentage of problems solved correctly, with the treatment (adaptive practice versus no practice) as between-subjects factor and pretest-post-test as repeated measure. Our findings were:

- The main effect for pre-test versus post-test was tending to statistical significance [$F(1,111) = 3.45$, $p = 0.066$] - post-test scored higher than pre-test.
- There was a significant interaction between the treatment (adaptive practice versus no practice) and time repeated measure [$F(1,111) = 7.837$, $p = 0.006$]: while average score with no practice declined modestly, with adaptive practice, it showed a significant increase.

In fall 2004, we evaluated *for* and *while* loop tutors. We used a within-subjects design: the same group of students used the non-adaptive version of the tutor on *while* loops one week, and the adaptive version on *for* loops the next week. In the non-adaptive version, the tutor presented problems for all the concepts, regardless of the learning needs of the student, in a round-robin fashion, with $p = 3$. Table 6 lists the average on the pre-test and post-test for the non-adaptive and adaptive versions of the tutor. One-way ANOVA analysis showed that the difference from the pre-test to the post-test was statistically significant in both the groups.

Table 6. Evaluation of non-adaptive versus adaptive versions of loop tutors – fall 2004

Average correctness of answers	Pre-Test	Post-Test	Change	Significance
Without adaptation (N = 15)				
Average	0.47	0.65	0.17	p = 0.014
Standard Deviation	0.24	0.20	0.24	
With adaptation (N = 25)				
Average	0.55	0.69	0.14	p = 0.0002
Standard Deviation	0.21	0.20	0.16	

Table 7. Problems Solved by the Control and Experimental Groups during 15-minute Practice

Problems Solved	Non-Adaptive Group	Adaptive Group	Statistical Sig.
Minimum	28	1	
Maximum	86	60	
Average	45.80	24.22	p= 0.00017
Std-Dev	15.44	14.56	

However, students solved far fewer problems during practice with the adaptive tutor than with the non-adaptive tutor, and this difference was statistically significant ($p < 0.05$) - the minimum, maximum and average number of problems solved by the two groups during practice is listed in Table 7. Given that the improvement in learning was similar for both the groups, this supports our hypothesis that associative adaptation helps students learn with fewer practice problems. Our results are in accordance with earlier results in computer-aided testing, where adaptive systems were shown to more accurately estimate a student's knowledge, and with fewer questions than non-adaptive systems [2, 19]. For this evaluation, we did not consider the time spent by the students on practice since all the students were required to practice for 15 minutes with the non-adaptive (control) tutor.

5 Conclusions

We proposed an associative mechanism for adaptive generation of problems in web-based intelligent tutors. Our evaluations show that:

1. Associative adaptation targets concepts less well understood by students - the average pre-test score on the concepts targeted by adaptation is significantly lower than the average on the concepts not targeted by adaptation.
2. A tutor with associative adaptation helps students learn with significantly fewer practice problems than a non-adaptive tutor.

Associative adaptation is easier to build and is scalable. Unlike vector spaces [17] and learning spaces [10], there is no need to exhaustively enumerate and organize all the problem templates. New concepts and problem templates can be added to the tutor without affecting any existing templates and/or modifying the previously constructed vector/learning space. This feature permits incremental development of tutors, which is invaluable when developing tutors for large domains.

Acknowledgements

Partial support for this work was provided by the National Science Foundation's Educational Innovation Program under grant CNS-0426021.

References

[1] Aimeur, E., Brassard, G., Dufort, H., and Gambs, S. CLARISSE: A Machine Learning Tool to Initialize Student Models. S. Cerri, G. Gouarderes, F. Paraguacu (eds.), Proc. of ITS 2002, Springer (2002). 718-728.
[2] Arroyo, I., Conejo, R., Guzman, E., & Woolf, B.P. An Adaptive Web-Based Component for Cognitive Ability Estimation., Proc. of AI-ED 2001, IOS Press (2001). 456-466.
[3] Bloom, B.S. and Krathwohl, D.R.: Taxonomy of   Educational Objectives: The Classification of Educational Goals. Handbook I: Cognitive Domain, New York, Longmans, Green (1956).
[4] Bloom, B.S.: The 2 Sigma Problem: The Search for Methods of Group Instruction as Effective as One-to-One Tutoring. Educational Researcher, Vol 13. 1984. 3-16.
[5] Brown, J.S. and Burton, R.R. Diagnostic models for procedural bugs in basic mathematical skills. Cognitive Science, Vol 2 (1978). 155-191.
[6] Czarkowski, M. and Kay, J. Challenges of Scrutable Adaptivity. U. Hoppe, F. Verdejo and J. Kay (eds.), Proc. of AI-ED 2003, IOS Press (2003). 404-406.

[7]   Dancik, G. and Kumar, A.N., A Tutor for Counter-Controlled Loop Concepts and Its Evaluation, Proceedings of Frontiers in Education Conference (FIE 2003), Boulder, CO, 11/5-8/2003, Session T3C.

[8]   Kay, J.: Stereotypes, Student Models and Scrutability. Proc. of ITS 2000. G. Gauthier, C. Frasson and K. VanLehn   (eds.). Springer (2000). 19-30.

[9]   Kalyuga, S. Rapid Assessment of Learner's Knowledge in Adaptive Learning Environments, Proc. of AI-ED 2003, IOS Press, (2003). 167-174.

[10] Kurhila, J., Lattu, M., and Pietila, A. Using Vector Space Model in Adaptive Hypermedia for Learning. Proc. of ITS 2002, Springer (2002). 129-138.

[11] Kumar, A.N. Using Enhanced Concept Map for Student Modeling in a Model-Based Programming Tutor. International FLAIRS conference on Artificial Intelligence, Melbourne Beach, FL, May 11-13, 2006,

[12] Kumar, A.N., Explanation of step-by-step execution as feedback for problems on program analysis, and its generation in model-based problem-solving tutors, Technology, Instruction, Cognition and Learning (TICL) Journal, to appear.

[13] Martin, B. and Mitrovic, A. Tailoring Feedback by Correcting Student Answers. Proc. of ITS 2000. Springer (2000). 383-392.

[14] Melis, E., Andres, E., Budenbender, J., Frischauf, A., Goguadze, G., Libbrecht, P., Pollet, M. and Ullrich, C. ActiveMath: A Generic and Adaptive Web-Based Learning Environment. International Journal of Artificial Intelligence in Education, Vol 12 (2001). 385-407.

[15] Millan, E., Perez-de-la-Cruz, J.L., and Svazer, E. Adaptive Bayesian Networks for Multilevel Student Modeling. Proc. of ITS 2000. Springer (2000), 534-543.

[16] Reiser, B., Anderson, J. and Farrell, R.: Dynamic student modelling in an intelligent tutor for LISP programming, Proc. of IJCAI 1985. Los Altos CA (1985).

[17] Salton, G., Wong, A. and Yang, C.S. A Vector Space Model for Automatic Indexing. Communications of the ACM, Vol. 18(11), (1975). 613-620.

[18] Weber, G. and Brusilovsky, P. ELM-ART: An Adaptive Versatile System for Web-Based Instruction. International Journal of Artificial Intelligence in Education, Vol 12 (2001). 351-384.

[19] Wainer, H. Computerized Adaptive Testing: A Primer. Lawrence Erlbaum Associates. Hillsdale, NJ, 1990.

Interactions Between Stereotypes

Zoë Lock[1] and Daniel Kudenko[2]

[1] QinetiQ, Malvern Technology Centre
St Andrews Road, Malvern, WR14 3PS, UK
zplock@qinetiq.com
[2] Department of Computer Science, University of York
Heslington, York, YO10 5DD, UK
{kudenko, lock}@cs.york.ac.uk

Abstract. Despite the fact that stereotyping has been used many times in recommender systems, little is known about why stereotyping is successful for some users but unsuccessful for others. To begin to address this issue, we conducted experiments in which stereotype-based user models were automatically constructed and the performance of overall user models and individual stereotypes observed. We have shown how concepts from data fusion, a previously unconnected field, can be applied to illustrate why the performance of stereotyping varies between users. Our study illustrates clearly that the interactions between stereotypes, in terms of their ratings of items, is a major factor in overall user model performance and that poor performance on the part of an individual stereotype need not directly cause poor overall user model performance.

1 Introduction

Since it was first proposed by Rich in 1979, stereotyping has been used many times in recommender systems. A stereotype represents a set of attributes that hold for a set of users. In user modelling, the concept of a stereotype strongly relates to its meaning in English — a body of default information about a set of people which may or may not accurately reflect the similarities between the people. Stereotyping has been used many times, mainly in the entertainment domain, as the "exploitation of sociological stereotypes seems to be usual in the mass-media world" [3]. The primary motivation for stereotyping is the new user problem — a purely individualised or *single-component* user model cannot be constructed until a user has provided some ratings of items. By appealing to a pool of stereotypes, each one representing the interests of a set of users with common socio-demographic attributes, and eliciting enough information from the user to select a set of applicable stereotypes, these can be combined and used to recommend items to the user.

In studying and comparing the performance of single-component and stereotype-based user models in two real group settings, we found that the performance of stereotype-based user models differed widely between users in both populations[1].

---

[1] Partly funded by the UK Ministry of Defence Corporate Research Programme.

V. Wade, H. Ashman, and B. Smyth (Eds.): AH 2006, LNCS 4018, pp. 172–181, 2006.

This led to us investigating the reasons behind this and this paper presents some of our findings.

The remainder of this paper is organised as follows. Section 2 presents an overview of previous work in the two areas of stereotype-based user modelling and data fusion. Section 3 briefly describes the two main data sets used in our research. Section 4 details our approach to constructing stereotype-based user models. Section 5 details our evaluation methodology. Section 6 presents our experiment results and Section 7 gives our conclusions.

2   Related Work

Little comprehensive evaluation of stereotype-based user models has been reported in the literature particularly with regards the relative performance of individualised and stereotype-based models and the reasons why some stereotypes combine to create good models while other do not. In their research into stereotyping for TV program recommendation, Ardisonno et al. [1] found that stereotyping performed poorly and attributed this to an incomplete stereotype collection and unstereotypical users. However, this was not explored in detail at the level of the individual user.

To date, stereotypes have been manually constructed by the system designer. Not only is this time-consuming, but it can introduce bias into the system as it is the designer's perception of a group of people that guides stereotype construction. Shapira et al. [7] differentiate between the behavioural (manual) and mathematical (automatic) construction approaches. By using a mathematical approach, as we have (see Section 4), alternative stereotype construction methods can easily be used and the relationship between the performance of individual stereotypes and that of the entire model can be assessed.

Combining of multiple stereotypes is related to combining multiple information retrieval (IR) systems, a topic that has been explored previously in a field known as *data fusion* [2, 4, 8]. We therefore looked to this research to help explain stereotype interaction. The motivation of data fusion is to derive an overall IR system that outperforms any of its component systems.

Diamond (as cited by Vogt and Cottrell [8]) offered three reasons why fused systems may perform better than individual ones:

- **The Skimming Effect:** If a set of individual IR approaches each retrieve a unique set of relevant documents then the fused system will retrieve more documents than any of the individuals and will therefore be more accurate.
- **The Chorus Effect:** If a document is correctly deemed relevant by a number of the individual approaches, then it will be ranked higher than those documents deemed to be relevant by fewer approaches by the fused system so it will outperform the individual ones.
- **The Dark Horse Effect:** By using a range of approaches, it is more likely that one of them will perform extremely well for at least a subset of items and its results will enhance the overall, fused ranking (if its voice can be heard above the others).

Until now, concepts from data fusion had not been applied to user modelling. There is a critical but subtle difference between an IR system and a stereotype. In systems in which many stereotypes may apply to an individual user, a stereotype is implicitly interpreted as a partial model of a user's interests from a single perspective and all the stereotypes assigned to a user are required to construct a complete model of the user's interests taking all perspectives into account. An IR system, on the other hand, is usually interpreted as a complete model of the target concept and a set of IR systems are combined to derive a more accurate complete model. This suggests that the Chorus and Dark Horse Effects may not feature in stereotype-based recommender systems.

3   Data Sets Used

For our investigation we obtained two data sets, both from team-role settings in which users belong to a set of teams and are assigned to roles within those teams. Each data set consists of a set of text documents, the relevance feedback on those documents provided by different users and the assignment of users to stereotypes (which in our case correspond to teams and roles). Note that here stereotype assignment is specified in advance rather than being triggered by events (as in Grundy [6]) so users cannot be said to be unstereotypical as such.

The first data set was obtained from a military HQ team experiment setting involving 2 teams of 5 officers, each with a single and defined military role (the roles were mirrored across the two teams). This set therefore involves 7 stereotypes altogether — 2 team stereotypes and 5 roles stereotypes. The 10 users were each asked to rate 133 text documents which were provided to them (though not all of them were read and rated by every user). These documents corresponded to segments of background material about a simulated operation e.g. the geographical features and political situation of the area in which the simulated operation was set.

The second data set was derived from a civilian source. Members of a business group at QinetiQ make use of an internal Wiki environment to store and share textual information about ongoing and past projects as well as some aspects of administration. Business group members belong to various project teams and fulfil different functional roles. Feedback on 84 pages covering a wide range of projects[2] was obtained from 13 users in all, covering 6 complete project teams. Within these teams, 4 functional roles were identified. This made 10 stereotypes in all for the Wiki domain. In this domain, unlike the previous one, some users assumed multiple roles across multiple teams.

4   Approach or Methodology

We have developed a tool called *Germane* which can automatically construct both single-component and stereotype-based user models from the following information:

---

[2] No example pages are given here as they contain proprietary information.

1. a set of textual information items — as separate plain text files;
2. relevance feedback from a set of users — in the form of XML fragments;
3. stereotype assignments of users — specified in a text file.

Germane's user models can then be used capture the users' interest levels in the information items and to recommend new text items for users according to how relevant they are. A single-component user model for a recommender system is constructed as a classifier that can be used to rate a new item according to its relevance to a user. A stereotype is constructed as a classifier that can be used to rate a new item according to its relevance to a group of users.

There are many existing classification techniques that could be used for constructing single-component user models, including decision trees and artificial neural networks. Germane currently uses three classification techniques that are particularly popular in text classification: *weighted feature vectors*; *k nearest neighbour* and *Naïve Bayes*. As we are only concerned here with the relative performance of stereotypes and the overall model, only one is considered here.

A *weighted feature vector* is a simple linear classifier represented as two corresponding vectors — one of features (words in this case) and one of their assigned weights:

$$c_f = f_1, f_2, ..., f_n \qquad c_w = w_1, w_2, ..., w_n$$

where n is the number of features selected to represent the class. The features used to represent the class are chosen from the complete set of unique features in the set of text items that remain after stop words and punctuation marks are removed and all text is converted to lower case. Then, the statistical measure $\chi^2(t, c)$ is used to measure the extent to which each feature indicates the pre-classification of items. $\chi^2(t, c)$ measures the lack of independence between a term (*i.e.* a word) t and a relevance category c. Its value is 0 if the t and c are independent. In this context, t is a word and c is either relevant or irrelevant. A high value of $\chi^2(t, c)$ indicates that t is strongly indicative of relevance category c.

$$\chi(t, c)^2 = \frac{N \times (AD - BC)^2}{(A + B) \times (B + D) \times (A + B) \times (C + D)}$$

where: N is the total number of documents rated, A is the number of times a word t and c co-occur, B is the number of times t occurs without c, C is the number of times c occurs without t and D is the number of times neither t or c occurs. The n top scoring features are used for the initial group model. The choice of n can be tuned by experimentation for most consistent performance and in the experiments reported in this paper, $n = 10$. After feature scoring, the top n scoring features are used to represent the class and their $\chi^2(t, c)$ scores are normalised to sum to one to form the corresponding weight vector. The selected features and their normalised weights are stored in a file which constitutes the user's user model.

Once a class profile has been constructed then a new item is rated simply by taking the inner or dot product of the class profile and the instance:

$$F_c(d) = \sum_{i=1}^{n} p(f_i, d) \cdot w_i$$

where $p(f, d) = 1$ if feature f is present in document d and 0 otherwise.

Whereas a single-component user model is trained using the relevance feedback of a single user, a stereotype is trained in the same way using the feedback of the set of users assigned to that stereotype. The stereotypes for a given user are constructed independently from each other. The rating that an overall stereotype-based user model assigns to a new text item is the weighted sum of the ratings of the constituent stereotypes. Germane uses *incremental gradient descent* [5] to train the stereotype weights based on the predictive errors made by the stereotypes during training. In the experiments described in this paper, stereotype weights are not a factor so the stereotypes are equally weighted.

Figure 1 illustrates Germane's process model.

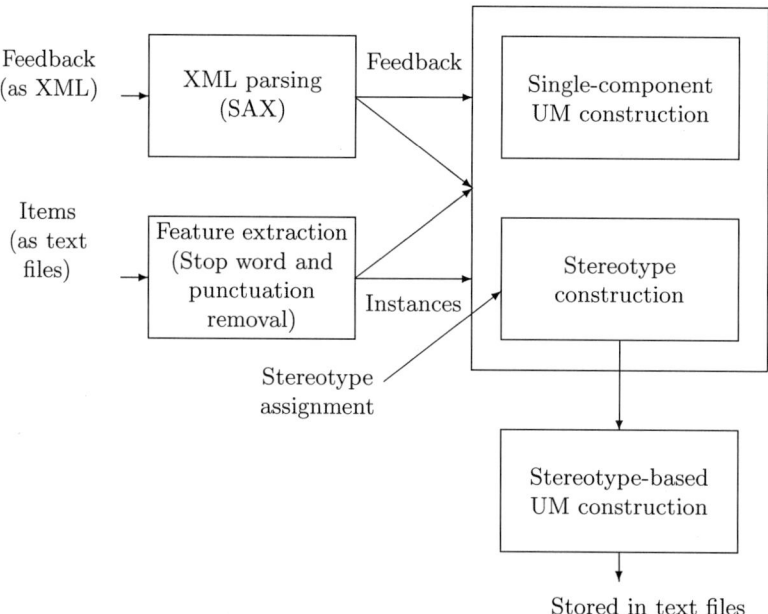

Fig. 1. Germane's overall process model

5   Evaluation Methodology

5.1   Cross-Validation

It is standard practise in machine learning, when assessing the prediction performance of a model, to divide the data set into two subsets: a training set on which a model can be constructed and a test set on which the model can be evaluated. Performance on the test set can provide an indication of the quality of the model. To ensure that this performance measure is stable, we have used *k-fold cross-validation* in which the relevance feedback data set for each user is divided into k disjoint subsets. In turn, each of the k subsets is used as a test set for an experiment while the remaining subsets are conjoined and used as the training set. The average performance over the k experiment runs is calculated to provide a more stable estimate of the quality of the model. To ensure that all test sets contain the same proportion of relevant and irrelevant documents (as rated by the user), the k test sets are *stratified* which means that each fold is composed of the same proportion of relevant and irrelevant documents as the overall data set [9].

5.2   Evaluation Metrics

The main metrics we have used for our investigation are the *F-measure* and *average precision*. These are described briefly below.

The *F-measure* (F_1) trades off the two metrics of *precision* and *recall*. Precision is the proportion of documents rated as relevant by the system that were also rated as relevant by the user. In our experiments, items rated above 0 are classified as relevant and all others as irrelevant. Precision measures how good the system is at correctly distinguishing between relevant and irrelevant documents. Recall is the proportion of documents rated as relevant by the user that the system also rates as relevant. Recall measures how good the system is at retrieving relevant documents.

$$Precision = \frac{TP}{TP + FP} \qquad Recall = \frac{TP}{TP + FN} \qquad F_1 = \frac{2 * precision \times recall}{precision + recall}$$

where: TP is the number of documents rated as relevant by both the user and the system (*true positives*), FP is the number of documents incorrectly rated as relevant by the system as they are rated as irrelevant by the user (*false positives*) and FN is the number of documents incorrectly rated as irrelevant by the system as they are rated as relevant by the user (*false negatives*). We assume here than precision and recall are of equal importance.

Uninterpolated Average Precision (AP) is used to assess how good a recommendation system is at ranking relevant items higher than irrelevant ones. AP is calculated by averaging the precision at each retrieved document (as shown below).

$$AP = \frac{1}{N} \sum_{i=1}^{N} P_i$$

where P_i is the precision at relevant retrieved document i and N is the number of relevant documents retrieved by the ranking algorithm (true positives). A ranking in which all relevant items are scored above all irrelevant items would be scored with $AP = 1.0$.

According to precision, a ranking in which all relevant items are retrieved and ranked below all retrieved irrelevant items would be scored the same as a ranking in which all retrieved relevant items are ranked above the retrieved irrelevant ones. The second ranking is clearly better from the point-of-view of a user of a recommender system and would be scored higher by *AP*.

6   Results

For the purposes of this analysis, it is necessary to define the Skimming, Chorus and Dark Horse effects in terms of the metrics we have used to assess user model performance:

- **Chorus Effect** — occurs when there is high overlap between the ratings of a set of stereotypes that all perform well and an overall AP higher than that exhibited by any of the individual stereotypes. This is because the items that are rated as relevant by multiple stereotypes are correctly rated higher by the overall model than items that are rated by just one of the stereotypes and this pushes up overall AP. Recall, and therefore, F_1 need not be affected.
- **Dark Horse Effect** — occurs when at least one of the individual stereotypes performs well and causes the overall performance (AP and F_1) to be high. No other stereotype interferes, by offering a significant proportion of false positives, to bring overall performance below that of the high performer(s).
- **Skimming Effect** — occurs when there is a low overlap between the ratings of a set of stereotypes that all perform well and the overall F_1 higher than that exhibited by any of the individual stereotypes. This is because each stereotype offers a unique subset of items that are indeed relevant to the user and so overall recall, and therefore, F_1 is pushed up. AP need not be affected.

Given these definitions, tailored to the metrics used in our investigation, it is possible to identify the users who benefit from these effects. Tables 1 and 2 provide a breakdown of the results of our experiments. For each user, the following information is offered:

- the standalone performance of each of his individual stereotypes;
- the proportion of items each stereotype uniquely retrieves with respect to every other stereotype in the model (U);
- the relevant overlap between each pair of stereotypes in the model (RO — as defined below);
- the overall performance of the entire stereotype-based user model;
- an indication of whether the Chorus, Dark Horse of Skimming Effect is seen.

$$RO(a,b) = \frac{nr_c \times 2}{nr_a + nr_b}$$

where nr_c is the number of common relevant documents retrieved, nr_a is the number of relevant documents retrieved by the IR system a and nr_b is the number of relevant documents retrieved by IR system b [4].

Table 1. Performance characteristics of SBMs (Military HQ)

User	Stereotypes			U	RO between	Overall		Effect		
		AP	F_1		(S_1, S_2)	AP	F_1	C	D	S
A2	Air	0.56	0.23	0.23	0.22	1.0	0.86		✓	✓
	Int	1.0	0.83	0.82						
A3	Air	0.7	0.56	0.32	0.34	0.6	0.61			✓
	Plans	0.52	0.53	0.7						
A4	Air	0.78	0.47	0.18	0.38	0.83	0.79			✓
	Logistics	0.79	0.68	0.66						
AC	Air	0.89	0.62	0.17	0.53	0.48	0.7			✓
	COS	0.38	0.66	0.57						
AL	Air	0.53	0.44	0.18	0.52	0.33	0.33			
	Liaison	0.22	0.32	0.56						
G2	Land	0.27	0.19	0.78	0.11	0.88	0.87			
	Int	0.99	0.87	0.92						
G3	Land	0.58	0.51	0.36	0.49	0.46	0.47			
	Plans	0.36	0.46	0.53						
G4	Land	0.34	0.35	0.26	0.6	0.49	0.47			
	Logistics	0.6	0.49	0.46						
GC	Land	0.93	0.55	0.22	0.38	0.68	0.69			✓
	COS	0.58	0.66	0.73						
GL	Land	0.8	0.53	0.1	0.55	0.84	0.81	✓		✓
	Liaison	0.84	0.8	0.57						

The Skimming Effect is clearly seen 12 out of 23 times in the results above whereas the Chorus and Dark Horse Effects are each only seen once (given the nature of stereotypes as stated in Section 2, each one typically characterising only a part of a user's set of interests, this is not surprising).

The data above shows that there are cases in which no stereotype particularly performs well in terms of both AP and F_1 but the overall performance is higher than any of the individuals. The Skimming Effect in particular leads to good stereotype-based user model performance. If a stereotype exhibits high performance then, as long as a poor stereotype does not offer a high proportion of unique retrieved items, overall performance will be higher than the component stereotypes. For users with mediocre stereotypes, high overall performance can be achieved if the overlap between them is low while they each retrieve a decent proportion of unique items.

Table 2. Performance characteristics of SBMs (Wiki)

User	Stereotypes	AP	F_1	U	RO between (S_1, S_2)	AP	F_1	C	D	S
1	TA	0.68	0.54	0.15	0.65 (TA, TC), 0.29 (TA, TB)	0.73	0.73			✓
	TC	0.6	0.54	0.0	0.53 (TA, PM), 0.21 (TC, TB)					
	TB	0.73	0.53	0.46	0.71 (TC, PM), 0.24 (TB, PM)					
	PM	0.74	0.54	0.09						
2	TD	0.78	0.63	0.31	0.69 (TD, Res)	0.72	0.6			
	Res	0.74	0.7	0.15						
3	TA	0.88	0.68	0.06	0.65 (TA, TD), 0.8 (TA, Res)	0.85	0.73			
	TD	0.8	0.63	0.29	0.65 (TD, Res)					
	Res	0.97	0.8	0.0						
4	TE	0.8	0.69	0.36	0.55 (TE, TA), 0.51 (TE, LR)	0.8	0.76			✓
	TA	0.81	0.59	0.14	0.51 (TE, Res), 0.63 (TA, LR)					
	LR	0.58	0.54	0.2	0.77 (TA, Res), 0.61 (LR, Res)					
	Res	0.89	0.68	0.06						
5	LR	0.47	0.49	0.45	0.57 (LR, TE)	0.61	0.6			✓
	TE	0.65	0.59	0.39						
6	TD	0.85	0.71	0.14	0.79 (TD, TC), 0.61 (TD, LR)	0.81	0.73			
	TC	0.89	0.73	0.14	0.55 (TC, LR)					
	LR	0.62	0.5	0.2						
7	TB	0.71	0.42	0.8	0.16 (TB, Imp)	0.53	0.53			✓
	Imp	0.42	0.34	0.87						
8	TD	0.98	0.78	0.22	0.71 (TD, TA), 0.71 (TD, LR)	0.97	0.86			✓
	TA	0.99	0.74	0.13	0.77 (TA, LR)					
	LR	0.99	0.65	0.16						
9	TC	0.55	0.53	0.36	0.59 (TC, Imp)	0.53	0.48			
	Imp	0.41	0.42	0.1						
10	TE	0.52	0.46	0.14	0.46 (TE, TD), 0.52 (TE, TC)	0.78	0.73			✓
	TD	0.84	0.69	0.14	0.57 (TE, Res), 0.48 (TE, PM)					
	TC	0.84	0.65	0.0	0.72 (TD, TC), 0.64 (TD, Res)					
	Res	0.63	0.47	0.05	0.51 (TD, PM), 0.58 (TC, Res)					
	PM	0.7	0.3	0.1	0.7 (TC, PM), 0.3 (Res, PM)					
11	TF	0.64	0.68	0.05	0.97 (TF, TB), 0.13 (TF, Res)	0.35	0.35			
	TB	0.71	0.72	0.0	0.13 (TB, Res)					
	Res	0.0	0.0	0.89						
12	TF	0.85	0.78	0.03	0.93 (TF, TB), 0.21 (TF, LR)	0.48	0.52			
	TB	0.87	0.77	0.0	0.15 (TB, LR)					
	LR	0.07	0.11	0.82						
13	TA	0.87	0.72	0.12	0.82 (TA, Res)	0.8	0.67			
	Res	0.73	0.73	0.18						

7   Conclusions

Our results clearly demonstrate that the performance of a stereotype-based approach depends as much on the interactions between stereotypes as the performance of them as individuals. We have applied findings from the distinct field of data fusion to explain some of the behaviour of stereotype-based systems. In particular, the Skimming Effect can be seen to cause good stereotype-based user model performance despite relatively poor performance on the part of individual stereotypes. It is necessary to apply our methodology to larger data sets in order to further validate our conclusions.

Our research raises the question of whether the performance of stereotyping can be predicted by designers from information about individual stereotypes. Our research suggests that as the combination of stereotypes is a critical factor, performance of stereotype-based systems cannot be predicted without the stereotype assignment and information about the relationship between stereotypes (in terms of the overlaps between the parts of the item space they cover — well or otherwise). In many domains, performance may be highly variable between users. For this reason, we recommend the construction and use of single-component models once relevance feedback has been collected. Stereotype-based user models could be maintained for new users.

References

1. Ardissono, L., Gena, C., Torasso, P., Bellifemine, F., Difino, A., Negro, B.: User Modeling and Recommendation Techniques for Electronic Program Guides. Personalized Digital Television. Targeting programs to individual users. L. Ardissono, A. Kobsa and M. Maybury editors. Kluwer Academic Publishers (2004).
2. Beitzel, S., Jensen, E., Chowdhury, A., Frieder, O., Grossman, D., Goharian, N.: Disproving the Fusion Hypothesis: An Analysis of Data Fusion via Effective Information Retrieval Stategies. ACM Eighteenth Symposium on Applied Computing (SAC) (2003).
3. Gena, C. and Ardissono, L.: On the construction of TV viewer stereotypes starting from lifestyle surveys. Proceedings of the 8th International Conference on User Modeling (UM'01) Workshop on Personalization in Future TV, Sonthofen, Germany (2001).
4. Lee, J.: Combining multiple evidence from different relevant feedback methods. Database Systems for Advanced Applications, 4(4) (1997) 421–430.
5. Mitchell, T.: Machine Learning. McGraw-Hill (1997).
6. Rich, E.: Building and Exploiting User Models. Carnegie-Mellon University, Computer Science Department (1979).
7. Shapira, B., Shoval, P., Hanani, U.: Stereotypes in Information Filtering Systems. Information Processing and Management, 33(3), (1997) 273–287.
8. Vogt, C. and Cottrell, G.: Predicting the Performance of Linearly Combined IR Systems. Proceedings of the 21st annual international ACM SIGIR conference on Research and development in information retrieval (1998) 190–196.
9. Witten, I. and Frank, E.: Data Mining. Morgan Kaufmann (2000).

Adaptation of Cross-Media Surveys to Heterogeneous Target Groups

Alexander Lorz

Dresden University of Technology
Multimedia Technology Group
Germany
Alexander.Lorz@inf.tu-dresden.de

Abstract. Adaptive surveys provide an efficient method for customizing questionnaires to the particular requirements of a study and specific features of the respondent. Hypermedia can enhance the presentation of questionnaires and enables interactive feedback. As comparability of survey results is crucial, adaptation is constrained by the requirement of cognitive equivalence. The scenario of a survey-based early warning system for virtual enterprises supplies a context for the discussion of further requirements concerning structure, markup, and adaptation of surveys. An XML markup for adaptive surveys is proposed that is applied within a survey system for virtual enterprises.

Keywords: survey adaptation, adaptive questionnaire, XML.

1 Introduction

Survey studies are a widely used, efficient and well understood scientific instrument for the acquisition of data, especially in the context of social sciences. After the initial investment in authoring and pre-tests they can be applied to large target groups at low additional costs. An important issue is however the payoff between generic applicability and therefore less specific or lengthy questionnaires on one side and the additional overhead of customization with all its ramifications on the other. Manual customization of surveys to the intent of a study, the applied distribution media, and to characteristic features of the target group is a tedious task, likely to be error-prone and leading to more complex distribution and evaluation processes.

Adaptive surveys offer a convenient way to avoid the horns of this dilemma by providing means to describe questionnaires at a semantic level in a more general, comprehensive way – and by defining rules that describe how and according to which parameters the questionnaire is to be customized. Although higher initial investments are required, this approach promises more versatile questionnaires that are easier to re-use and to maintain. Customization can be applied with low effort and without expertise in questionnaire authoring.

The intention of this paper is to point out basic requirements concerning adaptation, markup and presentation of surveys and to propose an XML markup

V. Wade, H. Ashman, and B. Smyth (Eds.): AH 2006, LNCS 4018, pp. 182–191, 2006.

language that emphasizes adaptation of presentation and interaction for different kinds of presentation media. Section 2 introduces an application scenario, providing the context for the description of requirements in Section 4. A brief overview of relevant applications, markup standards and research with relevance to adaptive surveys is given in Section 3 followed by a description of the proposed markup language in Section 5. The prototype survey system that provides the adaptation environment is introduced in Section 6.

2   Application Scenario

2.1   A Survey-Based Early Warning System for Virtual Enterprises

The concept of virtual enterprises (VE) depicts the cooperation of independent economic and organizational entities that aggregate into fluid and dynamic groups of interest for the purpose of pursuing a common goal. One goal of VE is to reduce risks, e.g. by pooling resources, connections, and intelligence. But new ones do arise due to the inherent challenges a cooperation between disparate partners yields. Whilst many risks are equivalent to those conventional enterprises will encounter, it is of emphasized interest to identify and understand the nature of those risks that arise from the cooperation itself.

The insights gained can be utilized to design an early warning system (EWS), which will support the involved partners in the assessment of possible risks and the selection of appropriate counter measures. Detailed research into this topic is an interdisciplinary field comprising i. a. psychology, economics and personal science in particular. Therefore efforts have been joined in the research project @VirtU [1] targeting the development of a computer assisted EWS. The applied scientific methods involve to a large extent the collection and analysis of data obtained by surveys and interviews.

2.2   The Role of Adaptive Surveys within the EWS

The early warning system (EWS) comprises recurring Web-based screenings and detailed surveys concerning mission critical aspects of virtual enterprises. Crucial factors include e.g. team-motivation, performance and job-satisfaction [2]. When implementing the EWS in a virtual organization aspects of the cooperation are defined that will be monitored. At first a basic coarse screening is applied to identify critical factors. Based on the results of this screening the supervisor selects which factors should be further analyzed. If necessary a consecutive survey is presented to the team to acquire more detailed information about identified critical aspects. These processes are repeated at regular intervals with frequency and level of detail depending on the result of prior surveys.

Due to the diversity of VE it is necessary to tailor surveys to the specific situation at hand. Surveys adapted to the needs of the investigations performed can be expected to be more efficient than a "one-size-fits-all"-approach. Adapted and therefore smaller and more appropriate questionnaires which take significantly less time to answer should also improve the compliance of the target group and yield a higher rate of return.

Although the focus of the chosen application scenario is on improving the cooperation in VE, the spectrum of possible applications for adaptive survey technologies is naturally much broader. In general these technologies will be useful in scenarios where:

1. Diversities within the target group can be anticipated and questionnaires shall go into more detail on topics concerning only parts of the target group.
2. Facts about the target group are already known and either the re-acquisition of these facts shall be avoided or more detailed feedback is required.

3   Related Work

Albeit a number of highly professional questionnaire systems, e.g. OPST from Globalpark[1] or the QEDML-products from Philology[2] exist, no known product covers the full scope of adaptation required in the scenario of Section 2. A comprehensive overview of available technologies is given at the website of the Association for Survey Computing[3].

Existing standards for questionnaire markup tend to be proprietary, viz. application-specific, hence lacking interoperability and extensibility toward adaptation. QEDML [3] rises the claim to be a universal markup standard for the interchange of cross-media surveys but is currently not open to the research community. Other attempts to establish generally accepted markup standards, e.g. IQML XML [4] or AskML, are not widely used by now. A well established and open standard for the markup and interchange of survey data and meta data is Triple-S [5]. However the strengths of Triple-S lie in providing interoperability for questionnaire results and not in the markup of the survey itself.

In scientific research one major application area of adaptive questionnaires is conjoint analysis. The works of Toubia et al. [6] and Abernethy et al. [7] aim at the development and evaluation of adaptation models for the optimization of questionaire design in this field. Lobach et al. [8] utilize adaptation for collecting clinical information from patients by customizing data acquisition to the respondent's native language, reading literacy and computer skills. In educational training and assessment Kurhila et al. [9] and Desmarais et al. [10] apply adaptation to match tasks to the skills of learners and to shorten assessment tests to the necessary minimum of questions required for obtaining the desired information, e.g. by omitting parts of the test when the score of the respondent can be determined with sufficient confidence.

The works mentioned above resemble only a small fraction of research areas where adaptive surveys are applied. However, there remains a conceptual gap between the presented application-specific solutions and more abstract, general and versatile means for providing survey adaptation.

---

[1] http://www.globalpark.de
[2] http://www.philology.com.au
[3] http://www.asc.org.uk

4   Requirements

To identify requirements it is necessary to examine the structure of questionnaires, the basic patterns of adaptation that apply to individual parts, and the constraints that arise from the composition of these parts with adaptation in mind.

Three distinct roles exist in the survey process. *Authors* develop and test questionnaires and define procedures for the evaluation. *Supervisors* select questionnaires, provide parameters for adaptation, conduct the actual survey and perform evaluation. *Respondents* fill out questionnaires.

4.1   Structural Requirements

Surveys mainly consist of a number of *items*, thus representing questions or statements. Respondents are expected to provide feedback in form of either arbitrary text, structured text (e.g. dates or numbers) or by selecting one or more given alternatives. The number of distinguishable item types varies depending on the applied classification scheme – McDonald [11] classifies nine *conceptually* different types. If variations in layout and presentation of items are to be taken into account a much larger number exists. However, to limit the complexity of adaptation, an efficient markup language has to provide a small number of basic components that are capable of describing a large variety of different items by combination and configuration. For highly specialized items that can not be described by these components an extension mechanism has to be provided.

The actual way of presenting items can differ. One constant concept of items is that respondents do assign values to variables defined within the item. These values can be constrained by predefined conditions and are possibly quantifiable or may require a manual expert rating for quantification.

In the evaluation process quantified items can be aggregated to *dimensions*, representing certain aspects of a psychological *constructs*, which are the top unit of aggregation. The necessary algorithms are to be defined by the author. Aggregation is not always required or intended. Therefore an additional concept for containment of arbitrary items that should be acquired together has to be provided. This will be referred to as *collections*.

4.2   Adaptation and Constraints

The comparability of survey results is the most crucial requirement for surveys to be a reliable instrument for data acquisition. Therefore adaptation can only be applied in a way that ensures *cognitive equivalence*. That is, the respondent should provide the same return values for variables, regardless of presentation media and composition of content. Indication exists, that the results of paper-pencil-surveys are equivalent to Web-based surveys [12]. Nevertheless, adaptation should be applied with caution to retain construct validity. Initially only established procedures for customizing paper-pencil-surveys will be applied to adaptive surveys. Customization is currently done by combining the acquisition of different constructs into one single questionnaire, by omitting inappropriate items, by adjusting wording to specifics of the target group, and by translating surveys into other languages.

Since altering the presentation of surveys beyond the scope of the established procedures is out of question, the following adaptation technologies according to Brusilovsky's taxonomy [13] are applicable: *Natural language adaptation, Inserting/removing fragments* and *Altering fragments*. Especially the latter is restricted by the requirement of cognitive equivalence. Authors usually have a particular notion about appearance, sequence, and grouping of items. But often they do not know or care about the ramifications of adaptation in detail. Therefore the markup language should provide a semantic concept of describing the authors ideas, leading to adapted documents that reflect the authors intentions as close as possible in any media. It is generally a bad idea to *force* authors to provide information and meta data. Therefore the amount of mandatory data to be specified has to be kept to a necessary minimum. As authoring is an iterative process, optional information, e.g. media-specific markup, can be supplied at a later stage to fine-tune the presentation.

Since e.g. print media provides no interactivity at all, interactive behavior has to be adapted to the capabilities of the presentation media. It is not surprising that there are interdependencies between the adaptation of content and presentation. Layout constraints and the media-dependent availability of presentation and interaction techniques require the presentation of alternative content or interaction elements.

5   An XML-Based Markup Language for Modular and Adaptive Surveys

For the specification of an appropriate XML-based markup language different surveys and their elements have been analyzed to determine the consequences that adaptation to selected presentation media implies. The scope of media adaptation considered shall be limited to rich-media HTML with client-side interaction (JavaScript) enabled, non-interactive HTML, accessibility-enhanced HTML and print media for paper-pencil-surveys. This limitation is not to affect the applicability of the underlying concepts, thus allowing to use adaptation in application scenarios e.g. comprising the use of cHTML for mobile devices or arbitrary media like audio-only for automated phone-interviews. In the following subsections the structure and the structural elements of adaptive questionnaires shall be depicted.

5.1   Overall Structure

The questionnaire markup language comprises four major sections with different semantic focus:

- General information about the questionnaire, e.g. version and authors, as well as background information for respondents that is to be presented before and after the presentation of actual content, viz. preamble and epilogue.

- The description of individual items, including one or more response-variables per item, value-constraints, presentation conditions, alternative content for different media and specific feedback that is given to the respondent in case of unmatched constraints. Items are encapsulated within blocks to define items that are to be presented together. Blocks contain additional markup that enables separation into sub-units of presentation, e.g. by defining page breaks or locations where content can be split into adjacent HTML forms.
- Markup of constructs, dimensions and collections with references to the associated items.
- The description of arbitrary parameters that can be referenced within the questionnaire definition but have to be provided by the runtime-environment that actually performs the adaptation. This includes parameters that determine if certain items are to be presented or if additional instructions are to be given.

5.2   Supported Response Types

Return variables within each item are typed according to the kind of question an item constitutes. In most cases one variable per item is sufficient, however items can be composed by specifying any number of return variables thus providing means to define more complex items. The following response types are supported:

ShortText. This response type is to denote short entries of arbitrary text that can be constrained by certain conventions (see Subsection 5.4). It is generally used to acquire explicit facts like names, dates, mail addresses etc.

LongText. When a more detailed feedback in the form of complete sentences is required long text items are applied. The only restrictions that exist concern size and presentation, allowing for arbitrary content.

SinglePunch. The respondent is expected to choose exactly one of several options provided.

MultiPunch. These items are a way to provide checklists where multiple options can be selected. The return value of multi punch questions is a set indicating the chosen options. Restrictions can apply to the minimum and maximum number of items that are to be selected.

Rating. Ratings contain a number of options that are attributed a natural order. They are often referred to as *Likert scales* which merely constitute a specific subset of rating scales. They are generally used to acquire the respondent's level of agreement to a given statement or to select a value that lies between two opposite poles.

5.3   Matrix Questions

Matrix questions provide a unit of containment for items that share response variables of the same types, thus permitting a condensed presentation by arranging questions and answers into a table. One row can contain one or more response variables of different type which can be constrained independently. To avoid errors in markup a grouping mechanism is applied that affixes response variables to a column set that determines the response type. If accessibility is to be granted, matrix question can easily be deconstructed into single items.

5.4 Markup for Adaptation

A detailed analysis of presentation and interaction techniques for the items above has been performed. From this work a specification of meta information that an author has to provide to enable an optimal presentation could be derived. The following comprises the functionality of the most commonly used features of the markup language:

All kinds of text elements and images contain attributes indicating the language of their content and the applicability for different presentation media. Additional text and images can be defined that are to be provided by the adaptation environment.

Optional conditions can be inserted at the level of blocks, items and individual response variables. Conditions are described as boolean expressions and determine if the associated element is to be presented. The free variables of these expressions do refer either to external parameters or to return values of items defined in preceding items.

If conditions refer to the values of prior items, non-interactive media require additional instructions to be given to the respondent, i. e. "Please fill in the following fields if . . . ".

Short text responses can be attributed with value constraints comprising either pre-defined types (date, integer, etc.) or regular expressions. The latter require the definition of specific feedback to be given to the respondent in case of erroneous input. For pre-defined types standardized feedback information is provided. Non-interactive media however need explicit instructions clarifying the desired input. In interactive media three levels of modality can be specified that defines if a user may leave the current unit of presentation or can even finish the questionnaire with erroneous input remaining.

For each item, or more precisely for each return variable, layout and presentation preferences can be defined by authors. In some cases, e.g. single punch questions, it can be defined which of several alternative interaction elements is to be used for a specific medium. More specific configuration parameters depend on the return type and the selected interaction element. Parameters include the alignment and arrangement of single and multi punch options and their corresponding labels or images, default content for text fields that can be used to illustrate the desired input format or the number of visible items for certain HTML form elements.

The following Example describes the configuration of the ShortText response that is used in Figure 1 for the date field. A restriction is applied to constrain the response to a date format and error feedback is provided for presentation in German and English. Example input text is provided as default value for the form field.

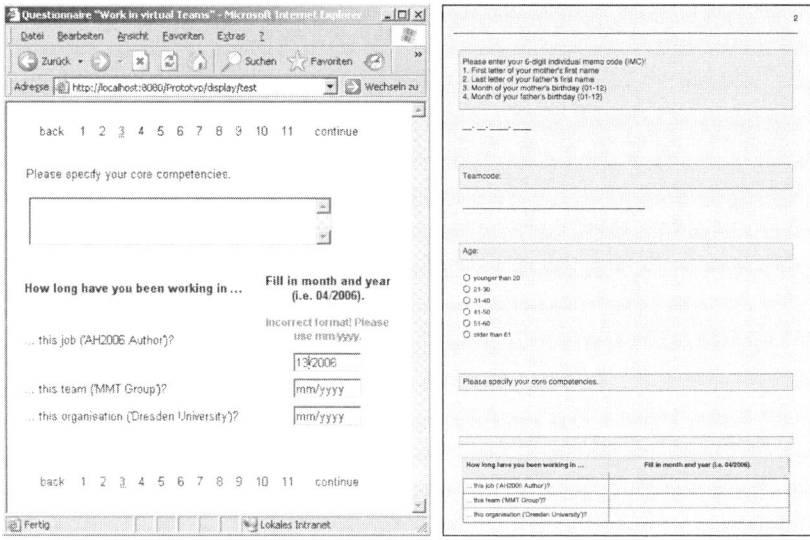

Fig. 1. Equivalent items presented as HTML-form and PDF document. Job description, team name and organization name have been adapted to the respondent.

```
<ResponseType>
 <ShortText visibleLength="7">
   <Restriction>
   <Date format="mm/yyyy"/>
     <RestrictInstruction>
       <Text lang="de" medium="all">Angaben in Monat und Jahr (z. B. 04/2006).</Text>
       <Text lang="en" medium="all">Fill in month and year (i.e. 04/2006).</Text>
     </RestrictInstruction>
     <RestrictError>
       <Text lang="de" medium="online">Bitte Eingabeformat MM/JJJJ beachten.</Text>
       <Text lang="en" medium="online">Incorrect format! Please use mm/yyyy.</Text>
     </RestrictError>
   </Restriction>
   <ExampleInputText>
     <Text lang="de">MM/JJJJ</Text>
     <Text lang="en">mm/yyyy</Text>
   </ExampleInputText>
 </ShortText>
</ResponseType>
```

6   Survey System Prototype

The described XML schema has been applied to mark-up several surveys used in the context of the @VirtU project. The Apache Cocoon Web development framework[4] is employed to construct a Web-based survey system acting as adaptation environment. Adaptation is performed by XSLT stylesheets, generating an on-line version consisting of multiple HTML forms connected by navigation elements and XSL-FO for PDF output.

---

[4] http://cocoon.apache.org/

The survey system is administered via a Web-based user interface. After a supervisor logs in to the system, he is presented a view consisting of team areas. Each team area is associated with a group of respondents, e.g. a project team of a virtual organization. The supervisor can add a questionnaire to a team area by selecting a survey definition from a library. In the next step a list of constructs and collections that can be acquired by the selected survey is presented. After choosing the desired elements from this list, the adaptation parameters have to be specified, e.g. the name of the project team and the desired language. The supervisor's view of the team area now contains links to the on-line version of the questionnaire and to a PDF document containing the print version. The actual adaptation of the survey and the generation of Web-pages or PDF documents is an automated process that requires no further manual intervention. It is initiated by the first access to the print version and every time a page of the on-line version is requested. The supervisor can either distribute the print version or grant access to respondents by generating a link.

When a respondent follows the supplied link, the preamble of the on-line version and a navigation bar is presented. Each time the respondent navigates to another page, the content of the form elements is submitted. The survey systems adds the content to a temporary user model and checks it against the constraints of the survey definition. Before presenting a page, adaptation to previously entered response values is performed. This includes the insertion of these values into form fields and showing/hiding elements that are constrained by a condition-node. If necessary, error-feedback is inserted as well. After completing all forms the respondent can submit the questionnaire. All submitted questionnaires are added to the supervisor's view of the team area. Since evaluation support is still an open issue, merely export functionality for acquired data is provided.

7   Conclusion and Future Work

Manual customization of questionnaires to specific features of the intended target group and to different distribution media is a tedious and error-prone task. The concept of adaptive surveys described in this paper can lower the effort for customization, re-use and maintenance of surveys. A conceptual gap exist between existing solutions and abstract, general, and versatile means for survey adaptation. Therefore requirements concerning structure and adaptation of surveys have been discussed, leading to the proposal of an XML markup language for adaptive surveys. This markup language has been used to describe surveys within the context of the interdisciplinary research project @VirtU. Adaptation of these surveys is provided by a prototype survey system, capable of generating paper-pencil-surveys as well as providing Web-based questionnaires.

Future work comprises extensive tests of the survey system as well as the integration of evaluation into the XML markup language and the survey system. The sustainability of the developed concept is to be proven by integrating more elaborate item types, by extending the existing stylesheets for generating accessibility enhanced HTML output and by conducting studies concerning cognitive equivalence of adapted questionnaires. Another targeted issue is the support of authoring by a Web-based authoring system to reduce the initial effort for providing survey adaptation.

The author would like to gratefully acknowledge the funding of the @VirtU project by the German Federal Ministry of Education and Research and the support from numerous colleagues and students contributing to this project.

References

[1] @VirtU: Participative Development of Diagnostic Early Warning Systems for Work in Virtual Corporations. http://www.atvirtu.de (2006)

[2] Meyer, J., Engel, A., Wiedemann, J., Richter, P.: Performance and Job Satisfaction in Virtual Teams. In: XII. European Congress of Work and Organizational Psychology - Convivence in Organizations and Society, Istanbul. (2005)

[3] Philology Pty. Ltd.: QEDML – Questionnaire Exchange and Deployment Markup Language. http://www.qedml.org (2004)

[4] IQML-Project Group: IQML – A Software Suite and XML Standard for Intelligent Questionnaires. http://www.epros.ed.ac.uk/iqml (2003)

[5] Triple-S Group: Triple-S – Open Survey Interchange Standard. http://www.triple-s.org (2005)

[6] Toubia, O., Hauser, J., Simester, D.: Polyhedral Methods for Adaptive Choice-Based Conjoint Analysis. Working papers 4285-03, Massachusetts Institute of Technology (MIT), Sloan School of Management (2003)

[7] Abernethy, J., Evgeniou, T., Vert, J.P.: An Optimization Framework for Adaptive Questionnaire Design. Working paper, INSEAD, Fontainebleau, France (2004)

[8] Lobach, D.F., Arbanas, J.M., Mishra, D.D., Campbell, M., Wildemuth, B.M.: Adapting the Human-Computer Interface for Reading Literacy and Computer Skill to Facilitate Collection of Information Directly from Patients. In: MedInfo. Volume 11 (Pt. 2). (2004) 1142–6

[9] Kurhila, J., Miettinen, M., Niemivirta, M., Nokelainen, P., Silander, T., Tirri, H.: Bayesian Modeling in an Adaptive On-Line Questionnaire for Education and Educational Research. In Ruokamo, H., Nyknen, O., Pohjolainen, S., Hietala, P., eds.: 10th International PEG Conference, Tampere, Finland (2001) 194–201

[10] Desmarais, M.C., Maluf, D., Liu, J.: Adaptive Training Based Upon Computerized Knowledge Assessment. In: Fourth International Conference on User Modeling. (1994) 102–112

[11] McDonald, R.P.: Test theory : a unified treatment. Lawrence Erlbaum Associates, Mahwah, New Jersey (1999)

[12] Kobrin, J.L., Young, J.W.: The Cognitive Equivalence of Reading Comprehension Test Items Via Computerized and Paper-and-Pencil Administration. Applied Measurement in Education 16(2) (2003) 115–140

[13] Brusilovsky, P.: Adaptive Hypermedia. User Modeling and User-Adapted Interaction 11(1-2) (2001) 87–110

The Effect of Adapting Feedback Generality in ITS

Brent Martin and Antonija Mitrovic

Intelligent Computer Tutoring Group
Department of Computer Science and Software Engineering,
University of Canterbury
Private Bag 4800, Christchurch, New Zealand
{brent, tanja}@cosc.canterbury.ac.nz

Abstract. Intelligent tutoring systems achieve much of their success by adapting to individual students. One potential avenue for personalization is feedback generality. This paper presents two evaluation studies that measure the effects of modifying feedback generality in a web-based Intelligent Tutoring System (ITS) based on the analysis of student models. The object of the experiments was to measure the effectiveness of varying feedback generality, and to determine whether this could be performed *en masse* or if personalization is needed. In an initial trial with a web-based ITS it appeared that it is feasible to use a mass approach to select appropriate concepts for generalizing feedback. A second study gave conflicting results and showed a relationship between generality and ability, highlighting the need for feedback to be personalized to individual students' needs.

1 Introduction

Intelligent tutoring systems (ITS) achieve much of their success by adapting to individual students. One potential avenue for personalization is feedback generality. Feedback in ITS is usually very specific. However, in some domains there may be low-level generalizations that can be made where the generalized concept is more likely to be what the student is learning. For example, Koedinger and Mathan [2] suggest that for their Excel Tutor (one of the cognitive tutors [1]), the concept of relative versus fixed indexing is independent of the direction the information is copied; this is a generalization of two concepts, namely horizontal versus vertical indexing. We hypothesized that this might be the case for our web-based tutor (SQL-Tutor). For example, an analysis of the feedback messages found that often they are nearly the same for some groups of concepts. Other concepts may differ only by the clause of the SQL query in which they occur (for example, the WHERE and HAVING clauses of an SQL query have substantially similar concepts).

Some systems use Bayesian student models to represent students' knowledge at various levels (e.g. [8]) and so theoretically they can dynamically determine the best level to provide feedback, but this is difficult and potentially error-prone: building Bayesian belief networks requires the large task of specifying the prior and conditional probabilities. We were interested in whether it was possible to infer a set of high-level concepts that generally represent those being learned while avoiding the

V. Wade, H. Ashman, and B. Smyth (Eds.): AH 2006, LNCS 4018, pp. 192–202, 2006.

difficulty of building a belief network, by analyzing past student model data to determine significant subgroups of knowledge units that represent such general concepts. Feedback can then also be attached to these more general concepts and selected according to students' needs.

One method of analyzing knowledge units is to plot learning curves: if the objects being measured relate to the actual concepts being learned, we expect to see a "power law" between the number of times the object is relevant and the proportion of times it is used incorrectly [6]. Learning curves can be plotted for all knowledge units of a system to measure its overall performance. They can also be used to analyze groups of objects within a system, or to "mine" the student models for further information. We used this latter approach to try to determine which groups of domain knowledge units appear to perform well when treated as a single concept. To decide which ones to group, we used a (man-made) taxonomy of the learning domain [3], and grouped knowledge units according to each node of the taxonomy. This enabled us to measure how well these units, when combined into more general ones of increasing generality, still exhibited power laws and hence represented a single concept that the students were learning. We then used this information as the basis for building a new version of the domain model that gave more general feedback.

In the next section we describe the system we used in the study. In Section 3 we present our hypotheses and discuss how we used the student models to predict the performance of groups of knowledge units. We then give the results for an initial experiment that tested a new feedback scheme based on these general concepts. Section 4 describes a second study, in which we modified the delivery of the generalized feedback, with some surprising results.   Section 5 then discusses differences between the results of the two studies, while the conclusions are given in Section 6.

2 SQL-Tutor

The initial goal of this research was to investigate whether we can predict the effectiveness of different levels of feedback by observing how well the underlying group of knowledge units appears to measure a single concept being learned. We performed an experiment in the context of SQL-Tutor, a web-based intelligent tutoring system that teaches the SQL database language to university-level students. For a detailed discussion of the system, see [4, 5]; here we present only some of its features. SQL-Tutor consists of an interface, a pedagogical module—which determines the timing and content of pedagogical actions—and a student modeler, which analyses student answers. The system contains definitions of several databases and a set of problems and their ideal solutions. SQL-Tutor contains no problem solver: to check the correctness of the student's solution, SQL-Tutor compares it to an example of a correct solution using domain knowledge represented in the form of more than 650 constraints. It uses Constraint-Based Modeling (CBM) [7] for both domain and student models.

Feedback in SQL-Tutor is attached directly to the knowledge units, or "constraints", which make up the domain model. An example of a constraint is:

```
(147
; feedback message
"You have used some names in the WHERE clause that are not from
this database."

; relevance condition
  (match SS WHERE (?* (^name ?n) ?*))

; satisfaction condition
  (or   (test SS (^valid-table (?n ?t))
        (test SS (^attribute-p (?n ?a ?t)))))

"WHERE")
```

Constraints are used to critique the students' solutions by checking that the concept they represent is being correctly applied. The relevance condition first tests whether or not this concept is relevant to the problem and current solution attempt. If so, the satisfaction condition is checked to ascertain whether or not the student has applied this concept correctly. If the satisfaction condition is met, no action is taken; if it fails, the feedback message is presented to the student. The student model consists of the set of constraints, along with information about whether or not it has been successfully applied, for each attempt where it is relevant. Thus the student model is a trace of the performance of each individual constraint over time. Constraints may be grouped together, giving the average performance of the constraint set as a whole over time, for which a learning curve can then be plotted. Figure 2 shows the learning curves for the two groups of the first study, for all students and all constraints. This is achieved by considering every constraint, for every student, and calculating the proportion of constraint/student instances for which the constraint was violated for the first problem in which it was relevant, giving the first data point. This process is then repeated for the second problem each constraint was used for, and so on. Both curves in Figure 2 (Section 3) show an excellent power law fit ($R^2 > 0.92$). Note that learning curves tend to deteriorate as n becomes large, because the number of participating constraints reduces.

3   Study 1: Does Feedback Generality Have an Effect?

We hypothesized that some groupings of constraints would represent the concepts the student was learning better than the (highly specialized) constraints themselves. We then further hypothesized that for such a grouping, learning might be more effective if students were given feedback about the general concept, rather than more specialized feedback about the specific context in which the concept appeared (represented by the original constraint). To evaluate the first hypothesis, we analyzed data from a previous study of SQL-Tutor on a similar population, namely second year students from a database course at the University of Canterbury, New Zealand. To decide which constraints to group together, we used a taxonomy of the SQL-Tutor domain model that we had previously defined [3]. This taxonomy is very fine-grained, consisting of 530 nodes to cover the 650 constraints, although many nodes only cover a single constraint. The deepest path in the tree is eight nodes, with most paths being five or six nodes deep. Figure 1 shows the sub tree for the concept "Correct tables present".

We grouped constraints according to each node in the taxonomy, and rebuilt the student models as though these were real constraints that the system had been tracking. For example, if a node N1 in the taxonomy covers constraints 1 and 2, and the student has applied constraint 1 incorrectly, then 2 incorrectly, then 1 incorrectly again, then 2 correctly, the original model would be:

(1 FAIL FAIL)
(2 FAIL SUCCEED)

while the entry for the new constraint is:

(N1 FAIL FAIL FAIL SUCCEED)

Note that several constraints from N1 might be applied for the same problem. In this case we calculated the proportion of such constraints that were violated. We performed this operation for all non-trivial nodes in the hierarchy (i.e. those covering more than one constraint) and plotted learning curves for *each* of the resulting 304 generalized constraints. We then compared each curve to a curve obtained by averaging the results for the participating constraints, based on their individual models. Note that these curves were for the first four problems only: the volume of data in each case is low, so the curves deteriorate relatively quickly after that. Overall the results showed that the more general the grouping is, the worse the learning curve (either a poorer fit or a lower slope), which is what we might expect. However, there were eight cases for which the generalized constraint had superior power law fit and slope compared to the average for the individual constraints, and thus appeared to

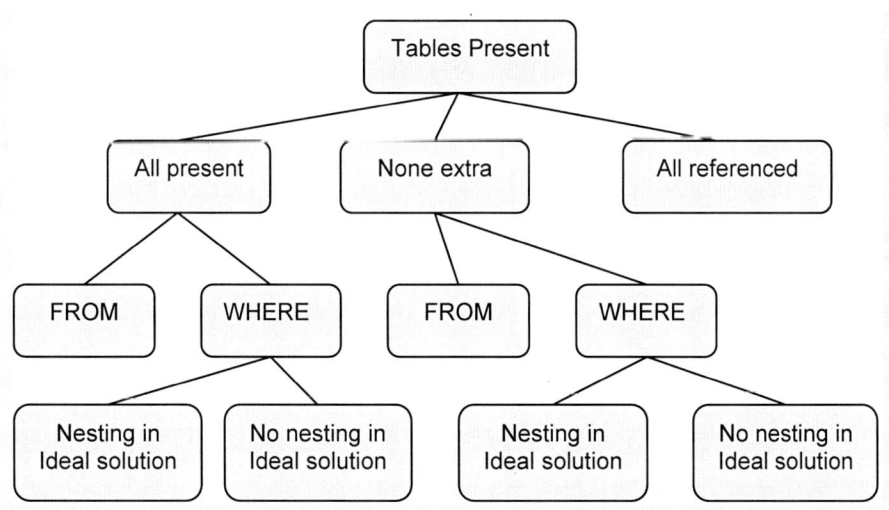

Fig. 1. Example sub tree from the SQL –Tutor domain taxonomy

better represent the concept being learned, and a further eight that were comparable. From this result we tentatively concluded that some of our constraints might be at a lower level than the concept that is actually being learned, because it appears that there is "crossover" between constraints in a group. In the example above, this means that exposure to constraint 1 appears to lead to some learning of constraint 2, and vice versa. This supports our first hypothesis.

We then tested our second hypothesis: that providing feedback at the more general level would improve learning for those high-level constraints that exhibited superior learning curves. Based on the original analysis we produced a set of 63 new constraints that were one or two levels up the taxonomy from the individual constraints. This new constraint set covered 468 of the original 650 constraints, with membership of each generalized constraint varying between 2 and 32, and an average of 7 members (SD=6). For each new constraint, we produced a tuple that described its membership, and included the feedback message that would be substituted in the experimental system for that of the original constraint. An example of such an entry is:

```
(N5 "Check that you are using the right operators in numeric
comparisons." (462 463 426 46 461 427 444 517 445 518 446
519 447 520 404 521 405 522))
```

This generalized constraint covers all individual constraints that perform some kind of check for the presence of a particular numeric operator. Students for the experimental group thus received this feedback, while those in the control group were presented with the more specific feedback from each original constraint concerning the particular operator.

To evaluate this second hypothesis we performed an experiment with the students enrolled in an introductory database course at the University of Canterbury. Participation in the experiment was voluntary. Prior to the study, students attended six lectures on SQL and had two laboratories on the Oracle RDBMS. SQL-Tutor was demonstrated to students in a lecture on September 20, 2004. The experiment was performed in scheduled laboratories during the same week. The experiment required the students to sit a pre-test, which was administered online the first time students accessed SQL-Tutor. The pre-test consisted of four multi-choice questions, which required the student to identify correct definitions of concepts in the domain, or to specify whether a given SQL statement is appropriate for the given context.

The students were randomly allocated to one of the two versions of the system. The course involved a test on SQL on October 14, 2004, which provided additional motivation for students to practice with SQL-Tutor. A post-test was administered at the conclusion of a two-hour session with the tutor, and consisted of four questions of similar nature and complexity as the questions in the pre-test. The maximum mark for the pre/post tests was 4.

Of the 124 students enrolled in the course, 100 students logged on to SQL-Tutor at least once. However, some students looked at the system only briefly. We therefore excluded the logs of students who did not attempt any problems. The logs of the remaining 78 students (41 in the control, and 37 in the experimental group) were then analyzed. The mean score for the pre-test for all students was 2.17 out of 4 (SD=1.01). The students were randomly allocated to one of the two versions of the

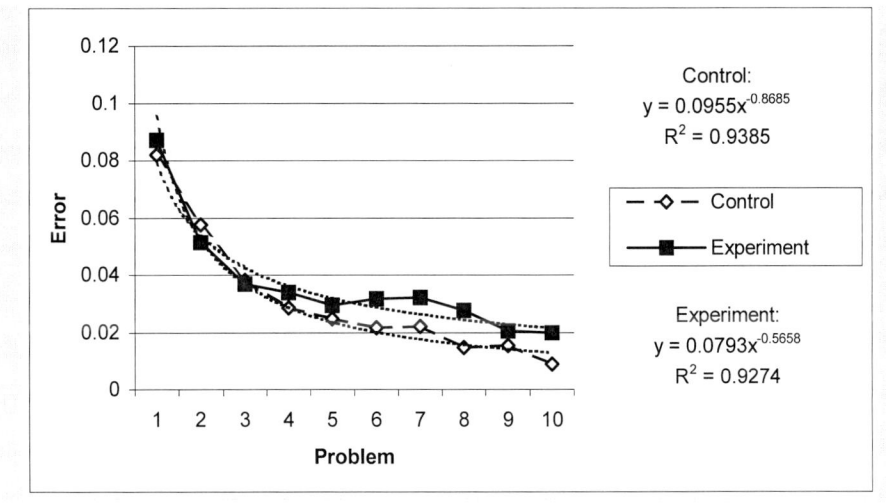

Fig. 2. Learning curves for the two groups

system. A t-test showed no significant differences between the pre-test scores for the two groups (mean=2.10 and 2.24 for the control and experimental groups respectively, standard deviation for both=1.01, p=0.53).

Figure 2 plots the learning curves for the control and experimental groups. Note that the unit measured for both groups is the *original* constraints, because this ensures there are no differences in the unit being measured, which might alter the curves and prevent their being directly compared. Only those constraints that belong to one or more generalized concepts were included. The curves in Figure 2 are comparable over the range of ten problems, and give similar power curves, with the experimental group being slightly worse (control slope = -0.86, R^2 = .94; experiment slope = -0.57, R^2 = 0.93).

Although the generalized constraints used were loosely based on the results of the initial analysis, they also contained generalizations that appeared feasible, but for which we had no evidence that they would necessarily be superior to their individual counterparts. The experimental system might therefore contain a mixture of good and bad generalizations. We measured this by plotting, for the control group, individual learning curves for the generalized constraints and comparing them to the average performance of the member constraints, the same as was performed for the *a priori* analysis. The cut-off point for these graphs was at n=4, because the volume of data is low and so the curves rapidly degenerate, and because the analysis already performed suggested that differences were only likely to appear early in the constraint histories. Of the 63 generalized constraints, six appeared to clearly be superior to the individual constraints, a further three appeared to be equivalent, and eight appeared to be significantly worse. There was insufficient data about the remaining 46 to draw conclusions. We then plotted curves for two subsets of the constraints: those that were members of the generalized constraints classified as better, same or 'no data' (labeled "acceptable"), and those classed as worse or 'no data' (labeled "poor"). Figure 3 shows the curves for these two groups.

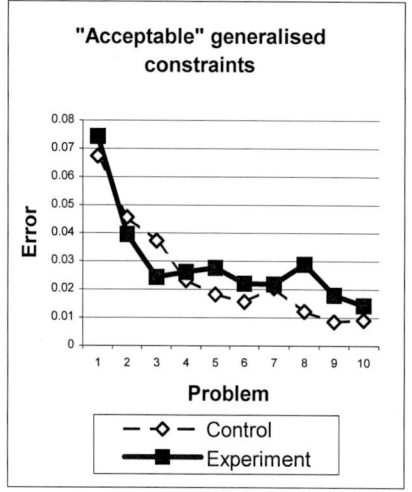
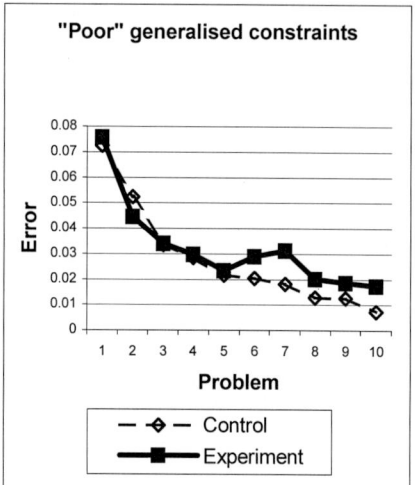

Fig. 3. Power curves based on predictions of goodness

For the "acceptable" generalized constraints, the experimental group appears to perform considerably better for the first three problems, but then plateaus; for the "poor" generalized constraints the experimental group performs better for the first two problems only. In other words, for the "acceptable" generalizations the feedback is more helpful than the standard feedback during the solving of the first two problems in which it is encountered (and so students do better on the second and third one) but is less helpful after that; for the "poor" group this is true for the first problem only. We tested the significance of this result by computing the error reduction between n=1 and n=3 for each student and comparing the means. The experimental group had a mean error reduction of 0.058 (SD=0.027), compared to 0.035 (SD=0.030) for the control group. The difference was significant at p=0.01. In contrast, there was no significant difference in the means of error reduction for the "poor" group (experimental mean=0.050 (SD=0.035), control mean=0.041 (SD=0.028), p>0.3). This result again suggests that the individual learning curves do indeed predict to some extent whether generalized feedback at this level will be effective. It also suggested that personalization may not be necessary; simply applying the same feedback to all students appeared to (initially at least) improve learning performance.

4   Study 2: Does Generalization Help?

Based on the results of the 2004 study, we concluded that generalized feedback seemed to work well initially but if feedback is needed too many times there reaches a point where it no longer helps the student. We hypothesized therefore that starting with more general feedback and later switching to specific feedback might yield the best results. We modified the experimental system to behave in this way: students in the experiment group received general feedback the first two times a constraint was

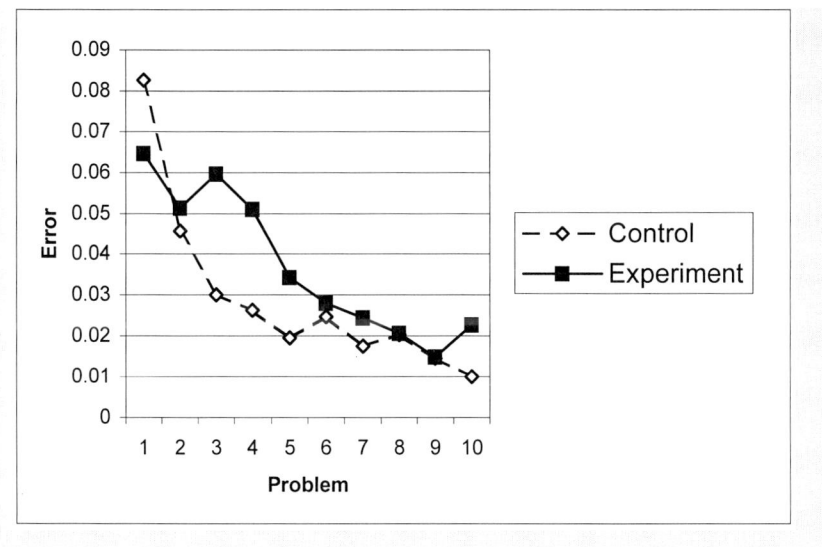

Fig. 4. Learning curves for the two groups

violated, then the same feedback as the control group (i.e. specific) thereafter. We included only those generalizations deemed "acceptable" in the previous study. If our hypothesis were correct we would expect the curve for the experimental group to be steeper at the beginning than the control, and then the same once the feedback has reverted to the same feedback as the control. Overall the experimental group should learn faster.

The experiment was run in October 2005, again using students from a year 2 database course at the University of Canterbury, New Zealand. The number of students participating in the experiment was lower this time; after we excluded those students who did not attempt any problems there were 21 students in the control group and 25 in the experimental group. The mean score for the pre-test for all students was slightly lower than in 2004: 2.02 out of 4 (SD=0.98) compared to 2.14 (SD=1.01) in 2004. The students were randomly allocated to one of the two versions of the system. The experimental group had a higher average than the control group (2.22, SD=1.04 Compared to 1.81, SD=0.87), although in an independent-samples T-test the result was not statistically significant (p=0.2).

Figure 4 again plots the learning curves for the control and experimental groups, for the first 10 problems that each knowledge unit was relevant. This time the experimental group performed much more poorly than the control; the control group reduced their error by 64% on average after receiving (specific) feedback for two problems, whereas the experimental group only reduced their error by 8% after receiving the more general messages. Further, on average they *increased* their error by 16% between the first and second problem. This result directly contradicts the previous experiment.

5 Discussion

At first glance the second study suggests that the method used to determine which concepts to make more general is not robust. However, another possibility is that feedback generality is not something that can be applied *en masse* to all students. Figure 5 plots error reduction over the first two problems versus pre-test score for the experimental group. Error reduction for this group is quite strongly correlated with pre-test score (slope = 23, R^2 = 0.67), indicating that poorer students may have difficulty understanding more general feedback. This trend was also observed for the 2004 study, although the effect was much weaker (slope = 3, R^2= 0.016). In contrast, for the control groups in both years error reduction is slightly *negatively* correlated: poorer students reduce their error more. The results for the control group for both years were nearly identical (slope = -4, R^2 = 0.015). This suggests that the system may need to adapt generality to the ability level of the student, perhaps varying the level over time as the student gains proficiency.

A difference in the experimental groups' experiences is that in 2004 the students received general feedback for the same subset of concepts *all of the time*, whereas in 2005 feedback switched back to specific messages after the general message had been shown twice. Perhaps this led to confusion; the student might have thought they had corrected an error because the feedback changed, and were now looking for a different error to fix; the error messages did not reference each other, so the student might quite reasonably infer that they referred to two different problems. For example, *"Check whether you have specified all the correct comparisons with integer constants"* might change to *"Check the constants you specified in WHERE!"* In particular, the second feedback message does not specify the *type* of constant (integer) whereas the first message does, so might equally apply to string constants for example. Less able students may have suffered this misconception, whereas the better students did not.

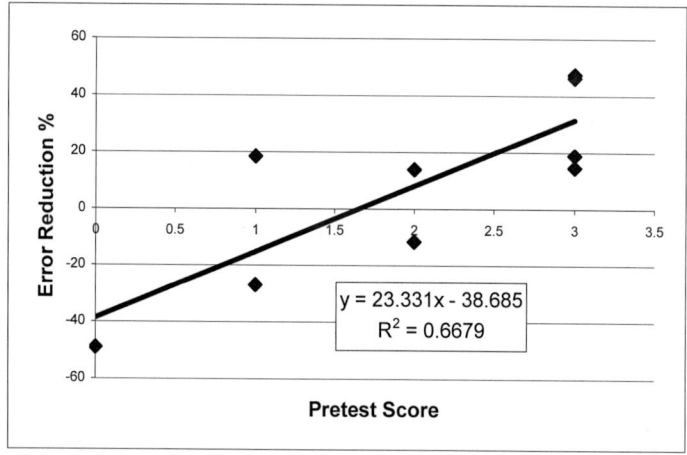

Fig. 5. Error reduction versus pre-test score for the experimental group, study 2

6 Conclusions

In this experiment we researched the effect of feedback generality on learning performance. We initially used past student model data for predicting the behavior of generalized feedback. We developed a more general feedback set that mapped to groups of underlying knowledge units, and found in an initial experiment that for some of these concepts learning performance appeared to improve, although only for the first two problems, after which it deteriorated. For other generalizations performance was worse. We also showed that we could predict to some extent which generalized constraints would produce better performance by analyzing their apparent performance in the control group. A second study contradicted the first; students given more general feedback initially exhibited *worse* performance. However, the experimental system differed between the two studies: in the first study generalized feedback was given all the time for selected concepts, while in the second it was only given initially and then the system reverted to giving specialized feedback.

In the second study the effect of the generalized feedback differed between students, with a strong trend indicating that less able students failed to cope with the feedback given. Since this trend was not observed in the first study, it also suggests that the less able students may have been confused when the feedback level *changed*. The problems observed with the second study might possibly have been obviated if it was made clear to the student that the feedback was still referring to the *same error*, e.g. if the later feedback included both messages, rather than switching from one to another.

The two studies show that feedback generality has a measurable effect on learning ability. Between them they also give hope that the general concepts can be inferred from past student model data, and indicate that the level of generality needs to be tailored to individual students. This motivates us to continue to explore how we can best personalize feedback to maximize student performance.

References

1. Anderson, J.R., Corbett, A.T., Koedinger, K.R., and Pelletier, R., *Cognitive Tutors: Lessons Learned.* Journal of the Learning Sciences, 1995. **4**(2): 167-207.
2. Koedinger, K.R. and Mathan, S. *Distinguishing Qualitatively Different Kinds of Learning Using Log Files and Learning Curves.* In: J. Mostow, P. Tedesco (eds) Proc. *Workshop on Data Mining of Student Logs at ITS2004.* 2004. Maceio, Brazil, pp. 39-46.
3. Martin, B., *Constraint-Based Modelling: Representing Student Knowledge.* New Zealand Journal of Computing, 1999. **7**(2): 30-38.
4. Mitrovic, A., *An Intelligent SQL Tutor on the Web.* Artificial Intelligence in Education, 2003. **13**(2-4): 173-197.
5. Mitrovic, A., Martin, B., and Mayo, M., *Using evaluation to shape ITS design: Results and experiences with SQL-Tutor.* User Modelling and User Adapted Interaction, 2002. **12**(2-3): 243-279.

6. Newell, A. and Rosenbloom, P.S., *Mechanisms of skill acquisition and the law of practice*, in *Cognitive skills and their acquisition*, J.R. Anderson, Editor. 1981, Lawrence Erlbaum Associates: Hillsdale, NJ. pp. 1-56.

7. Ohlsson, S., *Constraint-Based Student Modeling*, in *Student Modeling: The Key to Individualized Knowledge-Based Instruction*, J. Greer and G. McCalla, Editors. 1994, Springer-Verlag: New York. pp. 167-189.

8. Zapata-Rivera, J.D. and Greer, J.E., *Interacting with Inspectable Bayesian Student Models*. Artificial Intelligence in Education, 2004. **14**(2): 127-163.

An Authoring Tool for Building Both Mobile Adaptable Tests and Web-Based Adaptive or Classic Tests

Cristóbal Romero[1], Sebastián Ventura[1], Cesar Hervás[1], and Paul De Bra[2]

[1] Córdoba University, Campus Universitario de Rabanales, 14071, Córdoba, Spain
{cromero, sventura, chervas}@uco.es
[2] Eindhoven University of Technology (TU/e), PO Box 513, Eindhoven, The Netherlands
debra@win.tue.nl

Abstract. This paper describes Test Editor, an authoring tool for building both mobile adaptable tests and web-based adaptive or classic tests. This tool facilitates the development and maintenance of different types of XML-based multiple-choice tests for using in web-based education systems and wireless devices. We have integrated Test Editor into the AHA! system, but it can be used in other web-based systems as well. We have also created several test execution engines in Java language in order to be executed in different devices such as PC and mobile phones. In order to test them, we have carried out two experiments with students to determine the usefulness of adaptive tests and mobile tests.

1 Introduction

Computerized tests or quizzes are among the most widely used and well-developed tools in web-based education [7]. There are different types of computerized tests, depending on the type of items or questions (yes/no questions, multiple-choice/single-answer questions, fill-in questions, etc.) and there are two main types of control algorithms: classic or linear tests and adaptive tests [20]. The main advantage of computerized adaptive tests (CAT) is that each examinee usually receives different questions and their number is usually smaller than the number of questions needed in a classic test. Currently, there are several well-known commercial and free tools for developing adaptive and classic computerized test such as: QuestionMark [14], Webassesor [19], MicroCAT and FastTEST [2], SIETTE [1], Test++ [5], etc. Most of them are based on XML to record the information about assessments and some use the IMS Question and Test Interoperatiblity (QTI) international specification [4]. On the other hand, m-learning (mobile learning) and u-learning (ubiquitous learning) have started to emerge as potential educational environments [11]. In fact, there are nowadays several quiz systems [10] oriented to be used not only for PC users, but also for PDA and mobile phone users; and there are some interactive tests [12] specifically developed only for being used in mobiles phones. There are also several commercial tools such as Mobile EMT-B quiz [13], oriented to PDA devices and others such as Go Test Go's [9] oriented to be used in Java mobile phones. With the Test Editor described in this paper it is possible to author once and deliver on both mobile and Web-based platforms.

V. Wade, H. Ashman, and B. Smyth (Eds.): AH 2006, LNCS 4018, pp. 203 – 212, 2006.

2   Test Editor Author Tool

In order to facilitate computer tests creation and maintenance, we have developed the Test Editor tool for building computerized tests [16]. Currently, we have integrated it in the AHA! system [8] because that is a well-known adaptive hypermedia architecture used to build web-based courses, and because it uses the Java and XML languages. Test Editor is a (signed) Java Applet, just like other AHA! authoring tools: Form Editor, Concept Editor and Graph Editor.

As the first step for developing a test with Test Editor, the examiner has to create one or several (XML) *items* files. An *item* consists of a single question about a single concept (from an AHA! application or course), the answers (right and wrong) and explanations for the wrong answers. Several items/questions about the same concept can be grouped together into one items file. Figure 1 shows how to add questions to the items file, one by one. The examiner must also specify some required parameters (the enunciate flag, and for each answer a flag to indicate whether the answer is correct) and can add some optional parameters (an illustrative image, explanations and Item Response Theory (IRT) parameters [20]: item difficulty, discrimination and guessing). Using the Test Editor items can be added, modified or deleted. They can be imported/exported to/from other tests systems (currently only AHA! 1.0 and AHA! 3.0). Questions can thus be re-used from other test environments without needing to enter them again.

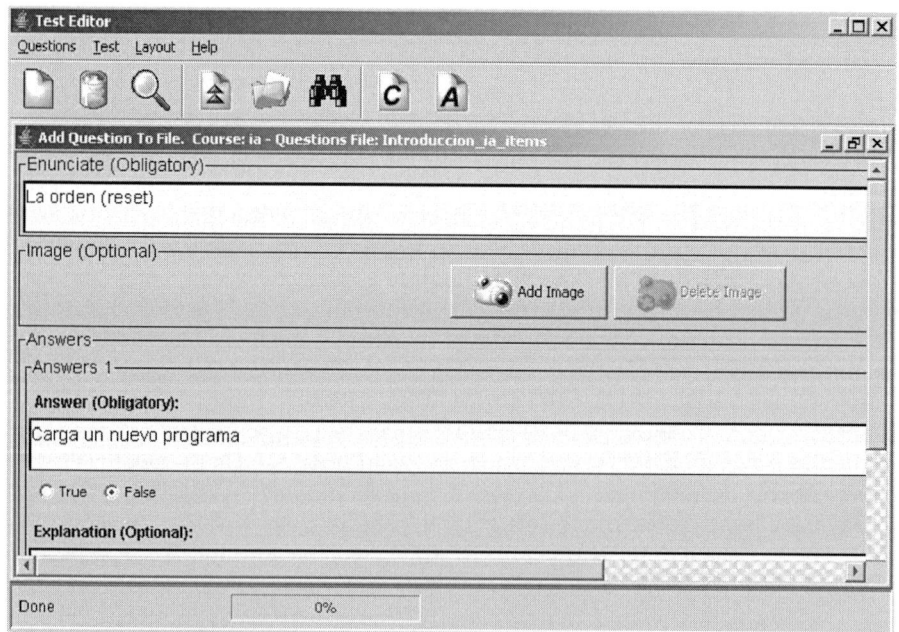

Fig. 1. Test Editor: Windows to introduce the obligatory parameters of an item

The second step is to build tests out of items. The examiner decides on the test type (classic test or adaptive test) he wants and whether to use just one or several items files. If the test evaluates only one concept, we consider it to be an "activity". If the test evaluates several concepts, it will be an "exam", about a chapter or perhaps a whole course. Next, the examiner can use different methods to select what specific items from these items files will be used in the test (the selection can be done manually, randomly or randomly with some restrictions). Then he sets presentation parameters (see Figure 2) about how questions are shown to examinees: the order in which questions and answers are shown, whether to show or hide explanations of the answers (through the "verbose" flag), the maximum time to respond, whether to show the correct answer or just a score, etc. In addition to these there are also parameters about evaluation: to penalize incorrect answers, to penalize unanswered questions and what percentage of knowledge the final score represents in the associated concept/concepts. If the test is adaptive, the examiner also has to set the adaptive algorithm parameters (questions selection procedure and termination criterion). Each test is stored in an XML file and that is exactly the same for both versions (PC and mobile). But for the mobile devices it also is necessary to create a *.jar* and *.jad* file [21] that includes both the multiple-choice test code (a Java Midlet test engine) as well as the questions and parameters (XML file).

The generated test can be downloaded (the *.jar* file) into a mobile phone and/or can be used directly (through a browser) in an AHA! course [8]. When used with AHA! a test is presented in an Java Applet, with a look and feel that is similar to the Java

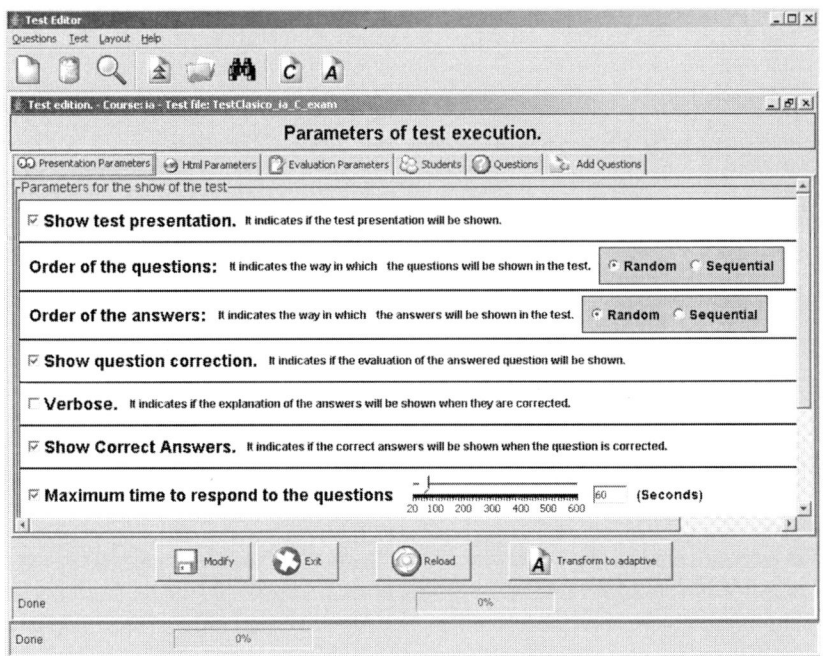

Fig. 2. Test Editor: Windows to select the questions presentation parameters

Midlet version. The results of tests are logged on the server. After a large number of examinees performed some tests, examiners can examine statistical information in the Test Editor (success rate per question, mean times to answer the questions, questions usage percentage, etc.) and use that information for maintenance/improvements to the tests. The examiner may decide to modify or delete bad items, add new items, but he can also modify the test configuration. Test Editor also can do items calibration [3], in order to transform a classic test into an adaptive one, or to optimize the IRT parameter of an adaptive test.

3   The Web-Based Adaptive and Classic Tests Engine

Our web-based tests engine is a signed Java Applet that uses Java Servlets to communicate with AHA! [8]. It can execute both classic and adaptive computerized tests with multiple-choice items [16]. A conventional (classic) test is a sequence of simple questions and normally the same questions are shown to all examinees. The algorithm to control the execution of a classic test is very simple: it shows a sequence of questions until either there are no more questions or the examinee has used up the maximum allowed time. On the other hand, a CAT [18] is a computer-based test where the decision about presenting a question or item and finishing the test is made depending on the examinee's performance in previous answers. The general adaptive tests algorithm (see Figure 3) consists of three main procedures: question selection, based on the most informative item for each student; proficiency estimation of each student; and checking the finalization criteria (maximum number of questions, maximum spent time or if the proficiency level has passed a confidence value).

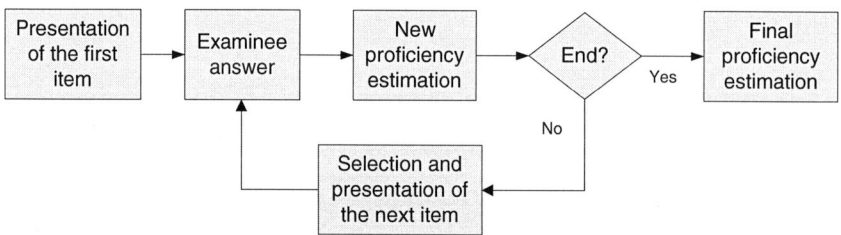

Fig. 3. Adaptive tests control algorithm

When a student starts a test (clicking on the test link), the engine connects to the server in order to obtain all the test information and to check if the student is allowed to take the test (or repeat it). If the test has "starting information" the engine will show it, and it will then start to show questions. The student has to select what the hopefully correct answer is (possibly more than one) and then presses the "Correct The Question" button (see Figure 4). This has to happen before the maximum response time has elapsed. The student can see if the submitted answer was correct or incorrect, if the author has set the parameter to show this. Finally, after the student replies to the last question he will see the obtained score and the total time spent.

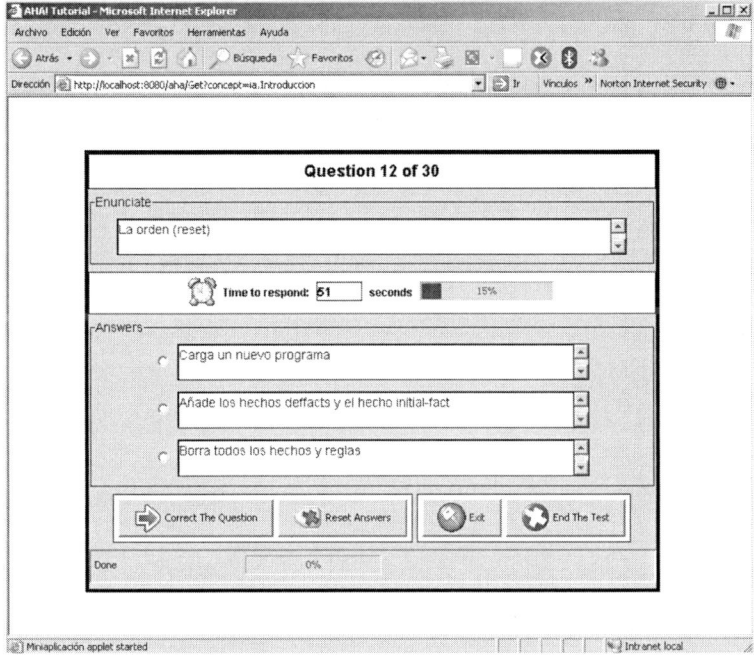

Fig. 4. Web-based tests execution engine interface with a question

4   Mobile Adaptable Tests Engine

Our mobile adaptable tests engine is a Java Midlet [21] with a specific tests interface designed for small wireless devices. Java Midlets are small applications that can be executed in the mobile phone. They have important advantages compared to WAP (Wireless Application Protocol) and browser based applications. For example, they can be used offline without connection cost, they have a more responsive and interactive interface and they are popular thanks to Java games [12]. Functionally, our mobile engine can read (XML) test files, present questions, check answers and send the score back to AHA! [8]. The user can download and install the *.jar* file (generated by the Test Editor) in the mobile device directly from Internet (by connecting to the *.jad* file), or he can download the *.jar* file to a PC first and then send it to the mobile using Bluetooth, Infrared, serial bus, etc. After installing, the execution of the test is totally off-line and it works as shown in Figure 5: the questions are shown on the mobile's screen in a linear or random order (depending on the test parameters), the answers have to be selected by the user with the phone keys and when the test ends the scores obtained and the used time are shown.

Mobile tests engine has some personalization characteristics for individualised execution [6]:

– When the user starts the application he/she has to identify himself/herself by introducing his/her personal login and password (the same as used in AHA!).

- When the user finishes the test execution the scores are physically stored in the mobile memory card by using RMS (Record Management System).
- If the user executes an exam, then the elapsed time in each question is shown.
- The user can send the obtained score to AHA! (in order to update his/her AHA! profile) through a GPRS (General Packet Radio Service) connection.
- Activities can be repeated several times by the same users, but exams cannot. The user cannot easily hack the downloaded .*jar* exam (for example, he can try to do it by uninstalling and installing the application again) because when an exam starts the application connects to AHA! in order to check that the user has never taken that exam before.

Fig. 5. Mobile tests execution interface with a question and the final score

Mobile tests engine also has some adaptable characteristics in the interface. The difference between adaptive and adaptable refers to the extent to which users can exert influence on the individualization process of a system [17]. Adaptable systems are customized by the users themselves. In our mobile tests application, the user can select the following preferences from the main menu (see Figure 6 at the left):

- The user can choose between different font types (see Figure 6 in the middle) and sizes, in order to improve the readability of the text of the questions.
- The user can choose to show questions and answers together on the same screen (see Figure 6 at the right) if he/she prefers to scroll, or to show them on two different screens (see Figure 5 at the left and in the middle) if he/she prefers to see the question on one screen and the answers on another.
- The user can choose to show the associated images that some questions have, if he/she has a screen big enough to show them, or not to show them if he/she has a small screen.

Fig. 6. Mobile tests main menu interface and preferences

5 Experimental Results

We have carried out two experiments to determine the usability of both adaptive tests (a calibrated version versus a non-calibrated version) and mobile tests (a PC version versus a Mobile version), using two different tests about the Java and CLIPS languages respectively.

In the Java Language test we compare the results students obtain when they use the same PC test but with adaptively calibrated items and with non-calibrated items. Each test has been carried out by a different group of 60 computer science engineering students at the Cordoba University, with a similar age, knowledge and experience. Both tests consisted of the same 27 items with 4 possible answers on which one answer was correct, and the same finalization conditions (if the standard error became lower than 0.33 or if all 27 questions were presented). The difference is that initially the IRT two-parameters (difficulty and discrimination) of the non-calibrated items are set manually by experts in Java, and after one group of students executes the test then the IRT two-parameters are calibrated using the maximum likelihood estimation estimator [3] to be used with the other group of students.

Table 1. Students tests execution results: adaptive non-calibrated versus calibrated test

	Time taken	Number of Items	Proficiency estimation	Standard error
Non-Calibrated Test	434.6±88.8	26.9±1.6	-1.3±0.3	0.6±0.1
Calibrated Test	182.4±81.2	11.5±2.6	-2.2±0.3	0.4±0.1

In the Table 1, we show the mean value and the confidence interval (95%) of the time taken (in seconds) to complete the test, the number of items attempted, the proficiency estimated and the standard error. We can see in the first table row, there was a reduction in the total number of questions used in the calibrated version versus the non-calibrated version. Secondly, we can see a reduction of the time needed to complete the test in the calibrated version precisely due to the reduction of questions. Finally, the estimated proficiency obtained in the calibrated version is lower than the non-calibrated version but the standard error is higher. It shows that the precision obtained in the calibrated version is higher, and the student's estimated proficiency is more accurate, as was expected.

On other hand, in the CLIPS Language test we compare the results students obtain when they execute the same test but on the PC or by the mobile phone. Each test has been carried out by a different group of 80 and 20 computer science engineering students (with Java mobile) at the Cordoba University, all with similar age, knowledge and experience. Both tests consist of the same 40 items with 3 possible answers of which one was correct. The questions were shown in random order.

Table 2. Students tests execution results: web-based classic test versus mobile test

	Time taken	Number of correct items	Number of incorrect items	Number of items without answer
PC Test	1157.8±75.2	19.8±0.8	6.3±0.6	3.8±0.5
Mobile Test	635.1±58.7	20±1.5	5.4±1.2	4.8±1.1

In the Table 2, we show the mean value and the confidence interval (95%) of the time taken (in seconds) to complete test, the number of correct items, number of incorrect items and the number of items without answer. We can see that the execution of the mobile test is much quicker than the PC test: students with the mobile test used only about half of the time that students with a PC needed. This can be because the user interface and input methods of this technology are simple and efficient (some examples are Java games and SMS applications) and so, the students show a great proficiency in using them (fast browsing through mobile interfaces). And the final scores were very similar in both versions with only small differences.

Finally, we have also carried out a survey among all the students of the CLIPS test in order to learn what their opinions are about the two versions of the test. The questionnaire had five questions (1.How much do you prefer it?, 2.How useful is it?, 3.How easy to use is it?, 4.How much do you like the user interface? and 5.How much do you like the data entry method?) that students have to answer with a range between 1 (a little) and 5 (much) for each version, and they can also write some comments.

Table 3. Student's opinion questionnaire: web-based classic versus mobile test

	More preferable	More useful	More easy to use	Best user Interface	Best data entry method
PC Test	3.57±0.34	3.78±0.55	4.78±0.18	4.05±0.23	4.36±0.37
Mobile Test	3.89±0.39	4.26±0.36	4.47±0.31	3.68±0.33	4.01±0.39

In the Table 3, we show the mean value and the confidence interval (95%) of the rating for preference, usefulness and ease of use of the test, and the rate of acceptance of the user's interface and the data entry method. We can see that the mobile test is more preferable and useful than the PC test, although the PC test is easier to use and it has a better user interface and data entry method. This can be because students are still more familiar with PC interfaces and their data entry methods for this type of applications. But, in general, students liked the experience to use a mobile application to execute tests that can evaluate their knowledge in a specific area. About the comments, students think that the main weaknesses of mobile phones are:

- Small screen size. In general, all students would prefer to be able to see questions, question and answer on the same screen and without needing to scroll although they are long, as they are written with the size of a PC screen in mind.
- Very expensive. Almost all the students think that Java mobile phones are very expensive at the moment, and it is necessary that they become cheaper in order for most of the students to be able to afford them. Once affordable the mobile tests and other m-learning tools will become really useful and usable in real life.
- Difficult input method. Some students with big fingers had some problems to press the correct button each time and they would like that mobile could have bigger buttons or some other alternative input method.

6   Conclusions and Future Work

In this paper we have described Test Editor, an authoring tool for building computerized tests. The main advantages of Test Editor in relation to other test tools are: modular (concepts, items and tests are clearly separated), easy to use (it has a friendly Java Swing graphical user interface); it facilitates the maintenance (it has statistical information and item calibration based on examinees' usage information), standard format (it uses XML files) and multi-device execution (it has several Java engines for executing tests on a PC and on wireless devices). We have resolved the problem of authoring once for delivery on two very different platforms using XML for storing test information and Java for developing the different test execution engines. Although we have integrated it within the AHA! system [8], it can be also used in other web-based educational systems that support the Java and XML languages. After the experimentation, the first impression is that students are generally highly motivated to use mobile technologies for testing and it can be possible and useful to use mobile devices for testing despite some limited possibilities of J2ME (Java 2 Micro Edition) such as small screen size, limited application size and no support for floating point numbers. But we have developed a user interface with preferences; we have tried to reduce the number of lines of code and we have used a Java floating point emulation library for J2ME [15].

Currently we are working on extending the interoperability with other tests formats. We want to allow import/export questions and tests to/from others computerized tests systems and standards such as IMS QTI [4], QuestionMark [14], SIETTE [1], etc. In the future, we want to add more adaptable characteristics and to develop an adaptive tests control algorithm for the test mobile engine.

Acknowledgments

The authors[1] gratefully acknowledge the financial support provided by the Spanish department of Research under TIN2005-08386-C05-02 Project.

References

1. Arroyo, I., Conejo, R., Guzman, E., Wolf, B.P.: An Adaptive Web-based Component for Cognitive Ability Estimation. Proc. of Artificial Intelligence in Education. Amsterdam:IOS (2001) 456-466
2. Assessment Systems Corporation: Microcat and Fasttest, http://www.assessment.com (2006)
3. Backer, F.: Item Response Theory, Parameter Estimation Techniques. Marcel Dekker (1992)
4. Bacon, D.: IMS Question and Test Interoperability. MSOR Connections, 3:3 (2003) 44-45
5. Barra, M., Palmieri, G., Napolitano, S., Scarano, V., Zitarosa, L.: Adaptive Testing by Test++. Proc. of the International Conference on Adaptive Hypermedia and Adaptive Web-Based Systems, Trento, Italy, (2000) 264-267
6. Bull, S., Reid, E.: Individualised revision material for use on a handheld computer. Proc. of the International Conference on MLEARN, UK (2003) 35-42
7. Brusilovsky, P., Miller P.: Web-based Testing for Distance Education. Proc. of the World Conference of WWW and Internet, Hawaii, USA, (1998) 149-154
8. De Bra, P., Aerts, A.. Berden, B., De Lange, B., Rousseau, B., Santic, T., Smits, D., Stash, N.: AHA! The Adaptive Hypermedia Architecture. Proc. of the ACM Hypertext Conference, Nottingham, UK, (2003) 81-84
9. Go test go: http://www.gotestgo.com (2006)
10. Goh, T., Kinshuk, Lin, T.: Developing an adaptive mobile learning system. Proc. of the International Conference on Computers in Education, Hong Kong, (2003) 1062-1065
11. Kinshuk: Adaptive Mobile Learning Technologies. GlobalEducator.com, (2003)
12. Mayorga, M.C., Fernández, A.: Learning Tools for Java Enabled Phones: An Application to Actuarial Studies. Proc. of the International Conference MLEARN, UK (2003) 95-98
13. Mobile EMT-B Quiz: http://www.emszone.com/mobilequiz (2006)
14. QuestionMark: http://www.questionmark.com (2006)
15. Real: http://sourceforge.net/projects/real-java (2006)
16. Romero, C., De Bra, P., Ventura, S.: An authoring tool for web-based adaptive and classic tests. Proc. of the World Conference on E-Learning in Corporate, Goverment, Healthcare and Higher Education, Washington, (2004) 174–177
17. Treiblmaier, H.: Measuring the Acceptance of Adaptive and Adaptable Systems. Proc. of the HHCCII, Hawai, USA, (2004) 1-8
18. Van der Linde, W. J., Hambleton, R. K.: Handbook of Modern Item Response Theory. Springer Verlag, Berlin (1997)
19. Webassessor: http://www.webassessor.com (2006)
20. Wainer, H.: Computerized Adaptive Testing: A premier. New Jersey, Lawrence Erlbaum Associates (2000)
21. Yuan, M.J.: Enterprise J2ME: Developing Mobile Java Applications. Prentice Hall, New Jersey (2003)

ASHDM – Model-Driven Adaptation and Meta-adaptation

Patricia Seefelder de Assis[1,2], Daniel Schwabe[2], and Demetrius Arraes Nunes[2]

[1] Grupo ROCA / Instituto Politécnico, Campus Regional de Nova Friburgo – Universidade
Estadual do Rio de Janeiro (UERJ) – Caixa Postal 97282 – 28610-974 – Friburgo – RJ – Brazil
[2] Departamento de Informática – Pontifícia Universidade Católica do Rio de Janeiro
(PUC-Rio) – Caixa Postal 38.097 – 22.453-900 – Rio de Janeiro – RJ – Brazil
`patricia@iprj.uerj.br, dschwabe@inf.puc-rio.br,`
`demetriusnunes@gmail.com`

Abstract. In this work we propose a general purpose architecture for adaptation and meta-adaptation in hypermedia systems, using the Adaptive Semantic Hypermedia Design Model together with the Hypermedia Development Environment, extended to include adaptation. This architecture is model-driven and ontology-based, so data and model may be handled in the same way.

1 Introduction

Adaptive applications are able to alter some of their characteristics, such as their navigation model (NM) or presentation model (PM), according to the adaptation context. This context may include information about the user, such as his/her preferences, navigation history, etc., and about the execution environment, such as access device, bandwidth, etc. This occurs at document-level. Meta-adaptive applications are able to alter both its models and its adaptation process according to the adaptation context. The need for meta-adaptation is spurred by the observation that some adaptation techniques are more (or less) efficient depending on the context.

The proposed architecture is model-driven, allowing direct manipulation of its metamodels and generated models, as well as the relations between them, thus making meta-adaptation easy. This architecture extends the metamodel used by the Hypermedia Development Environment (HyperDE) [11] with the Adaptive Semantic Hypermedia Design Model (ASHDM).

2 ASHDM

The initial idea of ASHDM is based on the Reference Metamodel for Adaptive Hypermedia Systems [1,2], which considers the separation of conceptual, navigational and presentation concepts proposed by OOHDM (Object Oriented Hypermedia Design Method) [12] enriched with the three models: Domain Model (DM), User Model (UM) and Adaptation Model (AM) proposed by AHAM (Adaptive Hypermedia Application Model) [4]. The resulting metamodel is composed by Domain, User, Adaptation,

V. Wade, H. Ashman, and B. Smyth (Eds.): AH 2006, LNCS 4018, pp. 213–222, 2006.

Navigation, Presentation, Integration (to integrate domains) and User Context[1] models, providing a framework for comparison between Adaptive Hypermedia Systems (AHSs) , analyzing what is adapted, based on what the adaptation occurs (including the granularity of time), and how the adaptation is achieved.

In order to enable the use for a common language both for describing data and models, the approach used in SHDM (Semantic Hypermedia Design Method) [13] is applied to the reference metamodel proposed in [1,2]. Next we present an overview of each model that composes the ASHDM proposal. We observe that, with respect to the reference metamodels, the terminology Domain and Presentation is substituted, respectively, by Conceptual and Interface, to maintain the consistency with SHDM. The Integration Model is not defined because we consider that the integration of domains can be done through the Navigation Model. The Adaptation Context Model (ACM) generalizes the idea of User Model and User Context Model.

2.1 Conceptual Model

The Conceptual Model is considered to be any ontology defined for the Semantic Web that uses concepts and relationships between them to represent the real world. This representation is supposed to be application-independent, and it may overlap with the UM (see section 2.4.1). Since it is a representation it will not be adapted itself; specific views are achieved through the navigation model.

2.2 Navigation Model

Navigational objects are considered to be views over conceptual objects. These views are based on user's tasks and user's profile. The Navigation Model can be understood as an Integration Model in the sense that navigational views can be constructed over conceptual ontologies defined for different domains.

The Navigation Model is specified by an ontology-based vocabulary that defines navigational classes, links, navigational contexts, access structures and landmarks. Views are defined by mapping a conceptual ontology into this navigational ontology.

Some types of adaptation that may occur are: in the mapping from conceptual to navigational; in the definition of the attributes which define the navigational class and in attributing values to them; in the definition of links; in the selection of the nodes that will compose a context and how they can be navigated; and in the definition of access structures.

2.3 Interface Model

The Interface Model (IM) represents the interaction between users and system through Abstract and Concrete Widgets Ontologies, and the mapping from abstract to concrete as proposed by [10]. Essentially, this interaction occurs through events which can be "activators" (Button/Link); "exhibitors" (Image/Label) and "capturers" (widgets such as CheckBox, ComboBox, RadioButton or an element composed by Link). This mapping may be adapted, as well as the CSS used to render nodes.

---

[1] This terminology is obsolete. In reality, the context represents the situation in which the application is used, and is not only related to the user.

2.4   Adaptation Context Model

Usually, AHSs are used for domains where the user exists as an individual and is typically modeled by a class in the domain model. So the UM contains an overlay model representing the relationship between the user and the domain concepts. An example is in the e-learning domain, to represent what the user (i.e., student) knows about the subject. In the e-commerce domain this relationship may represent if the user (i.e., customer) already bought a given product. In these cases, the adaptation depends on the *domain user* or simply, *user*. In the examples above, user is modeled by the "student" or "customer" classes in the domain model.

Sometimes, however, there is no need to consider the user as an individual for adaptation purposes. If the adaptation is based on the bandwidth, on display size, on the place where it occurs and so on, the result of the adaptation is the same for every *adaptation user* or *meta-user*.

We consider that the *meta-user* is represented by a UM which is a component of a general adaptation context. A User Representation (UR) is used to model the representation of the *user* in the domain (e.g., "student" or "customer"), and may be related to other domain concepts. Figure 1 (a) shows the relationship between these models and how they influence the Navigation and Interface Models.

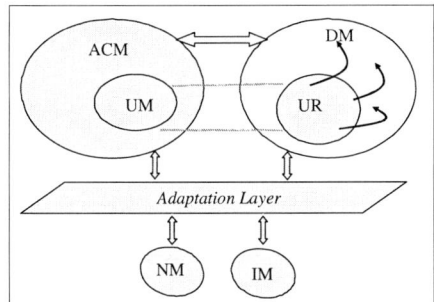 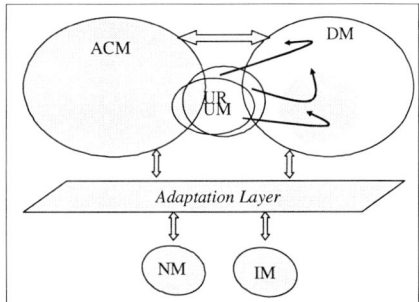

Fig. 1. (a) User relationship w/ respect to ACM, DM and other models. **(b)** UM/UR unification.

To avoid redundancy, we need to unify the data in the UM and in the UR. A simple way of doing this is by inheritance. In ASHDM the UR is defined as a subclass of the UM metaclass. Thus the UR may have its own attributes as well as the attributes inherited from UM. Figure 1 (b) shows the user unification schema.

The unified user information has to be integrated with other context and domain data. We use the notion of view to create a virtual context with all needed information.

Figure 2 shows an example of a virtual museum with a class User which has five attributes: ID (identifier), name, address, birthday and favorites (to record the rooms selected by the user). The ACM contains the attribute display, the UM also stores ID and name, together with cognitive style and presentation preferences. The overlay attribute history represents rooms already visited by the user. For adaptation, the Context View has the attributes: age, interest categories, history and display. The interest category could be inferred from age, for example.

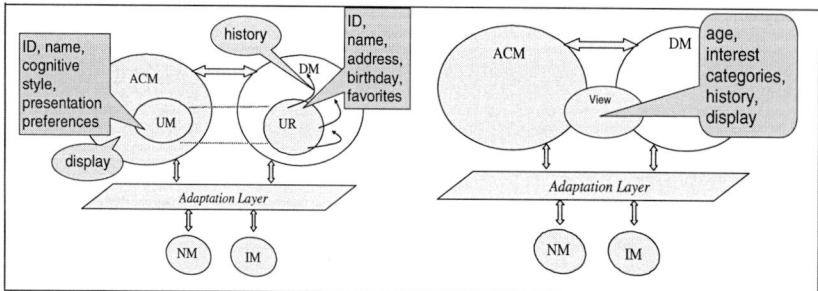

Fig. 2. Example of Adaptation Context View

2.4.1 User Model Schema

Research in user modeling area states that the User Model should be independent from AHSs, facilitating the tasks of constructing and maintaining the UM and enabling the reuse of the model. Application from the same domain or from similar domains could cooperate using the same part of the UM [9]. The semantics of a UM must be known, and the identification of which part is domain-independent and which one is common for all domains must be done in order to share a UM [9]

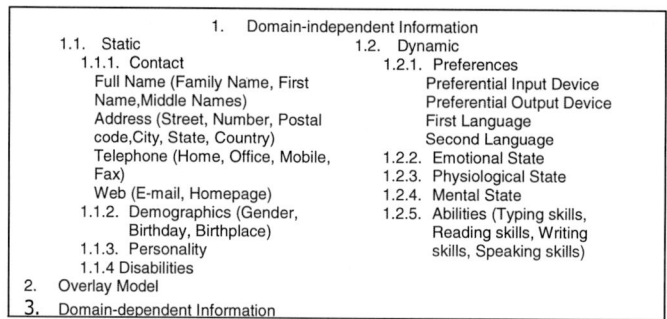

Fig. 3. User Model Structure: Domain-independent Information

The use of ontologies helps to structure the UM, but which information should be represented in the UM, and which one in the DM is an open question. As far as the adaptation mechanism is concerned, it actually makes no difference where (UM or DM) the data is stored, because the adaptation context view joins all this information. However, structuring user-related data independently from the domain may enable reuse across domains and applications.

We consider that information useful for any application independently from the domain-specific semantic, such as preferred input device, should be stored in the UM, whilst others, such as learning style, in the DM. However, since the domain ontology may be arbitrary, it must be considered that some user information may be represented in the domain ontology. For example, IMS LIP [7], a typical UR used in the DM of educational applications, stores user identification information, which in principle should be in the UM.

We propose a modular structure for the UM divided in three main categories: Domain-independent data; Overlay model, and Domain-dependent data. The general idea is based on GUMO (General User Model Ontology) [6]. The proposal, presented in Figure 3, is only a core structure. New information may be added as needed, and some information may be ignored in some applications.

In the proposed structure, static information is used for customization, as it does not change during system use. Contact information is mostly used for administrative tasks. Demographic and Personality are information suitable for most domains, although not all applications have mechanisms to deal with it.

Whereas GUMO models the five senses and the ability to walk and speak, we assume them as default. The absence of one or more of them is modeled as a deficiency. Information about emotional, physiological and mental states as well as some abilities is theoretically suited for all domains, although only specific applications deal with it. Furthermore, such user characteristics are difficult, if not impossible, to extract automatically, making them less likely to be used in most applications. We include them only for completeness.

In many domains, adaptation is based not only on user and environment characteristics, but also on relations between the user model and the domain model. The existence of a relationship between the user model and the domain concepts is represented in an Overlay Model. This relationship is in the sense of knowing or having a previous experience with the modeled concept. This model is not mandatory; even in e-learning the designer could state that the content must always be seen and the adaptation may be based on other parameters.

Preferences and data about the user which do not make sense for all domains – such as performance, preferred musical style, salary and so on – are classified as Domain-dependent information. They can be obtained from known ontologies like IMS LIP by eliminating all user-related classes that do not have a "knowledge meaning". This is possible because the use of metamodels and ontologies enable the definition of a metarule that queries the ontology definition e.g., "retrieve all resources whose domain belongs to user-class and whose property is not 'knows'".

This schema proposes a way to organize the UM so that the UM core together with some modules could be shared between applications of the same kind and same domain. This structure also allows the definition of metarules which select rules according to the model properties. For example, "if the UM has the property nationality, include news about the user's country".

This modular structure satisfies the requirements proposed by [8]: (a) different views of the UM may be available for each adaptive application, which will define only the UM components it needs; (b) a user may define which parts of the UM will be available to which applications; (c) users may want to have their personal data stored locally and may choose which data will be outside his/her direct control.

We consider the proposed UM as a task ontology that can be integrated with the application domain ontology. According to [3], "task ontology" defines a vocabulary for modeling a structure inherent to problem solutions for all tasks in a domain-independent way whereas the vocabulary defined for "domain ontology" specifies object classes and relationships that exist in certain domains.

2.5 Adaptation Model

The Adaptation Model uses rules following PRML (Personalization Rules Modeling Language) [5], where <body> may represent an action, or an action associated to a condition:

```
When event do        When event do         When event do
        <body>                  action        If condition then action
endWhen              endWhen                endWhen
```

In ASHDM, *events* are interactions between users and systems, represented in the Interface Model. *Actions* may adapt the content, navigation or presentation and may also update the ACM, including the UM. *Conditions* refer to the parameters for adaptation (based on what the adaptation occurs).

2.5.1 Execution Model
Events captured by the IM trigger the adaptation process. ACM and data that may be inferred as the system is used (such as navigation and interaction history) are used to select the set of rules that will be used. Then either the actions are applied to all required models, interface events are interpreted in the updated models and the cycle begins again, or updates in one model trigger adaptation in others, and the adaptation process is triggered every time the IM is activated.

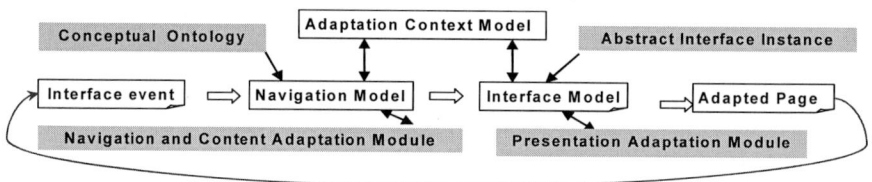

Fig. 4. Example of a possible Execution Flow

Figure 4 shows an example of the Execution Flow that represents the maximum granularity in a chain adaptation process, where the adaptation process is triggered by every click and the adaptation is done step by step. Note that, in ASHDM, content adaptation is considered to adapt the actual content (attribute values) defined in the NM. Hence rules for content and navigation adaptation are represented in the same module that interacts with the NM. This is one possible way of representing the Execution Model; rules could also be grouped all in the same module adapting the page in one single step.

2.6 Meta-adaptation

The selection of the Adaptation Model to be used, including the Execution Model, can be made based on user's role, goals and tasks, thus characterizing a kind of meta-adaptation. The adaptation strategy can be chosen based on a navigation pattern (e.g., the user browses repeatedly the same concept), for example. In educational domain, the choice could be based on learning style and/or on the user's goals (learning or referencing). The decision whether the presentation is adapted only the first time a concept is presented or at every session is another example of meta-adaptation.

Another kind of meta-adaptation is when models are adapted. The model-driven architecture allows the testing of conditions over a set of RDF triples, for example, as well as including or excluding triples from each of the models. In particular, since the model itself is represented as RDF, rules can easily change the model itself, exactly as they can also change the actual data values. The exhibition of a security-alert the first time the user accesses a concept, for example, may be implemented by presentation-adaptation rules (a heavier font the first time), by content-adaptation rules (exhibition only the first time) or by not including adaptation rules (exhibition always) according to the user profile. Even the choice about the triples to be included in the UM could be made according to user's goals.

3   Implementation Architecture

The HyperDE extended with adaptation mechanisms was chosen to implement the ASHDM, since it is a framework and development environment for hypermedia application, driven by ontologies. Figure 5 shows the general HyperDE architecture.

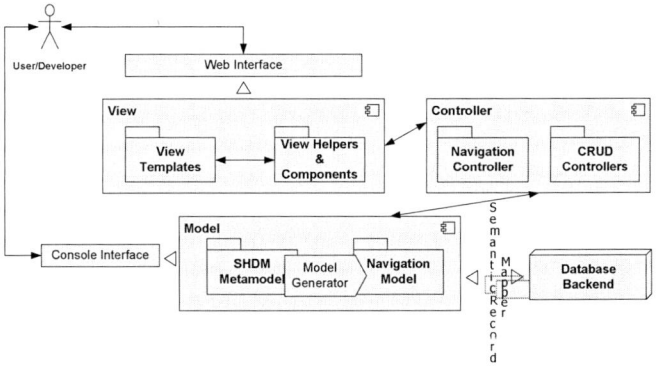

Fig. 5. HyperDE General Architecture

HyperDE allows program code to be passed as function parameter (closure). Thus, hooks may be defined to associate adaptation rules to the control, model or view layers, according to the desired adaptation type. PRML rules conditions usually test attribute values according to aspects on which the adaptation is based, whereas actions alter content, navigation or presentation and may also update the models.

HyperDE's navigation model layer provides SHDM primitives: navigational classes with its attributes and operations; links; (navigational) contexts; indexes with its attributes; landmarks and nodes with its relationships. These primitives are handled by object classes defined according to SHDM's Metamodel. The application navigation model is built by instantiating these generated classes. Thus a navigational class User, for example, is an instance of the metaclass NavClass composed by the metaclass NavAttribute whose instances could be ID, name, and birthday.

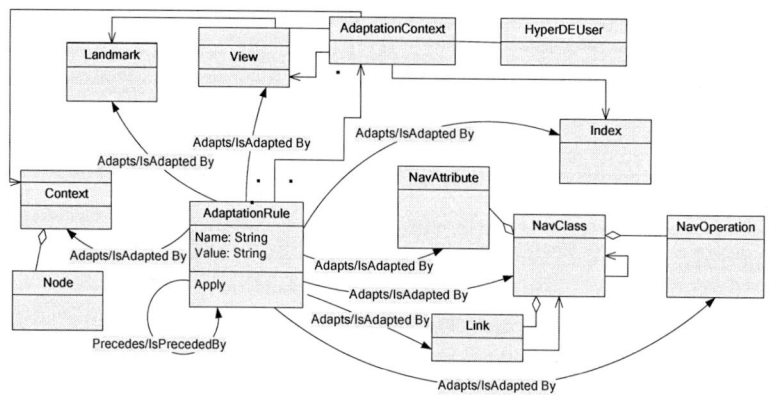

Fig. 6. Extended HyperDE Metamodel including Adaptation Model according to ASHDM

Figure 6 shows the HyperDE Adaptation Model, the extension of HyperDE Metamodel according to ASHDM principles. The `AdaptationContext` metaclass implements the ACM, and `HyperDEUser` is one of its components. If a UR exists (for example, `Customer` or `Student`), it should be declared as subclass of `HyperDEUser`. A navigational context is composed by a set of nodes (represented by the aggregation relationship between `Context` and `Node` metaclasses). A navigational class (`NavClass`) is composed by attributes (`NavAttribute`), `Links` between classes and operations (`NavOperation`). There is a "subclass of" relationship between navigational classes. The `AdaptationContext` provides data requested by the adaptation rules to create an adapted application navigation model based on the instantiation of `Node`, `NodeAttribute`, `NavOperation`, `Link`, `Landmark`, `Index` and `Context`. Since adaptation occurs at runtime, there is no direct adaptation of `NavClass` and `NavAttribute`. Instead, the adaptation occurs in the instantiation of its subclasses, respectively, `Node` and `NodeAttribute`.

The presentation adaptation as proposed by ASHDM has not yet been implemented, since HyperDE currently does not use the abstract and concrete ontologies proposed by [10]. Instead, it provides generic views for navigation. Personalized views (templates) may be defined and associated to navigational templates, overriding generic views. At runtime, the appropriate view is selected. The template sources use style sheets to format its elements, and use helper functions (provided by HyperDE) for accessing the primitives, thus achieving a similar result as the abstract interface definition. Presentation adaptation may occur both in the selection of the appropriate view, or at CSS level, by changing the applicable style sheet definition dynamically.

HyperDE is suitable for meta-adaptation since it uses a semantic database based on RDF and RDFS, which stores application data, the SHDM metamodel and the metadata that describes the application navigational model. Both vocabulary and instances are treated in the same way.

3.1 Execution Flow

Whereas events from PRML rules are captured by the IM in the ASHDM Adaptation Model, in HyperDE they are captured by the control layer. When a user triggers an event (clicking on an anchor), the control layer is activated. Usually, this event represents the selection of an anchor that points to an access structure (index) or to an element in a navigational context. If rules are associated to the selected index or context element, they are executed. Then the control layer triggers events at the model layer (which is built over SHDM primitives) passing the parameters needed to instantiate the models, i.e., which metaclass will be instantiated and with which values. If the metaclass has associated rules, they will be executed (conditional instantiation) and the result is the adapted application navigation model. Next, the control layer activates (selects) the view to render the application. This selection may be conditional and the CSS code associated to the view may change if existing associated rules alter them. The adapted page is then presented to the user.

We exemplify this process by considering a metaclass Publication with three attributes (abstract, short_abstract and extended_abstract) and one rule (Rule1) associated with abstract. When the user clicks on an anchor pointing to a specific publication, the control layer is activated and triggers the model layer passing the instance of Publication that was selected. Rule1 is executed and the value of abstract will be the content of short_abstract or of extended_abstract according to user's expertise. The Domain Specific Languages (DSL) used looks like:

```
Classes:
 Publication:
  attrs:
   abstract:
    rule1:
     hook: pre
     value: if AdaptationContext.current.user.expertise == "novice"
       attr_name = "short_abstract"
     else
       attr_name = "extended_abstract"
     end
```

Notice that this rule actually changes the abstract attribute definition, turning it into a façade for the other two attributes, short_abstract and extended_ abstract. The pre hook specification indicates that the adaptation rule is evaluated before accessing the attribute. Alternatively, a post hook would change the attribute *value* to be the desired one depending on the user's expertise.

4 Conclusions

This paper presents a proposal of a general architecture for adaptation and meta-adaptation in hypermedia systems. Being completely driven by models and ontologies, this architecture allows handling data and model in the same way thus facilitating meta-adaptation. The concern of a UM as a component of a general ACM is also discussed and a structure for a modular UM is presented.

5 Future Work

The mechanisms used to integrate domains through NM should be elaborated. The HyperDE should be extended to adapt the Interface Model as proposed by ASHDM. There is also the need to implement a complete case study in order to evaluate the results obtained with the several adaptation and meta-adaptation techniques available.

Acknowledgement. Daniel Schwabe was partially supported by a grant from CNPq.

References

1. Assis, P.S. and Schwabe, D. "A General Meta-Model for Adaptive Hypermedia Systems" In.Third International Conference, AH 2004, the Netherlands. p.433-436. 2004
2. Assis, P.S., Schwabe, D., Barbosa, S.D.J. "Meta-modelos para Aplicações de Hipermídia Adaptativa e Meta-adaptação". PUC-RioInf.MCC45/04, 2004.
3. Chen, W. and Mizoguchi, R. "Learner Model Ontology and Learner Model Agent". Cognitive Support for Learning - Imagining the Unknown, P. Kommers, Ed., IOS Press, pp.189-200, 2004.
4. De Bra, P., Houben, G.J. Houben and Wu, H. "AHAM: A Dexter-based Reference Model for Adaptive Hypermedia". In: Proceedings of the ACM Conference on Hypertext and Hypermedia, Darmstadt, Germany. p. 147-156, 1999.
5. Garrigós I., Gómez J., Barna P., Houben G.J. "A Reusable Personalization Model in Web Application Design". International Workshop on Web Information Systems Modeling (WISM 2005) (Held in conjunction with ICWE 2005). Sydney, Australia. 2005
6. Heckmann, D., Schwartz, T., Brandherm, B., Schmitz, M. and von Wilamowitz-Moellendorff, M. "GUMO - The General User Model Ontology", in Proceedings of UM 2005: International Conference on User Modeling, Edinburgh, UK, 2005. www.gumo.org
7. IMS Learner Information Packaging Best Practice & Implementation Guide. Final Specification, V. 1.0, 2001. Available at http://www.imsglobal.org/profiles/lipbest01.html.
8. Kay, J, Kummerfeld, R. J. and Lauder, P. "Personis: a server for user models", De Bra, P, P Brusilovsky, R Conejo (eds), Proceedings of AH'2002, Adaptive Hypertext 2002, Springer, 203 – 212, 2002.
9. Kuruc, J. "Sharing a User Model between Several Adaptive Hypermedia Applications", IIT SRC, 2005. Available at: http://www.fiit.stuba.sk/iit-src/38-kuruc.pdf.
10. Moura, S. S. "Desenvolvimento de interfaces governadas por ontologia para aplicações hipermídia", Dissertação de Mestrado, PUC-Rio, 2004.
11. Nunes, D.A. "HyperDE - um Framework e Ambiente de Desenvolvimento dirigido por Ontologias para Aplicações Hipermídia". MSc.Dissertation, PUC-Rio, 2005. HyperDE is available at http://server2.tecweb.inf.puc-rio.br:8000/projects/hyperde/trac.cgi/wiki
12. Rossi, G., Schwabe, D. and Lyardet, F; "Web application models are more than conceptual models", Lecture Notes in Computer Science 1727, pp. 239-252. Proceedings of the World Wide Web and Conceptual Modeling'99 Workshop, ER'99 Conference, Paris, 1999.
13. Szundy, G., "Especificação e Implementação de Aplicações Governadas por Ontologias na Web Semântica". Dissertação de Mestrado, Departamento de Informática, PUC-Rio, 2004 (in Portuguese).

Visualizing Personal Relations in Online Communities

Andrew Webster and Julita Vassileva

Computer Science Department, University of Saskatchewan, Canada
asw292@mail.usask.ca, jiv@cs.usask.ca.

Abstract. A hard challenge facing developers of online communities is attaining a critical mass of members and subsequently sustaining their participation. We propose a new mechanism for motivating participation in interest-based online communities, which engages non-contributing members (lurkers) by modeling and visualizing the asymmetrical relations formed when reading, evaluating, or commenting other community members' contributions. The mechanism is based on ideas from open user modeling, a new concept of "community energy," with a mechanism of rating contributions and visualizing the rank of contributions in the community interface.

1 Introduction

An online community is a virtual social space where people can meet and interact [1]. The purposes of such interactions are diverse and may include exchanging information or social support [2], fostering social ties [3], supporting learning [4], extending real-world relationships/communities [5], or a combination of these. The crux of building successful online communities is on managing to entangle people together around a common purpose that is usually reflected in the developer's agenda.

It is a well-known dilemma that a certain amount of interaction/contribution must occur in an online community before members start perceiving the benefits of the system and become active participants themselves. This problem is especially acute and frustrating for developers who must reconcile that the majority of their membership (45-90%) never participates [6] within systems understood to be gift economies [7;8]. In a gift economy, information is exchanged for the benefit of the whole community with the generalized understanding that the contributing individuals will receive some benefit from others later on. Hidden, non-participating members (lurkers) do not reciprocate the benefits they have received and have been generally seen as destructive to the health of online communities [8]. However, more recent research [9;10] has shown that this is not the case. Lurkers were interviewed [9] and reported feeling a sense of belonging to the community even though they had lower satisfaction with the community than participating members. The interviewed participating members viewed lurkers as legitimate members of the community (akin to the importance of having an audience in theater performances). It was suggested that "lurking should be recognized as a bona fide activity and supported more effectively" [9] (p 216).

However, in the early stages of a developing an online community, participation is needed and motivating lurkers (and the membership at large) to become active

V. Wade, H. Ashman, and B. Smyth (Eds.): AH 2006, LNCS 4018, pp. 223 – 233, 2006.

contributors is crucial. We propose a mechanism to motivate participation through making explicit and visible the process of developing networks of interpersonal relationships among the community members (both active participants and lurkers) aiming to "weave" in lurkers with participant members. The resulting visualizations of relationships should be applicable in a wide range of online communities.

2 Related Research

The question of what motivates or triggers individuals to join and participate in online communities and how to design the technical features of the community software accordingly rests on the particular rationale from a wide range of perspectives. Preece et al. [11] identifies research in social psychology, sociology, communication studies, computer-supported cooperative work (CSCW) and human-computer interaction as main areas which can help inform designers about how and why people interact in online communities. Consequently, there are many guiding directions on which interactions to support and how to support them. The variety of online communities with their own specific sets of interactions (e.g. a mailing list for cancer-sufferers vs. an interactive, educational website for teens) and specific purposes makes it very hard to choose appropriate guidelines for interaction design.

An area dealing with social issues in interaction design is CSCW and its application of theories from social psychology to the problems of group work [12]. Collective effort, social identity, and social categorization [13] are all theories which have provided direction in the design and evaluation of technical features to support the work of groups [14]. These theories have also been used in the design and study of online communities [15;16]. For example, earlier research from our lab [17] suggested awarding or revoking social status based on contribution levels would motivate higher levels of contribution because people would be motivated by social comparison (i.e. their status in the community) and would fear losing their current standing within the community if they did not continue participating.

However, there is no unified theory in social psychology and most theories are "mid-level," i.e. only the behaviour of individuals within groups is explained. Also, online groups have only recently received attention from social psychologists, and it is not completely clear what similarities and differences exist between face-to-face and online groups [13]. Finally, the CSCW agenda is one of supporting groups that primarily exist to achieve specific work-related goals (typically relatively short term, requiring close collaboration by the group members). Therefore, not all online communities can take straightforward advantage of these fields of knowledge, especially those that are interest-driven rather than goal-driven. For example, in investigating whether the theory of collective effort could potentially aid in increasing participation (the number of movie ratings) in the interest-based MovieLens community, Beenen et al. [7] did observe increase in the number of contributed ratings but failed to attribute it directly to the implementation of the theory. The authors offer several reasons for this including "a deeper mismatch of goals and values of HCI and CSCW research with those of social psychology" (p 220).

We suggest that the failure to apply the theory may also be due to the tendency to link non-participation with free-riding. This is a connection which is hard to avoid within a collaborative work context where individuals must work on their tasks to be of value to the group or community. Therefore, from the perspective of CSCW, non-participants are treated as a problem to be fixed. However, in a community where people share common interest but not a task or goal, lurking is acceptable.

It is often difficult for new members to join a new or preexisting community. It takes time to uncover the structure, norms, and history of the community before making one's presence known. It would be useful to present the rudimentary relationship that lurkers form with others, even when they are simply reading or browsing information. Our hypothesis is that by making the structure of these relations explicit new communities will develop quicker by rapidly integrating newcomers, increasing the probability that they will become active contributors rather than remaining on the sidelines as lurkers. In the next section we describe a mechanism for modeling such relations.

3 Mechanism: Energy and Relations

We place value on the *act* of contributing in online communities and not just necessarily on *what* is contributed: information valuable today may be worthless tomorrow. It is important to have people who are invested in each other enough to share information, exchange support, etc.

3.1 Energy: The Building Block

First, we introduce the concept of *energy* in an online community which is a measure of the current level of contributions in the community. When an item (e.g. discussion post, movie review, blog entry, etc.) is contributed, it brings in a default number of new *energy units* into the system. For example, a new post in a discussion thread may produce 5 units.

Only a certain number of energy units are allowed to stay attached to the new contribution (e.g. by default a post may keep 3 of the 5 units). The number of these units determines the contribution's *visibility* in the community. Different levels of visibility are achieved through the scaled use of colour and font size. If a contribution possesses many units, then it will be rendered with hot colours (e.g. orange, yellow) and large fonts, advancing towards the viewer. Conversely, if an item has few or no units, then it will be rendered with cold colours (e.g. blue, purple), and small fonts, receding from the viewer (see Fig. 1).

Units kept by an item are considered to be in the *@work state* (i.e. the energy units work to make the item more visible) while units not kept are considered to be in the *stored state* (i.e. units available to be put into the @work state). Energy units can freely move between the stored and @work states; this movement is mainly dependent on the actions of the community's members. If a member positively evaluates an item (and stored energy is available) then she may decide to "heat it up" by moving a stored energy unit into that item (equivalent to rating the contribution). As a result, the item becomes a little more visible to all other members. Conversely, other members may negatively evaluate the same item and "cool it down" by moving energy units back into storage, one at a time. There are 4 simple rules governing how energy may be distributed:

1. A member cannot add or remove energy from items she has contributed
2. A member can only heat up and cool down an item once
3. Items can only be heated up if stored energy is available
4. There is a set upper limit on the number of energy units an item may hold

Community members should not be able to add energy to their own contributions as their judgment is biased (rule 1). It should not be possible for one member to have too much influence over the visibility of a particular contribution, i.e. each member has one vote per item (rule 2). Energy can be added to contributions only if there is stored energy in the community, i.e. the community must manage the shared, limited resource of what is and is not visible at any point in time (rule 3).

The concept of community energy provides a novel metaphor and system for rating content with a number of advantages:

- Energy is finite and depends on the number of contributions to the community, keeping the ratings always in proportion with the contributions (i.e. prevents inflation in the ratings).
- Using community energy units for evaluation encourages the user to reflect on the usefulness of the item to the community and not just to herself (i.e. "I want others to notice this item" or "I want others to ignore this item").
- Evaluation is cognitively less demanding than determining if an item deserves 1, 2, 3, 4, or 5 stars, for instance.
- Emphasis is placed on the act of contributing (i.e. each contribution brings in new energy—a useful resource to the community).

In combination, these features allow members to easily determine where activity in the community is occurring and what particular activities are relevant to the whole

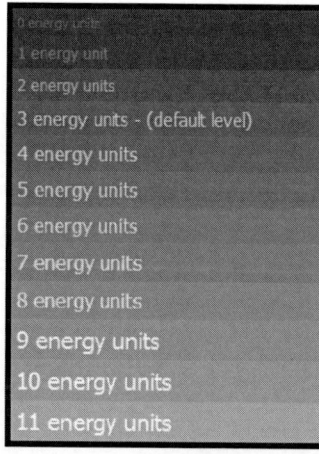

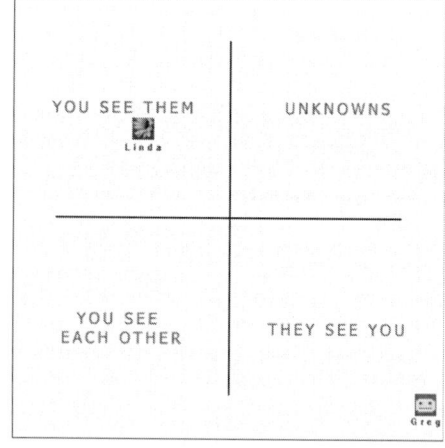

Fig. 1. The visual appearance of contributions at different levels of energy

Fig. 2. Example relation visualization (Relavis) from Ralph's viewpoint

membership (see Fig. 4). This should be of particular benefit to new members who are trying to decide what the community presently values in order to best introduce their contributions, opinions, values, etc.

3.2 Modeling Interpersonal Relations

Modeling and visualization for interpersonal relations aims at three goals: 1) connect lurkers and contributors, 2) give the viewer opportunity for reflection which can be beneficial, as suggested by open user modeling approaches [18], 3) influence the viewer to modify her behaviour in a desired way (to participate more). The visualization should also be dynamic to reflect that individual actions constantly modify relationships and in this way confirm and reward the user's actions.

The most common relationship found in online communities is the weakest (making it difficult to capture): the lurker-contributor relationship. The importance of weak ties has long been recognized [19] so defining a tenable connection between lurkers and contributors is a desirable feature of the visualization but also a challenge.

A relationship between two members A and B always has two sides: from A$\rightarrow$B and from B$\rightarrow$A, which are not necessarily symmetrical. We define the notion of *member visibility* to capture the inherent asymmetry in interpersonal relationships. The *member visibility* has a value ranging from 1 (invisible / unknown / opaque) to 0 (completely visible / transparent). For example, when a new member enters the community, she does not know or "see" any other member. Thus, from this member's perspective, visibility values of 1 are assigned to all other members, i.e. her relationships with all other members of the community have value 1. Conversely, as she is a new member, all other community members will assign a value of 1 to their relationships with this new member.

The visibility value at one end of the relation pair is dependent on actions performed by the member on the other end (see Section 3.4). For example, if a lurker reads several messages in a discussion forum, then the authors of these messages will become slightly more visible to the lurker (i.e. the value of the lurker's relationships with the authors of the posts will decrease), yet the lurker's visibility for the other members still remains unaffected (i.e. their relationships with the lurker will still have value 1).

3.3 Relation Visualization (Relavis)

The relation between two individual members can be visualized in a two-dimensional space which we call a Relaviz (Fig. 2). The horizontal axis (0 to 1) indicates the visibility of other members to the visualization's viewer (in this example, Ralph) while the vertical axis (0 to 1) indicates the visibility of the viewer to the other members. For example, in Fig. 2, the position of Linda's avatar icon (~0.3, ~0.7) describes the relation between Linda and Ralph.

To assist reading, the space is characterized by four relation quadrants: "you see them," "unknown," "you see each other," and "they see you." Insignificant relations (i.e. unknowns) are located in the top-right corner with coordinates (1, 1) while more significant relations (i.e. mutual awareness) are located in the bottom-left corner with coordinates (0, 0).

Let us return to the scenario where a lurker reads posts in a discussion forum. Let Ralph be an active contributor, checking his Relaviz once in a while to see how things stand. This time he notices "Greg" in the "they see you" quadrant (who did not appear the last time Ralph checked). Ralph can guess that Greg has read and rated positively most, if not all, of Ralph's contributions since the relation is so strongly asymmetric. Depending on the size of the community, Ralph may guess that Greg is new in the community or a chronic lurker who has recently discovered Ralph's contributions. This discovery gives an opportunity for Ralph, who has already received some benefit (i.e. Greg adding energy units to Ralph's contributions), to directly communicate with Greg, to search for Greg's contributions and perhaps evaluate them.

If Greg looks at his Relaviz, logically, he will see Ralph appear in the "you see them" quadrant. The important consideration is that both members now have some awareness of each other and can take actions to further define the relation. In order to encourage the use of the Relavis, whenever possible, a light-weight version is displayed alongside the contribution to give specific relation information (see Fig. 3).

3.4 Calculating Visibility Values

The calculation of visibility values is largely dependent on the features of the online community. Actions which are deemed to affect the visibility between members are assigned constant values which will either increase or decrease the overall visibility value (recall it ranges from 0, visible, to 1, invisible). In our implementation, accessing discussion thread subtracts a little (-0.005) from the opaqueness of each reader-author relationship regardless whether the reader actually looks at every post. Explicit actions that indicate preference (e.g. "heating" (-0.05) or "cooling" (+0.05) posts) have the most impact on visibility. For example, if a member comments on another's post (-0.08) and then cools down that post, the resulting decreased visibility is much greater (+0.15) had there been no comment. Also, energy units come into play to provide bonuses: "hot" items have stronger effect on changing visibility than "colder" ones.

The determination of these constants is an open question. Some initial intuition is required to say certain actions affect visibility between two community members more than others. The analysis of the results the evaluation (described in the next section) should provide direction into how these values should be best determined.

4 The Study: Comtella Discussions

Comtella Discussions (CD) is an online community for discussing the social, ethical, legal and managerial issues associated with information technology and biotechnology, available online at http://fire.usask.ca. The primary aim is to share and circulate information related to these topics through a discussion forum. Access to content is restricted to registered members, but anyone may create an account after consenting to the conditions of the study. A nickname (alias), e-mail address, and password are all that are required to create an account, so members are free to be relatively anonymous and create multiple identities, if they desire.

4.1 Participant Groups

CD is being used by students in two university courses at the University of Saskatchewan: Computer Science 408 and Philosophy 236, from January to April 2006. Both courses study the ethics of technology except the former emphasizes information technology while the latter emphasizes ethical theory and biotechnology.

Table 1. Subject groups in Comtella Discussions

Identifier	N	Description
Cα	10	Core members (computer science students required to participate) with test interface
Cβ	9	Core members who see a control (standard discussion forum) interface
Pα	15	Peripheral members (philosophy students and others not required to participate) with test interface
Pβ	17	Peripheral members who see a control interface

The computer science students, as part of their coursework, are required to submit five posts to the forum every week. Thus, they represent the core membership of the community. Conversely, philosophy students are not required to participate and are peripheral members: their instructor just recommended CD as an additional class resource. We denote the core members with C and peripheral members with P. Next, we divide the users (by the order in which accounts are created) into two orthogonal subgroups: a test group who receive the new (hot-cold) interface and Relaviz visualizations (α) and a control group who receive a standard discussion forum interface with no relation visualization (β). A summary of the groups is shown in Table 1. All groups use the same concept of community energy to evaluate postings, but the representation of the act of rating is different between groups (see Fig. 3). The model of relations for each participant computes visibility values towards the other participants as described in section 3.4; however, only the α-group participants receive visualizations displaying their relations. To the β-group participants, CD has the appearance and functionality typical of online discussion forums.

Fig. 3. A post header as seen by an α-group participant (left) and β-group participant (right)

4.2 Hypothesis

The hypothesis is that the subgroups using the α-interface, i.e. the test-subgroup, in both the core and peripheral user groups will show higher participation, will have less lurkers (or the number of non-actively participating members of the Pα group will be less than the corresponding number in the Pβ group) and will show increased satisfaction with the community. In order for the hypothesis to hold, participation rates p of each group should be ranked in the following order:

$$p(C\alpha) > p(C\beta) > p(P\alpha) > p(P\beta). \tag{1}$$

As a consequence, if the hypothesis holds, we expect the average interaction levels (and, of course, the corresponding mutual visibility values) between pairs of members of the four groups will be partially ordered so that the mutual visibility of members of the α-subgroup in both the core and the peripheral group is highest. Also we expect that the members of the β-subgroups will be more visible for the members of the α-subgroups than the reverse in both the core and peripheral groups. The lowest visibility and interaction levels will be between members of the β-subgroups in each of the core and peripheral groups.

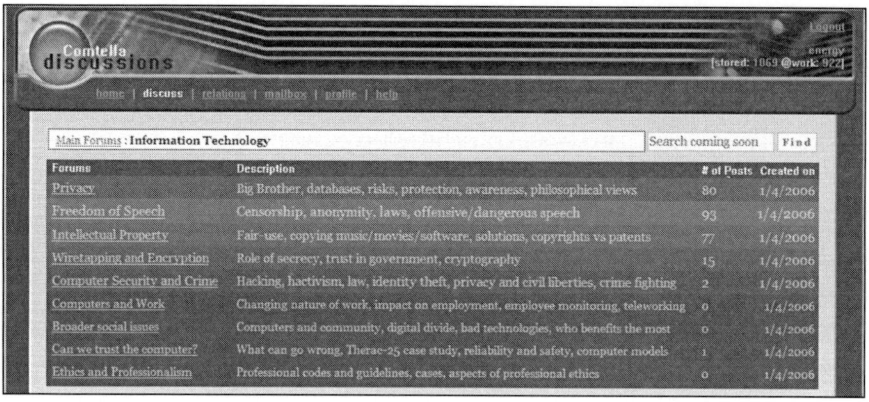

Fig. 4. The distribution of energy units when displaying forums in the α interface

5 Results

As shown in Table 2, for most participation metrics, the expected order (1) between the groups holds. However, the only observed significance was that Pα subjects logged into the system more than Pβ subjects did (p < 0.02).

Table 2. Subject Group Participation Data

Group	Contribution Counts				Average Access / Views		
	Threads	Posts	Comments	Evaluations	Logins	Threads	Relavis
Cα	72	326	17	55	66.3	233.6	4
Cβ	60	299	5	11	48.6	180.2	n/a
Pα	6	10	0	6	15.9	28.1	1.1
Pβ	1	6	1	4	7.9	19.2	n/a

Table 3 shows the relative ordering of average visibility of the participants from each subgroup. For an idea of the level of interaction these average visibility values capture, consider if all incoming relations to a particular participant averaged a visibility value of 0.75, then this participant can expect that *each* user connected with an incoming relation to her has viewed at least one of her posts approximately 50 times (ignoring other actions such as heating and cooling).

The results generally confirm our expectations. In particular, the Pα subjects interacted with the core group C more than Pβ subjects did ($p < 0.01$) which was our basic objective. Within the core group, the members of the α-subgroup engaged in more symmetrical relationships. Eight (8) relations of mutual recognition (i.e. 'you see each other') were made within the Cα group, compared to 3 such relations formed within the Cβ group. The interactions and visibility among the members of the peripheral group however do not confirm our predictions. Even though the differences are very small, the relationships of the Pβ group members among themselves and with members of the Pα group show that these users engaged in more interactions than the users of the Pα group.   We still need to do more thorough analysis and interpretation of the results. We are currently administrating a questionnaire which will help qualify the subjects' attitudes towards the visualizations.   Specifically, we are trying to determine if members changed their behavior in any significant way as a result of considering the visualization. A larger study, with more similar core and peripheral group will be done in the future.

Table 3. Interaction between Subject Groups

Grouping	Interaction (from → to)	Number of relations	Avg. Visibility
Core-to-Core	Cα → Cα	89	0.5988
	Cα → Cβ	90	0.5763
	Cβ → Cα	88	0.6125
	Cβ → Cβ	72	0.6573
Core-to-Periphery	Cα → Pα	11	0.9784
	Cα → Pβ	7	0.9860
	Cβ → Pα	11	0.9894
	Cβ → Pβ	3	0.9820
Periphery-to-Core	Pα → Cα	82	0.9624
	Pα → Cβ	87	0.9674
	Pβ → Cα	70	0.9711
	Pβ → Cβ	79	0.9742
Periphery-to-Periphery	Pα → Pα	42	**0.9713**
	Pα → Pβ	28	**0.9678**
	Pβ → Pα	40	**0.9688**
	Pβ → Pβ	33	**0.9667**

6 Summary

We propose a new mechanism for motivating participation in interest-based online communities which engages lurkers through modeling and visualizing the relations they build with other community members through reading, evaluating, commenting or replying to their contributions. The mechanism is based on ideas from open user modeling, a concept of community energy, and a new mechanism of rating contributions and visualizing the rank of contributions in the community interface. The results indicate that the new approach can draw increased participation for both active and non-active members.

References

[1] J. Preece, "Sociability and usability in online communities: determining and measuring success," *Behaviour & Information Technology*, vol. 20, no. 5, pp. 347-356, Sept.2001.

[2] D. Maloney-Krichmar and J. Preece, "A multilevel analysis of sociability, usability, and community dynamics in an online health community," *ACM Trans. Comput. -Hum. Interact.*, vol. 12, no. 2, pp. 201-232, 2005.

[3] D. Michele Boyd, "Friendster and publicly articulated social networking," in *CHI '04 extended abstracts on human factors in computing systems* Vienna, Austria: ACM Press, 2004, pp. 1279-1282.

[4] C. M. Johnson, "A survey of current research on online communities of practice," *The Internet and Higher Education*, vol. 4, no. 1, pp. 45-60, 2001.

[5] B. Wellman, J. Salaff, D. Dimitrova, L. Garton, M. Gulia, and C. Haythornthwaite, "Computer networks as social networks: Collaborative work, telework, and virtual community," *Annual Review of Sociology*, vol. 22, pp. 213-238, 1996.

[6] B. Nonnecke and J. Preece, "Lurker demographics: counting the silent," in *CHI 2000 Conference Proceedings. Conference on Human Factors in Computing Systems. CHI 2000. The Future is Here* The Hague, Netherlands: ACM, 2000, pp. 73-80.

[7] H. Rheingold, *The Virtual Community: Homesteading on the Electronic Frontier.* Reading, Mass.: Addison-Wesley Pub. Co., 1993.

[8] M. Smith and P. Kollock, *Communities in Cyberspace.* London: Routledge, 1999.

[9] J. Preece, B. Nonnecke, and D. Andrews, "The top five reasons for lurking: improving community experiences for everyone," *Computers in Human Behavior*, vol. 20, no. 2, pp. 201-223, Mar.2004.

[10] M. Takahashi, M. Fujimoto, and N. Yamasaki, "The active lurker: influence of an in-house online community on its outside environment," in *Proceedings of the 2003 international ACM SIGGROUP conference on Supporting group work* Sanibel Island, Florida, USA: ACM Press, 2003, pp. 1-10.

[11] J. Preece and D. Maloney-Krichmar, *Online communities: focusing on sociability and usability* Lawrence Erlbaum Associates, Inc., 2003, pp. 596-620.

[12] J. Grudin, "Groupware and social dynamics: eight challenges for developers," *Communications of the Acm*, vol. 37, no. 1, pp. 92-105, Jan.1994.

[13] *Blackwell Handbook of Social Psychology: Group Processes.* Malden, Massachusetts: Blackwell Publishers, 2001.

[14] R. E. Kraut, "Applying Social Psychology Theory to the Problems of Group Work," in *HCI Models, Theories and Frameworks: Toward a Multidisciplinary Science.* J. M. Carrol, Ed. New York: Morgan Kaufmann, 2003, pp. 325-356.

[15] G. Beenen, K. Ling, X. Wang, K. Chang, D. Frankowski, P. Resnick, and R. E. Kraut, "Using social psychology to motivate contributions to online communities," in *Proceedings of the 2004 ACM conference on computer supported cooperative work* Chicago, Illinois, USA: ACM Press, 2004, pp. 212-221.

[16] U. M. Dholakia, R. P. Bagozzi, and L. K. Pearo, "A social influence model of consumer participation in network- and small-group-based virtual communities," *International Journal of Research in Marketing*, vol. 21, no. 3, pp. 241-263, Sept.2004.

[17] R. Cheng and J. Vassileva, "Adaptive Incentive Mechanism for Sustainable Online Community," IOS Press, 2005, pp. 152-159.

[18] S. Bull, P. Brna, and V. Dimitrova, "LeMoRe http://www.eee.bham.ac.uk/bull/lemore/," 2006.

[19] M. Granovetter, "The Strength of Weak Ties," *Current Contents/Social & Behavioral Sciences*, no. 49, p. 24, Dec.1986.

A Comparative Study of Compound Critique Generation in Conversational Recommender Systems

Jiyong Zhang and Pearl Pu

Human Computer Interaction Group,
Ecole Polytechnique Fédérale de Lausanne (EPFL),
CH-1015, Switzerland
{jiyong.zhang, pearl.pu}@epfl.ch

Abstract. Critiquing techniques provide an easy way for users to feedback their preferences over one or several attributes of the products in a conversational recommender system. While unit critiques only allow users to critique one attribute of the products each time, a well-generated set of compound critiques enables users to input their preferences on several attributes at the same time, and can potentially shorten the interaction cycles in finding the target products. As a result, the dynamic generation of compound critiques is a critical issue for designing the critique-based conversational recommender systems. In earlier research the Apriori algorithm has been adopted to generate compound critiques from the given data set. In this paper we propose an alternative approach for generating compound critiques based on the multi-attribute utility theory (MAUT). Our approach automatically updates the weights of the product attributes as the result of the interactive critiquing process. This modification of weights is then used to determine the compound critiques according to those products with the highest utility values. Our experiments show that the compound critiques generated by this approach are more efficient in helping users find their target products than those generated by the Apriori algorithm.

Keywords: conversational recommender system, critiquing, compound critique, multi-attribute utility theory, interaction cycle.

1 Introduction

Critiquing techniques have proven to be a popular and successful approach in conversational recommender systems because it can help users express their preferences and feedbacks easily over one or several aspects of the available product space[1][2][3][4]. The simplest form of critiquing is unit critiquing which allows users to give feedback on a single attribute or feature of the products at a time[1]. For example, *[CPU Speed: faster]* is a unit critique over the *CPU Speed* attribute of the PC products. If a user wants to express preferences on two or more attributes, multiple interaction cycles between the user and the system

V. Wade, H. Ashman, and B. Smyth (Eds.): AH 2006, LNCS 4018, pp. 234–243, 2006.

are required. To make the critiquing process more efficient, a wise treatment is to generate compound critiques dynamically to enable users to critique on several attributes in one interaction cycle[2][3]. Typically, for each interaction cycle there are a large number of compound critiques available. However, the system is able to show only a few of them on the user interface. Thus a critical issue for recommender systems based on compound critiques is to dynamically generate a list of high quality compound critiques in each interaction cycle to save the users' interaction effort.

McCarthy et al.[5] have proposed a method of discovering the compound critiques through the Apriori algorithm used in the *market-basket analysis* method [6]. It treats each critique pattern as the shopping basket for a single customer, and the compound critiques are the popular shopping combinations that the consumers would like to purchase together. Based on this idea, Reilly et al.[2] have developed an approach called dynamic critiquing to generate compound critiques. As an improved version, the incremental critiquing[3] approach has also been proposed to determine the new reference product based on the user's critique history. A typical interaction process of both dynamic critiquing and incremental critiquing approach is as follows. First the system shows a reference product to the user. At the same time the system generates hundreds of compound critiques from the data set via the Apriori algorithm, and then determines several of them according to their support values for the user to critique. After the user's critique is chosen, the system then determines a new reference product and updates the list of critiques for the user to select in the next interaction cycle. This process continues until the target product is found.

The Apriori algorithm is efficient in discovering compound critiques from a given data set. However, selecting compound critiques by their support values may lead to some problems. The critiques determined by the support values can only reveal "what the system would provide," but cannot predict "what the user likes." For example, in a PC data domain if 90 percent of the products have a faster CPU and larger memory than the current reference product, it is unknown whether the current user may like a PC with a faster CPU and larger memory. Even though the system based on the incremental critiquing approach maintains a user preference model to determine which product to be shown in the next interaction cycle, some good compound critiques may still be filtered out before the user could choose because their support values do not satisfy the requirement. If the users find that the compound critiques cannot help them find better products within several interaction cycles, they would be frustrated and give up the interaction process. As a result, a better approach for generating compound critiques should allow the users to gradually approach the products they preferred and to find the target products with less number of interaction cycles.

In this paper we argue that determining the compound critiques based on the user's preference model would be more efficient in helping users find their target products. We propose a new approach to generate compound critiques for conversational recommender systems with a preference model based on multi-attribute utility theory(MAUT)[7]. In each interaction cycle our approach first determines a list of products via the user's preference model, and then generates compound critiques by comparing them with the current reference product. In our approach, the user's preference model is maintained adaptively based on user's critique actions during the interaction process, and the compound critiques are determined according to the utilities they gain instead of the frequency of their occurrences in the data set. We also carry out a set of simulation experiments to show that the compound critiques generated by our approach can be more efficient than those generated by the Apriori algorithm.

This paper is organized as follows. The related research work is reviewed in section 2. Section 3 describes our approach of generating compound critiques based on MAUT. Section 4 reports a set of simulation experiments to compare the performance of various critique approaches. Discussions and conclusions are given in section 5 and 6 respectively.

2   Related Work

Other than the unit critiquing and compound critiquing approaches that we have mentioned, a number of various critiquing approaches based on examples also have been proposed in recent years. The ATA system [8] uses a constraint solver to obtain a set of optimal solutions and shows five of them to the user (three optimal ones and two extreme solutions). The Apt Decision [9] uses learning techniques to synthesize a user's preference model by critiquing the example apartment features. The SmartClient approach[10] gradually refines the user's preference model by showing a set of 30 possible solutions in different visualizations to assist the user making a travel plan. The main advantage of these example-based critiquing approaches is that users' preferences can be stimulated by some concrete examples and users are allowed to reveal preferences both implicitly (choosing a preferred product from a list) and explicitly (stating preferred values on specific attributes). In fact, these example-based critiquing approaches can also "generate" compound critiques easily by comparing the critique examples with the current recommended product. But they are more viewed as tradeoff navigation because users have to state the attribute values that they are willing to compromise against those that they are hoping to improve[11]. The approach of generating compound critiques that we proposed here can be regarded as an example-based critiquing approach because we determine the compound critiques from a list of critique examples. However, the difference is that our approach concentrates on constructing user's preferences automatically through the choice of the compound critiques, and the user can save some effort in stating the specific preferences values during the interaction process.

Generating *diverse* compound critiques is also an important issue for conservational recommender systems as a number of researchers have pointed out that diversity has the potential to make the interaction more efficient[12][13][14]. For example, in [14] diversity is enhanced by reducing the overlap among those compound critiques generated by the dynamic critiquing approach. In our approach

PM— user's preference model; *ref*— the current reference product;
IS— item set; *CI*— critique items; *CS*— critique strings; *U*— utility value;
β— the weight adaptive factor

//The main procedure	//select the critique items by utilities
1. **procedure** Critique_MAUT ( )	20. **function** GenCritiqueItems (*PM, IS*)
2. *PM* = GetUserInitialPreferences ( )	21. *CI* = {}
3. *ref* = GenInitialItem (*PM*)	22. **for each item** O_i **in** *IS* **do**
4. *IS* ⟵ all available products – *ref*	23. $U(O_i)$ = CalcUtility(*PM*, O_i)
5. **while** not UserAccept (*ref*)	24. **end for**
6. *CI* = GenCritiqueItems (*pm, IS*)	25. IS' = Sort_By_Utility (*IS, U*)
7. *CS* = GenCritiqueStrings (ref, CI)	26. *CI* = Top_K (IS')
8. ShowCritiqueInterface (*CS*)	27. **return** *CI*
9. *id* = UserSelect (*CS*)	
10. *ref'* = CI_{id}	//Update user's preferences model
11. *ref* ⟵ *ref'*	28. **function** UpdateModel(*PM, ref*)
12. *IS* ⟵ *IS* – *CI*	29. **for** each attribute x_i **in** *ref* **do**
13. *PM* = UpdateModel (*PM, ref*)	30. $[pv_i, pw_i]$ ⟵ *PM* on x_i
14. **end while**	31. **if** $(V(x_i) \geq pv_i)$
15. **return**	32. $pw_i' = pw_i \times \beta$
	33. **else**
//user select the critique string	34. $pw_i' = pw_i/\beta$
16. **function** UserSelect (*CS*)	35. **end if**
17. *cs* = the critique string user selects	36. *PM* ⟵ $[V(x_i), pw_i']$
18. *id* = index of *cs* in *CS*	37. **end for**
19. **return** *id*	38. **return** *PM*

Fig. 1. The algorithm of critiquing based on MAUT

the weight of each product attribute is revised adaptively during the critiquing process, thus we believe that there is a certain degree of diversity between the compound critiques determined by our approach. The detail investigation of generating diverse compound critiques will be left in our future work.

3   Generating Compound Critiques Based on MAUT

MAUT[7] is a well known and powerful method in decision theory for ranking a list of multi-attribute products according to their utilities. Here we only use its simplified weighted additive form to calculate the utility of a product $O = \langle x_1, x_2, ..., x_n \rangle$ as follows:

$$U(\langle x_1, \cdots, x_n \rangle) = \sum_{i=1}^{n} w_i V_i(x_i) \qquad (1)$$

where n is the number of attributes that the products may have, the weight $w_i(1 \leq i \leq n)$ is the importance of the attribute i, and V_i is a value function of the attribute x_i which can be given according to the domain knowledge during the design time.

The general algorithm of the interaction process with this proposed approach (called Critique_MAUT) is illustrated by Figure 1. We use a preference model which contains the weights and the preferred values for the product attributes to represent the user's preferences. At the beginning of the interaction process, the initial weights are equally set to $1/n$ and the initial preferences are stated by the user. In each interaction cycle, the system generates a set of critique strings for the user to select as follows. Instead of mining the critiques directly from the data set based on the Apriori algorithm, the Critique_MAUT approach first determines top K (in practice we set $K = 5$) products with maximal utilities, and then for each of the top K products, the corresponding critique string is determined by comparing it with the current reference product. This "from case to critique pattern" process of producing compound critique strings is straightforward and has been illustrated in [5].

After the user has selected one of the critique strings, the corresponding critique product is assigned as the new reference product, and the user's preference model is updated based on this critique selection. For each attribute, the attribute value of the new reference product is assigned as the preference value, and the weight of each attribute is adaptively adjusted according to the difference between the old preference value and the new preference value. If the new preference value is equal or better than the old preference value, the current weight on the given attribute is multiplied by a factor β, otherwise it is divided by β (See line 30-36 on Figure 1). In practice we set the factor $\beta = 2.0$. Based on the new reference product and the new user preference model, the system is able to recommend another set of critique strings for the user to critique until the user finds the target product or stops the interaction process.

Figure 2 shows a screen shot of a personal computer recommender system that we have developed based on the proposed approach. In this interface, the user can see the detail of a reference product, and he or she can either conduct a unit critique or a compound critique to reveal additional preferences. It is very similar to the user interface proposed in [3] except that we show 5 different compound critiques generated by our approach in each interaction cycle.

4   Experiments and Results

We carried out a set of simulation experiments to compare the performance of the basic unit critiquing approach (Critique_Unit), the incremental critiquing approach which generates compound critiques with the Apriori algorithm (Critique_Apriori)[3], and our approach generating compound critiques based on MAUT (Critique_MAUT). In the The experiment procedure is similar to the simulation process described in [3] except for two differences. One is that we assume at the beginning the user will reveal several preferences to the system. We observed that an average user states about 3 initial preferences. Thus we randomly determine the number of the initial preferences from 1 to 5. Another difference is that in each interaction process we simply appoint a product as the target product directly instead of the *leave-one-out* strategy. Both the Critique_Apriori

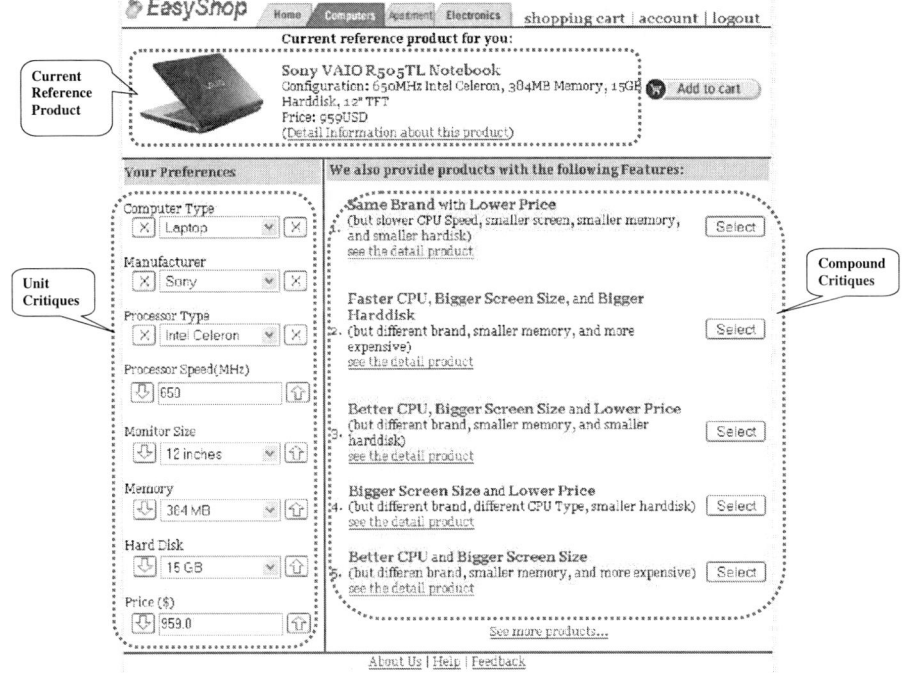

Fig. 2. The user interface with both unit and compound critiques

and the Critique_MAUT approaches generate 5 different compound critiques for user to choose in each interaction cycle. The Critiue_Apriori approach adopts the *lowest support* (LS) strategy with a minimum support threshold of *0.25* to generate compound critiques. In our experiments each product in the data set is appointed as the target choice for 10 times and the number of interaction cycles for finding the target choice are recorded. Two different types of data set are utilized in our experiments. The apartment data set used in [11] contains 50 apartments with 6 attributes: *type, price, size, bathroom, kitchen,* and *distance.* The PC Data set [2] contains 120 PCs with 8 different attributes. This data set is available at *http://www.cs.ucd.ie/staff/lmcginty/PCdataset.zip.*

Figure 3 (1) and (2) show the average interaction cycles of different approaches. Compared to the baseline Critique_Unit approach, the Critique_Apriori approach can reduce the average interaction cycles by 15% (for apartment data set) and 28% (for PC data set) respectively. This validates earlier research that the interaction cycles can be reduced substantially by utilizing compound critiques. Moreover, the results show that the proposed Critique_MAUT approach can reduce the interaction cycles over 20% compared to the Critique_Apriori approach (significant difference, $p < 0.01$).

We define the *accuracy* as the percentage of finding the target product successfully within a certain number of interaction cycles. As shown in Figure 3 (3)

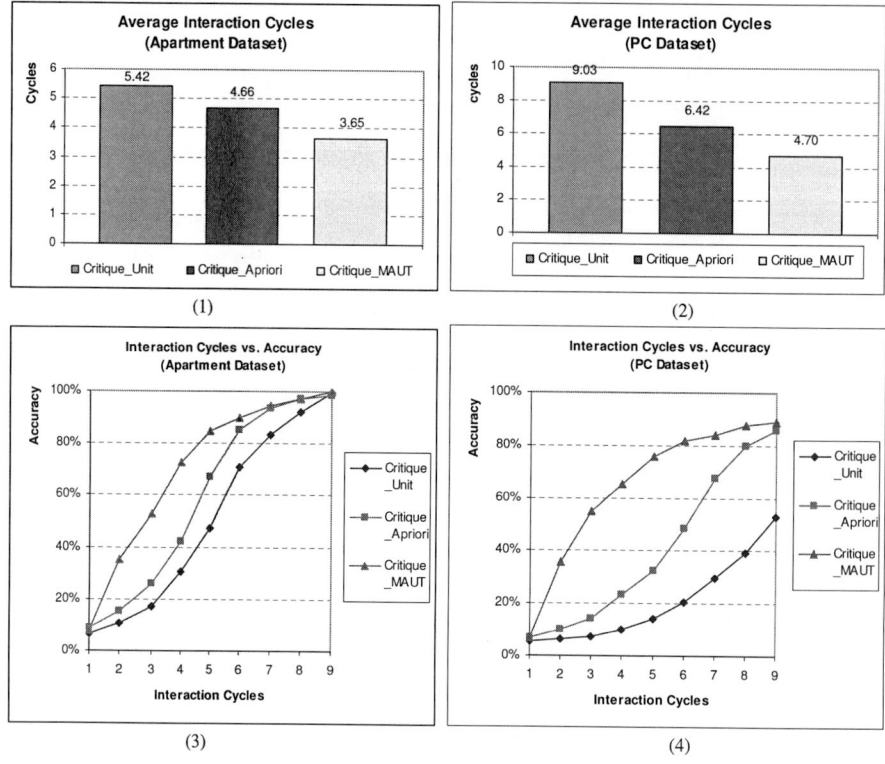

Fig. 3. The results of the simulation experiments with the PC data set and the apartment data set. (1)The average interaction cycles for the apartment data set; (2)The average interaction cycles for the PC data set; (3) the accuracy of finding the target choice within given number of interaction cycles for the apartment data set; (4) the accuracy of finding the target choice within given number of interaction cycles for the PC data set.

and (4), the Critique_MAUT approach has a much higher accuracy than both the Critique_Unit and the Critique_Apriori approach when the number of interaction cycles is small. For example, in the apartment data set, when the user is assumed to make a maximum of 4 interaction cycles, the Critique_MAUT approach enables the user to reach the target product successfully 85% of the time, which is 38% higher than the Critique_Unit approach, and 18% higher than the Critique_Apriori approach.

Compound critiques allow users to specify their preferences on two or more attributes simultaneously thus they are more efficient than unit critiques. When the compound critiques are shown to the user, it is interesting to know how often they are applied during the interaction process. Here we also compared the application frequency of compound critiques generated by MAUT and the

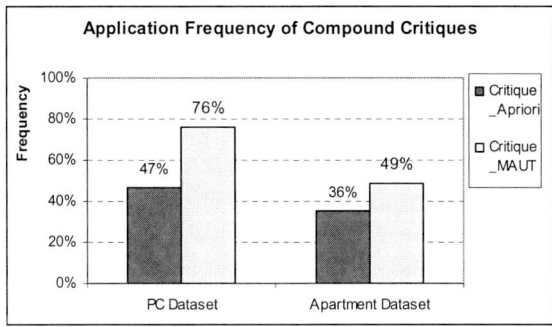

Fig. 4. Application frequency of compound critiques generated by MAUT and the Apriori algorithm

Apriori algorithm in our experiments. As shown in Figure 4, the application frequency of compound critiques generated by the Critique_MAUT method are much higher than those generated by the Critique_Apriori method for both the PC data set (29% higher) and the Apartment Data set (13% higher). We believe this result offers an explanation of why the Critique_MAUT method can achieve fewer interaction cycles than the Critique_Apriori method.

5   Discussions

The key improvement of the proposed Critique_MAUT approach is that the compound critiques are determined through their utility values given by MAUT instead of their support values given by the Apriori algorithm. Since a utility value measures the product's attractiveness according to a user's stated preferences, our approach has the potential to help the user find the target choice in an earlier stage. The simulation experiment results verified this advantage of the Critique_MAUT approach by comparing it with the Critique_Unit and the Critique_Apriori approaches.

Modeling user's preferences based on MAUT is not a new idea. In fact, MAUT approach can enable users to make tradeoff among different attributes of the product space. For example, Stolze has proposed the scoring tree method for building interactive e-commerce systems based on MAUT[15]. However, in our approach we designed an automatic manner to gradually update the user's preference model according to the critique actions. The users are not obliged to state their preference value or to adjust the weight value on each attribute explicitly thus the interaction effort can be substantially reduced.

There are several limitations in our current work. The user's preference model is based on the weighted additive form of the MAUT approach, which might lead to some decision errors when the attributes of the products are not mutually preferentially independent.[1] If some attributes are preferentially dependent, our approach is still able to generate the compound critiques. However, the user needs to spend some extra effort to determine the utility function which is more complicated than equation (1). Furthermore, currently the experiments are based on artificial users with simulated interaction processes. We assume that the artificial user has a clear and firm target in mind during the interaction process. In reality this assumption is not always true because the user may change his or her mind during the interaction process. Moreover, our approach determines the compound critiques only based on utility values. Some researchers have pointed out that the approach of combining similarity and diversity may provide better performance[12]. So far we haven't compared the Critique_MAUT approach with the approach based on similarity and diversity. Nevertheless, in this paper the newly proposed Critique_MAUT approach can generate compound critiques which are more efficient in helping users find their target product than those compound critiques based on the Apriori algorithm.

6   Conclusions and Future Work

Generating high quality compound critiques is essential in designing critique-based conversational recommender systems. The main contribution of this paper is that we propose a new approach in generating compound critiques based on the multi-attribute utility theory. Unlike the popular method of generating compound critiques directly by the Apriori algorithm, our approach adaptively maintains the user's preference model based on MAUT during the interaction process, and the compound critiques are determined according to the utility values. Our simulation experiments show that our approach can reduce the number of interaction cycles substantially compared to the unit critiques and the compound critiques generated by the Apriori algorithm. Especially when the user is willing to make only a few interactions with the system, our approach enables the user with a much higher chance in finding the final target product. In the future, we plan to organize a set of real user studies to compare the performance of these critiquing approaches in terms of the actual number of interaction cycles as well as the degree of users' satisfaction. We will also further improve the performance of our approach by integrating a certain degree of diversities into the compound critique generation process.

Acknowledgments

Funding for this research was provided by Swiss National Science Foundation under grant 200020-103490. The authors thank the anonymous reviewers for their helpful comments.

---

[1] The attributes $X_1, \cdots, X_n$ are *mutually preferentially independent* if every subset Y of these attributes is preferentially independent of its complementary set of attributes[7].

References

1. Burke, R.D., Hammond, K.J., Young, B.C.: The FindMe approach to assisted browsing. IEEE Expert **12**(4) (1997) 32–40
2. Reilly, J., McCarthy, K., McGinty, L., Smyth, B.: Dynamic critiquing. In Funk, P., González-Calero, P.A., eds.: Proceedings of the European Conference on Case-Based Reasoning (ECCBR-04). Volume 3155 of Lecture Notes in Computer Science., Springer (2004) 763–777
3. Reilly, J., McCarthy, K., McGinty, L., Smyth, B.: Incremental critiquing. Knowledge Based Systems **18**(4-5) (2005) 143–151
4. Faltings, B., Pu, P., Torrens, M., Viappiani, P.: Designing example-critiquing interaction. In: International Conference on Intelligent User Interfaces, Island of Madeira (Portugal), ACM (2004) 22–29
5. McCarthy, K., Reilly, J., McGinty, L., Smyth, B.: On the dynamic generation of compound critiques in conversational recommender systems. In: Proceedings of the Third International Conference on Adaptive Hypermedia and Adaptive Web-Based Systems(AH 2004). Volume 3137 of LNCS., Springer (2004) 176–184
6. Agrawal, R., Srikant, R.: Fast algorithms for mining association rules. In Bocca, J.B., Jarke, M., Zaniolo, C., eds.: Proceedings of the 20th International Conference Very Large Data Bases(VLDB), Morgan Kaufmann (1994) 487–499
7. Keeney, R., Raiffa, H.: Decisions with Multiple Objectives: Preferences and Value Tradeoffs. John Wiley and Sons, New York (1976)
8. Linden, G., Hanks, S., Lesh, N.: Interactive assessment of user preference models: The automated travel assistant. In: Proceedings of the 6th International Conference on User Modeling (UM97). (1997)
9. Shearin, S., Lieberman, H.: Intelligent profiling by example. In: Proceedings of the Conference on Intelligent User Interfaces, ACM Press New York, NY, USA (2001) 145–151
10. Pu, P., Faltings, B.: Enriching buyers' experiences: the smartclient approach. In: Proceedings of the SIGCHI conference on Human factors in computing systems, ACM Press New York, NY, USA (2000) 289–296
11. Pu, P., Kumar, P.: Evaluating example-based search tools. In: Proceedings of the ACM Conference on Electronic Commerce (EC'04), New York, USA (2004) 208–217
12. Smyth, B., McClave, P.: Similarity vs. diversity. In Aha, D.W., Watson, I., eds.: Proceedings of the 4th International Conference on Case-Based Reasoning (IC-CBR). Volume 2080 of Lecture Notes in Computer Science., Springer (2001) 347–361
13. McGinty, L., Smyth, B.: On the role of diversity in conversational recommender systems. In Ashley, K.D., Bridge, D.G., eds.: Proceedings of the 5th International Conference on Case-Based Reasoning (ICCBR). Volume 2689 of Lecture Notes in Computer Science., Springer (2003) 276–290
14. McCarthy, K., Reilly, J., Smyth, B., McGinty, L.: Generating diverse compound critiques. Artificial Intelligence Review **24**(3-4) (2005) 339–357
15. Stolze, M.: Soft navigation in electronic product catalogs. International Journal on Digital Libraries **3**(1) (2000) 60–66

Adapting Educational Hypermedia to Interaction Behaviors

Alessandro Assis, Michael Danchak, and Linda Polhemus

Rensselaer Polytechnic Institute
Troy, NY, USA, 12180
{assisa, danchm, polhel}@rpi.edu

Abstract. This research investigated learner interaction with presentation, content and navigation adaptivity and its effect on time spent (efficiency) and performance (effectiveness) with three online tutorials. The tutorials were developed using a learning cycle to address the needs of all learners. Adaptivity was gradually introduced according to the learner interaction behavior with the cycle. Results from an analysis of variance (ANOVA) indicate that the amount of time spent was significantly reduced in the third and fully adaptive tutorial with comparable performance.

1 Introduction

Interaction with a learning cycle formatted according to instructional design principles, specifically the OctoPlus™ [1], allows usage data, like time spent over the cycle and navigational sequence, to be collected and filtered, characterizing an individual interaction behavior. Other adaptive educational systems made use of learning cycles, i.e. INSPIRE [2] and EDUCE [3], but no other system proposed adapting the whole cycle organization according to the user interaction behavior. In general, adaptive educational systems give almost no attention to the learning cycle, an important aspect of learning style theory.

2 OctoPlus™

The OctoPlus™ provides the learner with a wide range of possible configurations and representations of content developed in a variety of ways, to create a continuously adaptive learning environment. The OctoPlus™ is composed of 8 instructional events [1], as described in part by McCarthy [4]. For example, the first instructional event is *Connect*. The purpose of this event is to engage students in a meaningful, concrete activity and/or to elicit prior knowledge. Within each instructional event are information blocks, made up of *raw assets* [5, 6]. Multiple information blocks are developed to reach a particular type of learner, the raw asset (or media type) varies, thereby building a hierarchical organization structure for the adaptive system [6].

V. Wade, H. Ashman, and B. Smyth (Eds.): AH 2006, LNCS 4018, pp. 244–248, 2006.

2.1 Sample Design

Figure 1 illustrates a typical OctoPlus™ interface. Clicking on a cycle bubble in the right top corner causes the corresponding instructional event (i.e. *connect*) content to be displayed in the main window. Within this instructional event (IE) an embedded information block, as designated by the instructional designer, is included. Next, two hyperlinks to the information blocks (IB) "Watch" and "You Try" are included. In this case, these two IBs represent the same content, but are presented in different ways. The information block "Read More" is an optional link, whose purpose is to add more content (depth) to this particular IE.

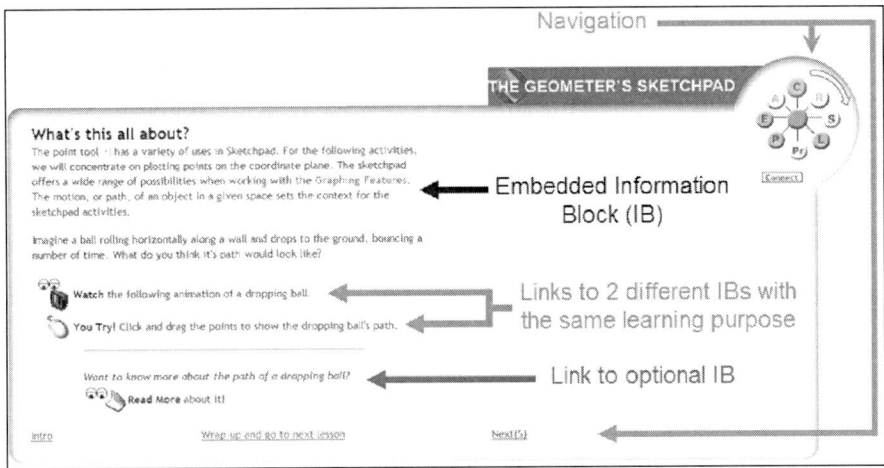

Fig. 1. OctoPlus™ adaptivity features

The OctoPlus™ learning cycle design provides a consistent framework with which to analyze learner interactions through observation and performance. Adaptivity led us to reflect on how we could transform a learning cycle into an interaction cycle, based on individual usage data. We hypothesized that performance could be improved and time spent reduced if learners could be guided somehow to attend to only the instructional events that match an individual interaction behavior, given data from past interactions with the cycle. Assis et al [5, 6] provide some pilot experiments that helped us identify which usage data could be relevant to define an individual interaction style:

- Performance in assessment tests and practical exercises;
- Normalized percentage (%) of time spent in each instructional event;
- Navigational sequence, i.e. order of instructional events visited;
- Information block class accessed. An information block is classified according to multimedia composition and instructional method. Each icon in Fig. 1 (preceding the "**Watch**", "**You Try!**", and "**Read More**" commands) is a link to an information block. A particular information block selected by the learner is considered accessed if its window remains open more than a minimum required amount of time.

3   The Adaptive Experiment

Three tutorials were developed according to the OctoPlus[TM] format, each one teaching a basic tool of The Geometer's Sketchpad[©] (http://www.keypress.com/sketchpad/) software. The sample was composed of 35 students from two different high school mathematics classes. The control group was composed of 18 students, where none of the 3 tutorials offered any kind of adaptivity. The adaptive group included 17 students where the adaptivity grew over time (see table 1).

Table 1. The Adaptive Group

Tutorial 1	Tutorial 2	Tutorial 3
No adaptivity	Adaptive Presentation	Adaptive Presentation + Content + Navigation

3.1 Data Collection

Presentation adaptivity was provided in the second and third tutorials for the adaptive group, using a Naïve Bayes Classifier (NBC) algorithm. Additionally, navigation and content adaptivity were implemented in the third tutorial for the adaptive group. A rule-based approach was implemented considering the following for each IE of the two previous tutorial cycles: 1) let tsl be an individual % time spent normalized by a domain expert % time spent; 2) let tse be the normalized domain expert % time spent.

- *Navigation adaptivity rule:* recommend IE if $tsl \geq 0.5tse$, considering average normalized % time spent in that specific IE during the previous two tutorials. The constant 0.5 was arbitrarily chosen to represent that, in a recommended IE, the individual average normalized % time spent is at least half of the expert's normalized % of time spent. Otherwise, IE is accessible from the OctoPlus[TM] cycle but it is not recommended (the correspondent IE bubble was grayed and faded out).
- *Content adaptivity rule:* Optional IB(s) should be automatically added to the default IE content window if $tsl \geq 1.5tse$, considering average normalized % time spent in that specific IE during the previous two tutorials. The constant 1.5 was chosen to represent that when an individual average normalized % time spent exceeds in more than 50% the expert's normalized % of time spent, it may be the case that individual is really interested in that specific IE. Therefore, system may facilitate interaction by embedding additional content to the default IE content window. Otherwise, optional IB(s) remain(s) available at the bottom of the page as optional link.

4   Experimental Results

The average time spent per instructional event and performance on assessments was compared between groups. Results from an analysis of variance (ANOVA) indicated that the adaptive group spent significantly less time ($\alpha = 0.05$) than the control group in the last and fully adaptive tutorial. No significant differences between time spent were detected in the first or second tutorial.

Performance data for practical exercises and assessment tests was also collected. Practical exercises were given to students during the cycle interaction and consisted of a task in each tutorial to be implemented with the Sketchpad software. Assessment tests were given at the end of a tutorial and consisted of open-ended retention and transfer questions. Overall, both groups scored higher in practical exercises, in other words, the tutorials were successful in teaching students how to use the Sketchpad software.

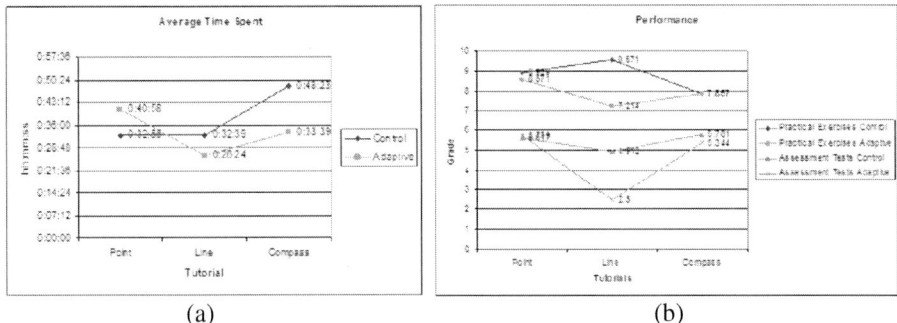

(a)   (b)

Fig. 2. (a) Average time spent (b) Practical exercises and assessment tests performance

For the second tutorial, the adaptive group was given adaptive presentation. Based on ANOVA results, the control group performed significantly better ($\alpha=0.01$) than the adaptive group on practical exercises and assessment tests in the second tutorial. When presentation, content, and navigation adaptivity was presented to the adaptive group for the third tutorial, no significant differences on performance were found. We are investigating if introducing adaptivity right after the very first OctoPlus[TM] cycle is indeed too early or if our problem is somehow related to the choice of the NBC algorithm. In a realistic scenario, adaptivity should only be applied if average learning performance in previous cycles is satisfactory.

Although performance for both groups was statistically comparable in the last tutorial, adaptivity significantly reduced time spent for the adaptive group over the control one. This might indicate that after two OctoPlus[TM] cycles students may be getting used to the model, increasing the chances of adaptivity success. Waiting for two interaction cycles also provides more data for inference engines making adaptivity decisions, increasing the likeliness of a positive outcome.

The sequence by which learners interact with the instruction event may also effect learner perceptions and/or performance. We are investigating how to integrate more advanced inference techniques, such as Markov chains and clustering analysis, into the OctoPlus[TM] adaptivity model. With that, we hope to achieve the goal of not only significantly reducing time spent with adaptivity but also significantly improving performance.

5 Conclusions and Future Work

Significantly reduced time spent for the adaptive group in the third and fully adaptive tutorial with comparable performance to the control group is an encouraging finding. Future work will explore adaptive presentation techniques different from link hiding to explore the shortcomings found in the second tutorial. Additionally, collecting data from at least two cycles before starting adaptivity may eliminate any degradation in student performance.

An analysis of individual interaction styles and experimentation with different inference techniques to better explore data (such as navigational sequence) to see how it can be useful in the adaptivity process is underway. In future work, we plan to integrate different inference techniques merging individual-based and collaborative-based approaches for guiding adaptivity in the OctoPlus^{TM}.

References

1. Polhemus, L., Swan, K., Danchak, M., Assis, A.: A Method for Describing Learner Interaction with Content. Journal of the Research Center for Educational Technology (2005) Available at: http://www.rcetj.org/?type=art&id=3523&sid=208832&iid=328
2. Papanikolaou, K., Grigoriadou, M., Kornilakis, H.: Instructional and Interface Design in an Adaptive Educational Hypermedia System. In: Proceedings of Panhellenic Conference on Human Computers Interaction. Patra, Greece. (2001) 223-228
3. Kelly, D., Tangney, B.: "Adapting to intelligence profile in an adaptive educational system", *Interacting with Computers*, pp. 1-25 (to be published).
4. McCarthy, B.: About Learning. Excel Inc., Barrington IL (1996)
5. Assis, A., Danchak, M., Polhemus, L.: Instructional Design and Interaction Style for Educational Adaptive Hypermedia. In: Proceedings of the Latin American Conference on Human-Computer Interaction. Cuernavaca, Mexico. ACM Press: New York (2005) 289-294
6. Assis, A., Polhemus, L., Danchak, M.: A Content Object Model for Personalizing Online Instruction. In: Presentation Proceedings of the 11th Sloan-C International Conference on Asynchronous Learning Networks. Orlando, FL (2005)

UbiquiTo-S: A Preliminary Step Toward Semantic Adaptive Web Services

Francesca Carmagnola, Federica Cena, Cristina Gena, and Ilaria Torre

Dipartimento di Informatica, Università di Torino, Corso Svizzera 185, Torino, Italy
{carmagnola, cena, cgena, torre}@di.unito.it

Abstract. In this paper we describe an approach to design an adaptive system as a Semantic Web Service. We focus on how adaptive systems can provide adaptive services through web service technologies. In particular, we concentrate on adding semantic information to enrich the service discovery phase. We present a recommender system, UbiquiTO-S, which exploits the technology of Web Services (WS) and Semantic Web to allow software agents to discover its services and use its adaptive services.

1 Introduction and Basic Principles

The past years have shown an enormous increase of efforts in standardization and development of interoperable Web technologies. In particular, with the number and diversity of Web Services (*WSs)* and Semantic *WSs* expected to grow, a recent trend is targeting the vision of offering adequate techniques for user-centric and preference-based services discovery and selection technologies that support personalization [2].

Adaptive techniques may be employed in the process of interaction among *WSs*. As underlined in [3], this issue leads to a number of research questions: How can Semantic *WSs* be used in adaptive environment? How can Adaptive Systems and *WSs* be joined to meet user needs? The most common approach is to add personalisation to the different stages of the process of interaction among *WSs*: discovery, querying, and execution [7,2]. In particular, a service can be searched according to user personal profile, which typically includes her individual preferences together with technical constraints on terminal and environment. A like-minded approach can be found in [3], which furthermore introduces the composition of Semantic *WS* by a domain expert, and the adaptive integration service in response to user needs using ontologies in order to capture and exchange models of the real world and making them available to automated agents.

Our approach moves from the same considerations, but the perspective is different: the focus is on Adaptive Systems that provide adaptive services using Semantic *WS* technologies. A similar approach is led by [6] that developed a mobile tourist application that offers information and services tailored to the context and the user plans. The platform is based on *WS* technologies combined with Semantic Web technologies, it is open and allows third parties to integrate new services and information into the platform. Similarly, in our approach we focus on the adaptation of an application that is designed to work as a Semantic Adaptive *WS*. In particular, in this preliminary

V. Wade, H. Ashman, and B. Smyth (Eds.): AH 2006, LNCS 4018, pp. 249–253, 2006.

work we concentrate on adding semantic information to enrich the service discovery phase. To extend WSDL[1] descriptions with semantic information we use WSSP (Web Service Semantic Profile) since it is specifically designed for the description of service profile and thus for the discovery phase [4,5]. Moreover, to describe ontologies and rules referenced in WSSP we use OWL[2] and RDF-RuleML[3].

In the next section we will present a usage scenario with the description of the corresponding platform to highlight that extending the expressive power of WSDL files is essential to implement a Semantic Adaptive WS. In particular, exploiting ontologies and semantic rules allow to express conditional inputs that are commonly necessary for user modeling and adaptation, in order to explain the reasons why such inputs are required and thus to explain the behaviour of the system. Moreover, semantic is essential to improve interoperability and to allow explanations, proof, user models sharing, etc. In the last part of the paper we will provide an example of a RDF-RuleML adaptation rule linked by a WSSP [4,5] file in UbiquiTO-S, a semantic tourist recommender.

2   Usage Scenario and Platform Description

USAGE SCENARIO
Carlo is a business traveler. He arrives in Torino and looks for events in the late afternoon. Thus, he runs the browser of his SmathPhone GPS-equipped and queries his preferred *matchmaker*[4] in order to find out a *WS* that satisfies his needs. From the matchmaker search interface he selects the categories tourism and events. The matchmaker already knows some information about Carlo, such as his position provided by his GPS-receiver and his profession and age provided by Carlo when he registered to the service the first time he used it. The matchmaker discovers UbiquiTO-S, invokes its services and finally Carlo receives a list of events in the city of Torino that mostly correspond to his interests and propensity to spend. He is satisfied about the recommendations and also because both the discovery of UbiquiTO-S and the personalization of the answers were carried out automatically.

PLATFORM DESCRIPTION
The above example presents a scenario where several *WSs* provide services to *end-users* and to *software agents*. As typical, they describe their services in WSDL files and advertise them in public UDDI[5] registries. UbiquiTO-S is a *WS*, and in particular a Semantic Adaptive *WS* that provides recommendations in the tourist domain. The matchmaker searches the UDDI registry and discovers several *WSs* (UbiquiTO-S is one of them) offering the information Carlo is interested in. The matchmaker evaluates the match between i) user requests and known user features and ii) the provided

---

[1] http://www.w3.org/TR/wsdl
[2] http://www.w3.org/TR/owl-features/
[3] http://www.w3.org/2004/12/rules-ws/paper/93/
[4] A matchmaker is a search engine a user can delegate to find services. It works performing a match between the user request and the service description typically advertised on UDDI registries.
[5] http://www.uddi.org/

outputs and *WS* requirements. The matchmaker decides to invoke UbiquiTO-S services since it is able to provide not only location based information, as done by other discovered *WSs*, but also information tailored to the provided user features.

UbiquiTO-S is designed as a Semantic *WS* that semantically annotates required input, provided output and their relationships. In particular, UbiquiTO-S enriches the WSDL service description by means of a WSSP file that specifies restrictions and constraints for WSDL parameters of input and output. WSSP, which has been introduced and successfully exploited by [4,5], is a discovery mechanism that semantically enriches the UDDI's search functionality and encodes semantic information with WSDL. It represents input and output semantics, as in the OWL-S profile[6], by describing the service capabilities with semantic information expressed in some ontology language (for example OWL). In addition to OWL-S profile, WSSP gives the possibility to link rules that allow to better specifying restrictions and constraints to inputs and outputs (for example in RDF-RuleML). Many other standards have been proposed (e.g., WSDL-S[7], WSML[8], SWSL[9]) but the choice of using WSSP in our proposal depends on the fact that it is compatible with the service ontology of OWL-S, and allows to use semantic rule languages, like RDF-RuleML, also in the description of service profile, and can be complementary used with the standard WSDL and UDDI structures. In particular, for the goal of adaptation, the possibility to define restrictions and constraints to input and output is quite interesting:

1. *Restrictions* to the required inputs can be specified by mapping the input parameter on ontologies. For example, an OWL ontology can be used to define the meaning of an input parameter (e.g., Profession), specifying its meaning and its relationships with other classes.
2. *Constraints* to input and output are expressed by means of semantic rules. Concerning the input, a rule can specify its allowed values, which in the above example are the subclasses of that particular class (e.g., Student, Manager). Concerning the output, rules are relevant to specify constraints that explain the reason why corresponding inputs are required. For example some rules exploited in the above scenario may specify that:
   - *if the user profession is provided* (input), *suggestions regarding events* (output) *have a Confidence Value (CV) of 0.5;*
   - *if the user profession and age are provided* (input), *suggestions regarding events* (output) *have a CV of 0.7;*

Thus we can state that *rules* try to justify the required input by explaining that the corresponding output information will be more precise and tailored to the specific needs. This not only increases the control over the adaptive service and its scrutability, but also offers to the requestor user-tailored information in addition to the purposes the web service is designed for. In order to show the relations between WSSP and rules, Fig. 1 presents a part of the WSSP file that shows the output message and the URI reference to the rule that specifies the constraints to the output. Then Fig. 1

---

[6] http://www. daml.org/services/owl-s/
[7] http://www.w3.org/2005/04/FSWS/Submissions/17/WSDL-S.htm
[8] http://www.wsmo.org/wsml/
[9] http://www.daml.org/services/swsl/

presents a part of the RDF-RuleML rule referred to the specified URI in the WSSP file. In particular, as it can be seen, it expresses in RDF-RuleML the second rule of the above examples, i.e. *"if the user profession and age are provided, suggestions have a CV of 0.7"*

```
WSSP constraints

<profile:output>
  <profile:message rdf:ID="ServiceResponse">
  ....
    <profile:constrainedBy rdf:resource="http://ubiquito-s /rules.rdf#ProvideAgeProfession"/>
  </profile:message>
</profile:output>
```

```
RDF-RuleMl

<Implies>
  <rdf:Description ref:about="http://ubiquito-s /rules.rdf#ProvideAgeProfession">
  <rdf:type resource="http://ubiquito-s/preds/Relation.owl#ProvideAgeProfession">
  <rdf:type resource="http://ubiquito-s/preds/Relation.owl#HasConfidence">
  ....
  </rdf:Description>
<body> <Atom>
    <oid><Ind wlab=http://ubiquito-s/UserModel.owl#User /></oid>
    <opr><Rel wref="http://ubiquito-s/preds/Relation.owl#ProvideAgeProfession"></opr>
    <slot><Ind wref=" http://ubiquito-s/onto/UserModel.owl#Age"/></slot>
    <slot><Ind wref=" http://ubiquito-s/onto/UserModel.owl#Profession"/></slot>
  </Atom> </body>
<head>   <Atom>
    <oid><Ind wlab="http://ubiquito-s"/></oid>
    <opr><Rel wref="http://ubiquito-s/preds/Relation.owl#HasConfidence"></opr>
    <slot><Ind wref=" http://ubiquito-s/onto/Output.owl#Events"/></slot>
    <slot><Ind wref="http://www.u2m.org/2003/situation#confidence"/><Data>0.7</Data></slot>
  </Atom></head>
</Implies>
```

Fig. 1. An example of WSSP constraints specified in a Rdf-RuleML rule

3   Conclusion and Future Works

In this paper we presented a recommender system, UbiquiTO-S, which exploits the technology of Web Services and Semantic Web to allow software agents to discover its services and invoke its adaptive services.

UbiquiTO-S has been developed as an extension of UbiquiTO [1], a mobile adaptive guide that provides personalized location-based tourist information. With respect to UbiquiTO, the main task is not changed, but its transformation into a *WS* and the choice to formally and semantically describe input requirements, outputs and especially their relationships introduces it in a cooperative environment for personalized services. With respect to common *WSs*, the advantage of this approach is that it allows a middle agent (e.g. the matchmaker in the scenario) to obtain services that i) better match the user request ii), fit specifically her features, iii) can be imported and processed to compose other services which take advantage of the personalization.

Moreover, considering the user point of view, while UbiquiTO provides adapted information without explaining the reason why it needs some data and its adaptive behaviour it is not transparent, UbiquiTO-S, on the contrary, is more scrutable for both end users and software agents.

As specified in the introduction, this is an ongoing work and this initial phase has been focused on the semantic discovery phase of the service, by adding semantic information to the service profile. The current work includes the definition of the WSDL file, the definition of the WSSP profile, and the definition of all the OWL ontologies and RDF-RuleML rules that are referred in WSSP to specify restrictions and constraints of the input and output messages.

Our next step will deal with adding semantic to the whole process that includes service composition, execution and monitoring.

References

1. Amendola, I., Cena F., Console L., Crevola A., Gena C., Goy A., Modeo S., Perrero M., Torre I., Toso A.: UbiquiTO: A Multi-device Adaptive Guide. Proc. of Mobile HCI 2004, Lecture Notes in Computer Science, 3160 (2004) 409-414.
2. Balke, W., Wagner, M.: Towards personalized Selection of Web Services. In *Proc. of the Int. World Wide Web Conf. (WWW)*, Budapest, Hungary, 2003.
3. De Bra, P., Aroyo, L., Chepegin, V.: The Next Big Thing: Adaptive Web-Based Systems. In Journal of Digital Information, Vol. 5 Issue 1 Article N.247, 2004-05-27.
4. T. Kawamura, J.-A. De Blasio, T. Hasegawa, M. Paolucci, K. Sycara, Preliminary Report of Public Experiment of Semantic Service Matchmaker with UDDI Business Registry, Lecture Notes in Computer Science, Volume 2910, Jan 2003, p 208– 224.
5. Kawamura T.; Hasegawa T.; Ohsuga A.; Paolucci M.; Sycara K.: Web services lookup: a matchmaker experiment. IT Professional Vol 7, Issue 2, Mar-Apr 05,,36-41.
6. Setten, M., Pokraev, S., Koolwaaij, J.: Context-aware recommendations in the mobile tourist application COMPASS. In Nejdl, W. & De Bra, P. (Eds.). AH 2004, 26-29 Aug 2004, Eindhoven, The Netherlands, LNCS 3137, Springer-Verlag, pp. 235-244.
7. Wagner, M., Balke, W., Hirschfeld, R., Kellerer, W · A Roadmap to Advanced Personalization of Mobile Services. In *Industrial Program of the 10th Int. Conference on Cooperative Information Systems (CoopIS 2002)*, Irvine, USA, 2002.

Considering Additional Adaptation Concerns in the Design of Web Applications

Sven Casteleyn[1], Zoltán Fiala[2], Geert-Jan Houben[1,3], and Kees van der Sluijs[3]

[1] Vrije Universiteit Brussel, Pleinlaan 2, 1050 Brussels, Belgium
{Sven.Casteleyn, Geert-Jan.Houben}@vub.ac.be
[2] Dresden University of Technology, Chair for Multimedia Technology,
01062 Dresden, Germany
Zoltan.Fiala@inf.tu-dresden.de
[3] Technische Universiteit Eindhoven, PO Box 513, 5600 MB Eindhoven, The Netherlands
{g.j.houben, k.a.m.sluijs}@tue.nl

Abstract. The design of Web applications traditionally relies heavily on the navigation design. The Web as it evolves now brings additional design concerns, such as omni-presence, device-dependence, privacy, accessibility, localization etc. Many of these additional concerns are occurrences of user- or context-dependency, and are typically realized by transformations of the application (design) that embed adaptation in the navigation. In this paper we focus on how to extend an application with new functionality without having to redesign the entire application. If we can easily add functionality, we can separate additional design concerns and describe them independently. Using a component-based implementation we show how to extend a Web application to support additional design concerns at presentation generation level. Furthermore, we demonstrate how an Aspect-Oriented approach can support the high-level specification of these (additional) design concerns at a conceptual level.

1 Introduction

Part of the popularity of the Web is due to its omni-presence and accessibility: mobile devices (mobile phones, PDA's etc.) make the Web accessible 'anywhere and any-time'. A broad range of organizations, e.g. in e-government, e-health, e-commerce, e-learning, currently offer (part of) their services through this omni-present WWW. In this evolution, designing and creating a Web application has become an increasingly complex task. Not only are the applications larger, they also have to take into account various (design) issues which were previously irrelevant: device-dependence, privacy, security, accessibility, localization, personalization etc. Many of these design issues require exhibiting a certain user- or context-dependency: the application becomes adaptive (to the user). When designing applications and taking into account all these separate issues, ad-hoc design obviously becomes unfeasible.

Web application design methods (e.g. Hera [1], OOHDM [2], WebML[3], WSDM[4], OO-H[5]), proposed in literature as a systematic and conceptual approach to Web application design, offer design and implementation (generation) support for engineering complex Web applications. Adaptation of data, navigation, and presentation that

V. Wade, H. Ashman, and B. Smyth (Eds.): AH 2006, LNCS 4018, pp. 254–258, 2006.
© Springer-Verlag Berlin Heidelberg 2006

suits the current user/context is specified by incorporating conditions in the relevant design models. This adaptation specification constitutes a significant part of the design of the Web application. Furthermore, it is closely intertwined with the (regular) design process, which complicates the Web engineering process and is in sharp contrast with the desired separation of concerns.

In this paper we first illustrate how to add adaptation to an existing (Hera-based) Web application, using a component-based implementation. We do so utilizing the Generic Adaptation Components (GAC [6]) provided by the AMACONT project, and exemplify this approach with a running example using Hera [1]. Furthermore, we illustrate how this adaptation can be specified at a higher-level of abstraction (i.e. at the design level), separately from the regular application, by applying aspect-oriented techniques. Using aspect-oriented techniques allows us to tackle cross-cutting design concerns, which adaptations typically are.

2 Implementing Additional Adaptation Concerns

Before explaining how to add adaptation to an existing Hera-based Web application, it is wise to recall the general architectural model behind such a Web application: under the direction of an application model (AM) it transforms domain content into a hypermedia presentation. When adding adaptation to such an application, each additional adaptation concern can be seen as a modification of the application, and thus, at implementation level all these additional adaptation concerns have to be incorporated into the overall hypermedia generation process (see Figure 1).

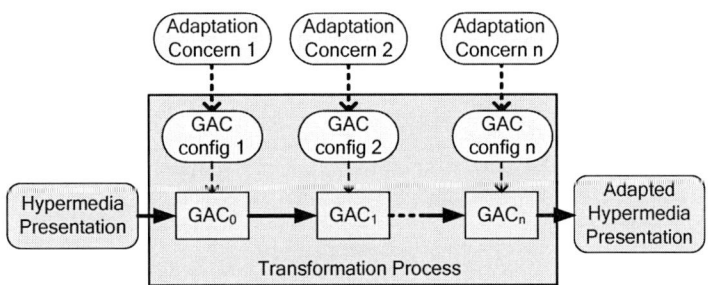

Fig. 1. Implementing Additional Concerns at Presentation Generation

For this implementation of additional adaptation concerns we exploit the Generic Adaptation Component (GAC), a transcoding tool for making Web applications adaptive. According to its rule-based configuration, it allows to perform instance-level adaptation operations on XML-based content (in our case the original hypermedia presentation underlying the initial application model) based on available user/context information is stored in its *adaptation context data* repository. The GAC is thus a particularly suitable solution for implementing adaptation for hypermedia presentation generation, independent of the regular application design. To illustrate this approach, consider the running example of (a part of) a research project's Web application. Figure 2 depicts the structure of the application according to the visual representation of a Hera AM. The starting page is the project homepage showing the project's name, its introductory project description and the project members' name and photos as thumbnails. Clicking on a member, one can navigate to the corresponding member's homepage containing the name, contacts, CV, image, as well as a link list showing the publications (title, conference, year of publication). Note that in this basic application model there is no adaptation embedded yet.

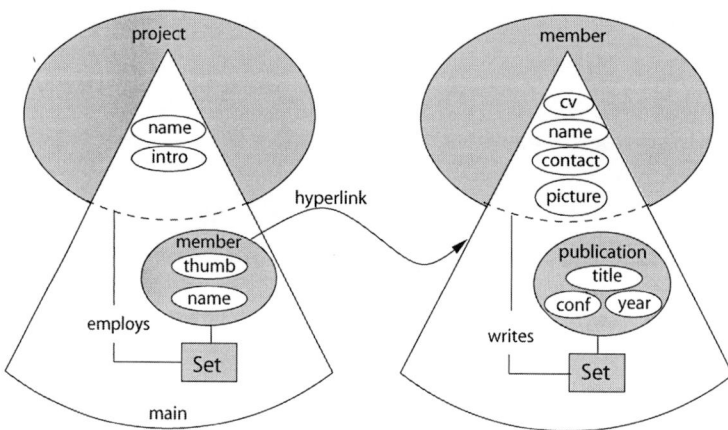

Fig. 2. Example Application Model

Now imagine we would like to express, in the context of an additional adaptation concern of device-dependency, that for pda-users no images will be shown, and on the member page, no publication-list will be given. The corresponding GAC rule for filtering images (which in this case will omit members' thumbs on the project page, and members' pictures on each member's page) looks as follows:

```
<gac:AppearanceRule gac:selector="//Slice/* [@mediatype = 'picture']">
   <gac:Condition gac:when="$device!='pda'"/>
</gac:AppearanceRule>
```

Figure 3 shows two versions of our running example's project member homepage. Based on the application model shown in Figure 2, the original (desktop) variant provides information of that member's title, name, CV, contacts but also a link list pointing to his publications. According to the above GAC rule, no pictures are shown on the PDA. Furthermore, the list of the member's publications is only shown on the desktop browser and filtered out on the handheld.

3 Specifying Additional Adaptation Concerns at Design Level

Using the GAC to specify additional adaptation concerns allows to specify adaptation separately from the regular Web application. However, this solution operates at the level of presentation generation, and requires detailed knowledge of the specific XML formats of the Web design method's implementation models (in our case, the Hera implementation models). Furthermore, the richness of these models is a determining factor for the specificity or generality of the GAC rules. A higher-level solution, which allows the designer to specify additional adaptation concerns at the design level exploiting their implementation independent semantics, yet still separate from the regular design, is thus desirable. Therefore, we will apply aspect-oriented techniques at design (model) level (see also [7] for a similar, yet lower level approach). From such a higher-level specification, one or more GAC rules for the specific XML (implementation) format can then be generated.

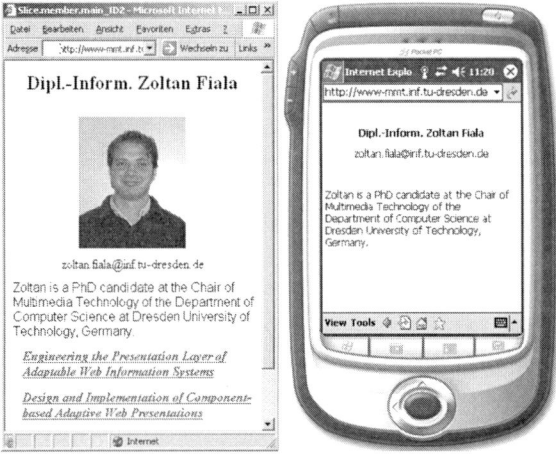

Fig. 1. Generated Member Page

As our "omit all pictures" example suggests, adaptation is, in most cases, not fixed to one particular element, yet distributed over the entire design. A similar observation was made in the programming community, when considering different design concerns of a software application: some concerns cannot be localized to a particular class or module; instead they are inherently distributed over the whole application. Such a concern is called a *cross-cutting* concern. To cleanly separate the programming code addressing this concern from the regular application code, Aspect-Oriented Programming was introduced. An *aspect* captures the code originating from the cross-cutting concern, and is split up in two parts: the *advice* (i.e. the programming code that needs to be injected in the regular code) and the *pointcut* (i.e. the particular place(s) in the regular code where the advice needs to be injected).

Returning to our running example, and applying aspect-oriented principles at the design level of a Web Application, we can express the required adaptation "for pda-users, remove all images from the application" as follows (using pseudo-code):

POINTCUT ALL ELEMENTS WITH mediatype = 'picture' **PROPERTY ADVICE ADD CONDITION** device != 'pda'

This pointcut/advice pair specifies that, for all design elements which are pictures (the pointcut), a condition is added which restricts visibility of these element to non-pda users only. Such an aspect-oriented specification can subsequently be (automatically) translated in one or more corresponding GAC rules, which perform the desired adaptation at implementation level, as described in the previous section. Note that both at design and implementation level, we strive for a separation of adaptation (concerns), from the regular design/application.

4 Conclusion

In this paper, we demonstrated how to add (additional) adaptation concerns to an existing (Hera-based) Web application, both at design and implementation (generation) level. Our approach is based on the observation that adaptation mostly boils down to transformations that realize a certain user- or context dependency. We showed how these transformations can be specified independently from the original application at presentation generation level, by using a generic transcoding tool GAC. We illustrated how higher-level support for this adaptation specification can be realized applying aspect-oriented techniques. We are experimenting with such aspect-oriented adaptation specifications, and with the required mapping to GAC rules.

References

[1] Vdovjak, R., Frasincar, F., Houben, G.J., Barna, P.: Engineering Semantic Web Information Systems in Hera. Journal of Web Engineering, Vol. 2, No. 1&2 (2003) 3-26.
[2] Schwabe, D., Rossi, G.: The Object-Oriented Hypermedia Design Model. In Communications of the ACM 38(8), ACM Press, ISSN 0001-0782 (1995) 45-46
[3] Ceri, S., Fraternali, P., Bongio, A., Brambilla, M., Comai, S., Matera, M.: Designing Data-Intensive Web Applications, Morgan Kaufmann (2003)
[4] De Troyer, O., Casteleyn, S.: Designing Localized Web Sites. In Proceedings of the 5th International Conference on Web Information Systems Engineering (WISE 2004), Brisbane, Australia (2004) 547-558
[5] Gómez, J., Cachero, C., Pastor, O.: Conceptual Modeling of Device-Independent Web Applications. In IEEE Multimedia Special Issue on Web Engineering, IEEE Computer Society Press (2001) 26-39
[6] Fiala, Z., Houben G.J.: A Generic Transcoding Tool for Making Web Applications Adaptive. In Proceedings of the CAiSE'05 FORUM, Porto, Portugal (2005) 15-20
[7] Bausmeister, H., Knapp, A., Koch, N., Zhang, G. Modelling Adaptivity with Aspects. In Proceedings of the International Conference on Web Engineering (ICWE2005), Sydney, Australia, 2005, 406-416

Towards Measuring the Cost of Changing Adaptive Hypermedia Systems

Nathalie Colineau, Cécile Paris, and Ross Wilkinson

CSIRO – ICT Centre
Locked Bag 17, North Ryde NSW 1670, Australia
{Nathalie.colineau, Cecile.Paris, ross.wilkinson}@csiro.au

Abstract. As applications evolve over time, it becomes increasingly desirable to be able to adapt a system, enabling it to handle situations in different ways and to handle new situations. We refer to this as the flexibility and maintainability of a system. These features come at a cost. We argue here that they are an important aspect of evaluation, and that we need to measure these costs. To start getting a handle on how one might evaluate these aspects of a system (or of an approach), we turned to our own approach to building AH applications and designed a specific study to allow us to look at these issues.

1 Introduction

The last decade has seen the development of approaches and reference models (e.g., [8] and [11]) for Adaptive Hypermedia (AH) systems, and the development of various methods to provide a range of adaptations to users. There are many AH systems in a various domains (e.g., [2], [6], [7], [5], [12], [4]), and the issue of evaluation has become crucial. Evaluation is a complex (and costly) problem, with multiple dimensions. Most evaluations to-date are empirical studies of specific applications under particular conditions, focussing on one dimension: the end-user. We argue that we must look at evaluation from a number of perspectives, including but not limited to the end-user. In particular, we are interested in a system-perspective.

In this paper, we propose to examine the flexibility and the ease of maintenance afforded by the design of a system. As a start towards this goal, we present a specific attempt to evaluate the flexibility of our system through a scenario in which we performed a series of changes requiring an existing application to produce new or different presentations and adaptations.

2 Current Evaluations of AH Systems

A great deal of work has focused on evaluating AH systems with a focus on usability (e.g., [1], [9] and [12]). In most cases, an experiment is set up to evaluate an adaptive system by comparing it to a standard system. While recent work started to look at the systems' performance and the validity of their design (e.g., [3] and [10]), we propose to look at yet another facet of a system-oriented evaluation, in particular the design of the underlying AH architecture with its impact on the maintenance of an application.

V. Wade, H. Ashman, and B. Smyth (Eds.): AH 2006, LNCS 4018, pp. 259–263, 2006.

This would provide insight into an AH architecture's customisability, its maintainability, its flexibility to be extended or modified, and the degree of reusability it allows. We believe this would help us understand the benefits and costs associated in developing AH applications and start comparing various architectures.

3 Evaluating the Flexibility of Adaptive Systems

Implementing adaptive systems able to handle specific situations in specific ways is important, but not enough. Most adaptive systems are built around a specific application. Using them in the context of a different application is difficult. As applications evolve over time, it is desirable to be able to change an application, enabling it to respond appropriately to new situations: this requires the ability to handle new situations or respond differently than originally envisaged to known situations. This is important for at least two reasons:

(1) We are designers not domain experts; it is thus difficult for us to know what is the most appropriate in each situation. The design of an application should allow the experts to take control and configure the application appropriately;
(2) Situations are dynamic – what is satisfactory today may be inadequate tomorrow. We must be prepared to take on board new requirements as they come in.

These requirements come at a cost. We thus believe that there is another side to evaluation: the ease or cost of developing applications that can be easily configured and maintained to meet changing requirements. Note that we are not talking here of computational learning models, but rather we refer to the manual cost of adapting and maintaining an application.

3.1 What Should Be Evaluated?

What should we take into account to evaluate the cost of maintaining adaptive applications? To get a handle on this issue, we started with our own architecture for AH applications. Our aim was to understand the ease with which an application built using our architecture could be maintained and extended. In particular, we looked at:

(1) *What changes are needed?* – When there are new requirements, do the modifications require the development of new resources, the implementation of additional functionality to the underlying architecture, or both?
(2) *Who can do it and what is the expertise required?* – Adaptive systems are now quite complex and require a lot of expertise that may be shared among several individuals (e.g., software engineering, HCI, domain expertise, etc.).
(3) *How hard it is?* – How much effort and time is required to modify the system to the new requirements?

The objective of this work was not to come up with an absolute figure nor a metric, but to start building an understanding of how flexible our system is, of the cost of extending an application, and of how one might evaluate approaches along these dimensions.

In the following sections, we outline our specific AH architecture, the Virtual Document Planner (VDP). We have already used this architecture to build various applications (e.g., [12] and [4]), and we felt that it was flexible and portable across domains and applications. Yet, we wanted to address our questions above more precisely, especially with respect to maintenance and cost.

3.2   The Virtual Document Planner Overview

The Virtual Document Planner (VDP) is a multimedia generation system that dynamically produces hypermedia documents. It is the main module of Myriad, our platform for Contextualised Information Retrieval and Delivery [11]. The VDP belongs to the class of AH systems working with an open set of (potentially heterogeneous) resources by opposition to AH systems based on a fixed and closed world (cf. [2] and [5]). Instead of providing navigation support and guidance through a (manually authored) hypermedia space, the VDP *creates* a tailored hypermedia space. The VDP generates hypermedia documents using discourse rules to select and organise the content, presentation rules to determine an appropriate way to realise the content and the structure of the presentation, and a set of templates to control the layout of the final document. In the two classes of systems, the adaptation methods used are different. For example, while AH systems with a fixed set of resources tailor the content by removing, inserting, altering or stretching fragments of text, open sources AH systems decide what needs to be included, retrieve the appropriate fragments from various sources and assemble them into a coherent whole. This process is done in our case by the VDP planning engine. In addition, while the former class of systems focuses on the development of adaptive navigation support techniques, the manipulation of links is not an issue in the latter class as systems have control over the generated hypermedia space. However, besides those differences, the two approaches present similarities in the way the adaptation is performed. In particular, they base the adaptation on the information recorded in the user profile, task model and other contextual models.

3.3   The Evaluation Study

To assess the flexibility of our system, we defined a scenario where our application was to generate three multimedia documents, taking into account a series of changes regarding both the content (varying the type and the amount of information provided) and the presentation (varying the way information is laid out). We wanted to evaluate: what needed to be done to enable the application to allow for the changes? Who could do it? And how easy/expensive it would be? Our study allowed us to put to the test our approach and architecture, and to assess its current flexibility to fit new requirements. We found that:

(1) By decoupling the engine/mechanisms from the resources, the changes were applied to the resources, at distinct layers of our architecture (content, presentation, or adaptation mechanisms). Indeed, while the planning engine used by the VDP is generic and can be reused in different applications, the resources (i.e., discourse and presentation rules) are domain and task dependent, and need to be specified and re-written for each application;

(2) It was hard to anticipate exactly the amount of work, especially for changes involving content. We realised that the cost of providing new content was not related to the amount of new material to be added. It depends both on the role in the discourse structure of the new content and how it fits with existing content, and on the granularity at which the new content is represented, as this influences the number of discourse rules to be written; and,

(3) The expertise needed to perform these changes was complex. Although the VDP's resources are highly modular and declarative, all expressed in XML, creating and modifying them requires some expertise. The person authoring a target document needs to understand the syntax in which the discourse rules are written, and, more importantly, how they can be combined to generate a particular document.

We realised that the latter was potentially a significant cost of our approach. As a result, we are now undertaking work to provide domain experts with authoring tools that generate automatically the appropriate discourse rules from the specification of a document structure, thus reducing that aspect of cost. Having the authoring tool coupled with our AH architecture, we can now revisit the cost of changing an application, as illustrated in Table 1.

Table 1. Comparative cost of introducing an authoring tool enabling the system to automate content changes from the author's specifications

	VDP without Authoring Tool	VDP with Authoring Tool
What needs to be changed?	Discourse Rules	Specifications of the document structure
Who is doing the changes?	System designers with discourse expertise	Authors for content
How much effort is required?	Several hours	15 to 30 min

Referring back to our original questions (What? Who? How hard?), we have now significantly reduce the complexity of the expertise and the amount of manual effort required (the new or modified discourse rules are derived automatically from the authoring tool). We thus believe that our analysis, albeit only a starting point, has already allowed us to get a handle on the cost of using our approach and has led us to improvements.

4   Conclusion

Situations and requirements evolve; nobody wants to rebuild a system each time a new need comes in. Thus, maintenance of adaptive systems for new situations is an important issue. While the flexibility of tailoring the provision of information to a wide range of situations is key, we must also understand the cost of adapting an application to new situations. Thus, we must understand the cost of extending an application to enable it to generate new tailored hypermedia presentations and applications. We have attempted to understand these costs for our approach. This is only a first step towards our goal: articulate a framework for evaluating various approaches to AH applications by addressing issues of flexibility and maintainability.

References

[1] Boyle, C. and Encarnacion, A.O. MetaDoc: an adaptive hypertext reading system. *User Modeling and User-Adapted Interaction* 4(1), 1-19, 1994.

[2] Brusilovsky, P. Methods and Techniques of Adaptive Hypermedia. *User Modeling and User Adapted Interaction*, 6(2-3): 87-129, 1996.

[3] Brusilovsky, P., Karagiannidis, C., and Sampson, D. Layered evaluation of adaptive learning systems. *International Journal of Continuing Engineering Education and Lifelong Learning*, 14 (4/5), 402–421, 2004.

[4] Colineau, N., Paris, C. and Wu, M. Actionable Information Delivery. In *Revue d'Intelligence Artificielle* (RSTI – RIA), 18(4), 549-576, Sept. 2004.

[5] De Bra, P., Aerts, A., Berden, B., de Lange, B. and Rousseau, B. (2003). AHA! The Adaptive Hypermedia Architecture, In *Proc. of the 14th ACM Conference on Hypertext and Hypermedia*, 81-84, Nottingham, 2003.

[6] De Carollis, B., De Rosis, F., Andreoli, C., Cavallo, V. and De Cicco, M.L. The Dynamic Generation of Hypertext Presentations of Medical Guidelines. *The New Review of Hypermedia and Multimedia* 4, 67-88, 1998.

[7] Fink, J., Kobsa, A. and Nill, A. Adaptable and Adaptive Information Provision for All Users, Including Disabled and Elderly People. *The New Review of Hypermedia and Multimedia* 4, 163-188, 1998.

[8] Halasz, F. G. and Schwartz, M. The Dexter Hypertext Reference Model, *Communications of the ACM*, 37(2), 30-39, 1994.

[9] Hothi, J. and Hall, W. An Evaluation of Adapted Hypermedia Techniques Using Static User Modelling. In *Proc. of the 2nd Adaptive Hypertext and Hypermedia Workshop at the 9th ACM International Hypertext Conference (Hypertext'98)*, Pittsburgh, PA. 1998.

[10] Paramythis, A., Totter, A. and Stephanidis, C. A Modular Approach to the Evaluation of Adaptive User Interfaces. In *Proc. of the workshop on Empirical Evaluation of Adaptive Systems at UM'2001*, 9-24, Sonthofen, Germany, 2001.

[11] Paris, C., Wu, M., Vander Linden, K., Post, M. and Lu, S. Myriad: An Architecture for Contextualized Information Retrieval and Delivery. In *Proc. of the International Conference on Adaptive Hypermedia and Adaptive Web-based Systems (AH2004)*. 205-214, The Netherlands, 2004.

[12] Paris, C., Wu, M., Vercoustre, A., Wan, S., Wilkins, P. and Wilkinson, W. An Empirical Study of the Effect of Coherent and Tailored Document Delivery as an Interface to Organizational Websites. In *Proc. of the Adaptive Hypermedia Workshop at UM'03*, Pittsburgh, USA, 2003.

Adaptive Patient Education Framework Featuring Personalized Cardiovascular Risk Management Interventions

Selena Davis and Syed Sibte Raza Abidi

Health Informatics Laboratory, Faculty of Computer Science, Dalhousie University,
Halifax, NS, Canada, B3H 1W5
{sdavis, sraza}@cs.dal.ca

Abstract. The PULSE project objectives are to generate and evaluate a web-based personalized educational intervention for the management of cardiovascular risk. We present a web-based adaptive hypermedia system to create and deliver the personalized education material to the patient. The adaptive personalization framework is based on a patient profile created by combining an electronic patient data capture template, the Systematic COronary Risk Evaluation (SCORE) algorithm, and a Stage of behaviour Change determination model. The interventions are designed to address both medical and psychosocial aspects of risk management and, as such, we combine staged lifestyle modification materials and non-staged messages based on Canadian clinical guidelines to motivate personal risk management.

1 Introduction

Patient education, especially for chronic health conditions, is becoming increasingly complex because the educational content needs to conform to the longitudinal healthcare needs of the patient. Computer based patient education allows for the delivery of educational content to the patient; lately the emergence of health web-portals allows for the dissemination of generic healthcare information [1]. However, patients prefer healthcare information that is personalized to their individual needs and situation [2], and evidence shows that personalized information is more likely to be read, remembered, experienced as personally relevant and in turn has a greater impact in motivating patients to make a behaviour change [3]. Adaptive hypermedia systems offer the functionality to support the composition and delivery of personalized healthcare educational programs.

Cardiovascular diseases (CVD) place a significant burden on health professionals, patients and their care-givers, and extract significant health care costs. Thus, there are important gains in its prevention that can be achieved through risk factor modification and healthy lifestyle changes [4]. Risk factor modification is addressed through patient education to empower patients to self-manage disease risk and improve their quality of life [2]. However, it is argued that educational interventions may not necessarily have the desired impact if they do not take into account the patient's behavioural attitudes towards self-management and self-improvement. Personalization of educational

V. Wade, H. Ashman, and B. Smyth (Eds.): AH 2006, LNCS 4018, pp. 264–268, 2006.
© Springer-Verlag Berlin Heidelberg 2006

interventions, therefore, should not only account for the patient's current health profile but in addition the patient's perceptions to health and readiness to change. We hypothesize that the above elements can realize objective user profiles and lead to the provision of personalized web-mediated interventions in terms of interest, knowledge, and compliance to the suggested lifestyle modifications of patients.

In this paper, we present our approach and proposed system - PULSE (Personalization Using Linkages of SCORE and behaviour change readiness to web-based Education). Our approach is grounded in the observation that the efficacy of any patient educational intervention is contingent on the patient's behaviour change readiness. As such, we use both CVD risk assessment and behavioural change readiness tool—in particular the Transtheoretical Model (TTM)—to determine the patient's profile; based on the profile, our personalization algorithm selects relevant messages to compose the educational material for an individual patient. We use Systematic COronary Risk Evaluation for risk assessment and Stages of Change for behaviour change readiness assessment. The educational material is derived from Pro-Change Behavior Systems Inc. and Canadian clinical guidelines. The personalization decision logic is represented in terms of Medical Logic Modules (MLM), implemented in Java. Finally, a web-based adaptive hypermedia system is being developed to generate and deliver the personalized education material to the patient.

2   Information Personalization for Healthcare

Patient education involves a set of planned, educational activities designed to improve patients' health behaviours and/or health status [5]. Personalization of healthcare information with respect to the patient's characteristics and health needs is an increasing trend as patients are taking an active interest and charge of their healthcare needs. The literature suggests that patients want: more information about their illness and treatment plan than they typically receive during physician visits; information that is *custom-tailored* to their own situation; information when they formulate questions about their health issues, which is generally after leaving the clinic and not during the physician visit; information that is endorsed by their physician as credible and applicable to their specific problem; information from other sources, such as journal articles and websites; and, information that they can retain for future reference [6].

Computer-tailored education programs, using adaptive hypermedia methods, generate comprehensive assessments of health-related behaviours at an individual level and compose personalized healthcare information by adapting the message, source of information, and/or the method of delivery. According to Jones et al., [7]computer-based information personalization requires at least five components, including: 1) a user profile, 2) a digital library containing all messages, 3) a mapping schema that generates the appropriate messages, 4) a document template for appropriate allocation and display of messages, and 5) a medium to deliver the message to the intended user. Web dissemination of tailored health interventions has demonstrated positive impact on determinants of behaviour change [8].

In our work we have incorporated behavior change considerations within the information personalization framework. The rationale being that the impact of any personalized information can be maximized if it aligns with the patient's state of readiness to uptake the recommended information. Research and experience reveal that initiating and maintaining positive behaviour changes is challenging for most people. Prochaska's TTM of intentional behaviour change is a stage-based model founded on 25 years of research. The model matches the change principles and processes to each individual's current stage of change, in order to guide them through the process of modifying problem behaviours and acquiring positive behaviours [9].

The use of fully integrated TTM constructs to inform the design of personalized messages has been effective for intervening across a broad range of health-related behaviors [10]. More specifically, results in tobacco control studies with interventions tailored to a smoker's stage were successful more often than non-tailored interventions in promoting forward stage movement [11].

3 PULSE: Design and Development

3.1 Patient Data Capture and Profile

We use the validated, commercially available Wellsource Coronary Risk Profile as the basis of our Data Capture Template (DCT) for collecting patients' demographic, behavioural, and clinical risk factor characteristics. The global INTERHEART Study [12] indicates that the nine risk factors of smoking, lipids, hypertension, diabetes, obesity, diet, physical activity, alcohol consumption, and psychosocial factors account for over 90% of the risk of acute MI. These factors are captured in our DCT to design an objective patient profile.

We represent the patient profile in three parts as each component collects patient parameters for specific personalization purposes: (1) *CVD Risk Profile* determined through the SCORE algorithm that estimates the 10-yr total cardiovascular risk of death. Patient data on age, gender, smoking, systolic BP, and total cholesterol and HDL cholesterol ratio is used to calculate the patient's risk category [13]; (2) *Staged Risk Factor Profile* depicts the patient's Stage of Change for specific modifiable risk factor behaviours. The Staged Risk Factor Profile is determined by a patient's response to questions relating to her/his readiness to change modifiable risk factor behaviours - smoking, being overweight, stress, depression, and exercise; and (3) *Non-staged Risk Factor Profile* determined by risk factor values—i.e. diet, alcohol, LDL cholesterol, Triglycerides, diastolic BP, glycemic control, and personal and family health history.

3.2 Message Library

In the PULSE program, the educational interventions are specifically designed to address both the medical and psycho-social aspects of CVD risk management. As such, we use a combination of staged lifestyle modification materials and risk-specific messages based on clinical guidelines to provide a valid use of behaviour change theory and Canadian sources of clinical and lifestyle modification education.

The various sourced materials are broken down into small "snippets of information", <tagged>, and stored in an SQL database. The XML <tag> for each snippet follows an indexing schematic which provides mapping ease to the patient profile for personalization purposes (e.g. <smoking>).

3.3 Decision Logic

Given a patient profile and a message library containing an assortment of education interventions, the personalization mechanism involves the selection of the most relevant set of messages based on the patient's profile. We design a personalization matrix to summarize the patient parameters assessed and describe specific combinations of characteristics that lead to a certain message. Personalization is achieved through the processing of a set of symbolic rules based on decision logic that maps the profile elements to specific messages. We develop a rule-based inferencing engine that incorporates the decision logic. To represent our medical knowledge we use MLMs, a standard for independent units composing a series of rules in health knowledge bases. The entire decision logic, sets of MLMs, is implemented in Java and represented as a comprehensive decision tree describing each of the risk factors and risk conditions contained in the patient profile. Each MLM consists of four parts: an evoking event, logic, action, and data mapping. The logic contains "if-then" rules, where the IF part of the rules contains variables for the patient profile. Using case statements, if the IF part of the rule *is not* satisfied then the engine directs the execution of the next case statement. If the IF part of the rule *is* satisfied—i.e. the patient's profile matches the rule constraints then the rule fires and the THEN part of the rule becomes available for execution. Typically the THEN part contains a list of messages that are to be selected as the patient's personalized educational material.

3.4 Presentation and Delivery

We pre-designed a hypermedia template for the output whereby relevant messages selected for an individual patient are structured and presented in a consistent manner. Such content adaptation ensures each patient's personalized document is coherent and contains only the information that is pertinent to the patient. A web-based delivery medium is used to deliver the information to the patients via the practitioners. A print version is available for patients without computer access.

4 Concluding Remarks

In this paper we have presented the preliminary design of our computer-tailored patient education strategy that features: (a) Usage of SCORE for risk assessment; (b) Incorporation of behaviour change inputs in determining the educational content as opposed to just relying on medical data; (c) Usage of an objective DCT currently operational; (d) Leveraging Canadian clinical guidelines for both deriving the decision logic and the corresponding educational intervention; and (e) Personalization of educational material. The realization for personalized education information compared to generic information has led to various computer-tailored healthcare educational programs [14]. The project is underway and we would be reporting detailed implementation and evaluation studies in a separate publication. Here, we state a case for the application of adaptive personalization methods for patient education programs; such programs can help reduce disease risks and deal with risk management by influencing patient behaviour changes through the provision of pertinent lifestyle modifications and change strategies.

References

[1] H.Q. Nguyen and V.C. Kohlman, "Internet-based patient education and support interventions: A review of evaluation studies and directions for future research," Computers in Biology and Medicine, vol. 34, pp. 95-112, 2004.

[2] T. Hoffmann, T. Russell and K. McKenna, "Producing computer-generated tailored written information for stroke patients and their carers: system development and preliminary evaluation," International Journal of Medical Informatics, vol. 73, pp. 751-758, 2004.

[3] J. Brug, M. Campbell, and P. van Assema, "The application and impact of computer-generated personalized nutrition education: A review of the literature," Patient Education and Counseling, vol. 36, pp. 145-156, 1999.

[4] D.G. Manuel, M. Leung, K. Nguyen, P. Tanuseputro and H. Johansen, "Burden of cardiovascular disease in Canada," Canadian Journal of Cardiology, vol. 19, pp. 997-1004, 2003.

[5] K. Lorig, T.R. Prohaska et al., Patient education: a practical approach. Sage Publications, 2001.

[6] M.W. Kreuter and R.J. Wray, "Tailored and targeted health communication: strategies for enhancing information relevance," American Journal of Health Behaviour, vol. 27, pp. S227-S232, 2003.

[7] B. Jones, S.S.R. Abidi and W. Ying, "Using Computerized Clinical Practice Guidelines to Generate Tailored Patient Education Materials," in 38th Hawaii IEEE International Conference on System Sciences, 2005, pp. 139b.

[8] A. Oenema, J. Brug and L. Lechner, " Web-based tailored nutrition education: results of a randomized controlled trial," Health Education Research, vol. 16, pp. 647-660, 2001.

[9] Cancer Prevention Research Center, "Detailed Overview of the Transtheoretical Model," December 15, 2004. Available:
http://www.uri.edu/research/cprc/TTM/detailedoverview.htm

[10] J.A. Sarkin, S.S. Johnson, J.O. Prochaska and J.M. Prochaska, "Applying the Transtheoretical Model to Regular Moderate Exercise in an Overweight Population: Validation of a Stages of Change Measure," Preventive Medicine, vol. 33, pp. 462-469, 2001.

[11] L. Spencer, F. Pagell, M.E. Hallion and T.B. Adams, "Applying the transtheoretical model to tobacco cessation and prevention: a review of literature," American Journal of Health Promotion, vol. 17, pp. 7-71, Sept-Oct. 2002.

[12] S. Yusuf, S. Hawken, S. Ôunpuu, T. Dans, A. Avezum, F. Lanas, M. McQueen, A. Budaj, P. Pais and J. Varigos, "Effect of potentially modifiable risk factors associated with myocardial infarction in 52 countries (the INTERHEART study): case-control study," The Lancet, vol. 364, pp. 937-952, 2004.

[13] R.M. Conroy et al., "Estimation of ten-year risk of fatal cardiovascular disease in Europe: the SCORE project," European Heart Journal, vol. 24, pp. 987-1003, 2003.

[14] U.S. National Institutes of Health, "Trial of a Tailored Message Program to Implement CHF Guidelines," Jan. 6, 2006. http://www.webcitation.org/1143495385123127 [accessed 2006 Jan 9]

Using Contexts to Personalize Educational Topic Maps

Christo Dichev and Darina Dicheva

Winston-Salem State University, 3206 E J Jones Computer Science Building,
Winston Salem, NC 27110, USA
{dichevc, dichevad}@wssu.edu
http://compsci.wssu.edu/iis/

Abstract. In this paper we discuss the support for personalization in TM4L - an environment for building and using Topic Maps-based learning repositories. Our approach is based on the idea of using different views to access a learning collection depending on the *context* of its use. We propose an extension of the Topic Map model with contexts and discuss its implementation in TM4L aimed at supporting context-based personalization.

1 Introduction

It is largely agreed that the exploration of information resources is affected by users' context. In the case of concept-driven access to learning material, concepts can be looked at from different perspectives. In order to account for that, the conceptual structure should not be predetermined on the base of too many assumptions, but should rather reflect different perspectives depending on the context in which the learning collection is being used. For a conceptual structure to be interoperable and resources to be shareable, this contextual information must be *explicit*.

We have been advocating the idea that concept-driven access to learning material implemented as a topic map [5] can bridge the gap between learning and knowledge. As a result, we have developed TM4L – a topic map-based environment for building, maintaining, and using standards-based, ontology-aware e-learning repositories [3]. Among the original goals of TM4L was to support efficient retrieval of learning content tailored to the needs of a learner working on an educational task. In this paper we discuss the latest development of TM4L where the focus is on the added functionality for supporting personalization. Our approach is based on the idea of using different views for accessing a learning collection depending on the *context* of its use.

In order to account for personalization in topic map navigation, we propose the access to the learning collection to be mediated by a set of *contexts*. Contexts can be considered as specific views on a domain, dependent on users' information needs. Our approach is based on the assumption that a successful information support application should not force users to change their way of looking at the learning repository, as an externally imposed schema might be perceived either as oppressive or irrelevant [1]. Thus, from our perspective, a context plays the role of a lens through which the users look at the learning repository.

V. Wade, H. Ashman, and B. Smyth (Eds.): AH 2006, LNCS 4018, pp. 269–273, 2006.
© Springer-Verlag Berlin Heidelberg 2006

2   Contexts in Topic Maps

In standard applications the notion of context is just assumed in the background of a conceptualization that is often created from the perspective of an author or a group of authors. However, the increased requirements for personalization in the information seeking applications need the representation of multiple views within a single framework, and this requires explicit mechanisms enabling filtering out or grouping of pieces of information according to *context*. We are modeling the world of the informational support by using the Topic Map model, where all objects of interests are mapped to topics, associations, occurrences and scopes. For this particular task we define context as a set of entities sharing a common set of topics, relations, occurrence types or scope, determined by a given information seeking task. The set of all topics related to a given topic is an example of such a context where all its objects share a common topic. The set of entities is a subset of topics and/or occurrences and is evaluated to a set of occurrences (defined by the context). To make this context definition effective, we need to specify the means for defining and evaluating contexts.

According to the definition, the common set of features defining a context of user's information needs is a combination of topics, relations, occurrence types, and scopes. This set represents user's current goals, interests, preferences, knowledge, etc. Assume, for example, that the set of entities sharing the common property "Advanced material" specifies a context of learning resources typically presented with less details, "External resources" specifies a set of resources originating outside the department, while "Examples" specifies a set of resources classified as examples. Then, the set of entities described by the combination of the features "Advanced material", "External resources", "Examples" specifies a context of external learning resources typically presented with less details and explanations, and limited to examples. The collection of those resources can be interpreted as a specific *viewpoint* of the collection.

It is clear that each individual has its own conceptualization of the world, which is partial (covers a portion of the domain) and represents user's own view of the domain, i.e. *user's semantics*. The views of different users will overlap when they share common knowledge. In this case the relations between the views can be seen as possible mappings between partially different individual conceptualizations. An infrastructure that enables the sharing of knowledge, without centralizing it, should have the capability of representing local contexts and mapping between their overlapping parts [1].

In general, a context is an individual depiction of a portion of a domain, but it is not completely independent from what holds in other contexts. The representation of two separate contexts can *overlap*, i.e. describe a common part of the domain. This overlapping can be detected during a process of meaning negotiation. For instance, the context describing "List Processing" and the contest describing "Recursion" overlap on "Recursive List Processing". However, it is not certain that the common part is defined *identically* in both contexts. On the other hand, the concepts in the two contexts are not independent and can be related to each other [2]. Such dependences can be observed, for example, when users (based on their context) are interested in importing information represented in the context of another agent. To enable such a process, the overlapping information in both contexts should be related directly through *context mapping*.

3 Contexts in TM4L

Context-aware applications typically *capture* user's context by monitoring their interactions with the system and store them in a context model. For example, in Myriad architecture for contextualized information retrieval, the contextual information is divided in five categories: user model, domain model, task model, device model, and discourse model [4]. It follows the traditions of building and use of *standard* user models. However, the lessons learnt from system-built student models are not too encouraging with regard to the applicability and efficiency of this approach in real systems. Such models are difficult to built and have serious scalability and maintenance problems. Thus, we propose *user-built* contextual models. Since the typical use of TM4L is for supporting users in their task of finding relevant resources, we constrain our consideration to contextual support for information retrieval. Our contextual support has two important components: supporting users to build their personal context, and mapping user's context to system's current context (i.e. author's context).

In our approach authors and users share the TM vocabulary without the restriction to share contexts. Users are provided the following primitives for defining their contexts: *topics, relation types, resource types,* and *themes.* From these primitives they build their context, which is interpreted as a query for *topic resources* that represents a person's current information need. Each context is defined in terms of a sequence of topics, a (possible) sequence of relations, a (possible) sequence of resource types and ranges.

The term *range* refers to the level of resource inclusion with regard to the topic hierarchy built on a specified (transitive) relation. It requires the generation of a set of children topics from the set of topics specified in the context. The range can be "full" or "terminal". "Full" denotes the set of resources linked to the full set of children topics, while "terminal" refers to the resources corresponding only to the terminal topics generated in each branch of the topic generation procedure.

For simplicity we restrict our consideration to binary relations. The intended use of relations in the context is for determining the children topics of the topics specified in the context. Generating children assumes some kind of directionality. For example, when using the *whole-part* relation we typically determine the *parts* from the *whole*. In a similar fashion, for all predefined relations TM4L applies a default directionality, which defines the order of topic traversal. For relations defined by the authors this order corresponds to the order of the roles in the definition of the corresponding relation type. For example, *simpler(less-simple, more-simple)* specifies that starting from the topic playing the role of *less-simple* we find its children playing the role of *more-simple*. If the context includes no relations, themes, or resource types, then the default is *all relation types*, *all resource types*, *no themes,* and *terminal range.*

The evaluation of a context results in a list of resources. The latter is obtained by adding to an initially empty list all qualifying (filtered by type) resources linked to the set of topics specified in the context, followed by generating all children topics of those topics by applying the specified in the context relations. This procedure is recursively applied to the list of the newly generated topics until no more new children can be generated. An additional filtering is performed at each step, using the themes included in the context.

As an example, let us assume that a Prolog topic map author has defined themes such as "Beginner", "Intermediate", etc. and has scoped appropriately resources in the topic map with them. Let us also assume that a user is interested in the topic "List Processing". If the user wishes to review resources containing introductory material on list processing with easy explanation of the key concepts, obviously, beside the topic "List Processing" he should include in his personal context the theme "Beginner". Further on, if the user is interested in resources of particular types, e.g., "Online notes" or "Examples", he should also add those resource types to the context. The user may then constrain the resources on the *resource coverage* of the topical structure generated by using the context. For example, if the topic "List Processing" includes subtopics "List Representation" and "Operations on Lists", the user can include a range value of "terminal" in the context, in order to get only resources linked to the terminal topics of the structure rooted by "List Processing", i.e. only resources for the topics "List Representation" and "Operations on Lists".

The list of resources resulting from the evaluation of the user context is intended to be used for additional support in terms of locating relevant resources. Suppose that a learner has defined his context as ("Prolog", "Whole-Part", "Advanced", "Examples") and has received the corresponding resources (see Fig. 1). If he selects a resource of interest that happens to be related to "Recursion" (e.g. http://ktiml.mff.cuni.cz/ ~bartak/prolog/learning.html), chances are for this resource to be shown under the topic "List Processing" in the "Partonomy" view of the collection (defined by the TM author). Then by using *neighborhood navigation*, the learner can find a number of relevant examples in the topic map author's original (default) context. Thus we realize the mapping between the user's and the author's context through resources.

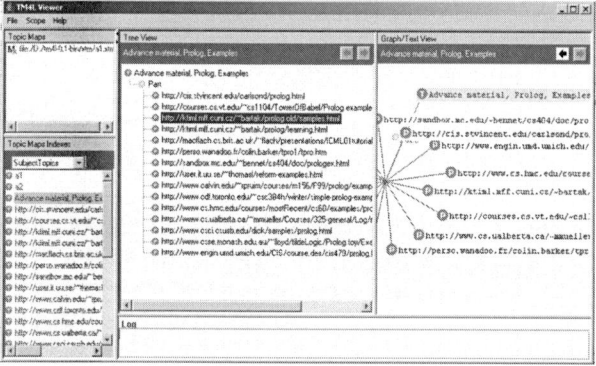

Fig. 1. Display of all resources in the AI topic map related to the context { "Prolog", "Advanced material", "Examples"}

The advantage of such a customized context is that it can provide a clue for searching in *unfamiliar* contexts/classifications. For example, if the user does not know where to look for resources of interest in a collection based on a standard taxonomy, this approach provides a starting point for exploration. When users have no idea how to drill down (e.g. looking for examples on recursion) in some of the predefined contexts, the provided functionality enables them to look into the collection from their own context. The contextual viewer will show where in the standard collection the resources selected from their context reside. This provides a good clue for further browsing. When learners have limited knowledge on the subject and are not able to specify their own exploration context, then even the online references supplementing a course lecture can be used as a simple context. Note that in human-to-human communication typically *both sides* try to meet a *matching* context.

The user context is built on-the-fly from its definition. The entities it contains will be different depending of the content of the repository at the particular time. TM4L builds the content of a specified user context following the described earlier procedure. After the context is built, TM4L maps it to its current context, so as to present the resources of interest in their default (designed by the topic map author) context.

4 Conclusion

In this paper we reported an extension of the TM4L environment that supports context-based personalization of educational topic maps. We extended the Topic Map model with a notion of context beyond scopes, and proposed and implemented an approach to mapping users' personal context to the default context of the information seeking system. Such a mapping provides the user with a clue for searching information in unfamiliar classifications. We believe that our approach will contribute to the development of efficient context-aware TM-based information seeking applications.

Acknowledgement

This material is based upon work supported by the National Science Foundation under Grant No. DUE-0333069 "NSDL: Towards Reusable and Shareable Courseware: Topic Maps-Based Digital Libraries" and Grant No. DUE-0442702 "CCLI-EMD: Topic Maps-based courseware to Support Undergraduate Computer Science Courses."

References

1. Bouquet P., Donà, A., Serafini, L., Zanobini, S.: Contextualized local ontologies specification via CTXML, AAAI-02 Workshop on Meaning Negotiation. Edmonton, Canada (2002)
2. Bouquet, P., Serafini, L., Zanobini, S.: Peer-to-Peer Semantic Coordination. Journal of Web Semantics, 2(1) (2005)
3. Dicheva, D. & Dichev, C.: TM4L: Creating and Browsing Educational Topic Maps, British Journal of Educational Technology - BJET, 37(3) (2006) 391-404
4. Paris, C., Wu, M., Vander Linden, K., Post, M., Lu, S.: Myriad: An Architecture for Contextualized Information Retrieval and Delivery. Proc. of the International Conference on Adaptive Hypermedia and Adaptive Web-Based Systems - AH 2004, The Netherlands (2004), 205-214
5. URL: XTM. Biezunski, M., Bryan, M., & Newcomb, S., ISO/IEC 13250:2000 Topic Maps: Information Technology, www.y12.doe.gov/sgml/sc34/document/0129.pdf

Combining Coherence and Adaptation in Discourse-Oriented Hypermedia Generation

Kateryna Falkovych[1], Federica Cena[2], and Frank Nack[1,3]

[1] Centrum voor Wiskunde en Informatica,
P.O. Box 94079, 1090 GB Amsterdam, The Netherlands
Kateryna.Falkovych@cwi.nl
[2] Department of Computer Science, Universita' degli Studi di Torino,
Corso Svizzera, 185, 10149 Torino, Italy
federica.cena@di.unito.it
[3] V2_, Institute for the Unstable Media,
Eendrachtsstraat 10, 3012 XL Rotterdam, The Netherlands
Frank.Nack@cwi.nl

Abstract. This paper provides a solution to discourse structure adaptation in the process of automatic hypermedia presentation generation. Existing approaches to discourse structure composition are based on the assumption that a user can comprehend relations between the elements in a discourse structure if the overall structure is semantically coherent. This assumption does not, so far, take into account specific user needs. In this paper we show that although discourse structure composition approaches significantly differ, a general model of the composition process can be derived. Within this general model we identify how adaptation can be applied. We formulate the problem of discourse adaptation with regard to the general model and present our proposed solution.

1 Introduction

One of the main goals in semantic-based hypermedia presentation generation research is to provide higher-level conceptual structures that ensure coherent organization of media assets for a particular presentation in the context of a dynamic heterogeneous environment [1,4,5,6]. This goal is achieved by creating discourse structures that are motivated by existing genre theories [2,7]. It is assumed that a user can comprehend relations between the elements in a discourse structure if the overall structure is semantically coherent. This assumption does not, so far, take into account specific user needs. For example, users with different knowledge in the domain might have different views on what organization of concepts in the discourse structure is more coherent.

To address this problem we propose a flexible adaptation layer that can handle a dynamic discourse composition process and that is independent of this process. Our goal is to provide adaptation to improve coherence in the discourse structure composition process that, on the one hand, preserves coherence of resulting discourse structures and, on the other hand, makes them more appropriate from the perspective of a particular user. Our scope is not in identifying which user features influence discourse structure

V. Wade, H. Ashman, and B. Smyth (Eds.): AH 2006, LNCS 4018, pp. 274–278, 2006.

composition. We focus on providing an approach for adapting coherence when such influences have been identified. Influences of the different levels of user knowledge on discourse coherence are used in our discussion as examples.

2 Discourse Composition in Hypermedia Presentation Generation

We describe related work with the goal of identifying a general model of the discourse composition process. Thus, we highlight similarities between the systems in the steps they follow to compose discourse structures.

A discourse structure contains domain concepts that are grouped and ordered to ensure coherence. Domain concepts and relations between them form a metadata structure that provides means for semantically annotating media items from a repository. A metadata structure together with annotated media items form a *semantic framework*. The selection of domain concepts for the discourse structure is done based on (1) relevance of each element in the discourse structure with regard to the complete discourse structure belonging to a certain genre (*global coherence*) and (2) the coherence relationships between a concept and other concepts in the discourse structure (*local coherence*).

In the **Artequakt project** [1] a developer creates templates for biographies of artists. A template consists of queries to the knowledge base. Each query retrieves data about one aspect of an artist's life. The author determines global coherence by selecting domain concepts for queries. S/he specifies local coherence by grouping and ordering queries using constructs that specify the preferred order of query appearances within the template. The *Context* construct allows for a certain level of adaptivity by identifying specific parts of a template available only to users with a necessary level of domain knowledge.

In **DISC** [6], discourse structures are represented by dynamic rule-based templates. A template specifies the main character and the genre and is divided into narrative units, e.g. a narrative unit about the professional life of a person. A narrative unit contains discourse rules that define which domain concepts can play a role of related characters in the discourse structure. For example, for a main character "Rembrandt", "Lastman" can play a role of the related character "teacher". Hence, narrative units determine global coherence of concepts for a discourse structure. In addition, discourse rules specify local coherence by defining what information about the related character can be presented. A dynamic template produces different discourse structures depending on what related characters can be found in the semantic framework.

Samp*Le* [4] uses discourse flow templates as an initial representation of a discourse flow for the genre. A discourse template is an analytical framework for building discourse structures for a particular genre. For example, a newspaper article discourse template consists of the components: *Main Event, Context, History, Comments* [8]. SampLe uses rules to specify the mapping between a discourse template and the semantic framework. These rules help to select domain concepts appropriate for each discourse template component. To create a coherent discourse structure, selected domain concepts are differentiated using coherence rules. Coherence rules take into account a part of the discourse structure which is already composed and a set of concepts that are appropriate for inclusion at the next step.

3   Problem of Discourse Adaptation

The descriptions in the previous section show that existing hypermedia presentation generation approaches create discourse structures following similar steps. They specify a *discourse flow* for a particular genre with human-authored templates (Artequakt) or rule-based templates (DISC, SampLe). Then they identify *relevant domain concepts* based on *global coherence* rules. *Local coherence* rules determine which domain concepts are *selected* to be used within each section of the discourse structure. These steps can be combined into a common model presented in Fig. 1.

The coherence achieved by hypermedia presentation generation approaches can be regarded as "general" coherence, since specific user features are not taken into account. We argue that discourse structures can be tailored to different users if we adapt decisions taken while evaluating local coherence to specific user needs.

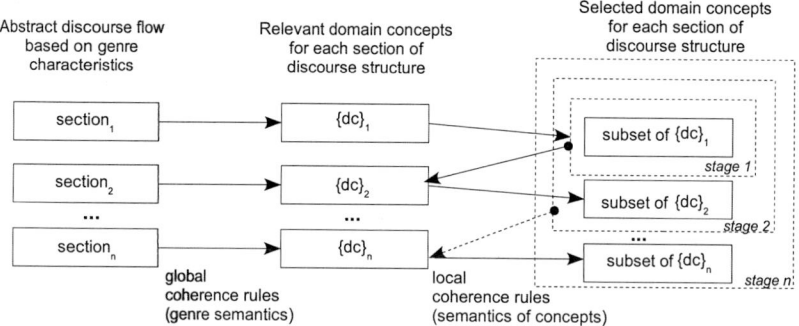

Fig. 1. A general model of the discourse structure composition process

Decisions about global coherence are guided by the notion of genre which represents established communication patterns [3] and is thus applicable among various user groups. Decisions about local coherence are guided by semantic relations between domain concepts. For different users the view on semantic relations between the concepts can vary. A user with little domain knowledge might be unfamiliar with one or more concepts in the discourse structure. The semantic relation between the two unfamiliar concepts will be unclear to the user and s/he might have difficulties in understanding why one concept follows another in the discourse. Thus, users with different domain knowledge have different views on the coherence relations between elements so the notion of local coherence can vary. Hypermedia presentation generation approaches do not take this aspect into account.

Adding adaptation to a discourse structure composition process results in *the problem of enabling modifications in evaluating local coherence between the concepts while preserving global coherence of the obtained discourse structure.*

4   Proposed Solution to Discourse Adaptation

To enable adaptation of local coherence rules we propose a mapping between the existing coherence rules and adaptation rules that we want to integrate in the discourse composition process. We define adaptation rules on top of the existing coherence rules. This allows specification of adaptation rules at an appropriate level of abstraction so that suggested adaptation strategies are independent from the particular strategies of traversing a semantic framework specified in the coherence rules.

To provide such a mapping we specify a set of common constructs that represent necessary means for both types of rules. As a result, coherence rules and adaptation rules operate with the same set of constructs that have agreed-upon datatypes. For each coherence rule there is a corresponding adaptation rule. An adaptation rule is written using variables as values of the common constructs. The corresponding coherence rule uses the functionality defined in the adaptation rule and instantiates the variables with specific instances found in the semantic framework.

We identify the set of common constructs based on the concepts involved in the evaluation of local coherence in the general model of the discourse composition process (Fig.1):

1. domain concepts that are already selected to represent the elements of the discourse structure - *current structure* (e.g. at the stage 2 of the composition process it is *subset of* $\{dc\}_1$);
2. domain concepts that are appropriate to appear inside a certain element of the discourse structure based on global coherence - *relevant concepts* (e.g. $\{dc\}_2$ at the stage 2);
3. one or more domain concepts that are selected to represent an element of the discourse structure - *selected concepts* (e.g. *subset of* $\{dc\}_2$ at the stage 2).

Coherence rules evaluate the *current structure* and *relevant concepts* and come up with *selected concepts* to be added to the *current structure*. For instance, for the stage n of the discourse composition process a coherence rule is defined as follows:

a_Rule(inputs=[currentStructure(subset of $\{dc\}_{n-1}$), relevantConcepts($\{dc\}_n$)], output=[selectedConcepts(subset of $\{dc\}_n$)]).

5   Conclusions

This paper explores an approach to add adaptivity into the discourse structure composition process used by automatic hypermedia presentation generation systems[1]. In order to evaluate our proposed solution, we implemented it within the SampLe system[2]. We choose SampLe as testing platform since it contains explicitly encoded local coherence rules, as described in Section 2. Explicit coherence rules provide the freedom in applying our approach to the necessary step in the discourse structure composition process, without having to modify other components. We tested the solution on the use case of composing discourse structures for the newspaper article genre. The main direction of our current work is to use a larger number of use cases with various local coherence

---

[1] The extended version of this paper can be found at
http://ftp.cwi.nl/CWIreports/INS/INS-E0601.pdf

[2] The SampLe demo can be found at
http://homepages.cwi.nl/~media/projects/CHIME/demos.html

rules and discourse structures belonging to different genres. These experiments should provide possible extensions to the rule-base. Besides, we aim at investigating whether particular genres have influences on coherence rules and their adaptation. Knowledge about such influences would allow fine-tuning the rules to make them even more suitable for a particular user case.

Acknowledgments

This research is funded by the Dutch National NWO ToKeN2000 CHIME project. The authors would like to thank Lynda Hardman, Jacco van Ossenbruggen, Stefano Bocconi and Alia Amin (CWI), Luca Console (Universita' degli Studi di Torino) and Lora Aroyo (Technische Universiteit Eindhoven) for the valuable comments and discussions during the development of this work.

References

1. H. Alani, S. Kim, D. E. Millard, M. J. Weal, W. Hall, P. H. Lewis, and N. R. Shadbolt. Automatic Ontology-based Knowledge Extraction from Web Documents. *IEEE Intelligent Systems*, 18(1):14–21, January-February 2003.
2. D. Duff. *Modern Genre Theory*. Pearson Education Limited, Edinburgh Gate, United Kingdom, 2000.
3. T. Erickson. Rhyme and Punishment: The Creation and Enforcement of Conventions in an On-Line Participatory Limerick Genre. In *Proceedings of the 32rd Hawaii International Conference on System Science*. IEEE Computer Society, January 5-8, 1999.
4. K. Falkovych and F. Nack. Composing Discourse based on Genre Semantics. Technical Report INS-E0502, CWI, December 2005.
5. K. Falkovych and F. Nack. Context Aware Guidance for Multimedia Authoring: Harmonizing Domain and Discourse Knowledge. *Multimedia Systems Journal, Special issue on Multimedia System Technologies for Educational Tools, S. Acton, F. Kishino, R. Nakatsu, M. Rauterberg & J. Tang eds.*, 11(3):226–235, 2006.
6. J. Geurts, S. Bocconi, J. van Ossenbruggen, and L. Hardman. Towards Ontology-driven Discourse: From Semantic Graphs to Multimedia Presentations. In *Second International Semantic Web Conference (ISWC2003)*, pages 597–612, Sanibel Island, Florida, USA, October 20-23, 2003.
7. A. Huxley. *Collected Essays*. Harper, New York, 1959.
8. T. A. van Dijk. *Handbook of Qualitative Methods in Mass Communication Research*, chapter The interdisciplinary study of news as discourse, pages 108–120. Routledge, London, 1991.

A Graph-Based Monitoring Tool for Adaptive Hypermedia Course Systems

Manuel Freire and Pilar Rodríguez

EPS-Universidad Autónoma de Madrid, Madrid ES-28049, Spain
{manuel.freire, pilar.rodriguez}@uam.es,
http://www.ii.uam.es/~mfreire

Abstract. Adaptive hypermedia courses are difficult to debug, validate and maintain. Logfile analysis is partly to blame. We propose a graph-based approach to both real-time student monitoring and logfile analysis. Students are represented at their current locations in a dynamically created map of the course. Selected parts of student user models are visually exposed, and more detail is available on demand. Hierarchically clustered graphs, automatic layout and focus+context techniques are used to keep visual complexity at a manageable level. This component has been developed for an existing AH course system. However we believe that our approach can be readily extended to a wide selection of adaptive hypermedia course systems, filling in an important gap during course creation and maintenance.

1 Introduction

Adaptive Hypermedia is an obvious choice for online courses. Adapting the course to the student surely sounds better than a one-size-fits-all approach. But a vast majority of online courses are not adaptive, because adaptation is difficult to design, test and maintain [1]. It is not easy to predict what users will find during browsing, and for online systems, direct observation is not an option. We propose the use of a graph-based interface to monitor and analyze course usage as an important aid to tutors and course authors.

2 Approach

The following figures illustrate our monitoring interface, which is tracking 5 users throughout a sample course. Users Alice and Bob are both in T2, while Carol, David and Edward are further along the course. In fig. 1, the current map is shown, with exactly enough detail to see the active users. In our visualization, courses are represented as maps, and particular nodes represent either specific activities (*tasks*) or decision points (*rules*). Most of the course is hidden, collapsed under the darkened task nodes marked with an asterisk. Students are represented as additional nodes connected to the last task they have accessed.

Tracking user progress is as simple as watching student nodes move throughout the map, with further details available on demand. In fig. 2, Alice has advanced a bit further,

V. Wade, H. Ashman, and B. Smyth (Eds.): AH 2006, LNCS 4018, pp. 279–282, 2006.

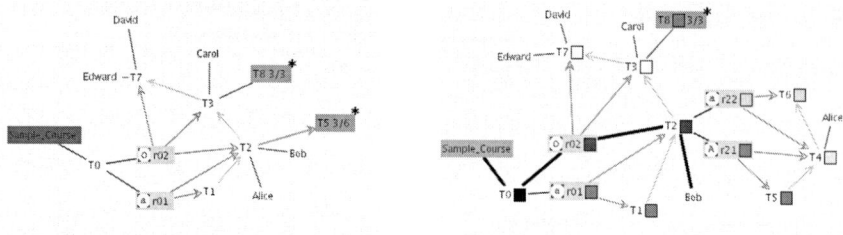

Fig. 1. Example course during monitoring; as-
terisks (*) represent clustered nodes

Fig. 2. Alice has advanced into T4; Bob is selected and his path becomes highlighted

and the map has been automatically expanded to display her progress. Additionally,
Bob's node has been selected: this causes Bob's past path to be highlighted. Color-
coded squares have appeared next to the labels of each task, rule and cluster, indicating
which parts of the course are, according to the system, recommended, available, or
disencouraged.

2.1 Interaction

The interface is built on top of the CLOVER framework [2], and inherits CLOVER's
implementation of hierarchically clustered graphs [3]. Clicking on a node selects it
and marks that node as the current *point of interest* (PoI). Nodes near to this PoI will
be presented in full detail, while nodes further away can be collapsed into clusters to
keep the level of visual complexity within the desired bounds. Whenever the set of
visible nodes changes, automatic layout is performed, and the old view is smoothly
animated to transform into the new one, in an effort to preserve the users mental map
[4]. PoI focusing and automatic layout can be toggled on and off, allowing nodes to
be moved around to suit the user (marquee selection and *Ctrl+click* are also available).
Both manually modified and automatic layouts are stored in a layout cache, and are
later reused if the same view is revisited.

Selecting individual tasks and user nodes triggers additional visual cues. When nothing is currently selected, the map simply tracks user position. Selecting a course task
annotates the users that are currently eligible to perform it, using a color-coded scheme:
red for "not allowed", blue for "started", black for "finished", and a color from yellow to
green to indicate a "degree of recommendation" for all other cases. Conversely, selecting a student annotates all currently-visible tasks with the same color-coding scheme.
In addition, the path that this student has followed throughout the course is highlighted
via increased thickness edges that have been transversed. Our system does not constrain users to following recommended links, and therefore the actual path can fall outside existing edges. An artificial, faded path is used for these cases, connecting the
unexpectedly-visited task to the nearest completed task (the course graph is guaranteed
to be connected, so this is always possible). Finally, double-clicking on a student node
displays a dialog with the student's current user model, color-coded again to reflect the
latest changes.

Popups are available when hovering over a node, without need to select it. Currently, they have only been defined for student nodes, displaying the tasks they have started but not completed, along with a percentage indicating degree of completion and their current "grade" for that task. Since in our system tasks form a hierarchy and the whole course is subsumed under a single task, this is displayed as a tree and allows a quick assessment of the student's performance.

2.2   Events

Changes to the graph are driven by *events*. A task change, an exercise submission or a new student logging in all trigger events. Once it is received by the monitor, it translated into a series of transformations on the graph, which can then be rendered on the interface. Undo support is also present, allowing both forward and backward event navigation.

Two event sources are currently available: a real-time source that monitors a running course on our AH system, and an offline source that reads its events off a log file generated during system execution. Events are not self-contained; instead, they only carry enough information so that the monitoring tool can replay them locally on copies of all user models involved, using the same adaptation engine found in the system itself, arriving at the same changes to these models. This results in smaller logs and an efficient monitoring protocol, at the expense of a heavier monitoring tool and the burden of synchronizing user models before a monitoring session. However, we believe that the benefits greatly outweigh the drawbacks: full user models are available at the monitor, and it is free to inspect the internal state of the adaptation engine. Events can be delivered preserving their time of occurrence, or issued at a constant pace (only if produced from non-realtime source types). The latter is the default for logfile playback. In logfile playback mode, additional controls have been implemented to "pause", "play" and "reverse" the event stream. Further video-like playback control is still work-in-progress.

2.3   Implementation

Our work is centered on the WOTAN adaptive hypermedia course system, a new version of TANGOW[5][6]. WOTAN courses are created and maintained with a graph-based authoring tool [7], which has been recently extended to allow course monitoring and logfile analysis; essentially the same interface is used for authoring and monitoring, with different hints and user interaction in each mode. Both the authoring/monitoring tool and the WOTAN AH course system have been implemented entirely in Java, and a large portion of the codebase is shared.

3   Concluding Remarks and Future Work

We have implemented a graph-based monitoring tool for the WOTAN system. Although our tool is heavily geared for use with this system, this integration only provides added value (in our case, full access to user models and system state, while keeping an efficient monitoring protocol); it is by no means necessary. Graph-based interfaces can be used to monitor usage of almost any hypermedia application, and are specially suited if complex user models are in use, because of the variety of visual hints that can be presented to users.

Work is ongoing in several areas, including new event sources (such as simulated, "random" students for course stress-testing), better event stream control (video-like positioning and playback control), and mental map preservation issues when many students are logging in and out at widely separated parts of a course.

An interesting idea is to integrate tutoring into the tool, allowing tutors monitoring a course to open instant-messaging sessions with students that appear to be stuck, maybe even presenting aid requests as small notes directly on the interface. Student collaboration could also use a simplified monitoring interface to stay aware of each other's virtual location.

Acknowledgments

This work has been sponsored by the Spanish Ministry of Science with project code TIN2004-03140.

References

1. Cristea, A., Aroyo, L.: Adaptive authoring of adaptive educational hypermedia. Lecture Notes in Computer Science **2347** (2002) 122–132
2. Freire, M., Rodriguez, P.: A graph-based interface to complex hypermedia structure visualization. In: Proceedings of AVI'04, ACM Press (2004) 163–166
3. Eades, P., Huang, M.L.: Navigating clustered graphs using force-directed methods. J. Graph Algorithms and Applications: Special Issue on Selected Papers from 1998 Symp. Graph Drawing **4** (2000) 157–181
4. Eades, P., Wei Lai, Misue, K., Sugiyama, K.: Layout adjustment and the mental map. Journal of Visual Languages and Computing **6** (1995) 183–210
5. Carro, R.M., Pulido, E., Rodriguez, P.: Dynamic generation of adaptive Internet-based courses. Journal of Network and Computer Applications **22** (1999) 249–257
6. Carro, R.M., Pulido, E., Rodriguez, P.: TANGOW: a Model for Internet Based Learning. International Journal on Continuing Education and Life-Long Learning **11** (2001)
7. Freire, M., Rodriguez, P.: Comparing graphs and trees for adaptive hypermedia authoring. In: Proceedings of the 3rd International Workshop on A3EH, AIED'05 (2005) 4–12

Much to Know About History

Eelco Herder[1], Harald Weinreich[2], Hartmut Obendorf[2], and Matthias Mayer[2]

[1] L3S Research Center, Hannover, Germany
herder@l3s.de
[2] University of Hamburg, Germany
{weinreich, obendorf, mayer}@informatik.uni-hamburg.de

Abstract. Users often revisit pages while browsing the Web, yet little is known on the character of these revisits. In this paper we present an analysis of various revisit activities, based on results from a long-term click-through study. We separate backtracking activities from recurrent behavior, discuss the impact of the use of multiple windows, and show that in particular infrequently reoccurring activities are poorly supported by current history support mechanisms. We conclude with a discussion on design implications for more personalized history support.

1 Introduction

Web users frequently return to pages visited before [6]. However, the revisitation tools of current Web browsers still have many known shortcomings. The *back button* is the most important history tool, yet its stack-based behavior is shown to be inefficient and confusing [3]. The temporally or lexically ordered *history list* is hardly used, as its presentation is poor, the filtering options are insufficient, and it requires several user actions to access it [6]. Manual maintenance and organization of *bookmarks* is problematic and time-consuming, which results in overly large, unorganized, and outdated bookmark lists [4].

In this paper we present an analysis of user page revisit behavior, based on results from a long-term client side Web usage study. The results indicate that users have various different reasons and strategies for revisiting pages. We conclude with several design implications for Web browsers to be more adaptive, and to consider the current requirements and behavior of Web users.

2 The Study: Data Collection and Preparation

In Winter 2004, we conducted a long-term client-side study with 25 participants from Germany and the Netherlands [8]. Nineteen participants were male and six female. Their ages ranged from 24 to 52 years (mean: 30.5). Sixteen participants had a background in computer science, nine had different backgrounds. The average time span of the logging periods was 104 days, ranging from 51 to 195 days. The data was collected using an intermediary system based on the framework Scone [7]. The system inserted JavaScript events into every Web page to capture many browser events and parameters. The recorded data included times of

V. Wade, H. Ashman, and B. Smyth (Eds.): AH 2006, LNCS 4018, pp. 283–287, 2006.

page requests, the browser action that led to the request, the document address, title and size, as well as the time spent on it. After removal of artifacts caused by advertisements, automatic reloads, redirects, and frame sets, 137,272 request actions were left for analysis.

3   Results: Categorizing Page Revisits

We found an average *recurrence rate* [6] of 47% ($\sigma = 11\%$); per-subject rates ranged from 20% to 71%. The results confirmed the dominance of revisits to a limited set of highly popular pages, as well as the dominance of revisits to pages visited very recently before [6]. The majority of the top n most popular pages could be categorized as search engines, news sites, participants' personal or institutional Web sites, and individual interest sites.

The two sets of dominant pages represent two different forms of page revisits: *backtracking* - visits to pages visited before in the same session, and *recurrent behavior* - visits to pages visited before in earlier sessions. Following [2] we used a 25.5 minute time-out mechanism for defining session boundaries.

In order to explore the relations between these two distributions in detail, the page requests were broken down into the following revisit categories:

- visits to pages not visited before;
- visits to pages visited before in the same session, but not yet in earlier sessions;
- visits to pages visited before in the same session and in earlier sessions;
- visits to pages only visited before in - one or more - earlier sessions.

The leftmost bar of figure 1 shows the distribution of the page visit categories. 47.7% of all pages are visited only once, backtracking was the most common form of revisitation, covering 73.5% of all revisits; only 26.5% of the revisits involved visits to pages not visited before in the same session.

The second to fifth bar show the transition probabilities between the four categories. An interesting aspect of revisitation behavior emerges: first-time visits, backtracking, and recurrent activities tend to occur in clusters. First-time visits will most likely be followed by another unexplored page. Backtracking activities are mostly followed by another backtracking action, or a first-time page visit. This supports the observation that users frequently backtrack to explore new paths from pages visited before [6]. It can also be observed that in recurrent activities, users backtrack to a similar extent as in first-time visit situations.

3.1   Support for Recent and Frequent Revisits

Page popularity and recently visited pages yield support in different situations: the lists of the top n most popular pages and the top n most recently visited pages cover a majority of the pages to be revisited. In order to estimate the performance of the two lists, we calculated the rate of pages that were present in the list of 15 - the number of items presented in the back button pop-up list - most popular and most recently visited pages for each revisit category

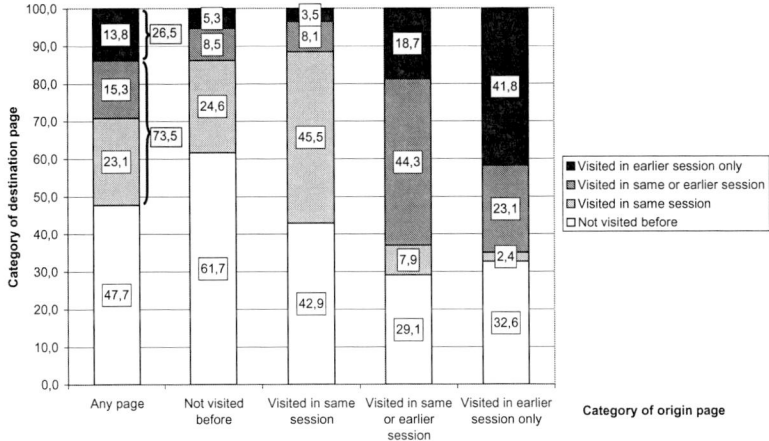

Fig. 1. Transition probabilities from one visit category to another

(table 1). The results confirm the assumption that the list of the 15 most recently visited pages supports backtracking remarkably well with a coverage of about 90%. As a comparison, we calculated to what extent within-session revisits are covered by the list of pages accessible in the pop-up menu of the back button: the average was only 52% ($\sigma = 10.8$). The list of popular pages supports recurrent behavior with a moderate 72%, mainly due to the long tail of pages that are revisited only a couple of times. However, revisits to pages from earlier sessions that have *not* been visited yet in the current session, are far better supported by the list of most popular pages - 51.2% versus 21.6% - for the 15 most recent pages.

Table 1. Revisit support of the 15 most recently visited and the 15 most popular pages

revisit type	15 most recent pages		15 most popular pages	
	average	st.dev	average	st.dev
same session	94.6%	2.97	42.3%	31.05
earlier session	21.6%	9.74	51.2%	13.05
same and earlier	87.9%	6.25	71.6%	14.10

Another drawback of the current back button implementation appeared when we analyzed the application of multiple browser windows and tabs. Our participants tended to use multiple windows to a large extent: 10.5% of all navigation activities involved the opening of a new window or tab [8] - in earlier studies this value was less than one percent [2][6]. The top third group of participants who opened new windows most often, employed the back button to a lesser extent (10.2%) than the bottom third (16.4%); this confirms that multiple windows are used as an alternative to backtracking (t=2.509, $p < 0.05$). A disturbing consequence of this behavior is that it disrupts the concept of the back button: If a user follows trails in multiple windows, the backtracking history is split into separate unrelated stacks. Hence, one often needs to remember what action was performed in which window or tab to relocate a recently visited page.

3.2   Support for Rare Revisits

Figure 2 illustrates that the average interval between two subsequent revisits is longer for less popular pages; for the pages with a popularity ranking below 10 it was not uncommon that more than a week had passed between two visits.

During an interview we asked every participant about specific situations in which they found it difficult to revisit a page. Most pages that were considered difficult to relocate provided specific information to be reviewed rather than online applications. Situations mentioned by our participants included 'finding a soccer results list in an unstructured club Web site', and 'locating a physician's home page'. They had either no bookmark, forgot the query or the Web address.

Our results showed that only a few very popular pages are visited on a frequent - often daily - basis. Our participants used different methods to return to these pages: they made use of the bookmark menu or toolbar, or they typed the URI into the address bar, making use of the automatic URL completion function of the browser. Ironically, the longer the interval between two subsequent revisits - and the more likely that the user will not remember the address - the less presumable it is that the action is still present in the browser history. Hence, users had to find other ways to relocate the page; search engines were stated as a key alternative.

We analyzed the revisit category of pages navigated to from search result pages: the far majority (79%) of all page visits following a result page were first-time visits and only 9% were followed by a revisit to a page known from an earlier session. Although only 2% of all queries were entered more than once, 24% of all long-term revisits were preceded by an earlier query. Whereas this suggests that query-based search is a common strategy for relocating pages, our participants stated that they often had problems in remembering the original query for relocating a page and had to resort to wayfinding strategies.

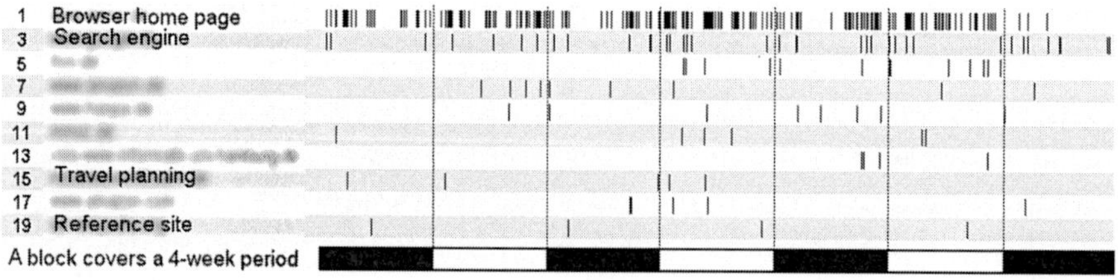

Fig. 2. Distribution of revisits to some of the 19 most popular pages of one participant. URIs have been blurred for privacy reasons.

4   Design Implications for Future Browsers

The more prominent use of multiple windows and browser tabs requires a major rethinking of the history mechanisms of browsers. A linear history of most recent revisits, as proposed by [6], does not reflect the character of parallel trails, and the unrelated back button stacks do not take the temporal relations between the trails into account. An alternative solution would be a 'branching history', which shows the trails in temporal order, but separates the activities in different windows. In an earlier laboratory study [5] we found that users who backtrack using links in Web pages often find informations more quickly than users who rely on the back button. Therefore, we think that adaptive hypermedia techniques, such as automatic link annotations, should be considered to visually identify the anchors that point to recently visited pages, in particular those that serve as hubs.

For rare long-term revisits, users often need to rely on finding waypoints that lead to the desired page. Web search appears to be an ineffective manner to find these waypoints, as people seem not to have problems to replicate exact queries. Given the large amount of infrequently visited pages, a manually organized list of bookmarks will be incomplete or too time-consuming to handle. A strategy that is likely to be more effective to support relocating information, would comprise explicit history search, with support for recognizing related earlier queries, and annotated *trails* [1] that users can follow from a waypoint to the desired location. For previously followed trails, shortcuts to the destination pages could save much effort from the user.

The results from our study show that there is much to know about a user's Web history than is currently used for providing effective support for page revisits. A key challenge for the adaptive hypermedia community is to find effective means to put this knowledge into use.

References

1. V. Bush. As we may think. *The Transatlantic Monthly*, July, 1945.
2. L.D. Catledge and J.E. Pitkow. Characterizing browsing strategies in the world wide web. *Computer Networks and ISDN Systems*, 27 (6):1065–1073, 1995.
3. A. Cockburn and S. Jones. Which way now? analysing and easing inadequacies in www navigation. *Intl. J. Human-Computer Studies*, 45 (1):105–129, 1996.
4. A. Cockburn and B. McKenzie. What do web users do: An empirical analysis of web use. *Intl. J. Human-Computer Studies*, 54 (6):903–922, 2001.
5. E. Herder and I. Juvina. Discovery of individual user navigation styles. In *Workshop on Individual Differences in Adaptive Hypermedia, AH2004*, pages 40–49, 2004.
6. L. Tauscher and S. Greenberg. How people revisit web pages: Empirical findings and implications for the design of history systems. *Int. Journal Human-Computer Studies*, 47:97–137, 1997.
7. H. Weinreich, V. Buchman, and W. Lamersdorf. Scone: Ein framework zur evaluativen realisierung von erweiterungen des webs. In *KiVS 2003*, pages 31–42, 2003.
8. H. Weinreich, H. Obendorf, E. Herder, and M. Mayer. Off the beaten tracks: Exploring three aspects of web navigation. In *Proc. WWW 2006*, 2006.

Learning Object Context for Adaptive Learning Design

Jelena Jovanović[1], Dragan Gašević[2], Colin Knight[2], and Griff Richards[2]

[1] FON, School of Business Administration, University of Belgrade, Serbia and Montenegro
jeljov@gmail.com
[2] School of Interactive arts and Technology, Simon Fraser University Surrey, Canada
{dgasevic, cjk2, griff}@sfu.ca

Abstract. The paper presents an ontology-based framework for capturing and explicit representation of the actual context of use of a specific learning object (LO) in a specific learning design (LD). Learning context related data represented in such a manner provides a solid ground for personalization of both LOs and LDs. The core part of the proposed framework is a LO Context ontology, that leverages a range of other kinds of learning ontologies (e.g. user modeling ontology, domain ontology, LD ontology etc.) to capture the information about the real usage of a LO inside a LD. Additionally, we present the architecture of an adaptive educational system based on the suggested framework, in order to illustrate the benefits of our proposal for personalization of LD.

1 Introduction

Learning design (LD) is about identifying necessary learning activities and assigning Learning Objects (LOs) to those activities in order to achieve a specified learning objective. IMS Learning Design (IMS-LD) Specification [1] provides a common set of concepts for representing LDs, enabling one to specify LDs targeted for different learning situations, based on different pedagogical theories, comprising different learning activities where students and teachers can play many roles, and carried out in diverse learning environments.

However, neither IMS LD nor other learning specifications (e.g. IEEE LOM) capture enough information that can be used to provide advanced levels of learning process personalization, such as personalization in accordance with the students' objectives, learning styles, and knowledge levels. As a result, the annotations of the developed LOs and LDs do not contain explicitly represented information that is important for personalization. Effective personalization requires [2]: 1) direct access to low-granularity content units comprising the structure of a LO; 2) recognition of the pedagogical role played by each content unit in a specific context (i.e. learning activity in terms of IMS LD); 3) awareness of learner's evaluations about usefulness of a specific content unit within a specific LD; 4) characteristics of learners that best fit a specific LD.

In order to alleviate at least some of the recognized deficiencies of the present learning specifications, we introduce the notion of the *Learning Object Context* (LOC) as a mean for capturing information relevant for personalization of both LOs and LDs. Furthermore, we argue for using ontologies to explicitly represent this information, hence increasing their consistency and potential for exchange. Ontologies

V. Wade, H. Ashman, and B. Smyth (Eds.): AH 2006, LNCS 4018, pp. 288–292, 2006.
© Springer-Verlag Berlin Heidelberg 2006

also enable the use of the Semantic Web technologies, such as reasoning and recommendation. The number of different kinds of ontologies employed in the learning domain is growing - domain ontologies covering diverse subject domains, competency ontologies, user model ontologies, etc. These different kinds of ontologies can be integrated in an ontological framework in order to enable personalization of the learning process. Our proposal for such a framework is presented in the paper. The architecture of an adaptive educational system (AES) based on this ontology framework is illustrated as well.

2   Ontologies-Based Framework for Learning Design Adaptation

When learning content is assembled into a larger object or design to be presented to learners, many assumptions are made about the learners and the learning situation: assumptions about the learners' experiences, skills, and competences; about their personal preferences, learning styles, goals, and motivation; about the available time, to name but a few. This is what we refer to as the "context" – the unique situation-related assumptions and rules that implicitly govern how content (LOs) is structured into a flow of interaction (LDs).

2.1   LOCO-Cite Ontology

The LOCO-Cite ontology was initially developed as a formal expression of the linkage between a LD and the LOs the design references. More precisely, it was originally defined as a part of an ontology-based framework for bridging LDs and LOs [3]. The framework includes: ALOCoM Content Structure (ALOCoMCS) ontology formalizing LO content structure; LOCO–an ontology for LD based on the IMS-LD specification; and LOCO-Cite ontology aimed at formalizing learning object context. Here we describe how the LOCO-Cite ontology evolved to capture information about learners, learning activities, user evaluations and the like.

Aiming to further enhance the proposed formalization of the LOC, the LOCO-Cite ontology is related to and makes use of a number of other types of the ontologies relevant for the e-Learning domain. Specifically, connections with those ontologies are established via an additional set of properties introduced in the LOCO-Cite ontology.

The *contentUnitRef* property refers to the actual unit of (learning) content that the context is about. The range of this property is the abstract *alocomcs:ContentUnit* class defined in the ALOCoMCS Ontology to formally represent a (learning) content unit of any granularity level. Therefore, the ontology design enables one to represent context-relevant (meta)data for content units of diverse levels of granularity.

The *subjectDomain* and *domainTopic* properties are aimed at representing the subject domain and the domain topic, respectively, that best describe the context of use of a specific LO. These properties link a LOC with an appropriate domain ontology and its concept(s) represented in accordance with the SKOS Core Specification.

The *usedInLD* and *usedInActivity* properties are introduced to keep references to the actual LD and its learning activity that the LO was used within. Both LD and learning activity are represented in accordance with the LOCO ontology, i.e. the range of these properties are *loco:LearningDesign* and *loco:Activity*, respectively.

The *isOfInstructionalType* property relates the LOC with the instructional/pedagogical role the LO assumed in the learning activity it was used in. The range of this property is any class of the ALOCoM Content Type ontology developed to formally represent different instructional types a content unit might have [8].

The *userRef* property refers to the user model of the learner who actually used the LO in that specific learning context. The user model is compliant with the user model ontology developed for the TANGRAM project (see the next section).

The *dateTimeStart* and *dateTimeEnd* properties store data about the date and the time when the learner started and finished working with the LO. Hence, the time period the learner spent dwelling on the LO can be deduced.

The *userEvaluation* property reports on the usefulness of the LO in the given context. We intend to capture evaluations from all relevant 'players' in the learning process: instructional designers, teachers and learners.

2.2 User Model Ontology

In the scope of the TANGRAM project we developed a User Model (UM) ontology to help us formally represent relevant information about TANGRAM users. To enable interoperability with other learning applications and exchange of users' data, we based the ontology on official specifications for user modeling: IEEE PAPI Learner (http://edutool.com/papi) and IMS LIP (http://www.imsglobal.org/profiles). Even though the UM ontology enables formal representation of relevant information about both authors (designers) and learners, from the perspective of the LOCO-Cite ontology the representation of the learners' features are of primary importance. The ontology defines formalisms for representing the learners' basic personal data, their preferences regarding language, domain topics and content authors, their performance, as well as different dimensions of their learning styles. Detailed description of the ontology is given in [4].

2.3 Ontological Representation of Competences

Since competences play essential role in expressing learners' achievements, as well as requirements and objectives of learning activities, we developed a tiny ontology to enable formal representation of competences. The design of the ontology was partially inspired by the work of Rogozan & Paquette presented in [5]. The *Competency* class is introduced and the following properties are assigned to it:

1. *skillRef* property pointing to a concept from a skills ontology. We are currently building such an ontology out of the skills taxonomy proposed in [6]. The ontology is made compliant with the W3C's proposal for representing conceptual schemas, namely the SKOS Core ontology (http://www.w3.org/2004/02/skos/core/).
2. *domainTopicRef* property refers to a concept from a domain ontology represented in accordance with the SKOS Core ontology (i.e. *skos-core:Concept* class).
3. *description* property is a human readable description of the competency; it is made equivalent to the *dc:description* property.

This ontology is essential for representing a learner's performance in the UM ontology, as well as prerequisites and learning objectives of a learning activity/design in the LOCO.

3   Architecture for Learning Design Adaptation

In this section we describe the architecture of an adaptive educational system that leverages the capabilities of the presented ontologies for discovery, reuse and adaptation of LOs and LDs. The architecture comprises a repository of LOs (LOR) and its accompanying repository of LOCs (LOCoR). The LOR use the ALOCoMCS ontology as the model (schema) for storing LOs, whereas the LOCoR stores LOs' context-related data in accordance with the LOCO-Cite ontology. The idea is that each LO from the LOR has its corresponding LOCs in the LOCoR..

Besides a LOR and a LOCoR, the architecture also comprises a repository of LDs represented in accordance with the LOCO. LDs stored in the repository, do not directly reference concrete LOs, but instead they contain a query specifying the key features of the current learning context (i.e. LOC). Such a query provides the learner with a custom 'view' (or a 'virtual subsection') of the LOR, generated in accordance with the requirements (prerequisites, learning objectives etc.) of his/her current learning activity. The introduced notion of the custom 'view' is analogous to the well known concept of view in databases that is used to protect the database users from the complexity of the underlying database schema. The learner is free to search and/or browse through that 'virtual subsection' of the LOR. This way the learner is given a substantial level of control over their learning process (we believe in the active learning approach), whereas, at the same time, the usage of custom 'views' over the LOR protects him/her from the cognitive overload. The learner's searching/browsing behavior is tracked and that data is mined to infer the learner's preferences, as well as some dimensions of his/her learning style. Based on the acquired insights into the learner's preferences, the virtual subsection of the LOR for every subsequent activity the learner performs is further customized. In other words, the customization is not based only on the requirements of the learning activity, but also on the inferred information about the learner's preferences/style. One should also note that each time a learner selects a LO from the LOR, a LOC instance of that LO is created in the LOCoR and all relevant context-related data for that usage are stored in it.

The proposed ontological framework facilitates visualization of the learning process, hence providing learners' with visual clues of their current situation and learning progress. An ontology-based LD can be easily visualized as a semantic network (graph) having activities as its nodes, whereas edges represent connections between 'compatible' activities. Those edges (i.e. connections) are inferred from a set of pedagogy-based rules that determine for each activity which other activities can be taken next. Additionally, a modified version of conventional adaptation techniques, such as link annotation and hiding, can be used to further personalize the visualization of the network. For example, different colors can be used to differentiate activities the learner has already passed from those that (s)he can undertake now, as well as those that (s)he is not prepared for. Likewise, network edges can be colored differently, depending whether the learner has followed them or not; also the edges representing the path that the system assumes to be optimal for the learner can be specially colored. Alternatively (or even in parallel), different colors (or annotations) of nodes or edges can be used to reflect the learner's satisfaction with the activity (s)he has taken (assuming that the learner's evaluations of the performed activities are available).

These visual clues help the learner choose the next step to take, by reminding him/her on the experiences with the previously undertaken activities.

4   Conclusions

Researching the potentials of personalized use of the two most prominent learning technology efforts, namely LOs and LDs, we have developed a novel ontology (LOCO-Cite) for bridging them. The ontology makes use of several other kinds of learning-related ontologies (user modeling ontology, competences ontology, content structuring ontology etc.) in order to capture the information about specific context of use of a LO inside a LD (referred to as learning object context - LOC). Information of this kind can be rather useful for personalization of LDs – for example, during the runtime a query specifying the main features of the current learning situation can be sent to the repository of LOCs in order to identify LOCs representing similar learning situations and from them infer the most suitable LOs for the present circumstances (learning objectives, learner's preferences, available time, etc.). Furthermore, the ideas of personalized views over LOs repository, as well as, visualization of the learning process in the form of a semantic network are presented as benefits resulting from the proposed ontology-based framework. Our future research will be focused around the implementation of the suggested architecture, as our aim is to leverage the presented ontologies to enable personalization and reuse of LOs and LDs.

References

1. IMS Learning Design Information Model. Version 1.0 Final Specification, rev.20, 2003, http://www.imsglobal.org/learningdesign/ldv1p0/ imsld_infov1p0.html.
2. Cristea, A., "Authoring of Adaptive Hypermedia," *Educational Technology & Society*, Vol. 8, No. 3, 2005, pp. 6-8.
3. Knight, C., Gašević, D., & Richards, G., "An Ontology-Based Framework for Bridging Learning Design and Learning Content," *Educational Tech. & Society*, Vol. 9, No. 1, 2006.
4. Jovanović, J., et al, "Dynamic Assembly of Personalized Learning Content on the Semantic Web," *3th European Semantic Web Conf.*, Budva, Serbia & Montenegro, 2006 (accepted).
5. Rogozan, D. & Paquette, G., "Semantic Annotation in e-Learning Systems based on Evolving Ontologies," *Int. SW-EL Workshop*, Amsterdam, The Netherlands, 2005.
6. Conole, G., et al. (2005). Pedagogical review of learning activities and use cases, LADIE project report. [online]. Available at:
   www.jisc.ac.uk/uploaded_documents/ PedVocab_VocabsReport_v0p11.doc.

Personalised Navigation System with Multidimensional Linkbases

Panchit Longpradit, Christopher Bailey, Wendy Hall, and Gary Wills

Intelligence, Agents and Multimedia Group
School of Electronics and Computer Science
University of Southampton, SO17 1BJ
United Kingdom
Tel.: +44 (0) 23 8059 3255; Fax: +44 (0) 23 8059 2865
{pl01r, cpb, wh, gbw}@ecs.soton.ac.uk

Abstract. Adaptive hypermedia techniques provide users with personalisation of contents and links. Some of the criticisms of adaptive systems are that users do not always understand why the system is adapting the content and links [14], and that the adaptation process can lead to prolific or out of place linking. This paper introduces the concept of a multi-dimensional linkbase to describe a single linkbase containing links annotated with metadata that places them in several different contextual dimensions at once. We also allow users to have control over personalisation by enabling direct manipulation of the linkbase. We argue that this approach answer some of the criticisms of adaptive hypermedia.

1 Introduction

Adaptive hypermedia (AH) techniques [3] enhance how information can be presented online: the same information adapted in the forms of contents and/or navigational hyperlinks based on individual users. Many frameworks and systems to date have been proposed [4,7,10].

The link augmentation technique, which originated from the open hypermedia community, is defined as *the process of inserting additional links dynamically into an existing web page* [1]. The links are separated from the body of a hypermedia document and stored independently in a link database (linkbase). A link service is required to insert dynamically additional links from a linkbase or a variety of linkbases into a web page. These links can be filtered so that they correspond to a user model. At the University of Southampton, open hypermedia (OH) research was commenced in the late 1980's with the creation of Microcosm [8], the Distributed Link Service (DLS) [5] and the Fundamental Open Hypermedia Model (FOHM) [12]. The link augmentation process is not a new technique and can be found in several other systems [1,15], and although it is not present in Brusilovsky's AH methods and techniques, there have been attempts to bringing the concept of OH to the field of AH [2,10].

FOHM, is a model of open hypermedia with contextual structures used to describe the structure of hypertext objects and their associations between data. It has a notion of n-dimensional context which can be attached to the hyperstructure, and defines the contexts in which that structure is visible. FOHM has also been used to implement

V. Wade, H. Ashman, and B. Smyth (Eds.): AH 2006, LNCS 4018, pp. 293–297, 2006.

AH by encoding adaptive rules in the context mechanism. Auld Linky (formerly Auld Leaky), is a contextual link server designed to store and serve FOHM structures [13]. Auld Linky can be used to respond to requests for link matching dynamically and to provide flexibility in modelling hypermedia structures such as navigational links, tours, level of detail and concept structures and as such is particularly useful for the implementation of adaptive hypermedia.

In this paper we introduce the concept of a multi-dimensional linkbases to represent different dimensions of expertise in a single linkbase. This concept builds on and extends the contextual structures of FOHM and is implemented using Auld Linky.

2   A Multi-dimensional Linkbase (MDL)

The motivation for this research stemmed from our hypothesis that in a domain where there are many different categories of users such as novice, beginners, and advanced learners (and some stages in between) within a given context, or where there are many expertise dimensions required in the subject domain, the concept of a multi-dimensional linkbase can be beneficial. For instance, a user who is a skilled English historian but has no expertise in Asian history requires a different links presentation from a user who might be an Asian historian but has limited knowledge about English history. Within this context, we believe that it is essential to take into account the representations of links from different dimensions of expertise. We regarded this as the concept of multi-dimensional linkbases. It is defined as a concept that different sets of links or linkbases are treated as different dimensions of expertise. So for example one Link could be annotated as a member of the expert group while another in the same linkbase could be annotated as a member of the novice group. At the same time users are provided with control over the presentation and personalisation of links.

3   Personalised Navigation System with MDL(s)

The concept of a MDL has been put into practice by the development of a web-based personalised navigation system, called an inquiry-led personalised navigation system (IPNS). Users are provided with navigational tools that map properties about their expertise onto contextual dimensions, each of which can be enabled or disabled, facilitating flexibility and reducing the problem of link overload. In IPNS the links are classified by types of information and their relationships [11] and by the functions of links. In addition to the *Expertise MDL*, we have introduced two more linkbases; namely *Inquiry* and *Glossary*. Although these are implemented using the same FOHM structures they are not multidimensional in our current implementation. Both provide the user with more navigational functions.

- *An Expertise MDL* comprises referential links that relate a keyword in a context to its additional explanation. The Expertise MDL comprises three dimensions of expertise – Subject links (sub classified into raw materials, operations and output, which the user has the option of having 'beginner', 'advanced', 'no links', and 'all links'), Language links (allow users to observe some of the keywords in a chosen language, English, Latin or Spanish), and Learning Style (simply implemented to provide users with a selection between inter-active and non-interactive versions). These Expertise links are augmented into existing pages based on user's levels of expertise and individual user model.

- *An Inquiry linkbase* consists of structural and/or associative links depending on a keyword it is representing in the author's own defined ontology. Based on the 'keyword-based retrieval system', these links are to help users find what they want to know through searching.
- *A Glossary linkbase* embodies another set of referential links. Based on Microcosm philosophy, the user can highlight a word/phrase and request matching links.

The links in the IPNS application are all held in one of the three linkbases. If no links are chosen by using the provided tools users will only notice the ordinary structural links to navigate between pages. Links within the document are dynamically added depending on their selection in the MDL and other linkbases. A single MDL contains the source and destination information for all links in its group. Individual links within MDL can have one or many sources and/or destination. The Context object in FOHM determines the visibility of links. Auld Linky performs the context culling process and returns the remaining links in a given context for a particular user. Figure 1 describes an overall picture of how different arrays of MDLs are provided in the system.

4 Discussion

The benefits of the link augmentation technique are that the separation of links from documents enables the links to be created, added, or modified without any effect on the original document, and that despite the text being modified or moved around, the links still function [1]. However, its conventional process centres the link insertion on known or visited keywords, which can inevitably result in common problems such as too many links inserted into an existing hyperdocument – 'prolific linking' [6], a situation when every keyword becomes a generic link [1], and irrelevant or out of place links where the links fail to support the document's context [9]. Furthermore, despite AH techniques offering personalisation of contents and links to users, one of the criticisms of adaptive systems is that users are prevented from having the control of the system's action [14]. With these issues in mind, we hypothesise that representing the different dimensions of expertise and allowing users to have direct control of the visibility of links can rectify the traditional problems with link augmentation and AH systems. In addition, this concept provides users with greater flexibility as the links displayed are chosen by the users and not automatically detected and generated by the system. We believe that presenting links based on the users' own selection allows them to perceive the behaviour of the working system and empower them by letting them decide whether or not to make use of the functionality offered.

5   Conclusions and Future Work

This paper presents an inquiry-led personalised navigation system based on a concept of a multi-dimensional linkbase. It is a concept where arrays of links signify dimensions of expertise and each of these offers links presentation based on the user profile. IPNS is an attempt to offer navigational links according to users dimensions and levels of expertise. We have developed three linkbases based on our link classification, namely an Expertise MDL and Inquiry and Glossary linkbase, and consider that representation of links from different dimensions of expertise will resolve the problems with prolific and out of place links and facilitate the flexibility. Users are also provided with the inquiry-led tools which enable them to personalise links presentation, each of which can be enabled or disabled; hence facilitating flexibility and reducing user's 'too-many-irrelevant-additional links' syndrome. It was implemented in a specific domain as a personalised web-based system; however, it can also be enhanced to facilitate shareability and reusability issues when it is further developed in a web services environment. FOHM and Auld Linky are the main technologies of our implementation. Future work will be looking at a more formal evaluation of the prototype to confirm whether our concept is applicable and meaningful to users and to establish what is the extent and limit of this understanding.

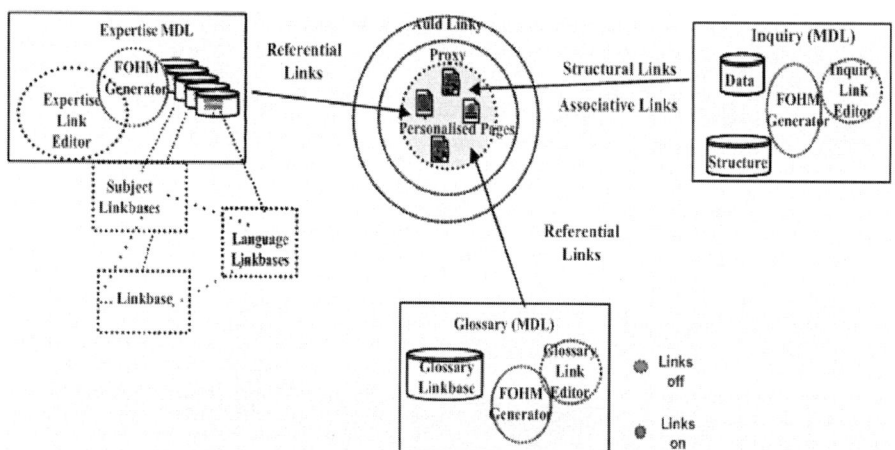

Fig. 1. Multi-Dimensional Linkbases (MDLs)

References

1. Bailey, C., El-Beltagy, S. R., and Hall, W.: Link Augmentation: A Context-Based Approach to Support Adaptive Hypermedia. In: Proceedings Hypermedia: Openness, Structural Awareness, and Adaptivity, Århus, Denmark (2001)
2. Bailey, C., Hall, W., Millard, D. E. and Weal, M. J.: Towards Open Adaptive Hypermedia. In Proceedings of the Second International Conference on Adaptive Hypermedia and Adaptive Web Based Systems, Malaga, Spain (2002)

3. Brusilovsky, P.: Adaptive Hypermedia. In User Modeling and User-Adapted Interaction, 11 (2001) 87-110
4. Brusilovsky, P., Eklund, J., and Schwarz, E.: Web-based Education for All: A Tool for Developing Adaptive Courseware. In Proceedings of Seventh International World Wide Web Conference, 14-18 April, 30 (1-7)(1998) 291-300
5. Carr, L, DeRoure, D, Hall, W and Hill, G.: The Distributed Link Service: a tool for publishers, authors and readers. Fourth World Wide Web conference, Boston, (1995) see http://www.w3.org/Conferences/WWW4/Papers/178/
6. Carr L., Kampa S., Hall W., S. Bechhofer, Goble C, Horal B.: Ontological Linking : Motivation and Case study. In WWW Proceedings (2002)
7. De Bra, P., Aroyo, L., and Chepegin, V.: The Next Big Thing: Adaptive Web-based Systems. Journal of Digital Information, 5 (2004)
8. Davis, H., Hall, W., Heath, I., and Hill, G.: Towards An Integrated Information Environment With Open Hypermedia Systems. In: Proceedings of the Fourth ACM Conference on Hypertext, Milan, Italy (1993) 181-190
9. El-Beltagy, S., Hall, W., De Roure, D., and Carr, L.: Linking in Context. In Journal of Digital Information, Issue 2, Vol 3 (2002)
10. Henze, N.: Open Adaptive Hypermedia: An approach to adaptive information presentation on the Web. First International Conference on Universal Access in Human-Computer Interaction (UAHCI 2001), 5-10 August 2001, New Orleans, USA (2001)
11. Lowe, D. and Hall, W.: Hypermedia & the Web: An Engineering Approach, Wiley (1999)
12. Millard, D.E., Moreau, L., Davis, H.C., and Reich, S.: FOHM: A Fundamental Open Hypertext Model for Investigating Interoperability between Hypertext Domains. In: Proceedings of the Eleventh ACM Conference on Hypertext and Hypermedia, San-Antonio, Texas, ACM, 6 (2000) 93-102.
13. Michaelides, D.T., Millard, D.E., Weal, M.J. and De Roure, D.C.: Auld Leaky: A Contextual Open Hypermedia Link Server. In: Proceedings of the 7th Workshop on Open Hypermedia Systems, ACM Hypertext Conference, Åarhus, Denmark (2001)
14. Tsandilas, T., schraefel, m.c.: Usable Adaptive Hypermedia Systems. New Review of Hypermedia and Multimedia, 10(1)(2004) 5-29
15. Yankelovich, N., Haan, B. J., Meyrowitz, N., and Drucker, S.M.: Intermedia: The Concept and the Construction of a Seamless Information Environment. IEEE Computer, 21(1)(1988) 81-96

Personalized Navigation in Open Information Space Represented by Ontology*

Katarína Matušíková and Mária Bieliková

Institute of Informatics and Software Engineering, Faculty of Informatics
and Information Technologies, Slovak University of Technology
Ilkovičova 3, 842 16 Bratislava, Slovakia
cakanka@gmail.com, bielik@fiit.stuba.sk

Abstract. In this paper we deal with personalized navigation in an open information space in order to support effective orientation in increasing amount of information accessible through the web. We present a method for personalized navigation based on social navigation where information space is represented by an ontology. We discuss potential contributions of using the ontology representation for the navigation in open information spaces and for the navigational ability to deal with frequent change of the information contents.

1   Introduction

Assisting a user in finding relevant information by navigating in a large information space through a web-based application is a key requirement today. We follow the following research directions for improving navigation: *semantic web* that focuses on adding semantic layer into the web information space for possibility of automatic information processing [8], techniques for *adaptive navigation* that enable personalization [1], and *social navigation* that uses the collective knowledge of large community of users [4] for improving navigation. This combination is important in order to overcome problems related to navigation in open information spaces such as difficult orientation in the information space due to complex informational potential or frequent change of the information content.

There exist several techniques that provide effective support of navigation in a closed information spaces (such as educational book or digital library) [1]. They are successful in an attempt to navigate a user to his goals especially because of the known structure of the information space. However, navigation within open spaces deals with complex informational potential and frequent changes of the content. Existing approaches supporting navigation in open information spaces gain information from resources by an analysis of the content [7] or by sharing knowledge within users with similar interests (social navigation [3]). Content-based and social navigation are far from the precision of closed information

---

* This work was supported by Science and Technology Assistance Agency under the contract No. APVT-20-007104 and State programme of research and development "Establishing of Information Society".

V. Wade, H. Ashman, and B. Smyth (Eds.): AH 2006, LNCS 4018, pp. 298–302, 2006.

space techniques when offering the most relevant information. Despite of their ability to work with large information spaces they do not provide the full power of navigation support in such a scale as it was provided by closed information space oriented adaptive hypermedia systems.

The aim of this paper is to present a method for personalized navigation support based on mentioned approaches. It is proposed for the usage in large information spaces with frequent change of the information content. We use information about a user group behavior for coloring interesting parts of the information space represented by an ontology.

2   Method Overview

Proposed method for personalized navigation:

- *is based on semantics description by an ontology:* this enables to split an information fragment from its characteristics; thus we can bind personalized ratings not only to the particular information fragment, but also to its characteristics;
- *uses social navigation:* navigation is realized using group "footprints" of users with possibly similar goals and preferences;
- *uses techniques for effective navigation:* we use maps and landmarks to support user orientation in the information space [2]; we also use techniques developed for closed information spaces such as adaptive annotation, adaptive link generation and adaptive sorting [1].

Personalization comprises of two processes: acquiring navigational information and using this information to navigate user through information space. Process of acquiring navigational information consists of two steps:

1. *Record user access* – we create a new ontology object representing the user access and describing the attributes of this access.
2. *Infer and update navigational information* (rating) for the user and for his group – ratings are maintained not only for the target information fragment but also for its properties and related information fragments according the ontology definition. This way we bound the navigational information to the information fragment and also its properties. Consequently, even when the target information fragment is no more current we are still able to use gained navigational information and apply it for similar information fragments.

Process of using navigational information consists of the following steps:

1. *Find all values of selected dimension* and find corresponding subspace for every one of them.
2. *Get groups ratings* of these subspaces.
3. *Get actual user ratings* of these subspaces.
4. *Display navigational map* containing results of navigation enriched with personalized ratings.

Our method works with user, domain and observation models. Each model is represented by an ontology. Using an ontology for models representation allows to explore user goals and preferences similarity to create groups, define informational fragments hierarchy in different dimensions and their relations, record navigational information (ratings), and use them for personalization.

3   Creating Navigational Information

Navigation is realized using properties and relations that describe target navigational class in the domain model. Every property of the target navigational class can represent a dimension and its values constitute a range of this dimension. The information space map shows the information space divided according to the selected dimensions (properties) by displaying a set of target information fragments for every value the dimension can take. In every such set there are visualized all target information fragments that have the property (represented by dimension) with particular value characterizing the set.

The information space map provides also a navigation among multi dimensions. Sets created according previously selected dimensions are displayed within the sets of the last selected dimension (e.g., see the *full time* dimension on the Figure 1). Thus, the whole information space is divided into sets according to the last selected dimension. Every set on this level contains other sets representing dimensions selected one step before the last and so on.

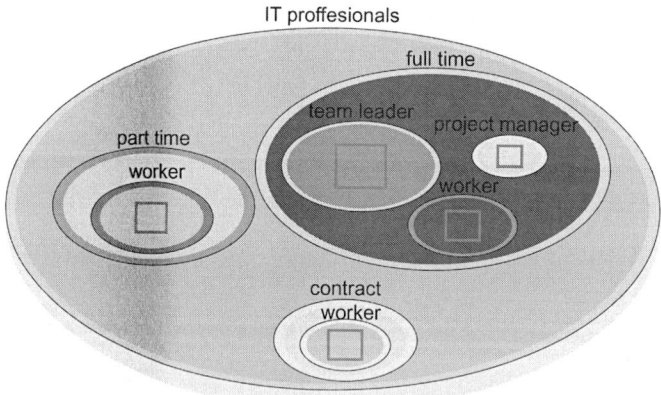

Fig. 1. Presentation of several dimensions

We record every user interaction (e.g., the selection of the dimension, its property or the information fragment selection) and use this information to create and update recommendations or rates. The record of the information about the user interaction is realized in the object of the *Access* class (from the Observation model).

Despite the navigational information a user can get lost in the information space. In such case the user is typically looking for his way until several probes among wrong subspaces. We do not consider the information about these "confused" accesses to create a recommendation. We perform the transformation of the access information into ratings only after the user proves he has really found the relevant information. As a proof we consider the user access to the target information fragment (and his visit of it for a certain time). Then we use all previously recorded accesses to create recommendations. In this way we bind the recommendations not only to target information fragments but also to every of their properties and values that has been selected on the way to find this target.

4   Using Navigational Information

The crucial part of personalized navigation lies in a visualization of navigational information to guide a user to his desired information fragments. The map of the personalized information space contains the following navigational information:

- *selected dimensions:* list containing selected outlines of properties;
- *other dimensions:* list of properties that can be selected as a dimension;
- *dimensions rates:* the *rateValue* of the rate of every not yet selected dimension for the user and his group; graphical expression of these values by color intensity represents user's "footprints" and the "footprints" of his group;
- *information space map:* a map containing sets, their labels, rates and links to target information fragments;
- *multidimensional view:* the information space structured into sets and subsets according to a few dimensions; every dimension corresponds to particular set level;
- *mutual set position:* location of sets on the map expresses their mutual relation;
- *set size:* reflects the number of items in a set in comparison with other sets;
- *set label:* markings of sets by keywords that show the common property value for all items in particular set;
- *set rates:* the *rateValue* of the rate of every set for the user and his group (likewise dimensions rates); graphical expression of these values is accomplished by color intensity represents the user's "footprints" (the outline color) and "footprints" of his group (the fill color).

The user and group "footprints" from previous searching in the information space are the crucial elements of personalized navigation. The user traffic fulfills the task to navigate user by confrontation with the group traffic – the user sees the differences in exploration of particular information subspace between himself and his group.

5   Conclusions

In this paper we have presented a method for personalized navigation that deals with support of navigation in open information spaces. The method is based on social navigation principles with employing semantics of an application domain represented by the ontology. It is able to resist frequent information content changes and preserves gained navigational information despite of the changes. We developed a navigation support tool PENA [5] that is based on proposed method. We tested its applicability in labor supply domain within the scope of a larger project at the Slovak University of Technology [6].

To solve the problem of acquiring navigational information we used social navigation principles. "Collective knowledge" navigate a user to a job offers sets showing him, which set his group has considered as the "interesting" one (in comparison with his characteristics presented in the user model). The use of ontology enabled us to split information fragments and their characteristics. We bind the acquired navigational information to both information fragments and their characteristics. Thus the navigational information is preserved even when the source information fragment is no more available or actual – it is still valid for fragment characteristics and we can use it to navigate user to information fragments with similar characteristics.

One of the most important parts of navigation is the visualization of navigational results. We use the ontology potential to structure the information space into subspaces (sets) to make the navigation more effective. This structure is visualized for the user on the information space map enriched by intuitive annotations with labels and colors.

References

1. Brusilovsky, P. Methods and techniques of adaptive hypermedia. *User Modeling and User Adapted Interaction*, 6 (2-3) 1996, 87-129.
2. Brusilovsky, P., Rizzo, R. Using maps and landmarks for navigation between closed and open corpus hyperspace in Web-based education. *The New Review of Hypermedia and Multimedia* 9, 2002, 59-82.
3. Brusilovsky, P., Chavan, G., Farzan, R. Social Adaptive Navigation Support for Open Corpus Electronic Textbooks. In *Proc. of 3rd Int. Conf. on Adaptive Hypermedia and Adaptive Web-Based Systems – AH 2004.* P. De Bra, W. Nejdl (Eds.). Springer LNCS 3137, 2004, pp.24 -33.
4. Dieberger, A., et. al. Social Navigation: Techniques for Building More Usable Systems. *Interactions*, 7, 6, 2000, 36-45.
5. Matušíková, K. Personalized Navigation in an Information Space. Master Thesis. Slovak University of Technology in Bratislava. 2005.
6. Návrat, P., Bieliková, M., Rozinajová, V. Methods and Tools for Acquiring and Presenting Information and Knowledge in the Web. In *Proc. of Int. Conf. on Computer Systems and Technologies – CompSysTech'2005.* June 2005, Varna, Bulgaria.
7. Polčicová, G., Návrat, P. Semantic Similarity in Content-Based Filtering. In *Proc. of Advances in Databases and Information Systems – ADBIS 2002*, Y. Manolopoulos, P. Návrat (Eds.), Springer LNCS 2435, 2002, pp. 80-85.
8. W3C Semantic Web. 2004. http://www.www.org/2001/sw/

A Unified Approach to Adaptive Hypermedia Personalisation and Adaptive Service Composition

Ian O'Keeffe, Owen Conlan, and Vincent Wade

Knowledge and Date Engineering Group,
School of Computer Science and Statistics, Trinity College Dublin, Ireland
{Ian.OKeeffe, Owen.Conlan, Vincent.Wade}@cs.tcd.ie

Abstract. Adaptive Hypermedia is utilised in several domains, such as eLearning and professional training, where there is a growing movement towards the use of cognitively richer and more 'active' approaches to user engagement. In order to support this move, it is vital that adaptive personalisation systems, in these domains, are capable of integrating adaptively composed activities into adaptively personalised content compositions [1]. Through the integration of the approaches that are used in the automated composition of web services with those found in Adaptive Hypermedia, we believe that it will be possible to support a unified approach to the adaptation of content and services through the leveraging of the characteristics that are common to both adaptive application domains.

1 Introduction

Research in the area of Adaptive Hypermedia (AH) has focused on the adaptive selection, at run-time, of multimedia content in tandem with the personalised sequencing and presentation of that content. Examples of such systems include: AHA! [2], KnowledgeTree [3] and APeLS [4]. In parallel, the Semantic Web community has seen a growing focus on the application of adaptivity to Web Service Composition (WSC). Here the approach involves the dynamic selection, sequencing and choreography of services that is typically based on the completion of a desired application goal or objective.

Their is a growing move towards the application of pedagogical strategies, such as WebQuest and Action Mazes, in eLearning. Such strategies aim to provide cognitively richer learning experiences through the use of interactive activities, which engage the learner. This has highlighted a need for the integration of activities into more traditional hypermedia solutions. Furthermore, authoring tools such as LAMS [5] and ACCT [6] also promote the use of activities as the basis for eLearning. As such, they require learning environments that support both content delivery and the provision of interactive services [7]. By utilising web service technology and the associated service composition approaches it is possible to provide services that are adaptively selected and composed [8] in a manner that complements the goals of AH.

V. Wade, H. Ashman, and B. Smyth (Eds.): AH 2006, LNCS 4018, pp. 303–307, 2006.

The necessary functionality can be achieved through the integration of adaptive web service composition techniques with those of AH. In order for this integration to carry significant benefits it should be carried out based on the common approaches to adaptation used in both domains and should also recognise the inherent differences that exist between AH and service composition. This leads to the need for an analysis of both domains to be carried out.

The rest of this paper is structured as follows, section 2 presents an overview of the approaches used in both AH and adaptive web service composition. This is followed, in section 3, by an analysis of the features that are common to both domains as well as those which differentiate them. Finally, section 4 discusses the conclusions drawn from this research.

2   Approaches to Adaptation and Personalisation

In both AH and Adaptive Web Service Composition (AWSC), the aim is to achieve a desired outcome through the composition of available resources while taking into account the requirements of the user, as well as other contextual information. In both application domains many different approaches exist, each of which has its own advantages and limitations.

2.1   Adaptive Hypermedia

Adaptive Hypermedia Systems (AHS) focus on providing two main adaptive behaviours, the adaptive selection and sequencing of content (adaptive navigation) and the adaptive presentation of resources to the user [9]. Traditionally, the goal of AH is to present the user with appropriate material from a much larger hyperspace while maintaining the associated benefits of hypermedia.

Adaptive navigation can be realised in several different ways, these include: direct guidance; link sorting; link hiding; link annotation. Adaptive presentation traditionally involves the use of techniques such as conditional text and stretch text to expand the verbosity of a piece of text as necessary. More recent AH systems have combined the use of adaptive navigation and presentation in order to provide more advanced personalisation behaviours, for example the application of learning styles [10, 11] or device attributes [12, 13] as adaptive axes.

AHS can be described using an abstract model consisting of four main components: a domain model, a user model, an adaptation model and an Adaptive Engine. The domain model provides the AHS with information about the knowledge domain in which it is operating. The user model represents the system's current view of the user, containing information about key attributes of the learner, which the system can use to inform the adaptation process. The final component is the adaptation model, which consists of a set of rules describing how the adaptation will be carried out. This is used by the Adaptive Engine to reconcile the user model with the domain model.

2.2   Adaptive Web Service Composition

AWSC aims to provide previously unavailable functionality through the composition of many heterogeneous services. Current work in this area can be generalised into two approaches, the use of workflow composition and the use of AI planning techniques. Workflow based approaches rely on the manual composition of services using languages such as BPEL4WS. AI planners, attempt to deal with the dynamic nature of service orientated environments through the dynamic composition of services based on their meta descriptions and functional properties as well as the initial state of the 'world' and the desired goal state. This paper will focus on the AI planning approaches to AWSC as these compliment those used in AH.

Planning approaches to service composition generally consist of four components, a planning engine, a semantically rich description of the available services, a definitions of the 'worlds' current state and the required goal state.

Service selection and composition is not only informed by the functional characteristics of services, but also by non-functional properties and it is these properties that allow the composition to be personalised [14]. Information captured in a user model can affect the selection process in order to ensure that the resulting composition not only has the desired functionality but that it also carries out that functionality in a manner that is most suitable to the user.

The planner described by McIlraith et al. in [15] uses situation calculus (preconditions and effects) to describe services and which uses a procedural programme to compose services based on these descriptions. The Unpop [16] system uses a rule based approach that infers over machine readable service descriptions which focus on the messages (parameters) sent and received by the service. SHOP2 [17] takes an alternative approach, using OWL-S ontologies to describe services and employing a Hierarchical Task Network planner to devolve a high level task/goal into atomic actions which can be mapped to individual services as described by the ontology.

3   Commonalities and Differences

It is clear, from the approaches described above, that AH and AWSC are very similar in some respects and that lessons can be learned from each. AH can be used to compose a set of concepts in order to facilitate the comprehension of a specific topic. Similarly, AWSC attempts to combine a set of services into a plan which will achieve a specific goal, for example to carry out a learning activity or to achieve a knowledge state. Prior knowledge and prerequisite knowledge are often used in AH as adaptive axes. In web service composition functional and non-functional service properties can be considered analogous.

At a more concrete level, AH and AWSC share several common features, key to both AH and AWSC systems is the utilisation of semantic models to describe the 'elemental' resources that are available for composition in the respective approaches, for example learning objects in adaptive content composition and service descriptions in adaptive service composition. In both domains the composition process is based on the inference of sequencing logic to compose the respective elements. Furthermore, this inference process is influenced or 'informed' by external information, for example user or context models.

Despite the commonalities, AWSC and AH are not the same and as such there are some significant differences which must be accommodated in a system which combines both. Unlike traditional content, web services are parameterised, that is they take inputs and return values. This is important as the behaviour of a web service can be influenced by its parameters to the extent that a single service can have several very different outcomes. The existence of parameters also imposes requirements on a composition, it is necessary to capture the flow of information between web services in the composition as well as the sequencing of the services. Unlike traditional AH content, web services are capable of returning errors when they fail to execute correctly.

The integration of AH and adaptive service composition can be approached in different ways. Existing AH techniques could be utilised through treating the services as content, for example by embedding a service into a piece of content, and carrying out the composition as normal. However, this approach is simplistic as it ignores the differences that exist and as such cannot take advantage of the benefits that web service composition presents. For example, the parameterisation of the service must either be ignored or 'hand crafted' with little room for information to flow between services. A more transparent approach to the problem, based on the common feature of both, in which the differences between services and content are acknowledged would be a more interesting solution. This solution would allow the strengths of web services and of service composition to be fully utilised in conjunction with those of AH.

4   Discussion and Future Work

This paper has presented the approaches supported in AWSC and AH. Through an analysis of the existing approaches in both AH and AWSC, the commonalities that exist in both have been identified. Both domains adaptively select their respective 'elemental' components based on semantically rich metadata and combine these components by inference based on sequencing logic. Furthermore, in both cases the selection and composition are guided by information, for example user preferences or contextual data, that are modeled outside of the adaptation process. Although differences do exist, the common features identified suggest that web services and hypermedia can be adaptively composed in an integrated manner.

We believe that a combination of AWSC and AH techniques would be highly relevant in next generation eLearning, as we move to more 'active' learning events, where presonalisation is concerned not only with content composition, but also the personalisation and sequencing of activities. The ability to deliver interactive and engaging activity based, personalised offerings has many advantages.

References

1. Hodgins, W.: Leadership in learning: Accelerating the arrival of the future. Closing presentation at the Innovations in eLearning Symposium (2005)
2. De Bra, P., Aerts, A., Berden, B., De Lange, B., Rousseau, B., Santic, T., Smits, D., Stash, N.: AHA! the adaptive hypermedia architecture. In: Proceedings of the ACM Hypertext Conference. (2003) 81–84
3. Brusilovsky, P.: KnowledgeTree: A distributed architecture for adaptive e-learning. In: Proceedings of The Thirteenth International World Wide Web Conference, WWW 2004 (Alternate track papers and posters), ACM Press (2004) 104–113
4. Conlan, O., Hockemeyer, C., Wade, V., Albert, D.: Metadata driven approaches to facilitate adaptivity in personalized eLearning systems. Journal of the Japanese Society for Information and Systems in Education **1**(1) (2002) 38–45
5. Dalziel, J.: Implementing learning design: The learning activity management system (LAMS). In: Proceedings of ASCILITE Conference. (2003)
6. Dagger, D., Wade, V., Conlan, O.: Personalisation for all: Making adaptive course composition easy. Journal of Educational Technology and Society **8**(3) (2005) 9–25 Special Issue on "Authoring of Adaptive Hypermedia".
7. Wilson, S., Blinco, K., Rehak, D.: An E-Learning framework. In: Proceedings of the Advaning Learning Technology Interoperability Lab Conference. (2004)
8. Rao, J., Su, X.: A survey of automated web service composition methods. In: Proceedings of the First International Workshop on Semantic Web Services and Web Process Composition SWSWPC, Springer-Verlag (2004) 43
9. Brusilovsky, P.: Methods and techniques of adaptive hypermedia. User Modeling and User-Adapted Interaction **6**(2-3) (1996) 87–129
10. Bajraktarevic, N., Hall, W., Fullick, P.: Incorporating learning styles in hypermedia environment: Empirical evaluation. Workshop on Adaptive Hypermedia and Adaptive Web-Based Systems (2003) 41–53
11. Papanikolaou, K.A., Grigoriadou, M., Kornilakis, H., Magoulas, G.D.: Personalizing the interaction in a web-based educational hypermedia system: the case of INSPIRE. User Modeling and User-Adapted Interaction **13**(3) (2003) 213–267
12. Herder, E., van Dijk, B.: Personalized adaptation to device characteristics. In Bra, P.D., Brusilovsky, P., Conejo, R., eds.: Adaptive Hypermedia and Adaptive Web-Based Systems, Second International Conference. Volume 2347 of Lecture Notes in Computer Science., Springer (2002) 598–602
13. Brady, A., Conlan, O., Wade, V.: Dynamic composition and personalization of PDA-based eLearning - personalized mLearning. In Richards, G., ed.: Proceedings of World Conference on E-Learning in Corporate, Government, Healthcare, and Higher Education 2004, Washington, DC, USA, AACE (2004) 234–242
14. Higel, S., Lewis, D., Wade, V.: Realising personalised web service composition through adaptive replanning. In: 1st Int'l Workshop on Agents, Web Services and Ontologies Merging (AWeSOMe'05). Volume 3762., Springer-Verlag (2005) 49–58
15. McIlraith, S., Son, T.: Adapting Golog for composition of semantic web services. In: Proceeding of the Eighth International Conference on Principles of Knowledge Representation and Reasoning. (2002)
16. McDermott, D.: Estimated-regression planning for interactions with web services. In: Proceedings of the Sixth International Conference on AI Planning and Scheduling, AAAI Press (2002)
17. Wu, D., Sirin, E., Hendler, J., Nau, D.: Automatic web services composition using SHOP2. Workshop on Planning for Web Services (2003)

Can Adaptive Systems Participate in Their Design? Meta-adaptivity and the Evolution of Adaptive Behavior

Alexandros Paramythis

Johannes Kepler University,
Institute for Information Processing and Microprocessor Technology (FIM)
Altenbergerstraße 69, A-4040 Linz, Austria
alpar@fim.uni-linz.ac.at

Abstract. This paper discusses the opportunities arising from the employment of meta-adaptivity as a tool that can facilitate the design of adaptation. The discussion is structured around a specific example problem in the domain of adaptive course delivery systems. The paper builds upon this example to argue that meta-adaptivity is a viable solution to the "ground up" design of adaptive systems, and may be especially suited for cases where there is little empirically validated evidence to support design decisions.

1 Introduction

As any researcher or practitioner in the field of adaptive hypermedia systems will readily admit, designing adaptive behavior is hard. Some of the difficulties stem from the lack of established and proven practices in this respect; others are due to the lack of sufficient empirical evidence to support the design of adaptation. Furthermore, although adaptive systems are inherently interactive systems, the design approaches, methods and tools available from the field of human-computer interaction do not suffice in themselves in addressing the aforementioned problems, as they have not been devised to design systems that dynamically change their behavior to suit the (changing) requirements of individuals. At the same time, increased attention is being paid to adaptation meta-data, and, specifically, their generation and incorporation into the adaptation design / authoring process. This is both spurred by the goal of achieving meta-adaptivity *per se*, and a natural consequence of the introduction of semantic web technologies for the attainment of adaptivity in modern adaptive systems (which, to a large extent, provide an "enabling" layer for meta-adaptivity). In the context of this paper, the term "meta-adaptivity" will be used to refer to the capacity on the part of an adaptive system to observe, assess and modify its own adaptive behavior, towards a (set of) adaptation design goal(s). Furthermore, we will be exclusively focusing on a specific type of meta-adaptivity, namely self-regulation (in short, self-regulation assumes the capability for an adaptive system to perform self-evaluation and learn from that) [2]. This paper argues and provides an example of how meta-adaptivity offers a design tool, or vehicle, that potentially facilitates the design of adaptive systems.

V. Wade, H. Ashman, and B. Smyth (Eds.): AH 2006, LNCS 4018, pp. 308–312, 2006.
© Springer-Verlag Berlin Heidelberg 2006

2 Example Adaptive System

This section presents an example design case study of an adaptive system. The basis of our exemplary system design is a simple, yet quite popular, adaptive function in the area of adaptive hypermedia systems: the annotation of links within learning content. For our needs we will assume a system that exhibits characteristics common to a large range of adaptive systems in the field (e.g., NetCoach [5]). The system's most important features are as follows:

- The system's domain model is a small, course-specific ontology comprising: learning concepts, corresponding modules / pages, and semantic relations between these.
- The user model is an overlay model (over the domain), with a number of discrete, user-specific "states" with respect to each of the concepts in the domain model.
- Individual user models are updated on the basis of observable user activities.
- Adaptation logic is expressed through adaptation rules, such as in the case of [4].
- Further to the above, the user model may contains other user attributes, some of them explicitly provided by the user, and others inferred from user activity.
- Based on the user model, the system can decide on recommendations regarding the future visits of different modules / pages. It is exactly on the basis of these recommendations that link annotation is being considered in the context of our example.

The design question at hand is whether and in what way to annotate links to concepts or modules to convey the semantics of the system's recommendations. Although there is a considerable body of research on this question, for the purposes of this example, we will assume that the system's designer has no empirical evidence to support the considered design alternatives. The alternatives themselves are encapsulated in five different strategies as far as link annotation is concerned: *Strategy A: No annotation.* This can be considered the base-line strategy, and would simply involve not exposing the user to the system's recommendations. *Strategy B: Annotation using different link colors.* In this strategy different colors are used directly on the links to signify system recommendation. *Strategy C: Annotation using bullets of different colors.* This is very similar to strategy B above, with the exception that the colors are applied externally to the links. Annotations (i.e., the bullets) are dynamically added to the document. *Strategy D: Annotation using custom icons.* A variation of strategy C above, with the bullets replaced by icons intended to carry more semantic information. *Strategy E: Link hiding.* This strategy involves hiding (but not disabling) links [1], for which the system's recommendation is that the user is not yet ready to visit them.

Given the strategies above, the design question at hand is which one(s) to use, and for a given user and context of use. Note that the strategies are not necessarily mutually exclusive. Also note that it would be desirable to identify situations that might justify a transition from one strategy to another.

3 Evolution of Adaptive Behavior

The designer starts out with no evidence about when and under what conditions to use each strategy, or whether, indeed any one strategy is "better" than all the rest. Each strategy has obvious trade-offs as far as flexibility and user control over the navigation process is concerned. The designer's goal however, is clear: students should encounter concepts that they are not "ready" for as little as possible, and this should be achieved with the least possible restrictions on interaction / navigation. Continuing with the example introduced above, we will look at three potential iterations that the design process could have gone through.

The first step of the design would involve the encoding of the strategies as sets of adaptation actions (e.g., as in [3]). Since the designer has no evidence regarding the applicability of the different strategies, these cannot be directly assigned to adaptation logic. The system would need to be able to recognize these strategies and apply them (separately or combined) in more or less a trial-and-error fashion. The design information that already exists, and can be conveyed to the system, is which strategies are mutually exclusive, and which ones can be applied in combination. Given these constraints, and a suitably encoded representation of the design goal stated earlier as self-regulation metric, the system is then ready to undergo the first round of user testing.

We will assume that the results of the first round of testing do not yet suffice for building a comprehensive body of adaptation logic to guide the system's adaptive behavior. They do, however, provide enough evidence for the following:

- Eliminating strategies (and combinations thereof) that do not seem to meet the desired design goal under any circumstances. In the context of the ongoing example we can assume this includes strategy B and all its combinations (e.g., because changing links' colors seems to be confusing for users).
- Categorizing and providing a tentative "ranking" of the remaining combinations, based, respectively, on their design / interaction semantics, and on the rate of success they have exhibited during the first round of testing.

The aforementioned categorization and ranking process, might result in something like the following in the case of our example: *Category I*: Includes only strategy A and corresponds to absolute freedom in navigation, with no system assistance / guidance whatsoever. *Category II*: Includes the uncombined strategies C and D and corresponds to absolute freedom in navigation, but this time with explicit system assistance / guidance. *Category III*: Includes all combinations that include strategy E and corresponds to the application of restrictions on the navigation, to enforce a path through the learning material. The preceding categorization and ranking is, obviously, only one of several possibilities. It does, nevertheless, serve to demonstrate the following points:

- Although it is a ranking, it is not obvious in which "direction" it should be applied. For example, should the system start with the most "liberal" (in terms of navigation freedom) category and move to the more "restrictive" one?
- Applying such a ranking incorporates two concepts that may need to be extricated and made explicit: the concept of the "default" category of strategies that might be applicable for a new user; and the concept of a "fallback" category that gets applied when none of the available categories / strategies has the desired effect.

For our example, we will assume that the designer has opted to use the ranking in the order presented above (i.e., "liberal" to "restrictive"), and to let the default and fallback categories be the first and last ones respectively. With these additional constraints, the system would be ready for a second round of user testing.

The introduction of additional structure in the adaptation design space effected in the previous phase, along with more results from user testing, based on that structure, can be expected to finally provide detailed enough results to start building more concrete and comprehensive adaptation logic around the alternative strategies.

According to results from related research in the literature, this phase might result in user model-based adaptation logic along the following lines:

− For users that are novice or unfamiliar with the knowledge domain of the learning material, the more restrictive category (III) of strategies would be applicable.
− Within Category III, a ranking between strategies would be possible, such as: (i) strategy E − link hiding, no explicit recommendations by the system, (ii) combination D+E − link hiding and icons to "explain" the rationale behind provided guidance, and (iii) combination C+E − same as previous, but with less visual clutter.
− Category II (uncombined strategies C or D) would be reserved for users that are sufficiently familiar with the system and the recommendation mechanism, and Category I for users that already have familiarity with the knowledge domain, or exhibit behavior aimed at circumventing constraints applied on their navigation freedom.

Please note that the above adaptation logic is only exemplary in nature and might differ significantly from the actual results one might get with a specific system and learning material. Also note that, although the example case study is ending here, there is no reason why in real-world settings this would be the last design iteration.

4 Adaptive System Design Revisited

Based on the design evolution outlined in the previous section, we will now move on to an overview of the meta-adaptive facilities being utilized behind the scenes, and their effects on the design process.

To start with, the basis of the design iterations has been the derivation of new knowledge regarding their suitability for different users (or contexts of use) given the overall design goal / self-regulation metrics. This knowledge, in its simplest form, is derived by applying alternative (combinations of) adaptation strategies, and assessing the extent to which the self-regulation metrics are satisfied, always in connection to the current user's model. Knowledge derivation, then, is achieved by analyzing all recorded cases where a particular strategy has had similar results, and identifying common user model attributes among the respective users. This is the core of the "learning" facilities in the context of self-regulated adaptivity, and their output could be expressed in various forms, including for instance as preliminary adaptation logic, intended to be reviewed, verified and incorporated into the systems by the designers. Although rather straightforward, the above step may already suffice to provide valuable input to the design process. For example, it should be capable to identify strategies that are not suitable for any (category of) users, in any context of use. This was assumed to be the case in the elimination of strategy B and all its combinations in the previous section.

A second set of capabilities alluded to in the previous section is the categorization, or "clustering" of adaptation strategies, as well as their "ranking". Categorization can take place mainly along two dimensions: (a) The system can try to identify strategies that have similar effects with respect to the self-regulation metrics, given sufficiently similar user models; the output of this process would be a provisional clustering of strategies, based on their "cause and effect" patterns. (b) The system can try to identify the differentiating subsets of user models that render some strategies more effective than others. These dimensions give, respectively, two semantically rich measures of similarity and differentiation of adaptation strategies. When sufficient meta-data about the user model itself is available, the system can combine that with the measures to provide provisional rankings of alternatives within categories.

Before closing it is important to note that the example in the previous section, as well as the analysis in this section, only assume three types of analytical assessment capabilities on the part of a self-regulating adaptive system. Although these are by far not the only ones possible, they are already adequate for the type of design support put forward in this paper. Space constraints do not permit going into a discussion of additional possibilities, or of the requirements placed on the adaptation infrastructure by this type of self-regulation; interested readers are referred to [2] for details on the later.

In conclusion, this paper has presented a case for the use of meta-adaptivity as a facilitator in the design of adaptive systems. The applicability of the proposed approach is of course not universal: it requires that a self-regulating adaptive system (or infrastructure) is already operational, and that the cost of authoring the alternative adaptive behaviors is not prohibitive. It is also mainly intended for cases where there exist several alternative adaptive behaviors, with little or no empirical evidence as to their suitability for different categories of users, or different "states" of a single user. Within these confines, however, it is argued that meta-adaptivity does not represent only the next logical step in the evolution of adaptive systems, but also a potentially irreplaceable tool in how we design such systems in the future.

References

[1] Brusilovsky, P. (1996). Methods and techniques of adaptive hypermedia. *User Modeling and User-Adapted Interaction*, 6(2-3), 87-129.
[2] Paramythis, A. (2004). Towards Self-Regulating Adaptive Systems. In Weibelzahl, S., & Henze, N. (Eds.), *Proceedings of the Annual Workshop of the SIG Adaptivity and User Modeling in Interactive Systems of the German Informatics Society (ABIS04)*, Berlin, October 4-5 (pp. 57-63).
[3] Paramythis, A., & Stephanidis, C. (2005). A Generic Adaptation Framework for Hypermedia Systems. In Chen, S. Y., & Magoulas, G. D. (Eds.) *Adaptable and Adaptive Hypermedia Systems* (pp. 80-103). Idea Group, Inc.
[4] Stephanidis, C., Paramythis, A., Zarikas, V., & Savidis, A. (2004). The PALIO Framework for Adaptive Information Services. In A. Seffah & H. Javahery (Eds.), Multiple User Interfaces: Cross-Platform Applications and Context-Aware Interfaces (pp. 69-92). Chichester, UK: John Wiley & Sons, Ltd.
[5] G. Weber, H.-C. Kuhl, and S. Weibelzahl. Developing adaptive internet based courses with the authoring system NetCoach. In S. Reich, M. Tzagarakis, and P. de Bra (Eds.), *Hypermedia: Openness, Structural Awareness, and Adaptivity*, (pp.226-238), Berlin, 2001.

A System for Adaptive Information Retrieval

Ioannis Psarras and Joemon Jose

Department of Computing Science, University of Glasgow, Glasgow, G12 8QQ

Abstract. In this paper, we describe the design and development of personal information assistant (PIA), a system aiming to meet individual needs of the searchers. The system's goal is to provide more up-to-date and relevant information to users with respect to their needs and interests. The main component of the system is a profile learner for capturing temporal user needs, based on implicit feedback gathering techniques. It monitors the system usage, the documents viewed and other user actions in order to infer users' changing needs.

1 Introduction

Web search engines, designed for discovering documents online, are very popular and generally perceived to do a good job in finding relevant information on the web. However, recent studies, such as [4, 5], have highlighted that users interact only with a limited number of search results usually among the first page. [4, 5] also demonstrated that, searchers usually choose some relevant information within the first page of results having viewed very few documents. Uncertain about the availability of other relevant documents most users end their search sessions after one or two iterations. In fact, most of the time, they keep looking for information regarding the same topics, for example things that relate to their work. Often such information requirements change by sliding into new topics, based on the changes of user interests. Only way to satisfy such needs is to search on a continuous basis, that is keep looking for information regularly.

In this paper, we argue that a personal information assistant will improve search experience recommending additional documents, relevant to the interests of users. We have developed a system, called PIA (Personal Information Assistant), which makes it easier for people to locate information regarding their needs. Our system adapts to the changing needs of users, manages their multiple search interests, and pro-actively fetches and presents relevant documents on a regular basis. The aim was to build a system capable of modeling people's evolving needs, in an effective way, and use the information provided in order to create a personalized information source for users. The main feature of the system's design, that supports this, is the profiling learning algorithm responsible to discover users' interests. Another key aspect of PIA's design is the extractor algorithm that facilitates implicit information gathering from the sources the user showed some interest. More details, about profile creation and the various algorithms used, are provided in later sections.

V. Wade, H. Ashman, and B. Smyth (Eds.): AH 2006, LNCS 4018, pp. 313–317, 2006.
© Springer-Verlag Berlin Heidelberg 2006

2   Motivation

With the growth of the World Wide Web the need for tools to address problems with information overload, [6], has become more apparent. However, in many situations the information seeking experience is less than satisfactory: often searchers have difficulty finding relevant information. The main reason for this is the lack of effective search interaction and retrieval tools. The existing tools are often ineffective for all but the most simple search tasks [2]. There are three main areas of user interaction with a search engine: selection of initial query words, the assessment of retrieved pages and query modification [3]. To build an effective search tool one has to address the problems of query formulation and support the formation of information needs that are prone to develop or change during a search.

Past solutions, like [1], used mostly explicit feedback gathering to model the user's searching behavior. WebMate [1] is a search agent that supports both Internet searching and browsing. Using multiple vectors to keep track of user's interests, relevant documents can be suggested to the user. The system automatically attempts to learn the user's categories of interest by requiring the explicit marking of pages during normal browsing. However, this form of relevance feedback increases the user's responsibility which can cause inconvenience or introduce confusion. Other such systems are aimed to pro-actively find and filter relevant information that matches our interests. New interests are stored in a simple profile, containing terms related to different interests and hence resulted in poor performance.

We need a pro-active search assistant that addresses these issues, identifies the multiple facets of user needs and can fetch relevant information. In order to reduce the cognitive load in the feedback issues a combination of implicit and explicit feedback gathering can be much more powerful, since they only require minimal user interaction.

3   PIA - Main Components

Personal Information Assistant was developed as an adjunct to the current web search engines. The system was developed using JAVA Enterprise Edition (J2EE) and is based on a three-tier architecture. User queries and other interaction data is captured and processed at the server. The queries are forwarded to Google, and the results are parsed and presented to the browser. At this stage, the user's profile gets updated to exploit the information gathered from the previously issued search. At some future point, the assistant will analyze the information stored and attempt to retrieve additional relevant documents regarding the user's evolving needs.

In order to help the user in judging relevant information PIA uses a summarization system. We have implemented a version of the system described in [7]. It generates summaries of result pages based on the queries and known as query biased summaries. As demonstrated in [7], such summaries will facilitate more interaction with the system.

The main user interface features a personalized homepage for each user and a profile editor. Each user's home page is similar to a portal, where people can view the documents recommended by the system with respect to their interests. Interests are displayed on a priority basis aiming to improve the retrieval performance of the system, since high-priority facets are likely to be more attractive for the user. The other components of the system are the term extractor algorithm and the profile generation scheme, described in subsequent sections.

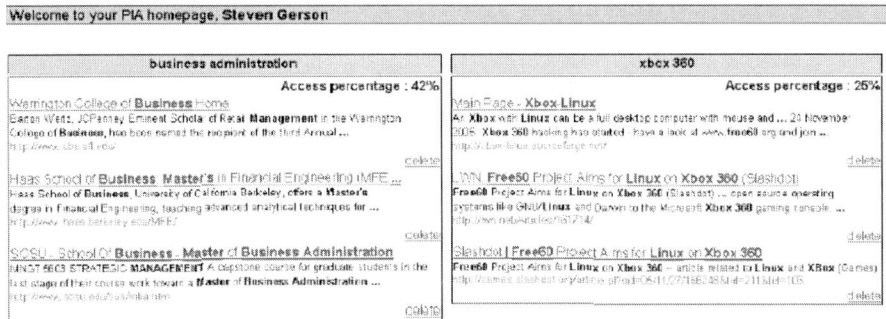

Fig. 1. The personalized home page, displaying additional documents discovered by the system

3.1 Profile Representation and Management

A profile consists of a set of interests that relate to the user requirements. PIA recognizes that user interests are multiple and hence their profile contain multiple facets of user needs. Fundamentally, an interest constitutes a weighted keyword vector, distinguished by a representative name. Such interests can be temporal, which will be eventually discarded, or long-term needs. As discussed in [4], people usually interact very little with information retrieval tools, such as search engines, so forcing them to add their own profiles would definitely decrease the functionality and usability of our system. Therefore, PIA features techniques to make it possible to modify a user's profile implicitly. Using a term extraction algorithm and a profile learning scheme, interests can be discovered and populated without any user interaction. Explicit profile creation is possible, as well as modification of the system's suggested interests, available through the profile editor interface, but it only constitutes an optional feature.

3.2 The Extractor Algorithm

The extraction algorithm strives to extract a set of representative words, from user search iterations, with respect to their information needs. Apart from the search terms, it takes into consideration the search engine snippets and summaries of recently viewed documents, since these directly reflect to the user's information need. Query terms directly express the user's search requirements and are applied an extra weight compared to the other words in the set. For experimentation purposes, three retrieval models have been made available: A boolean model, a frequency model and the well-known TF-IDF model.

After performing thorough tests with all schemes and measuring their performance in a variety of circumstances, we deduced that the frequency model gives the best results for out application. Taking into account the frequency model's formula, where the weight of each term equals to the number of times it occurs in the collection, it is easy to observe that the extracted set of terms is less likely to be random.

3.3   The Profiling Generation Algorithm

The profile learning model is based on the assumption that users will always visit documents related to their search requirements. Therefore, after the user performs a search, web pages that have been viewed are considered to be more relevant than the rest in the result collection. The profiler extracts the most representative words for a query, by continuously monitoring user interaction and exploiting this information to discover representative terms. Before providing a more detailed description of how profiles are created implicitly, some knowledge is needed regarding the extractor algorithm.

We used clustering techniques to detect various facets of users' interests. Having extracted a set of terms from the visited documents in the result set, a single-pass clustering algorithm is applied, using using cosine coefficient as the similarity matching function.

As discussed earlier on, the aim was to profile users' requirements with the least possible effort from them. One of the main issue, that arises, is labeling interests. Asking users to fill in interests' names explicitly is not an option, because we want to go beyond this explicit feedback gathering model. Cluster labeling is one of the most major information retrieval issues. Due to time constraints, simple, but efficient, cluster and interest labeling algorithms were used for this purpose. The most frequent terms, appearing in an interest or a cluster, are most likely to describe it correctly. So, by labeling the interest using the n most popular terms seems to work effectively enough and hence used.

3.4   Finding Additional Documents

The reason for implementing all these algorithms is to present to the user adequate additional relevant documents related to his interests. When the user re-visits the portal, he will get a listing of new documents associated with his interests in a personalized home page, illustrated in figure 1 above. The system takes advantage of the profiler algorithm and formulates a new query by extracting n most frequent words from an interest. During the implementation and evaluation of our system, it was observed that 4-6 query terms are adequate to retrieve additional relevant documents from the web. Finally, it issues an online search using the query formulated and adds m documents retrieved to the related interest.

This process occurs whenever a user logs in to the system, but at most once a day to avoid updating the suggested documents too often. In fact, the whole document updating procedure is completely transparent to the user with no slow-down at all. The system suggests them some documents that might be of interest and they decide whether they want to delete them or not.

4 Conclusion

We have designed, deployed and evaluated a system aiming to supply users with up-to-date information regarding their personal needs. By using an implicit information gathering model we eliminate the necessity of forcing users to create their profiles explicitly. By formulating queries based on the users' interests and automatically seek more information on the web, the assistant recommends additional documents that might be of interest to the users. We also present techniques to keep up with users' evolving needs effectively such as the term extractor scheme and the profile management algorithm.

Acknowledgments

The work reported in this paper is partly funded by the Engineering and Physical Research Council (EPSRC), UK grant number EP/C004108/1.

References

1. Chen, L., & Syraca, K., Webmate: A Personal Agent for Browsing and Searching, Proceedings of the 2nd International Conference on Autonomous Agents, 132-139
2. Dennis, S., McArthur, R. and Bruza, P. (1998). Searching the WWW made easy? The Cognitive Load imposed by Query Refinement Mechanisms. Proceedings of the 3rd Australian Document Computing Symposium.
3. Ingwersen, P. and Willett, P. (1995). An introduction to algorithmic and cognitive approaches for information retrieval. Libri. 45(3/4), 160-177.
4. Jansen, B.J. and Pooch, U. (2000). A Review of Web Searching Studies and a Framework for Future Research. Journal of the American Society for Information Science and Technology. 52(3), 235-246
5. Jansen, B.J., Spink A. and Saracevic, T. (2000). Real life, real users, and real needs: a study and analysis of users on the Web. Information Processing and Management. 36(2), 207-227.
6. Nelson, M.R. (1994). We Have the Information You Want, But Getting It Will Cost You: Being Held Hostage by Information Overload. ACM Crossroads. 1(1).
7. White, R. W., Jose, J. M. and Ruthven, I. (2003). A task-oriented study on the influencing effects of query-biased summarisation in Web searching. Information Processing & Management, 39(5), 707- 733.

Describing Adaptive Navigation Requirements of Web Applications*

Gonzalo Rojas[1,2], Pedro Valderas[1], and Vicente Pelechano[1]

[1] Technical University of Valencia, Camino de Vera s/n 46022 Valencia, Spain
[2] University of Concepcion, Edmundo Larenas 215 Concepcion, Chile
{grojas, pvalderas, pele}@dsic.upv.es

Abstract. This work introduces a proposal to capture adaptive navigation characteristics of a Web Application in the Requirements Specification stage. Tasks that users must be able to achieve are identified and described, considering the navigational adaptations that are needed to fulfill them. By applying a given code generation strategy, it is possible to obtain fully operative prototypes of the adaptive web application from its requirements specification.

1 Introduction

The specification of adaptivity requirements of Web applications has received little attention by Web development proposals. In the case of adaptive navigation requirements, there is a gap between their textual specification and the definition of adaptivity restrictions over navigational primitives, which makes difficult to trace these requirements along the development process. To tackle this problem, we propose a systematic process of requirements specification that supports the description of adaptive navigation requirements. We identify the tasks that users can achieve when interacting with the application, and incorporate user-centered constraints in the task descriptions. These constraints define different access levels to information and functionality for different users. From the requirements specification, we can derive the navigational schema of the application, in terms of the OOWS Navigational Model [1], and from this generate adaptive prototypes by applying a given automatic code generation process [2].

2 Development Process of Web Applications

OOWS [1] is a web engineering method that allows obtaining fully operative prototypes of Web applications from a requirements model. To specify the system requirements, this method proposes to: (1) identify and specify the potential users of the web application; (2) detect the tasks that each user must be able to achieve when interacting with the application; and (3) describe these tasks in terms of the user-application interactions that are required to fulfill them.

* This work has been developed with the support of MEC under the project DESTINO TIN2004-03534 and cofinanced by FEDER.

V. Wade, H. Ashman, and B. Smyth (Eds.): AH 2006, LNCS 4018, pp. 318–322, 2006.

Next, a set of model-to-model transformations are applied to the obtained specification in order to generate an OOWS conceptual schema [1]. Static structure and behaviour of the system are described through a class diagram and dynamic-and-functional models. Navigation is captured by the OOWS navigational model, which incorporates conceptual structures with different implementation alternatives for different users. Finally, fully operative prototypes of the adaptive Web application can be obtained from the OOWS conceptual schema, extending a strategy of automatic code generation for non-adaptive Web applications [2].

3   Deriving Adaptive Navigation Specifications

To specify the adaptive navigation features of a Web application, we firstly need to describe its intended users and the tasks that are provided to them. We propose the definition of a **Diagram of User Stereotypes**, based on the concept introduced by Rich in [3]. This diagram comprises the application-relevant user groups (stereotypes), ordered in a hierarchical structure. User attributes are also defined, comprising personal information, user application-related information (expertise, preferences, etc.) and navigational behaviour. Stereotypes allow specifying a common coarse-grained adaptive solution for similar users, based on their general, shared characteristics; whereas constraints over the defined user attributes determine a fine-grained navigational adaptation, based on specific characteristics of the user.

For the task descriptions, we propose the building of a **Task Taxonomy**, by defining a hierarchical tree that contains the full set of tasks that the system provides. From the *statement of purpose* of the system, which is the most general task, a progressive refinement is performed to obtain more specific tasks, until the level of *elementary tasks*, which are composed by atomic actions. The achievement of an elementary task can be restricted to specific user stereotypes, which implicitly defines the navigational structures that users can access.

3.1   Task Description and Adaptive Navigation Features

Each elementary task is described through a UML-compliant Activity Diagram, defining how users can achieve it. This diagram includes restrictions and preconditions that allow describing different ways to fulfill the same task by different users. We adopt the concept of *Interaction Point (IP)* (introduced in [2]) to represent the moment in which the system provides the user with information and/or operation access, both related to an entity (object of the system domain). Each node of the activity diagram represents an *IP* (solid line) or a *system action* (dashed line); the number of entity instances of an IP (cardinality) is depicted in the upper right corner of the primitive. Each arc represents: (a) a *user action* (information selection or operation activation) if the arc source is an IP or (b) a *node sequence* if the arc source is a system action. In this work, we have incorporated the following primitives to describe adaptive navigation requirements, in terms of entity features and user attributes:

- *Accessibility conditions* over arcs. If the arc source is an *IP*, these conditions must be fulfilled by the user to access the target node; if the arc source is a *system action*, they must be satisfied to continue with the sequence.
- *Select Precondition* of IPs (expressed as a UML *"localPreCondition"*), which must be fulfilled by the set of instances provided in the IP.
- *Sorting Precondition* of IPs (expressed as a UML note stereotyped with the ≪*sorting*≫ keyword). This precondition defines the order in which the entity instances must be provided to the user.

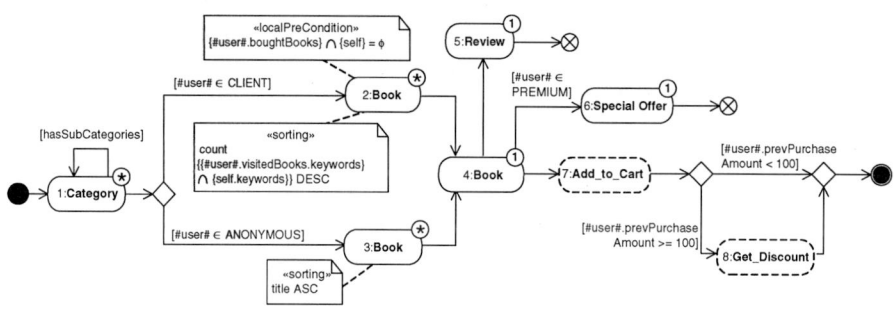

Fig. 1. Activity Diagram of an elementary task

Let us consider an example of a Web-based bookstore. Figure 1 shows the activity diagram of the *"Add Item to Cart"* elementary task. When the user selects one of the book categories presented in (*1:Categories,**) IP, the system gives a list of books that belong to the selected category. If the user belongs to CLIENT stereotype (Fig. 1, upper arc accessibility constraint), this list includes only those books that a user has not already bought (*"localPrecondition"* constraint of (*2:Book,**) IP) and must be ordered according to the number of keywords that displayed books have in common with those books whose pages the client has visited (≪*sorting*≫ condition). If the user belongs to ANONYMOUS stereotype (Fig. 1, lower arc accessibility constraint), there is no restriction to the list of books and they are ordered alphabetically by their titles ((*3:Book,**) IP). Once a book is selected, its description is provided by (*4:Book,1*) IP, from which the user is able to: access a specialized review of it ((*5:Review,1*) IP); check an special offer associated to the book ((*6:Special Offer,1*)), if the user belongs to PREMIUM stereotype; or activate the *7:Add_to_Cart* system action, adding the selected book to the shopping cart. Finally, the system applies a discount (*8:Get_Discount* system action) for a limited group of users, according to their previous purchases.

The features of each entity and the IPs in which they must be shown are defined through *information templates*. Inclusion of these features in a given IP can be ruled by conditions on user attributes, e.g., the full review of a book will be only shown if the connected user has visited information of at least 20 books and accessed the full review of at least an 80% of them.

4   Obtaining an Adaptive Web Application Prototype

By applying a set of mapping rules [4], it is possible to obtain the OOWS navigational schema of the application from the Requirements Specification, supporting adaptive characteristics. Once this is done, a web application prototype is automatically generated. This prototype can be used to verify whether adaptive navigation requirements have been correctly captured.

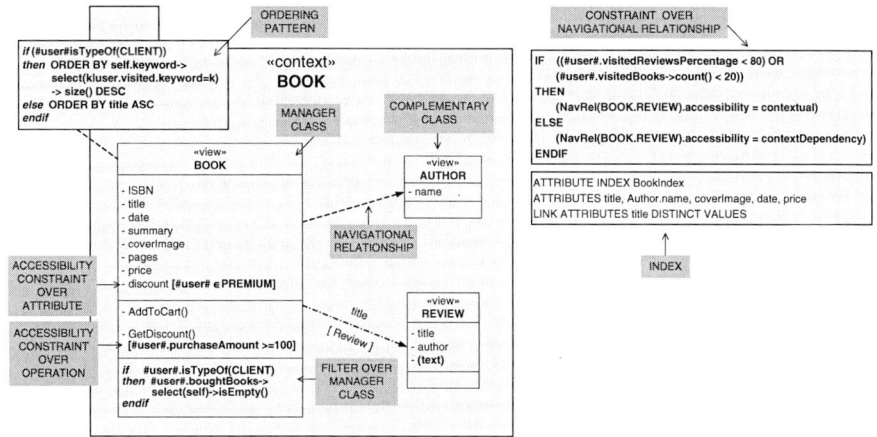

Fig. 2. Adaptive Navigational Context

A *Navigational Context* is the OOWS structure that represents a navigational view of the class diagram. Figure 2 shows the navigational context derived to fulfill the *Add Item to Cart* task. This context shows information about a particular *Book*, its *Author* and *Review*. An index (Fig. 2, middle right side) provides an indexed access to the population of books. Attributes are derived from the features included in information templates, while operations are derived from the *system actions*. In both cases, accessibility constraints defined in the task description have been incorporated in navigational structures. An *Ordering Pattern* (Fig. 2, upper left corner) is defined from the ≪*sorting*≫ constraints; a *Filter* over the main class, derived from the "*localPreCondition*" restrictions, selects the instances shown in the index. Finally, the adaptive access to the *text* feature of the *Review* is expressed through a constraint (Fig. 2, upper right corner), which allows including the corresponding attribute in the current navigational context or transferring it to another one, to which navigation is provided.

Figure 3 shows two Web pages generated from the navigational context in Fig. 2, and accessed by an ANONYMOUS user (hereafter "*User1*") and a PREMIUM user ("*User2*"), respectively. The link to the *Special Offers* page is only available to *User2*. This user fulfills the previously mentioned condition of the number of visits to book reviews, so the page includes the corresponding review, whereas *User1* needs to access another page to access it. The *discount* value associated

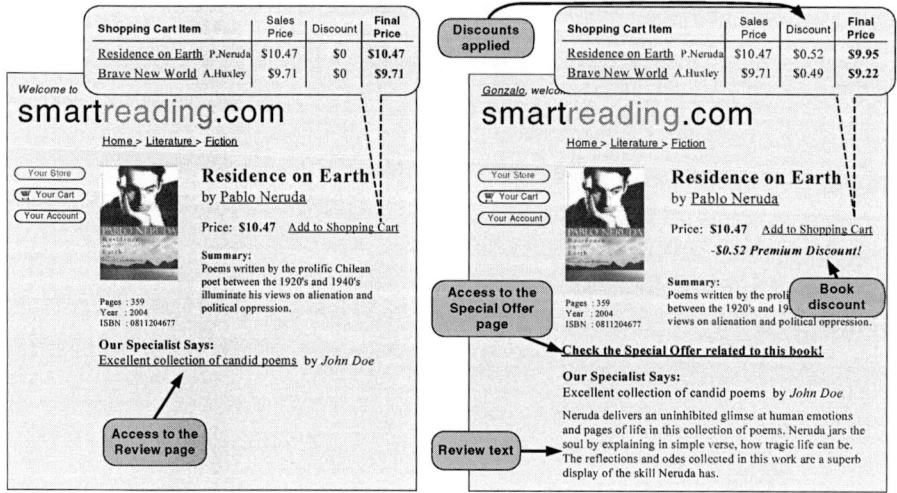

Fig. 3. Web pages derived from one navigational context, accessed by different users

to the book is only valid to *User2*, according to the accessibility restriction of the previous purchases. The shopping cart state after adding the product (balloons in Fig. 3) shows how discounts are only applied to the items added by *User2*.

5   Conclusions

This work introduces an approach to describe the adaptive navigation requirements of a Web Application, and derive the conceptual description of the navigational structures that allow their fulfillment. Adaptive prototypes can be automatically generated, which makes possible a rapid validation of adaptivity requirements, with development time and effort saving. Different granularity levels of navigational adaptivity are provided by the proposed user description: a coarse-grained adaptation based on user stereotypes; and a fine-grained adaptation, based on restrictions on more specific user attributes.

References

1. Fons, J., Pelechano, V., Albert, M., Pastor, O.: Development of Web Applications from Web Enhanced Conceptual Schemas. In: Proc. of ER 2003. LNCS 2813, Springer (2003) 232–245
2. Valderas, P., Fons, J., Pelechano, V.: Transforming Web Requirements into Navigational Models: A MDA Based Approach. In: Proc. of ER 2005. LNCS 3716, Springer (2005) 320–336
3. Rich, E.: User Modeling via Stereotypes. International Journal of Cognitive Science **3** (1979) 329–354
4. Rojas, G.: Obtaining Adaptive Navigational Descriptions from Requirements Specifications. Technical report, DSIC - UPV, http://oomethod.dsic.upv.es (2006)

Learning Styles Adaptation Language
for Adaptive Hypermedia

Natalia Stash, Alexandra Cristea, and Paul De Bra

Faculty of Mathematics and Computer Science, Eindhoven University of Technology,
Postbus 513, 5600 MB Eindhoven, The Netherlands
{nstash, acristea, debra}@win.tue.nl

Abstract. Typically, the behavior of adaptive systems is specified by a set of rules that are hidden somewhere in the system's implementation. These rules deal with instances of the domain model. Our purpose is to specify the adaptive response of the system at a higher level (to be applied and reused for different domains or adaptive applications) in an explicit form, called *adaptation language*. For this purpose we have chosen learning styles (LS) as an implementation field. We defined an XML-based adaptation language LAG-XLS for the AHA! system. In this paper we focus on the empirical evaluation of LAG-XLS.

1   Introduction

Adaptive hypermedia (AH) systems (AHS) mostly focus on the delivery of adaptive applications to end-users and less on *authoring aspects* [2]. To allow a widespread use of AHS, more attention is needed for the authoring process [2], to make it as "simple" and intuitive as possible [5]. In [9], to alleviate the so-called "authoring problem" we discussed limiting repetitive work by reuse of previously created materials and other components. These include the *static parts* of the authored courseware (e.g., domain model content) and the *actual system dynamics* (adaptive behavior). Most existing standards (LOM, SCORM, etc.) address only static and not dynamic reuse [9]. In [9] we compared LAG-XLS ('LAG-excels'), a language developed for the AHA! (Adaptive Hypermedia Architecture) system [7], with a more generic language for AH, LAG [3,5], as its theoretical basis. LAG-XLS focuses on adaptation to various learning styles (LS), meaning here an individual's preferred way of learning. Here we outline what type of strategies can be created in LAG-XLS, how they are applied and visualized in AHA! applications, and we present some evaluation results of our approach.

2   Adaptation to Learning Styles in AHA!

LAG-XLS: allows 3 types of adaptive behavior [9]: *selection of items* to present (e.g. media types); *ordering* information types (e.g., examples, theory, explanation); and creating *different navigation paths* (e.g. breadth-first vs. depth-first). LAG-XLS also allows for the creation of *meta-strategies,* tracing users' preferences for certain types

V. Wade, H. Ashman, and B. Smyth (Eds.): AH 2006, LNCS 4018, pp. 323–327, 2006.
© Springer-Verlag Berlin Heidelberg 2006

of information or reading order. Strategies are defined as XML files using a prede-fined DTD. XML was chosen as it is an extensible language and a W3C standard.

Creating an AHA! adaptive application: consists of defining the domain/adaptation model and writing application content (XHTML pages [7]). The extended system allows applying *adaptive strategies,* specified in LAG-XLS, to the domain model. Authors can create their own strategies or reuse existing ones. We pre-defined *adaptation strategies* for the following LS [8,3]: active vs. reflective, verbalizer vs. imager (visualizer), holist (global) vs. analytic, field-dependent vs. field-independent; strategies for inferring user preferences (*adaptation meta-strategies*) for textual or pictorial information, and navigation in breadth-first or depth-first order (BF vs. DF). Authors can change the predefined strategies. For this, they have to use elements defined in the LAG-XLS DTD, and ensure that the domain model concepts have the attributes required by the strategies [9]. Authors choose which strategies to apply to a particular application, and in which order (in case of several strategies, order can be important).

Visualization of strategies application in AHA!: The learner sets his preferences (e.g., LS) via a form or selects preference tracing. Later a user can inspect his user model and make changes to it (e.g., to try a new strategy corresponding to other LS).

3   Empirical Evaluation LAG-XLS

3.1   Evaluation Settings

We tested the application of LAG-XLS (meta-)instructional adaptation strategies to AHA! in an AH course [1], with 34 students: 4th year undergraduates in Computer Science and 1st year Masters students in Business Information Systems.

3.2   The Experimental LAG-XLS Assignment Steps

1. The students had to perform the assignment in groups of 2-3 people in 4 weeks.
2. They installed the AHA! system version supporting LS on their notebooks. It con-tained two example applications (courses) and some predefined strategies to apply.
3. Students had 2 roles: *authors*; using the Graph Author tool [7] to see course con-cept structure and select strategies to apply; *end users*: visualizing strategy appli-cation results; analyzing the same course with different LS settings and automatic tracing.
4. Next, the students filled out a questionnaire about their experience with the system.
5. The students also filled out the Felder-Solomon "Index of Learning Styles Ques-tionnaire" (ILS) [8]. ILS maps a set of 44 questions over 4 LS dimensions. For the assignment, 3 dimensions were of interest: *active* vs. *reflective, visual* vs. *ver-bal* and *sequential* vs. *global.* We examined if the students' preferred settings (explicitly selected by them whilst using the system) corresponded to the LS re-vealed by the ILS questionnaire and if the system's inferred preferences matched the ILS questionnaire.
6. Finally, students were asked to create their own strategies, or variations of existing strategies, in the LAG-XLS language, and apply them in the provided applications.

3.3 Experimental Quantitative Results

The quantitative results of the assignment are presented in the integrated table 1.

Table 1. Experimental quantitative results

1. Students' average stated preferences (%)	verbal	visual	active	reflective	global	analytic
	9	68	24	56	24	41
2. ILS questionnaire average results (%)	verbal	visual	active	reflective	global	sequential
	1	49	19	9	26	5
3. Students' prior knowledge (%)	pre-knowledge LS			pre-knowledge XML		
	24			79		
4. Overall impression of instructional strategies and experiments (%)	useful	pleasant			easy	
	82	67			54	
5. Working with the system (%)	understand Graph Author	no problem editing?	understand application strategies	satisfied with presentation	strategy change worked?	
	88	47	77	76	75	
6. Students' satisfaction with the strategies (%)	verbalizer vs. imager	active vs. reflective	global vs. analytic	text vs. image pref.	BF vs. DF pref.	
	87	67	73	87	71	

Students' stated preferences vs. ILS questionnaire results. Table 1 (row 1, 2) shows that students are rarely aware of their LS. Note the difference between stated "analytic" (equivalent here with "sequential") preference and the ILS results (showing "global" tendency). Further on, for "active vs. reflector", the former tendency is stronger in ILS, whilst the latter dominates in actual use. Results coincide in the students' strong image preference. Still, the intensity is different in praxis and theory.

Students' prior knowledge (row 3). As most were from computer science, unsurprisingly, their XML prior knowledge was far greater than the LS one (79 vs. 24%). Many had never heard of LS before. This may explain fluctuations in learning preferences.

Students' general impression of their first encounter of LS in combination with AH (row 4). Students considered the implementation of *adaptive instructional strategies* and *(monitoring) meta-strategies* for adaptive educational systems *useful* (82%). Less strong, but still positive was their conviction about this experimental process being *pleasant* (67%). A (smaller) majority of students considered the work *easy* (54%). This difference shows that, although students realized the necessity and importance of adaptive strategies in AH, and enjoyed the assignment, they did not consider it trivial. Thus reuse of ready-made, custom-designed strategies is vital for AH authors, to reduce creation time and costs.

Working with the system (row 5). The students understood how the application of strategies works (77%) – the core of the LAG-XLS language understanding – and are greatly satisfied with the presentations (76%). They understand the AHA! Graph Author very well (88%). However creation of their own strategies was the most difficult problem. Only 47% did not have a problem with editing. The strategy changes worked well for 75% of the students.

Students' satisfaction with the (meta-)strategies (row 6). All strategies and meta-strategies were deemed appropriate by the majority (over 65%) of students. The "winning" *strategy* is the "verbalizer vs. imager", considered most accurate (87%). Following is the "global vs. analytic" (73%) and "activist vs. reflector" strategy (67%). From the *meta-strategies*, the one liked best by students was the "text vs. image preference" meta-strategy. For the latter, most students noticed that it traced their behavior within *3 steps*. The "BF vs. DF" strategy is more complex. For a user with a breadth-first preference, the system analyzes a larger number (between 7-14, with an *average:13*) of steps till the LS was detected. 71% were satisfied with the strategy.

3.4   Experimental Qualitative Results: Selection of Questions and Answers

Due to the of lack of space, we only provide a summary of some of the comments.

1. *Do you find the application of different instructional/monitoring strategies for educational adaptive hypermedia useful?* Most students gave a positive reply. They considered it a good aid in the learning process, as presentation of material suiting the user's need allows working more efficiently and saves time. However, some correctly noticed that it is quite easy to fool the system, as it does not check whether material is really understood when the user browses through it (this is a typical AH problem).

2. *Compare the preference induced by the system with the ILS questionnaire results.* For the majority of students the induced preference corresponded with the ILS results. If this was not the case the students provided us with some comments. One student replied: "*I generally like to see the global picture first and then go into the details. However in the tutorial, ... If I read the high level concepts first and then go into the details, I have forgotten what the high level concepts were.*" This problem may be caused by the fact that the authors of the example application do not have enough psychological knowledge about how to fully support the global and analytic LS (beyond the recommended breadth-first and depth-first processing). Another student commented that he has a textual preference according to ILS, but he so much liked the pictures in the tutorial that he preferred the imager version. Also, some students correctly noticed that LS preferences may vary in different domains.

3. *Can you think of more strategies that you would like to apply but are not able to express using LAG-XLS?* Most students were only able to create variations of the existing strategies by using different names for presentation items and by increasing/decreasing the number of steps required by the monitoring strategies to achieve a threshold. The students did not come up with any completely new strategies.

4   Discussion and Conclusion

From the evaluation results we can say that designing an application in such a way that different types of users get equivalent information appropriate to them is a useful endeavour. Students understood the process and liked being involved in it, in spite of the fact that it wasn't a simple task. It is very reassuring that our students understood the basics of LS application, as they were computer science students, with little or no knowledge in this field prior to the course. This exercise shows also the challenges of the *end-user* side, the *learner*: theory and praxis do not always match in identification of LS. The end-user rarely has meta-knowledge of this type.

This was a small-scale exercise in *authoring the dynamics of AH*, from the point of view of *tasks* involved (the group size was average). The results and comments show that LAG-XLS allows a quick grasp on the adaptation process (for computer science students), as well as relatively easy handling and small modifications of existing adaptation strategies. Still, some students couldn't create new strategies from scratch.

It is clear that the creation process of adaptive behaviour in itself requires a lot of psychological and/or pedagogical knowledge. As we are no psychologists, the main aim of our research is to allow the authors with experience in pedagogical psychology to design different types of strategies and apply these strategies to the applications. Moreover, the question about how to structure the application and organization of the materials to correctly suit different LS is left for the author of the application or psychologist. Therefore, from a future evaluation point of view, it would be interesting to test LAG-XLS with LS specialists, instead of computer scientists, focusing more on the *qualitative aspects* instead of the *technical aspects* of the language.

Acknowledgements

This work is supported by the PROLEARN network of excellence, the NLnet Foundation and was initiated by the EU Minerva ADAPT project.

References

1. Adaptive Hypermedia course (TU/e, 2ID20) winter trimester 2004/05, http://wwwis.win.tue.nl/~acristea/AH/
2. Brusilovsky, P., Developing adaptive educational hypermedia systems: from design models to authoring tools. "Authoring Tools for Advanced Technology Learning Environments", Eds. T. Murray, S. Blessing, S. Ainsworth, Kluwer (2003).
3. Coffield, F , Learning Styles and Pedagogy in post-16 learning: A systematic and critical review. Learning & Skills research centre. http://www.lsda.org.uk/files/pdf/1543.pdf
4. Cristea, A.I., and Calvi, L. The three Layers of Adaptation Granularity. UM'03. Springer.
5. Cristea, A.I., and Verschoor, M. The LAG Grammar for Authoring the Adaptive Web, ITCC'04 April, 2004, Las Vegas, US, IEEE (2004).
6. Cristea, A. Authoring of Adaptive Hypermedia; Adaptive Hypermedia and Learning Environments; "Advances in Web-based Education: Personalized Learning Environments". Eds.: S. Y. Chen & Dr. G. D. Magoulas. IDEA Publishing group (2006).
7. De Bra, P., Stash, N., Smits, D., Creating Adaptive Web-Based Applications, Tutorial at the 10th International Conference on User Modeling, Edinburgh, Scotland (2005)
8. R. M. Felder & B. A. Soloman 2000. Learning styles and strategies. At URL: http://www.engr.ncsu.edu/learningstyles/ilsweb.html
9. Stash, N., Cristea, A., De Bra, P. Explicit Intelligence in Adaptive Hypermedia: Generic Adaptation Languages for Learning Preferences and Styles, HT'05, CIAH Workshop, Salzburg, (2005)

Context-Based Navigational Support in Hypermedia

Sebastian Stober and Andreas Nürnberger

Institut für Wissens- und Sprachverarbeitung,
Fakultät für Informatik,
Otto-von-Guericke-Universität Magdeburg, D-39106 Magdeburg, Germany
{stober, nuernb}@iws.cs.uni-magdeburg.de

Abstract. In this paper, we present the system "DAWN" (direction anticipation in web navigation) that helps users to navigate through the world wide web. Firstly, the purpose of such a system and the approach taken are motivated. We then point out relations to other approaches, describe the system and outline the underlying prediction model. Evaluation on real world data gave promising results.

1 Introduction

Navigating through hypermedia can be a hard task, especially if the resource is as dynamic as the world wide web that is steadily growing and constantly changing. Users that browse the web often need to choose between multiple options on how to continue navigation. Depending on how well they choose the hyperlinks they follow, it will take them less or more time to finally get to the information they desire. Whilst some users might find this task quite easy, others may get lost, especially if they are facing unfamiliar web content. Although there is most likely no general rule on how to most efficiently navigate to the desired information, there may be certain navigational patterns that can be used as heuristics. Users may unconsciously develop such patterns. A system that watches users navigating the web could learn the users' navigational patterns. During a browsing session, the system could perform a lookahead crawl in the background and suggest the hyperlinks that best match the previously learned patterns.

This paper introduces a prototype of such a system, named DAWN (direction anticipation in web navigation). In the following sections, differences to related work are pointed out and a brief system overview is given. In Sect. 4 we present some promising results of a first evaluation of the system with real-world data. Finally, we summarize our work and give an outlook on future developments.

2 Related Work

The general idea to support users browsing the world wide web is not new. Systems that accomplish this task by suggesting hyperlinks or web pages are e.g.

V. Wade, H. Ashman, and B. Smyth (Eds.): AH 2006, LNCS 4018, pp. 328–332, 2006.

discussed in [1, 2, 3, 4, 5]. The system presented here has much in common with these systems: Like Webmate [3], Broadway [4] or Personal Webwatcher [5] it uses an HTTP-proxy to log user actions and to manipulate the requested web pages. Documents are, according to common practice, represented as term vectors with TF/iDF-weights. Letizia [1] was one of the first systems that used background lookahead crawling. However, Letizia was designed as a plug-in for the Netscape Navigator 3 and heavily relied on its API whereas the proxy-architecture chosen for DAWN allows the users to use their browsers of choice. Moreover, bandwidth and computational expensive tasks can be performed on the server which reduces the burden on the client machine. In contrast to DAWN, which uses a combination of navigational patterns and document similarities, Webmate, Personal Webwatcher and Letizia are purely content-based systems that rely on document-similarities to decide which web pages are interesting. Broadway relies on case-based reasoning to recommend web pages using a special similarity measure on ordered sequences of past accessed documents. For this, a special similarity measure on ordered sequences of past accessed documents had been developed, combining temporal constraints with similarities of URLs and page content represented by page title, HTML headers and keywords. Webwatcher [2] uses a collaboration-based approach by asking a user about the desired information and then suggesting links that users with similar information needs have followed previously. Furthermore, Webwatcher is a server-side application that is restricted to one specific website, whereas DAWN works on a client-side proxy and therefore has no such local restriction. DAWN stores the navigational patterns in a Markov Model. Such models have been, e.g., successfully used for prediction of HTTP-requests to optimize web-caches [6]. Recently, they have been proposed to model user navigational behavior in the context of adaptive websites [7, 8, 9] and web-usage mining [10]. However, these are solely server-side applications that are inherently locally confined. To our knowledge, there have not been any client-side systems that use Markov Models so far.

3   System Overview

An overview of the system is shown in Fig. 1. All HTTP-requests made by the user during a browsing session are recorded in a database. This information

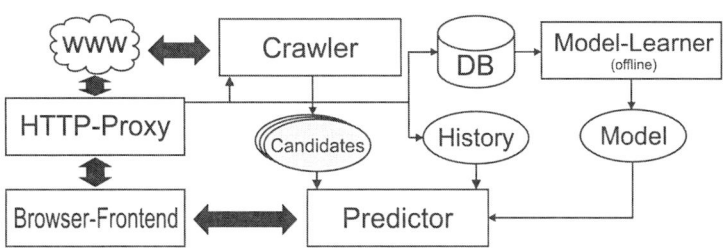

Fig. 1. DAWN: System Overview

is used by the model-learner that generates a model of navigational patterns using an algorithm that has been derived from the one presented by Borges and Levene in [10]. This algorithm has been originally designed to represent a collection of user navigation sessions of a website. It iteratively constructs an nth-order Markov Model by making use of the state cloning concept where a state is only duplicated if the nth-order probabilities diverge significantly from the corresponding 1st-order probabilities. Apart from several small modifications we introduced an additional clustering step prior to model induction. In this step similar pages are grouped into clusters according to standard TFiDF-similarity. Each cluster corresponds to a single context represented as a weighted term vector. This drastically reduces the size of the model's state space but more importantly it combines different browsing paths (consisting of web pages) into an abstract navigational pattern (consisting of contexts). The additional abstraction level accomplished by the introduction of the preliminary clustering step makes it possible to detach the original approach from its server-side application, i.e. the prediction model can be applied to arbitrary web sites.

It is possible to learn a separate model for each user as well as a global one. Based on an nth-order Markov Model candidate pages can be assessed given a user's current history of the last n accessed web pages. Mapping the history onto

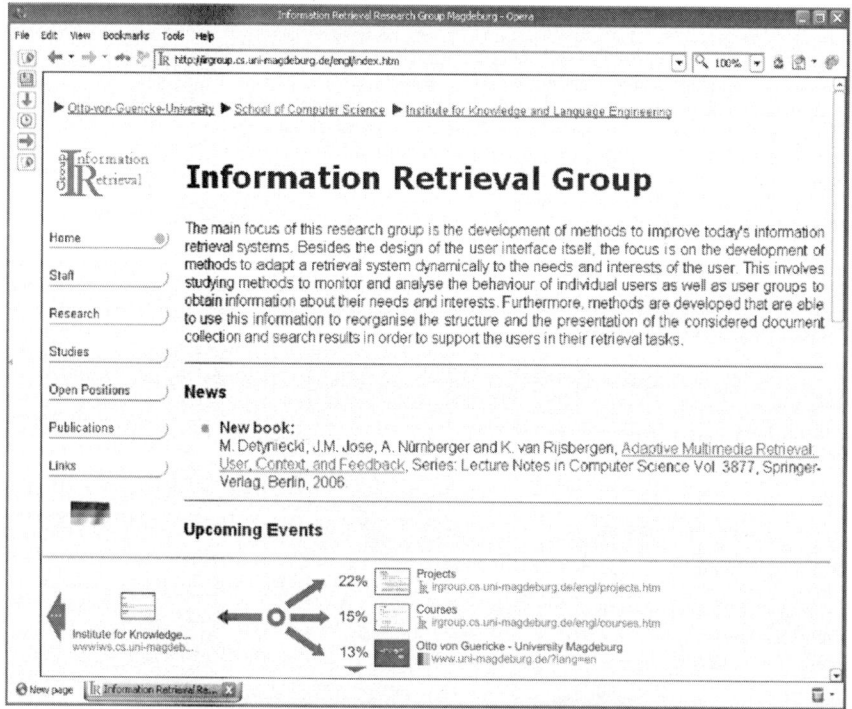

Fig. 2. Browser-Frontend. Suggestions for possible next links in the users navigation path are recommended at the bottom of a web page.

the model by identifying similar navigational paths, a probability distribution for the next state (i.e. a cluster of web pages) is derived. Having mapped the candidate pages onto the model's states in an analogous manner, the probability distribution can be used to rank the candidate pages. Eventually, title, URL and automatically generated thumbnails of the three most probable candidates are displayed in the browser-frontend shown in Fig. 2. The thumbnails allow a general visual impression of the page layout and provide visual information that can help the user in addition to the usual ranking and content information to assess a list of candidate pages collected by a lookahead crawler.

4 Evaluation

Aim of the system presented here is to support users to navigate through the world wide web. Consequently, the usefulness of the system can only be truly assessed by a user study. This however involves considerable effort and costs. We therefore decided to do a first evaluation of the prediction model on web server log files assuming that every link that a user followed led to a page satisfying the user's information need. Obviously, this assumption may not hold in all cases. Furthermore, predicting a link that a user did not follow does not necessarily implicate poor performance as recommending the link still might have been useful. Thus, the accuracy of the predictions can only be interpreted as an indicator for the system's usefulness.

As the content of the accessed web pages is required in the clustering step, only web server log files that did not contain outdated URLs could be utilized for the evaluation. We therefore used anonymized log files containing requests on web pages hosted by the University of Magdeburg recorded during 6 consecutive days. These logs were filtered as follows: Any requests with a response status code other than 200 (OK) and 304 (not modified) were removed as well as requests of URLs with non-HTML content. Additionally, several possible denial of service attacks on specific URLs were detected and removed. Afterwards, sessions were identified as, e.g., described in [11]. The prediction model was learned from the data of the first 5 days. For the evaluation of the model the data of the 6th day was used. Table 1, left shows the number of sessions, requests and unique URLs in the data.

Table 1. Left: Number of sessions (sequences of pages accessed by a user), requests (page accesses) and unique URLs in the data used for training and evaluation. Right: Evaluation results. The number of candidates (number of different outbound links in a page) ranged from 1 to 607 with a mean of 10.77.

	sessions	requests	URLs	rank	1st	2nd	3rd	1st–3rd	in 1st third
train	58314	237098	25771	absolute	6788	2113	3328	12229	22716
test	13437	60461	5657	relative	16%	5%	8%	30%	56%
total	71751	297559	27877						

The requested web pages in the training data were clustered into 250 clusters resulting in an average cluster size of about 100. From the 250 clusters and the sessions extracted from the training data, a 2nd-order Markov Model was induced. This model was used to estimate the probability of all outgoing links for each web page in the test sessions. Table 1, right shows the results. In about 30% of all test cases, the candidate that had actually been chosen by the user was amongst the 3 highest ranked candidates. In these cases it would have been displayed in the browser-frontend and could have helped the user.

5   Conclusions and Future Work

In this paper, we have presented a prototype system that provides navigation support for users browsing the world wide web. It combines ranking, content and visual information to make it easier for users to assess the relevance of suggested hyperlinks. A first evaluation of the prediction accuracy on real-world data has shown promising results. However, the evaluation results should only be interpreted as an indicator for the system's usefulness. As future work we plan an evaluation of the system in a user study.

References

1. Lieberman, H.: Letizia: An Agent That Assists Web Browsing. IJCAI, 1995.
2. Joachims, T., Freitag, D., Mitchell, T.: WebWatcher: A Tour Guide for the World Wide Web. In: IJCAI, 1997.
3. Chen, L., Sycara, K.: WebMate: A Personal Agent for Browsing and Searching. In: Proc. 2nd Intl. Conf. on Auton. Agents and Multi Agent Sys., AGENTS '98, 1998.
4. Jaczynski, M., Trousse, B.: Broadway, A Case-Based Browsing Advisor for the Web. In: ECDL '98: Proc. of the 2nd Europ. Conf. on Research and Adv. Technology for Digital Libraries, 1998.
5. Mladenic, D.: Machine learning used by Personal WebWatcher. In: Proc. of ACAI-99 Workshop on Machine Learning and Intelligent Agents, 1999.
6. Sarukkai, R.: Link Prediction and Path Analysis using Markov Chains. Computer Networks, Vol. 33, pp. 337–386, 2000.
7. Anderson, C., Domingos, P. Weld, D.: Relational Markov Models and their Application to adaptive Web Navigation. In: Proc. 8th ACM SIGKDD Intl. Conf. on Knowl. Discovery and Data Mining, 2004.
8. Zhu, J., Hong, J., Hughes, J.: Using Markov Chains for Link Prediction in Adaptive Web Sites. In: Soft-Ware 2002: Comp. in an Imperfect World: 1st Intl. Conf., 2002.
9. Cadez, I., Heckerman, D., Meek, C., Smyth D., White, S.: Model-Based Clustering and Visualization of Navigation Patterns on a Web Site. Data Min. Knowl. Discov., Vol. 7, pp. 399–424, 2003.
10. Borges, J., Levene, M.: A Clustering-Based Approach for Modelling User Navigation with Increased Accuracy. In: Proc. of the 2nd Intl. Workshop on Knowl. Discovery from Data Streams (IWKDDS) & PKDD, 2005.
11. Cooley, R., Mobasher, B., Srivastava, J.: Data Preparation for Mining World Wide Web Browsing Patterns. Knowl. and Information Sys., Vol. 1, No. 1, pp. 5–32, 1999.

Contextual Media Integration and Recommendation for Mobile Medical Diagnosis

David Wilson[1], Eoin McLoughlin[2], Dympna O'Sullivan[2],
and Michela Bertolotto[2]

[1] Department of Software and Information Systems
University of North Carolina at Charlotte, USA
[2] School of Computer Science and Informatics
University College Dublin, Dublin 4, Ireland
davils@uncc.edu,
{eoin.a.mcloughlin, dymphna.osullivan, michela.bertolotto}@ucd.ie

Abstract. Hospitals everywhere are taking advantage of the flexibility and speed of wireless computing to improve the quality and reduce the cost of healthcare. Caregivers equipped with portable computers now have levels of interaction at the bedside not possible with paper charts and can leverage accurate real-time patient information at the point of care to diagnose and treat patients with greater speed and efficiency. We present a mobile medical application that integrates heterogenous medical media (e.g. textual patient case descriptions, relevant medical imagery, physician dictations and endoscopies) into encapsulated patient profiles. This paper provides an overview and initial evaluation of the MEDIC mobile healthcare recommender system that facilitates decision support for expert diagnosis.

1 Introduction

Mobile computing solutions are revolutionizing the way in which medicine is delivered and practiced [1]. Physicians can now access complete and accurate patient information efficiently and securely from any location, at any time. For example, caregivers have access to many resources including up-to-the-minute laboratory test results directly at the bedside or a specialist located away from the hospital can help with diagnostics from a mobile device. These solutions can help improve patient safety, reduce the risk of medical errors and increase physician productivity and efficiency.

In this research we have developed a task-based knowledge management environment (MEDIC - MobilE Diagnosis for Improved Care) that facilitates caregivers as they interact with disparate patient information contained in electronic patient profiles during the course of a diagnosis. The application supports healthcare professionals in diagnostic tasks that involve recording details, analyzing patient information (including medical imagery, the latest laboratory test results, medication and prescription data and other media such as endoscopies), summarizing important findings and accessing online or other electronic hospital resources. The system integrates all such explicit heterogeneous data and

V. Wade, H. Ashman, and B. Smyth (Eds.): AH 2006, LNCS 4018, pp. 333–337, 2006.

media for each patient in an electronic records system [2], as well as any tacit knowledge provided by healthcare professionals they interact with patients [3]. Our task-based environment enables capture of and access to human expertise and proficiency in diagnosing and treating particular illnesses through diagnostic media annotation and implicit profiling, which in turn allows us to understand why relevant information was accessed and investigated. By incorporating this implicit expert knowledge with case-based reasoning techniques [4] we have developed a decision support system for expert physicians: entire patient profiles with known diagnoses can be automatically filtered, retrieved, recommended and displayed to compare symptoms, diagnoses, treatments and outcomes for patients with similar presenting complaints or care records. These profiles, including all constituent media from which they are composed are presented in an adaptive medical Graphical User Interface (GUI) [5] which can tailor presentation content depending on the context of the interacting expert user [6]. This paper provides an overview of the MEDIC mobile healthcare recommender system and an initial evaluation of system recommendation capabilities.

2   The MEDIC Application

The MEDIC application consists of two clients: a desktop application used by radiologists and a mobile component used by physicians. The radiologist employs a suite of image processing tools (e.g. sketching, filters and multimedia tools), to annotate medical imagery with relevant notes regarding a patient's condition. The image retrieval component can be queried to display previously annotated patient images from a knowledge base of previous patient profiles for comparative studies to aid with more effective diagnosis and treatment. Physicians use the mobile application on a Personal Digital Assistant (PDA) or Tablet PC to retrieve and view electronic profiles and to quickly document patient progress in real-time. The PDA provides increased mobility and flexibility and allows physicians to view textual abstractions of current/previous patient data. The Tablet PC has a higher processing power and so provides a more comprehensive user interface and additional functionality such as the ability to view and annotate medical imagery. Both mobile devices may be used to query the central repository of patient profiles with information specific to particular illnesses to retrieve similar patient case histories for comparative assistance.

The MEDIC application enables integration of complex medical imagery with other patient data by creating encapsulated patient profiles from all available patient information. It also captures high-level concepts provided by healthcare professionals as they interact with these patient profiles and stores this information as parcels of expert experience that are also encapsulated within the patient profiles. For example, capturing a measure of human proficiency involved in making a diagnosis from an X-Ray allows us to understand why relevant information was selected (highlighting a particular organ) and how it was employed in the specific diagnosis (inferred from an added annotation).

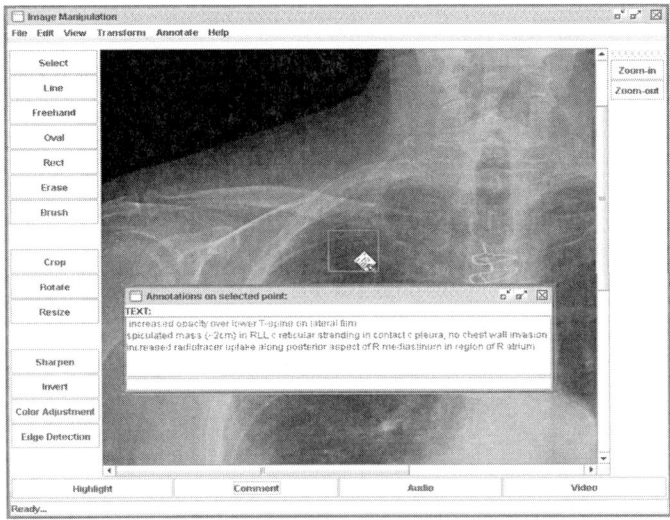

Fig. 1. Annotating Medical Imagery

If a caregiver wishes to annotate an image it is displayed in the interface depicted in Figure 1.

From the radiologist's perspective, the image interaction tools support them in carrying out their task. However from a system perspective they record the radiologist's actions and capture diagnostic knowledge that can improve the ability of the application to recommend similar patient profiles for diagnostic and treatment procedures. As the system builds up encapsulated user interactions the retrieval of entire previous patient case histories is enabled. This allows a physician or radiologist to look for images/patient profiles that are most similar to those of the presenting patient. Our retrieval metrics combine structured patient data (e.g. demographics) with unstructured textual diagnostic and annotation data (e.g. clinical data, diagnostic notes, recommended treatments and image annotations). We employ Information Retrieval metrics across all individual fields of a patient profile as a basis for retrieval. Given a textual representation of a patient profile we can match textual queries to previous patient contexts. Queries are generated from current user context, but users may also formulate their queries by specifying which spaces to search as well as assigning weights to these fields. Entered queries are matched against other patient profiles and a weighted average is used to compute similarity. For more details on how similarity is calculated the reader is referred to [7].

Figure 2 shows an example of retrieved case histories. Each row represents a similar patient case history and is summarized to show the most important information for that patient. It includes the matching percentage score between the current query and the similar case, symptoms, diagnosis, applied treatments, outcomes and relevant medical imagery. This interface, as well as the interface for retrieved imagery (not shown here due to space constraints), adapt their content presentation in response to actions performed by the interacting caregiver. For

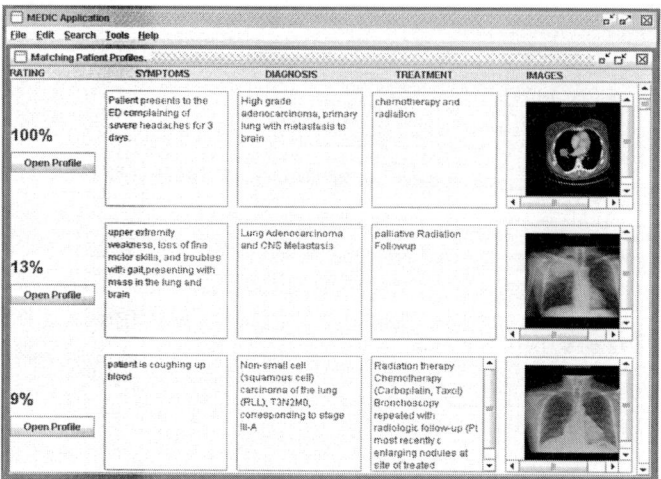

Fig. 2. Retrieved Case Histories

example, if a user clicks on the symptoms field, the system deems that the caregiver is particularly interested in the current patient's symptoms as a basis for diagnosis and recomputes their query by combining it with the symptoms from the case history. The interface is then adapted and redrawn dynamically to reflect this updated context.

3   Evaluation

In this initial evaluation we have tested the case retrieval capabilities of the application with a dataset of 300 encapsulated patient profiles and associated medical imagery from the dermatology domain. We were interested in showing that the system is capable of capturing and deciphering expert medical knowledge and that recommendations made by the system based could be used to support physician decision making. We initiated our evaluation by selecting ten cases corresponding to different skin diseases from the dataset. These cases were then eliminated from the dataset for the evaluation. The remaining cases in the database were clustered as being either "relevant" or "not relevant" to each of the 10 selected cases based on the diagnosis. The 10 cases were then input as search parameters to the application and the retrieved profiles we analyzed. Each returned case was marked as either "relevant" or "not relevant" to the query and the ratings were then compared to the clusters outlined earlier.

Our results are graphed in Figure 3 using precision and recall metrics. We observe that the system is performing case retrieval accurately. The precision remains high for the first few cases retrieved showing that the most relevant results are being retrieved first (particularly important for mobile interaction) and we also observe a linear increase in recall as the number of results returned increases indicating retrieval accuracy across the dataset.

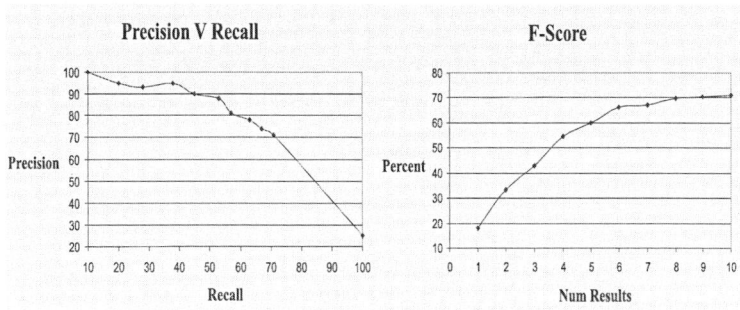

Fig. 3. Precision V Recall and F-Score

4   Conclusions and Future Work

The current practice of recording patient data using paper charts is cumbersome, time-consuming and does not facilitate knowledge sharing. Disparate information, is stored in different locations and valuable time is often lost trying to correlate such data. The MEDIC system addresses such issues by providing doctors with instant access to patient information; it supports them to make critical decisions and diagnoses with greater speed and efficiency by combining relevant diagnostic information in an adaptive mobile medical recommender interface. The initial evaluation results reported here show that MEDIC provides relevant results for real medical data. We plan to conduct expanded trials with expert users to evaluate accuracy and quality both in results and interface usability.

References

[1] Gillingham, W., Holt, A. and J. D. Gillies "Handheld computers in health care: What software programs are available?," New Zealand Medical Journal (2001).
[2] Abidi, S. S. R. "Medical Knowledge Morphing: Towards Case-Specific Integration of Hetrogeneous Medical Knowledge Resources," Proceedings of CBMS (2005).
[3] Wyatt, J.C. "Management of Explicit and Tacit Knowledge," Journal of the Royal Society of Medicine (2001).
[4] Nilsson, M. and Sollenborn, M. "Advancements and Trends in Medical CBR: An Overview of Systems and System Development," Proceedings of FLAIRS (2004).
[5] Plaisant, C., Mushlin, R., Snyder, A., Li, J., Heller, D. and Shneiderman, B. "Life-Lines: Using Visualization to Enhance Navigation and Analysis of Patient Records," American Medical Informatic Association Annual Fall Symposium (1998).
[6] Maes, P. and Rhodes, B.J. "Just-in-time information retrieval agents.," IBM Systems Journal (2000).
[7] McLoughlin, E., O'Sullivan, D., Bertolotto, M. and Wilson, D. "MEDIC MobilE Diagnosis for Improved Care," Proceedings of ACM Symposium on Applied Computing (2006).

User Modelling: An Empirical Study for Affect Perception Through Keyboard and Speech in a Bi-modal User Interface*

Efthymios Alepis and Maria Virvou

Department of Informatics, University of Piraeus, 80 Karaoli & Dimitriou St.
18534 Piraeus, Greece
{talepis, mvirvou}@unipi.gr
http://www.unipi.gr

Abstract. This paper presents and discusses an empirical study that has been conducted among different kinds of computer users. The aim of the empirical study was to find out how computer users react when they face situations which generate emotions while they interact with a computer. The study has focused on two modes of human-computer interaction namely input from the keyboard and the microphone. The results of the study have been analyzed in terms of characteristics of users that have taken part (age, educational level, computer knowledge, etc.). These results were used to create a user modeling component that monitors users silently and records their actions (in the two modes of interaction) which are then interpreted in terms of their feelings. This user modeling component can be incorporated in any application that provides adaptive interaction to users based on affect perception.

1 Introduction

Multi-modal interfaces may provide more convenience and flexibility to users than conventional interfaces since they allow users to benefit from multiple modes of interaction. However, in multi-modal interfaces, adaptivity remains a desired feature since it can provide interaction which is dynamically tailored to each user's needs. Adaptive hypermedia systems build a model of the goals, preferences and knowledge of each individual user and use this model throughout the interaction with the user in order to adapt to the needs of that user [1]. Yet another user's feature that has been recently acknowledged as quite important is associated with users' emotions.

Multimodal affect-sensitive human computer interaction is likely to become one of the most widespread research topics of the artificial intelligence (AI) research community [4]. On the other hand the exploration of how we as human beings react to the world and interact with it and each other remains one of the greatest scientific challenges [2][3].

---

* Support for this work was provided by the General Secretariat of Research and Technology, Greece, under the auspices of the PENED program.

V. Wade, H. Ashman, and B. Smyth (Eds.): AH 2006, LNCS 4018, pp. 338–341, 2006.

In view of the above in this paper we present and discuss an empirical study leading to the requirements specification of adaptive user interfaces that recognize emotions through a combination of user input from the keyboard and the microphone.

2 Settings of the Empirical Study

The empirical study involved 50 users (male and female) of varying educational background, ages and levels of computer experience. These users were given questionnaires to fill in concerning their emotional reactions to several situations of computer use in terms of their actions using the keyboard and what they say.

People's behavior while doing something may be affected by several factors concerning their personality, age, experience, etc. For example, experienced computer users may be less frustrated than novice users or older people may have different approaches in interacting with computers, comparing with younger people, etc. Thus for the purpose of analyzing the results of our empirical study we categorized them in several groups.

In particular there were 12,5% of participants under the age of 18, approximately 20% of participants between the ages of 18 and 30. A considerable percentage of our participants were over the age of 40. Mentioning the participants' computer knowledge level a 18% of them claimed to be novice users, 28% had little experience, 20% of the participants where using computers for a few years, while 34% could be characterized as "computer experts". Concerning the educational level of the participants, most of them (40%) were university level arts track graduates, 17% university level science track graduates, 20% of the participants had high school knowledge and a 33% of the participants were at the postgraduate level of education.

In the study, participants were asked to answer questions considering their behavior while interacting with personal computers. Specifically the participants had to imagine an interaction with a computer while they were using an educational application and the affect on their voice and keyboard actions. An example of a question in the questionnaire is the following:

While interacting with a personal computer, what happens in the following cases (usually)?
1) When you get upset one can notice it:
A) with the keyboard: …………………………………….............
B) in your voice (you say something)……………………………………………………
     ☐ I raise the tone of my voice
     ☐ The pitch of my voice changes
     ☐ I just say something
     ☐ Nothing

Participants were also asked to determine possible actions in certain emotional states during their interaction. Our aim was to be able to recognize changes in the user's behavior and then to associate these changes with emotional states like anger, happiness, boredom, etc. Within a more general scope we tried to recognize positive and negative feelings from the bi-modal interaction.

3   Results of the Empirical Study

The results of the empirical study have been collected and analyzed in terms of the categories of the participants as explained above and then they were analyzed in terms of each mode of interaction examined, namely speech and keyboard input as well as the combination of the two modes.

After collecting and processing the information of the empirical study we came up with considerably interesting and promising results. In some cases not only can we have evidence of the emotional state of a user using a bi-modal interface, but we can also use that information to re-feed our system in order to make it more accurate. Considering the users' answers to questions about hypothetical situations we found that the percentages are showing more noticeable information if they are filtered by using the participants main characteristics (sex, age, computer knowledge, educational level). Therefore the results are discussed using these characteristics. An exhaustive account of all the results for all the combinations of categories of users is beyond the scope of this document. Therefore, we present a part of the results that corresponds to common stereotypes of users.

A small percentage of the participants say something with anger when they make a spelling mistake. However from the participants who do say something, 74% of them consider themselves having little or moderate (2-6 months of practice) computer knowledge. Only 2% of the computer experts say something when making a minor mistake. One very interesting result is that people seem to be more expressive when they have negative feelings (figure 3), than when they have positive feelings.

Another important conclusion coming up from the study is that when people say something either expressing happiness or anger it is highly supported from the changes of their voice. They may raise the tone of their voice or more probably they may change the pitch of their voice.

Moreover it is interesting to notice that a very high percentage (85%) of young people (below 30 years old) who are also inexperienced with computers find the oral mode of interaction very useful. On the contrary participants belonging to the "postgraduate level of education" group and who also are used to computers dislike the oral communication with their computer.

While using the keyboard most of the participants agree that when they are nervous the possibility of making mistakes increases rapidly. This is also the case when they have negative feelings. Mistakes in typing are followed by many backspace-key keyboard strokes and concurrent changes in the emotional state of the user in a percentage of 82%. Yet users under 20 years old and users who are over 20 years old but have low educational background seem to be more prone to making even more mistakes as a consequence of an initial mistake and lose their concentration while interacting with an application (67%). They also admit that when they are angry the rate of mistakes increases, the rate of their typing becomes slower 62% (on the contrary, when they are happy they type faster 70%) and the keystrokes on the keyboard become harder (65%). Of course the pressure of the user's fingers on the keyboard is something that can not be measured without the appropriate hardware. Similar effects to the keyboard were reported when the emotion is boredom instead of anger.

One conclusion concerning the combination of the two modes in terms of emotion recognition is that the two modes are complementary to each other to a high extent. In many cases the system can generate a hypothesis about the emotional state of the user with a higher degree of certainty if it takes into account evidence from the combination of the two modes rather than one mode. Happiness has positive effects and anger and boredom have negative effects that may be measured and processed properly in order to give information used for a human-computer affective interaction. For example, when the rate of typing backspace of a user increases, this may mean that the user makes more mistakes due to a negative feeling. However this hypothesis can be reinforced by evidence from speech if the user says something bad that expresses negative feelings.

4   Conclusions and Future Work

The exploration of human emotions for the purposes of user modeling and adaptivity is a relatively new research topic that is not mature yet and many improvements are allowed. Recording and analyzing human experience in an empirical study provides very useful insight for further research. In this paper we have described the results of an empirical study that was conducted among computer users. The results of the empirical study were used for affective user modeling.

In future work we plan to improve our system by the incorporation of stereotypes concerning the users' characteristics. Moreover, there is on-going research work-in progress that exploits a third mode of interaction, visual this time [5].

References

1. Brusilovsky, P.: Adaptive Hypermedia, User Modeling and User-Adapted Interaction Vol.11, Springer Science+Business Media B.V. (2001) 87-110
2. Oviatt, S.: User-modeling and evaluation of multimodal interfaces. Proceedings of the IEEE (2003) 1457-1468
3. Pantic, M., Rothkrantz, L.J.M.: Toward an affect-sensitive multimodal human-cumputer interaction. Vol. 91, Proceedings of the IEEE (2003) 1370-1390
4. Sharma, R., Yeasin, M., Krahnstoever, N., Rauschert, I., Cai, G., Brewer, I., Maceachren, A.M., Sengupta, K.: Speech-Gesture driven multimodal interfaces for crisis management. Vol. 91, Proceedings of the IEEE (2003) 1327-1354
5. Stathopoulou, I.O., Tsihrintzis, G.A.: Detection and Expression Classification System for Face Images (FADECS), IEEE Workshop on Signal Processing Systems, Athens, Greece, November 2-4 (2005)

The AHES Taxonomy: Extending Adaptive Hypermedia to Software Components

Frank Hanisch[1], Meike Muckenhaupt[1], Franz Kurfess[2], and Wolfgang Straßer[1]

[1] WSI/GRIS University of Tübingen, Sand 14, 72072 Tübingen, Germany
{hanisch, strasser}@gris.uni-tuebingen.de
meike.muckenhaupt@student.uni-tuebingen.de
[2] California Polytechnic State University, Computer Science Department,
San Luis Obispo, CA 93407

Abstract. Hypermedia has matured to XML-based specifications and Java/Flash software componentry. In this contribution we extend known adaptation methods and techniques to software programs and classify them by component type. We consider adaptation of internal multimedia structures, graphics elements, interactions, and included algorithms. Methods are illustrated with a prototype system that implements matching, component-based adaptation techniques. It is available for free and includes an XML authoring schema, an adaptation layer for third-party Java applets, and a server-side adaptation engine.

1 Introduction

Adaptive hypermedia must keep up with the evolving Web technologies [1]. We therefore introduce concepts of software componentry to an accepted taxonomy of adaptation technologies [2]. By targeting components within multimedia instead of text fragments, we show how internal software structures, spatial/time-based graphics, interactions, and included algorithms can be presented adaptively in a Web-based system. In effect, these components can be inserted, removed, altered, sorted, dimmed, stretched, and annotated like text fragments. With components, adaptive navigation support can be offered granularly: instead of attaching links to text/XML fragments and multimedia entities only, navigation help and links can be placed within non-XML media, at the accurate position and time.

Adaptation techniques are implemented in our Adaptive Hypermedia Educational System (AHES). Authors mark adaptive content with an XML schema. In contrast to other approaches, authors present included software partly in XML. A server-side adaptation engine then compares stated concept requirements with the current user model and transforms the XML according to a set of adaptation rules. It also generates parameters for a Java adaptation layer, which wraps around the actual software and executes the final software adaptation. Other software languages, e.g. Flash, could be supported similarly. The AHES is available, together with installation and editing instructions, at http://regal.csc.calpoly.edu/~mmuckenh/packages.

V. Wade, H. Ashman, and B. Smyth (Eds.): AH 2006, LNCS 4018, pp. 342–345, 2006.

2 Related Work

Adaptation within multimedia currently focuses 3D navigation support in virtual environments [4,5]. Methods adapt the user's viewpoint and path, i.e. a single camera component. However, there are more components. Today's interactive software separates multimedia components by design patterns [6]. The Model View Controller encapsulates internal representation (model) from external presentation (view) and from interaction, i.e. the mapping of user gestures to model/view functionality (controller). They are aggregated into widgets, components of the user interface. Views in turn are made of graphics items (spatial geometry, e.g. Java) or movie clips (time-based, e.g. Flash). Programming can also be encapsulated into algorithm components, either within software (strategy) or outside (script, e.g. JavaScript). In principle, any of them could be adapted for presentation *and* navigation.

Web technology represents multimedia in XML, e.g. mathematics (MathML), 2D/3D graphics (SVG, X3D), and synchronization (SMIL). Formats can be styled (CSS) and mixed. Future software programs might also be stored in XML [7]. The AHA! system [1] demonstrates how XML can be utilized to markup concepts and adaptation rules. But it repurposes specific XHTML/SMIL tags, which complicates the integration of other XML multimedia languages. Single multimedia components cannot be adapted. XML content could therefore be paired with a separate description that identifies adaptable components and variables [8], but adaptation semantics are dropped. So we developed an adaptation XML schema that supports components – it can be transformed, validated, and edited in standard XML writing tools.

3 Component-Based Adaptation

We augment Brusilovsky's taxonomy [3] with the component types models, views, controllers, widgets, graphics items, movie clips, scripts, and strategies (see Fig. 1).

Inserting or removing components matches presentation best to individual knowledge and preferences by adapting XML content or CSS styling. We can do the same for any visual component. Inserting/removing single views or high-level widgets sets up a matching user interface. Applying the method to graphics items changes the 2D/3D scene and their spatial setup; selecting movie clips changes timing and sequencing. When removing a controller component, we remove an interaction facility, which corresponds to dimming (see below). Inserting controllers adaptively can in turn be used to adapt to specific input devices or provide different help, e.g. by inserting drag-snapping to grids or other relevant objects. Scripts are embedded into the software's surrounding; therefore, inserting or removing them steers the degree of interlinking and the amount of functionality provided. The system can also decide to present programming assignments by removing parts of an algorithm.

Component altering presents a given piece of information by component variants. The system can then change its internal representation (model), its specific view, and the offered control. Switching equivalent widgets changes the graphical user interface – the same effect can then be achieved with different control elements, e.g. to support handicapped users. Alternative graphical items can support rendering preferences and

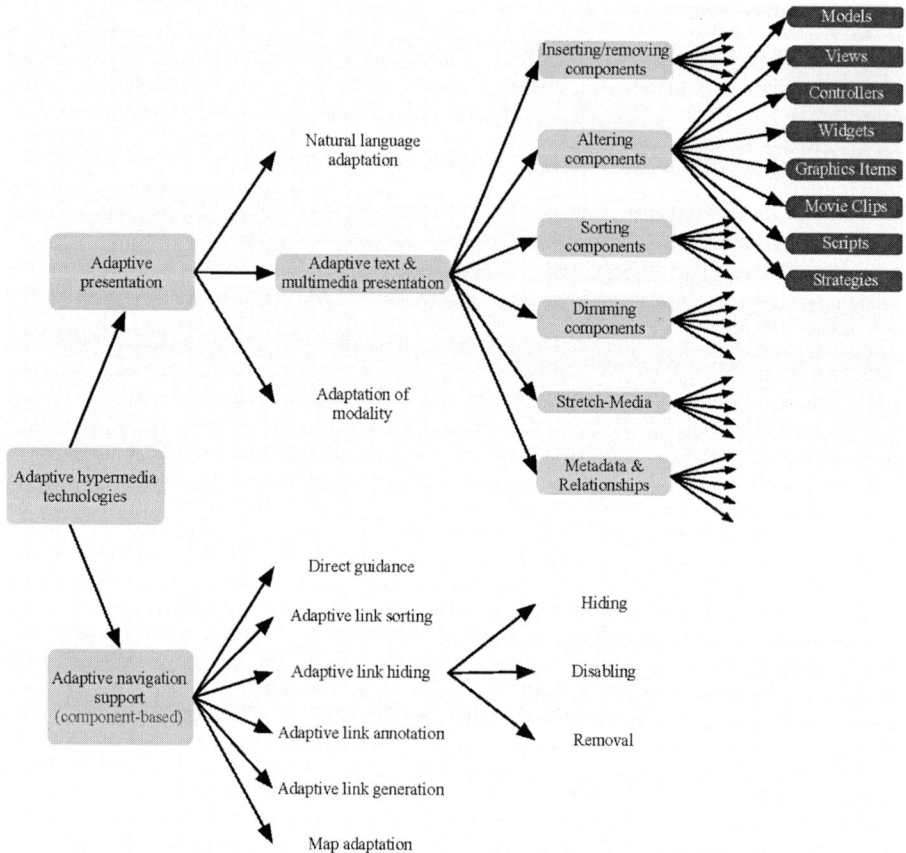

Fig. 1. We extend Brusilovsky's taxonomy [3] to components within multimedia. Adaptive presentation may now target internal multimedia structures, graphics items, interactions, and included algorithms. Adaptive navigation observes component location and relevance. Components are colored blue, affected classes grey. The component tree is attached to all presentation classes; for clarity, it is printed once only.

different graphics hardware (e.g. OpenGL vs. DirectX), whereas alternative movie clips alter an animation. Strategy altering can use a specific algorithm that is known to the user, or use one that is not known, depending on the learning objective. Scripts with the same functionality can be altered to adapt to the browser technology, or target other components and parameters in the software. In many cases, variants can be generated by a parameter set.

The *sorting* technology arranges components depending on their current relevance. When applied to widgets, the layout is reconfigured to support for example left/right handed users, or cultural differences in horizontal/vertical alignment. The system can also resort the widget's view and model in cases where the user chooses from a list of options, either textual or graphical. Inside 2D/3D graphics, the method executes spatial (graphics items) or temporal (movie clips) sorting, for example to rearrange occluded elements, or move uninteresting elements to the back.

Dimming components marks component relevance without changing it. This reduces the cognitive load and can be accomplished by toggling specific views and/or controllers. Dimming is often indicated by a grey background or blurred graphics.

Stretch-Media varies the component's level of detail continuously. Computer graphics has brought out multi-resolution models that naturally provide a matching 2D/3D technique: for a given model, they capture a wide range of levels of detail from which the system chooses the level currently needed.

Adaptive navigation support can now be attached directly, conceptually and visually, to the component it belongs to. Because components may change dynamically in location, size, sorting, view, level of detail, and other aspects, the given help must be sorted and placed, too. Direct guidance within multimedia can for example inserts a navigation widget to targets other components in the same media. This can be used in a known sequence of interactions, e.g. in a guided tour. Usually, the next component will get the input focus. If components belong to multiple guided tours, some of them could be hidden adaptively. Links can deliver parameters to the target component, so components can be set up to match the visited path.

4 Conclusion

Adaptive hypermedia technologies should target within-multimedia components instead of text fragments. To make them available for Web-based adaptation, they can be marked in XML. The free AHES engine includes examples for Java components.

References

1. De Bra, P., Stash, N.: Multimedia Adaptation using AHA!. Educational Multimedia, Hypermedia & Telecommunications, Vol. 1, Association for the Advancement of Computing in Education (2004) 563-570
2. Brusilovsky, P.: Methods and techniques of adaptive hypermedia. User Modeling and User-Adapted Interaction, Vol. 6, No. 2-3. Kluwer Academic Publishers (1996) 87-129
3. Brusilovsky, P.: Adaptive hypermedia. User Modeling and User-Adapted Interaction, Vol. 11, No. 1/2. Kluwer Academic Publishers (2001) 87-110
4. Hughes, S., Brusilovsky, P., Lewis, M.: Adaptive navigation support in 3D ecommerce activities. Recommendation and Personalization in eCommerce (2002) 132-139
5. Chittaro, L., Ranon, R.: Dynamic generation of personalized VRML content: a general approach and its application to 3D E-commerce. Web3D, ACM Press (2002) 145-154
6. Gamma, E., Helm, R., Johnson, R., Vlissides, J.: Design Patterns. Elements of Reusable Object-Oriented Software. Addison-Wesley (1995)
7. Wilson, G.: Extensible Programming for the 21st Century. ACM Queue Vol. 2, No. 9. ACM (2004-2005)
8. Chittaro, L., Ranon, R.: Using the X3D Language for Adaptive Manipulation of 3D Web Content. Adaptive Hypermedia and Adaptive Web-based Systems, Lecture Notes in Computer Science Vol. 3137, Springer-Verlag Berlin (2004) 287-290

Web-Based Recommendation Strategy in a Cadastre Information System

Dariusz Król, Michał Szymański, and Bogdan Trawiński

Wrocław University of Technology, Institute of Applied Informatics,
Wybrzeże S. Wyspiańskiego 27, 50-370 Wrocław, Poland
{Dariusz.Krol, Trawinski}@pwr.wroc.pl

Abstract. Web-based recommendation strategy implemented in a cadastre information system is presented in the paper. This method forms the list of page profiles recommended to a given user. The idea of page recommendation uses the concept of a page profile for system pages containing forms with search criteria. The calculation of rank values for page profiles is based on the usage frequency and the significance weights of profile elements determined by users.

1 Introduction

Due to the growth of the Web systems the users impose new methods for predicting their needs. This requirement is fulfilled by personalization [2]. The personalization process consists of (a) the collection and preprocessing of Web data, including content data, structure data, usage data and user profile data, (b) the analysis and discovery of correlations between such data, (c) the determination of the recommendation methods for hyperlinks [4], queries [1], and user interface [6].

Authors present many recommendation techniques identified in [5] non-personalized, attribute based, item-to-item or people-to-people correlation. In paper [3] authors present a model that uses the visiting time and frequencies of pages without considering the access order of page requests in use sessions. To capture the relationships between pages they extract information from log data.

In this work we focus on Web Usage Mining by user profiling and content analysis to recommend queries profiles.

2 The Idea of the List of Page Profiles

The idea of page recommendation is based on the concept of a page profile, which concerns the pages with search criteria. The page profile is characterized by the option of the main menu e.g. by the function of the system and also by the type of search criteria (simplified or extended) and finally by a section chosen during retrieval process. A formal model of page profiles can be presented as follows.

Let $O = \{o_1, o_2, ...,o_{No}\}$ is a set of options, where N_o is the number of options, $S = \{s_1, s_2, ...,s_{Ns}\}$ is a set of sections registered in the system, where N_s is the number of sections, then $P = \{p_1, p_2, ...,p_{Np}\}$ - the set of page profiles can be expressed as

V. Wade, H. Ashman, and B. Smyth (Eds.): AH 2006, LNCS 4018, pp. 346–349, 2006.
© Springer-Verlag Berlin Heidelberg 2006

$$P \subseteq (O \times S).$$ (1)

where $N_p = N_o * N_s$.

The recommendation mechanism analyses previous activity of a user and calculates and assigns a rank value to each page profile used. The rank value is based on the frequency of usage and is automatically calculated for each user separately. In order to lower the importance of prior uses the factor $1 - k/D$ has been introduced, where k is the number of days which past up to the moment of calculation and D is the period of usage. The value of D should be determined by each user as the component of his set of preferences. It is of essential importance to select the best total rank value of the page profile, with the following elements taken into account.

2.1 Rank Value of a Page Profile

Rank value $r_i(p_j)$ of a page profile p_j used by user i can be calculated in the following way

$$r_i(p_j) = \left(\sum_{k=1}^{D_i} f_{ik}(p_j) * (1 - \frac{k}{D_i}) \right) * N_{pu}.$$ (2)

where $f_{ik}(p_j)$ is the usage frequency of page profile j by user i and k days back before the day of rank calculation and N_{pu} means the coefficient compensating the frequency scattering, which can be equal to the number of page profiles used.

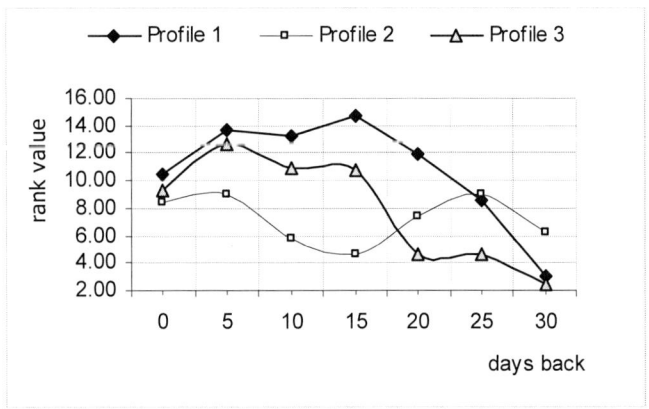

Fig. 1. Rank values of page profiles for a selected user on December 20th 2005

In order to reveal the nature of this element web server logs and application logs have been analyzed for one of the most active user in a chosen information center. Fig. 1 shows how the rank value of three profiles changes in function of k value.

2.2 Rank Value of an Option

Rank value $r_i(o_j)$ of an option oj used by user i can be calculated in the following way

$$r_i(o_j) = \left(\sum_{k=1}^{D_i} f_{ik}(o_j) * (1 - \frac{k}{D_i}) \right) * N_{ou} . \tag{3}$$

where $f_{ik}(o_j)$ is the usage frequency of option j by user i and k days back before the day of rank calculation and N_{ou} means the coefficient compensating the frequency scattering, which can be equal to the number of options used.

2.3 Rank Value of a Section

Rank value $r_i(s_j)$ of a section sj used by user i can be calculated in the following way

$$r_i(s_j) = \left(\sum_{k=1}^{D_i} f_{ik}(s_j) * (1 - \frac{k}{D_i}) \right) * N_{su} . \tag{4}$$

where $f_{ik}(s_j)$ is the usage frequency of section j by user i and k days back before the day of rank calculation and N_{ou} means the coefficient compensating the frequency scattering, which can be equal to the number of sections used.

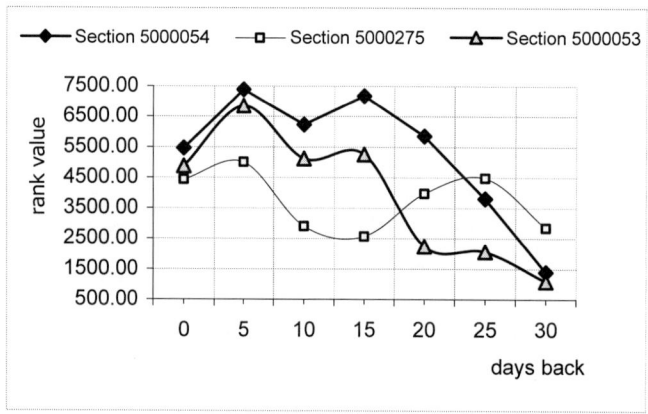

Fig. 2. Rank values of sections for a selected user on December 20th 2005

Similarly, in order to reveal the nature of this element analogous analysis for the same user and the same period has been carried out. Fig. 2 shows how the rank value of chosen sections changes in function of k value.

2.4 Total Rank Value of a Page Profile

Total rank value of a page profile assumes that the rank value primarily calculated is modified by rank values of other elements according to user preferences. So it can be calculated as follows

$$R_i(p_j) = r_i(p_j) + w_{oi} * r_i(o_j) + w_{si} * r_i(s_j).$$ (5)

where

- w_{oi} – significance weight of an option determined by i-user,
- w_{si} – significance weight of a section determined by i-user.

3 Conclusion and Future Works

The recommendation mechanism presented in the paper has been implemented and provided to the users of the ISEG2000-INT system, an internet information system designed for the retrieval of real estate cadastre data. The system has been deployed in about 50 intranets and extranets in local governments throughout Poland.

Future work will focus on observing how users will use the recommendation mechanism and what values will gain the ranks depending on different values of parameters. It will be interesting to investigate the behavior of system users using association rules and fuzzy logic methods.

References

1. Baeza-Yates R., Hurtado C., Mendoza M.: Query Recommendation Using Query Logs in Search Engines. LNCS, Vol. 3268. Springer-Verlag (2004) 588–597
2. Eirinaki M., Vazirgiannis M.: Web Mining for Web Personalization. ACM Transactions on Internet Technology, Vol. 3, No. 1 (2003) 1–27
3. Gunduz S., Ozsu T.: A User Behavior Model for Web Page Navigation. University of Waterloo (2002)
4. Kazienko P.: Multi-agent Web Recommendation Method Based on Indirect Association Rules. LNAI, Vol. 3214. Springer-Verlag (2004) 1157–1164
5. Nasraoui O., Pavuluri M.: Complete this Puzzle: A Connectionist Approach to Accurate Web Recommendations based on a Committee of Predictors. WebKDD Workshop on Web Mining and Web Usage Analysis, Seattle, WA (2004)
6. Sobecki J.: Web-Based Systems User Interfaces Recommendation Using Hybrid Methods. International Series on Advanced Intelligence, Vol. 10 (2004) 95–111

Topic-Centered Adaptive Curriculum for E-Learning

Yanyan Li and Ronghuai Huang

Knowledge Science & Engineering Institute, Beijing Normal University,
100875, Beijing, China
Liyy1114@hotmail.com, huangrh@bnu.edu.cn

Abstract. This paper proposes an approach to dynamically compose an adaptive curriculum for e-learning based on a topic-centered resource space. By exploiting the semantic relationships that characterize learning objects (LOs) and learner profile, the approach dynamically selects, sequences, and links learning resources into a coherent, individualized curriculum to address learners' focused learning needs. We developed an active learning system with semantic support for learners to access and navigate through learning resources in an efficient and personalized manner, while providing facilities for instructors to manipulate the structured learning resources via a convenient visual interface.

1 Introduction

E-Learning is just-in-time education integrated with high velocity value chains. It is the delivery of individualized, comprehensive, dynamic learning content in real time, aiding the development of communities of knowledge, linking learners and practitioners with experts [1]. But the production of learning content for e-learning is demanding and expensive. It is therefore a necessity to reuse e-learning materials for producing Web-based courses with less time and efforts. Unfortunately, existing electronic courses are seldom reused, as there is usually always a need to change some part for a new course to be held.

The notion of learning objects (LOs) has been introduced in the e-learning field to enhance the portability, reusability, and interoperability of learning resources. Ideally, Web-based course developers could quickly and easily assemble learning objects into coherent and effective organization for instruction to address a learner's focused learning needs [3]. However, current Web-based courses are still developed largely manually. Additionally, they are often designed for general users and thus not adapt to individual learners. [2] presents an approach to assemble learning objects into coherent and focused learning paths from a repository of XML Web resources. It simply relies on the learner's query to select matching LOs but not consider learner's learning history and background. Therefore, a more automatic and flexible approach is needed that is sensitive to each learner's unique needs and context, providing focused and structured learning resources.

V. Wade, H. Ashman, and B. Smyth (Eds.): AH 2006, LNCS 4018, pp. 350–353, 2006.
© Springer-Verlag Berlin Heidelberg 2006

2   Semantic Modeling of Learning Resources

The conceptual model of learning resources organization is shown in Fig. 1. Assets refer to any of the media files, such as Web pages, PDF documents, and videos. They can be uniquely identified with URI, and their semantic description is embedded in the corresponding learning objects. The distributed huge amounts of learning assets are stored separately, and related assets are grouped together as a learning object. Learning objects tagged with metadata represent any chunk of learning material regardless of its form, granularity and functionality. Knowledge Map (KM) describes the domain-specific knowledge schema, which provides a semantic view of the linking learning objects [4]. A Knowledge map uses a network structure to cover the knowledge structure in a specific domain, which includes nodes and typed semantic links between nodes.

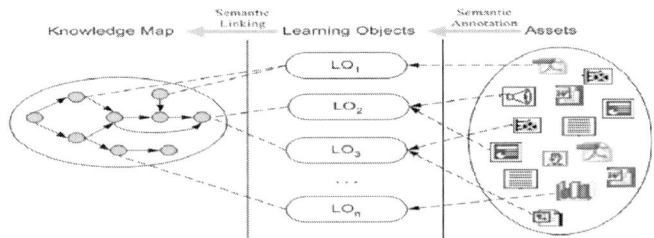

Fig. 1. Conceptual model of learning resources organization

3   Adaptive Composition Mechanism

The process flow of the curriculum composition comprises the following steps.

- Step1: Query annotation. The first step is to automatically process the query and annotate the query with possible semantic information to expedite the search for LOs in a large repository.
- Step 2: LOs searching. Ssearch the LO repository for relevant learning objects based on the keyword matching of the learning objects content and metadata to the query term. The search results are a set of learning objects.
- Step3: Topic mapping. Identify the target topics by mapping the LOs in the search results to the topics in the knowledge map. The simple way is to follow the links preset by the instructors if there exist links from learning objects to topics, otherwise, use the topic clustering to find the mapping topic based on the metadata of returning learning objects.
- Step4: Learning syllabus planning. Learning syllabus is represented as a sequence of semantically interrelated topics that a learner can follow to address his focused learning needs. Taken the mapping topics as anchor nodes, the learning syllabus is generated based on the graph traversal approach according to topic relationships.

- Step5: LOs sequencing. Substantiate each topic of the syllabus with one or more LOs. Pedagogical rules are used to select and sequence the learning objects about the same topic based on their metadata description.

To the end, serving as components of a learning curriculum, the target learning objects are sequenced and provided for the learners.

4 Implementation

We have developed an e-learning platform WebCL (available at http://www. webcl.net.cn/) that has been used in more than twenty universities or high schools, and the total number of registered users exceeds 10000. The adaptive curriculum application is built on top of the WebCL Workbench that offers a plug-in interface for extension modules. Fig. 2 shows the resulting curriculum for the query "Lattice homomorphism" proposed by a novice. As the learner has little knowledge on this topic, the generated curriculum contains the basic and comprehensive content. The componential learning objects are displayed in a sequence with hypertext navigation structure.

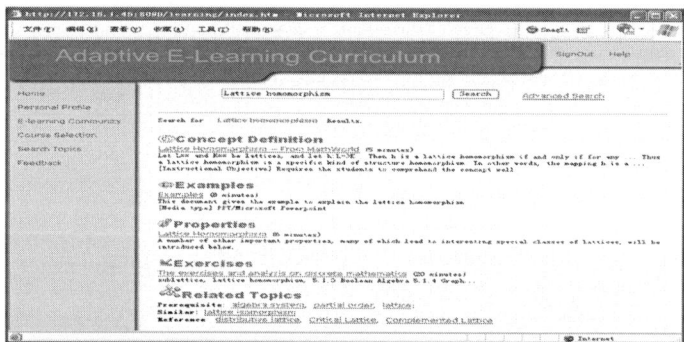

Fig. 2. The interface for displaying e-learning curriculum

5 Conclusions

By incorporating the learning objects and the learner profile, this paper proposes an adaptive curriculum composition approach for e-learning. Driven by the specific queries from learners, adaptive e-learning curriculum is dynamically generated by selecting and structuring the semantic relevant learning objects according to knowledge map, LOs metadata, and learner profile. In this way, the generated curriculum with tailored content and flexible structure caters for different learners with different backgrounds, capabilities and expectations, at different time and venue.

References

1. Drucker, P., Need to Know: Integrating e-Learning with High Velocity Value Chains, A Delphi Group White Paper, 2000, http://www.delphigroup.com/pubs/whitepapers/20001213-e-learning-wp.pdf.
2. Farrell, R., Liburd S.D. and Thomas, J.C., Dynamic Assembly of Learning Objects, in Proceedings of The thirteenth International World Wide Web Conference, May, New York, USA, 2004.
3. Wiley, D.A. (ed.), The Instructional Use of Learning Objects. Agency for Instructional Technology, Bloomington, 2002.
4. Zhuge, H. and Li, Y., Learning with Active E-Course in Knowledge Grid Environment, Concurrency and Computation: Practice and Experience, 2006.

Semantic-Based Thematic Search for Personalized E-Learning

Yanyan Li and Ronghuai Huang

Knowledge Science & Engineering Institute, Beijing Normal University,
100875, Beijing, China
Liyy1114@hotmail.com, huangrh@bnu.edu.cn

Abstract. This paper describes one solution to the problem of how to collect, organize, and select Web learning resources into a coherent, focused organization for instruction to address learners' immediate and focused learning needs. By exploiting the semantic relationships that characterize learning resources and learner profile, the proposed semantic-based thematic approach supports both semantic querying and conceptual navigation of learning resources pertaining to specific topics. A system has been developed and deployed within an academic setting, enabling learners to organize, search, and share the learning resources in a flexible and personalized manner.

1 Introduction

More and more instructors are developing multimedia learning materials, such as lecture notes, software simulations, and videos, to support distance learning. As a result, the amount of multimedia resources available to learners is increasing continuously. The wealth of resources presents a great challenge: how to provide a coherent, structured, shareable collection of resources to cater for learners' specific needs. Some systems have been proposed intending to effectively support resources searching and exploitation [1], [2], [3]. However, they are still in infancy and have two weaknesses. One is that the terminology used by different sources is often inconsistent and there is no common overarching context for the available resources, so maintaining huge weakly structured resources is a difficult and time-consuming activity. The other is that existing keyword-based search without semantic annotations retrieves much irrelevant information, so navigation through a large set of independent sources often leads to learners' being lost.

By incorporating the Semantic Web technologies, this paper proposes a semantic-based thematic search approach. It is to select Web learning resources into a coherent, focused organization for instruction to address learners' immediate and focused learning needs.

2 General Architecture

The general architecture is illustrated in Fig. 1, which comprises the following core modules. User interface enables learners to access the learning resources and instructors

V. Wade, H. Ashman, and B. Smyth (Eds.): AH 2006, LNCS 4018, pp. 354–357, 2006.

to maintain the resource organization model by means of visual operations. Domain ontology describes the common knowledge schema in a specific domain. Learner profile is used as the adaptive user model representing the interests and knowledge of individual learners. Resource collecting module is responsible for collecting learning resources from the Web and from people, and then all the collected documents are classified and stored in the resource space. Thematic search is to search for a collection of resources that provide the user with comprehensive information he is trying to find on specific topics. Conceptual navigation engine shows the resource structure in tree-view or map-view pattern through which users can freely navigate through the resources by simply clicking the nodes.

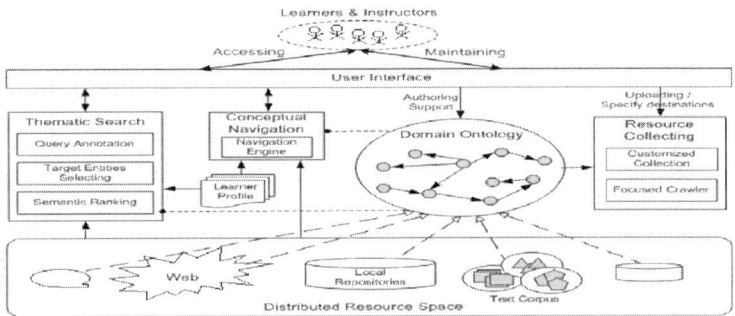

Fig. 1. The general architecture

3 Thematic Search Strategy

For the given query proposed by the learner, the search is conducted by following the three-step process.

Step1: Query Annotation. For a given query, the first step is to map the search term to one or more entities of the resource space. This might return no matches, a single match or multiple matches. If there is no matching entity, then we are not able to contribute anything to the search results. As for the case of multiple matches, one reason is that the query is divided into several terms. The other reason is the linguistics ambiguity (e.g. synonym), in this context, users' profiles are taken as the reference to select the proper annotation. Additionally, the search context and the popularity of the term as measured by its frequency of occurrence in a text corpus can also give hints for selecting the proper annotation for the search terms.

Step2: Target Entities Selecting. Taken the matching entities as the anchor ones, this step is to find semantic relevant entities. The simple approach for selecting the target entities for the one matching entity, purely based on the structure of the graph, is to collect the first N triples originated from the anchor entity, where N is the predefined traversal constraints. As for the case of two matching entities corresponding to the query, it is the key problem to find all the semantic association paths between the two entities so as to select the relevant instances on the paths. The basic idea of the algorithm is to traverse the graph in a breadth-first order starting from the two entities.

Step3: Semantic Ranking. This step is to rank the target entities in terms of their association weights. Our approach to ranking the semantic associated results is primarily based on capturing the interests of a user. This can be accomplished by enabling a user to browse the ontology and mark a region (sub-graph) of nodes and/or properties of interest. If the discovery process finds some semantic association paths passing through these regions then they are considered relevant, while other associations are ranked lower or discarded.

4   Implementation

Assuming a student inputs the query "Knowledge Grid", and Fig. 2 shows the searching results. As the student is only interested in the research domain, so the search results related to the research domain are selected and displayed in a structured manner. In addition to the general information about the item (e.g. introduction, link-address), more related resources are given for learners' reference, and thus learners can click any topic to get more focused information. To the right of each item title is the type of the learning resource. In this way, the search results augmented with semantic information do help to guide user's navigation. The student can click the related item to get more focused information.

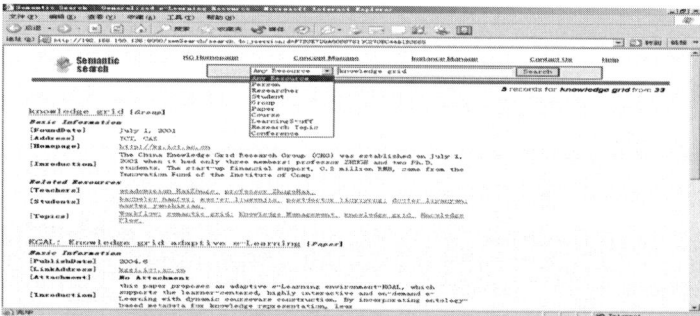

Fig. 2. Search results augmented with referenced information

5   Conclusion

Our semantic oriented system has the following advantages. First, the knowledge structure is separated from the media resources, which enables effective resource organization and reusing. Second, learners benefit from the thematic search that discovers and provides semantic associated resources to address the learners' focused and personalized learning needs. Third, the adaptive learning resources delivered in a coherent structure empower learners to efficiently explore the learning resources at their own paces.

References

1. Goecks, J. and Cosley, D., NuggetMine: Intelligent groupware for opportunistically sharing information nuggets, Proceedings of the Intelligent User Interfaces Conference, pp. 87-94, 2002.
2. Jari, K., Stroulia, E., EduNuggets: an intelligent environment for managing and delivering multimedia education content, In Proceedings of the 8th international conference on Intelligent user interfaces, Miami, Florida, USA, pp: 303 - 306, 2003, ACM Press.
3. Young, R.L., Kant, E., and Akers, L.A., A knowledge-based electronic information and documentation system, Proceedings of the Intelligent User Interfaces Conference, pp. 280-285, 2000.

Adaptation in Adaptable Personal Information Environment

Thanyalak Maneewatthana, Gary Wills, and Wendy Hall

IAM Group, School of Electronics and Computer Science
University of Southampton, SO17 1BJ, UK
{tm03r, gbw, wh}@ecs.soton.ac.uk

Abstract. In order to support knowledge workers during their tasks of searching, locating and manipulating information, a system that provides information suitable for a particular user's needs, and that is also able to facilitate annotation, sharing and reuse information is essential. This paper presents Adaptable Personal Information Environment (a-PIE); a service-oriented framework using Open Hypermedia and Semantic Web technologies to provide an adaptable web-based system. a-PIE models the information structures (data and links) and context as Fundamental Open Hypermedia Model (FOHM) structures which are manipulated by using the Auld Linky contextual link service. a-PIE provides an information environment that enables users to search an information space based on ontologically defined domain concepts. The users can add and annotate interesting data or parts of information structures into their information space, leaving the original published data or information structures unchanged. a-PIE facilitates the shareability and reusability of knowledge according to users' requirements.

1 Introduction

In a community of practice people are often willing to develop and share knowledge. They could use a repository for this purpose, but often the context and relationship between information chunks will be lost. Knowledge management and the associated tools aim to provide such an environment in which people may create, learn, share, use and reuse knowledge, for the benefit of the organisation, the people who work in it, and the organisation's customers. However, instead of helping users, many systems are just increasing the information overload. Adapting the information chunks and/or the links (associations) to the needs of individual users greatly enhances navigation and comprehension of an information space, and reduces the information overload.

In this paper we propose an adaptable Personal Information Environment system (a-PIE) that brings together knowledge technologies and adaptive hypermedia to facilitate the reuse and sharing of information. a-PIE aims to provide a system in which members of the community or organisation are able to browse information tailored to their needs, store relationships to content of interest in their own information repository, and are able to annotate the relationships for reuse. This paper briefly presents the technologies and a system overview of a-PIE, focusing on the support for adaptation of information. Finally related work and some conclusions are presented.

V. Wade, H. Ashman, and B. Smyth (Eds.): AH 2006, LNCS 4018, pp. 358–361, 2006.

2 Motivation and Background

A brief scenario helps explain the motivation behind this research. A user in a virtual community is looking/searching for information from a community or organisation's web site. They find an interesting piece of information and would like to keep it for reference later in a personal repository. On occasions, they would like to add annotation to particular information snippets and would like to record the context before storing it in their personal repository. They would also like to share this information, with others in the community. As this is a diverse community they annotate the information with the level of expertise (e.g., experts, intermediate or beginners) the reader requires in order to understand the information. Then depending on reader's profile (e.g., knowledge background, expertise) only those authorised by the original user will see the information and its annotations.

In Open Hypermedia Systems, links are considered as first-class objects. The Fundamental Open Hypermedia Model (FOHM) [1] is a protocol for open hypermedia with additional context-awareness features. It is a data model for expressing hyperstructure by representing associations between data. Auld Linky [1] is a context based link server which supplies links from specified linkbases by parsing FOHM structures. FOHM also provides a Context modifier object, which can be attached to any part of the FOHM structure. Context objects define conditions for the visibility of particular objects and are used by Auld Linky to distinguish which bindings should be returned to the user.

3 System Overview

The adaptable Personal Information Environment (a-PIE) aims to provide a system in which members of the community are able to browse information suitable to their particular needs, identify and store FOHM structures in their own information repository which users may enhance prior to reuse. a PIE further enhances these functionalities by using ontologies [2] to define the associations and facilitate interoperate between components.

a-PIE consists of several services. The domain concept service provides the relevant concept. The user model service updates user model. The data item and association service manipulates data and structures, as FOHM objects, from linkbases through the contextual link server (Auld Linky). The user service or adaptive engine provides the facilities for reconciling the data content, FOHM structures, and user model, to present the individualised document to the user through a web browser.

Figure 1 illustrates the system architecture of a-PIE. The functionality of the system is made available to software agents through a Web Service interface (WSDL), and to end-users through a Web browser. The system separates these components; domain concept, data, structure, user information and context. Each model has an ontology as a means for interoperation.

- *Domain concept*: represents the basic structure of concept schemes.
- *Domain data model*: represents the data in the form of FOHM Data objects.

- *Structure model*: connects FOHM Data objects as a series of FOHM Association structures which can be Navigational Link, Tour, Level of Detail and Concept.
- *User model:* represents user-related information, such as background knowledge.
- *Context model*: represented by FOHM Context objects which can be attached to a Data or Association object for describing the context in which the data item or association is visible (or hidden) from the user.

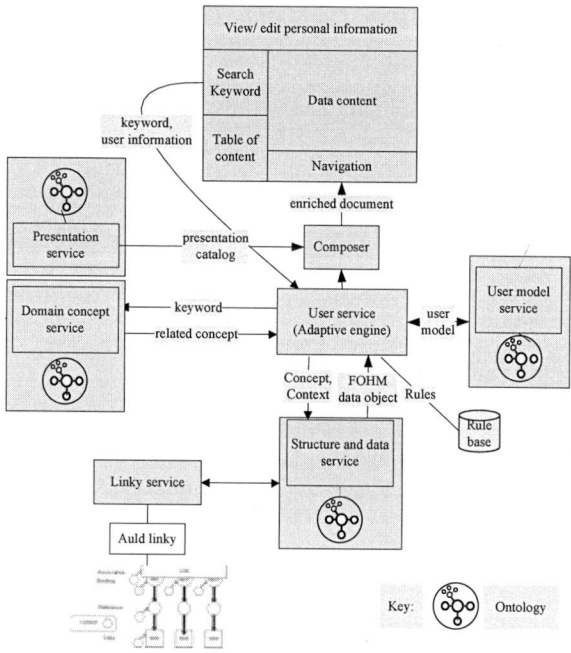

Fig. 1. a-PIE System Architecture

a-PIE provides adaptive hypermedia support through the use of Auld Linky as a contextual link server to integrate FOHM structure and data objects according to the context. Context objects define conditions for the visibility of particular objects and are used by Auld Linky to distinguish which bindings should be returned to the user. FOHM structures can be combined to implement a range of adaptive hypermedia techniques [3].

The ontologies are used to enrich links and data content, and to enable other users to share and reuse the content or structure of the FOHM representation. In addition to browsing and searching the site the user can; add data, add additional specialist information, and change the context or behaviour of the FOHM structures.

4   Related Work and Discussion

There are several formal models proposed which focus on the mechanisms and structures based on adaptive hypermedia systems such as Adaptive Hypermedia

Application Model (AHAM) [4]. Hunter gatherer is a tool that allowed people to browse the web and identify pieces of information and group these as a collection of links [6], while, Piggy Bank is a browser enabled tool that re-constructs Web page content into a Semantic Web format [7]. The tool also allows user to save and share pages as links represented in RDF. Unlike a-Pie, the tool does not use an ontology to organise the pool of pages but a *folksonomies*. COHSE [8] is a non-adaptable ontological hypertext system that allow semantic annotations of webpages.

This paper describes a-PIE as a Web-based system aimed to provide adaptable information and support sharing and reuse of information which are achieved by using FOHM and Auld Linky and Semantic Web technology. The a-PIE system conforms to the generic architecture for an Adaptive Hypermedia System proposed by Ohene-Djan *et al.*[5].

Acknowledgement

Our thanks to The Royal Thai Government for funding this work.

References

[1] D. T. Michaelides, D. E. Millard, M. J. Weal, and D. C. De Roure, "Auld Leaky: A Contextual Open Hypermedia Link Server," presented at Proceedings of the seventh Workshop on Open Hypermedia systems, ACM Hypertext Conference, Aarhus, Denmark, 2001.
[2] T. Berners-Lee, J. Hendler, and O. Lassila, "The Semantic Web," *Scientific American*, vol. 279, pp. 35-43, 2001.
[3] C. Bailey, W. Hall, D. E. Millard, and M. J. Weal, "Towards Open Adaptive Hypermedia," presented at Proceedigns of the second International Conference on Adaptive Hypermedia and Adaptive Web-Based System, Malaga, Spain, 2002.
[4] P. De Bra, P. Brusilovsky, and G. J. Houben, "Adaptive Hypermedia: From Systems to Framework," *ACM Computing Surveys*, vol. 31, 1999.
[5] J. Ohene-Djan, M. Gorle, C. Bailey, G. Wills, and H. Davis, "Is It Possible to Devise a Unifying Model of Adaptive Hypermedia and Is One Necessary?," presented at Workshop on Adaptive Hypermedia and Adaptive Web-Based Systems, 14th Conference on Hypertext and Hypermedia, Nottingham, UK, 2003.
[6] m. c. schraefel, D. Modjeska, D. Wigdor, and S. Zhao, "Hunter Gatherer: Interaction Support for the Creation and Management of Within-Web-Page Collections," presented at Proceedings of International World Wide Web Conference, Honolulu, Hawaii, USA, 2002.
[7] D. Huynh, S. Mazzocchi, and D. David Karger, "Piggy Bank: Experience the Semantic Web Inside Your Web Browser," presented at Proceedings of the fourth International Semantic Web Conference, Galway, Ireland, 2005.
[8] L. Carr, S. Kampa, D. C. De Roure, W. Hall, S. Bechhofer, C. G. Goble, and B. Horan, "Ontological Linking: Motivation and Analysis," presented at CIKM, 2002.

Towards Formalising Adaptive Behaviour Within the Scope of E-Learning

Felix Mödritscher

IICM, Graz University of Technology, Inffeldgasse 16c, A-8010 Graz, Austria
fmoedrit@iicm.edu

Abstract. As there are a lot of approaches and projects within the area of adaptive e-learning, several theoretical models have been developed in the last 15 years. Against this background, the AdeLE team implemented a first prototype on basis of informal descriptions given by literature research as well as concrete circumstances of the research project. Nevertheless, a theoretical model fulfilling certain requirements for our approach is still missing. This paper points out possibilities and limitations of existing models in the scope of the AdeLE project. Further, the authors own attempt towards formalising adaptive behaviour in e-learning environments is denoted.

1 Introduction

Despite various approaches and systems arisen within the scope of adaptive e-learning in the last 15 years (e.g. see [2]), the research project AdeLE aims at developing another framework in this area by tying up to well-founded theories and trying to realise innovative features such as an improved learner observation through eye-tracking or the application of a dynamic background library. As a first step of dealing with the basics of adaptive e-learning, we examined historical approaches as well as system types given in this scope and introduced an model applicable for the AdeLE project [1]. This model was implemented in the first prototype as pointed out in [4]. Nevertheless, this theoretical approach is merely informally described. Thus, I attempt to adopt or build up a theoretical model for adaptive e-learning fulfilling certain requirements given within the AdeLE project. Therefore, the next section gives a short overview about the AdeLE project and outlines problems requiring specific features of a theoretical model. Thereafter, existing approaches in this area are examined with respect to our needs. Concluding this paper, I propose a solution for describing the adaptive behaviour of the AdeLE system.

2 The AdeLE Project and Its Unclear Initial Direction

The research project AdeLE, which stands for "Adaptive e-Learning with Eye Tracking", aims on two important issues in the context of adaptive e-learning. On

V. Wade, H. Ashman, and B. Smyth (Eds.): AH 2006, LNCS 4018, pp. 362–365, 2006.

the one side we try to exploit eye-tracking technology for an improved learner observation and an enhanced adaptation mechanism. On the other side it is planned to apply a so-called Dynamic Background Library (DBL) to adapt the learning process by providing accurate and topical background information. Considering these two directions, it was the task of the IICMs researcher group to realise a server-sided adaptive e-learning environment which allows processing any data about learning behaviour as well as offering the learner background knowledge via DBL. In particular, my own research work deals with the conception and implementation of the adaptive e-learning platform consisting of a LMS and an Adaptive System, adapting the learning process on basis of didactical and pedagogical rules, exploiting the user model given by the Modelling System as well as providing background information supplied by the DBL.

In the context of AdeLE, I faced the following problems with defining clear requirements for the development of the system: At the beginning of the project, our psychologist could not estimate which information the eye-tracking device can infer about the learner behaviour. Thus, it was unclear to which aspects should be adapted. Secondly, the elements of the virtual learning process to adapt were not determined. According to the projects aims, adaptation might affect navigational elements, the path though the course, instructions as well as single assets. Furthermore, the input of the DBL should also be offered in some way. Thirdly, we tried to consider the users interaction with the system as well as other sensory data, e.g. provided by the eye-tracking device. Yet, it was also discussed to apply further sensors in the future. Fourthly, we distinguished between didactical and pedagogical issues in e-learning. While didactics focuses on the teachers intentions of running a course, pedagogy deals with the suitability of an instruction within a certain context or for a certain learner. Thus, we propose two kinds of adaptation rules, didactical and pedagogical ones.

Due to this lack of a clear direction in the initial phase of the project, I chose a holistic approach towards adaptive e-learning trying to avoid didactical restrictions and to consider all kinds of pedagogical aspects of the virtual learning process. After all, I came to the conclusion that we need a theoretical model to describe adaptive behaviour in the AdeLE system and evaluate its benefits for learning. Therefore, the next section examines existing models with respect to our special needs.

3   Possibilities and Limitations of Existing Models

Adaptive e-learning, as stated e.g. in [9], comprises a research and development stream dealing with educational systems that adapt the learning content as well as the user interface with respect to pedagogical and didactical aspects. Adaptive educational hypermedia is meant to be relatively new by commonly known researchers (e.g. see [2]). Nevertheless, [7] state that certain ideas of adapting instructions (e.g. Presseys teaching machine) can be tracked back to the early 20th century, while first systems were realised in the 1960s. [7] also provide an excellent model to characterise adaptive instructional systems summing up the historical mainstreams: Firstly, the macro-adaptive instructional approach comprises didactical aspects of learning content such as the students' achievement levels, dependencies between instructional units, etc. A model behind this mainstream can be reduced to the sequencing rules, as specified e.g. in SCORM. Secondly, the aptitude-treatment interactions (ATI) approach focuses on instructional design on basis of students aptitudes, which originated various heuristics for instructional design and UI principles. Thirdly, the micro-adaptive instructional approach comprises adaptation during instruction and on basis of a diagnose process, whereas a real adaptation model, e.g. based on mathematics, trajectory, Bayesian probability, algorithms and rules, etc., is needed.

In practice, these three mainstreams for adaptive instructional systems can be found in various types of systems. Macro-adaptive and computer-managed instructional systems focus on typical aspects as explained for the macro-adaptive instructional approach, but these technological solutions do not allow on-task adaptation, nor do they consider UI elements of the e-learning platform. The ATI approach mainly affects courseware design as well as navigational elements of the platform, but also influences micro-adaptive instructional technologies such as intelligent tutoring systems (ITS) and adaptive educational hypermedia systems (AEHS). ITS are based on AI techniques and include an expertise, a student, and a tutoring model. The application of these systems are mostly restricted to a certain domain or context or fail to incorporate valuable learning principles and instructional strategies [7]. Younger mainstreams, such as AEHS or adaptive/personalised e-learning, tie up to the foundations of ITS and comprise the following models: (a) a content model semantically enriching the learning content, (b) a learner model specifying learner characteristics, (c) an instructional (or tutoring) model providing the teaching strategy, and (d) an adaptation model determining rules to adapt the learning process.

While a lot of excellent approaches e.g. [9] or [7] in this scope are of informal nature, I inspected three formal models for the application for the AdeLE system and identified the following possibilities and limitations: First of all, the Adaptive Hypermedia Application Model (AHAM) by [3] focussing on hypertext and hypermedia systems allows specifying didactical issues and pedagogical rules. Yet, this formal model restricts the possibilities of teachers, e.g. by addressing merely the cognitive domain (read, learned) or not separating between learning materials and learning activities. Further, to a high extent AHAM deals with architectural issues, which is, in my opinion, not a requirement for designing and evaluating adaptive behaviour within an e-learning environment. Secondly, [5] came up with an innovative sequencing methodology for AEHS considering also the suitability of a path through the course. Although this approach would allow specifying and examining all possible didactical and pedagogical issues of adaptive e-learning, it only addresses the learning content and, thus, I did not figure out the way how elements of the platform can be directly adapted according to specific rules. Thirdly, [6] introduces the Munich Model representing a rather technological approach and specifying the single models, such as the domain model, the user model, etc., with UML and formal methods. Nevertheless,

I think that this model is much too complex, because the design is too detailed, and it can hardly be of benefit for describing adaptive behaviour in e-learning environments. Notwithstanding the existence of a high number of other formal models, I have to state at this point that the these three formal models miss the requirements of our research project. Further, I have not found an formal approach providing a flexible way to describe adaptation of instructions and platforms elements on basis of relevant aspects of e-learning.

4   Conclusions and a Solution Approach

Concluding this paper and as a general statement, I assume that most models miss important didactical or pedagogical aspects or drive our attention in the wrong direction e.g. by focusing too strongly on software development issues. To define and evaluate adaptive behaviour in the scope of an e-learning platform, a formal model has to allow the specification of the systems underlying adaptation principles without regarding issues of lower priority. Thus, I propose a(nother) formal approach, namely FORMABLE, which stands for "FORmal Model for Adaptive Behaviour in e-Learning Environments" and consists of four models: (a) the Domain Model dealing with the domain, the context, and the learning content, (b) the Pedagogical Model specifying states in relation to learners, the domain, and the context, (c) the Didactical Model comprising all aspects of e-teaching, and (d) the Adaptation Model realising different adaptation methods and defining rules to offer the learner more relevant and suitable instructions. As there is only limited space within this paper, the FORMABLE model, fully described with the formal specification language VDM++, will be presented in the poster session at the conference.

References

1. AdeLE: Website of the research project. http://adele.fh-joanneum.at (2006-03-30)
2. Brusilovsky, P.: Adaptive Educational Hypermedia: From Generation to Generation. Proc. of ICTE (2004) 19–33
3. De Bra, P., Houben, G.-J., Wu, H.: AHAM: A Dexter-based Reference Model for Adaptive Hypermedia. Proc. of ACM Hypertext (1999) 147–156
4. Gütl, C., Mödritscher, F.: Towards a Generic Adaptive System applicable for Web-based Learning Management Environments. Proc. of ABIS (2005) 26–31
5. Karampiperis, P., Sampson, D.: Adaptive Learning Resources Sequencing in Educational Hypermedia Systems. Educational Technology & Society **8(4)** (2005) 128–147
6. Koch, N.: Software Engineering for Adaptive Hypermedia Systems: Reference Model, Modeling Techniques and Development Process. Ludwig-Maximilians-Universität München (2000)
7. Park, O., Lee, J.: Adaptive Instructional Systems. Educational Technology Research and Development (2003) 651–684
8. Shute, V.J., Psotka, J.: Intelligent tutoring systems: Past, present and future. Handbook of research on educational communications and technology (1996) 570–600
9. Shute, V., Towle, B.: Adaptive E-Learning. Educational Psychologist **38** (2003) 105–114

Informing Context to Support Adaptive Services

Alexander O'Connor and Vincent Wade

Knowledge and Data Engineering Group,
Department of Computer Science,
Trinity College,
Dublin 2, Ireland
{oconnoat, Vincent.Wade}@cs.tcd.ie

Abstract. A common trend in modern applications is the move towards more mobile, adaptive, customisable software. The evolution of software from static, invariant tools for narrow portions of a task to adaptive, open interaction frameworks is embodied in the use of a variety of technologies for creating a reconfigurable application. Perhaps the two most important techniques are Adaptive architectures and Ubiquitious Computing. However, many techniques employed merging these two technologies to form the vision of a truly ubiquitous, adaptive environment have so far failed to take full account of the expressive quality of both context and adaptivity. This paper presents a new, semantic interopration-based approach to creating context-informed adaptive applications that make maximum use of the rich content that can be found in both technologies.

1 Introduction

Adaptive Applications are characterised by their variable behaviour in response to their information models[1]. Adaptivity allows for applicationsto make considerable changes for personalisation and customisation preferences as defined by the user and the content being adapted. This mechanism is extremely powerful in providing tailored presentation of information to the user.

Adaptivity also permits this class of applications to leverage Contextual information very effectively, employing additional axes of information to better inform customisation and personalisation. Many of the current approaches to Contextual support for Adaptivity are, however, focused on a mechanism whereby the application itself does a large proportion of the work by querying external sources of information and integrating the results by treating contextual data as separate and distinct. By placing the responsibility for managing and querying and integrating context on the application, this approach can place extra burden on the application programmer, who must design an integration strategy for Context, and on the application itself which potentially makes the information models larget and more complex.

This paper presents a Context-Informed approach to enriching Adaptive applications. In this architecture, the adaptive application is served by a contextual broker, which enriches the application based on a broader spectrum of concerns,

V. Wade, H. Ashman, and B. Smyth (Eds.): AH 2006, LNCS 4018, pp. 366–369, 2006.

and which makes use of a model-oriented approach for indirect querying and direct integration. This approach provides and innovative solution using Topic Maps to manage a semantic interoperation process.

2 Context

There are a great many[2] definitions and descriptions of what exactly constitutes context, both in general and for particular application domains. For the purposes of this work, it is most important to be aware that contextual information is knowledge about the user, their environment or their task which is not known to the application being used for the task, but which is available at run-time through other services. This extra knowledge can be recognised by a semantic description offered by services surrounding the user and their application, even though the application itself may not know of such information directly.

The system presented follows the context-*informed* model: the aware environment informs the application. This means that neither the target application nor the sources need to be aware of each other, and that the Target application need only be designed to know that it has the opportunity to gain some extra information, not what that information might be or how it might be acquired.

The principal challenges associated with context-informed support for adaptive services are:

1. To Identify the information need of the adaptive service.
2. To Identify the possible external sources of information.
3. To Identify matching information in sources and infer on its influence on the adaptive service.
4. To determine how to amend the adaptive service both in terms of data and model.

These challenges comprise a broad solution to the process of enhancing adaptive services. Of particular interest in this work are the third and fourth challenges. The process of determining possible sources of context through exploring the information space is, in itself, a very interesting problem. It is likely one made more difficult if the nature of the information and the process by which it is incorporated is not known.

3 Architecture

The Architecture is composed of three tiers: the Target Application, which is the system to be enriched; the Sources of Context, which are services that offer additional information to be combined as context, and the Context Exchange, which brokers and manages the process. In proposing this form of architecure, the roles of each participant are clearly defined: it is the Target Application which is enriched by the integrated content returned by the Context Exchange. The enrichment process is performed using a semantic, model-based exchange.

The internal model of the Target Application is exposed via a schema, and the schema labels are populated by the current state of the application's knowledge. This can then be compared to the information known to Sources of Context via a joined schema that forms the Information Space.

A number of approaches have been suggested[3] for managing contextual information, and enabling transfers. The semantic interoperation approach, as opposed to a planned or workflow model, is desirable because it natually accounts for the dynamic and composite nature of contextual data, as well as generally giving a better responsiveness to change. Topic Maps represent a lightweight 'index' linking the semantically close elements of the different participant ontologies. This provides a navigable framework for creating an enriched model for the Target Application that can be generated based on the definitive underlying ontologies. This system employs Topic Maps to represent the shared schema between the Target Application and the Sources of Context within the Environment. This allows the Context Exchange to create an expressive shared schema that is still lightweight and composable, without the need for the detailed formality that ontologies require. In addition, the ability of the system to alter the Target Applications *models* as well as data will be dependant on the design of the Target and the Environment.

3.1   Enhancing Adaptivity

The underlying benefit to the Adaptive System is that a Context-informed environment facilitates the leveraging of additional information known by external services with minimal *a-priori* knowledge on the part of the developer. This assists both the content designer and system developer by enabling them to focus on the core concerns of the adaptive application, the remaining information being handled as context. The developer remains in control of the enrichment process by being responsible for determining how and when models are submitted to the Context Exchange.

This approach to deciding what information to treat context can vary greatly for different usage scenarios, depending on the configuration provided at design-time, as well as the properties of the environment at runtime.

4   Analysis and Future Work

Currently, the system is in the early stages of implementation. It is intended to employ the system in trials in both the eLearning and corporate collaboration application domains. These areas provide a spectrum of cognitive depth and application adaptivity useful in measuring the generality of this solution and the nature of the tailoring process required by different systems. As an interim approach, it is proposed initially to investigate the properties of this system in a static, pre-determined service environment.

The topic of semantic matching is, in itself, an area of considerable research interest. There are many challenges associated with the process of linking separate, possibly disjoint perspectives, even with the considerable assistance provided by ontologies and other semantic techniques. Physical[4] and semantic[5] techniques provide a basis for locating these links, but it is possible that the best achievable solution, in practice, will be a semi-automatic system where the link list is corrected and improved by the user. This has additional advantages in that it assists in maintaining the scrutability of the overall adaptive system - a feature vital in maintaining user interests[6].

The Degree to which the adaptivity of the Target Application affects how this system can be employed. In particular, the process of amending and integrating data and models will likely require some design-time tailoring, depending on the particular properties of the target application and the sources.

5   Conclusion

This paper has presented a model-driven, context-informed framework for supporting adaptive applications. The system is based on the principles of semantic interoperation, which provide for the generation of a lightweight aggregate semantic view of the information space which a user, and their application, occupy.

Acknowledgements

This work is funded by the Irish Research Council for Science, Engineering and Technology: funded by the National Development Plan. Portions of this work are in collaboration with the IBM Centre for Advanced Studies, Dublin.

References

1. De Bra, P., Aroyo, L., Chepegin, V.: The next big thing: Adaptive web based systems. Journal of Digital Information (**5**(247, 2005-05-27))
2. Chen, G., Kotz, D.: A Survey of Context-Aware Mobile Computing Research. Technical Report TR2000-381, Dartmouth College, Computer Science, Hanover, NH (2000)
3. Noy, N.F.: Semantic integration: a survey of ontology-based approaches. SIGMOD Rec. **33**(4) (2004) 65–70
4. McGuinness, D.L., Fikes, R., Rice, J., , Wilder, S.: The chimaera ontology environment. In: Proceedings of the Seventeenth National Conference on Artificial Intelligence (AAAI 2000). (2000)
5. O'Sullivan, D., Power, R.: Bridging heterogenous, autonomic, dynamic knowledge at runtime. In: 1st International Workshop on Managing Ubiquitous Communications and Services (MUCS). (2003)
6. Czarkowski, M., Kay, J.: How to give the user a sense of control over the personalization of ah? In De Bra, P.e.a., ed.: AH2003: Workshop on Adaptive Hypermedia and Adaptive Web-Based Systems; Workshop proceedings from the Ninth International Conference on User Modeling. (2003)

eDAADe: An Adaptive Recommendation System for Comparison and Analysis of Architectural Precedents

Shu-Feng Pan and Ji-Hyun Lee

Graduate School of Computational Design, NYUST,
123 University Road, Section 3,
Douliou, Yunlin 64002, Taiwan, R.O.C
{g9334701, jihyun}@yuntech.edu.tw

Abstract. We built a Web-based adaptive recommendation system for students to select and suggest architectural cases when they analyze "Case Study" work within the architectural design studio course, which includes deep comparisons and analyses for meaningful architectural precedents. We applied hybrid recommendation mechanism, which is combining both content-based filtering and collaborative filtering in our suggested model. It not only retains the advantages of a content-based and collaborative filtering approach, but also improves the disadvantages found in both. We expect that the approach would be helpful for students to find relevant precedents more efficient and more precise with their preferences.

1 Introduction

The process of an architectural design studio course includes deep comparisons and analyses for meaningful architectural precedents, which are related to the design concept. There are several websites (e.g., GreatBuildings.com[1] and archINForm[2]) providing online architectural case searching for students and architects. The Web searching and navigation problems, however, require an intelligent educational recommendation mechanism that is adaptive based on user's various needs and explicit and implicit user feedback in the task of finding relevant information in the complicated structure of website [1].

Such a recommendation mechanism can be embodied by using several kinds of information filtering approaches. Balabanovic and Shoham [2] and Popescul et al. [3] proposed a mechanism of combining *Collaborating Filtering* approach with *Content-based Filtering* approach for information recommendation. The content-based filtering approach analyzes user's preference and measures the similarity of different items to the user's preference. The items that have a high degree of similarity to user's preference are recommended to the users. Unlike the content-based filtering which considers only an active user's preference, the collaborating filtering approach considers other user's preferences. The degree of items usually needs to be rated by the user based on user likes or dislikes. However, explicit rating maybe has a rating sparsity

---

[1] http://www.greatbuildings.com/
[2] http://www.archinform.net/

V. Wade, H. Ashman, and B. Smyth (Eds.): AH 2006, LNCS 4018, pp. 370–373, 2006.

problem. The hybrid approach, therefore, retains the advantages of a content-based and collaborative filtering approach, thus we wanted to apply this approach in our proposed system.

In this paper, we built eDAADe (e-learning Dynamic Adaptive website in Architectural Design education), a Web-based adaptive recommendation system for students to compare and analyze the precedents in the "Case Study" phase of the architectural design process and to prove our concepts by several concrete examples.

2 Hybrid Recommendation Approach in eDAADe

To apply the hybrid approach in our eDAADe system, the process of the recommendation system can be explained as follows:

(1) Identify the features of architectural precedents: each precedent can identify the following four feature categories: a) *name*, b) *description*, c) *builder* and d) *keywords*.

(2) Analyze the content of precedents based on explicit and implicit user feedback: the *explicit feedback* can be measured from students by rating the degree of preference based on their likes and dislikes. We use the 5-Point Likert Scales methodology to measure students' ratings for each precedent. However, students perhaps are not willing to rate (rating sparsity). Therefore, we can find out the *implicit feedback*. We write a spider (cookie) program to record the data we need and apply data mining techniques to discover the students' behavior patterns when they navigate the website. From the information, we are able to know students' viewing time and frequency for each architectural precedent. If the precedent were viewed by students frequently and if they spent a lot of time at this site, we can assume the students have high interest in that precedent. Since each architectural precedent also includes four features as we mentioned above, we are able to know the student's preferences according to each feature appearing on the web page by frequency rate. Based on this, we can build content-based profiles of each student tendency and interest.

(3) Measure similarity between different students by computing *Pearson-r* Correlation Coefficient: The similarity between an active student s_x and another student s_y using the Pearson-r correlation coefficient is calculated as:

$$\text{sim}(s_x, s_y) = \frac{\sum_i^m (x_i - x_{avg})(y_i - y_{avg})}{\sqrt{\sum_i^m (x_i - x_{avg})^2} \sqrt{\sum_i^m (y_i - y_{avg})^2}} \tag{1}$$

Here x_i denotes the preference rating of the student s_x on architectural precedent i, x_{avg} is the average preference rating of the student s_x, and n is the number of architectural precedents co-rated by both student s_x and user s_y.

(4) According to the result in step (3) recommend architectural precedents to the active student.

The eDAADe manages a *user model* that stores the estimates of the student's preferences for architectural design cases. The user model is constructed by student explicit feedback (e.g., student to rate those precedents) and implicit feedback (e.g., students' navigation behaviors for collecting architectural precedents).

3   The eDAADe System

The eDAADe system is implemented by several technologies: PHP scripting language; MySQL, a relational database; Apache web server. Fig. 1 shows the architecture of our system.

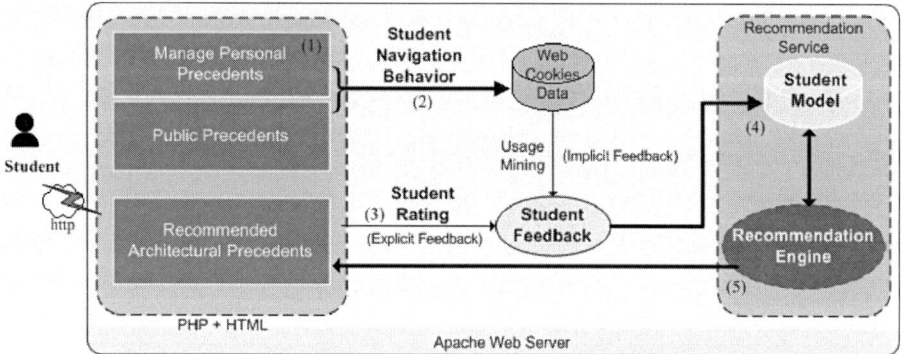

Fig. 1. The system architecture of eDAADe system

The system is divided into five parts: *(1) Preferences management module*: students' architectural cases collected in their personalized web pages; *(2) Implicit feedback module*: students' navigation behavior data stored in Web cookies in terms of date, duration time, frequency, etc. Time thresholds for duration offer a feasible way of determining whether the page is interesting or not; *(3) Explicit feedback module*: students' rating of the precedents based on their preferences; *(4) User (student) model module*: combining explicit and implicit feedback; *(5) Recommendation engine module*: the results of the similarity measurement.

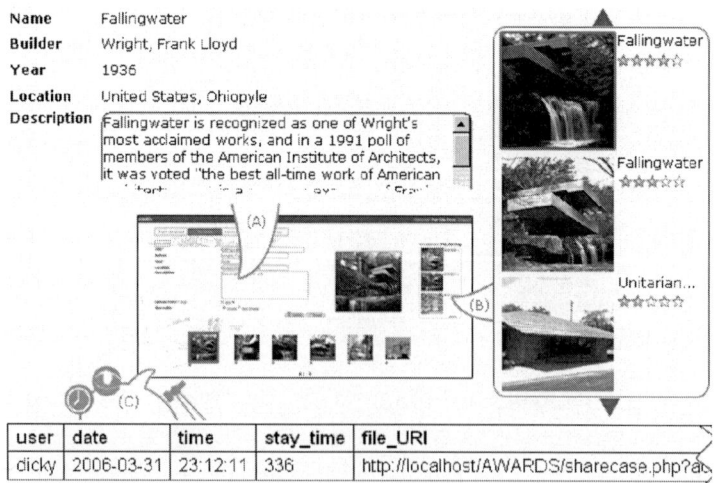

Fig. 2. A snapshot of the interface: (A) The features of architectural precedents; (B) Student to rate the recommend precedents based on their likes or dislikes; (C) Usage mining from cookies to know student's implicit feedback

From the highest sum of the rated precedents will be recommended to the student (see Fig. 2). The recommendation is presented to the students with two kinds of adaptations. One is *adaptive presentation*. The most helpful and relevant recommended precedents are presented, sorted by an ordered list with photo links to students. The photo links are helpful for students to follow the descriptions of the recommended precedents to learn more about them. The other is *adaptive navigation*. It can assist to students in hyperspace orientation and navigation by the appearance of visible links. For example, we use visual cues such as colors and icons to show different meanings and significances of a recommendation. The adaptation in recommendation system is helpful for students to navigate the Web, from both feedbacks, explicit feedback (e.g., rating task) and implicit feedback (e.g., students' navigation behaviors).

4   Conclusion

This paper proposed a hybrid approach, combining collaborating filtering and content-based filtering, to apply our eDAADe, a Web-based adaptive recommendation system. We have implemented this approach using explicit and implicit feedback modules from students (see Fig. 2). This recommendation mechanism is presented to the students with two kinds of adaptations, adaptive presentation and adaptive navigation. The system would be helpful for architectural students who want to find, compare and analyze relevant precedents more *efficient* [time wise] and more *precise* with their preferences in the "Case Study" phase. An empirical study to measure students' performance will be tested in the future work.

References

1. Buono, P., Costabile, M. F., Guida, S. Piccinno, A.: Integrating User Data and Collaborative Filtering in a Web Recommendation System. *Lecture Notes in Computer Science (Hypermedia: Openness, Structural Awareness, and Adaptivity)* **2266** (2002) 315-321
2. Balabanovic, M., Shoham, Y.: Fab: Content-Based, Collaborative Recommendation. *Communications of the ACM* **40**(3) (1997) 66-72
3. Popescul, A., Ungar, L. H., Pennock, D. M., Lawrence, S.: Probabilistic Models for Unified Collaborative and Content-Based Recommendation in Sparse-Data Environments. Proceedings of the Seventeenth Conference on Uncertainty in Artificial Intelligence (UAI-01) (2001) 437-444

On the Dynamic Adaptation of Computer Assisted Assessment of Free-Text Answers*

Diana Pérez-Marín[1], Enrique Alfonseca[1,2], and Pilar Rodríguez[1]

[1] Computer Science Department, Universidad Autonoma de Madrid
[2] Precision and Intelligence Laboratory, Tokyo Institute of Technology
{Diana.Perez, Enrique.Alfonseca, Pilar.Rodriguez}@uam.es

Abstract. To our knowledge, every free-text Computer Assisted Assessment (CAA) system automatically scores the students and gives feedback to them according to their responses, but, none of them include yet personalization options. The free-text CAA system Atenea [1] had simple adaptation possibilities by keeping static student profiles [2]. In this paper, we present a new adaptive version called Willow. It is based on Atenea and adds the possibility of dynamically choosing the questions to be asked according to their difficulty level, the students' profile and previous answers. Both Atenea and Willow have been tested with 32 students that manifested their satisfaction after using them. The results stimulate us to continue exploiting the possibilities of incorporating dynamic adaptation to free-text CAA.

1 Introduction

Computer Assisted Assessment (CAA) studies how to use effectively computers to automatically assess students' answers. Traditionally, it has been done just with objective testing questions. However, it is considered a quite limited type of assessment [3]. Hence, several other kinds have been proposed. In particular, in the mid-sixties, the possibility of assessing free-text answers was presented [4]. Since then, advances in Natural Language Processing (NLP) have made possible a favorable progress of this field [5].

The approach described in this paper is based on the free-text scoring system called Atenea [1] and its new version called Willow able to dynamically adapt the assessment process for the first time. Willow considers the students' personal profiles in the evaluation section and adjusts the difficulty level of the questions to the students' knowledge. Two experiments have been done with 32 students of our home university to study how well the adaptation in the assessment is appreciated and which adaptive techniques are more valuable.

The article is organized as follows: Section 2 describes Atenea and Willow. Section 3 details the experiments performed with the students. Finally, the conclusions and the open lines for future work are drawn out in Section 4.

---

* This work has been sponsored by Spanish Ministry of Science and Technology, project number TIN2004-0314.

V. Wade, H. Ashman, and B. Smyth (Eds.): AH 2006, LNCS 4018, pp. 374–377, 2006.
© Springer-Verlag Berlin Heidelberg 2006

2   Atenea and Willow

Atenea [1] is an on-line CAA system for automatically scoring free-text answers [1]. It is underpinned by statistical and NLP modules. Its main aim is to reinforce the concepts seen during the lesson with the teacher. It compares the student's answer to a set of correct answers (the references) by using the wraetlic toolkit[2]. The more similar a student's answer is to the references, the higher the score the student achieves.

Atenea randomly chooses the questions to ask the student until the end-of-session condition is fulfilled as a fixed number of questions has been completed or as a limited amount of time has expired. Recently, simple adaptation capabilities based on stereotypes were added to the system [2]. However, this kind of adaptation was very limited as it does not allow the system to dynamically adapt the assessment. Thus, we have created Willow, a new version of Atenea that, keeping all previous features, modifies dynamically the order in which the questions are presented to the students.

During the assessment session, as the students answer the questions of the different topics, which are chosen according to their difficulty levels, the values are modified to adjust the level of the questions to the level of knowledge that each student has in each topic addressed in the collection. When the students successfully answer a certain (configurable) percentage of the questions in a collection they are promoted to a higher level. On the other hand, a certain percentage of failures will demote them to the lower level. A topic is considered successfully passed when a student is in the highest level and has exceeded the percentage necessary to be promoted even further. In this way, a session may finish as soon as the student is considered apt in all the chosen topics.

3   Experiments with Students

Atenea and Willow have been used in two different experiments by the students in the *Operating Systems* course, in the Telecommunications Engineering degree, Universidad Autonoma de Madrid[3]. The teachers of that subject (none of whom was involved in the development neither of Atenea nor of Willow) introduced twenty different questions of different levels of difficulty and topics from real exams of previous years. The use of the system was voluntary, but the teachers motivated the students by telling them that the questions had been taken from previous exams and that the practise would positively help them towards the final score in the subject.

A total of 32 students took part in the first experiment, from which two subgroups were randomly created each one with 16 students: group A that used Atenea, and group B that used Willow. The score to pass a question was set to

---

[1] Available at http://orestes.ii.uam.es:8080/ateneaAdaptativa/jsp/loginAtenea.jsp

[2] Available at www.ii.uam.es/~ealfon/eng/download.html

[3] The authors would like to thank to Manuel Cebrián, Almudena Sierra, and Ismael Pascual for their collaboration in the experiments with the students.

Table 1. Average results for the first experiment

Question	group A	group B
Familiarity with on-line applications	4.3	3.8
Difficulty of use	4.1	4.1
Intuitiveness of the interface	4.0	3.5
System's answer time	4.1	3.8
Fitness of students' needs	3.4	3.2
Order of the questions	3.2	3.4
Level of difficulty	2.3	2.9
Number of references	3.0	3.0
Number of questions answered	7.0	8.5
Time to study this course	less than 5 h.	less than 5 h.
Recommendation of using Atenea/Willow	yes	yes

50% of the maximum score, and the percentage to be promoted or demoted was set to 40% of the total number of questions. At the beginning all the students received a brief talk (5 minutes) about Atenea and Willow, its aim and how to use the system. Next, they were required to take a 5-minute test with five multiple-choice questions corresponding to the five topics under assessment. In a 0–5 scale, the average score was 2.8 for group A, and 3.2 for group B. Once finished the test, the students were allowed to start using the indicated version of the system during 20 minutes. After that, they were asked again to complete the same test to check if they had acquired new knowledge during the assessment session. The average score for the group A did not change at all, whereas the average score for the group B increased slightly up to 3.4. Finally, the students were asked to fill a non-anonymous Likert-type scale items satisfaction questionnaire. The results are summarized in Table 1.

In the second experiment students could use Atenea and/or Willow during a week from anywhere, at anytime, and feel free to choose any option. In particular, they were asked to compare Atenea and Willow and fill a non-anonymous comparison questionnaire at the end of the week. In total, seven students (22%) volunteered to take part in the experiment and six of them filled the questionnaire. The results are as follows: all the students agree that Willow fits better their needs; they think that the promotion-demotion feature is quite good; and, in general, they agree with the schema of starting with easy questions and next having them increasingly harder.

4   Conclusions and Future Work

The free-text CAA systems Atenea and Willow have been tested in two different experiments. The students were mostly familiarized with on-line applications but none of them had used before a system that automatically scores open-ended questions. The adaptation was focused on the dynamic selection of the questions according to the procedure of promotions and demotions of difficulty levels as described in Section 2.

According to the comments given by the students, it can be confirmed that they like the idea of having an interactive system with questions from exams of previous years and the teachers' answers. 91% of the students would recommend to use the system to other friends in Operating System and other subjects. 80% of the students with Internet access at home prefer to log into the system from their home because they feel more comfortable. All the students find easy to use the system irrespectively of the version. Besides, they think that it is very useful to review concepts.

The students who used Willow were able to lightly increase their score the second time the test was presented after using the system just 20 minutes, whereas the students who use Atenea kept the same score. As expected, in average, the students of the first experiment who used Atenea answered less questions and they felt that the questions were more difficult than those who used Willow who declared that the order of the questions were more adequate.

When the students are directly asked if they prefer Atenea or Willow, there is not a clear answer. However, when they are asked about the system's features one by one, it can be seen that most prefer Willow, because it fits better their needs, the order of the questions is more adequate, and they feel more satisfied as the system controls their progress. In particular, the students who use Willow find its use more amusing and they feel more engaged to keep answering questions. On the other hand, some students say that they feel that they were learning less because the questions presented were less varied and that they find the interface less intuitive.

Including more dynamic adaptation in the system is a promising line of work that could be further exploited by updating dynamically the level of difficulty of each question according to the answers given by most of the students; giving the option of moving freely between the questions, with a color code to warn the students whether each question belongs to their knowledge level or not; and repeating the experiment with more students, maybe as a compulsory and anonymous experiment, to gather more results.

References

1. Alfonseca, E., Pérez, D.: Automatic assessment of short questions with a BLEU-inspired algorithm and shallow NLP. In: Advances in Natural Language Processing. Volume 3230 of Lecture Notes in Computer Science. Springer Verlag (2004) 25–35
2. Pérez, D., Alfonseca, E., Rodríguez, P.: Adapting the automatic assessment of free-text answers to the students profiles. In: Proceedings of the CAA conference, Loughborough, U.K. (2005)
3. Birenbaum, M., Tatsuoka, K., Gutvirtz, Y.: Effects of response format on diagnostic assessment of scholastic achievement. Applied psychological measurement **16** (1992)
4. Page, E.: The imminence of grading essays by computer. Phi Delta Kappan **47** (1966) 238–243
5. Valenti, S., Neri, F., Cucchiarelli, A.: An overview of current research on automated essay grading. Journal of Information Technology Education **2** (2003) 319–330

An Adaptive Hypermedia System Using a Constraint Satisfaction Approach for Information Personalization

Syed Sibte Raza Abidi and Yan Zeng

NICHE Research Group, Faculty of Computer Science, Dalhousie University Halifax, B3H
1W5, Canada
sraza@cs.dal.ca

Abstract. Adaptive hypermedia systems offer the functionality to personalize
the information experience as per a user-model. In this paper we present a novel
content adaptation approach that views information personalization as a
constraint satisfaction problem. Information personalization is achieved by
satisfying two constraints: (1) relevancy constraints to determine the relevance
of a document to a user and (2) co-existence constraints to suggest comple-
menting documents that either provide reinforcing viewpoints or contrasting
viewpoints, as per the user's request. Our information personalization framework involves: (a) an automatic constraint acquisition method, based on
association rule mining on a corpus of documents; and (b) a hybrid of constraint
satisfaction and optimization methods to derive an optimal solution—i.e. personalized information. We apply this framework to filter news items using the
Reuters-21578 dataset.

1 Introduction

The WWW provides access to a massive amount of information through web portals,
websites, mailing lists, distribution lists, bulletin boards and newsgroups. As the
volume of information for public consumption increases it is becoming increasingly
difficult to selectively search and consume information as per a user's specific
interest. *Information Personalization* (IP) methods allow the dynamic adaptation of
generic information content to generate personalized information content that is
specifically tailored to suit an individual's demographics, knowledge, skills,
capabilities, interests, preferences, needs, goals, plans and/or usage behavior [1, 2].
To date, there are a number of web-mediated information services that provide
customized information regarding healthcare [3], customer relationships [4], product
promotions, education [5], tourism and so on.

Information personalization is largely achieved via *adaptive hypermedia systems*
[6] that provide an umbrella framework incorporating hypermedia, artificial
intelligence, information retrieval and web technology to develop and deploy personalized web-based information and E-service systems. Information personalization
through content adaptation can be achieved via the selection of multiple information
items based on the user-model and then synthesizing them based on a pre-defined
document template to realize a personalized hypermedia document.

V. Wade, H. Ashman, and B. Smyth (Eds.): AH 2006, LNCS 4018, pp. 378–388, 2006.
© Springer-Verlag Berlin Heidelberg 2006

We believe that information personalization systems offering content adaptation can extend their information coverage by providing additional information items that are (a) 'topically consistent' with the user's specified topic(s) of interest in order to provide a more comprehensive information outlook; or (b) 'topically inconsistent' with the user's specified topic(s) of interest in order to provide contrasting viewpoints. In each case, the content adaptation requirement is to establish the *topical consistency/inconsistency* between two information items.

We approach information personalization as a constraint satisfaction problem that entails the satisfaction of two constraints: (1) *relevancy constraints*—given a set of information items, the constraint is to select only those information-items that correspond to the user-model; and (2) *co-existence consistency constraints*—given a set of user-specific information items, the constraint is to select additional information items that are topically consistent (to a degree specified by the user). Our information personalization strategy involves the satisfaction of the abovementioned constraints such that: (i) given a large set of documents we select only those documents that correspond to the user-model; (ii) given the selected user-compatible documents, we collect additional documents based on the type and degree of co-existence consistency specified by the user; and (iii) we maximize the information coverage by selecting the largest possible set of documents that satisfy the above two constraints. In our work, information personalization is achieved without deep content analysis, rather by leveraging the pre-defined classification of documents along a list of topics.

In this paper, we build on our previous work [7] to present an intelligent information personalization framework that comprises (a) an automatic constraint acquisition method based on association rule mining [8] to derive co-existence consistency constraints from the corpus of documents (indexed on topics); (b) a hybrid of constraint satisfaction methods to satisfy a variety of constraints to personalize information as per the user model; and (c) a user preference setting mechanism whereby users can set their personalization criteria: (i) choose to seek additional documents that are topically consistent, inconsistent or a mix of both; (ii) determine their tolerance to topical consistency/inconsistency, and (iii) set the degree of information comprehensiveness. We demonstrate the working of our information personalization framework for news item selection for a personalized news delivery service using the Reuters-21578, Distribution 1.0 data-set.

2   Information Personalization: An Overview

IP research offers interesting insights into ways for (a) profiling users based on information about the user's demographic data, knowledge, skills, capabilities, interests, preferences, needs, goals, plans and/or usage behaviour; and (b) pro-actively adapting hypermedia objects based on the user's profile. There are three levels of IP:

Content adaptation involves the adaptation of the actual content via page variants [5], fragment variants [9, 4], adaptive stretchtext [10] and language processing.

Structure adaptation involves the dynamic changing of the link structure of hypermedia documents. Collateral structure adaptation [11], link sorting [12], link annotation, and link removal/addition are some of the methods used.

Presentation adaptation leads to changes in the layout of the hypermedia document. Typically, the changes involve text positioning (or focusing), graphics and multimedia inclusion/exclusion, background variations and GUI interface.

Our work involves content adaptation based on fragment variants, whereby multiple information fragments are selected with respect to a particular user's model, and at runtime they are synthesized to yield a personalized information document.

3   Constraints for Information Personalization

Constraint satisfaction methods allow the efficient navigation of large search spaces to find an optimal solution that entails the assignment of values to problem variables subject to given constraints [13]. *Constraint programming* solves problems by stating constraints about the problem area and consequently finding solutions that may 'satisfy' all the constraints. A *Constraint Satisfaction Problem* (CSP) is defined by a tuple $P = (X, D, C)$ where $X=\{X1, ... , Xn\}$ is a finite set of *variables*, each associated with a domain of discrete values $D = \{D1, ..., Dn\}$, and a set of constraints $C = \{C1,..., Cl\}$. Each constraint Ci is expressed by a relation Ri on some subset of variables. This subset of variables is called the *connection* of the constraint and denoted by *con(Ci)*. The relation Ri over the connection of a constraint Ci is defined by $Ri \subseteq Di1 \times...\times Dik$ and denotes the tuples that satisfy Ci. A solution to a constraint satisfaction problem is an assignment of a value from its domain to every variable, in such a way that every constraint is satisfied [13].

3.1   Our Approach for Constraint Acquisition

We believe that when information is composed it entails some inherent constraints about which topics can meaningfully co-occur in a coherent discussion. Typically, as informed users, we intuitively determine the co-existence consistency between topics, and then filter documents based on our need to either retrieve a set of documents that reinforce a viewpoint (i.e. documents that have a positive co-existence constraint between them) or a set of documents that present an alternate or divergent viewpoint (i.e. documents that have a negative co-existence constraint between them).

We pursue the acquisition of co-existence constraints, between the topics of news items, as an association rule mining problem [8]; human experts finally validate the constraints. The frequency of co-occurrence of topics reflects the degree of co-existence consistency between two topics. We treat topics as items and use the Apriori algorithm to find 2-itemsets [8]. We calculate the correlation between the two items, A and B, as follows:

$$corr(A, B) = \frac{p(AB)}{p(A)p(B)} \tag{1}$$

The correlation value is used to distinguish between positive and negative co-existence constraints as follows:

- If $0 < corr(A, B) < 1$, A and B are correlated negatively it means these two topics are topically inconsistent to each other, so a *negative co-existence constraint* can be established between these two topics.

- If *corr(A, B)* > 1, *A* and *B* are positively correlated and they reinforce the co-occurrence of each other, so a *positive co-existence constraint* can be established between these two topics.
- If *corr(A, B)* = 1, *A* and *B* are independent to each other.

Negative co-existence constraints are used to either filter out topically inconsistent documents or to present documents that suggest divergent views. The positive co-existence constraints are used to recommend the simultaneous presentation of multiple topically consistent documents. For example, with the football world cup in Germany in 2006, the topics *Germany* and *football* will co-occur more frequently in news articles, leading to a positive co-existence constraint between Germany and football. Using such a positive co-existence constraint we can recommend information about football if the user has a interest in Germany, and vice versa.

From the Reuters-21578 dataset we acquired 913 frequent 2-itemsets that were further filtered by applying the Chi-Square statistical significance test; 177 item-sets with 95% interestingness were retained. The item-set correlation measure was used to divide the rules into 120 positive (with high item correlation) and 57 negative (with low item correlation) co-existence constrains that are represented as *const(topic1, topic2, correlation)*, e.g. -*const* (*earn, ship, 0.0093*) and +*const* (*barley, grain, 17.76*).

4   Constraint Satisfaction Based IP Framework

4.1 The User-Model

The user-model comprises three elements: (a) user's interests represented as a list of topics, (b) user's tolerance towards inter-document co-existence inconsistency, selected by a sliding bar with a scale of 0-100%. A tolerance of 0% means that the user wants only those documents that offer a topically consistent viewpoint, whereas a tolerance of 100% means that the user is seeking documents that offer a divergent view—i.e. topically inconsistent documents. Any setting in between allows for the respective mix of both; and (c) user's preference towards the coverage of the solution—i.e. whether to satisfy all the user-interests or the co-existence constraints.

4.2 The Information Items

The information items (i.e. document) comprise two sections: (i) the *content* section contains the information; and (ii) the *context* section contains a list of topics that are used to characterize the information in the document. The topics in the context section are compared with the user's interests specified in the user-model to determine the relevance of the said document to a particular user.

4.3 Information Personalization Requirements

Our information personalization solution needs to satisfy the following requirements (ordered decreasing priorities):

1. The personalized information should be relevant to the interests of the user.
2. The personalized information should reflect the topical co-existence constraints specified by the user.
3. The personalized information should cover the largest set of relevant documents.

4.4 Defining Information Personalization as a Constraint Satisfaction Problem

In our CSP approach for information personalization, the topics representing the user's interest are viewed as variables, and domains of the variables comprise any combination of available documents. Requirement 1 is a unary constraint to the variables and represented by constraint c_1. Requirement 2 is a unary constraint c_2 and a binary constraint c_3. Requirement 3 is reflected in the objective function O. We define our information personalization problem as $P(V, D, C, O)$.

- Variable set $1 \leq i \leq n$ $V = \{v_1, v_2, \dots, v_n\}$, where n is the number of topics of a user's interest; v_i, , represents the $i\, 1 \leq i \leq n$ topic of a user's interest.
- Domain set $D = \{d_1, d_2, \dots, d_n\}$; d_i, , represents the domain of v_i. Suppose $s = \{t_1, t_2, \dots, t_m\}$ is a set consisting of all documents, then d_i is the power set of s without the empty set $\emptyset$. E.g. If $\{t_1, t_2\}$ is the set of documents, the domain of the variable will be $\{\{t_1\}, \{t_2\}, \{t_1, t_2\}\}$.
- Constraint set $C = \{c_1, c_2, c_3\}$; $c_1 = rel(v_i)$, where $1 \leq i \leq n$, is a unary constraint, and means the value of v_i must be relevant to users' interest (Requirement 1). Suppose v_i represents the $i\,$ topic of a user's interest, and the domain of v_i is $\{\{t_1\}, \{t_2\}, \{t_1, t_2\}\}$. By checking the topics of t_1 and t_2, we know t_1 is relevant to the $i\,$ topic of the user's interest, but t_2 is not. To satisfy c_1, $\{t_2\}$ and $\{t_1, t_2\}$ will be removed from the domain of v_i. $c_2 = con1(v_i)$, where $1 \leq i \leq n$, is a unary constraint, and means the documents assigned to v_i must be consistent to each other (Requirement 2). Suppose the system is trying to assign $\{t_1, t_2\}$ to v_1. To decide whether c_2 is satisfied or not, we check the co-existence constraint between t_1 and t_2. Suppose $t_1 = \{$acquisition' and 'stocks'$\}$, and $t_2 = $ 'acquisition' and 'gold'$\}$. We take one topic from t_1 and t_2 respectively to form pairs of topics ordered alphabetically—i.e. *(acquisition, acquisition)*, *(acquisition, gold)*, *(acquisition, stocks)* and *(gold, stocks)*. We check these four pairs against the negative/positive co-existence constraints.

  When checking c_3, take a document from the value of both variables to form pairs of documents. If any pair meets the personalization conditions specified by the user, c_3 is satisfied.
- $O = \sum_i (n_i * weight_i)$ is the objective function, where i is a member of the set of satisfied positive co-existence constraints. n_i is the frequency of the constraint i being satisfied. $weight_i$ is the correlation value of the constraint i. The target is to find a complete valuation that maximizes the objective function. This function is used to maximize the coverage of the personalized information.

4.5   Solving the Constraint Satisfaction Problem for Information Personalization

From the specification of our CSP, it can be seen that information personalization is an over-constrained problem—i.e. a complete valuation that satisfies all hard constraints cannot be guaranteed. There are a number of possible reasons, e.g. the only document that can be assigned to a topic is topically inconsistent to another document that is assigned to another variable. Solving an over-constrained problem can be viewed as a partial constraint satisfaction problem (PCSP) in which a complete valuation is made with some constraints unsatisfied—the valuation with the smallest distance is selected as the final solution. Distance is defined as the number of constraints violated by a valuation [15]. In our framework, users can set up their information personalization preferences to guide the process in case a complete satisfaction of the constraints cannot be achieved. If a user prefers maximum coverage of the topics of interest then the solution that covers all the topics but violates the least number of co-existence constraints will be selected. If the user prefers a certain degree of co-existence consistency, then the solution satisfying the respective co-existence consistency whilst not assigning documents for the least number of topics will be selected. To solve information personalization through PCSP in an efficient manner, we employ a hybrid of constraint satisfaction and optimization techniques. Our information personalization process is shown in Fig. 1. In the forthcoming discussion, we discuss our information personalization process using a working example, whereby the user has interest in four different topics (see table 1) and has selected to be provided topically consistent documents—i.e. asking to solve the positive co-existence constraint. The documents used in the example are shown in Table 2.

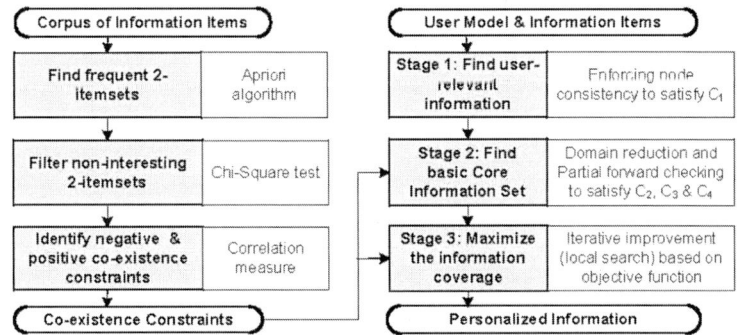

Fig. 1. An illustration of our information personalization strategy

Table 1. The user model used in the example

Component	Value
Interests	acquisition, gas, income, jobs
Tolerance	20% tolerance to negative co-existence constraints
Preference	Satisfy the co-existence constraints (instead of finding documents for all topics of interest)

Based on the user-profile, we get four variables corresponding to the four topics of the user's interest. We call them v_{acq}, v_{gas}, v_{income} and v_{jobs}. The domain of four variables is the power set of the 15 news items that are shown in Table 2.

Table 2. The dataset used for the example

News Item	Topics	News Item	Topics
t1	Acquisition	t9	Jobs
t2	acquisition, crude, nat-gas	t10	bop, cpi, gnp, jobs
t3	acquisition, gold, lead, silver, zinc	t11	jobs, trade
t4	gas	t12	gnp, jobs
t5	cpi, crude, fuel, gas, nat-gas	t13	acquisition
t6	fuel, gas	t14	fuel, gas
t7	crude, gas	t15	jobs, trade
t8	gnp, income, ipi, retail, trade		

Step 1: User-relevant information selection

In this step we filter all documents that are relevant to the user's interest by applying a node consistency method. We satisfy the unary constraint $c1= rel(vi)$ by comparing the topics of the various documents against a user's interest. For our example, any document that does not have topic '*acquisition*' will be filtered out from *vacq* 's domain (the same is true for *vgas*, *vincome* and *vjobs*). The resultant set of documents for each variable (see Table 3) is called the *user-specific information set*.

Table 3. Relevant items for the variables—i.e. the *user-specific information set*

Variable	Retained Relevant item	Removed Relevant Item	Variable	Retained Relevant item	Retained Relevant item
V_{acq}	t1, t2, t3	t13	V_{income}	t8	
V_{gas}	t4, t5, t6, t7,	t14	V_{jobs}	t9, t10, t11, t12,	t15

Step 2: Domain reduction

Typically, after step1 the set of relevant documents is quite large. The task at step2 is to reduce the domain of the variables by searching the solution space and eliminating redundant documents from the domain of variables in three stages.

1. Delete duplicate documents from the user-specific information set.
2. Delete values with multiple documents from the domain of variables. The rationale is that when trying to find solutions violating the least number of co-existence constraints, values with multiple documents will violate more co-existence constraints as compared to values with a single document. In this way, the domain size of a variable that has k relevant document will be reduced from 2^k to $k+1$.
3. Delete dominating values (sets) from the domain. If the topic set of item *t1* is *a* subset of the topic set of item *t2*, we say *t2* dominates *t1*, and *t2* is a dominating item. Because a dominating item presents some extra topics

besides the topics presented by an item dominated it, the dominating item only has the chance to violate more consistency constraints than the dominated item does.

For the working example, we show the outcome of deleting values with multiple documents and dominating values for $vacq$ in Table 4. The reduced domain of the four variables is given in Table 5.

Table 4. Outcome of deleting multi-document and dominating values for $Vacq$

Retained	Removed (dominating values)	Removed (multi-element values)
$\emptyset, \{t_1\}$	$\{t_2\}, \{t_3\}$	$\{t_1, t_2\}, \{t_1, t_3\}, \{t_2, t_3\}, \{t_1, t_2, t_3\}$

Table 5. The reduced domain for the four variables in the user-model

Variable	Domain	Variable	Domain
v_{acq}	$\{\emptyset, \{t_1\}\}$	v_{income}	$\{\emptyset, \{t_8\}\}$
v_{gas}	$\{\emptyset, \{t_4\}\}$	v_{jobs}	$\{\emptyset, \{t_9\}\}$

Step3: Topically consistent information selection
After domain reduction, co-existence consistency is enforced through constraints $c2$ and $c3$. We apply Partial Forward Checking (PFC) algorithms to our Partial CSP using two different distances: (i) the number of variables assigned to the empty set; and (ii) the number of times the co-existence constraints are violated. The application of PFC algorithms to our working example yields two solutions, as shown in Table 6. Since the user has preferred the satisfaction of all co-existence constraints as opposed to having at least a single document for each topic of interest, for both the solutions one topic cannot be assigned a document without violating the co-existence constraints. Note that $\{t1\}$ and $\{t8\}$ cannot coexist due to the negative co-existence constraint nc(acquisition, trade, 0.034) Each solution is referred as the *core information set*.

Table 6. Topically consistent solutions

Solution #	acquisition	gas	income	jobs
1	$\{t1\}$	$\{t4\}$	NULL	$\{t9\}$
2	NULL	$\{t4\}$	$\{t8\}$	$\{t9\}$

Step 4: Information coverage maximization
To maximize the coverage of the personalized output (i.e. requirement3), we apply optimization techniques to add more documents from the *user-specific information set* to the *core information set*, whilst maintaining the coexistence constraints.

We use local search methods [16] to iteratively improve the solutions in table 6 as follows: Assign the core information set as the base-solution and then search its neighborhood for a better solution. The neighborhood of the base-solution consists of all solutions that differ with it by just the value of one variable. A solution is better than the base-solution if it has a higher value for the objective function. If a better solution is found then it is deemed as the base-solution and search continues to find an even better base-solution. For our example, Table 7 shows the results of the information coverage maximization applied to the solutions shown in table 6.

Table 7. Optimized solutions with maximum information coverage

Solution #	acquisition	gas	income	jobs	Objective function
1	{ t1}	{ t4, t6}	NULL	{ t_9, t_{10}, t_{12}}	45.28
2	NULL	{ t4, t6}	{ t8}	{ t_9, t_{10}, t_{11}, t_{12}}	121.65

It may be noted that solution2 has higher objective function value than solution1, hence it is selected as the best solution and it represents the best possible personalized information as per the user-model. In total 7 documents, each corresponding to the user's interest and offering the desired co-existence consistency degree, will be synthesized and presented as personalized information to the user.

5   Evaluations of Heuristics for Search Methods

In general, variable and value ordering heuristics affect the efficiency of systematic search methods. For our problem, we compared the performance of partial forward checking (basic_pfc), partial forward checking with variable ordering (order_pfc), partial forward checking with variable and value ordering (full_pfc). Note that performance is measured in terms of the number of constraint checked.

Given the Reuters-21578 dataset and the user's topics of interest, we compared the performance of these algorithms by varying the user's preference and co-existence consistency tolerance. The results (see Fig. 2 and Fig. 3) indicate that amongst the three variants of PFC, full_pfc always gives the best performance, hence vindicating our approach. We performed a number of other experiments to test the effectiveness of our framework for different user-models and preferences, and noted that for each exemplar user-setting unique personalisation was generated.

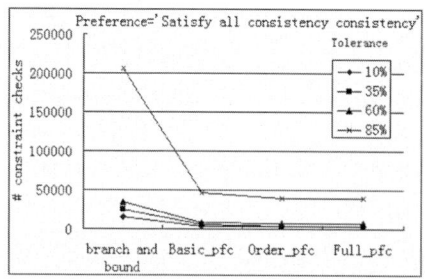 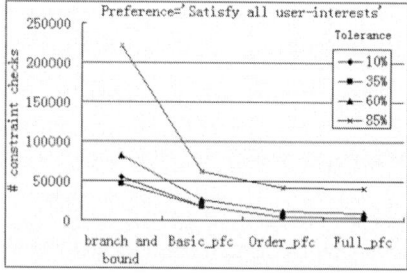

Fig. 2. Performance of search algorithm: User preference is satisfy all co-existence constrains

Fig. 3. Performance of search algorithm: User preference is satisfy all user interests

6 Concluding Remarks

Intuitively, information personalization is a constraint satisfaction problem—the user's interests and preferences impose a set of constraints towards the selection, filtering and composition of information items—whereby the satisfaction of the user's constraints yield personalized information as per the user-model. We have presented a novel information personalization strategy that addresses the underlying personalization constraints using standard constraint satisfaction techniques. Our information personalization framework allows (a) the user to easily set their personalization preferences in a flexible manner (which can be repeated if they are not satisfied with the output); (b) establishes a core information set—i.e. the smallest set of documents that meets all the user's interests and preferences—as the baseline personalized information; and (c) maximizes the information coverage of the core information set, through a recursive local search method, by including additional documents that satisfy the user-model. We have incorporated co-existence constraints that aim to provide users with information that either reinforces or contradicts the information pertaining to their topics of interest. In addition, the negative co-existence consistency constraints ensure that the combination of two documents does not inadvertently lead to the generation of factually inconsistent information—i.e. one document stating a certain fact/recommendation whilst the other document simultaneously contradicting the same fact/recommendation.

In this paper, we demonstrated our framework in the field of news service, however it can be applied to other fields where mutually exclusive information items need to be selected and presented to users vis-à-vis personalized information.

References

[1] Fink J, Kobsa A, Putting personalization into practice, *Communications of the ACM*, Vol. 45(5), 2002.

[2] Bogonikolos N, Makris C, Tsakalidis A, Vassiliadis B, Adapting information presentation and retrieval through user modeling. International Conference on Information Technology: Coding and Computing, 2-4 April 2001, pp. 399-404.

[3] Abidi SSR, Chong Y, Abidi SR, Patient empowerment via 'pushed' delivery of customized healthcare educational content over the internet. *10th World Congress on Medical Informatics*, 2001, London.

[4] Kobsa A, Customized hypermedia presentation techniques for improving online customer relationships. *Knowledge Engineering Review,* Vol. 16(2), 1999, pp. 111-155.

[5] Henze N, Nejdl W, Extendible adaptive hypermedia courseware: integrating different courses and web material. In *P. Brusilovsky, O Stock & C Strappavara (Eds.) Adaptive Hypermedia and Adaptive Web-based Systems*, Springer Verlag, 2000, pp. 109-120.

[6] Brusilovsky P, Kobsa A, Vassileva J (Eds.), *Adaptive Hypertext and Hypermedia.* Kluwer Academic Publishers, Dordrecht, 1998.

[7] Abidi SSR, Chong Y. An adaptive hypermedia system for information customization via content adaptation. *IADIS Intl. Journal of WWW/Internet*, 2004 2(1), pp. 79-94.

[8] Han JW, Kamber M. *Data Mining: Concepts & Techniques*. Morgan Kaufmann, 2000.

[9] Kobsa A, Muller D, Nill A, KN-AHS: an adaptive hypermedia client of the user modeling system BGP-MS. *Fourth Intl. Conf. on User Modeling*, 1994, pp. 99-105.

[10] Boyle C, Encarnacion AO, MetaDoc: An adaptive hypertext reading system. *User Models and User Adapted Interaction,* Vol. 4(1), 1994, pp. 1-19.

[11] Hohl H, Bocker HD, Gunzenhauser R, HYPADAPTER: An adaptive hypertext system for exploratory learning and programming, *User Modelling and User Adapted Interaction,* Vol. 6(2), pp. 131-155.

[12] Kaplan C, Fenwick J, Chen J, Adaptive hypertext navigation based on user goals and context, *User Modelling and User Adapted Interaction,* Vol. 3(3), pp. 193-220.

[13] Tsang E, *Foundations of constraint satisfaction.* Academic Press, London, UK. 1993.

[14] Padmanabhuni S, You JH, Ghose A. A framework for learning constraints. *Proc. of the PRICAI Workshop on Induction of Complex Representations,* August 1996.

[15] Freuder E, Wallace R. Partial constraint satisfaction. *Artificial Intelligence*, Vol. 58, 1992, 21-70.

[16] Aarts E, Lenstra, JK. (Eds). *Local search in combinatorial optimization.* Princeton University Press, Princeton, NJ, 2003.

My Compiler Really Understands Me: An Adaptive Programming Language Tutor

Kate Taylor and Simon Moore

University of Cambridge Computer Laboratory, Cambridge, United Kingdom
{kate.taylor, simon.moore}@cl.cam.ac.uk
http://www.cl.cam.ac.uk/intelligent-verilog/

Abstract. We describe an intelligent interactive online tutor for computer languages. The tutor uses an ontology of programming language terms together with a language-specific ontology. These ontologies are embedded in web pages structured at different levels of student expertise to provide a web front end that can be re-assembled in many different ways to suit a particular student's attempt to compile a particular program. This dynamic reassembly copes well with the initial learning curve for a language as well as revision a few months later. We argue that such a dynamic solution is more appropriate in this case than user profiling as a student's capabilities are not the same for all parts of the language to be learnt or from one session to the next. Our system gives the student control over the learning process by the use of question answering techniques on the same ontology. Our system tracks what the user is doing in the programming exercises to understand what they are trying to write. Early trials with a real student audience have produced positive results and feedback for more research.

1 Introduction

Our aim is to produce an e-tutor that behaves like an experienced colleague looking over your shoulder as you learn a language. Our e-tutor, the Intelligent Verilog Compiler (IVC) is embedded in a web tutorial that on the face of it looks much like any other, explaining the syntax of the language and providing some examples. The IVC teaches a second year undergraduate the Verilog hardware description language by moving between teaching, checking, correcting and reminding. The IVC uses a compiler to check the syntax and a model checker to check the dynamic semantics of predefined exercises. The student is able to ask questions as well as being taught, allowing them to move the focus to what they want to ask to create a dialogue rather than a monologue.

The programming exercises bring to light areas where the student needs to complete ideas or correct misunderstandings. The compiler output and the student's program are passed through an explainer which deduces what is helpful to read from the ontology as well as suggesting the underlying cause of the error as a mistake or as an omission.

Layering the ontology allows different computer languages to be taught in the same framework. Adapting the framework to teach a new language L requires new

V. Wade, H. Ashman, and B. Smyth (Eds.): AH 2006, LNCS 4018, pp. 389–392, 2006.
© Springer-Verlag Berlin Heidelberg 2006

language web page fragments and the language ontology i.e. the words used to describe programming in language L but not in any other. Common concepts such as *variable, module* etc are in the programming ontology.

2 Ontology Design

IVC includes a programming ontology, the Verilog-specific ontology and links into WordNet [2]. Adding synonyms creates richness of vocabulary to support the question answering in unrestricted English. A Prolog program, voogle (**verilog google**), provides automatic generation of text from the tutorial web content from a variety of viewpoints based on a subset of those used in WordNet. It uses a variety of levels of text from glossary entry to full explanation. Selection of text to display in each situation is guided by an appreciation of the task that the student is trying to perform.

Displaying the line of source code with an error message works well for errors in statements or expressions. We have rewritten some of the grammar that generates the compiler to provide more detailed error messages at a lower level. However, errors in blocks need more context, so here we have taken the approach of several extra passes over the code. The explainer "understands" what language constructs the code actually represents, and remedies the inability of a chart parser to use much context in its error handling.

Another issue is how to detect what is missing from incorrect code. For example, the explainer component understands that a particular compiler error can arise from a missing *endcase* keyword. If the explainer cannot find *endcase* in the source code, then this is explicitly pointed out to the user. The voogle component generates suitable help text explaining what a case statement requires, i.e. omitting much of the detail as the problem is with the structure of the case rather than its contents.

3 Dialogue Planning

Dialogue planning aims to keep track of the overall progress towards a correct answer. The focus is determined by keeping track of which line the student is working on and hence which construct they are thinking about.

We are using the data collected from the questionnaire for previous versions of IVC to generate a graph as in Figure 1 below. There are many possible graphs depending on how people construct their code, but we have continued the established pedagogical approach that emphasises using sequential and combinational logic together to avoid an imperative style of writing Verilog. We believe all languages have style issues like this to consider, and that using these graphs to plan the dialog allows different styles to be supported.

These graphs are effectively syntax graphs, often called railway diagrams, which form the basis of the chart parser used by the compiler. One of the equivalent snippets of the grammar, expressed in Extended Backus-Naur format is:

```
conditional_statement ::= if (expression) state-
ment_or_null [else statement_or_null|if_else_statement
```

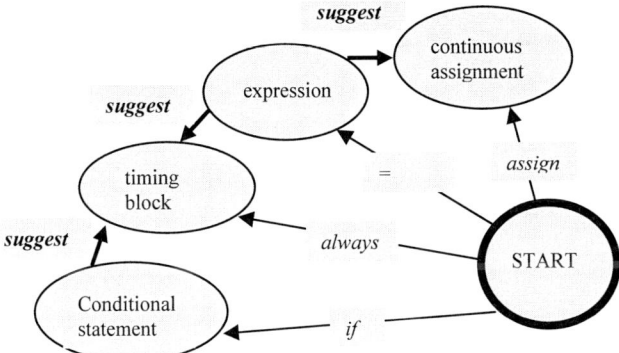

Fig. 1. Dialogue management graph for IVC2.1 with student input shown in (*italics*) and system (*suggest*) *e.g.* now think about wiring your design into the outputs

We have extended them in two ways: the student can start at *any* point rather than strictly left-to-right, and each transition has a prompt text to advise them where they can get to from where they are. We have considered whether the dialogue graph should be visible, fading it out as the student becomes more proficient, or whether the student should know where they are: at present it remains hidden to promote deep learning.

4 Results

The student feedback from [1] indicates that they prefer to keep code, explanation and help in one window, resulting in a *pop-in* rather than a *pop-up* style of handling the user interface. Figure 2 overleaf shows the explanation between the code and the errors. The *ask a question* button replaces the help text with a dialogue.

5 Conclusions and Future Work

IVC is a shallow system in the sense that it takes a simplistic approach to a number of active research areas in adaptive hypermedia, too many to describe in this format. It has shown that introducing an ontology opens up opportunities to follow the focus of the student's activities without the constraints of a user profile or hard-coded dialog.

There are many learning scenarios where this approach has difficulties: we observed in the user trials in [1] the complication of two partially correct answers muddled into one incorrect one, but we have also demonstrated that there are many where it is effective. We aim to allow *the student* to control how much help is being given to promote deep learning through a conversation with the IVC.

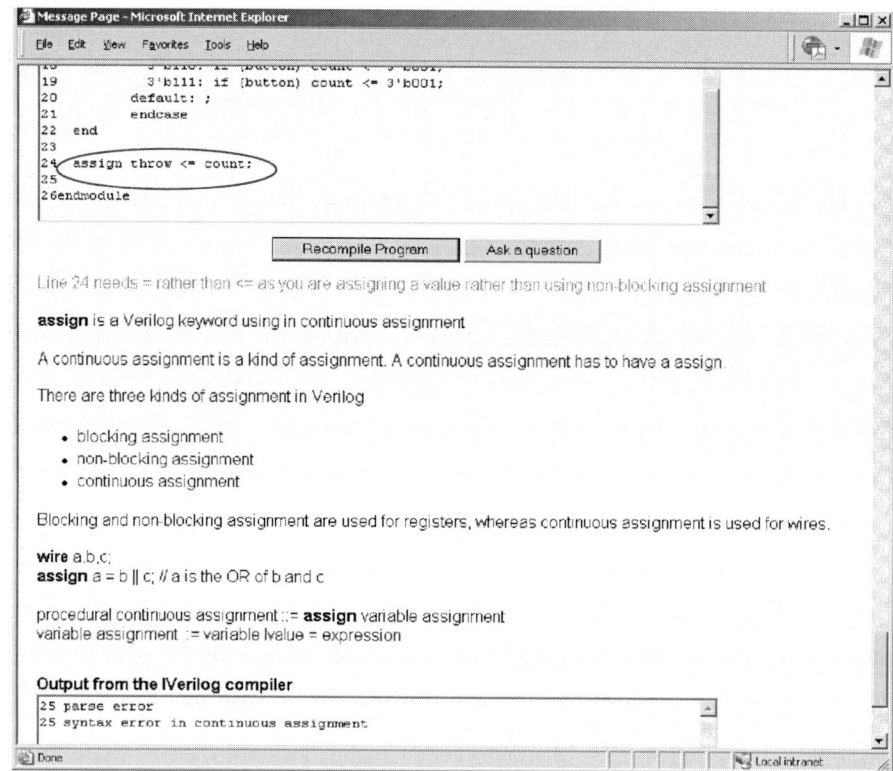

Fig. 2. The student has typed (<=) instead of (=) at line 24. The voogle component generates links back into the tutorial whilst the explainer (in red text) points out the error.

This work was funded by the Cambridge MIT Institute (CMI) and the evaluation performed with the Centre for Applied Research in Educational Technology (CARET). We wish to thank the students for their enthusiasm and commitment.

References

1. Moore, S, Taylor K An Intelligent Interactive Online Tutor for Computer Languages, 25th Annual International Conference of the British Computer Society's Specialist Group on Artificial Intelligence (SGAI) (2005).
2. WordNet an Electronic Lexical Database May 1998 ISBN 0-262-06197-X

Adaptive Learning for Very Young Learners

J. Enrique Agudo, Héctor Sánchez, and Mercedes Rico

University of Extremadura. Centro Universitario de Mérida, c/ Santa Teresa de Jornet, 38
06800, Mérida (Badajoz) Spain.
{jeagudo, sasah, mricogar}@unex.es

Abstract. The use of Information and Communication Technologies (ICTs) is spreading inside the classrooms at all educational levels. As this integration has extended to young learners (3 to 5 years), the authorities have recommended their use so that children can acquire knowledge and dexterities they will use all their lives. Keeping in mind that it is at this age when very young learners acquire abilities and basic dexterities at their own pace, the more personalized the better. From all the premises above, we can claim that whereas other computer assisted language learning systems do not account for differences in children's cognitive development when designing computerized applications, the introduction of AHS (Adaptive Hypermedia Systems) is aimed at adapting and personalizing content to children's needs and abilities.

1 Introduction

Nowadays, ICTs are a common resource used in all educational levels as a way to improve and enrich the teaching process.

However, the effective incorporation of ICTs in the classroom and the suitable use of educational software for early ages is not exempt from important challenges. In this period, children have not developed yet all the language and cognitive abilities that older learners have. These circumstances demand from the system an exclusively visual interface and require, in addition, previous training in the use of computers and input devices (mouse and keyboard).

According to Haugland [1], the appropriate use of computers as well as the educational software may increase creativity and self esteem in children. He also claims that children exposed to software that tends to boost their development may successfully increase their intelligence, verbal /non verbal skills, visual and movement related abilities, structural knowledge, long term memory, problem solving, decision making, abstraction and conceptual formation skills. On the contrary, the uncontrolled use of ICTs in the classroom could infer a negative impact on children.

Thus, it is necessary to consider several factors which could affect the successful integration of ICTs in pre-school education [2]: how to integrate the computer in the classroom, the features of the educational software at these ages, the use of adequate input devices, the interaction styles and the teacher's active role as organizer of the learning process.

V. Wade, H. Ashman, and B. Smyth (Eds.): AH 2006, LNCS 4018, pp. 393–397, 2006.
© Springer-Verlag Berlin Heidelberg 2006

We claim that an adaptive hypermedia system adapts to young learners´ educational software demands because:

- Thanks to their hypertext structure, the necessary level of freedom is achieved so that the children develop their curiosity and explore the knowledge.
- The multimedia tasks provide the necessary motivation to make children feel attracted by software content [3].
- The intelligent tutoring system carries out the adaptation to the student's characteristics, which provides a personalized teaching and adaptation to the level of the student's knowledge, as well as to the student's learning style.
- It is also in charge of providing the necessary support and help to reach the learning objectives.

2 Adaptive Hypermedia System for Children

Our objective is to use ITCs for teaching a foreign language at early ages. Bearing in mind the considerations dealt with in the previous section, we seek, therefore, to develop an AHS for English teaching in pre-school education (3 to 5 years). This system will be a Web-based system, since the election of Web-like development of adaptive platforms in educational hypermedia is becoming standard. [4] This environment allows the teacher to carry out observations and evaluate all the students. In addition, not only do we seek to develop an AHS, but also evaluate the use of ICTs at early ages and the benefits derived by adaptating to this type of user and evaluate which Web platform will allow us to know the results of the children's interaction with the system.

Adapting to children is different to adapting to adults because children at this age still cannot read or write and most AHS are text-based systems. Also, in this period children have not yet developed all the language and cognitive abilities that older learners have.

Under the name of SHAIEx (Adaptive Hypermedia System for English learning at pre-school in linEX), this system is being designed to integrate information technology in relation to certain learning traits at early ages. From the whole system, we have already developed the following phases /subsystems:

- **Content and structure of the pedagogical domain.** The content consists of nine didactic units and comprises points of interest of Infant school. The didactics units have been elaborated starting from preschool curriculum, books and surveys to the teachers. The decomposition of each didactic unit in blocks of multimedia activities and the dependency among them is based on the task-based paradigms[5].
- **User model.** For the adaptation, SHAIEx stores the following child's characteristics:
- Educational level: For 3, 4 and 5 years will be the corresponding levels 1, 2 and 3, based on the curriculum for infantile education. The different levels are associated with the contents of the curriculum, which implies that a 3 year old child, for example, can be in level 2 or that a 5 year old child begins from level 1. Because multimedia activities are addressed to heterogeneous groups of students, such tasks should be developed by accounting for all students' needs and preferences.

– Knowledge: The contents will adapt as the child progresses. Different itineraries will be available for those didactic units which show a varying degree of complexity for different users.
– Dexterity with the mouse: The device elected for interaction with the system is the mouse since it is the most efficient device for this age [6]. The children are learning to use the mouse and considering that operations like "double click" or "drag and drop" can be complicated for them, we will adapt the use of the mouse in the activities and games to the dexterity they have.
– Language: Although our objective is to develop an English learning system, we will allow the inclusion of other languages (French, Spanish, etc.) that the children can learn in the school.
– Difficulty of the activities: The complexity of the activities and games will be adapted increasing or diminishing the number of elements of the same ones.
– Text information: We include a text label together to a picture (or a sound) so that the children associate the text with the visual (or auditory) information.

This user model is created for defect to the beginner level for the system and the teacher can improve the initial information. Once the user model is created the system update this user model with the progress of the children.

3   Methods and Techniques of Adaptation

The system adapts both the navigation support and the presentation [4]. For the navigation support, the links, represented as graphical icons, are generated and ordered according to the educational level and knowledge of children. The mechanism based on teaching task and rules developed by Carro [5], [7] is used to provide the navigation support.

For presentation, adaptive multimedia presentation is used, by which the system adapts the different task to the user. The scene presented to a child is generated by building the most suitable version according to his/her profile (adaptive scene).

Fig. 1. Adaptive Scene of SHAIEx

In Figure1, a scene of the unit "Happy Birthday" is shown. The appearance or not of these characters, the textual information and their associated dialogue are described in the table above. For level 1characters 1 and 2 will appear saying only their names. For level 2 characters1, 2 and 3 will appear and saying this time their names and the animal type they are. Finally, in level 3 all the characters will appear telling us their names and nationalities. The textual information only appears for level 3.

The difficulty and the mouse interaction style of the activities will be adapted to the educational level and psychomotor skills. The location of the multimedia elements inside these activities is randomly determined to produce different variations. Thus, the child will successfully complete the activity according to his/her knowledge, not to their memory capabilities. In the activity showed in figure 2, the child is asked to place the character in the corresponding shadow after listening to information and descriptive hints. Likewise, the adaptation will be carried out according to five parameters: the number of characters (difficulty), the audio information related to each character (language and level), to show the text information or not and the mouse interaction style.

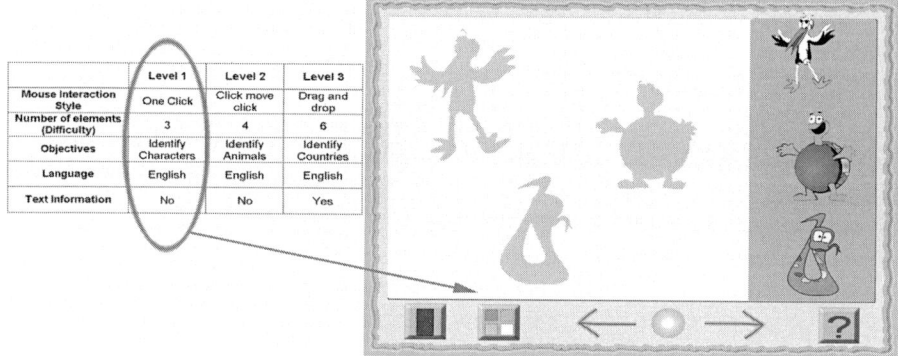

	Level 1	Level 2	Level 3
Mouse Interaction Style	One Click	Click move click	Drag and drop
Number of elements (Difficulty)	3	4	6
Objectives	Identify Characters	Identify Animals	Identify Countries
Language	English	English	English
Text Information	No	No	Yes

Fig. 2. Dynamically generated adaptive activity

The audio attached to each character depends on the language and educational level he/she has. For level 1 the character's name will be identified; for level two the animal type will be chosen and for level 3 the information to be identified is the character's origin. The textual information only appears for level 3. Finally, the way of carrying out the activity for each level of dexterity with the mouse will be also adapted (one click, click move click, drag and drop).

4 Future Work

For the completion of the whole hypermedia system, there are some phases which are being currently developed and some others to develop in 2006:

- Design and development of the whole system. The user's interface is being implemented in Macromedia Flash, since this tool allows us to design attractive animations and motivating games for children. The intelligent tutor's implementation will implement this by means of Java Servlets

- User's Evaluation. Evaluating the child's progress is crucial so that the system can adapt to his/her learning needs. Most educational systems evaluate this progress by means of tests and activities based on reading skills. Considering our learners cannot read or write and are slightly familiar with the use of computers, in order to assess progress and language acquisition, we should design activities adapted to such characteristics.
- System evaluation in the classroom. Whether the whole system is an efficient learning resource will be evaluated in a real environment, the preschool classroom. From the children's feedback, improvements to the initial prototype will be added

5   Conclusions

This paper aims to present how the integration of ICTs is more than advisable at all educational levels and claim it is important to introduce them at early ages to make children familiar and involved with their use. Our research has also attempted to demonstrate when developing software for such an early age it is necessary to keep in mind children are learning simultaneously how to communicate in natural languages and developing most of their cognitive and psychomotor abilities. From these assumptions we can state that AHS is surely the best solution to develop software for early ages, since, covering all children's needs, they offer the most personalized and adapted teaching hypermedia method. As for the software design, AHS can also provide adaptation in different areas: knowledge, educational level and dexterity with the mouse, consequently achieving the adaptation and necessary motivation so that the preschool children can get the highest benefits from the learning process [8].

References

1. Haugland, S.W.: The best development software for young children. Early childhood education journal, Vol. 25. (1998) 247-254
2. Agudo, J.E. and Sánchez H.: Development and implantation of an adaptive hypermedia system for young learners. Eurocall Conference. Cracow, Poland (2005).
3. Panagiotakopoulos C. T. and Ioannidis G. S.: Assessing children's understanding of basic time concepts through multimedia software. Computers&Education, Vol.38. (2002) 331-349
4. Brusilovsky, P.: Adaptive hypermedia. User Modeling and User-Adapted Interaction, Vol. 11, No 1-2. (2001) 87-110
5. Carro, R. M., Pulido E. and Rodríguez P.: TANGOW: Task-based Adaptive learner Guidance on the WWW. Proceedings of Second Workshop on Adaptive Systems and User Modeling on the WorldWideWeb, Toronto and Banff, Canada. Computer Science Report 99-07, Eindhoven University of Technology. (1999) 49-57
6. Wood, E., Willwughby, T., Schmidt, A., Porter, L., Specht, J. and Gilbert, J.: Assesing the Use of Input Devices for Teachers and children in early childhood education programs. Information Technology in Childhood Education Annual. (2004) 261-280
7. Carro, R.M., Breda, A.M., Castillo, G., Bajuelos, A.L.: A Methodology for Developing Adaptive Educational-Game Environments. Adaptive Hypermedia and Adaptive Web-Based Systems. Lecture Notes in Computer Science 2347, Springer-Verlag. (2002) 90-99
8. Costabile, M., Angeli, A., Rossell, T., Lanzilotti, R., Plantamura, P.: Evaluating the educational impact of a tutoring hypermedia for children. Information Technology in Childhood Education Annual 2003, Vol. 1. (2003) 269-308

A Collaborative Constraint-Based Adaptive System for Learning Object-Oriented Analysis and Design Using UML

Nilufar Baghaei

Intelligent Computer Tutoring Group
Department of Computer Science and Software Engineering
University of Canterbury, Private Bag 4800, New Zealand
n.baghaei@cosc.canterbury.ac.nz

Abstract. This paper presents COLLECT-$\mathcal{UML}$, a constraint-based ITS that teaches object-oriented (OO) design using Unified Modeling Language (UML). We have developed a single-user version that supports students in learning UML class diagrams. The system was evaluated in a real classroom, and the results show that student performance increases significantly. We present our experiences in extending the system to provide support for collaboration and describe the architecture, interface and support for collaboration in the new, multi-user system.

1 Introduction

E-learning is becoming an increasingly popular educational paradigm as more individuals who are working or are geographically isolated seek higher education. As such students do not meet face to face with their peers and teachers, the support for collaboration becomes extremely important [3]. There have been several definitions for collaborative learning. The broadest (but unsatisfactory) definition is that it is a *situation* in which *two* or *more* people *learn* or attempt to learn something *together* [4]. A more comprehensive definition states as follows: "... a coordinated, synchronous activity that is the result of a continued attempt to construct and maintain a shared conception of a problem". Effective collaborative learning includes both learning to effectively collaborate, and collaborate effectively to learn, and therefore a collaborative system must be able to address collaboration issues as well as task-oriented issues [6].

In the last decade, many collaborative learning environments have been proposed and used with more or less success. Researchers have been exploring different approaches to analyse and support the collaborative learning interaction. However, the concept of supporting peer-to-peer interaction in Computer-Supported Collaborative Learning (CSCL) systems is still in its infancy, and more studies are needed to test the utility of these techniques. Some particular benefits of collaborative problem-solving include: encouraging students to verbalise their thinking; encouraging students to work together, ask questions, explain and justify their opinions; increasing students' responsibility for their own learning and increasing the possibility of students solving

V. Wade, H. Ashman, and B. Smyth (Eds.): AH 2006, LNCS 4018, pp. 398–403, 2006.
© Springer-Verlag Berlin Heidelberg 2006

or examining problems in a variety of ways. These benefits, however, are only achieved by active and well-functioning learning teams [8].

This paper describes COLLECT-$\mathcal{UML}$, a web-based Intelligent Tutoring System (ITS) that takes a Constraint-Based Modeling (CBM) approach to support both problem-solving and collaborative learning. The CBM approach is extremely efficient, and it overcomes many problems that other student modeling approaches suffer from. CBM has been used successfully in several tutors supporting individual learning [7]. We provide a brief overview of the single-user version which we have finished developing [1, 2] and describe extensions being made to this tutor, to support multiple students solving problems collaboratively.

2   Related Work

Three categories of CSCL systems can be distinguished in the context of the collaboration support [6]. The first category includes systems that reflect actions and make the students aware of their team-mates' actions. The systems in the second category monitor the state of interactions; some of them aggregate the interaction data into a set of high-level indicators and display them to the participants, while others internally compare the current state of interaction to a model of ideal interaction, but do not reveal this information to the users (e.g. EPSILON [8]). In the latter case, this information is either intended to be used later by a coaching agent, or analysed by researchers in order to understand the interaction. Finally, the third class of systems offer advice on collaboration. The coach in these systems plays a role similar to that of a teacher in a collaborative learning classroom. The systems can be distinguished by the nature of the information in their models, and whether they provide feedback on strictly collaboration issues or both social and task-oriented issues. COLER [3] is an example of such systems.

Although many tutorials, textbooks and other resources on UML are available, we are not aware of any attempt at developing a CSCL environment for UML modeling. However, there has been an attempt [8] at developing a collaborative learning environment for OO design problems using Object Modeling Technique (OMT) – a precursor of UML. The system monitors group members' communication patterns and problem solving actions in order to identify (using machine learning techniques) situations in which students effectively share new knowledge with their peers. The system does not evaluate the OMT diagrams and an instructor or intelligent coach's assistance is needed in mediating group knowledge sharing activities. In this regard, even though the system is effective as a collaboration tool, it would probably not be an effective teaching system for a group of novices with the same level of expertise, as it could be common for a group of students to agree on a flawed argument.

3   COLLECT-$\mathcal{UML}$: Single-User Version

COLLECT-$\mathcal{UML}$ is a problem-solving environment, in which students construct UML class diagrams that satisfy a given set of requirements. It assists students during problem-solving, and guides them towards a correct solution by providing feedback. The feedback is tailored towards each student depending on his/her knowledge. COLLECT-$\mathcal{UML}$ is designed as a complement to classroom teaching and when providing assistance, it assumes that the students are already familiar with the fundamentals of OO design. For details on system's architecture, functionality and the interface refer to [1, 2]; here we present only the basic features of the system.

At the beginning of interaction, a student is required to enter his/her name, which is necessary in order to establish a session. The session manager requires the student modeler to retrieve the model for the student, if there is one, or to create a new model for a new student. Each action a student performs is sent to the session manager, as it has to link it to the appropriate session and store it in the student's log. The action is then sent to the pedagogical module. If the submitted action is a solution to the current problem, the student modeler diagnoses the solution, updates the student model, and sends the result of the diagnosis back to the pedagogical module, which generates appropriate feedback.

COLLECT-$\mathcal{UML}$ contains an ideal solution for each problem, which is compared to the student's solution according to the system's domain model, represented as a set of constraints. The system's domain model contains 133 constraints that describe the basic principles of the domain. In order to develop constraints, we studied material in textbooks, such as [5], and also used our own experience.

We conducted an evaluation study in May 2005 [2]. The study involved 38 volunteers enrolled in an introductory Software Engineering course at the University of Canterbury. The students had learnt UML modeling concepts during two weeks of lectures and had some practice during two weeks of tutorials prior to the study.

The study was conducted in two streams of two-hour laboratory sessions. Each participant sat a pre-test, interacted with the system, and then sat a post-test and filled a user questionnaire. The pre-test and post-test each contained four multiple-choice questions, followed by a question where the students were asked to design a simple UML class diagram. The participants spent two hours interacting with the system, and solved half of the problems they attempted. The average mark on the post-test was significantly higher than the pre-test mark ($t = 2.71$, $p = 4.33E-08$).

We also analyzed the log files, in order to identify how students learnt the underlying domain concepts. Figure 1 illustrates the probability of violating a constraint plotted against the occasion number for which it was relevant, averaged over all constraints and all participants. The data points show a regular decrease, which is approximated by a power curve with a close fit of 0.93, thus showing that students do learn constraints over time. The probability of violating a constraint on the first occasion of application is halved by the tenth occasion, showing the effects of learning.

The results showed that COLLECT-$\mathcal{UML}$ is an effective learning environment. The participants achieved significantly higher scores on the post-test, suggesting that they acquired more knowledge in UML modeling. The learning curves also proved that students did learn constraints during problem solving. Subjective evaluation showed that most of the students felt spending more time with the system would have resulted in more learning and that they found the system to be easy to use. The questionnaire responses suggested that the participants found the hints helpful.

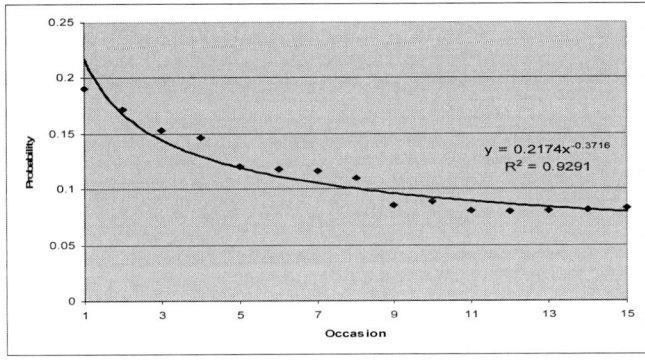

Fig. 1. Probability of constraint violation

4   COLLECT-$\mathcal{UML}$: **Collaborative Version**

The collaborative version of COLLECT-$\mathcal{UML}$ is designed for sessions in which students first solve problems individually and then join into small groups to create group solutions. The system has a distributed architecture, where the tutoring functionality is distributed between the client and the server. The interface, which is an extension of the single-user interface, is shown in Figure 2. The problem description pane presents a design problem that needs to be modeled by a UML class diagram. Students construct their individual solutions in the private workspace (right). They use the shared workspace (left) to collaboratively construct UML diagrams while communicating via the chat window.

The private workspace enables students to try their own solutions and think about the problem before start discussing it in the group. The group area is initially disabled. When all of the students indicate readiness to work in the group, the shared workspace is activated, and they can start placing components of their solutions in the workspace. The *Group Members* panel shows the team-mates already connected. Only one student, the one who has the pen, can update the shared workspace at a given time. The chat area enables students to express their opinions regarding objects added to the shared area using sentence openers. The student needs to select one of the sentence openers before being able to express his/her opinion.

The group moderator can submit the solution, by clicking on the *Submit Group Answer* button. The feedback messages on the individual solutions as well as contribution to the group solution and collaboration will appear on the frame located in the right-hand side. The system gives collaboration-based advice based on the content of the chat area, students' participation on the shared diagram and the differences between students' individual solutions and the group solution being constructed. The task-based advice is given to the whole group based on the quality of the shared diagram.

The ultimate goal of COLLECT-$\mathcal{UML}$ is to support collaboration by modeling collaborative skills. The system is able to promote effective interaction by diagnosing

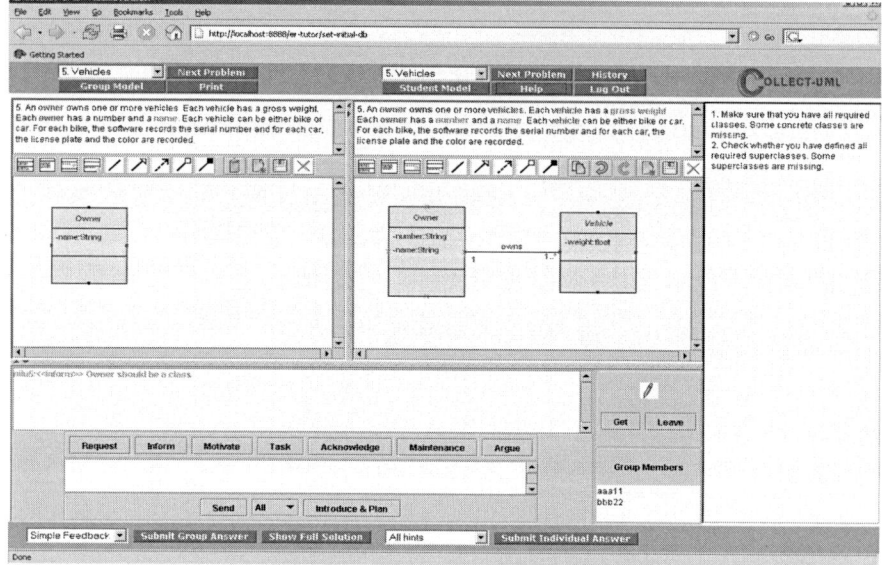

Fig. 2. COLLECT-*UML* interface

students' actions in the chat area and group diagram using a set of 22 meta-constraints, which represent an ideal model of collaboration. These constraints have the same structure as domain constraint, each containing a relevance condition, a satisfaction condition and a feedback message. The feedback message is presented when the constraint is violated. Figure 3 illustrates an example of a meta-constraint. The student model records the history of usage for each constraint (both from the domain model and the collaboration model) and the group model records the history of group usage for each constraint from the domain model. This information is used to select problems of appropriate complexity for the student, and generate feedback.

```
(235
"Some methods in the group diagram are missing from your individual solution. You
   may wish to discuss this with other  members."
(and  (match GS METHODS (?* "@" ?tag ?name ?c1_tag ?*))
      (match SS CLASSES (?* "@" ?c1_tag ?*)))
(match SS METHODS (?* "@" ?tag ?name2 ?c1_tag ?*))
"methods"
(?c1  tag))
```

Fig. 3. An example of a meta-constraint

5   Conclusions and Future Work

This paper presented the single-user version of COLLECT-*UML,* and the results of the evaluation study performed. The results of both subjective and objective analysis showed that COLLECT-$\mathcal{UML}$ is an effective educational tool. We then presented the multi-user version of the same intelligent tutoring system. We have extended the interface and developed meta-constraints, which provide feedback on collaborative activities. The goal of future work is to complete the implementation of the multi-user version and conduct a full evaluation study in April 2006, aiming to evaluate the effect of using the system on students' learning and collaboration.

CBM has been used to effectively represent domain knowledge in several ITSs supporting individual learning. The contribution of the project presented in this paper is the use of CBM to model collaboration skills, not only domain knowledge. Comprehensive evaluation of the collaborative version of COLLECT-$\mathcal{UML}$ will provide a measure of the effectiveness of using the CBM technique in intelligent computer-supported collaborative learning environments.

References

[1] Baghaei, N., Mitrovic, A. and Irwin, W. *A Constraint-Based Tutor for Learning Object-Oriented Analysis and Design using UML.* In Looi, C., Jonassen, D. and Ikeda M. (eds.), ICCE 2005, pp.11-18.

[2] Baghaei, N., Mitrovic, A. and Irwin, W. *Problem-Solving Support in a Constraint-based Tutor for UML Class Diagrams*, Technology, Instruction, Cognition and Learning Journal, 4(1-2) (in print), 2006.

[3] Constantino-Gonzalez, M., and Suthers, D. *Coaching Collaboration in a Computer-Mediated Learning Environment.* CSCL 2002, (NJ, USA, 2002), pp.583-584.

[4] Dillenbourg, P. *What do you mean by "Collaborative Learning".* In Dillenbourg, P. (eds.), Collaborative Learning: Cognitive and Computational Approaches, Amsterdam: Elsevier Science. pp.1-19, 1999.

[5] Fowler, M. *UML Distilled: a Brief Guide to the Standard Object Modelling Language.* Reading: Addison-Wesley, 3rd edition, 2004.

[6] Jerman, P., Soller, A. and Muhlenbrock, M. *From Mirroring to Guiding: A Review of State of the Art Technology for Supporting Collaborative Learning.* CSCL 2001, (Netherlands, 2001), pp.324-331.

[7] Mitrovic, A., Mayo, M., Suraweera, P. and Martin, B. *Constraint-based Tutors: a Success Story.* IEA/AIE-2001, (Budapest, 2001), Springer-Verlag Berlin Heidelberg LNAI 2070, pp.931-940.

[8] Soller, A. and Lesgold, A. *Knowledge acquisition for adaptive collaborative learning environments.* AAAI Fall Symposium: Learning How to Do Things, Cape Cod, MA, 2000.

Decentralized Mediation of User Models
for a Better Personalization

Shlomo Berkovsky*

University of Haifa, 31905, Haifa, Israel
slavax@cs.haifa.ac.il

Abstract. The growth of available personalization services and the heterogeneity in content and representation of therein exploited User Models (UMs), raise a need for a mechanism allowing to aggregate partial UMs generated by other services. Such a mechanism will allow reuse of partial UMs in multiple personalization services that may need it. This paper discusses the details of a decentralized mediator for cross-domain and cross-technique translation and aggregation of partial UMs. The mediator facilitates enriching UMs managed by personalization services and improving the quality of the provided personalization.

1 Introduction

Providing accurate personalized information services to consumers requires modeling their preferences, interests and needs. This data is referred to in the literature as the User Model (*UM*) [7]. Typically, service providers build and maintain proprietary UMs, tailored to the specific contents offered by the service, and the personalization technique being exploited. Since the quality of the provided personalized service depends largely on the characteristics and richness of the UMs, different services would benefit from enriching their UMs through importing and aggregating partial UMs, i.e., the UMs built locally by other, possibly related, services. This can be achieved through *mediation* of partial UMs.

UM mediation raises a number of issues. The first issue is the commercial nature of the nowadays information world. Due to competition, personalization services usually neither cooperate, nor share their partial UMs. The second issue is customer's privacy. Partial UMs built by service providers may contain customer's private data, which should not be disclosed to untrusted parties [4]. The third and fourth issues are the structural heterogeneity and incompleteness of the UMs contents, since every service refers to a specific application domain only. The lack of standard representation, and specific requirements imposed by different personalization techniques, result in personalization services building their models in different, ad-hoc forms. As a result, large amounts of heterogeneously represented and possibly overlapping (or conflicting) data are scattered among various service providers.

Generation of a central UM, as a composition of partial UMs stored by various personalization services, is discussed in [6]. For this, each service maintains a mechanism

---

* The author would like to thank his advisors, Tsvi Kuflik and Francesco Ricci, for their valuable comments on this paper.

V. Wade, H. Ashman, and B. Smyth (Eds.): AH 2006, LNCS 4018, pp. 404–408, 2006.

capable of accessing the relevant parts of the central UM. To provide personalization, each service extracts the required data from the central UM and later updates the central UM. However, the centrality of the UM poses a severe problem that should be treated. In [8], the authors discuss agent-based sharing and management of partial UMs, which are centrally aggregated into a global UM. However, neither the sharing policy, nor the translation between different representations is defined, such that UMs sharing between the services should be implemented explicitly.

Unlike the above studies, this work aims at handling the aggregation through a *decentralized UM mediator*, capable of aggregating partial UMs. The mediator provides a scalable platform for privacy-enhanced data exchange and facilitates an ad-hoc (i.e., for a specific purpose, and not derived from a general, continuously maintained UM) generation of the UMs for the target service through translation and aggregation of partial UMs built by other services. Thus, the mediator bootstraps empty UMs, or enriches the existing UMs, leveraging the quality of the provided personalization.

2   Mediation of User Models

Principal architecture of the mediator was discussed in [1], whereas this paper elaborates on the mediation process and the ways of applying the mediator in a decentralized distributed environment. The main functionality of the mediator is to facilitate aggregation of partial UMs built by different services. Thus, it provides a common interface for user modeling data exchange. Figure 1 illustrates the mediation process.

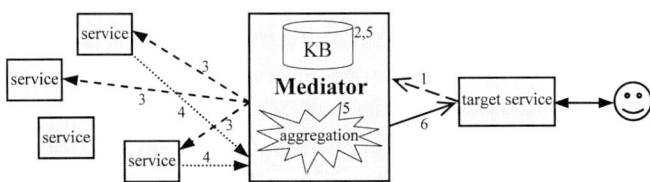

Fig. 1. Architecture and stages of the UM mediation

The mediation process is partitioned to the following stages:

1. A target service, required to provide personalization to a user, queries the mediator for the UM related to the application domain of the provided service.
2. The mediator identifies the required personalization domain and the UMs representation in the target service.
3. The mediator determines a set of other services that can potentially provide partial domain-related UMs of the given user and queries them.
4. Services, actually storing the needed data, answer the query, and send to the mediator their partial UMs of the given user.
5. The mediator translates and aggregates the acquired partial UMs (using the KB) into a single domain-related UM, represented according to the target service.
6. The generated domain-related UM is sent to the target service, which is capable of providing more accurate personalized service.

Two major issues that should be resolved to facilitate proper functionality of the mediator are: (1) "Which services can provide valuable partial UMs?", and (2) "How to translate and aggregate the acquired heterogeneous UMs?", i.e., stages *3* and *5* in figure 1. Thus, in the rest of the paper we focus on these stages.

First, let us analyze the distribution of partial UMs among the services. Nowadays, personalization services are exploited in a wide variety of application domains (e.g., movies, music, tourism, etc...). The contents of the UMs may vary between application in the same domain, and certainly between applications in different domains. Thus, the UM is considered as an aggregation of partial domain-related UMs: $UM=aggr(UM_1,UM_2,...,UM_k)$. Moreover, within a given domain, the services may exploit various personalization techniques (e.g., collaborative, content-based, case-based reasoning, etc) that impose different representations of the UMs. As a result, domain-related UM is considered as an aggregation of partial technique-related UMs: $UM_d=aggr(UM_d^1,UM_d^2,...,UM_d^n)$, where UM_d^t denotes the partial UM referred to application domain d, built by a service exploiting personalization technique t.

Stage *3* of the mediation aims at determining the set of services that should be queried by the mediator. We assume that three groups of services will provide valuable partial UMs for building UM_d^t for a service from domain d exploiting technique t: (1) other services from d that also exploit t, (2) services from d that exploit another technique t', and (3) services from another, relatively similar, domain d' that also exploit t. Although other services, i.e., with different combinations of techniques and domains, can potentially provide valuable partial UMs, we refrain from querying them, since their mediation requires multiple translations, which may 'contaminate' the data.

To alleviate the task of determining and querying the relevant services, we propose to organize the available services in a hierarchical semantically demarcated structure. The upper level of the hierarchy represents different application domains of the services. The domains are represented by the nodes of an undirected graph, where the weights of the edges reflect the similarity between the respective domains. The similarity values allow determining whether partial domain-related UM_j can be valuable for aggregating another domain-related UM_i. The bottom layer represents specific services within the domains, such that the services are grouped according to the personalization techniques they exploit. This organization of services inherently restricts the queries for partial UMs only to the services referring to the same application domain, or to different but relatively similar domains, and exploiting the same personalization technique (or both, i.e., the same domain and technique). Analyzing

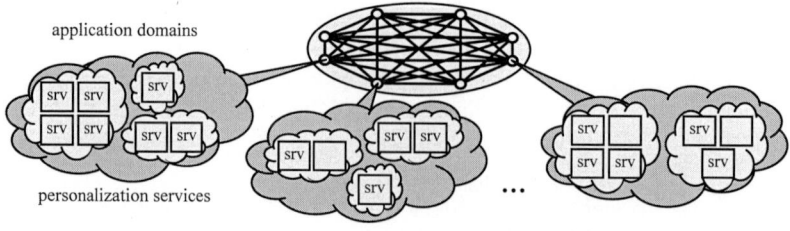

Fig. 2. Organization of services: graph of domains and grouping by the techniques

UM representations in various techniques will allow determining the applicability of partial UM_d^m for aggregating in another UM_d^n, and further restricting querying of services. Figure 2 illustrates the organization of the personalization services.

Another important issue is translating and aggregating the acquired partial UMs (stage 5). Clearly, different application domains require different information to be stored in the UMs. Even within the same domain, different services may store different information in their partial UM, according to the exploited technique (e.g., ratings vector in collaborative UM vs. a list of interest topics in content-based UM). Moreover, partial UMs from the same domain and technique may use different terms to de-scribe equivalent semantic concepts. Thus, successful translation of partial UMs requires rich inter- and intra-domain *Knowledge Base* (KB) that allows identifying commonalities between partial UMs and inferring the required data. According to the above-mentioned groups of services providing valuable partial UMs, we define 3 types of possible translations: (1) simple concatenation of partial UMs, (2) *cross-technique* translation, and (3) *cross-domain* translation. Clearly, each type of translation requires specific inference mechanism and exploits different data from the KB.

In addition to the main task of UMs translation, stage 5 of the mediation process is also responsible for aggregating partial UMs, i.e., resolving conflicts and inconsistencies. This is not unreasonable that different services will provide partial UMs with different levels of accuracy, relevance and 'freshness'. Although we highlight the importance of resolving these issues, they are beyond the scope of the current work.

Consider an example scenario where content-based movie recommender requests the mediator for a UM of a given user (stage 1). The mediator identifies the domain and the representation of the UM, and queries other services that can potentially provide valuable partial UMs (stages 2 and 3). Let us assume that other content-based movie recommenders, movie recommenders exploiting other techniques, and TV, books and music recommenders are queried. Services, storing the user's UMs, answer the query and send their partial UMs (stage 4). The mediator exploits various KBs to translate and aggregate the acquired partial UMs into a single movie-related content-based UM (stage 5). For example, cross-technique translation from collaborative to content-based movies UM exploits a KB of movies data (e.g., genres, directors and actors), which allows the mediator to generalize a set of collaborative ratings into the content-based UM, containing a list of genres, directors and actors liked/disliked by the user. Conversely, cross-domain translation from books to movies content-based UMs exploits a KB of books and movies genres that facilitates the translation through identifying the correlations between the contents of the UMs (e.g., liked/disliked genres, common to movies and books). Then, the aggregated UM is sent to the movies recommender, which provides the user more accurate personalization (stage 6).

Finally, we would like to highlight three hypothesized advantages of the proposed mediation mechanism: (1) the designed one – better personalization provided by the target service, (2) scalability and robustness – achieved due to the lack of a centralized user modeling mechanism and UM representation, (3) data encapsulation and privacy – achieved due to an independent management of domain-related data by the services, and direct communication between them, where attacking a single service will expose partial UMs only. Nonetheless, we should raise the main disadvantages: necessity of strong inference mechanisms and rich inter- and intra-domain KBs.

3 Preliminary Results and Future Research

Preliminary evaluations of cross-domain mediation in collaborative movie recommender were reported in [2]. There, the datasets from different (but similar) domains were simulated by splitting movies UMs according to the genres of the movies. The accuracy of the recommendations over the aggregated UMs was similar to the accuracy of centralized collaborative recommendations, providing an initial validation to the feasibility of cross-domain UMs mediation. In the future, we plan to investigate the applicability of cross-domain mediation in less similar application domains.

Cross-technique mediation between collaborative and content-based movie recommenders was discussed and evaluated in [3]. To achieve this, we exploited IMDB database (*www.imdb.com*) for extracting the features of the movies (e.g., genres, actors, directors, etc) and building a weighted content-based UM that served as a basis for generating content-based recommendations. Experiments showed that for small UMs, accuracy of the recommendations using the translated content-based UMs is better than of the recommendations using the original collaborative UMs.

Currently, we are also working on UMs mediation between case-based reasoning and content-based tourism personalization systems. For this, we exploit IR techniques for analyzing the contents of the UMs built by Trip@dvice tourism planning system (*tripadvice.itc.it*) and initializing the UMs of museum visitors. In parallel, we exploit similar IR techniques for analyzing textual contents of Web-sites classified in Web-directories for devising distances between different application domains.

In the future, we plan to investigate the possibility of exploiting UM ontologies, e.g., GUMO [5], for the purposes of using parts of generic UM representations in the mediation process. Finally, we will extensively evaluate the proposed approach through combining cross-technique and cross-domain mediations, and will deduce the conditions, where UM mediation improves the quality of provided personalization.

References

[1] S.Berkovsky, "*Ubiquitous User Modeling in Recommender Systems*", in proc. of the UM Conference, 2005.
[2] S.Berkovsky, P.Busetta, Y.Eytani, T.Kuflik, F.Ricci, "*Collaborative Filtering over Distributed Environment*", in proc. of the DASUM Workshop, 2005.
[3] S.Berkovsky, T.Kuflik, F.Ricci, "*Cross-Technique Mediation of User Models*", in proc. of the AH Conference, 2006.
[4] L.F.Cranor, J.Reagle, M.S.Ackerman, "*Beyond Concern: Understanding Net Users' Attitudes about Online Privacy*", Technical Report, AT&T Labs-Research, 1999.
[5] D.Heckmann, T.Schwartz, B.Brandherm, M.Schmitz, M.von Wilamowitz-Moellendorff, "*GUMO – the General User Model Ontology*", in proc. of the UM Conference, 2005.
[6] J.Kay, B.Kummerfeld, P.Lauder, "*Managing Private User Models and Shared Personas*", in proc. of the UbiUM Workshop, 2003.
[7] A.Kobsa, "*Generic User Modeling Systems*", in User Modeling and User-Adapted Interaction, vol.11(1-2), pp.49-63, 2001.
[8] A.Lorenz, "*A Specification for Agent-Based Distributed User Modeling in Ubiquitous Computing*", in proc. of the DASUM Workshop, 2005.

From Interoperable User Models to Interoperable User Modeling

Francesca Carmagnola and Federica Cena

Dipartimento di Informatica, Università di Torino,
Corso Svizzera 185, Torino, Italy
{carmagnola, cena}@di.unito.it

Abstract. Currently, there is an increasing demand user-adaptive systems for various purposes in many different domains. The development of such systems requires computational efforts which is often challenging and off-putting. The main contribution of our work is the idea to go one step further from sharing user model data (interoperable user models) towards the exchange of user model reasoning strategies (interoperable user modeling). In this paper we discuss, exemplified in a concrete scenario, how Semantic Web techniques may be applied to the field of the Adaptive Systems in order to have a more effective and reliable user model interoperability, considering both the perspectives of User Modeling Servers and Web Servers.

1 Introduction

Personalization features are becoming popular and are being integrated in various domains, e.g. e-commerce, e-learning, tourism and cultural heritage, travel planning, interaction in instrumented environments. Users can nowadays interact with a great number of personalised systems, so there is the great opportunity to acquire wider knowledge about a user and use it in order to reach a better adaptation. This possibility is exemplified trough the so called "Ubiquitous user modeling"[7]. Ubiquitous user modeling describes ongoing modeling and exploitation of user behavior with a variety of systems that share their user models.

This possibility can be carried out by user model servers (e.g. [9], [10], [4]) which have made a significant advancement by offering flexible server-client architectures where a user model, stored as a central repository, is maintained by and shared across several applications.

These shared user models can be either used for mutual or for individual adaptation goals and can be just exchanged or integrated [10] .

Sharing user models across applications has many advantages [8], for instance it lets to speed up the phase of user model initialization [10] and it lets the "increased coverage", since more aspects can be covered by the aggregated user model, because of the variety of the contributing systems. The "increased level of detail" and the "increased reliability", including in the user model features that one system could not acquire by itself, lead to a deeper understanding of the user, letting better adaptation

V. Wade, H. Ashman, and B. Smyth (Eds.): AH 2006, LNCS 4018, pp. 409–413, 2006.

results. What statements can be retrieved and exchanged in respect to privacy regulations and how they are integrated depends on several layers of metadata attached to the statements [8].

Our approach moves from these considerations and is aimed to explore how interoperability of user models can be improved by sharing semantically annotated rules.

In the paper we will provide a justification of the need and the challenge of this approach which represents our thesis and our research activity. To test its applicability and value we move from U2M [8], a framework for ubiquitous user modeling focused on the exchange and the semantic integration of partial user models, with the aim to extend this framework by introducing the exchange of semantically described rules that represent the reasoning strategies implemented by the applications to model users, following the principles described in MUSE [5]. In Sec. 2 we specify the problem we want to face, by showing an example with existing applications that share user models data, and explaining how these problems can be solved through the approach of the interoperability of User Modeling`   Sec. 3 concludes the paper and specify which will be the next steps of our researches.

2   Interoperability of User Modeling Reasoning Strategies

The main focus of our work moves from interoperability of user data but focuses on the possibility to make the user modeling reasoning strategies interoperable among systems.

Starting Problem

To better specify the problem we want to address in our proposal, we take into consideration two systems, UbiquiTO [1] and Specter [11]. Both these applications interact with the same user and for her they define a user model according to the application goals. What they wish to do is to communicate and share/exchange knowledge regarding user models. UbiquiTO is an adaptive and mobile tourist guide for the city of Turin, while Specter addresses the exploitation of user actions captured in an intelligent environment to define a memory for situated user support. Imagine a shopping scenario wherein a system tries to predict whether or not the user should be presented an advertisement of a nearby store. In this context, UbiquiTO wants to provide personalized suggestions to a user that has already interacted with Specter. To perform adaptation in a shopping environment, UbiquiTO needs to know the user's "propensity to spend" (that indicates the user's availability of money), which it infers on the basis of user age and profession. Being the features age and profession not directly related to the propensity to spend, the value inferred by UbiquiTO could be not much reliable. UbiquiTO knows that the user interacts with Specter as well, so it decides to verify if Specter calculates a value for the user's "propensity to spend". Specter computes this value (by the direct observation of user actions), thus UbiquiTO asks Specter for it.

The interoperability of user models data outlined in this scenario, leads to many issues:

i) Does UbiquiTO trust Specter? Is the value provided by Specter calculated in a way that UbiquiTO believe reliable?

ii) If the value "propensity to spend" inferred by Specter for the same user is different from the one calculated by UbiquiTO, which is the most reliable? If also another application infers the user "propensity to spend" but stores a very different value for the same user, how can UbiquiTO decide which value trust?

UbiquiTO needs to manage all these conflicts.

Proposed Solution

We state that sharing the user modeling reasoning strategies exploited by the applications could bring relevant contributions to address these problems and can extend the U2M framework approach.

In particular, the basic idea of the proposal is to exchange reasoning strategies described by means of rules and using a semantic web rule language to represent them[1]. The choice of using rules to express knowledge is related to their role in the semantic web. As underlined in [2] rules can add expressiveness to description logic-based ontology languages and thus they can be used to draw inferences, to express constraints, to transform data, etc.

In detail, considering these questions, we can sketch how exchange reasoning strategies and not only value about user model could address them.

i) When UbiquiTO asks Specter for the value of the user "propensity to spend", it has no way to check nor if Specter or the values provided by it are reliable before using it to perform adaptation (and so before having a direct feedback of its validity from the user). Knowing the value itself is not enough, since an application may have many different ways to derive it. Knowing the reasoning process that lead to the definition of "propensity to spend" gives UbiquiTO an explanation regarding how this value is obtained in Specter, letting the chance of evaluating its reliance, according with some heuristics.

ii) If the value calculated by UbiquiTO is different we would have a problem of "conflict resolution" and UbiquiTO should choose between the values. However, knowing the mere values is not enough since they do not provide a mean to take the decision. Thus, if UbiquiTO could know the rule describing the reasoning process that led Specter to this value, it could understand how that value has been defined. However, this is not yet sufficient to take the decision. UbiquiTO needs a set of strategies that allow to understand if process itself is good or not. Therefore, we hypothesize that for each class of the user's ontology of each system there is a property (provenance) that describes the modality of acquisition of the value of the

---

[1] Candidates are SWRL [www.daml.org/2003/11/swrl/], which combine OWL DL, OWL Lite and the Unary/Binary Datalog RuleML and extend the set of OWL axioms to include Horn-like rules, and RDF/RuleML [http://www.ruleml.org/w3c-ws-rules/implementing-ruleml-w3c-ws.html], which combines XML Schema definitions, translators, and bidirectional interpreters written in Java.

corresponding feature. For example, the value of the feature "Interest For Art" may be inferred by the system or declared by the user herself, it may be recent or out-of-date, and the combination of these values influences the reliability of the values they are referred to. Hence, UbiquiTO checks the rule that produces this user feature and, in particular, analyzes every term of the rule, which is mapped to the class of the user ontology, and the values of the corresponding property "provenance", and on the basis of its heuristics, it will be able to choose which of the conflicting values are more reliable, and then import this value. This approach can be extended to a situation with more than two systems, wherein there could be an higher possibility that more than one application infers different value for the same user feature.

3   Conclusions and Future Work

The main contribution of our work is the idea to go one step further from sharing user model data (interoperable user models) towards the exchange of user model reasoning strategies, thus some reasoning mechanisms to both update the model and decide about adaptation strategies (interoperable user modeling).

The main focus of our research concerns the possibility to explore how to make the user modeling reasoning strategies interoperable. In this line, our two thesis will follow two directions: (i) *how* can user modeling strategies be defined as rules that can be shared across applications; and (ii) *what* has to be shared in order to acquire more knowledge of a user and improve the adaptation process.

Regarding the first aspect, our proposal follows principles and goals of the Semantic Web representation of rules [6], and we want to demonstrate how interoperability of user models can be improved by sharing semantically annotated rules that describe the reasoning strategies for user modeling implemented by the applications that share user models statements.

Regarding the second aspect, there are two open issues that have to be investigated. The first one regards the problem of the *semantic match*: in the scenario, how UbiquiTO may be sure that Specter offers a values that really semantically corresponds to the one it is looking for? In other words, how can UbiquiTO be sure that Specter has the same understanding of the concept "propensity to spend"? The second one deals with the issue of provide proof to the user: in the scenario, how UbiquiTO can provide its final user with the justification of the results obtained?

In order to test our approach, the next step will be the development of a framework for the sharing of the knowledge among Adaptive Systems (data and reasoning strategies about UM) exploited with semantic web service technology [3]. All the adaptive applications of the framework will be designed as semantic web services that take as input user data and give in output (i) user modeling dimensions (ii) adaptive services and (iii) reasoning strategies related with user and adaptation modeling.

Furthermore we are working on the definition of suitable evaluation methodologies to verify the achievement of the interoperability of reasoning strategies, in particular (i) what may be considered a success and (ii) how to measure it.

Acknowledgements

We are very grateful to Cristina Gena, Ilaria Torre and Luca Console for their contribution in the project.

We would like to thank also Dominik Heckmann, Vania Dimitrova, Lora Aroyo, and Alexander Kröner for their help, support, discussions and research material.

References

1. Amendola, I., Cena F., Console L., Crevola A., Gena C., Goy A., Modeo S., Perrero M., Torre I., Toso A.: UbiquiTO: A Multi-device Adaptive Guide. Proc. of Mobile HCI 2004, Lecture Notes in Computer Science, 3160 (2004) 409-414
2. Antoniou, G., Baldoni, M., Baroglio, C., Patti, V., Baumgartner, R., Eiter, T., Herzog, M., Schindlauer, R., Tompits, H., Bry, F., Schaffert, S., Henze, N., May, W.: Reasoning Methods for Personalization on the Semantic Web. Annals of mathematics, Computing & Teleinformatics, Vol.1, N.2, 2004, pp 1-24
3. Ardissono, L., A. Goy, G. Petrone, M. Segnan, Interaction with Web Services in the Adaptive Web, Adaptive Hypermedia and Adaptive Web-Based Systems. 3rd Int. Conf., AH 2004, Eindhoven, Springer Verlag, pp. 14-23, 2004
4. Brusilovsky, P., Sosnovsky, S., and Yudelson, M. (2005) Ontology-based framework for user model interoperability in distributed learning environments. In: G. Richards (ed.) Proceedings of World Conference on E-Learning, E-Learn 2005, Vancouver, Canada, October 24-28, 2005, AACE, pp. 2851-2855
5. Carmagnola, F., Cena, F., Gena, C., Torre, I.. MUSE: A Multidimensional Semantic Environment for Adaptive Hypermedia Systems. In the proceedings of ABIS 2005.
6. Cirstea, H., Kirchner, C. Types for Web Rule Languages: a preliminary study, REWERSE EU Network of Excellence, technical report I3-D2, 2005.
7. Heckmann, D., B. Brandherm, M. Schmitz, T. Schwartz, and B. M. Von Wilamowitz-Moellendorf. GUMO - the general user model ontology. In Proceedings of the 10th International Conference on User Modeling, Edinburgh, Scotland, Jun 2005. LNAI 3538: Springer, Berlin Heidelberg, pp 428–432,
8. Heckmann, D. UbiquiTOus User Modeling. PhD thesis, Department of Computer Science, Saarland University, Germany, 2005.
9. Kay, J., B. Kummerfeld, and P. Lauder. Personis: A server for user models. In P. de Bra, P. Brusilovsky, and R. Conejo, editors, Proceedings of AH 2002, LNCS 2347, pages 203–212. Springer-Verlag Berlin Heidelberg, May 2002.
10. A. Kobsa, J. Koenemann, and W. Pohl. Personalised hypermedia presentation techniques for improving online customer relationship. The Knowledge Engineering Review, Vol.16(2):111–115, 2001.
11. Kröner, A., Heckmann, D., Wahlster, W. SPECTER: Building, Exploiting and Sharing Augmented Memories in the proc. of Workshop on Knowledge Sharing for Everyday Life, Kyoto, Japan, KSEL 2006

Assessment of Motivation in Online Learning Environments

Mihaela Cocea

National College of Ireland, Mayor Street, Dublin 1, Ireland
mihaela_cocea@yahoo.com

Abstract. This research outline refers to the assessment of motivation in online learning environments. It includes a presentation of previous approaches, most of them based on Keller's ARCS model, and argues for an approach based on Social Cognitive Learning Theory, in particular building on self-efficacy and self-regulation concepts. The research plan includes two steps: first, detect the learners in danger of dropping-out based on their interaction with the system; second, create a model of the learner's motivation (including self-efficacy, self-regulation, goal orientation, attribution and perceived task characteristics) upon which intervention can be done.

1 Introduction

Motivation has always been one of the most important factors for learning (Bandura, 1986), i.e., it plays a crucial role in e-learning and especially with regard to drop-out and quality of learning. In a classical interaction between a human tutor and students in the classroom, the assessment of motivation is done by tutors, who then act according to their findings. In the case of an Intelligent Tutoring System (ITS), the assessment of motivation is also needed in order to interact with students according to their level of motivation.

We propose an approach to assessment of motivation in two stages: first, indirect assessment/observation – the aim of this stage is to identify learners that are in danger of dropping out or giving up as early as possible using unobtrusive observation methods; second, explicit elicitation: in order to inform a personalized and suitable intervention, the system would explicitly explore and verify the learners' motivational level (self-efficacy, self-regulation, goal orientation, attribution, perceived characteristics of the task etc). Thus, we are addressing the following research questions: Which factors in the learning behavior can predict drop-out? How to assess/create a learner model of his/her motivation?

2 Background

Human tutors usually infer motivation from observational cues – like mimics, posture, gesture, conversational cues etc. which are difficult to be processed by adaptive systems (although there are efforts in this direction – i.e.: Kapoor, Picard and Ivanov, 2004; D'Mello et al., 2005; Fernandez and Picard, 2005). Thus, most of the research

V. Wade, H. Ashman, and B. Smyth (Eds.): AH 2006, LNCS 4018, pp. 414–418, 2006.

is directed towards finding a way to assess motivation from cues that can be easily processed automatically (e.g. learner's interactions with the system, time spent on a task, his/her statements about his/her level of motivation etc.).

Three previous works are of particular interest for our research. All of them are related to Keller's ARCS model (Keller, 1987), briefly presented here: ARCS stands for Attention, Relevance, Confidence and Satisfaction. Gaining and retaining the learner's *attention* is necessary for an efficient learning, *relevance* (of the learning content) is a condition for attention and motivation, *confidence* determines the level of effort invested in learning and *satisfaction* refers to the reward gained from the learning experience. The three mentioned works came up with interesting approaches. One of these approaches has been presented by de Vicente & Pain (2003); they proposed several rules to infer motivational states from two sources: the *interactions* of the students with the tutoring system and their *motivational traits*. A second approach was developed by Qu, Wang & Johnson (2005) and infers three aspects of motivation – *confidence*, *confusion* and *effort* from several sources: the learner's focus of attention, the current task and expected time to perform the task.; they were interested in particular in low confidence, high confusion and low effort, as these are strong indicators of the student giving up. A third approach was introduced by Zhang, Cheng, He& Huang (2003); they also started from ARCS model and assessed two of the model's variables: *attention* and *confidence*.

All three approaches focus on motivational states and a way to measure them without asking the learner. The ambition to build a system that is able to assess motivation without specifically asking the learners about it seems too high for our current knowledge. The assessment of motivation classically includes either observation or self-report or both. The idea of getting a system to do what humans do is a goal that seems quite far – at least when we talk about emotions, feelings, motivation and will. And as these aspects are important for learning, they need to be taken into consideration.

That is why our approach for the assessment of motivation is based on Social Cognitive Learning Theory and especially related to self-efficacy (SE) and self-regulation (SR) concepts. SE is generally described by Bandura (1986) as the confidence that the individual has in his/her ability to control his/her thoughts, feelings and actions; more specifically, it refers to a person's belief/ expectancy in his/her capacity to successfully complete a task. SR refers to a person's ability to control his/her actions, in our case learning (Schunk & Zimmerman, 1994; Zimmerman, 1994). Karoly (1993, p.25) defines SR as "those processes (…) that enable an individual to guide his/her goal-directed activities over time and across changing circumstances (contexts)".

We argue that Social Cognitive Learning Theory is a sound theoretical base for assessment of motivation. It is a well established construct in the literature. There is broad evidence that this theory has good application in classroom (Tuckman, 1999; Schraw & Brooks, 2000), as well as in online learning (Hodges, 2004; Irizarry, 2002) and blended learning (Wang & Newlin, 2002). The theory offers a variety of possibilities to intervene in order to motivate the learner in a personalized way. It also offers a framework for influencing the learner's subjective control of the task through *motivational beliefs* (SE) and *cognitive learning strategies* (SR/ self-monitoring).

3   Methodology

In accordance with the two stages of assessment proposed above, this project is split into: the prediction of drop-outs and the dialog-based creation of learner model.

3.1   Which Factors in the Learning Behavior Can Predict Drop-Out?

The approach for this first research question will build upon and elaborate Johnson's approach (Qu, Wang & Johnson, 2005): This research aims at identifying the learners with the risk of dropping out. Rather than directly inferring particular motivational states from the observed behavior, we propose to use behavioral cues as indicators that can predict the giving-up risk. These indicators related to the concept of SR include: browsing fast rather than reading, skipping sections, non-systematic progression, and answering questions quickly (in less time than the minimum required time for at least reading the questions). Another indicator is how often and how insistent the learner seeks for help from peers/instructor. Also if the learner is searching external content for a related topic it may be a sign of getting lost in the course content; it may also be a sign of an elaboration cognitive strategy.

Perhaps the most intuitive and easy to use indicator is time (time required higher than predicted time). It is interesting that de Vicente & Pain (2003) used it to infer confidence or lack of interest, while Qu, Wang & Johnson (2005) used it to infer effort. Time is probably a component of each of the three mentioned aspects, but is not sufficient to infer any of them. We use time as a general indicator of drop-out risk: a too short or a too long focus on an issue may indicate "problems". Of course, both could be due to other factors: a too short time spent on a task might be explained by a good knowledge and exceeding time could be justified by factors like breaks or deep thought. These situations can be clarified by asking the learner.

To evaluate the drop-out risk prediction two comparison studies will be conducted that compare the ITS' prediction against the learner's performance and continuity with the course, on one hand, and human tutors' prediction (based on the learner's interactions with the ITS), on the other hand. The benefits from the second approach are: human teachers can provide explanations for the learners' behavior; they can identify and explain contradictory situations (i.e. the learner's behavior indicates drop-out/good performance, but the actual behavior of the learner is different).

The next step after spotting the learners in danger of giving-up is interacting with them in order to identify the ones really in danger (as situations like the ones mentioned above can occur) and engage them in a dialog in order to explicitly elicit information about their motivation and build a learner model. Figure 1 illustrates the steps involved in our approach.

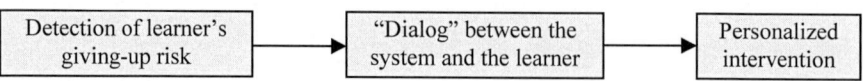

Fig. 1. The assessment process

3.2   How to Build a Learner Model of Motivation?

The second research question will be approached based on a dialog with the learner. The dialog deals with the following aspects: a) Inform and explain the learner about the dialog: the learners identified to be in danger of giving up will be informed by the system that it has noticed some "confusing" behavior and informs the learner about the next questions that he/she will be asked in order to identify "the problem"; b) Ask the learners about their SE, SR, goal-orientation (GO), attribution of their performance and perceived characteristics of the task at hand.

To elicit the level of SE, SR and GO, adapted versions of existing questionnaires will be used. To elicit the attribution of their performance, learners will have to choose from the following options (depending on the level of performance): my (lack of) ability; my (lack of) effort; (bad) luck; task reasonable (hard) difficulty. Perceived characteristics of the task include difficulty, cognitive interest, sensory interest (structure/ presentation), controllability and challenge. From the attribution choice we can infer the locus of control and the control-non control dimension. This information together with the other measured aspects will be included in a learner model.

An experiment will be conducted to investigate the reliability and construct validity of the adapted SE, SR and GO questionnaires. The construct validity of the attribution measurement is assured by the fact that the options given for answering are from the theory of attribution (Heider, 1958; Weiner, 1974). A random group of students will participate in the experiment. They will be required to complete the questionnaires and the gathered data will be analyzed in three ways: reliability coefficients will be calculated; a confirmatory factor analysis (for the types of GO) and goodness-of-fit of the model will be investigated.

4   Summary

Social Cognitive Learning Theory offers a frame for a deep knowledge of a learner's motivation and several possibilities for intervention. It can, thus, serve as a sound theoretical basis for assessment of motivation in online learning environments. Our research includes two aspects: the predictions of the giving-up risk and the development of a learner motivational model (including SE, SR, GO, attribution and perceived task characteristics).

By the actual time, our research has covered the research questions, the literature review and partially the methodology. Future work includes: define the methodology in detail, conduct a study to predict and validate the dropping-out risk assessment and one to build and validate the learner's model of motivation; collect and analyse the data and draw conclusions about this approach.

References

1. Bandura, A.: Social foundations of thought and action: A social cognitive theory. Englewood Cliffs, NJ: Prentice Hall (1986)
2. De Vicente, A., Pain, H.: Informing the Detection of the Students' Motivational State: an empirical Study. In Cerri, S. A.; Gouarderes, G.; Paraguau, F: Intelligent Tutoring Systems, 6th International Conference. Berlin: Springer-Verlag., (2002) 933-943

3. De Vicente, A., Pain, H.: Validating the Detection of a student's Motivational State. In Mendez Vilas, A.; Mesa Gonzalez, J. A.; Mesa Gonzalez, J. (eds): Proceedings of the Second International Conference on Multimedia Information & Communication Technologies in Education (m-ICTE2003), number 15 of "Sociedad de la Informacion" Series, Volume III, (2003)
4. D'Mello, S. K., Craig, S. D., Gholson, B., Franklin, S., Picard, R. W., Graesser, A. C.: Integrating Affect Sensors in an Intelligent Tutoring System, In Affective Interactions: The Computer in the Affective Loop Workshop at 2005 International conference on Intelligent User Interfaces (pp. 7-13) New York: AMC Press (2005)
5. Fernandez, R., Picard, R. W.: Classical and Novel Discriminant Features for Affect Recognition from Speech, Interspeech 2005 - Eurospeech 9th European Conference on Speech Communication and Technology pp. September 4-8, Lisbon Portugal (2005)
6. Heider, F.: The Psychology of Interpersonal Relations, N.Y.: John Wiley & Sons, (1958)
7. Hodges, C. B.: Designing to Motivate: Motivational Techniques to Incorporate in E-Learning Experiences, The Journal of Interactive Online Learning, Vol. 2, No 3 (2004)
8. Irizarry R.: Self-Efficacy & Motivation Effects on Online Psychology Student Retention. USDLA Journal, Vol. 16, No 12. (2002)
9. Karoly, P.: Mechanisms of self-regulation: a systems view. Annual Review of Psychology, Vol. 44, (1993) 23-52
10. Kapoor, A., Picard, R.W., Ivanov, Y.: Probabilistic Combination of Multiple Modalities to Detect Interest, International Conference on Pattern Recognition, Cambridge, U.K. (2004)
11. Keller, J. M.: Development and use of the ARCS model of instructional design. Journal of Instructional Development, 10(3), (1987), 2-10
12. Qu, L., Wang N., Johnson, W. L.: Detecting the Learner's Motivational States in an Interactive Learning Environment. Artificial Intelligence in Education. C.-K. Looi et al. (Eds.), IOS Press (2005) 547-554
13. Qu, L., Wang N., Johnson, W. L.: Using Learner Focus of attention to Detect Learner Motivation Factors. In Ardissono, L., Brna, P., Mitrovic, A.: User Modelling 2005. Springer-Verlag Berlin Heidelberg (2005) 70-73
14. Schraw, G., Brooks, D. W.: Helping Students Self-Regulate in Math and Sciences Courses: Improving the Will and the Skill (2000) http://dwb.unl.edu/Chau/SR/Self_Reg.html
15. Schunk, D. H., & Zimmerman, B. J.. Self-regulation of learning and performance: Issues and educational applications. Hillsdale, NJ: Lawrence Erlbaum (1994)
16. Tuckman, W. B.: A Tripartite Model of Motivation for Achievement: Attitude/Drive/ Strategy (1999) http://dwb.unl.edu/Chau/CompMod.html
17. Wang, A. Y., Newlin, M. H.: Predictors of web-student performance: The role of self-efficacy and reasons for taking an on-line class. Computers in Human Behavior, 18 (2002)151-163
18. Weiner, B.: Achievement motivation and attribution theory. Morristown, N.Y.: General learning Press (1974)
19. Zhang, G., Cheng, Z., He, A., Huang, T. A WWW-based Learner's Learning Motivation Detecting System. Proceedings of International Workshop on "Research Directions and Challenge Problems in Advanced Information Systems Engineering", Honjo City, Japan, September 16 – 19, 2003, http://www.akita-pu.ac.jp/system/KEST2003/
20. Zimmerman, B. J.: Dimensions of academic self-regulation: A conceptual framework for education. In Schunk, D. H., Zimmerman, B. J. (eds.):Self-regulation of learning and performance: Issues and educational applications. Hillsdale, NJ: Erlbaum (1994) 3-22.

User-System-Experience Model for User Centered Design in Computer Games

Ben Cowley, Darryl Charles, Michaela Black, and Ray Hickey

University of Ulster, Cromore Rd, Coleraine, Northern Ireland
{cowley-b, dk.charles, mm.black, rj.hickey}@ulster.ac.uk

Abstract. This paper details the central ideas to date, from a PhD entitled 'Player Profiling for Adaptive Artificial Intelligence in Computer and Video Games'. Computer and videogames differ from other web and productivity software in that games are much more highly interactive and immersive experiences. Whereas usability and user modelling for other software may be based on productivity alone, games require an additional factor that takes account of the quality of the user experience in playing a game. In order to describe that experience we describe a model of User, System and Experience (USE) in which the primary construct for evaluation of a player's experience will be the Experience Fluctuation Model (EFM), taken from Flow theory. We illustrate with a straightforward example how this system may be automated in real-time within a commercial game.

1 Introduction

The majority of modern commercial video games distinguish between players in a rather shallow manner. For example, it is common practice to offer players a choice of three distinct difficulty levels, through which advancement is pre-set and linear. This practice assumes a player model based on "an ideal user and so some players may feel somewhat discontented when they advance in a manner that is counter to the ideal" [1]. This paper outlines the central ideas from a PhD project that sets out to address this issue. We propose an approach to effectively model the users of commercial computer & video games (hereafter called games) so that a game's play structure may automatically adapt to the preferences and skills of each individual player. The motivation is to improve the experience of mainstream game playing, and to broaden the appeal of games generally since the mainstream gaming audience has a rather narrow demographic.

Variation between players can be seen in Electronic Arts and iHobo audience models of gamer 'clusters' with differing skill levels and lifestyle priorities for games [2]. These levels of game playing ability, combined with personality types, have been refined into player types in models such as Demographic Game Design (DGD) 1 and 2 [2] (based on Temperament Theory and the Myers-Briggs Type Indicator). These refinements illustrate that gamers have differing personality qualities such as attention span, temper, reasoning faculties, spatial skills; and differing attitudes to game hardware such as the mechanistic/anthropomorphic split between hardcore PC gamers and casual gamers. Games too come in different flavours, such as the four game types of

V. Wade, H. Ashman, and B. Smyth (Eds.): AH 2006, LNCS 4018, pp. 419–424, 2006.

Callois – agon (competitive play), alea (games of chance), mimicry (impression of altered identity) and illinx (sensation of vertigo) [3] – for each of which gamers will have differing preferences. This variation seems to be of low priority in the industry. Paradoxically, developers are generally unconcerned with broad accessibility for their games. Accessibility should be designed in from the beginning, as "many of the games which are afforded vast budgets have no potential to tap the higher sales figures" [4] – because they only feature one mode of play (often agon). Most of the all-time top-selling games contain multiple modes of play (i.e. Halo) – achieved with massive budgets and world-class game design. It would be easier implemented with adaptive player modelling.

This project builds on existing User Centered Design (UCD) principles and procedures, as evidenced in such user modelling applications as Intelligent Tutoring Systems. Most other research on User Modelling is focused on productivity software where less import is placed on experiential factors. We propose incorporating the user's play experience in the real-time User Model, to suit game systems. A cornerstone of this approach, and the focus within this paper, is on the use of Experience Fluctuation Model (EFM) [5] and Flow Theory [5] to describe and measure players' (optimal) experience. Flow theory proposes that the key attribute of optimal experience for an individual is a balance between the challenges perceived in the experience, and the skills deployed respectively. It views optimal experience as autotelic and task/goal-oriented, similarly to gaming.

We illustrate a new approach for the automation of Flow measurement in-game, and propose a new experience-description construct – the USE model, shown in Figure 1 and described in Section 2. Section 3 details a method for automating Flow evaluation which is illustrated in Figure 2. Section 4 lays out the plan for future work in the PhD.

2 Adapting the PAT Model for Computer Game Play

In order to conceptualise the major elements of task-oriented computer use, [6] proposed the Person-Artefact-Task (PAT) model. The PAT model provides a framework for the relationships between the constructs used for measuring a person working with an artefact, and their consequent experience. The aim was to create a propositional model to help researchers operationalise Flow in the context of a computer-mediated experience (CME). The study of the interactions between Person, Artefact and Task provides logical propositions describing how a Flow experience is produced.

We contend that PAT was designed to describe production-oriented systems, and falls short when it comes to game systems. As pointed out in [7], research in UCD has mostly focused on productivity software and there is an important difference between usability and playability. When playing a game, experience not production becomes the ultimate point of the task, and must thus be a part of the Task section of the model. Flow also has a dependency relationship with learning, which has a profound effect on gameplay. Therefore Flow cannot be an extrinsic part of the model, nor completely describe the playing experience, as in PAT – it must be intrinsic to the interaction space, with other constructs. To achieve this we propose a new model, the User-System-Experience (USE) model, derived from the PAT model but with an important structural-emphasis shift.

The experience description construct used in PAT, and most other CME research, is Flow. For games also, Flow is the best-fit experiential construct, as we can see remarkable similarity between its attributes and antecedents [5] and those of play [8]. Flow can be viewed as a balance between external complexity and internal information processing, and so we have illustrated roughly how complexity may be related to engagedness [11].

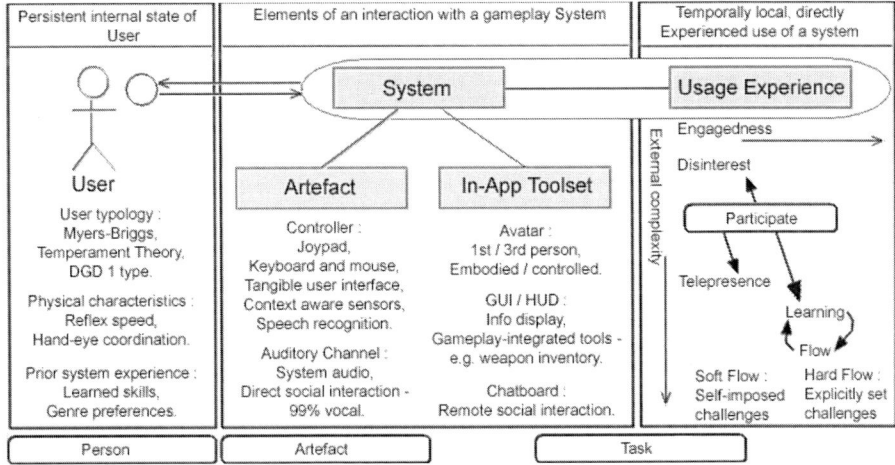

Fig. 1. The USE model for virtual interactive entertainment, e.g. computer gaming

However, not all computer gaming experiences fit the 'challenge vs. skill' model of Flow. For a number of game types, and for other games in limited contexts, a construct designed for more passive experience is necessary – namely, Telepresence [9]. This describes the "experience of presence in an environment by means of a communication" [9], and is defined by the vividness of the experience – i.e. breadth (number of senses involved) and depth (degree of involvement) – and the responsiveness of the system.

Thus these two constructs form the basis for describing experience in the USE model. In any given gaming experience, Flow will occur depending on the user's degree of engagement, and learning potential. The EFM implicitly presupposes learning – viz clear goals and immediate feedback – and a lack of learning will necessarily rule out a Flow type experience. A user who is either totally familiar with, or unable to master, the system will have little or no capacity for learning or Flow – here Telepresence may occur given a sufficiently immersive set of stimuli. If there is neither engagement nor immersion, the game offers no intrinsic reward and will likely be given up. Note that games have a very high dimensionality of interaction. It is no trivial matter to completely learn any game.

Should learning commence, the possibility of a Flow experience is raised, and the user will have an experience corresponding to some part of the EFM. This implies that games are learning-based experiences, and that game software is educational. We see support for this in USE: gameplay depends on both the design of a game and the player's state while playing, just as quality of learning is tied to the experience had while learning. The authors contend that learning is what distinguishes games from productivity software.

Our USE model can be seen as a refinement of the PAT model, describing the relationships between User, System and Experience. The Experience boundary models the causal formation of a user's experience, includes the Flow and Telepresence relationship, and is mediated to the Player via the usage channel of the System boundary, which comprises the hardware and software facilitating gameplay. USE could be used to facilitate the operationalisation of Flow evaluation in a player modelling algorithm.

3   Automating Experience Evaluation Models Such as Flow

The methodology proposed to achieve player modelling includes automating the evaluation of Flow, guided by the EFM, over the course of a gameplay session and ideally with reference to previous Flow experiences via a persistent gamer profile.

It has been proposed [10] that the cognition and emotion of gamers can be mapped from the attributes of the state of Flow, to a corresponding set of attributes of gameplay.

Table 1. List of attributes of Flow and corresponding gameplay attributes

Flow Attributes	Gameplay attributes
A task to be completed	Gaming experience (inc. social interaction)
Perceived Challenges	Mastery and completion of game
Skills w.r.t. challenges	Familiarity with controller, genre & game
Ability to concentrate	Telepresence, isolated environment
Clear goals	Clearly presented contingencies (reward patterns)
Immediate feedback	Well-timed, suitable and desirable rewards
Altered sense of time	Immersion in gameplay

In the scheme proposed, a testbed game would be developed with appropriate adaptive mechanisms for gameplay. Then each of the above elements would be identified in the testbed's gameplay mechanism, assigned a utility metric, and evaluated at some periodicity of game cycles congruent to acceptable computational overhead. Principle to Flow are two elements – challenges and skills. Given their causal relation and temporal synchronicity, reasoning about their operation within a testbed game is simpler than for the other elements above.

Gameplay attributes describing the concepts of challenge and skill would be monitored in the evaluation module – for example, consider the game of Pacman:

- **Challenges**   Avoid ghosts   Eat dots quickly   Tactical use of fruit
- **Skills**   # Lives left   # Dots eaten   Use fruit when threatened

Based on this simple evaluation, the game adaptation engine would have a knowledge base of choices with which to decide its course of action – for instance, if #Lives left is low, increase the averaged Manhattan distance of all ghosts to make

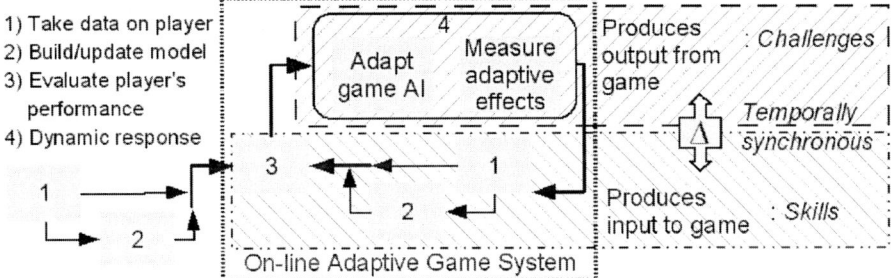

Fig. 2. A schema diagram of the game engine for adaptivity and Flow automation

avoidance easier. Pacman shows capacity for telepresence, but its gameplay is about producing Flow through the perceived-challenge/skilled-response cycle – that is what personalised adaptivity would be used to improve – this game is more about mechanics than aesthetics.

4 Conclusion and Future Work

This PhD aims to model game players in order to improve their playing experience, and it is hoped, broaden the demographic appeal of games. One part of the approach will be to automate the evaluation of a player's experiential state as described by the EFM, a model derived from Flow theory. In this paper we proposed the USE model to format the relationships between user experience measurement constructs, user typologies and gaming preferences, and the system which provides the CME. This model is based on the PAT model, and is intended to facilitate player modelling for mainstream games.

Our short-term goal is to define in detail, and then encode, the schematic relations shown in the USE model using only simple data capture methods – and then test the hypothesis that measuring and adapting to Flow can improve the gameplay experience. Current research suggests that Information Theory could be used to evaluate in-game decision making, within the framework of a formal system describing gameplay. This formal system is currently a type of categorical grammar, but that may change after the first implementation has been evaluated. The initial testbed game will be a version of Pacman, which offers a classic example of the Predator/Prey game, has been used in similar research [12], and is still both familiar to and popular with modern gamers.

References

1. Gilleade K M, Dix A, Using frustration in the design of adaptive videogames. ACE '04, vol. 74. ACM Press, New York, NY, 228-232, 2004.
2. Bateman C M, Boon R, 21st Century Game Design, Charles River Media, 2005.
3. Caillois R, Barash M (translation), Man, Play and Games, London: Thames & Hudson, 1962.

4. Bateman C M, Only A Game weblog, posted 20/01/06, last accessed 05/02/06, http://onlyagame.typepad.com/only_a_game/2006/01/the_imagination.html
5. Csikszentmihalyi M, Flow: The Psychology of Optimal Experience. Harper & Row Publishers Inc., New York, NY, USA, 1990.
6. Finneran C, Zhang P, A Person-Artefact-Task (PAT) Model of Flow Antecedents in Computer-Mediated Environments. Journal of Human Computer Studies, 2003.
7. Charles D, McNeill M, McAlister M, Black M, Moore A, Stringer K, Kucklich J, Kerr A, Player-Centred Game Design: Player Modelling and Adaptive Digital Games, presented at DIGRA 2005, Simon Fraser University, Canada.
8. Huizinga J, Homo Ludens: a Study of the Play Element in Culture, London: Temple Smith, 1970
9. Steuer J, Defining virtual reality: dimensions determining telepresence. 33-56, Communication in the Age of Virtual Reality, Biocca F and Levy M R, Eds., 1995.
10. Sweetser P, Wyeth P, GameFlow: A Model for Evaluating Player Enjoyment in Games, ACM Computers in Entertainment 3 (3), 2005.
11. Rauterburg M, About a framework for information and information processing of learning systems, Proceedings: Conference on Information System Concept, 1995.
12. Yannakakis G, Hallam J, A Scheme for Creating Digital Entertainment with Substance, Workshop on Reasoning, Representation and Learning in Computer Games, IJCAI, Edinburgh, 2005

Adaptive Support for Cross-Language Text Retrieval

Ernesto William De Luca and Andreas Nürnberger

Otto-von-Guericke University of Magdeburg
Universitätsplatz 2, 39106 Magdeburg, Germany
Tel.: +49-391-67-18290; Fax: +49-391-67-12018
deluca@iws.cs.uni-magdeburg.de

Abstract. In this paper we discuss ideas for adaptive support of cross-language text retrieval. In order to enable users to access multilingual information, different problems have to be solved: disambiguating and translating the query words, as well as categorizing and presenting the results appropriately. After giving a brief introduction to cross-language text retrieval, word sense disambiguation and document categorization, actual achievements of the research project are described and future work is discussed. We focus especially on the problem of browsing and navigation of the different word senses in a source and target languages.

1 Introduction

The Internet comprises of mainly English documents, but the amount of documents in other languages grows daily. Therefore, the internet is likely to change very quickly from an English language medium to a multilingual information and communication service. Most people have a good passive understanding of a foreign language, but are not usually in the situation to formulate search queries in this foreign language as good as in their mother tongue. Considering that people want to access multilingual information, the importance of their ability of language understanding increases rapidly. At the moment the support provided to navigate multilingual information is not yet so sophisticated that users can access documents over the internet in the seamless and transparent way as they do in their mother tongue.

In order to enable users to access multilingual information, different problems have to be solved: disambiguating the query words (Section 1.1), translating the query words (Section 1.2), categorizing and presenting the results appropriately (Section 1.3). In the following we briefly discuss these aspects.

1.1 Disambiguating the Query Words

Humans often use polysemous words for searching for documents; a distinction of the related word senses is difficult [9]. A word is polysemous if it has different meanings (polysemy from Greek poly = *many* and semy = *meanings*). When people search for documents related, e.g., to the word *bank*, they will find different documents related to different meanings of this word (bank as a financial institution, bank as a seat, etc...). Humans are able to disambiguate these polysemous words using their knowledge about

V. Wade, H. Ashman, and B. Smyth (Eds.): AH 2006, LNCS 4018, pp. 425–429, 2006.

the related context, but mostly they can do this using their linguistic context knowledge related strictly to the language [9]. Reading the documents retrieved, they can assign the word sense to its linguistic context. In order to identify the meaning of a polysemous word in a Word Sense Disambiguation task, this has to be considered. Working in a multilingual context, words have to be disambiguated both in the native and in other languages (See Section 2.1).

1.2 Translating the Query Words

Retrieving documents in other languages, we have to translate the concepts of the search keywords. Machine translation should help in processing and delivering this information. But as discussed in [10], this approach cannot be viewed as a realistic answer to the problem of query translations right now. The problem of automatically matching documents and queries over languages is not properly solved yet, and therefore it has to be done manually to a great extent. In Section 2 the use of query-related word senses retrieved from the lexical resources and their translation as an alternative solution to this problem is discussed.

1.3 Categorizing and Visualizing the Results

User studies have shown that categorized information can improve the retrieval performance for a user. Thus, interfaces providing category information are more effective than pure list interfaces for presenting and browsing information as shown in [6], where the effectiveness of different interfaces for organizing search results was evaluated. Users were 50% faster in finding information organized into categories. Similar results based on categories used by Yahoo were presented in [8]. Motivated by these evaluations, we developed methods in order to provide additional disambiguating information to the documents of a result set retrieved from a search engine in order to enable categorization, restructuring or filtering of the retrieved document result set. Since we cannot expect a perfect word sense disambiguation or categorization of results, an adaptive and error tolerant visualization is required. Thus, the retrieval of information should be supported by an appropriate interactive visualization of results and categories.

2 Cross-Language Text Retrieval

In general an information retrieval system tries to find and retrieve relevant documents related to a user query, with documents and query being in the same language [1]. Dealing with a multilingual document collection naturally brings up new questions. Being able to read a document in a foreign language does not always imply that a user can formulate appropriate queries in that language as well.

In [10] three main approaches for multilingual information access are described: machine translation, corpus-based and knowledge-based techniques. Since we want to avoid the use of large corpora and translation methods that are not yet providing sufficient quality, our focus is on the use of lexical resources to enable multilingual information access. Thus, we are using so-called knowledge-based approaches. We first try to disambiguate word senses, then retrieve the appropriate translation from the lexical resource and finally categorize documents using the proper word sense. Then we have to visualize the results according to the user needs.

2.1 Word Sense Disambiguation (WSD) and Translation (WST)

For disambiguating word senses a variety of association methods (knowledge-driven, data-driven or corpus-based WSD) can be used [7]. So far, we only used the knowledge-driven WSD approach, i.e. we make use of linguistic information contained in lexical resources [11], like machine readable dictionaries, thesauri or computational lexicons, in order to obtain a linguistic context description of different word senses. Therefore, lexical resources have to be (automatically) explored using the query words, selecting the concepts based on the linguistic relations that define the different word senses and their linguistic context.

In order to use such resources for a multilingual approach we have to retrieve not only the concept (word sense) with its linguistic relations, but also its related translations. EuroWordNet [12] provides such a list of word senses for each word, organized into synonym sets (SynSets), and an Inter-Lingual-index (ILI) is used to access the concepts (SynSets) of a word sense in different languages. However, different problems related to the use of (Euro)WordNet for this purpose have been encountered as discussed in more detail in [2]. One main problem is that the differentiation of word senses is very often too fine grained for typical information retrieval tasks [3]. One way to obtain a higher granularity is to merge SynSets if they describe a very similar meaning of the same word [5]. For web search, such methods could be used for creating a reduced structure of the ontology hierarchy, having fewer word senses that are carrier of a more distinctive meaning, in order to categorize the documents retrieved [2]. We described a first approach to solve this problem in [5].

2.2 Prototypical Implementations

So far, we have developed several tools [3, 4] and evaluated different disambiguation approaches [2, 5]. In the following, we briefly discuss some of the most important aspects. For more details see the referenced publications.

Multilingual exploration of lexical resources

We implemented a user interface with a focus on multilingual explorative search. The interface can help users in discovering languages using lexical resources for disambiguating meanings, combining words and their translation. The translations of all possible source language senses are provided in the target language based on the ILI entries of EuroWordNet (see Section 2.1). In this way we can recognize the word senses of the different word combinations and disambiguate them with the help of the lexical resource.

Categorization of Documents Using the Sense Folder Approach

An approach to classify documents in *Sense Folders*, which are defined based on context descriptions obtained by merging information from word senses (retrieved from WordNet) with associated linguistic relations is proposed in [2]. These context descriptions are used in order to categorize and annotate retrieved documents with their best matching Sense Folder. Every document is first assigned to its most similar Sense Folder and afterwards this classification is revised by a clustering process in order to improve the disambiguation performance [2]. Labels defining the disambiguating classes are then added to each document of the result set. The visualization of such additional information (Fig. 1) should enable a simple navigation through the huge number of documents and, if possible, should restrict information only to the relevant query-related results. More details about this approach can be found in [2, 3] and [4].

Figure 1 shows the implemented categorization techniques combining the knowledge-driven WSD with the knowledge-based text retrieval approach integrated in the developed user interface. The lexical resources are used in order to disambiguate documents (retrieved from the web) given the different meanings (retrieved from lexical resources, in this case EuroWordNet [12]) of a search term having unambiguous description in different languages. These techniques were combined with clustering processes that strongly improved the overall classification performance. While the pure Sense Folder based approach correctly classified 42% of the documents, the clustering process was able to assign approximately 70% of the documents to the correct class [2].

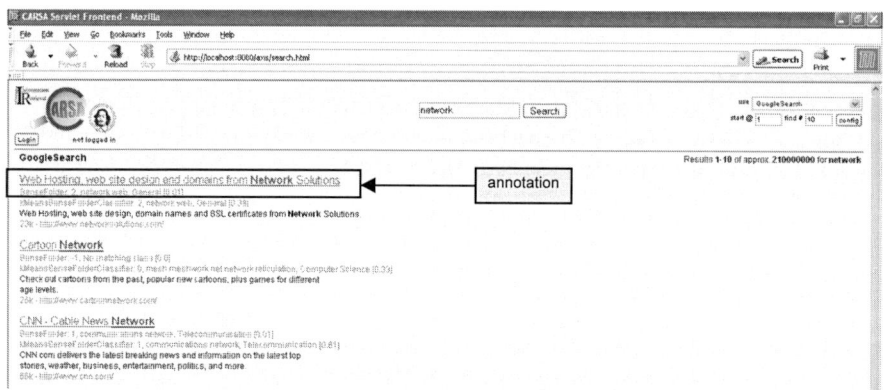

Fig. 1. Desktop User Interface

3   Conclusions and Future Work

The main goal of this work is to develop an adaptive user interface that helps users in the search process considering the languages they can speak and the word senses they want to navigate in order to retrieve the documents they are looking for. The retrieved web documents are automatically categorized using different methods as described above. The results are not yet presented in groups that can be accessed interactively. However, a first approach to visualize the relations of word senses and search results for language exploration has been implemented.

A better integration of all techniques (word sense disambiguation, word sense translation and classification approaches) in an interactive, user and context adaptive retrieval tool is one main goal of future work. At the moment these techniques are separated and should be put together in a combined user interface. Furthermore, the usability of the current user interface should be evaluated in order to better understand the needs of users working in a multilingual environment.

References

1. A. Abdelali, J. Cowie, D. Farwell, B. Ogden and S. Helmreich. Cross-Language Information Retrieval using Ontology In: *Proc. of the Conference TALN 2003*, France, 2003.
2. E. W. De Luca and A. Nürnberger. Improving Ontology-Based Sense Folder Classification of Document Collections with Clustering Methods, In: *Proc. of the 2nd Int. Workshop on Adaptive Multimedia Retrieval (AMR 2004)*, pp 72-86, Valencia 2004.
3. E. W. De Luca and A. Nürnberger. 2005. Supporting Mobile Web Search by Ontology-based Categorization. In: *Proc. of GLDV 2005*, pp. 28-41, Bonn, 2005.
4. E. W. De Luca and A. Nürnberger. A Meta Search Engine for User Adaptive Information Retrieval Interfaces for Desktop and Mobile Devices In: *Proc. of the PIA 2005*, UK, 2005.
5. E. W. De Luca and A. Nürnberger. 2006. The Use of Lexical Resources for Sense Folder Disambiguation. In *Workshop Lexical Semantic Resources (DGfS-06)*, Bielefeld, Germany.
6. S. T. Dumais, E. Cutrell and H. Chen. Bringing order to the web: Optimizing search by showing results in context. In: *Proc. of the CHI'01*, 2001, 277-283.
7. N. Ide and J. Véronis. Word Sense Disambiguation: The State of the Art. In: *Computational Linguistics*, Volume 14, Part 1, 1998.
8. Y. Labrou and T. Finin. Yahoo! as an ontology: using Yahoo! categories to describe documents. In: *Proc. of 8th Int. Conf. on Information and Knowledge Management*, 1999.
9. G. A. Miller. Ambiguous Words. In: *Impacts Magazine*. Publ. on KurzweilAI.net, 2001.
10. C. Peters and P. Sheridan. Multilingual Information Access. In: *Lectures on Information Retrieval, Third European Summer-School*, ESSIR 2000, Varenna, Italy, 2000.
11. W. Peters. Lexical Resources, In: *NLP group Department of Computer Science*, University of Sheffield, http://phobos.cs.unibuc.ro/roric/lex_introduction.html, 2001.
12. P. Vossen. EuroWordNet: a multilingual database for information retrieval. In: *Proceedings of the DELOS workshop on Cross-language Information Retrieval*, Zurich, 1997.

Some Ideas for a Collaborative Search of the Optimal Learning Path*

Sergio Gutiérrez Santos, Abelardo Pardo, and Carlos Delgado Kloos

Department of Telematic Engineering
University Carlos III of Madrid, Spain
{sergut, abel, cdk}@it.uc3m.es
www.it.uc3m.es

Abstract. One of the challenges of adaptive hypermedia educational (AHE) systems is that of adapting the sequencing of learning units presented to the student. One approach is to model the set of possible sequencings with a graph, but the process of designing and maintaining the graph may be tedious and error-prone. This paper presents some ideas to overcome this, inpired by swarm intelligence techniques. Problems that may arise, as well as possible solutions, are presented.

1 Introduction

Web based education is becoming more popular in recent years, as many learning activities are moving to the web. One of the main challenges of web-based systems is their ability to be adaptive, i.e. to adapt to different user requirements. Adaptation is achieved through several means. One of them is sequencing adaptation, that is, to adapt the order in which the learning content units are presented to the student.

A possible approach to the problem is to define a set of sequencings using a graph in which every node is equivalent to a learning unit or to another graph. The traversal of the student through the graph determines the actual sequencing of units for her. This approach for the definition of adapting sequencings has proven to lead to positive results [1], but has some drawbacks as it is explained bellow. A way to extend this idea is proposed in this paper, based on swarm intelligence techniques.

The rest of the paper is organised as follows. Section 5 makes a survey of initiatives related to the work presented here. Sections 2 and 3 explains its theoretical foundations, putting emphasis on the new contributions. An overview of lines for future work and how these ideas will be experimentally tested are presented in Section 4.

2 Definition of Paths

For the definition of the posible sequencings available to the student, we use Sequencing Graphs (SG). Topologically, a SG is a hierarchical directed multigraph [2]. Details specific to SG are depicted in this section.

---

* Work partially funded by Programa Nacional de Tecnologias de la Informacion y de las Comunicaciones, project TIC2002-03635.

V. Wade, H. Ashman, and B. Smyth (Eds.): AH 2006, LNCS 4018, pp. 430–434, 2006.

Nodes of a SG can be associated to actual learning units, or to other sequencing graphs of a lower level of hierarchy. There may be multiple edges from one node to another one. The edges have always one and only one condition associated to them, and there could be a set of actions on each one to modify the student model.

Conditions are boolean conditions connected by negation, conjuction (&) and disjuction (|) operators. These conditions are evaluated against data in the student model. Operators allowed for integer comparison are $=, <, \leq, >, \geq$. Strings (including booleans) can only be checked for equality. Actions may add a new variable to the environment, modify the value of an existing one, or delete it. They can be used to record the history of the student as she traverses the graph.

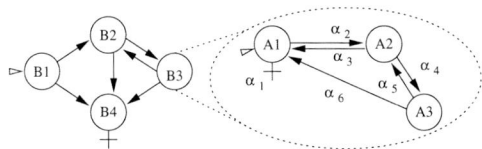

Fig. 1. An example of Sequencing Graph

3   Selection of the Best Paths

Not all possible sequencings are well suited for learning. That's why some of them are permitted and some of them are not. (i.e. it would make no sense to deliver a student the last assesment if she has not been presented the former theory units.) That is why some arcs exist between units and some do not. Moreover, the arcs have conditions to match before the student is allowed to travel from one unit to the next one, and this is how the sequencing is adapted to different students with different capabilities or needs (this brings some similarities with link hidding [3]).

This approach has two weaknesses. First, it relies on some human designer/teacher to design the graphs. While this gives the opportunity of reusing the expertise of a teacher, it makes it harder to maintain the system in the long term. The use of hierarchy mitigates the problem, as some lower-hierarchy graphs can be remade from scratch without affecting the general graph, but it still requires a lot of work to add new learning units to a existing graph.

Additionally, student groups change over time. Different generations have, as a group, different capabilities and needs. It would be desirable that graphs offered the possibility of adapting themselves to different populations of students, and not only adapting the sequencing of learning units to every student according with some rules. As it is pointed out in [4], the set of paths designed at first could not be adequate.

We have tried to overcome these problems with the addition of some stigmergic capabilites to our system. Thus, succesful paths are reinforced in order to guide students through the optimum path for their learning. The mechanism is similar to the one used by ants for reinforcing the paths leading to food sources through the use of pheromones. When a unit is delivered to the student, his sucess or failure is recorded. If there was a success, information is stored about the actual activity and the former one. Thus, the

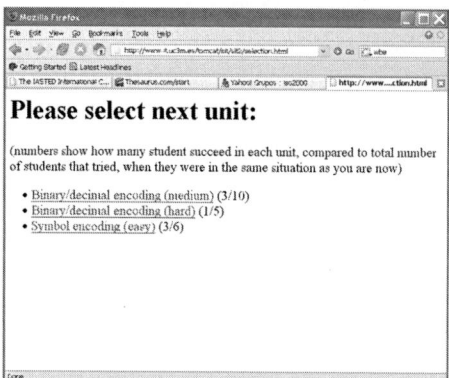

Fig. 2. An example of a selection screen

edges have both a conditions to be met by students and information about how many students were succesful when following it.

This information is presented to the student every time she finishes one unit. All the available units (those at the end of an edge with a fulfilled condition) are presented to her. Each of them has information attached, about how many students have gone to each of them starting from the same unit as the student has just finished. The total number of students that have gone there is also showed. That way, the student has the 'ratio of success' for each unit, according to the data collected from her peers. As it can be seen in Figure 2, the result brings some similarities to a collaborative filtering system [5], but applied to adaptive sequencing.

A student that knows that she is above average compared with her classmates can select to do a unit that has a lower ratio of success but represents a higher challenge. A not-above-average student will be able to select those units in which many of her classmates were succesful. This represents an additional degree of adaptation. Its big advantage is that it is achieved in a distributed and automatic manner, and gives a sensation of freedom and self-control to the students about its own learning, which is very positive.

As more and more students use the system, learning paths appear in the same way as natural paths are created in the wilderness. These learning paths are created with no interference from the human teacher. They are created distributedly and automatically, using indirect communication between classmates. It is an stirmegic process.

4   Future Work and Experimental Tests

As many collaborative filtering systems, the platform proposed in this paper is susceptible to the 'cold-start' problem. In any case, this should not be critical as the system has inherent adaptability capabilities because of the underlying graph (see [1] for results of a similar system with no swarming techniques involved).

There are some issues to be concerned about, though. As with every other stigmergic process, there exists the possibility of local 'not-really-better' optima. This happens when students reinforce some paths in excess, so everybody follows the same paths, even if they are not optimal for them. This could happen as the first steps of aggregation are almost random, but once a path is reinforced the process is positively reinforced and accelerated [6]. A possible way to overcome this problem is the clustering of students, so a student only produces reinforcements on arcs for some of her mates, those that have similar capabilities and needs as her; this has the drawback of making the 'cold-start' problem even worse, as the system evolves more slowly.

This process of "student clustering" can be directed by the student themselves. The system presented in this paper shows only how students have performed so far as a homogeneous group. If the names of students is shown (e.g. "A, B and F suceeded here"), next students have the oportunity of following those students (i.e. classmates) with whom they feel more identified. This approach presents some social concerns (e.g. privacy) that need to be solved.

Another possibility to be studied in the future is that of extending the information stored to more than one step. Thus, students would not be compared with those peers that visited the same node as they are now, but to those that visited the same sequence of nodes up to this point. In a sense, this is similar to what is proposed in [7]. Again, the 'cold-start' could get worse, as more data are needed.

We are preparing some experiments to be conducted on our platform. The students will be able to interact with the tutor for some months. As time progresses, arcs will be reinforced and the students will have more information available to them about the following learning units. We plan to see the influence of differents factors as: presence of the reinforcement information, importance of the reinforcement information (i.e. cold start very notorious or not), influence of first or more capable student on the results of their classmates (presence of leaders [8]), appearance of local optima. Based on the collected data, an improved version of the platform will be developed. Results will be compared to former experiments on which there was no reinforcement of paths, only a graph-defined set of sequencings.

5   Related Work

Some authors have used the Unified Modelling Language (UML) for the definition of adaptive sequencings [9, 10]. The drawback of this approach is that it makes it harder for non-technical course designers to create courses with adaptive sequencings.

Collet et al. use a graph metaphor very similar to the one used in this paper, but the transitions between nodes are decided according to some probabilities associated with the arcs, and there are not any conditions or prerrequisites. This work has been succesfully applied to the Paraschool system [7]. There is another similarity between that work and the one presented here, as Collet uses swarm intelligence techniques to modify the graph. There are two main differences. First, swarm-based adaptation in the Paraschool system is absolutely invisible to the student, as they do not notice how the positive and negative feromones are modifying the probabilities in the arcs of the underlying graph. Second, positive and negative pheromones are used (depending on students actions) and they reinforce several arcs leading to the current node; the nearer ones being reinforced (or penalised) more than the further ones.

Tattersal et al. use a Transition Matrix, in which they record how well the students have interacted with a set of learning units in a Learning Network [11]. There is no graph in this case, as students have to deal with all the units in any order[1]. Depending on how well they perform in each one, the path 'coming' from the former unit is reinforced (e.g. if you solve correctly exercise 3 and formerly you saw the video in activity 5, the index (5,3) in the Transition Matrix in increased). Next activities are decided randomly, but probabilities are weighted according to the indexes in the matrix. This is invisible to students.

Our approach gives the students the opportunity to see what are the 'reinforcements' on each arc. This bears similarities with collaborative-filtering applications. COFIND [5] is such a tool that has been used in web-based education. In that case, students had to select between educational resources giving more weight to the more useful ones. There was no sequencing involved, just a distributed filtering of the most valuable resources (e.g. web pages, multimedia presentacions, etc) from the point of view of the students.

References

1. Gutiérrez, S., Pardo, A., Kloos, C.D.: An adapting tutoring system based on hierarchical graphs. In: Adaptive Hypermedia. Volume 3137 of Lecture Notes in Computer Science., Springer (2004)
2. Gutiérrez, S., Pardo, A., Kloos, C.D.: Finding a learning path: Toward a swarm intelligence approach. In: Web Based Education, Acta Press (2006)
3. Brusilovsky, P.: Methods and techniques for adaptive hypermedia. User Modelling and User Adapted Interaction 6 (1996) 87–129
4. Semet, Y., Yamont, Y., Biojout, R., Luton, E., Collet, P.: Artificial ant colonies and e-learning: An optimisation of pedagogical paths. In: 10th International Conference on Human-Computer Interaction. (2003)
5. Dron, J., Boyne, C., Mitchell, R.: Footpaths in the stuff swamp. In Lawrence-Fowler, W.A., Hasebrook, J., eds.: Proceedings of WebNet 2001 - World Conference on the WWW and Internet, AACE (2001)
6. Bonabeau, E., Dorigo, M., Theraulaz, G.: Swarm Intelligence: From Natural to Artificial Systems. Oxford University Press, Inc., New York, NY, USA (1999)
7. Semet, Y., Lutton, E., Collet, P.: Ant colony optimisation for e-learning: Observing the emergence of pedagogical suggestions. In: IEEE Swarm Intelligence Symposium. (2003)
8. Dron, J.: Achieving self-organisation in network-based learning environments (PhD thesis). Brighton University (2002)
9. Papasalouros, A., Retalis, S., Avgeriou, P., Skordalakis, M.: An integrated model for the authoring of web-based adaptive educational applications. In: AH2003: Workshop on Adaptive Hypermedia and Adaptive Web-Based Systems. (2003)
10. Dolog, P.: Model-driven navigation design for semantic web applications with the uml-guide. Engineering Advanced Web Applications (2004)
11. den Berg, B.V., Es, R.V., Tattersall, C., Janssen, J., Manderveld, J., Brouns, F., Kurvers, H., Koper, R.: Swarm-based sequencing recommendations in e-learning. In: International Workshop on Recommender Agents and Adaptive Web-based Systems. (2005)

---

[1] This could be seen as a perfectly connected graph.

Interception of User's Interests on the Web

Michal Barla[*]

Institute of Informatics and Software Engineering
Faculty of Informatics and Information Technologies
Slovak University of Technology in Bratislava
Ilkovičova 3, 842 16 Bratislava, Slovakia
barla@fiit.stuba.sk

Abstract. Current adaptive systems acquire information about users mainly by simple tracking of resources, a user has requested and by asking users to supply the needed information. In this paper, we discuss user modeling based on observing a user's interaction with the system. We propose to collect usage data on the server side as well as on the client side. Collected data are then processed into knowledge about user's intentions and preferences. This processing relies on a set of heuristics, which help to interpret the usage patterns found in the collected data.

1   Introduction

Adaptivity is becoming ever more important feature of web-based systems. An adaptive system reflects the particular needs of an individual user in a particular context and improves the efficiency of the user – system interaction. It is a response to the permanent information growth on the Internet, where finding the right information becomes difficult and time consuming.

Each adaptive system can only perform personalization if it already has some knowledge about the user. This knowledge is stored in various attributes in the user model. As the user continues to use the system, additional knowledge is acquired and added to the user model resulting in better adaptation. This leads to the cyclic loop "user modeling – adaptation" in an adaptive system, as mentioned in [1].

Our work focuses on the user modeling part of adaptive systems. Many user modeling systems gain information about users by simply asking them, however we chose to focus on an approach based on user observation. This includes the collection of data about user activity and the transformation of this data into knowledge about the user – creating the user model. We identify the main problems in this area and discuss possible solutions. Results of our work, as part of the project [2] are verified in the domain of job offers in a system used for job finding.

The paper is structured as follows. Section 2 discusses the approaches of gathering information about user actions in the information space in a non-intrusive manner. Next, in Section 3, we describe the methods used to transform acquired usage data to the user model. Finally, we draw some conclusions.

---

[*] Supervisor: prof. Mária Bieliková.

V. Wade, H. Ashman, and B. Smyth (Eds.): AH 2006, LNCS 4018, pp. 435–439, 2006.
© Springer-Verlag Berlin Heidelberg 2006

2   Data Collection

There are several ways to acquire information about a user which serve for user model constructing. One is to monitor the user's interaction with the system – logging each user action for further analysis. One main drawback is the unreliability of user characteristics deduced from the acquired information, because there is no explicit relation between user actions and characteristics in the user model. However, this approach has the advantage that the system does not force the user to provide information explicitly, but instead it implicitly gathers the sequence of user actions during a session and interprets the acquired data to make statements about the user.

There are several approaches to user monitoring, which can either be performed on the server side or on the client side of the system. As a third option, one can combine both of these approaches.

Server side monitoring tracks user requests for resources. Its main drawback is that it does not provide precise time-related data, because it relies on the behavior of web browsers, which usually do not re-demand an already visited page from the server, but instead use the copy stored in the local cache. Thus the system does not know the exact time that the user spent viewing a certain page. The current most widespread web browsers do not respect the cache-control directives of the HTTP protocol forbidding the use of the local cache, so they cannot be used to bypass the cache problem. It is also mentioned in [3] that client side monitoring is necessary to get the precise records about a user's interaction with a system. Despite this, server side monitoring is still suitable for many adaptive systems. For example, AHA![1] uses server side logging to track what reading material is presented to the user [4].

Client side monitoring allows for the creation of a detailed log of user actions with exact timestamps. It can be performed by a specific client side application (e.g., User Action Recorder in [5]) or by employing a client web technology like JavaScript or Java applets. Since we consider the first approach as very invasive and not flexible enough, we focus on the second approach. The mentioned web technologies are common in the majority of web browsers on all major platforms. The possible drawbacks are that not every user accepts this kind of detailed monitoring and some of them block the execution of embedded scripts. Furthermore users may not have the necessary software installed on their computers (e.g., Java virtual machine).

Several tools with support for client side logging exist that exploit JavaScript such as WebVip[2] or WET[3]. Both tools are primarily designed for the purpose of web site usability evaluation. These tools are either too focused on the evaluation process or demand the entire copy of the web site for their operation. Therefore, we developed our own client side logging tool based on JavaScript combined with

---

[1] Adative Hypermedia for All, http://aha.win.tue.nl/
[2] Web Variable Instrumenter Program,
   http://zing.ncsl.nist.gov/WebTools/WebVIP/overview.html
[3] Web Event-logging Tool, [6].

the DOM2 event handling and asynchronous server communication using AJAX technology.

To summarize, it is not possible to gather any data if the user is not willing to enable client side user monitoring, which is a strong argument against the sole use of the above mentioned tools. On the other hand, server side monitoring is more reliable since it always acquires some data, but carries the risk of loosing precious time-related information. Our approach is based on the idea of combining the two aforementioned approaches – on the extraction of a maximum amount of data from the server log and on the use of the client log as a source of optional additional, precise information about the user's activity.

3   Data Analysis

After the data collection stage, we are supposed to transform the sequence of user's activities into statements about her cognitive processes. In another words, we have to determine non-behavioral meanings, which are either implied by or associated with the users' behavior [7] (e.g., to find out user goals, estimate user knowledge about certain concepts). The binding between actions and cognitive processes is not deterministic and is never definite. This is why the problem is widely discussed in the user modeling community (e.g., [8, 7]).

Patterns and Heuristics. When interpreting the data we look for interesting usage patterns, which describe the implicit feedback of the user. We analyze the sequences of "clicks" on the web-site and usage of the *back* button in the browser. We use sequential pattern mining algorithms to find such sequences of actions that differ only slightly from the predefined ones. For the initialization of the system, we plan to define patterns related to the user's goal and evaluate these patterns as the system will be used by real users.

We assign higher weights to the "first click" of the found sequence, as it usually has stronger relation to the user's intentions than the rest of the sequence. Successively we identify the appropriate usage pattern and use heuristics to infer user characteristics (see fig. 1).

An example of a simple heuristic in the domain of job offers is: "If a user chose to view at least "sufficient number" of offers from sector A (e.g., health-care or IT), raise the relevance level of this sector in the model of the user's ideal job offer".

During the analysis stage we also consider the navigation model of the system, which actually determines the possible sequences of user actions and thus makes all heuristics system-specific. Educational systems with sequential structure of pages forming an e-course, would have different usage patterns compared to a job offer portal, whose content is not sequential. The system must support easy navigation and searching in the information content, what results in a hierarchically organized navigation structure of the portal.

Relations between concepts. User actions in the context of adaptive web-based systems can be regarded as navigation between concepts. Our idea is that by

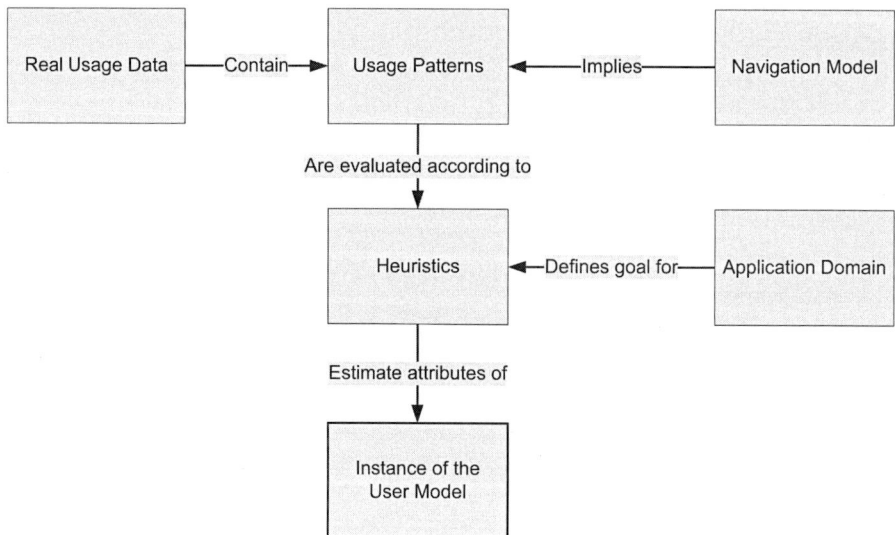

Fig. 1. Sources for creating an instance of the user model. We search for interesting *Usage Patterns* in the *Usage Data*. These patterns are determined by the *Navigation Model*. Knowing the related *Heuristics*, we can evaluate the located *Usage Patterns* to estimate attributes of an *Instance of the User Model*. *Heuristics* are bound to the goals of the user, determined by the *Application Domain*.

comparing the visited concepts and finding out their common and different aspects, we may gain knowledge about reasons (user preferences), why a user reacted differently to each of them. This comparison can either point out the values of different attributes of two concepts or compute their distance.

The distance represents the measure of dissimilarity of two concepts. For instance, C# is different from JAVA but it is definitely closer – less different to JAVA than to Lisp. A heuristic, which use the differences of two concepts must consider the distance of these concepts and its impact on the user model.

Afterward, it is possible to estimate user characteristics from the different or similar user actions related to the compared concepts. For instance, if the user "refuses" one offer but "accepts" another and these offers are quite close to each other, with their main difference being in the duty location, we can surmise that the user prefers the region from the second offer.

4   Conclusion

We described our research in the field of user modeling that is focused on user modeling based on user observation, which comprises the collection of information about the user activities within an information system and the successive analysis of the acqired information to create a user model.

We have identified several ways of user activity data acquisition, where client side monitoring appears to be the most efficient based on the richness of data, but also has a serious drawback in the unreliability of execution. Therefore, we use a combination of client and server side monitoring to achieve good results.

Analysis of the acquired data transforms the acquired user behavior into the knowledge about user characteristics or about user goals. We identified aspects, which influence the creation of heuristics that estimate some user characteristics from the recorded usage patterns.

Future work includes the design and verification of a method for the creation of an instance of the user model based on analysis of server and client side logs. This method would map the preferences of a user to a particular sequence of actions, use the comparison of the visited concepts to reveal user preferences and semi-automatically fill the user model with relevant data. To verify our design, we evaluate it with the user model used in the project [2] for adaptation in the domain of job offers.

Acknowledgments

This work was partially supported by the Science and Technology Assistance Agency under the contract No. APVT-20-007104 and the State programme of research and development "Establishing of Information Society" under the contract No. 1025/04.

References

1. Brusilovsky, P.: Methods and techniques of adaptive hypermedia. User Modeling and User-Adapted Interaction 6(2-3) (1996) 87–129
2. Návrat, P., Bieliková, M., Rozinajová, V.: Methods and tools for acquiring and presenting information and knowledge in the web. In: International Conference on Computer Systems and Technologies – CompSysTech' 2005, Varna, Bulgaria (2005)
3. Paganelli, L., Paterno, F.: Intelligent analysis of user interactions with web applications. In: IUI '02: Proceedings of the 7th international conference on Intelligent user interfaces, New York, NY, USA, ACM Press (2002) 111–118
4. Bra, P.D., Calvi, L.: AHA: a generic adaptive hypermedia system. In: 2nd Workshop on Adaptive Hypertext and Hypermedia. (1998) 5–12
5. Thomas, R., et al.: Generic usage monitoring of programming students. In Crisp, G., Thiele, D., Scholten, I., Barker, S., Baron, J., eds.: 20th Annual Conference of the Australasian Society for Computers in Learning in Tertiary Education (ASCILITE). (2003)
6. Etgen, M., Cantor, J.: What does getting wet (web event-logging tool) mean for web usability? (In: 5th Conference on Human Factors & The Web)
7. Judd, T., Kennedy, G.: Making sense of audit trail data. Australasian Journal of Educational Technology 20(1) (2004) 18–32
8. Kay, J., Lum, A.: Creating user models from web logs. In: Intelligent User Interfaces Workshop: Behavior-Based User Interface Customization. (2004)

Intervention Strategies to Increase Self-efficacy and Self-regulation in Adaptive On-Line Learning

Teresa Hurley

National College of Ireland, Mayor Street, Dublin 1, Ireland
teresa.hurley@gmail.com

Abstract. This research outline refers to the validation of interventional strategies to increase the learner's motivation and self-efficacy in an on-line learning environment. Previous work in this area is mainly based on Keller's ARCS model of instructional design and this study argues for an approach based on Bandura's Social Cognitive Theory – especially the aspects of self-efficacy and self-regulation. The research plan envisages two phases: The first phase will extract rules for interventional strategy selection from expert teachers. The second phase aims to validate these rules by providing to the learner the selected strategy and observing the resulting behavior.

1 Self-efficacy in Adaptive On-Line Learning

On-line education is one of the most dynamic and potentially enriching forms of learning that exists today. However, attrition rates for on-line learning courses, which tend to be 40% to 50% higher than traditional classroom courses (Dille & Metzack, 1991) is a serious problem resulting in personal, occupational and financial implications for both students and academic institutions. Motivation to learn is affected by a student's self-efficacy, goal orientation, locus of control and self-regulation. In a traditional classroom tutors can infer the level of motivation of a student from several cues, including speech, behavior, attendance, body language, or feedback and can offer interventional strategies aimed at increasing self-efficacy and self-regulation. Intelligent Tutoring Systems (ITS) need to be able to recognize when the learner is becoming demotivated and to intervene with effective motivational strategies. Such an ITS would comprise two main components, an assessment mechanism that infers the learners' level of motivation from observing the learning behavior and an adaptation component that selects the most appropriate intervention strategy. This study aims to inform the development of the adaptation component by extracting and validating selection rules for motivational intervention strategies to increase learners' self-efficacy.

2 Background

2.1 Learner Modeling

Studies on the assessment of motivation in on-line learning to date include Del Soldato, 1994, de Vicente & Pain, 2002; 2003; Qu, Wang & Johnson, 2005; and

V. Wade, H. Ashman, and B. Smyth (Eds.): AH 2006, LNCS 4018, pp. 440–444, 2006.
© Springer-Verlag Berlin Heidelberg 2006

Zhang, Cheng & He, 2003. These studies primarily focus on similar motivational states, mainly derived from the ARCS model (Keller, 1987a, 1987b), such as *attention, relevance, confidence*, and *satisfaction*. These states are inferred from behavioral cues in the interaction such as *time taken, effort, confidence,* and *focus of attention*. However, the theoretical basis for these models seems to be weak. We argue that a model of motivational states of learners should build upon a well established theory of motivation in learning. Accordingly, we propose a model that is based on Social Cognitive Theory (Bandura, 1986) and in particular the constructs of self-efficacy, goal orientation, locus of control and self-regulation. As learners differ widely in these constructs, intervention strategies must be adapted to suit the individual and the task. Such interventions may take the form of verbal persuasion, vicarious experience, mastery experience or scaffolding.

2.2 Motivation

Motivation in general is defined as "the magnitude and direction of behavior and the choices people make as to what experiences or goals they will approach or avoid and to the degree of effort they will exert in that respect" (Keller, 1993). Pintrich and De Groot (1990) report that students with higher levels of intrinsic motivation and self-efficacy achieve better learning outcomes. Malone (1981) states that intrinsic motivation is created by three qualities: challenge, fantasy and curiosity.

Social cognitive theory provides a framework for understanding, predicting, and changing human behavior. The theory identifies human behavior as an interaction of personal factors, behavior, and the environment.

Self-efficacy. Bandura (1986) described self-efficacy as "individuals' confidence in their ability to control their thoughts, feelings, and actions, and therefore influence an outcome". Individuals acquire information to help them assess self-efficacy from (a) actual experiences, where the individual's own performance, especially past successes and failures, are the most reliable indicator of efficacy; (b) vicarious experiences, where observation of others performing a task conveys to the observer that they too are capable of accomplishing that task; (c) verbal persuasion, where individuals are encouraged to believe that they possess the capabilities to perform a task; and (d) physiological indicators, where individuals may interpret bodily symptoms such as increased heart rate or sweating as anxiety or fear indicating a lack of skill. Perceptions of self-efficacy influence actual performance (Locke, Frederick, Lee, & Bobko, 1984), and the amount of effort and perseverance expended on an activity (Brown & Inouye, 1978).

Attribution Theory. Attribution Theory (Heider, 1958; Weiner, 1974) has been used to explain the difference in motivation between high and low achievers. Weiner identified ability, effort, task difficulty, and luck as the most important factors affecting attributions for achievement. High achievers approach rather than avoid tasks relating to achievement as they believe success is due to ability and effort. Failure is attributed to external causes   such as bad luck or a poor exam. Thus, failure does not affect self-esteem but success builds pride and confidence. Low achievers avoid success-related tasks because they doubt their ability and believe success is due to luck or other factors beyond their control. Success is not rewarding to a low achiever because he/she does not feel responsible, i.e. it does not increase his/her pride or confidence.

Locus of Control. Locus of control (Rotter, 1966) is a relatively stable trait and is a belief about the extent to which behaviors influence successes or failures. Individuals with an internal locus of control believe that success or failure is due to their own efforts or abilities. Individuals with an external locus of control believe that factors such as luck, task difficulty, or other people's actions, cause success or failure.

Goal Orientation. One classification of motivation differentiates among achievement, power, and social factors (McClelland, 1985). Individuals with a learning goal orientation (mastery goals) strive to master a particular task regardless of how many mistakes they make. Their primary goal is to obtain knowledge and improve skills. Individuals orientated towards performance goals are concerned with positive evaluations of their abilities in comparison to others and focus on how they are judged by parents, teachers or peers. It is possible for students to have learning and performance goals at the same time.

Self-Regulation. Self-regulation refers to students' ability to understand and control their learning by employing cognitive strategies that assist in construction of meaning and retention of information and by using metacognitive strategies such as planning and monitoring to control their progress (Zimmerman, 1994).

3   Research Question and Study Design

This study aims to inform the development of the intervention component of an adaptive educational system. An assessment component that creates an accurate model of the motivational states of the learner is currently being developed in a related project being carried out by a fellow researcher and it is planned to use this assessment component in the validation stage of this study.   The fact that this automatic assessment component has not yet been developed is currently a limitation for us. However, the intervention strategies will remain valid and can be incorporated as soon as the assessment component becomes available. In the meantime, a learner model will be created manually. With this model we propose to extract expert views on selection rules for intervention strategies that increase learners' self-efficacy and self-regulation and these rules will be validated in a subsequent phase.

The research will have two separate phases: The first phase will extract rules for strategy selection from experts. The second phase aims to validate these rules.

A learner model has been developed based on the Social Cognitive Theory constructs of self-efficacy, goal orientation, locus of control, and self-regulation. The learner model contains twenty-three learner personas which have been systematically developed using the above constructs. In order to identify rules to determine which interventional strategy - verbal persuasion, vicarious experience, mastery experience or scaffolding - is the most appropriate for each learner's persona when low motivation is observed from the behavior of the learner, the assistance of expert teachers will be sought. If, for example, a learner with low self-efficacy ("I believe I cannot pass this quiz") and external locus of control ("The quiz items are too hard") is involved, teachers might indicate that verbal persuasion ("This quiz is similar to the one that you just passed. Most students that passed the first quiz also passed the second.") would be the strategy to adopt. In this way, a set of rules could be extracted.

Second, these expert rules need to be validated in a real learning environment to see if the intervention strategies adopted actually increase the self-efficacy of the learner. This will take the form of a Wizard of Oz study where an intervention based on the extracted rules will be applied to a learner who has become demotivated. A human tutor will observe the learning behavior of students in an online course. Demotivated students will receive an intervention in accordance with the expert rules. The outcome will be assessed based on a subjective report from the learner (e.g., motivation and satisfaction) and on an observation of the learner's behavior and progress.

In conclusion, this study offers a way to elicit and validate explicit rules from experts on intervention strategies to increase self-efficacy and self-regulation. These rules will then be used by an Intelligent Tutoring System to select the most appropriate intervention strategy for a demotivated learner and the results will be monitored.

4 Summary

Social Cognitive Theory offers a theoretical framework for a deep knowledge of a learner's motivation by utilising the concepts of self-efficacy, goal orientation, locus of control and self-regulation as a base for interventional strategies to increase the level of the level of the learner's motivation.

This research outline has been defined as the first step of a two-year project. A literature review has been conducted. The learner model is currently being developed which will be used to extract the rules and to validate the interventional strategies. Future work includes conducting the studies, analysing the data and drawing conclusions. It is anticipated that the first results will be available for presentation at the conference in June 2006.

References

1. Bandura, A.: *Social foundations of thought and action: A social cognitive theory.* Englewood Cliffs, NJ: Prentice-Hall (1986).
2. Brown, I. Jr., & Inouye, D. K.: Learned helplessness through modeling: The role of perceived similarity in competence. *Journal of Personality and Social Psychology* (1978) *36*, 900-908.
3. De Vicente, A., Pain, H.: Informing the Detection of the Students' Motivational State: an empirical study. In Cerri et al. (2002) 933-943.
4. De Vicente, A., Pain, H.: Validating the Detection of a student's Motivational State. In A. Mendez Vilas, J. A. Mesa Gonzalez, J. Mesa Gonzalez, editors, *Proceedings of the Second International Conference on Multimedia Information & Communication Technologies in Education (m-ICTE2003)*, number 15 of *"Sociedad de la Informacion" Series*, Volume III, (2003) 2004-2008, Merida, Junta de Extremadura (Consejeria de Educacion, Ciencia y Tecnologia).

5. del Soldato, T.: *Motivation in Tutoring Systems*. PhD thesis, School of Cognitive and Computing Sciences, The University of Sussex, UK, 1994. Available as Technical Report CSRP 303

6. Dille, B., & Mezack, M.: Identifying predictors of high risk among community college telecourse students. *The American Journal of Distance Education,* (1991) *5(1)*, 24-35.

7. Heider, F. *The Psychology of Interpersonal Relations.* New York: Wiley. (1958).

8. Keller, J.M.: Strategies for stimulating the motivation to learn. *Performance and Instruction, 1987a,* 26 (8), 1 – 7.

9. Keller, J.M.: The Systematic Process of Motivational Design. *Performance and Instruction, 1987b,* 26 (9), 1 – 8.

10. Keller, J.M.: Motivational design of instruction. In C.M. Reigeluth (Ed.) *Instructional design theories and models: An overview of their current status.* Hillsdale, NJ: Erlbaum (1993).

11. Locke, E. A., Frederick, E., Lee, C., & Bobko, P.: Effect of self-efficacy, goals, and task strategies on task performance. *Journal of Applied Psychology,* (1984) *69*, 241-251.

12. Malone, T.: Towards a theory of instrinsically motivating instruction. Cognitive Science, 4, 333-369. (1981).

13. McClelland, D.: *Human motivation.* New York: Scott, Foresman. (1985).

14. Pintrich, P.R., & De Groot, E.V.: Motivational and self-regulated learning components of classroom academic performance. *Journal of Educational Psychology,* (1990) 82(1), 33-40.

15. Qu, L., Wang N., & Johnson, W. L.: Detecting the Learner's Motivational States in an Interactive Learning Environment. Artificial Intelligence in Education. C.-K. Looi et al. (Eds.), IOS Press (2005) 547-554.

16. Rotter, J. B.: Generalized expectancies for internal versus external control of reinforcement. *Psychological Monographs* (1966) *80*(Whole No. 609).

17. Weiner, B. (1974). *Achievement motivation and attribution theory.* Morristown, N.J.: General Learning Press.

18. Zhang, G., Cheng, Z., He, A., & Huang, T.: A WWW-based Learner's Learning Motivation Detecting System. Proceedings of International Workshop on "Research Directions and Challenge Problems in Advanced Information Systems Engineering", Honjo City, Japan, September 16–19, 2003, http://www.akita-pu.ac.jp/system/KEST2003/

19. Zimmerman, B. J.: Dimensions of academic self-regulation. In D. H. Schunk & B. J. Zimmerman (Eds.), *Self-regulation of learning and performance: Issues and educational applications* (pp. 3-21). Hillsdale, NJ: Lawrence Erlbaum (1994).

Dynamic Content Discovery, Harvesting and Delivery, from Open Corpus Sources, for Adaptive Systems

Séamus Lawless and Vincent Wade

Knowledge and Data Engineering Group
Trinity College, Dublin, Ireland
{slawless, Vincent.Wade}@cs.tcd.ie
http://www.cs.tcd.ie/~slawless

Abstract. Personalised elearning is being heralded as one of the grand challenges of next generation learning systems, in particular, its ability to support greater effectiveness, efficiency and student empowerment. However, a key problem with such systems is their reliance on bespoke content developed for, and only used by, these systems. The challenge for adaptive systems in scalably supporting personalised elearning is its ability to source, harvest and deliver open corpus content to adaptive content services and personalised elearning systems. This paper examines the issues involved in implementing such an adaptive content service. The paper seeks to explore the accurate extraction of content requirements from the adaptive system, the sourcing and identification of suitable learning content, the harvesting and customisation of the content for delivery to adaptive elearning systems.

1 Motivation

eLearning environments are attempting to respond to the demand for personalised on-demand distance/on-line learning by providing increasing support for such functionality as personalisation, adaptivity and on-demand learning object generation [1]. Adaptive Hypermedia is seen as one of the key areas of delivering personalised "just-for-you" eLearning. The benefit of such learning is that it can be dynamically tailored to the individual's experience, goals, preferences etc. This empowers the learner as the learning experience and activities are more suited to that individual.

One of the most significant problems with personalised eLearning systems (PeLS) is that they are traditionally restricted to using bespoke proprietary content. This is particularly the case with Intelligent Tutoring Systems (ITS) where, in fact, the personalisation is embedded in the content itself [2]. However in the second generation of adaptive systems the sequencing for adaptivity has been separated from the physical content. This provides the opportunity whereby content can be selected, to create a learning offering, in a sequence that suits each individual learner. This would allow the developers of online learning offerings to concentrate on the pedagogical design of such offerings, rather than on content development. However, in such systems (Knowledge Tree, Aha!, APeLS) the content is, in most cases, still sourced from a private repository of learning resources. This paper discusses ongoing

V. Wade, H. Ashman, and B. Smyth (Eds.): AH 2006, LNCS 4018, pp. 445–451, 2006.

research into the provision of dynamic adaptivity using open corpus content rather than content uniquely created for each system involved.

The paper begins with a brief introduction into the state of the art in Adaptive Hypermedia Systems (AHS), how they currently source and utilize learning content, and how this has evolved over the generations of AHS. The paper proceeds by identifying the key issues and challenges in the discovery, harvesting, and delivery of open corpus content for AHS. The paper concludes by presenting a proposed system architecture of an open corpus content service, in its initial stages. The areas where, and methods by which, key challenges will be addressed are detailed.

2   State of the Art

The first generation AHS were stand alone systems with knowledge rules and content entwined in a single model. The AHS reconciled this model with a user model to produce personalised content. Two of the most successful systems that emerged from this generation were AHA! [3] and ELM-ART [4]. However as personalisation rules and content were intertwined, there was little scope for content reuse or the use of externally developed content.

The second generation of AHS attempted to alleviate some of the difficulties encountered in the first generation by implementing a multi-model approach. This approach created a distinct separation of content from the personalisation rules of the system [5]. In these systems the adaptive tool is more generic and relies upon separate knowledge models to adapt the system for each individual. The user-model is used to represent attributes such as Prior Knowledge, User Preferences, Cognitive and Learning Style, Aims and Goals etc. Successful second generation AHS include APeLS [6], KnowledgeTree [7], various prototype systems based on the AHA! architecture and KBS-Hyperbook [8].

The current, or third, generation of AHS is moving toward a service-oriented architecture. The systems are attempting to support adaptive personalisation through the use of individual services for the sourcing of learning content, the personalisation of learning offerings, and the presentation of such offerings. One of the main challenges in scalably supporting personalised elearning for this generation of AHS, is its ability to source and harvest open corpus content and make it available to adaptive content services and thus to PeLS.

3   Challenges and Direction

The fact that AHS, ITS and PeLS have traditionally been reliant on bespoke proprietary content has severely restricted the ability of these systems to reuse content or to use externally developed content. The move in second generation AHS to make content and knowledge sources discreet has provided an opportunity whereby content developed externally to an AHS can be used in the creation of personalised learning offerings. By implementing a content service whereby open corpus content may be used to supply suitable learning content to AHS, a situation is created where such systems can improve their ability to reuse content and improve the quantity and variety of content available to the user. There are several key issues and challenges involved in the creation of such a content service, which will be detailed in this section.

- The provision of accurate content requirements by the AHS and the structuring of these requirements into queries that can be used to source relevant learning content.
- The performance of the AHS must not be detrimentally affected by the use of a content service rather than using bespoke proprietary content.
- Content Metadata - Interoperability between metadata standards, the vocabulary used in metadata descriptions and the generation of metadata descriptions for open corpus content.
- Once content has been sourced and harvested, the manner and format in which it is delivered to the AHS from the content service needs to be addressed.

Issues such as digital rights management, intellectual property, security and ensuring the conceptual and aesthetic flow of learning offerings will also arise when utilising open corpus content. However, it is felt that these issues are out of the scope of this current research and as such will not be addressed by this work.

Requirements for desired content must be specified by the sourcing AHS. A course developer's knowledge can be leveraged through their personalised elearning designs. The ontological knowledge representation of the subject matter area provides information on the learning concepts involved, the relationships of those concepts, such as prerequisites, and the semantic granularity of those concepts. When personalisation information is incorporated into learning designs it provides information on pedagogy, context and subject matter area.

The technical requirements found in elearning designs relate to the syntactic layers of learning content, namely the representation layer and the description layer. Requirements from the representation layer relate to the metadata standard implemented and in the case of some open corpus content, the absence of metadata information. Requirements relating to the description layer include the vocabulary and taxonomies used to describe the learning content, also the format of the metadata information. Granularity is an issue that affects both the semantic and syntactic layers of learning content. The granularity of learning content refers to its size, conceptually and technically, its aggregation and its ability to be reused and repurposed [12].

These requirements, both semantic and syntactic, can be extracted from the AHS learning designs without manual intervention from the author and passed to the content service for incorporation into queries that are used to source suitable content. By satisfying requirements that are both semantic and syntactic in nature, more accurate identification of suitable content is achieved. [13]

To support Dynamic Contextual eLearning, content requirements from the AHS will need to be satisfied at run-time during the personalisation of an elearning offering. This leads to concerns over system performance. The time taken to source and deliver suitable content for incorporation into the elearning offering must not unduly inhibit the performance of the AHS. If the performance of the system is slow or tedious, student empowerment will be sacrificed. To combat this and unsure suitably expedite content search queries, a metadata cache will be generated.

A web crawler will be instantiated that will create and continually maintain a cache of metadata pertaining to the learning content that is sourced. An entry will be made for all sourced learning content. When a query is executed, the search will be performed against this metadata cache to source suitable candidate content. Once found, the true location of the content can be extracted from the metadata information and the content can be harvested for customisation before being delivered to the AHS for incorporation into the learning offering in question.

The ability of AHS to use open corpus content and the reusability of content in AHS is restricted by the fact that not all systems employ the same metadata standards. Not all metadata standards are interoperable and thus some systems may be unable to accurately decipher or comprehend content that uses conflicting metadata standards. Mappings to a canonical metadata model will need to be implemented. This involves customising the existing metadata before entry into the cache so that all metadata descriptions are structured in a standard fashion. This ensures that when searching for content the correct metadata tags are referenced for requirements matching.

The lack of a standard vocabulary in describing content also makes semantic matching of searches to relevant content a difficult task. Such an interoperability issue not only effects the sourcing of content but also the re-use of any learning objects generated by the service. It will be necessary to map to a fixed ontology of terms during the customisation of the metadata. This will ensure consistency of content metadata descriptions and increase the semantic accuracy of searches.

No assumptions can be made regarding metadata descriptions of content sourced on the WWW. The content may have insufficient metadata descriptions or have no associated metadata information. This impedes the ability of AHS to comprehend and categorize sourced content. When learning content is discovered and lacks sufficient metadata information, a metadata description of the content will need to be generated before the learning content can be classified and added to a cache of candidate content. Thoroughness and consistency in this metadata generation is essential to ensure accurate searching and retrieval of content. Metasaur [9], Semtag [10] and IBM's LanguageWare [11] are all tools that are attempting to resolve this problem using various methods of lexical analysis and metadata tag generation.

When suitable content has been retrieved it needs to be delivered to the AHS in a format that can be used during the generation of a personalised eLearning offering. To enable this, the content needs to be structured into a learning object. The generation of learning objects and their structuring is deemed to be outside the scope of this research, however there are research projects focused on addressing such issues. For example, the iClass project suggested the development of a component called the Learning Object Generator [14]. The open corpus content service could provide appropriately grained and suitably tagged content to such a learning object generation environment which could then deliver the learning object back to the AHS.

4   Proposed Architecture

It is proposed to provide an open corpus content facility as a stand-alone service that can replace the current method of content sourcing in the architecture of AHS. The system that will be used for the purposes of this research will be APeLS [6], which is an adaptive system developed by KDEG, Trinity College Dublin.

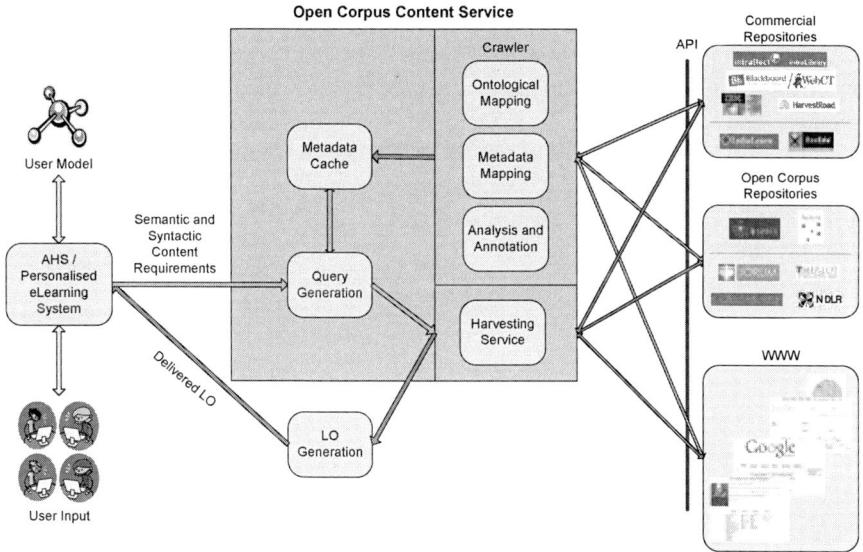

Fig. 1. Proposed Architecture of Open Corpus Content Service

Content identification will be the first issue that the system must address. A web crawler will be implemented to traverse selected digital repositories and the WWW. As content is sourced, a metadata cache will be created, updated and maintained. Mappings to a canonical metadata model will be implemented using a fixed ontology of terms to create the metadata descriptions used in the cache. These mappings are required to ensure both accuracy and consistency in content description and the results of searches performed on the cache. In cases where metadata descriptions are insufficient or do not exist, automatic/semi-automatic analysis of the content and generation of metadata descriptions will need to take place, before an entry can be made in the candidate content cache. An analysis of the tools available to perform this tag generation will take place before that methodology of automatic analysis and tagging is adopted by the system.

Semantic and Syntactic content requirements will be extracted from course learning designs contained within APeLS, which have been created by a course developer. An interface will be provided whereby the learning design can be analysed, and the necessary information regarding the nature of the content required, both technical and semantic, can be extracted without manual intervention by the user. These requirements are then customised by the open corpus content service, and restructured into a search query. This search query is then used to identify suitable learning content in the metadata cache of candidate learning content.

Once suitable content has been identified, the physical location of the content, be it in a digital repository or on the WWW, is extracted from the metadata information and the actual content is harvested. The content is then passed to either an LO Generation service or to the adaptive system itself, depending on how the delivered content needs to be structured for incorporation into the learning offering. If passed to an LO Generation Service it will be structured and sequenced into a learning object. This learning object is then passed back to the AHS. However if the content is passed directly back to the AHS, then that system will be responsible for ensuring that conceptual and aesthetic flow is maintained. Once the content is delivered to the AHS, the course developer will assess its suitability for the learning offering. If the course developer is not satisfied, the content requirements can be manually refined and the search query regenerated to improve the suitability of the content returned. When the content developer is satisfied with the content retrieved, it can then be integrated into the adaptive learning offering for which it was sourced.

References

[1] Brusilovsky, P. Adaptive Hypermedia. In: User Modelling and User-Adapted Interaction, Springer, March 2001, 87-110.
[2] Urban-Lurain, M. Intelligent Tutoring Systems: An Historic Review in the Context of the Development of Artificial Intelligence and Educational Psychology. In: Technical Report, Department of Computer Science and Engineering, Michigan State University, 1996.
[3] De Bra, P., Calvi, L. AHA: A Generic Adaptive Hypermedia System. In: Proceedings of the 2nd Workshop on Adaptive Hypertext and Hypermedia, Pittsburgh, 1998, 5-12.
[4] Brusilovsky, P., Schwarz, E., Weber, G., (1996). ELM-ART: An Intelligent Tutoring System on the World Wide Web. In: Proceedings of Third International Conference on Intelligent Tutoring Systems, ITS-96, Montreal, June 12-14 1996. Berlin: Springer Verlag, 261-269.
[5] Duval, E., Hodgins, W., Rehak, D., Robson, R. Learning Objects 2003 Symposium: Lessons Learned, Questions Asked. In: Proceedings, Learning Objects 2003 Symposium, Honolulu, HI, Association for the Advancement of Computing in Education, ISBN: 380094-49-5, June, 2003.
[6] Conlan, O., Wade, V. Evaluation of APeLS - An Adaptive eLearning Service based on the Multi-model, Metadata-driven Approach. In: Proceedings of 3rd Int. Conference on Adaptive Hypermedia & Adaptive Web-Based Systems AH2004, Eindhoven, The Netherlands, August 23-26 2004, 291-296.
[7] Brusilovsky, P. KnowledgeTree: A Distributed Architecture for Adaptive E-Learning. In: Proceedings of the 13th International World Wide Web Conference, WWW 2004, New York, NY, 17-22 May, 2004, ACM Press, 104-113.
[8] Henze, N., Nejdl, W. Extendible adaptive hypermedia courseware: Integrating different courses and Web material In: Proceedings of Adaptive Hypermedia and Adaptive Web-based Systems, AH2000, Trento, Italy, August 28-30 2000, 109-120.
[9] University of Sydney's Metasaur Project. Demonstration available online at www.it.usyd.edu.au/~alum/demos/metasaur_hci/
[10] Dill, S., Eiron, N., Gibson, D., Gruhl, D., Guha, R., Jhingran, A., Kanungo, T., Rajagopalan, S., Tomkins, A., Tomlin, J., Zien, J. SemTag and Seeker: Bootstrapping the semantic web via automated semantic annotation. In: 12th International Conference on World Wide Web, Budapest, Hungary, 2003, 178-186.
[11] IBM LanguageWare Linguistic Platform. http://www-306.ibm.com/software/globalization/topics/languageware/index.jsp

[12] Dagger, D., Conlan, O., Wade, V. Fundamental Requirements of Personalised eLearning Development Environments. In: Proceedings of World Conference on E-Learning in Corporate, Government, Healthcare, and Higher Education, Vancouver, CA, 2005 E-Learn 2005, 2746-2754

[13] Kobayashi, M., Takeda, K. Information Retrieval on the Web. In: ACM Computing Surveys (CSUR), v.32 n.2, 144-173, 2000.

[14] Brady, A., Conlan, O., Wade, V. Towards the Dynamic Personalized Selection and Creation of Learning Objects. In: Proceedings of World Conference on E-Learning in Corporate, Government, Healthcare, and Higher Education, Vancouver, CA, 2005 E-Learn 2005, 1903-1909

Personalised Multimodal Interfaces for Mobile Geographic Information Systems

Eoin Mac Aoidh

School of Computer Science and Informatics, College of Engineering, Mathematical
and Physical Sciences, UCD Dublin, Ireland.
eoin.macaoidh@ucd.ie

Abstract. HCI in GIS is complicated by information overload and inap-
propriately designed user interfaces considering the task at hand. Implicit
user profiling makes it possible to personalise both the data displayed
by the GIS, and the interface used to display this data. The advance of
mobile computing in recent years has put a great demand on mobile GIS
to be made more efficient and user-friendly, as GIS are best experienced
in the field. While operating in the field, it is quite conceivable that one's
hands would be otherwise occupied, thus the advancement of a multimodal system is imperative for field operation. This doctoral consortium
paper addresses the personalisation of the HCI with such a mobile GIS.

1 Introduction

The two main areas addressed by this paper are personalisation of HCI (Human
Computer Interaction) and mobile GIS (Geographic Information Systems). Geographic Information Systems display maps to a user, and allow him to interact
with them. In particular, the goal of our research is to improve HCI for mobile GIS applications by way of personalisation. There is a massive amount of
GIS data available at many levels of detail, mapping every kind of feature from
detailed, specialist data such as the topography and local rainfall distribution
in some remote river catchment, to general, local tourist information, such as
the location of all the restaurants and hotels in Manhattan. This wealth of data
inevitably leads to the problem of information overload.

The maps displayed by GIS applications are a form of hypermedia - hypermaps. The individual elements (rivers/roads/parks etc.) comprising the map can
be interacted with independently of one another. Their independence and flexibility can be exploited to produce personalised maps corresponding to the users
needs for his task at hand, and to reduce the problem of information overload.
This monitoring of HCI for user profiling in GIS has been explored to some
extent. Zipf [1] and Weakliam et al. [2] explore the reduction of the dataset
presented to the user by generating user profiles, and implicitly capturing user
preferences in order to personalise their dataset, thus reducing information overload. Data describing user preferences can be ascertained based on the frequency
and location of mouse clicks over the displayed data. This information is then
used to personalise the dataset. Research has been concentrated on reducing

V. Wade, H. Ashman, and B. Smyth (Eds.): AH 2006, LNCS 4018, pp. 452–456, 2006.

and improving the dataset by personalisation based on contextual information [1][3][4] or on user profiles [1][2], but comparatively little research has been carried out in the way of using this information to improve the HCI interface for the users future interactions.

Making use of the user's context is very important in GIS. There are many contexts which can be taken into account; Location, operating system, user goals, experience and social contexts are some of the contexts which can be used to build a clearer picture of the user. Users with distinctly different contexts will have distinctly different goals and interaction requirements when they interact with the GIS, e.g. A professional surveyor with years of GIS experience sitting at his desktop PC and a tourist with little GIS experience using a hand-held PC would require a very different interfaces (and datasets) while browsing the same area. The presentation of different maps of the same area to each of these two users, using one application and offering them both the functionality they desire to perform their respective tasks would be the ideal scenario. However there is a gap to be bridged before that situation is achieved.

The goal of this research is to develop a framework which focuses on improving the current levels of HCI in GIS to bring them nearer this ideal, to tackle the issues of improving usability by focusing the user on his task, in a multimodal, mobile environment. We aim to achieve this by means of implicit and explicit profiling to personalise the user's multimodal, mobile experience. The advancement of mobile computing in recent years and the need to use GIS in the field has placed a high demand on the improvement of Mobile GIS. The use of mobile systems goes hand in hand with the development of multimodal systems. When using a mobile device in the field, it is conceivable that one's hands/eyes might be otherwise occupied, thus necessitating the development of alternative I/O such as speech and device tilting. We hope to enrich GIS user's HCI experiences as much as possible by allowing them to interact multimodally in a mobile environment.

2   Related Work

CRUMPET [1] and CoMPASS [2] both generate personalised maps for mobile applications. The contents of the maps reflect the user's interests. CRUMPET is aimed primarily at once-off users, it uses explicit profiling, while CoMPASS is aimed at repeated users. It's user profiling is entirely implicit. We aim to focus on implicit profiling, with the introduction of a "first-time use" explicit profiling wizard, similar to [3] to make our system viable to both once-off tourists, and professional users who will repeatedly return to the system.

Mueller and Lockerd [5] developed a system called Cheese, which tracks and records mouse movements on a web page. The user's positioning of the mouse allows them to make certain inferences and assumptions as to the user's interests. The system posts mouse movement data (position and time) automatically by embedded scripting. The data is analyzed and stored on a server. The system made predictions on user preferences for a particular item shown on a web site with an accuracy of up to 75%. Cheese focused on web pages, however we believe that this method of implicit profiling has potential to be explored further in terms of GIS.

Fischer [6] provides an overview of HCI. Originally, HCI was primarily focused on making systems easier to use. As a result some of the more expressive notions were curtailed. While accommodating novices, the systems became laborious for experienced users, and prevented them from exploiting applications to their full potential. However as things have developed, it is now possible to focus on improving functionality and to use applications as expressive extensions of the human. High functionality applications can interpret contextual factors in the user's environment and adapt the software to the individual users in order to provide the most productive environment for the user. Oviatt [7] has conducted much research into multimodal HCI in GIS. User trials have shown that multimodal interaction in GIS is preferred by 95% of users tested. Doyle et al. [8] have conducted user trials on the CoMPASS multimodal GIS system which show that the introduction of combined speech and pen commands yield an increase in efficiency of 12.21% over non-multimodal commands. One of our system's goals is to personalise the level of multimodal functionality available to the user, based on their profile.

Crow et al. [9] discuss the notion of task-oriented interface construction, in contrast to the more traditional tool-centered interface. DB_Habits provides an adaptive user interface. The system uses pattern recognition techniques to profile users. It remembers the tasks a user performs from observation of a user's behavior, the tasks are then made available to the user as macro scripts. This simple form of programming by example makes effective, accurate personalisation possible. We believe it could be combined seamlessly with profile and context based personalisation.

These systems all provide various important aspects of an adaptive multimodal GIS interface. However, no aspect alone resolves the provision of such a system. We propose a framework to provide such a system. Research will be focused on the intersection of these topics, optimizing the user's multimodal interaction experience by focusing him on the task at hand using personalisation. It is imperative to design the GIS interfaces of the future to suit the user's requirements, as it produces a more user-friendly interface for the end user.

3   Work Developed so Far

Work to date has been developed within the CoMPASS (Combining Mobile Personalised Applications with Spatial Services) project. The project is comprised of a number of components. Of primary interest are the personalisation and mobile HCI components. The personalisation component profiles users implicitly based on their interactions with the map data. Their interactions with specific features are monitored - such as turning on/off a feature and zooming in/out on feature(s). By gathering this information the system can determine which features are of most interest to a user and can personalise his future sessions by returning more detail related to the features that interest him, and less detail on the ancillary features. The mobile HCI component is concerned with migrating the CoMPASS application to the mobile environment, that of the tablet PC and PDA. Smaller screen sizes and slower download speeds have lead to a rethink of the interface design, and the introduction of multimodal interaction. CoMPASS benifits from the introduction of mutlimodal interaction, as it makes the application more versatile [7], easier to use [8], and will reduce the clutter of buttons on the interface as some functionality is ported to other modalities.

As part of the introduction of multimodal interaction to CoMPASS, the option of giving voice commands to interact with some of the basic map functionalities [2] was integrated into the system. This improves HCI for the mobile GIS environment by allowing simple tasks to be carried out in a hands-free environment [8]. The multimodal commands were integrated into the user profiling and personalisation component.

Work was carried out on improving the feedback from the system to the user. The prototype interface developed to date has been largely functional, to demonstrate all the available functionality to the user. From a user's point of view, the interface was not very well designed. Employing a user centered design approach, we re-implemented the loading of the map data to the users device on a feature by feature basis, and included a status bar to inform the user as to the percentage of the overall map loaded.

A comparison study was carried out comparing the CoMPASS system, which is based on non-proprietary open-source software to a professional mobile GIS application. A number of things were learned from this comparison. It is intended that recognised comparison techniques such as in [10] be used in the future to carry out an evaluation of the suggested framework.

4   Plans for Future Research

The advantages of multimodal interaction with hypermaps [7][8][4], and the reduction of information overload in GIS by personalisation [1][2][6] have been clearly documented by many sources. These elements, fused with implicit profiling [5], and the flexibility of an adaptive user interface [9] would provide a valuable human-computer interface for a GIS. We propose the development of a framework to provide an adaptive multimodal GIS interface.

Research will be primarily focused on creating an adaptive user interface. User data extracted from implicit profiling of the user's interactions with the hypermaps will be recorded and stored in a database. The appearance and functionality of each individual's custom interface will be determined by the weighted frequency of the implicitly collected data, for instance, if a heavily weighted functionality appears frequently in the user's profile data, then it should appear prominently on the GUI for that user's future sessions. Incorporating personalised multimodal interaction capabilities into the mobile interface will compliment the primary research to produce a personalised, user-friendly mobile GIS. Following the system's development, recognised interface evaluation techniques

[10] will be employed to evaluate the interface. The interface will be evaluated in terms of both its suitability and adaptability to a given user, and its adaptability to other GIS applications.

The intersection in the topics of personalisation, mobile GIS, and adaptive interfaces provide an interesting research area. An area with a growing demand for development due to the ever-growing cache of geographic data, and its recognised uses. Our proposed framework will broach the advancement of adaptive multimodal interfaces.

References

1. Zipf, A.: User-adaptive Maps for Location Based Services (LBS) for Tourism. In: Proceedings of the 9th International Conference for Information and Communication Technologies in Tourism, Innsbruck, Austria (2002) 329–338
2. Weakliam, J., Lynch, D., Doyle, J., Min Zhou, H., Aoidh, E.M., Bertolotto, M., Wilson, D.: Managing Spatial Knowledge for Mobile Personalized Applications. In: Proceedings of Knowledge-Based Intelligent Information and Engineering Systems: 9th International Conference, KES, Melbourne, Australia, Springer-Verlag GmbH (2005)
3. Cheverst, K., Davies, N., Mitchell, K., Friday, A. Efstratiou, C.: Developing a Context-aware Electronic Tourist Guide: Some Issues and Experiences. In: Proceedings of the Conference on Human Factors in Computing Systems (CHI'2000), Hague, Netherlands, ACM Press (2000) 17–24
4. Baus, J., Kruger, A., Wahlster, W.: A Resource-Adaptive Mobile Navigation System. In: Proceedings of IUI'02, San Francisco,California,USA., ACM (2002) 15–22
5. Mueller, F., Lockerd, A.: Cheese: Tracking Mouse Movement Activity on Websites a Tool for User Modeling. In: Proceedings of the Conference on Human Factors in Computing System (CHI'2002). (2002)
6. Fischer, G.: User Modeling in Human-Computer Interaction. In: Proceedings of the 10th Anniversary issue of User Modeling and User-Adapted Interaction (UMUAI). (2000)
7. Oviatt, S.L.: User-Centered Modeling for Spoken Language and Multimodal Interfaces. IEEE Multimedia **(Winter)** (1996) 26–35
8. Doyle, J., Weakliam, J., Bertolotto, M., Wilson, D.: A Multimodal Interface for Personalising Spatial Data in Mobile GIS. In: 8th International Conference on Enterprise Information Systems. ICEIS. In Press, Paphos, Cyprus (2006)
9. Crow, D., Smith, B.: The Role of Built in Knowledge in Adaptive Interface Systems. In: Proceedings of the 1993 International Workshop on Intelligent User Interfaces, Orlando, Florida, ACM Press (1993)
10. Jeffries, R., Miller, J.R., Wharton, C., Uyeda, K.: User Interface Evaluation in the Real World: A Comparison of Four Techniques. In: Proceedings of CHI'91, New Orleans, LA, ACM (1991) 119–124

A Model for Personalized Learning Through IDTV*

Marta Rey-López, Ana Fernández-Vilas, and Rebeca P. Díaz-Redondo

Department of Telematic Engineering, University of Vigo, 36310, Spain
{mrey, avilas, rebeca}@det.uvigo.es

Abstract. Interactive Digital TV (IDTV) opens new learning possibilities where new forms of education are needed. In this paper we explain a new conception of t-learning experiences where TV programs and learning contents are combined. In order for its creation to be possible we will use Adaptive Hypermedia techniques and Semantic Reasoning to design an Intelligent Tutoring System (ITS) whose tasks consist in selecting, combining and personalizing the contents to construct these learning experiences.

1 Introduction

The arrival of IDTV makes the access to distance education easier, since about 98% of European homes have at least one television set, whereas the penetration of Internet-enabled computers is lower than 60% [1]. Apart from wide-world usage, TV is considered by the viewer trustworthy in reference to broadcast content and easy to operate. These conditions are an ideal starting point for TV-based interactive learning, referred to as t-learning.

In fact, education has always been present on TV, embedded in documentaries or programs for children—e.g. *Sesame Street*. To designate this form of entertainment designed to be educational, in 1973, Robert Heyman coined the term *edutainment*. Today, some TV channels have developed t-learning contents in this direction. In the UK, we can find some examples of games and interactive stories for children, as well as documentaries with additional contents, e.g. *Walking with beasts* produced by the BBC [1]. In Portugal, TV Cabo has developed several *edutainment* applications, some of them adapted from existing web sites, like *Ciberdúvidas* —resolving doubts regarding the Portuguese language [2].

Apart from introducing education into TV programs, transferring traditional structured courses to IDTV is also possible, using this medium solely as a means of transmission for education: transmitting on TV the image of the teacher to the students and vice versa [3] or broadcasting on TV typical e-learning courses, based on text and images [4]. One step further, the scenario for t-learning developed by our research group [5] has improved on these, since learning resources are designed especially for TV and so are based on audio and video content.

However, the approaches mentioned above isolate learning elements from TV programs. The approach we propose looks for a new conception of learning through TV,

---

* Partly supported by the R+D project TSI 2004-03677 (Spanish Ministry of Education and Science) and by the EUREKA ITEA Project PASSEPARTOUT.

V. Wade, H. Ashman, and B. Smyth (Eds.): AH 2006, LNCS 4018, pp. 457–461, 2006.

so as it not only acts as a means of transmission for the courses, on the contrary, the education offered is specific for this medium, taking into account its restrictions and making the most of its potential. Concerning the restrictions, we have to bear in mind both social and technological ones. As the student has just been a viewer for a long time, he/she will probably have a passive attitude when interacting with TV, that is why we have to make education attractive to activate him/her. On the other hand, the contents shown should be in accordance with the technological constraints of IDTV, such as the low resolution of the screen, the fact of using a simple remote control to interact with the programs or the limited features of a set-top box compared with a computer.

Considering these limitations, we will take advantage of the fact that viewers have always conceived TV as a pastime and we will try to offer them education without forgetting entertainment. For this to be possible, we will create learning experiences that combine learning elements and audiovisual ones, i.e. TV programs.This way, we obtain two different types of experiences, those having a TV program as its central axis and the ones whose core is a learning element. Another characteristic of these experiences is their personalization according to user's preferences and learning background, which is essential in t-learning. In this environment, personalization permits the user to access those contents that are interesting for him/her and prevent him/her from getting lost in the huge amount of contents received, compensating in some extent the typical passivity of the viewer. To compose these experiences, we propose the creation of an Intelligent Tutoring System (ITS), which selects, relates and personalizes audiovisual and learning contents. The design of this ITS constitutes the main goal of the Ph.D. work described in this paper, whose objectives will be presented in Section 2. The process to achieve them is explained in Section 3. Finally, in Section 4 we discuss some related research to this topic.

2   Research Objectives

We distinguish two types of experiences that our ITS should be able to create. The first one deals with '*entertainment that educates*'. Its central element is a TV program, which will be complemented with learning elements (Fig. 1a). To refer to these experiences, we have applied the term **entercation**. The construction of *entercation* experiences is initiated by the selection of a TV program interesting for the viewer. In this moment, the ITS has to choose the most appropriate learning elements —from those ones it has access— related to the characteristics of the program and perceived level of interest for the user. We have to take into account user's peculiarities to make effective the learning experience and avoid him/her getting bored. The selected learning objects will be offered to the user at the appropriate moment during the program and he/she could access them from this moment on. In these experiences, the TV program acts as a hook to engage viewers in education.

The second type refers to '*education that entertains*'. Its central axis is a learning element (Fig. 1b), which will be complemented with TV programs (or segments of these ones) in order for the experience to be more entertaining and attractive for the student. We have used the term **edutainment** for these experiences. The ITS will create an *edutainment* experience from a learning element it considers appropriate for the

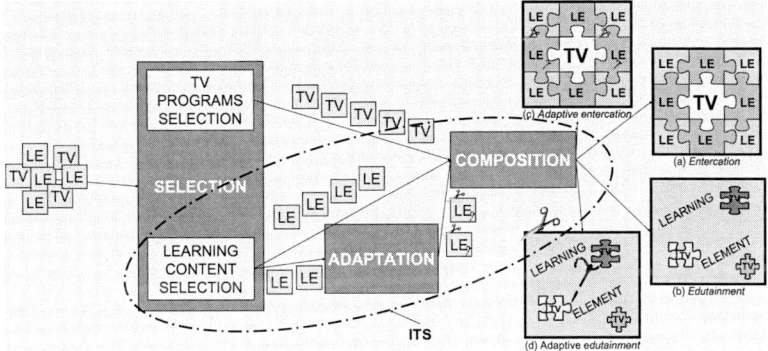

Fig. 1. Creation of t-learning experiences

student, according to his/her learning interests. At the appropriate point, it will add some relevant audiovisual elements (that may be of interest to the student), according to learning content, in order to make the experience more entertaining.

In order to go a step further towards the personalization of learning experiences for IDTV —the main goal of this Ph.D. work— we intend to add adaptivity to these experiences, obtaining **adaptive** *entercation* and *edutainment* experiences (Figs. 1c and 1d). In these experiences, we introduce adaptive elements, which are adapted in order for the student to achieve its objectives in an appropriate way according to his/her characteristics [6].

3   Research Methodology

To achieve the project objectives, an environment based on widely accepted standards is advisable in order for reusability of components and interoperability between systems to be possible. The ITS will work within the technological context defined by the MHP (Multimedia Home Platform) standard [7], which is consolidating worldwide as one of the technical solutions that will shape the future of IDTV. It defines an open interoperable solution that normalizes the characteristics of the set-top boxes and the applications they can execute. On the other hand, the learning elements used by this ITS will comply with the ADL SCORM (Sharable Content Object Reference Model) standard [8], which brings together the works of several normalization initiatives into a consistent body of specifications that is achieving global acceptance.

In Fig. 1, we can see the different stages needed to create the proposed learning experiences. The first stage refers to the **selection** of those contents that are appropriate for the user's preferences stored in his/her profile. In t-learning, this profile is double-sided since it takes into account the user's characteristics as a viewer and a student. The system in charge of selecting audiovisual content is a recommender for TV programs. For our work, we will use AVATAR [9], a recommender based on semantic reasoning designed by our research group. For our Ph.D., AVATAR's most relevant elements are a viewer profile and an ontology based on the TV-Anytime metadata [10], which permits classifying TV programs.

Regarding learning content, its selection is one of the tasks that our ITS has to perform. For this to be possible, we have to define a user model that reflects his/her preferences and background as a student. To relate this profile with the appropriate learning elements, we have to define an ontology based on SCORM, where the ITS creates the instances of all the elements it can access, thus allowing semantic reasoning.

When finalizing the selection process, those elements that are not appropriate for the student have already been discarded. The next phase consists of creating learning experiences from TV programs and learning elements. First, **adaptation** should be performed for adaptive learning elements, selecting the most appropriate way —among those possible— for the user to achieve the intended objective. Since SCORM does not currently permit adaptivity, we are working on an extension to this standard to achieve learning contents adaptation. This extension should include some structures that provide adaptation rules. This rules allow the ITS to decide which organizations and elements are more appropriate for the characteristics of the user.

The last stage is the **composition** of learning experiences. In this phase, the contents are linked to be shown to the user, semantically relating the instances of learning and audiovisual elements using the aforementioned ontologies, by means of a gateway ontology that contains the concepts of the subject domain.

4   Related Work and Discussion

In terms of related work, there are several relevant research fields, including Adaptive Hypermedia, User Modelling and Semantic Reasoning.

Adaptive Hypermedia (AH) is one of the most promising areas to offer personalization on the e-learning field. It tries to overcome the problem of having users with different goals and knowledge by using the information represented in the user model to adapt the contents [6]. This is the objective we want to achieve by defining adaptable learning elements appropriate for IDTV. As stated in [11] the techniques used in AH can be extended to audiovisual contents in the field of interactive television. To achieve this adaptation, we are working on extending the SCORM standard with adaptation rules. In this sense, the proposals exposed in [12] and [13] are close to ours since they try to offer adaptivity by including dedicated adaptation-specific constructs in the course definition. However they do not offer different possibilities for users with different needs.

With reference to **User Modelling**, we can find several proposals. One method widely used to represent this one is the overlay model, where the learner knowledge is represented as a subset of the expert knowledge [14]. Another popular method is classifying users into categories and making predictions about them based on a stereotype associated with each category [15]. Regarding the viewer profile, the user model defined for AVATAR stores those branches of the TV ontology that contain the programs the user has already watched [16]. We intend to design our user profile by taking these proposals into account as well as the most relevant standards concerning learner information: IMS LIP (Learner Information Package) [17] and IEEE PAPI (Personal and Private Information) [18].

Regarding **Semantic Reasoning**, for the selection of learning elements, we take as a starting point the work developed by our group [9], with experience in collaborative filtering and semantic inference that perfectly apply to our needs. To establish relationships between TV programs and learning content, we need a gateway ontology, e.g. SUMO (Suggested Upper Merged Ontology) [19].

To conclude, in this paper we look for a new conception of learning experiences for IDTV combining audiovisual and learning contents, essential requisites for t-learning, taking advantage of its potential instead of using it as a simple means of transmission for the courses. To construct these experiences we will design an ITS to select, relate and personalize the contents, which will be developed using an agent-based architecture. Up to now, we have already designed the SCORM ontology, we are putting the final touches to the SCORM extension and we have developed an authoring tool to create adaptive elements. In the future, we should work on relating learning contents and TV programs to produce *entercation* and *edutainment* experiences.

References

1. Bates, P.J.: A Study into TV-based Interactive Learning to the Home. http://www.pjb.co.uk/t-learning (2003)
2. Damásio, M.J., Quico, C.: T-Learning and Interactive Television Edutainment: the Portuguese Case Study. In: Proc. of ED-MEDIA 2004. (2004)
3. Zhao, L.: Interactive Television in Distance Education: Benefits and Compromises. In: Proc. of ISTAS'02. (2002) 255–261
4. Aarreniemi-Jokipelto, P.: Experiences with an Interactive Learning Environment in Digital TV. In: Proc. of ICALT'04. (2004)
5. Pazos-Arias, J.J., et al.: ATLAS: A framework to provide multiuser and distributed t-learning services over MHP. Software: Practice and Experience. (In press)
6. Brusilovsky, P.: Methods and techniques of adaptive hypermedia. User Modeling and User Adapted Interaction 6(2-3) (1996) 87–129
7. DVB Consortium: Multimedia Home Platform 1.2.1. ETSI TS 102 812 V1.2.1 (2003)
8. ADL: Sharable Content Object Reference Model. http://www.adlnet.org (2004)
9. Blanco-Fernández, Y., et al.: AVATAR: An advanced Multi-Agent Recommender System of Personalized TV Contents by Semantic Reasoning. In: Proc. of WISE 2004. (2004)
10. The TV-Anytime Forum: Broadcast and On-line Services: Search, select and rightful use of content on personal storage systems. ETSI TS 102 822 (2004)
11. Masthoff, J., Pemberton, L.: Adaptive hypermedia for personalized TV. In: Adaptable and Adaptive Hypermedia Systems. IDEA group publishing (2005) 246–263
12. Conlan, O.: The Multi-Model, Metadata Driven Approach to Personalised eLearning Services. PhD thesis, Trinity College, Dublin (2005)
13. Mödritscher, F., et al.: Enhancement of SCORM to support adaptive E-Learning within the Scope of the Research Project AdeLE. In: Proc. of ELEARN 2004, USA (2004)
14. Weber, G., Brusilovsky, P.: ELM-ART: An Adaptive Versatile System for Web-based Intruction. International Journal of Artificial Intelligence in Education 1 (2001) 351–384
15. Kobsa, A., et al.: Personalised hypermedia presentation techniques for improving online customer relationships. The Knowledge Engineering Review 16(2) (2001) 111–155
16. Blanco-Fernández, Y., et al.: AVATAR: Modeling Users by Dynamic Ontologies in a TV Recommender System based on Semantic Reasoning. In: Proc. of EuroITV-05. (2005)
17. IMS: Learner Information Package (LIP). http://imsproject.org (2001)
18. IEEE LTSC: Private and Public Information. http://edutool.com/papi/ (2001)
19. Niles, I., Pease, A.: Towards a Standard Upper Ontology. In: Welty, C., Smith, B., eds.: Proc. of FOIS-2001, USA (2001)

Performance Enhancement for Open Corpus Adaptive Hypermedia Systems

Lejla Rovcanin[1,2], Cristina Hava Muntean[1], and Gabriel-Miro Muntean[1]

[1] School of Electronic Engineering, Dublin City University,
Glasnevin, Dublin 9, Ireland
{lejlar, havac, munteang}@eeng.dcu.ie
[2] School of Electronic and Communication Engineering, Dublin Institute of Technology,
Dublin 2, Ireland
lejla.rovcanin@dit.ie

Abstract. Adaptive Hypermedia Systems adjust the content to best suit users' personal characteristics, but rarely consider delivery performance. Performance issues are even more significant in distributed architectures such as that of an Open Corpus Adaptive Educational Hypermedia System (OAEHS). This paper introduces a Performance Oriented Adaptation Agent (POAA) that enhances OAEHS by taking into consideration not only user personal characteristics but also network delivery conditions in the content selection process. The usage of POAA is expected to bring significant delivery performance improvements in terms of learner satisfaction and learning outcome.

1 Introduction

1.1 Adaptive Hypermedia Systems

The delivery of informational content to heterogeneous e-users presents significant challenges, which have been addressed in various areas of research. Adaptive Hypermedia Systems (AHS) identify user categories and deliver differentiated content tailored to individuals or groups based on user characteristics such as skills, goals, capabilities, knowledge, interests and preferences [1]. The AHS approach involves monitoring of the user's interactions with the system, building of a user profile and, based on it, adapting various aspects of the delivered content to suit the user [2]. Possible adaptations include content modifications (the content is adapted to best suit the users) and link adjustments (the link structure is tailored to guide the users towards relevant and interesting information) [1]. A comprehensive review of techniques used by the proposed AHS is provided in [2].

AHS proposed in education aim to improve both the overall learning outcome and the quality of user interaction with the system. Adaptive Educational Hypermedia Systems (AEHS) such as AHA! [3], InterBook [4], and ISIS-Tutor [5] seek to optimize learner experience with their online course material by personalizing this material to the learner's individual learning requirements.

V. Wade, H. Ashman, and B. Smyth (Eds.): AH 2006, LNCS 4018, pp. 462–466, 2006.
© Springer-Verlag Berlin Heidelberg 2006

1.2 Open Corpus Adaptive Hypermedia Systems

Existing AHS and especially AEHS are stand-alone systems dealing with a limited number of well-structured resources known at system design time. They are so-called *closed corpus* systems that use proprietary repositories to store the information to be delivered based on users' characteristics and requests. The design and the development of such a repository are difficult and time-consuming tasks. These systems, although deployed in the Web context, provide no support to incorporate information from arbitrary Web locations.

The Web plays a key role in information access and dissemination, and it has become an integral part of the learning environment. Some issues, such as intellectual property rights, privacy, peer review, validity and quality of Web information are still to be addressed. These issues are addressed to a limited extent within existing Digital Educational Repositories (DER) that allow for safe storage, delivery, reuse and sharing of information. The reuse of existing information makes economic sense, improves efficiency, allows for interdisciplinary sharing of expertise and provides up-to-date and accurate learning resources.

Open Adaptive Educational Hypermedia Systems (OAEHS) are AEHS that operate with existing information resources such as DER. These systems use an *open corpus* of documents and adapt hypermedia documents to the individual needs of the user regardless of the origin or location of the materials. For example, the materials may be part of a tutorial, may refer to content from a personal Web page or could be learning objects (LOs) that belong to a digital repository of learning material. Such information space must be searchable, interoperable and accessible. OAEHS interoperability and content reusability have been addressed with a number of communication protocols (e.g. Open Hypermedia Protocol), guidelines and standards for the representation of resources (e.g. CMI). Many of the OAEHS separate links from documents. Links are kept in centralized locations for easy maintenance and are processed separately from the media to which they relate [6].

1.3 Performance Issues for OAEHS

Distributed computing, including devices for user input and display, the network capacity, connectivity, and costs may all change over time and place. The performance of distributed systems, including OAEHS is determined by both network conditions and end-user devices. Currently, Open AH research in the area of education places very little emphasis on delivery performance and its effect on the learning process. Context-related issues are addressed by Smith [7] and Dagger [8] who focus on the end-user device and Muntean [9] who considers network-related factors.

Existing DERs are large collections of LOs. In consequence oversupply of information may occur, disorienting the learner. In this context OAEHS are of significant benefit as they provide support for the selection of the best LOs for a particular learner, based on the learner's interests, goals, background knowledge, learning style, etc. An issue that may arise is the network connection performance between the OAEHS front-end server and the source of the LO or the learner.

OAEHS can select an LO that perfectly coincides with the given learner's profile, however, due to network performance issues, the user might perceive an unacceptable download time and be unhappy with their experience. Therefore learners have different perceptions of the same content and performance factors.

The delivery network conditions can change significantly, sometimes even within the duration of a given learning session. Metrics such as delay, jitter, loss, download time, etc. reflect the state of the network and can be monitored in order to determine performance-based adaptation measures. Such measures can be used to guide the selection of the LOs in response to existing network conditions. Therefore there is a need for performance-aware OAEHS that select the best LOs based both on performance and the learner specific characteristics.

In this context, this paper introduces a Performance Oriented Adaptation Agent (POAA) that enhances OAEHS by considering network delivery conditions along user personal characteristics in the content selection process. The POAA and the simulation setup are presented in the following section.

2   Performance Oriented Adaptation Agent

OAEHS selection of LOs should be based not only on learner's personal characteristics but also on network connectivity properties in order to allow for performance-efficient delivery. To address this issue, a Performance Oriented Adaptation Agent (POAA) is proposed. POAA calculates a network performance rating, which is subsequently factored into the process of selecting the LOs to be delivered.

In a typical example of an existing OAEHS, the learner requests content on the client side. The OAEHS front-end server processes the request, selects appropriate LOs from various sources, builds a presentation suitable for the learner and delivers it. This relies on the fact that different sources may contain LOs with the same learning objectives.

We extend this architecture by deploying a POAA on the OAEHS front-end server. The POAA monitors network conditions between the OAEHS front-end server and DER servers. Network parameters considered are related to the delivery performance, such as download time, loss, delay and jitter. The values of these parameters are collected and stored separately for each DER in a sliding window-like structure. The POAA uses this data to calculate performance ratings. Every time a LO is selected and new performance information is acquired, the relevant DERs sliding window is updated.

The three-step LOs selection process is depicted in Fig. 1. The first step is relevance selection where the OAEHS identifies the learning outcome and selects LOs providing that learning outcome. These LOs may be distributed across several DER servers. The second step is personalization selection where the OAEHS shortlists a number of suitable LOs based on the user's profile. Each LO is assigned a suitability rating for that learner. The third step is performance selection where POAA agent estimates performance rating for each suitable object. An LO is assigned a performance rating based on the average computed on the performance values collected for the DER on which it resides. Suitability and performance ratings are combined. The LO with the highest cumulative rating is delivered to the learner. Some adaptive systems, such as SASY [10] inform the user on omitted content. In the proposed system the learner cannot directly interfere in the selection process.

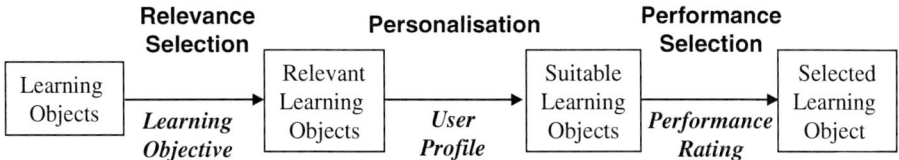

Fig. 1. POAA-based learning objects selection process

Preliminary tests are currently performed using Network Simulator version 2.27 – NS2 [11]. NS2 is a discrete event simulator, with substantial support for simulation of protocols at various levels of the TCP/IP networking model over wired and wireless networks. The test setup is presented in Fig. 2. Clients (C_1, C_2, ..., C_N) and DER servers (S_1, S_2, ..., S_M) are connected to a OAHES server (P) on which POAA was deployed. The initial simulations focus on the connections between the server and the DER servers (P-S_i) consequently the network links between the clients and the server (C_i-P) are over-provisioned such that no loss or significant delays are expected. The network connections (P-S_i) differ in terms of bandwidth and propagation delay. Communication between S_1 and C_1 benefits from POAA deployment, whereas that between S_i-C_i, i>1 consists of background traffic.

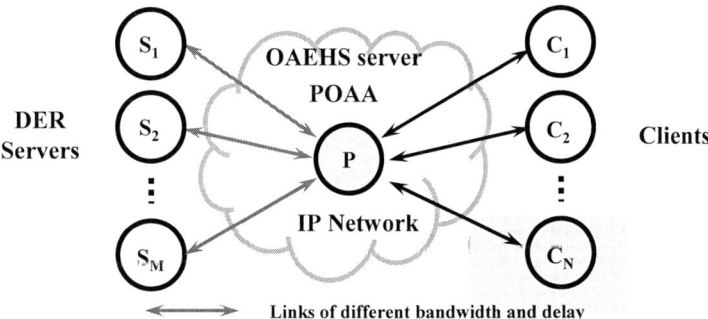

Fig. 2. Simulation topology

We assume that the system would be aware of servers that contain different LOs. The aim of these tests is to compare the delivery performance in terms of download time for a system that deploys the proposed POAA against those measured for a system that does not employ any intelligent selection of the content based on performance. Results are expected to indicate a significant improvement in performance when using the POAA-based system in comparison with the classic system.

3   Conclusion and Future Work

This paper proposes a Performance Oriented Adaptation Agent (POAA) for Open corpus Adaptive Educational Hypermedia Systems (OAEHS). POAA enhances the existing selection process of learning objects (LOs) by taking into consideration not only the user personal characteristics but also network delivery conditions. The use of POAA for OAEHS brings significant delivery performance improvements and is expected to improve overall learners' satisfaction as well as their learning outcomes.

The proposed agent could be used with existing OAEHS such as Knowledge Tree [12] to augment the current adaptation process.

The proposed approach will be more extensively tested with a higher number of clients, in different network topologies, against background traffic that varies in type, shape and size.

References

1. Brusilovsky, P.: Adaptive Hypermedia. User Modeling and User Adapted Interaction, Vol. 11, No. 1-2, (2001) 87-110.
2. Brusilovsky, P.: Methods and Techniques of Adaptive Hypermedia. Special Issue on Adaptive Hypertext and Hypermedia, User Modeling and User-Adapted Interaction, Vol. 6, No. 2-3, (1996) 87-129.
3. De Bra, P., Calvi, L.: AHA! An Open Adaptive Hypermedia Architecture. The New Review of Hypermedia and Multimedia, Vol. 4, (1998) 115-139.
4. Brusilovsky, P., Eklund, P., Schwarz, E.: Web-based Education for All: A Tool for Developing Adaptive Courseware. 7th International World Wide Web Conference (1998), 291-300.
5. Brusilovsky, P., Pesin, L.: ISIS-Tutor: An Adaptive Hypertext Learning Environment. JCKBSE'94, Japanese-CIS Symposium on Knowledge-based Software Engineering, Pereslavl-Zalesski, Russia (1994) 83-87.
6. Bailey, C., Hall, W., Millard, D. E., Weal, M. J.: Towards Open Adaptive Hypermedia. 2nd International Conference on Adaptive Hypermedia and Adaptive Web Based Systems, Malaga, Spain (2002) 36-46.
7. Smyth, B., Cotter, P.: Content Personalisation for WAP-enabled Devices. Workshop Machine Learning in the New Information Age: Conf. on Machine Learning, Barcelona (2000)
8. Dagger, D., Wade, V., Conlan, O.: Towards "anytime, anywhere" Learning: The Role and Realization of Dynamic Terminal Personalization in Adaptive eLearning, Ed-Media 2003, World Conference on Educational Multimedia, Hypermedia and Telecommunications, Hawaii (2003)
9. Muntean, C.H. and McManis, J.: End-User Quality of Experience Layer for Adaptive Hypermedia Systems. 3rd International Conference on Adaptive Hypermedia and Adaptive Web-based Systems, Eindhoven, The Netherlands (2004), 87-96.
10. Czarkowski. M., Kay, J., Potts, S.: Web Framework for Scrutable Adaptation, Proceedings of Workshop on Learner Modelling for Reflection, International Conference on Artificial Intelligence in Education (2005), 11-18.
11. Network Simulator. Version 2 – http://www.isi.edu/nsnam/ns
12. Brusilovsky, P.: Knowledge Tree: A Distributed Architecture for Adaptive E-Learning. 13th International World Wide Web Conference, New York, New York, USA (2004)

Personalized Navigation in the Semantic Web[*]

Michal Tvarožek[**]

Institute of Informatics and Software Engineering
Faculty of Informatics and Information Technologies, Slovak University of Technology,
Ilkovičova 3, 842 16 Bratislava, Slovakia
tvarozek@fiit.stuba.sk

Abstract. Effective navigation and information retrieval is difficult and time consuming due to the increasing size of hyperspace. The introduction of the semantic web allows us to enhance traditional search methods with semantic search capabilities that take advantage of machine readable semantic information ideally stored in an ontology. Nevertheless issues concerning the user-friendly construction of search queries and a simple yet effective presentation of search results must still be addressed. The proposed approach takes advantage of adaptive hypermedia in an enhanced faceted browser capable of dynamically adapting the set of available facets with additional support for data retrieval from an ontology and adaptive annotation of search results.

1 Introduction

By definition, navigation is the process of following links and browsing web pages. At present, navigation is necessary because it is not (yet) normally possible to satisfy all user needs on a single web page or on the first visited web page. Generally speaking, user needs can be classified into the following types [1]:

- Informational, when the user seeks information
- Navigational, when the user seeks a starting point for further browsing
- Transactional, when the user wants to perform an action

In order to fulfill either type of need a user typically first enters a query into a search engine to find a list of the most relevant pages. Next, he selects the most promising links and initiates a navigation session that involves the browsing of the selected web pages. If the respective need cannot be satisfied, the user modifies the original query and starts from the beginning.

Several studies have shown that the recursion rate of navigation is roughly 60% [2] and describes the number of repeatedly visited pages to the total number of visited pages. Furthermore, the shift from the use of closed and relatively small information spaces towards large, open and ever growing information spaces is bound to further escalate this problem. Perhaps a good example of such an open information space is the domain of job offers on the Internet.

[*] This work was supported by Science and Technology Assistance Agency under the contract No. APVT-20-007104 and State programme of research and development "Establishing of Information Society".

[**] Supervisor: Professor Mária Bieliková, bielik@fiit.stuba.sk

V. Wade, H. Ashman, and B. Smyth (Eds.): AH 2006, LNCS 4018, pp. 467–471, 2006.
© Springer-Verlag Berlin Heidelberg 2006

Problems and Issues. We intend to address several contemporary navigation problems with the proposed approach. These include the navigation in open and relatively large information spaces, which is too time consuming and often results in the "lost in hyperspace" syndrome that occurs when users loose track of their position in hyperspace due to insufficient navigation aids or because the hyperspace is "too large".

While the problems of effective searching and information retrieval in these spaces can be addressed by semantic search [3, 4] this requires the use of more complex queries than full-text search. As a result, new user-friendly ways of query construction and simple yet effective methods for the presentation of search results must be employed. Adaptive hypermedia technologies [5] can be used to make it easy for users to read and understand the results and allow them to quickly choose the most promising ones for further navigation.

2   Research Agenda

2.1   Proposed Approach

We propose the use of a faceted browser[1] as a solution for the aforementioned problems. A faceted browser is a browser that supports faceted navigation that takes advantage of faceted classification defined by a classification ontology that describes important aspects of instances from a domain ontology. The attributes of instances correspond to facets and the values of attributes correspond to facet values. The user can reduce the total number of displayed instances by enabling one or more restrictions defined by facet values thus decreasing the size of the visible information space. Individual facet values can be further combined to form complex restrictions allowing the user to perform more precise queries.

While we are primarily interested in large information spaces with many similar instances represented by a domain ontology with semantic markup (e.g., OWL), the proposed approach should also be applicable to other areas. The advantages of ontologies are twofold. First, it is easier to create a classification ontology from a domain ontology than from unstructured data and it should also be possible to automate this process. Second, reasoning on ontologies allows us to perform "more complex" queries with higher quality results. Several reasoning tools are presently available. Simpler tools are supplied with ontological databases (e.g., Sesame), others are free or commercial such as RacerPro[2].

Large information spaces and additional data obtained by reasoning on ontologies would result in too much information thus overloading the user with information. To address this issue we propose personalization and user adaptation as means of reducing information overload by focusing on current user needs and goals defined by a user model. To simplify the process of adaptation and more importantly presentation of data, we propose the use of a presentation framework for ontological data based on the Fresnel presentation ontology [6].

---

[1] Use of Faceted Classification,
 http://www.webdesignpractices.com/navigation/facets.html (2.2.2006)
[2] http://www.racer-systems.com/products/racerpro/index.phtml (27.3.2006)

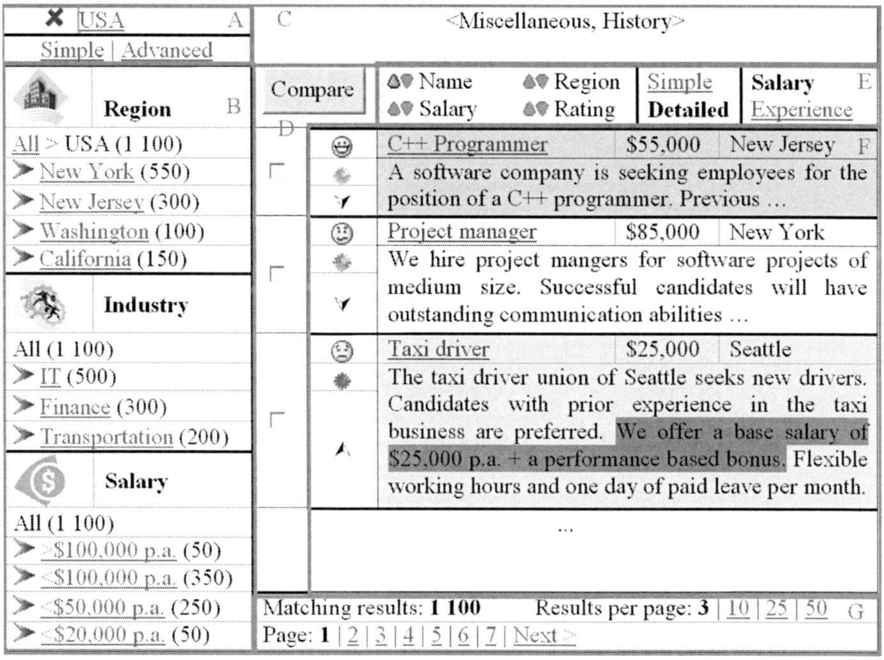

✖ USA A	C	<Miscellaneous, History>
Simple | Advanced		

Fig. 1. A sample user interface of an enhanced faceted browser. Area A shows the currently selected restrictions, area B contains the available set of facets (Region, Industry, Salary) and restrictions. Area C contains miscellaneous data, like navigation or query history and additional settings. Area D is used to compare a set of instances while area E allows the user to sort instances, change views or highlighting options. Area F displays individual instances (search results) and depicts instance data enriched with adaptive annotation techniques (emoticons, background color, traffic lights). Area G serves for navigation between different results pages

2.2   Progress to Date

We implemented a basic version of a faceted browser that supports the use of simple search queries and the browsing of search results (job offer instances). We use an ontological database of job offers, which was developed within the scope of a larger project conducted at the Slovak University of Technology [7].

Based on an initial evaluation of the usability of the browser, we see a strong need for adaptation due to the high number of available facets and facet values with the user's goals and background as the primary sources of adaptation stored in a user ontology. Furthermore, users have specific requirements which translate into the need and/or preference of some facets and facet values over others.

From a user's standpoint, the usability of a tool is not only defined by the array of available functions but also by the usability of its graphical user interface. While this concerns a somewhat different area of research we designed an initial outline of a user interface for an enhanced faceted browser (see Fig. 1).

2.3   Future Research Challenges

We intend to explore the adaptation of the faceted browser based on a user model. This includes the adaptation of facets and facet values and adaptation of search results e.g. by means of adaptive annotation techniques. Furthermore, the visual representation of navigation history in the form of a (hyper)graph appears to have some potential in improving a user's understanding of hyperspace.

Although the primary source of adaptation will be a user model, it appears to be an interesting research prospect to evaluate the usability of the observed user navigation and history data as an additional source of adaptation.

Adaptation of Predefined Facets. The adaptation of predefined facets includes adaptive navigation techniques like reordering, hiding [5] and the presentation of facets and facet values. Also interesting is the possibility to present facets as enumerated lists or as graphs created by OWL visualization tools.

For example, in the case of the job offer ontology, if a user was interested in high paying jobs with specific experience requirements, the facets including these restrictions would be displayed first. Less important facets or restrictions that are assumed to be irrelevant would be either shown later or completely hidden.

Dynamic Facet Generation. Dynamic generation of facets goes one step beyond simple adaptation as described above. Ideally it will be able to create new facets and the respective restrictions at run time based on the knowledge contained in the domain ontology and in the user model. This feature would also improve on the usability of the faceted browser with different domain ontologies which would thus not require extensive manual definition of facets.

Assuming that a facet for experience level requirements was not yet defined, dynamic facet generation would be able to create a new facet definition if experience levels were present in the domain ontology. This new facet would then be displayed together with the original facets in the top part of the facet list.

Advanced Query Mode. The selection of individual restrictions in facets is transformed into a query that is executed on an ontological database. In simple query mode, exactly one restriction per facet can be selected and all facets are combined with the logical AND function resulting in relatively simple queries.

The proposed advanced query mode allows users to create and execute more complex queries with multiple restrictions per facet thus resulting in a more precise description of the desired instances. We also plan support for additional facet combination functions, such as the logical OR function or braces. Thus if a user wanted a job either in the USA or in Canada, he would select both USA and Canada in one facet – "Region" and combine them with the OR function.

Presentation and Processing. The result of a search performed by a faceted browser is normally an unordered list of instances that satisfy the search criteria. This however is not ideal for effective evaluation of the search results by the user. Additional means for processing of the search results are necessary to improve usability. We intend to add simple ordering of search results as well as support for more complex external sorting tools and several adaptive views with different levels of detail [8]. The possibility to compare the attributes of the selected instances (search results) also seems to be good for improving usability.

While sorting only displays the rating of instances with regard to one attribute, a user will often be interested in ratings based on several attributes simultaneously. The use of adaptive annotation techniques [5] to present these attributes appears to be a promising direction for further research.

For example, in the domain of job offers background color can indicate how well a user satisfies the requirements of the employer, an emoticon can indicate how well a job offer satisfies user criteria, while the job offers are ordered in descending order based on the offered salary. A traffic light signal can indicate a composite suitability rating of a job offer based on a heuristic function or the overall rating of the employing company by previous applicants.

3   Summary

We proposed an enhanced faceted browser as a solution for several navigation and search related problems. The usability evaluation of a basic faceted browser, confirmed the need for its adaptation due to the high number of available facets and facet values. Further work will include enhancements to facets – their adaptive reordering, hiding and dynamic generation and support for adaptive annotation based on a user model and domain ontology. We will also continuously evaluate the usability of the browser and the viability of the proposed concept based on feedback from sample users in the domain of job offers [7].

References

1. Broder, A.: A taxonomy of web search. SIGIR Forum (2002)
2. Lavene, M., Wheeldon, R.. Navigating the World-Wide-Web. In Lavene, M., Poulovassilis, A., eds.: Web Dynamics, Springer (2003)
3. Guha, R., McCool, R., Miller, E.: Semantic Search. In: The 12th International Conference on World Wide Web. (2003) 700–709
4. Zhang, L., Yu, Y., Zhou, J., Lin, C.X., Yang, Y.: An Enhanced Model for Searching in Semantic Portals. In: WWW 2005, ACM Press (2005) 453–462
5. Brusilovsky, P.: Adaptive Hypermedia. In Kobsa, A., ed.: User Modeling and User-Adapted Interaction, Ten Year Anniversary Issue. (2001) 87–110
6. Bieliková, M., Grlický, V., Kuruc, J.: Framework for presentation of information represented by an ontology. In Vojtáš, P., ed.: ITAT 2005 – Workshop on Theory and Practice of Information Technologies, Račkova dolina (2005) 325–334
7. Návrat, P., Bieliková, M., Rozinajová, V.: Methods and Tools for Acquiring and Presenting Information and Knowledge in the Web. In: International Conference on Computer Systems and Technologies – CompSysTech' 2005, Varna, Bulgaria (2005)
8. Domingue, J., Dzbor, M., Motta, E.: Magpie: Supporting Browsing and Navigation on the Semantic Web. In: Intelligent User Interfaces. (2004) 191–197

Author Index

Vol. 3998: T. Calamoneri, I. Finocchi, G.F. Italiano (Eds.), Algorithms and Complexity. XII, 394 pages. 2006.

Vol. 3997: W. Grieskamp, C. Weise (Eds.), Formal Approaches to Software Testing. XII, 219 pages. 2006.

Vol. 3996: A. Keller, J.-P. Martin-Flatin (Eds.), Self-Managed Networks, Systems, and Services. X, 185 pages. 2006.

Vol. 3995: G. Müller (Ed.), Emerging Trends in Information and Communication Security. XX, 524 pages. 2006.

Vol. 3994: V.N. Alexandrov, G.D. van Albada, P.M.A. Sloot, J. Dongarra (Eds.), Computational Science – ICCS 2006, Part IV. XXXV, 1096 pages. 2006.

Vol. 3993: V.N. Alexandrov, G.D. van Albada, P.M.A. Sloot, J. Dongarra (Eds.), Computational Science – ICCS 2006, Part III. XXXVI, 1136 pages. 2006.

Vol. 3992: V.N. Alexandrov, G.D. van Albada, P.M.A. Sloot, J. Dongarra (Eds.), Computational Science – ICCS 2006, Part II. XXXV, 1122 pages. 2006.

Vol. 3991: V.N. Alexandrov, G.D. van Albada, P.M.A. Sloot, J. Dongarra (Eds.), Computational Science – ICCS 2006, Part I. LXXXI, 1096 pages. 2006.

Vol. 3990: J. C. Beck, B.M. Smith (Eds.), Integration of AI and OR Techniques in Constraint Programming for Combinatorial Optimization Problems. X, 301 pages. 2006.

Vol. 3989: J. Zhou, M. Yung, F. Bao, Applied Cryptography and Network Security. XIV, 488 pages. 2006.

Vol. 3987: M. Hazas, J. Krumm, T. Strang (Eds.), Location- and Context-Awareness. X, 289 pages. 2006.

Vol. 3986: K. Stølen, W.H. Winsborough, F. Martinelli, F. Massacci (Eds.), Trust Management. XIV, 474 pages. 2006.

Vol. 3984: M. Gavrilova, O. Gervasi, V. Kumar, C.J. K. Tan, D. Taniar, A. Laganà, Y. Mun, H. Choo (Eds.), Computational Science and Its Applications - ICCSA 2006, Part V. XXV, 1045 pages. 2006.

Vol. 3983: M. Gavrilova, O. Gervasi, V. Kumar, C.J. K. Tan, D. Taniar, A. Laganà, Y. Mun, H. Choo (Eds.), Computational Science and Its Applications - ICCSA 2006, Part IV. XXVI, 1191 pages. 2006.

Vol. 3982: M. Gavrilova, O. Gervasi, V. Kumar, C.J. K. Tan, D. Taniar, A. Laganà, Y. Mun, H. Choo (Eds.), Computational Science and Its Applications - ICCSA 2006, Part III. XXV, 1243 pages. 2006.

Vol. 3981: M. Gavrilova, O. Gervasi, V. Kumar, C.J. K. Tan, D. Taniar, A. Laganà, Y. Mun, H. Choo (Eds.), Computational Science and Its Applications - ICCSA 2006, Part II. XXVI, 1255 pages. 2006.

Vol. 3980: M. Gavrilova, O. Gervasi, V. Kumar, C.J. K. Tan, D. Taniar, A. Laganà, Y. Mun, H. Choo (Eds.), Computational Science and Its Applications - ICCSA 2006, Part I. LXXV, 1199 pages. 2006.

Vol. 3979: T.S. Huang, N. Sebe, M.S. Lew, V. Pavlović, M. Kölsch, A. Galata, B. Kisačanin (Eds.), Computer Vision in Human-Computer Interaction. XII, 121 pages. 2006.

Vol. 3978: B. Hnich, M. Carlsson, F. Fages, F. Rossi (Eds.), Recent Advances in Constraints. VIII, 179 pages. 2006. (Sublibrary LNAI).

Vol. 3977: N. Fuhr, M. Lalmas, S. Malik, G. Kazai (Eds.), Advances in XML Information Retrieval and Evaluation. XII, 556 pages. 2006.

Vol. 3976: F. Boavida, T. Plagemann, B. Stiller, C. Westphal, E. Monteiro (Eds.), Networking 2006. Networking Technologies, Services, and Protocols; Performance of Computer and Communication Networks; Mobile and Wireless Communications Systems. XXVI, 1276 pages. 2006.

Vol. 3975: S. Mehrotra, D.D. Zeng, H. Chen, B.M. Thuraisingham, F.-Y. Wang (Eds.), Intelligence and Security Informatics. XXII, 772 pages. 2006.

Vol. 3973: J. Wang, Z. Yi, J.M. Zurada, B.-L. Lu, H. Yin (Eds.), Advances in Neural Networks - ISNN 2006, Part III. XXIX, 1402 pages. 2006.

Vol. 3972: J. Wang, Z. Yi, J.M. Zurada, B.-L. Lu, H. Yin (Eds.), Advances in Neural Networks - ISNN 2006, Part II. XXVII, 1444 pages. 2006.

Vol. 3971: J. Wang, Z. Yi, J.M. Zurada, B.-L. Lu, H. Yin (Eds.), Advances in Neural Networks - ISNN 2006, Part I. LXVII, 1442 pages. 2006.

Vol. 3970: T. Braun, G. Carle, S. Fahmy, Y. Koucheryavy (Eds.), Wired/Wireless Internet Communications. XIV, 350 pages. 2006.

Vol. 3969: Ø. Ytrehus (Ed.), Coding and Cryptography. XI, 443 pages. 2006.

Vol. 3968: K.P. Fishkin, B. Schiele, P. Nixon, A. Quigley (Eds.), Pervasive Computing. XV, 402 pages. 2006.

Vol. 3967: D. Grigoriev, J. Harrison, E.A. Hirsch (Eds.), Computer Science – Theory and Applications. XVI, 684 pages. 2006.

Vol. 3966: Q. Wang, D. Pfahl, D.M. Raffo, P. Wernick (Eds.), Software Process Change. XIV, 356 pages. 2006.

Vol. 3965: M. Bernardo, A. Cimatti (Eds.), Formal Methods for Hardware Verification. VII, 243 pages. 2006.

Vol. 3964: M. Ü. Uyar, A.Y. Duale, M.A. Fecko (Eds.), Testing of Communicating Systems. XI, 373 pages. 2006.

Vol. 3963: O. Dikenelli, M.-P. Gleizes, A. Ricci (Eds.), Engineering Societies in the Agents World VI. XII, 303 pages. 2006. (Sublibrary LNAI).

Vol. 3962: W. IJsselsteijn, Y. de Kort, C. Midden, B. Eggen, E. van den Hoven (Eds.), Persuasive Technology. XII, 216 pages. 2006.

Vol. 3960: R. Vieira, P. Quaresma, M.d.G.V. Nunes, N.J. Mamede, C. Oliveira, M.C. Dias (Eds.), Computational Processing of the Portuguese Language. XII, 274 pages. 2006. (Sublibrary LNAI).

Vol. 3959: J.-Y. Cai, S. B. Cooper, A. Li (Eds.), Theory and Applications of Models of Computation. XV, 794 pages. 2006.

Vol. 3958: M. Yung, Y. Dodis, A. Kiayias, T. Malkin (Eds.), Public Key Cryptography - PKC 2006. XIV, 543 pages. 2006.

Lecture Notes in Computer Science

For information about Vols. 1–3956

please contact your bookseller or Springer